ETERNITY

AT THE END OF A ROPE

ETERNITY
AT THE END OF A ROPE

Executions, Lynchings and Vigilante Justice
in Texas 1819–1923

Clifford R. Caldwell and Ron DeLord

Foreword by Dave Johnson

SUNSTONE
PRESS

SANTA FE

Sunstone books may be purchased for educational, business, or sales promotional use.
For information please write: Special Markets Department, Sunstone Press,
P.O. Box 2321, Santa Fe, New Mexico 87504-2321.

Book and cover design › Vicki Ahl
Body typeface › Minion Pro
Printed on acid-free paper
∞
eBook 978-1-61139-437-5

Library of Congress Cataloging-in-Publication Data

Names: Caldwell, Clifford R., 1948- | DeLord, Ron.
Title: Eternity at the end of a rope : executions, lynchings and vigilante
   justice in Texas, 1819-1923 / by Clifford R. Caldwell and Ron DeLord ;
   foreword by Dave Johnson.
Description: Santa Fe : Sunstone Press, 2015. | Includes bibliographical
   references and index.
Identifiers: LCCN 2015033715| ISBN 9781632930880 (softcover : alk. paper) |
   ISBN 9781632930897 (casebound : alk. paper)
Subjects: LCSH: Punishment--Texas--History--19th century. |
   Punishment--Texas--History--20th century. | Lynching--Texas--History--19th
   century. | Lynching--Texas--History--20th century. |
   Vigilantes--Texas--History--19th century. |
   Vigilantes--Texas--History--20th century.
Classification: LCC HV9466 .C35 2015 | DDC 364.6609764--dc23
LC record available at http://lccn.loc.gov/2015033715

Sunstone Press is committed to minimizing our environmental impact on the planet. The paper used in this book is from responsibly managed forests. Our printer has received Chain of Custody (CoC) certification from: The Forest Stewardship Council™ (FSC®), Programme for the Endorsement of Forest Certification™ (PEFC™), and The Sustainable Forestry Initiative® (SFI®).

The FSC® Council is a non-profit organization, promoting the environmentally appropriate, socially beneficial and economically viable management of the world's forests. FSC® certification is recognized internationally as a rigorous environmental and social standard for responsible forest management.

WWW.SUNSTONEPRESS.COM
SUNSTONE PRESS / POST OFFICE BOX 2321 / SANTA FE, NM 87504-2321 /USA
(505) 988-4418 / ORDERS ONLY (800) 243-5644 / FAX (505) 988-1025

Dedicated to the innocent victims and to all of those
who were falsely accused and suffered the consequences.

Contents

Foreword
by
David Johnson

It may be the most feared word in whatever language it appears in—mob. In North American popular culture it has come to symbolize vigilante justice, particularly in the nineteenth century west. Walter Van Tilburg Clark's chilling novel *The Ox-Bow Incident* is one of the most graphic depictions of vigilante justice or, in this case, injustice.

Lynching is most common during times of economic and or social tension. It has never been confined to the United States as some might believe, but is rather a global phenomenon stemming from what psychologists term herd mentality. In more recent times, it is sometimes linked with the hedonistic phrase "the greater good." Whatever the justification, mob mentality is rarely, if ever, a good thing.

Law on the frontier, whatever frontier it may be, is always harsh. In the case of Texas where Mexican banditos, Anglo outlaws and savage Indian raiders of various tribes struck frequently with impunity during the 1800s, necessity frequently and perhaps necessarily outweighed the finer points of justice. After all, why should people along the Rio Grande risk their lives hauling a convicted murderer hundreds of miles for a legal hanging when there was a convenient tree limb close by?

Similarly, sentences were carried out swiftly. Jails during the early years of Texas history were notoriously unreliable and frequently absent from the frontier counties. Tales of prisoners being shackled to a tree are not uncommon. Further, jails were not always secure. After the Civil War mobs frequently liberated prisoners to either return them to their native haunts or to exact summary justice. Texas passed a law to construct Huntsville prison in 1848. Its second prison, Rusk Penitentiary, was not established until 1883. Both were in eastern Texas and far from the frontier counties.

The authors have done a great service to all those interested in Texas history. While they admittedly point to the fact that out of necessity their undertaking may not be totally complete, their work is a major contribution to both Texas and Americana history. The circumstances leading to each perpetrator's execution, legal or otherwise, are documented and their sources noted. Undoubtedly, it will be a classic work. While some may view it simply as a research tool, it is an entertaining read as well, documenting the cold-eyed predators to whom life and punishment were cheap. The frequently inhumanity of man upon himself and the need, then and now, for the citizens to be able to protect themselves, is clearly highlighted. As founding father George Mason once wrote, "To disarm the people is the most effectual way to enslave them."

Introduction

The use of capital punishment as a penalty or consequence when dealing with malefactors who have committed severe infractions of established laws, and as a vigilante tool, dates back to when societal groups were first formed. The United States of America, together with China, Japan, several Asian, Middle Eastern and African countries allow capital punishment. Lynching and vigilante justice occurs in practically every corner of the world.

At present, thirty-two states allow the death sentence. A total of sixty-nine countries maintain the use of capital punishment. Almost ninety per cent of all known executions take place in just five countries: China, Iran, Pakistan, Iraq, and Sudan. At least 1,722 people were sentenced to death in fifty-eight countries in 2012. That same year Amnesty International recorded executions in a total of twenty-one countries. Executions took place in Egypt and Syria as well, although the numbers could be confirmed. The United States accounted for only 2.5% of the total, logging thirty-five deaths by lethal injection during 2014, two of which were female.

The administration of capital punishment by hanging, by means of a rope fashioned into some form of a slipknot or hangman's noose dates back at least as far as 13th century England. Prior to the 13th century methods of executions were even more barbaric than hanging, and included practices like back breaking, boiling in oil, burying alive, crucifixion, keelhauling, stoning, drawing and quartering, beheading and impaling.

Hangings in the New World began basically as soon as colonists arrived. One of the first cases in involved a man named of John Billington. Billington arrived with the original band of pilgrims at Plymouth Colony aboard the Mayflower in 1620. According to reports, Billington was prone to blasphemous language. He got off to a bad start on his journey when, during the trip across the Atlantic he became involved in an altercation with the ship's captain, Miles Standish. Standish ordered crewmembers to tie Billington's feet and neck together as an example to others of "...a sin-struck man possessed of a Devil's tongue." Ten years after his arrival in the New World Billington became the prime suspect in the murder of a man named John Newcomen. In due course he was hanged by his neighbors in 1630, thus becoming the first American to be "lynched."

So far as how the gruesome process of execution by hanging actually works, the person to be finished customarily stood over a trapdoor on a platform that was purpose built for the occasion. A rope was secured to a wooden beam overhead

with the other end fastened around the individual's neck using a special slipknot known as a "hangman's noose" or "hangman's collar." The individual charged with the task of "executioner" pulled a lever that opened the trapdoor which, when sprung, allowed the subject to fall through the opening
in the floor.

In theory, the subject would travel downward until the length of rope allotted had expired. The sudden stop at the end would break their neck, killing them.

The length of the rope had to be carefully calibrated in proper proportion to the subject's weight. If the rope was too short, insufficient velocity was generated by fall and the neck would not be broken, resulting in a painful and protracted death by strangulation. If the rope was too long, excessive velocity was produced which could result in the victim being decapitated. That was an especially gruesome sight to observe. Even when care was taken to make certain that the rope was of the correct length a subject with an unusually large or strong neck may not die instantly, and be left dangling hopelessly at the end of their tether.

No form of execution at the time was completely painless. The prospect of a death by a hanging gone horribly wrong was high. In some cases the equipment failed. Such was the case with the hanging of James McLean. Sheriff Benjamin Barton of Genesee County, New York botched that job on 28 August 1807. The incident took place in front of a large crowd. When the executioner pulled the lever and actuated the trapdoor McLean fell through the opening. When he reached the end of his rope the thing snapped in two. McLean tumbled to the ground entirely unharmed. A new rope was quickly located and the process begun again. On the second try the desired results was achieved. As an aside, McLean had been sentenced to hang for the murder of two people. Many mused that it was entirely fitting that he should have been hanged twice.

The term "lynching" has its origin in the United States. In the late 18th century, in Pittsylvania County, Virginia, citizens were troubled by the difficulty of administering punishment to criminals because the closest courts were too distant. On 22 September 1780, a man named William Lynch, along with a group of his neighbors, argued that Pittsylvania had "...sustained great and intolerable losses by a set of lawless men...that...have hitherto escaped the civil power with impunity." The group agreed to respond to reports of criminality in their neighborhood by "repair[ing] immediately to the person or persons suspected...and if they will not desist from their evil practices, we will inflict such corporeal punishment on him or them, as to us shall seem adequate to the crime committed or the damage sustained."

In short William Lynch and his neighbors drew up a compact of vigilante punishment allowing them to become judge, jury and executioner. Fortunately Lynch's treatment for shortcutting justice did not catch on, but Lynch did have the misfortune of having his surname forever associated with this unsavory practice of unlawful execution.

Lynching was generally much less sophisticated than a legal hanging Webster's defines lynching as "...to put to death, especially by hanging, by mob action and without legal authority" and "...the administration of summary punishment, especially death, upon a suspected, accused, or convicted person by a mob acting without legal process or authority." By definition these "lynching's" were often carried out in the heat of the moment, by mobs of angry citizens outraged by the misdeeds of the subject.

Many were administered without benefit of a proper hangman's knot, and/ or without the use of a conventional gallows structure. One source claimed that they had pinpointed 2,805 victims of lynch mobs in the southern states between 1882 and 1930 alone. These figures do not include Texas, and focus mostly on Alabama, Mississippi, Georgia, Louisiana, Arkansas and Florida which together account for a whopping 76.5% of the cases. In terms of ethnicity, although 300 whites were strung up during that period almost 2,500 blacks met the same fate. The reader might be surprised to note that other sources have reported that there were roughly 1,200 cases of lynching, unlawful execution or man burning in Texas between 1819 and 1942.[1] The authors have documented at least an additional 650 additional incidents that had been overlooked, bringing the tally closer to 2,000.

Throughout Texas' history one can find examples of hangings and lynching in every corner of the state. Cattle King John Chisum related a tale of having chased a cattle rustler for miles. When his men finally overtook the fellow they were unable to find a tree of sufficient height to properly hang the outlaw, so they improvised by lashing the man's legs in a kneeling position to compensate for the diminutive hanging tree.

In a case that occurred in May 1930, involving the murder of Fannin County Deputy Sheriff George Forest Fortenberry by a black man named George Johnson, local citizens exacted a full measure of vengeance. After locating Johnson, who at the time was hiding in a cabin near town, a mob of posse members estimated to numbering 300 opened fire on the tiny structure. When the smoke cleared Johnson's bullet riddled body was found inside. Simple death was not sufficient. The crowd hurried into town with Johnson's lifeless corpse fastened to the bumper of a truck. There they dragged the corpse a distance of about two miles, circled the village and stopped in front of a black church. There they lynched the now mutilated and practically unrecognizable corpse of Johnson to a tree. Not yet content, the throng dowsed the battered cadaver with gasoline and set it ablaze.

The mob, estimated to have reached 1,000 souls, did not disburse until a rainstorm passed over.

As the United States entered the 20th Century, Texans can take some measure of comfort in the fact that the Lone Star State did not hold the record for lynching, flogging, and man burning. Georgia holds that grim distinction, logging the majority of the nearly 4,000 acts of human atrocity. Arkansas may have hit the high water mark for the most ingenious method employed, when citizens decided to torture a black man by twisting his arms and legs out of their sockets.[2] To be certain, no state can claim to not have taken part in the horrific practice of lynching and man burning.

In Texas, legally administered death by hanging came to an end at McKinney on 31 August 1923, with the execution of a man named Nathan Lee. Lee had been convicted of murder.

The only other lawful method of execution used in Texas during this period was death by firing squad, which was often used during the Civil War. In one such case a thirty year old black man named Pess White who had been convicted of attempted outrage in 1864 was executed by firing squad.[3]

The reader will find that African Americans were most often the victims of lynching, especially in post-Civil War Texas. Although this fact may not come as a shock to the studied historian, the number of incidents and the frailty of the evidence with which the individuals were found guilty was startling. When it came to impromptu executions, Mexicans were only slightly more fortunate than blacks. In Chapter I of *Decade of Disorder* the author Nicholas Villanueva states that:

> *Anglo men responded with threats to punish those who violated the color line with legal or extra legal punishment. Between 1848 and 1928 there were 597 known lynching cases of people of Mexican descent in the US; more than 47% occurred in Texas.*[4]

Villanueva's statistics came from William D. Carrigan and Clive Webb article "The Lynching of Persons of a Mexican Origin or Descent in the United States 1848-1928" which appeared in the Journal of Social History #37 in 2003. Carrigan's work on the subject is valuable, although not always precise or complete. Villanueva, on the other hand, does not consider the impact of the Mexican Revolution on Texas, nor does he take into account the prevalence of looting across the border by Mexican and Indian bandits. True enough, reciprocal pillaging was common, none-the-less, Mexicans in Texas stood in line immediately behind Blacks when it comes to being victims of vigilante justice.

An article in the *Beaumont Journal,* circa 1899, commented that, "The trouble about mobs is that when they are permitted to kill without any punishment they finally kill not for offenses, but because of beliefs and because of unpopularity." The piece went on to say, "let the law punish those who commit offenses. The courts are organized for the purpose." More true words have never been spoken.[5]

Cultured readers will be shocked at the barbarity of some of the incidents in this book. Many events were nothing short of morbid theater worthy of another era, perhaps the Dark Ages, but not multicultural, predominantly Christian Texas. One wonders about the thought process of a mother and father who gleefully pack a picnic lunch, load the children into the family carriage and raced off to the Friday hanging at the town square.

Many times these public executions were witnessed by thousands...not dozens. Often the onlookers had to secure a ticket to attend. In scenes reminiscent of "the lions versus the Christians" in the coliseums of ancient Rome, the unsophisticated technology of the day made each and every hanging a crap shoot, with bystanders wagering whether the victim would suffocate or have his or her neck snapped. Better yet, perhaps the head would be catapulted from the body like the wilted bloom of a marigold, adding greatly to the morbid spectacle.

This book covers legally sanctioned executions and non-legal actions that were done by means of hanging or lynching, man burning, and in a few select instances floggings and shootings. In the case of lawful hangings, some form of public record generally exists. Records of lynchings, on the other hand, run the gamut from well documented to little more than rumor or folklore. In the case of the latter, the authors have attempted to put forth whatever credible evidence exists while leaving the final verdict regarding the veracity of the incident to the reader's judgment.

Given that no previous historian has accurately documented all of the legal executions and vigilante actions in Texas, the authors were faced with a protracted and seemingly endless research project. Documented lynching cases, along with those that are mere folklore, dot the annals of Texas history. In order to complete the work in a reasonable time we acknowledge that there may be some cases yet to discover.[6]

Without question, capital punishment is a topic of heated debate. Those on both sides of the conversation have strong feelings to express. This book does not attempt to rationalize, justify or condemn capital punishment. The authors have simply recorded the incidents that took place in Texas chronologically, for the benefit of historians and researchers. We have undertaken the task without bias in terms of race, gender, religion, nationality or social class. No agenda is intended, nor should one be perceive. As one wise historians and authors once said, "It is best to gather the facts first, then form one's hypothesis...not the other way around."

Language and Construction

During the process of compiling this book the authors gave careful consideration to the matter of standardization of language, reference and construction. This book spans a century and a half, and for the most part covers incidents that took place over a hundred years ago. Subtle changes have occurred in the common use of the English language as it is spoken in the United States during that period. Terminology that was once commonplace is seldom heard in twenty-first century discourse. Equally, words that are now recurrently used were not a part of the vocabulary of the day, or in some cases may have had subtly different meanings.

Throughout this text the reader will find that although the authors have retained the style of the period for various terms. An effort has been made to avoid the numerous opportunities to reference or cite the gratuitously descriptive text of some newspaper accounts.

Certain expressions of the day are used. The period term "outrage" has been chosen in lieu of the hard-edged word "rape." Many of the condemned souls who went to the gallows or were lynched were African-Americans, Native Americans or Hispanics.[7] The more period-correct categories of Black, Mexican and Indian have been chosen instead, and are uniformly and respectfully used throughout.

In terms of style, the authors have used the Chicago Manual of Style, 14th Edition. Notes at a section in the back of the book provide the reader with background.

Acknowledgements

The list of names dates and summary of the incidents listed in this book took years to assemble. It is the product of untold hours of work, and contains the contributions of many historians, authors, researchers and dear friends who took time from their busy lives to lend a hand. The authors would like to believe that this book is the best, most complete and accurate work of its kind ever assembled, that owing in large part to the contributions of so many fellow historians.

The individuals involved in the research necessary to produce the dozens of historical books and reference materials cited in the bibliography are extensive. We acknowledge all for their valuable contributions to the field of history. Special recognition is due to Retired Dallas County Sheriff's Assistant Chief Deputy Terry Baker, who has generously shared his personal files as well as his and hard found research material, adding valuable detail to our work. Retired Fort Worth Police Sergeant Kevin Foster, author of several books on the history of the Fort Worth Police Department, gave valuable assistance by sharing his research as well.

Donaly E. Brice, former Senior Research Assistant at the Texas State Library and Archives Commission, and all of the volunteers there have provided needed material throughout the course of this undertaking. Our hats are off to them as always. Other friends and colleagues have contributed both research material and on some cases text. Readers will find quotes or summaries written by noted Texas authors including Dave Johnson, Bob Alexander and Chuck Parsons.

The oft-despised newspaper journalist deserves a word of thanks as well. Literally hundreds of tabloids from across the nation were used for source material and are cited in the bibliography. During an era that preceded the instantaneous communications and around-the-clock news cycle we have today, thousands of these journalists wrote volumes of articles over two centuries offering readers a glimpse into the events of the day. Some proved accurate and unbiased, others presented an agenda or point of view. All proved useful, even if only to be used as a bad example.

We thought that because we had power,
we had wisdom.
　　　　　　　—Stephen Vincent Benet

Texas Executions 1819 to1923
(In Chronological Order)

Brown, George
Born: (Unknown)—Date of Death: November 1819
Place: Galveston County
Event: Quasi-Legal Execution/Hanged

The first permanent European settlements on Galveston Island were constructed some time around 1816, by the pirate Louis Michel Aury as a base of operations to support Mexico's rebellion against Spain.[8] Following that insurrection, the Congress of Mexico issued a proclamation on 17 October 1825, establishing the Port of Galveston.

George Brown, notorious pirate and ship's captain, was the first person on record to have been executed in Texas. Brown, a white man, was convicted by Jean Lafitte's admiralty court of the crime of piracy. He was hanged on Pelican Island in November 1819. Lafitte, a notorious pirate and privateer, had established a brigand stronghold and settlement at Galveston Island which he called "Campeche" and nominated himself as its sovereign.

For a long time Laffite refused to commission George Brown as a captain. Speculation as to his hesitation center around the belief that he did not trust Brown, and it was vital that he have men under his command that he could rely on. Over time Laffite relented. Brown's first act was the theft of several slaves from a plantation near Lake Charles, Louisiana. This alerted the United States revenue cutter *Lynx*. In October 1819, Brown attempted to capture an unarmed American merchantman just offshore near the mouth of the Sabine River. The *Lynx* witnessed the incident and immediately engaged Brown. During the affray Brown, who is referred to as a "fierce character," ran his vessel aground and, in the company of four of his men, made good his escape. He returned to Galveston.[9] Laffite, fearing reprisal from the United States because of the Brown's actions, ordered that Brown be executed by hanging. The remainder of Brown's crew was turned over to the commander of the *Lynx*. According to legend, another man named Francois, who was a member of Lafitte's band of ne'er-do-wells, was hanged for his role in a plot to rob and murder a Louisiana sugar planter and slave buyer named Kuykendall. Kuykendall had come to Galveston Island to buy slaves from Lafitte. [10]

Brown is said to have been hanged from a conspicuous gallows at the east end of the island where the body was left swinging and was "picked by the birds on the sands of the bay."[11]

Finch, Barney
Born: (Unknown)—Date of Death: 8 February 1834
Place: Nacogdoches County
Event: Legal Execution/Hanged

Looney, Samuel

Born: (Unknown)—Date of Death: 8 February 1834

Place: Nacogdoches County

Event: Legal Execution/Hanged

Saunders, John

Born: (Unknown)—Date of Death: 8 February 1834

Place: Nacogdoches County

Event: Legal Execution/Hanged

Barney Finch, Samuel Looney and John Sanders, all white men, were executed by hanging at Nacogdoches County on Saturday, 8 February 1834.[12] The threesome went to the gallows together. All were murderers.

As an aside, Samuel Looney had been a delegate to the Convention of 1832. The group met at San Felipe de Austin on 1 October 1832, in response to an address issued there on 22 August 1832, by Horatio Chriesman, First Alcalde and John Austin, Second Alcalde of the Municipality of Austin. This address recommended that each town, precinct, and civil district in Texas elect five delegates. Stephen F. Austin was elected President, and F. W. Johnson, Secretary. The rules of the Senate of the State of Missouri, so far as applicable, were adopted for the government of the proceedings of the Convention.[13]

Clayton, Joseph

Born: (Unknown)—Date of Death: July 1834

Place: Fort Bend County

Event: Legal Execution/Hanged

Joseph Clayton, a white man, was tried of murder and found guilty. He was executed by hanging at Fort Bend County in July 1834.

Clayton had stabbed a man named Abner Kuykendall at San Felipe in June 1834. Kuykendall, who was a Stephen F. Austin Old 300 Colony Pioneer and noted Indian fighter of the era, died in late July 1834.[14] Kuykendall's grave has never been found.

One Unidentified Indian Woman

Born: (Unknown)—Date of Death: July 1835

Place: On Brazos River Central Texas

Event: Lynching/Decapitation

A posse of eighteen men decapitated an unidentified Indian woman for resisting capture. The exact location of the incident is not known.[15]

One Unidentified Indian Man
Born: (Unknown)—Date of Death: circa 1836
Place: Central Texas
Event: Lynching/Shot

A posse of ten to twelve white men killed an unidentified Indian horse thief.[16]

Jones, Bob
Born: (Unknown)—Date of Death: circa 1837 or 1838
Place: Unknown County
Event: Legal Execution/Hanged

The *Austin Journal* relates an interesting story involving an early legal hanging in Texas. The article lacked enough specificity to accurately pinpoint the county in which the episode took place, but it was a newly established venue that did not have much in the way of infrastructure or resources. It seemed that a known desperado named Bob Jones was tried for murder. The judge found him guilty. Owing to the fact that there was no jail or suitable lodging, no bed or blankets, Jones was ordered to be immediately removed from the court and hanged.

With a lariat borrowed from a bystander, Jones was led by the sheriff to a tree a few feet distant. The rope was looped around his neck and the thing done as prescribed...right then and there. All in order, just as the judge had decreed.[17]

Jones, David
Born: (Unknown)—Date of Death: 28 March 1838
Place: Harris County
Event: Legal Execution/Hanged

Quick, John
Born: (Unknown)—Date of Death: 28 March 1838
Place: Harris County
Event: Legal Execution/Hanged

David Jones and John Quick, both white men, were tried and convicted of murder. The men were escorted to their place of execution by a group of about 100 soldiers who had been drafted from several militia companies in the city. A large crowd gathered to witness the event.

The gallows had been constructed in a beautiful stand of timber on the prairie, about a mile south of Houston. Quick made a long and eloquent speech during which he condemned gambling and the wearing of concealed pistols. He went on to meet his fate with great firmness. Jones maintained his claim of innocence and silence, appearing to be stupefied with fear and shame.

At about 2:00 pm on Wednesday, 28 March 1838, both were executed by hanging and buried beneath the tree upon which they had met their end.[18]

Campbell, Michael
Born: (Unknown)—Date of Death: 28 April 1838
Place: Victoria County
Event: Legal Execution/Hanged

Michael Campbell, a white man, was indicted for murder by a grand jury on 26 April 1838. He was put on trial the next day and found guilty. District Judge James W. Robinson, who sentenced Campbell to death by hanging, denied a motion for a new trial.

Campbell was a native of New York. He had killed a man named Lindsay. Campbell had received a change of venue to Jackson County where, in the absence of a jail, he was chained to the sill of a house.[19] After the trial the sheriff delivered a bottle of whiskey to the jury. When two of the jurors had managed to consume a great deal of the ardent spirits, they laid down to sleep. Campbell asked for, and received, another change of venue. This time back to Victoria. Unfortunately for him it was at that place where he was convicted and hanged.

Legend has it that Campbell was hanged on the same day that he was sentenced, from the limb of a post oak tree in what later came to be known as the Diamond Hill section of Victoria. [20]

Six Unidentified Mexican Men
Born: (Unknown)—Date of Death: November 1838
Place: Nacogdoches County
Event: Legal Execution

In newspaper accounts of the day sources claim that six unidentified Mexican men were executed for high treason at Nacogdoches. They had been involved in a recent revolt against the Texas constitution.[21]

Morris, Given Name Unknown
Born: (Unknown)—Date of Death: 28 December 1839
Place: Travis County
Event: Legal Execution

A corporal named Morris, who was a member of the First Regiment of Texas Infantry, was charged and found guilty of assault with intent to commit murder on Captain Kenneymore. Kenneymore, who was acting as officer of the day at the time of the incident, served in the soldier's own regiment.[22]

Corporal Morris was executed at Austin on Saturday, 28 December 1839. According to the *Austin Gazette*, "...he met his fate with Roman firmness."[23]

Sloan, J.
Born (Unknown)—Date of Death: circa 1840-1841
Place: Colorado County
Event: Lynching/Hanged

Some time during March or April 1843, Samuel Damon and Captain Heard found the skeleton of a man, along with a horse, at San Bernard, just a few miles from the mill located along the banks of a stream. The man had obviously been hung since the lariat used to do the job was still looped around his neck. The horse had been shot in the head. A shaving box with the initials J. S. was discovered nearby. The subject remains were believed to have been those of J. Sloan who had disappeared two or three years earlier.[24]

Forbes, Henry
Born: (Unknown)—Date of Death: 13 November 1840
Place: Galveston County
Event: Legal Execution/Hanged

Henry Forbes, a black man, was captured and held at an old military brig building that was used as a jail called "The Elbe."[25] Forbes was arraigned before Judge A. B. Shelby on Friday, 10 April 1840, on charges of burglary. The jury was unable to agree on a verdict. He was returned to jail but managed to break free. Forbes was re-captured, and when district court convened in October 1840, was charged with jail breaking. Forbes was tried and convicted on 17 October 1840, and sentenced to death under Section 9 of the Texas Republic's criminal code, which carried the death penalty for either offense at that time.[26]

Escaped slaves were liable to recapture. Those legally free might be seized on fraudulent claims and enslaved by law. Free papers were by no means conclusive evidence that blacks were entitled to their freedom. Forbes admitted, on the gallows, that a white man had made-up the documents.

Sheriff William F. Wilson carried out Forbes' sentence on Friday morning, 13 November 1840. He was hanged "...on the bay shore in the eastern part of the city..." [27] Forbes was said to have been a bad character, and rode to his hanging sitting on his own coffin in the back of a wagon, singing a hymn as he traveled the route to his execution.

Humphreys, Given Name Unknown
Born: (Unknown)—Date of Death: circa 1841
Place: Galveston County
Event: Legal Execution/Hanged

Newspaper accounts of the day indicate that a man identified only by the surname of Humphreys was found guilty of stealing horses. Afterwards he was whipped harshly for his crime. Following that ordeal he was accused and found guilty of murdering a man named C. W. Jackson. For that infraction Humphreys was hanged.

Indications are that Humphreys may have been taken across the bridge to Logansport, Louisiana for the actual lynching. If that was the case then this incident should be categorized as a Louisiana lynching (although the crime as well as the vigilante sentence occurred in Texas).[28]

Yocum, Thomas D.
Born: (Unknown)—Date of Death: circa 1841
Place: Harris County
Event: Lynching/Shot

One or Two Unidentified White Men
Born: (Unknown)—Date of Death: circa 1841
Place: Harris County
Event: Lynching/Shot

Pine Island is located in Jefferson County. Thomas D. Yocum (identified as Yoakum by some newspapers) had a large land grant in the area. Yocum owned more than a hundred slaves and thousands head of horses and cattle. He was considered one of the richest men in Texas. Local residents suspected Yocum and his compatriots of being thieves and murderers who were being protected by his considerable wealth and influence.

Yocum's unraveling occurred when he was suspected of planning the murder of a man named Carey, a wealthy citizen from Houston County who was staying at his home. Yocum believed that Carey was transporting a large sum of money. A black servant of Carey's learned of the plot and warned him to flee. Carey, who only narrowly escaped, alerted local residents of Yocum's plan to rob him. A meeting that was attended by more than 100 local residents took place soon after, resulting in a decision to drive the gang out of the county.

Yocum got wind of the plan and decided to flee west, taking with him some of his cohorts and slaves. The mob overtook them in their flight at Big Cypress, near Houston. Yocum and one or two of his men were shot to death. The slaves were tied to trees and questioned, resulting in their confession of Yocum's criminal acts. A number of missing person cases were soon revealed to have been murders committed by the Yocum gang. A subsequent examination of Yocum's house revealed a well containing several human skulls. Apparently Yocum had been murdering travelers who stayed at his home and tossing their heads down the shaft.[29]

Two Unidentified White Men
Born: (Unknown)—Date of Death: circa 1841
Place: Red River County
Event: Lynching/Hanged

Newspaper accounts of the day indicate that two unidentified white men were lynched as horse thieves without benefit of a trial.[30]

Two Unidentified White Men
Born: (Unknown)—Date of Death: circa 1841
Place: Austin County
Event: Lynching

Newspaper accounts of the day indicate that two unidentified white men were killed at Austin County. No reason or circumstance was provided by the source.[31]

Two Unidentified White Men
Born: (Unknown)—Date of Death: circa 1841
Place: Jefferson County
Event: Lynching

Newspaper accounts of the day indicate that two unidentified white men were killed at Jefferson County and the home of one burned to the ground. A mob of self-styled regulators did the work.[32]

One Unidentified White Man
Born (Unknown)—Date of Death: circa 1841
Place: Washington County
Event: Lynching/Shot

Newspaper accounts of the day indicate that one man, claimed to have been a murderer, was shot to death.[33]

Harlow, Guy M.
Born (Unknown)—Date of Death: circa June1841
Place: Fort Bend County
Event: Lynching/Shot

Guy M. Harlow was incarcerated in the Fort Bend County jail on a charge of manslaughter. During the night a person or persons unknown fatally shot him through the jail house window. [34]

Unknown Number of Unidentified White Men
Born: (Unknown)—Date of Death: September 1841
Place: Harrison County
Event: Lynching/Shot

Newspaper accounts of the day speak of an unknown number of unidentified white men being lynched for having committed murder at Harrison County during September 1841.[35]

Reel, Henry
Born: circa 1805—Date of Death: 19 September 1841
Place: Refugio County
Event: Lynching/Hanged and Shot

Newspaper accounts of the day indicate that a white man named Henry Reel was hanged and subsequently shot to death by Mexican troops at the Mission of Refugio. Reel had killed a Mexican soldier and wounded several others when they had tried to enter his home. He was told to surrender and his life would be spared. When he complied, the troops tied a rope around his neck and pulled him behind a horse for ten miles, afterwards hanging him by his feet and shooting him full of holes. [36]

Reel was the local magistrate. He had come from North Carolina to Texas in about 1835. His name appears on the Williams Settlement Census, which was taken on 21 April 1835...the same day as the Battle of San Jacinto. [37] Some sources have recorded Reel's surname incorrectly, as Ryal.

Jackson, Given Name Unknown
Born (Unknown)—Date of Death: circa October 1841
Place: Shelby County
Event: Lynching/Shot

Lowler, Given Name Unknown
Born (Unknown)—Date of Death: circa October 1841
Place: Shelby County
Event: Lynching/Shot

Newspapers accounts of the day chronicle a civil disturbance in Shelby County between the Regulators and the Moderators. One tabloid described the Regulators as "Lynchers" having about 200 members and the Moderators as "decent people" having roughly 100 souls in their ranks. Political bias in reporting is apparently not a twenty-first century phenomenon after all.[38]

In about October of 1841, a party of Regulators headed by Captain Jackson burned two dwellings owned by Moderators to the ground. A band of Moderators said to number nearly 100 strong pursued Jackson, overtaking him and his traveling companion named Lowler. The

Moderators shot the pair, killing Jackson and leaving Lowler fatally wounded. Lowler's fate is not known. Newspaper reports claimed that during the previous year the men had refused to pay any tax, calling themselves "The Independent Republic of Tenehaw."[39]

Bledsoe, Given Name Unknown
Born (Unknown)—Date of Death: circa October 1841
Place: Shelby County
Event: Lynching/Shot

McFadden, Given Name Unknown
Born (Unknown)—Date of Death: circa October 1841
Place: Shelby County
Event: Lynching/Hanged

McFadden, Given Name Unknown
Born (Unknown)—Date of Death: circa October 1841
Place: Shelby County
Event: Lynching/Hanged

A group of five men were traveling in Shelby County when Regulators overtook them. One of the group, a man named Bledsoe, was shot and killed. Another fellow named Strickland was shot and seriously wounded when he tried to escape. Three others, all having the surname McFadden, were taken to Shelbyville where two of them were hanged on a Saturday night (precise date unknown).[40]

Boatright, Given Name Unknown
Born: (Unknown)—Date of Death: November 1841
Place: Harrison County
Event: Lynching/ Shot, Mutilated and Hanged

Marauders from the Republic of Texas crossed into Caddo Parish, Louisiana and took forcible possession of a man named Boatright. They carried him back into Texas and proposed to bury him alive. As his grave was being dug Boatright tried to escape into the thicket. A volley of musket fire brought him to the ground. His body was cut up and hung in trees as a warning to travelers. Boatright's transgression was not mentioned. It was not uncommon for gangs of men organized as Regulators or Moderators to exact vigilante justice during this period in East Texas.[41]

One Unidentified Mexican Man
Born: (Unknown)—Date of Death: circa 1842
Place: Jackson County
Event: Lynching/Hanged

Sometime in late June or early July 1842, an unidentified Mexican man who had been cohabitating with a black slave woman was taken out and lynched near Texana. The man had planned on escaping with the girl to Old Mexico. When the plot was uncovered, the punishment was swiftly administered.[42]

Lynch, Given Name Unknown
Born (Unknown)—Date of Death: circa May 1842
Place: Austin County
Event: Lynching/Hanging

A man named Lynch, who had been causing fear in the neighborhood of San Felipe, was hanged without trial. He had reportedly killed one or two citizens and threatened the lives of others. Civil authorities had been searching for him but fate intervened, resulting in his execution outside the bounds of the law. It is ironic that his surname was Lynch. One wonders if that coincidence played some role in his fate.[43]

Allen, Isaac
Born: (Unknown)—Date of Death: 21 April 1843
Place: At Sea - Aboard the Texas Navy Warship *Austin*
Event: Legal Execution/Hanged

Hudgins, James
Born: (Unknown)—Date of Death: 21 April 1843
Place: At Sea - Aboard the Texas Navy Warship *Austin*
Event: Legal Execution/Hanged

Landois, Antonio
Born: (Unknown)—Date of Death: 21 April 1843
Place: At Sea - Aboard the Texas Navy Warship *Austin*
Event: Legal Execution/Hanged

Simpson, William
Born: (Unknown)—Date of Death: 21 April 1843
Place: At Sea - Aboard the Texas Navy Warship *Austin*
Event: Legal Execution/Hanged

The navy of the Republic of Texas was on blockade duty off the Yucatan Peninsula in Mexico. Apparently a plot was fomented whereby two of the ships would be seized and taken to Vera Cruz where they would be turned over to Mexican authorities. The plan was never put into action. In February 1842, a mutiny broke out on the Republic of Texas schooner, *San Antonio* that, at the time, was anchored at New Orleans. Lieutenant Fuller was killed and two other officers wounded. Nine sailors were arrested and jailed. A courts martial was held on board the *Austin,* a 600-ton sloop-of-war that was under the command of Commodore Edwin Ward Moore. On Friday, 21 April 1843, Isaac Allen, James Hudgins, Antonio Landois and William Simpson were found guilty and executed for their treachery.[44]

Commodore Moore had resigned his commission in the US Navy at age twenty-nine to join the Republic of Texas Navy. Under his command, Texans blockaded the Mexican coast and controlled the Gulf of Mexico. Republic of Texas President Sam Houston dismissed Moore on 1 June 1843, charging him with disobedience and suspending his service. Later, Moore was found not guilty of those accusations by courts martial. He was, however, found blameworthy of four minor infractions.

Henniker, Charles
Born: (Unknown)—Date of Death: 8 December 1843
Place: Galveston County
Event: Legal Execution/Hanged

Henniker was a German immigrant farmer who operated a market garden a few miles from the town of Galveston. He was a man of notable bad disposition who often found himself at odds with his neighbors. He also made frequently appearances before the justice of the peace as a consequence of his vile comportment.

Henniker's neighbor, Benjamin Tyson, also raised vegetables for nearby markets. On Wednesday morning, 20 September 1843, Tyson's partner made a trip to town to sell produce. Upon his return he discovered Tyson dead and the house on fire. Henniker was brought to town and interrogated under suspicion of having committed both the murder as well as the house firing. He denied responsibility for either. A German woman who was living at his home at the time confessed to having knowledge of the incident, but only after being assured that she would be protected from Henniker's wrath. Apparently Henniker had gone to Tyson's home, struck him in the head with a mallet and threw him down the well. He robbed the residence of a few trifling article then set fire to the house and left.[45]

Henniker went to trial on Thursday, 2 November 1843, and was found guilty of murder robbery. On Friday morning, 8 December 1843, he rode to his execution seated on his coffin in the back of a wagon smoking his pipe. A gallows for the purpose of the hanging had been erected on the shore of the bay. Given an opportunity to address the crowd, Henniker called out a long list of those against whom he had bad feelings. After a lengthy display of animosity, some directed at Mr.

A. F. James for whom he had uniquely hostile regard, Henniker was halted in his endless oration and prepared for the hanging. Sheriff A. N. Smyth tried to place a black hood over the stubborn old man's head but Henniker asked that he be allowed to witness the event. His wish was granted. When the trapdoor fell Henniker swung down as planned, but his neck was not broken by the drop. He dangled there, swaying back and forth, eyes open and gazing at the crowd for a time before his movement ceased and, apart from a few kicks of the foot, his spirit flew from its mortal host.

Three Unidentified Indian Men

Born: (Unknown)—Date of Death: circa 1844
Place: Central Texas
Event: Lynching/Shot

A posse of ten to twelve white men reportedly killed three unidentified Indians who were horse thieves.[46] This incident, along with a number of similar cases that have been reported by this particular source, remains unconfirmed.

Wiles, William "Bill" or "Wild Bill"

Born: circa 1779—Date of Death: 8 May 1844
Place: Shelby County
Event: Lynching/Hanged

A white man named William Wiles who hailed from Maryland and who had come to Texas by way of Missouri wished to remain identified only as "Wild Bill" to conceal his identity. At home in Maryland Wiles had come from a respectable family. That fact did not protect him from the hangman's rope at Shelbyville, Texas when he was accused of murdering a man named Runnels.

"Wild Bill" confessed that he and another man had been employed by certain individuals in Texas to kill five men in exchange for a fee of $1,000. Runnels was on that list. "Wild Bill" was dispatched to his eternal reward without benefit of a formal trial, merely the vengeance of an outraged community.[47] Wiles left behind a wife, Sarah Elizabeth Bowman, and thirteen children.[48]

Jones, Andrew "Andy"

Born: (Unknown)—Date of Death: 8 June 1844
Place: Hunt County
Event: Legal Execution/Hanged

Mitchell, Given Name Unknown
Born: (Unknown)—Date of Death: 8 June 1844
Place: Hunt County
Event: Legal Execution/Hanged

Wray, L.
Born: (Unknown)—Date of Death: 8 June 1844
Place: Hunt County
Event: Legal Execution/Hanged

White, Harvey
Born: (Unknown)—Date of Death: 8 June 1844
Place: Hunt County
Event: Legal Execution/Hanged

A band of horse thieves had established themselves between the Mississippi and Sabine Rivers, headquartered at a place where the town of Lone Oak in Hunt County now stands. The leaders of the gang were two men named Wray and Mitchell.

In April 1844, two members of the outfit named Andy Jones and Harvey White, both white men, unwisely decided to relieve a band of Indians of their possessions by murdering three of the group. Local whites thought little of the matter until it became known that the Indians intended to extract their revenge by killing all of the local white settlers unless something was done about the atrocity.

Motivated by this very real threat, word went out to all surrounding regions to send representatives to Meredith Hart's place in Sulphur on the first Monday in June 1844. Accordingly, a large group gathered, including Judge John B. Simpson from Fannin County. After two days of hearings and three hours of deliberation a verdict of guilty was returned. The four outlaws were sentenced to death by hanging. That verdict was to be carried out on Saturday, 8 June 1844.

As decreed, a large pole was placed in the crotch of two trees standing close together and all four condemned men were loaded into a wagon that was positioned beneath. Nooses were fastened to the pole, the other ends to the four men respectively. Words of religious consolation were spoken and, at the appropriate signal, the wagon was pulled away leaving the men to hang until suffocated to death.

This story remained untold until a correspondent of the *Philadelphia Times* newspaper reported it in 1891. Henry Skidmore, in his seventies by 1891, was one of few persons still alive who had witnessed the hanging. Skidmore was a resident of Muskegon, Michigan at the time the article was published.[49]

Unidentified Black Man
Born: (Unknown) —Date of Death: July 1844
Place: Galveston County
Event: Lynching/Hanged

According to legend, a black man, the slave of an Englishman named R. P. Jones who was living near the waterfront, attempted to outrage a woman named Mrs. Helfenstein. As there was an imperfect organization of courts for handling such matters, a jury of twelve citizens was empanelled to try the offender. The alleged perpetrator was found guilty and sentenced to be hanged.

The trial was denounced by some as "mob law." None-the-less, the unfortunate black man was removed from confinement by force of arms and lynched from the rafters of Sylvester's Barroom. His head was hacked off and his body tossed into the bay.[50]

Smith, Abraham W.
Born (Unknown)—Date of Death: 5 August 1844
Place: Madison County
Event: Lynching/Hanged

Abraham Smith was convicted of murder during the June term of court at Madisonville. The court stayed his sentence so that his attorneys would have time to file an appealed to the Supreme Court and request a new trial. On Monday, 5 August 1844, a mob took Smith from the county jail by force and hung him. John Sinclair, reported to have been one of the members of the mob, placed the noose around Smith's neck and helped to string him up. When officers tried to arrest Sinclair he fled the county.

In October a man recognized Sinclair while he was walking down a street in St. Louis, Missouri. The man swore out a warrant and had Sinclair arrested and placed in jail where, at last report, he was awaiting extradition to Madison County. A man named Mays, who was one of the ringleaders, was said to have remained on the wanted list while eight or ten other participants were arrested and released on bond. It is not known if anyone was ever prosecuted for the lynching of Smith.[51]

Castro, Given Name Unknown
Born (Unknown)—Date of Death: 29 November 1844
Place: Harris County
Event: Legal Execution/Hanged

On Thursday, 6 June 1844, the body of a man named B. Canfield, who resided near Houston, was discovered in a nearby bayou. He had been shot in the face and neck with fourteen pellets of buckshot. A slave named Castro, who belonged to Judge Campbell, was arrested. Castro was subsequently convicted and sentenced to death during the term of the court. His execution was set for Friday, 29 November 1844, however no document has been uncovered confirming that the hanging actually took place.[52]

McDaniel, John
Born: (Unknown) —Date of Death: 14 June 1845
Place: Jackson County
Event: Legal Execution/Hanged

Brown, Joseph
Born: (Unknown) —Date of Death: 14 June 1845
Place: Jackson County
Event: Legal Execution/Hanged

Certain accounts of Texas executions list John McDaniel and Joseph Brown as having been legally hanged at Jackson County on Saturday, 14 June 1845. Confirmation of these executions has proven difficult to uncover.[53]

One Unidentified Black Man
Born (Unknown)—Date of Death: 23 July 1845
Place: Washington County
Event: Lynching/ Hanged

On Monday, 21 July 1845, Dr. D. A. Perry left his home on horseback riding to his plantation, which was located half-mile away. Several hours later, his horse returned without Perry. His family immediately began a search, eventually discovering his badly mutilated body nearby. A former slave was the suspect. Although there were no witnesses to the murder the black man allegedly confessed to the killing and was hanged on or about Wednesday, 23 July 1844.[54]

Simmons, Joseph
Born: (Unknown) —Date of Death: 28 November 1845
Place: Shelby County
Event: Legal Execution/Hanged

Joseph Simmons, a white man, was executed at Shelbyville on Friday, 28 November 1845. His crime was the murder of a man named James B. Tutt. The killing had taken place on 5 June 1845.[55]

Grinder, Jesse
Born: (Unknown)—Date of Death: 30 November 1846
Place: Fannin County
Event: Legal Execution/Hanged

A black slave known as Jesse who was the property of a Mr. Grinder was convicted of murder and sentenced to death for his crime. That verdict was carried out on Monday, 30 November 1846.[56]

Goodman, Given Name Unknown
Born: (Unknown)—Date of Death: 12 April 1847
Place: Montgomery County
Event: Lynching/Hanged

Samuel Grimmett was elected sheriff of Montgomery County on 13 July 1846. On Saturday, 27 March 1847, while Grimmett was in the discharge of his official duties he was shot and mortally wounded by a man named Goodman (or Goodwin). Grimmett lingered until Sunday, 11 April 1847, when he died from his wounds. The next day Goodman, who had been arrested and confined at the jail, was removed by force and hanged.[57]

Russell, Jean Baptist
Born: (Unknown)—Date of Death: 27 May 1847
Place: Colorado County
Event: Lynching/Hanged

Newspapers of the day indicate that a man named Jean Baptist Russell was lynched at Colorado County on 27 May 1847. Russell was charged with a murder.[58]

Jones, Given Name Unknown
Born: (Unknown)—Date of Death: circa June or July 1847
Place: Cherokee County
Event: Lynching/Hanged

A man named Jones from Cherokee County is said to have lived a rather unhappy home life, frequently at odds with his wife. He had threatened to take the couples child and give it to his mother because he believed his spouse to be unfit and unworthy. Sometime in June or July 1847, the couple began quarreling again. During the scuffle the child was accidentally killed. Jones then beat his wife to death and buried both her and the infant beneath some logs in a creek. Neighbors eventually learned of the murder and apprehended Jones.

Jones was brought to the county seat, but magistrates refused to accept him. He was then handed over to a mob that included the wife's brothers. Jones' father and brother were present but did not interfere. They did ask that he not be hanged until they were out of sight, and that they be given the body for burial afterwards.

Jones was strung up and lowered repeatedly until he confessed to the killings, then hanged a final time until he expired. Afterwards his father returned to claim the body and bury him.[59]

Wilkinson, Given Name Unknown

Born: (Unknown)—Date of Death: circa May or June 1847
Place: San Augustine County
Event: Lynching/Hanged

A man identified only as "Old Man" Wilkinson, said to have been a notorious hog thief, purloined some pigs from a neighbor named Sanders.

It seems that a man named Morris was to be the groom at a wedding ceremony that was to take place at the Sanders house. It is unclear from the documents as to why the Sanders home was the venue selected for the ceremony. The groom, Morris, had allegedly been whipped twice in Mississippi for "negro stealing."

"Old Man" Wilkinson sent food that was laced with poisoned to the wedding. As a result of consuming the tainted meal Mrs. Sanders, three children, several guests as well as a number of slaves died. It was claimed that Wilkinson had warned the bride and groom not to eat the food. Wilkinson, his wife and Morris' wife were arrested and released on bond. He tried to flee but was captured and hanged. Newspaper reports of the day claimed that he was a Moderator and Sanders a Regulator, thus establishing the motive for the poisoning. Some sources also claim that the incident occurred in Shelby County.[60]

Morris, Given Name Unknown

Born: circa 1829—Date of Death: circa October 1847
Place: Nueces County
Event: Lynching/Hanged

A young man identified only as Morris, aged about eighteen or nineteen, was sent to Corpus Christi to stand trial for murder. At the District Court he was found guilty of manslaughter and released on bail. Morris took up with a man from New Orleans. They later became involved in an argument during which Morris insisted that they settle the matter in a pistol duel. The gentleman declined. At his first opportunity, Morris shot him in the heart and killed him.

Morris was returned to jail. In due course he and two other men charged with murder escaped. Morris was soon captured, but the posse decided that since he was such a hard case they should go ahead and hang him on the spot..., which they did. The other two escapees surrendered and were returned to custody. [61]

Nelson, Given Name Unknown
Born (Unknown)—Date of Death: 9 June 1848
Place: Red River County
Event: Legal Execution/Hanged

At the fall term of the court at Clarksville a slave identified only as Nelson was charged with the murder of a man named Luckey. He was convicted, but his attorney appealed to the Supreme Court arguing that the jury had not been properly sworn in. The appeal was rejected. Nelson was found guilty on a Friday and hanged the following Friday, 9 June 1848. Before he met his fate Nelson expressed his displeasure that a fellow identified only as "Boy Alee," and others, who he had also been charged as having been involved in the killing were not being punished.

When the trap was sprung Nelson dangled at the end of his tether for about ten minutes before expiring. Newspaper opined that Nelson's appeal was a mere quibble, and the price tag for jailing Nelson for eighteen months would cost the county a great deal.[62]

Martin, Juan
Born: (Unknown)—Date of Death: 14 November 1848
Place: Nueces County
Event: Lynching/Hanged

On election night, Tuesday, 14 November 1848, a man named Samuel Righton was the instigator in a disagreement between Juan Martin and David Ivy. Martin killed Ivy during the fight that followed. For his role in the affray Righton was severely beaten.

Martin was arrested and confined in jail at Corpus Christi for what clearly appeared to have been self-defense. During the night, a mob of masked men seized Martin and hanged him.[63]

Fourteen Unidentified White Men
Born: (Unknown)—Date of Death: circa 1849
Place: Washington County
Event: Lynching/Hanged

An East Coast newspaper carried the fantastic story of fourteen men, members of what they called a "robber clan," being lynched for their nefarious deeds at Washington County. The source claimed that the incident had taken place sometime before September 1849. Surprisingly, this mass hanging seems to have escaped the view of all but a lone tabloid, giving rise to concerns about it's veracity.[64]

Shook, Parson

Born: (Unknown)—Date of Death: circa 1849
Place: Grayson County
Event: Lynching/Shot

A white man identified as Parson Shook was lynched at Paris, in Grayson County.[65] Shook was "outlawed up," and may have had an accomplice or two who met a similar fate at the same time.

It is presumed that Shook's given name was Parson, and that he was not a man of the cloth. There are no genealogical records of any kind for a person named Parson Shook...in Texas or elsewhere. There was, however, a man named Nathan Shook who hailed from Missouri and who died in Texas in 1849 at the age of thirty-one. Thus, one might hypothesize that either Nathan Shook was this man, the surname referenced is incorrect, or that this person named Shook was actually a preacher.[66]

Short, William

Born: 1 January 1820—Date of Death: 9 July 1849
Place: Washington County
Event: Lynching/Hanged

William Short, a white man, was lynched at Brenham, in Washington County, on Saturday, 9 July 1849. Sources claim that Short had taken up the outlaw way and paid the price at the end of a lynch mob's rope for his trouble.[67]

Mills, Jack

Born: (Unknown)—Date of Death: July 1849
Place: Starr County
Event: Lynching/Shot

Sometime in late July 1849, a white man named Jack Mills shot and killed a prominent Mexican gentleman at a fandango (dance) held at Rio Grande City. His actions were unprovoked. A meeting of citizens quickly took place, during which Mills' measures were condemned, along with Mills himself. A group of populace was appointed to carry out the sentence. They faithfully completed their charge by shooting Mills more than thirty times with musket balls, extinguishing his life as had been instructed.[68]

One Unidentified Indian Man
Born: (Unknown)—Date of Death: circa 1850
Place: Central Texas
Event: Lynching/Shot

A posse of twenty-nine white men killed an unidentified Indian horse thief sometime during 1850. This report, found in Carrigan's book The Making of a Lynching Culture, seems a bit peculiar considering that scores of Texas Indians who were killed during this era for stealing horses from settlers. A precise tally of the victims would be impossible to compile. Interested readers should consult a reliable source such as J.W. Wilbarger's book Indian Depredations in Texas.[69]

Guerra, Juan Chapa
Born: (Unknown)—Date of Death: January 1850
Place: Cameron County
Event: Lynching/Whipped

A Mexican man identified as Juan Chapa Guerra was whipped so severely that he died from the thrashing. The incident took place at Brownsville, in Cameron County, sometime in January 1850. As it turned out, Guerra's death was a tragic incidence of mistaken identity, as he had committed no crime.[70]

Two Unidentified Black Men
Born: (Unknown)—Date of Death: 15 April 1850
Place: Fayette County
Event: Legal Execution/Hanged

Two unidentified black men murdered a fellow named Gerard Haydon near La Grange on Friday, 5 April 1850. The pair was executed for the crime ten days later, on Monday, 15 April 1850.[71]

Flores, Francisco
Born: (Unknown)—Date of Death: July 1850
Place: Cameron Texas
Event: Lynching/Hanged

From accounts of the day, provided by a local newspaper called the *Flag,* a young Mexican man named Francisco Flores had shot and killed another Mexican at a Monte Bank. Afterwards he attempted to escape, back into Old Mexico. Flores was apprehended in the process, returned to Texas, and lynched by his captors...all this in the span of twenty minutes.[72]

Hardy, William "Bill"
Born: circa 1814—Date of Death: 12 July 1850
Place: Cameron County
Event: Lynching/Hanged

William "Bill" Hardy, a gambler who hailed from Kentucky, was a notorious malefactor and ruffian.[73] On Thursday, 11 July 1850, Hardy followed Captain John Brennan out of a bar at Brownsville and murdered him with a knife. Brennan, it seems, had refused to surrender his cash to Hardy, thus provoking Hardy to slay him. Still sporting the murder weapon which was covered with Brennan's blood, Hardy returned to the establishment saying, "I am a tart; and that's the way I will serve any man who follows me."

Once authorities became aware of Brennan's death men were sent to the various ferry crossings to prevent Hardy's escape into Mexico. He was subsequently apprehended the following morning, Friday 12 July 1850. On investigation, it was discovered that Hardy had also killed a man at St. Louis, one in Arkansas, and had attempted to kill several persons at Austin, Galveston and San Antonio as he worked his way south. This known, a committee of citizens decided to cut short his career as a highwayman and murderer and lynch him right away.

A crowd formed, seemingly up to the task. They stormed the jail, demanding the key that they might liberate Hardy to their custody. The jailor explained that he understood the circumstances, and was willing surrendered the keys without a struggle so long as Hardy would be allowed to deliver a final oration. . The mob agreed, and Hardy was transported to the intended site. Once there he explained that he understood that he had to die, but would prefer to be shot rather than hanged. Unfortunately for Hardy no one was willing to pull the trigger, thus the mob fell back to the original plan of lynching. Reverend Cravens came forth from the multitude and asked if Hardy had anything to say. The condemned man spoke briefly regarding the disposition of his possessions, then asked the Reverend to pray for him.

Next Hardy took the rope intended for his hanging and tied the noose, showing the novice crowd of vigilantes how the thing was to be done. Someone in the swarm, not trusting Hardy, untied the rope fearing a trick. Once done, the doubting fellow was then unable to duplicate the knot.

Frustrated with the inept rabble, Hardy clamored into the cart that was intended to be the gallows platform, climbed onto the plank and fastened the rope around his own neck. He asked to have his hands bound behind his back. The cart was then moved forward and Hardy, defiant as ever, met death in the same manner in which he had lived his life...bold and reckless.[74]

One Unidentified Black Man
Born: (Unknown)—Date of Death: August 1850
Place: Tyler County
Event: Lynching/Hanged

Newspaper accounts of the day indicate that sometime in early August 1850, a black slave who was the property of a man in Montgomery County tried to outrage a white woman in Tyler County. It seems that the victim, a girl identified as Miss Houston who was residing of Village Creek, had taken a stroll into the woods when the black man attacked her. He bound and gagged her then pummeled her body severely as he attempted to violate her honor. Miss Houston managed to avoid the outrage and sounded the alarm. The black man was subsequently chased to the Caney settlement when he took shelter in a schoolhouse.

When discovered and pressed by the pursuing posse he made a run for it, whereupon his trackers fired their weapons, wounding him seriously enough that he was unable to continue his flight. Word was sent to Mr. Houston who joined the captors in deciding to lynch the man. That decision was promptly carried out. Afterwards it was learned that the attacker had committed sundry lesser crimes during his flight from the attack on the young Houston woman. This, I am certain, gave the vigilantes further comfort that they had done the right thing by lynching the man without benefit of trial or verdict.[75]

Wiley, Taylor
Born: circa 1797—Date of Death: August 1850
Place: Rusk County
Event: Lynching/Shot

Taylor and Verlinda Fennel-Wiley, of Van Zandt County, had recently undergone a separation. Mr. Wiley proposed a property settlement, which apparently, seemed acceptable to Mrs. Wiley. The pair then traveled to their former residence to affect the bargain. Rather than culminating the deal, Mr. Wiley asked Mrs. Wiley to join him in the yard whereupon he shot her in the head with a pistol, killing her instantly.

A number of citizens tracked Wiley to Rusk County where they overtook him and executed him.[76] This incident occurred sometime in late July or early August 1850. The Wileys' had three sons who survived this ordeal.[77]

Fifteen Unidentified Men
Born: (Unknown)—Date of Death: circa 1851
Place: El Paso County
Event: Lynching/Hanged

One East Coast newspaper reported that "There have been some terrible examples of lynch Law at El Paso," claiming that fifteen had met their end by that means sometime prior to June 1851.[78]

As is so often the case, this particular tabloid failed to include sufficient information to validate their claim, leaving the ardent researcher to wonder if this incident is related to the legal hangings of Butler, Craig and Wade that took place on 31 January 1851.[79]

Reports such as this, although salacious, lack specificity and often credibility. They do, however, dot the annals of history and need to be acknowledged in an encyclopedic account of this nature. There were actually four men legally hanged at El Paso in 1851.

Two Unidentified Mexican Men
Born: (Unknown)—Date of Death: 10 January 1851
Place: Cameron County
Event: Legal Execution/Hanged

Slaughter, Howard
Born: (Unknown)—Date of Death: 10 January 1851
Place: Cameron County
Event: Legal Execution/Hanged

Howard Slaughter, a white man, and two unidentified Mexican men were all severally convicted of murder at the district court session proceeding January 1851. They were all sentenced to be hanged. That verdict was carried out on Friday, 10 January 1851 at Brownsville.

All three men confessed their respective guilt at the gallows. Reverend Chamberlain of the Presbyterian Church made an impressive prayer at the request of Slaughter. A Roman Catholic Priest addressed the gathered throng as well, expressing the sorrow and regrets of the culprits for their deeds in Spanish. As he met his fate, Howard Slaughter offered the following sound advice: "Beware of liquor, for it has brought me to this."[80]

It is not uncommon for convicted criminals sentenced to death to express sorrow for their deeds and repent, just at the instant when the Gates of Heaven come into view.

Butler, Marcus
Born: (Unknown)—Date of Death: 31 January 1851
Place: El Paso County
Event: Legal Execution/Hanged

Craig, William
Born: (Unknown)—Date of Death: 31 January 1851
Place: El Paso County
Event: Legal Execution/Hanged

Wade, John
Born: (Unknown)—Date of Death: 31 January 1851
Place: El Paso County
Event: Legal Execution/Hanged

Newspapers of the day were quick to report that armed bands of ruffians, teamsters, discharged soldiers, frontiersmen and all forms of rabble have been causing riot, disorder, murder and execution at Socorro. On the 28th and 29th of January, the rabble "...ranged like wild beasts..." throughout the town until citizens were compelled to send for troops from nearby San Elizario.[81]

On the evening of Wednesday, 29 January 1851, a particular group of malefactors went to a fandango in search of a man named E. C. Clark, son of a Senator from Rhode Island.[82] They fired off pistols, terrified the women and threatened the men, causing a very ugly uproar. Finally the leader of the group, Alexander Young, aided by three other ruffians, John Wade, Marcus Butler and Craig Young, gave Clark nine or ten mortal wounds. Another partier named Charles Gates was badly shot during the affray.

The morning following the incident members of the Boundary Commission sent for help from nearby San Elizario. This time the response was strong. A mounted band of Mexicans and Americans arrived within three hours and rounded up eight or ten of the evildoers including Wade, Butler and Craig. Young, the leader of the crowd managed to escape.

On 30 January the threesome were brought before Judge Berthold and arraigned. The following day they were tried and convicted of murder. A death sentence was ordered, and on Friday, 31 January 1851, they were strung up from the branches of trees and executed. At about 2:00 pm the three men were buried alongside their victim Mr. Clark.[83]

Young, Alexander
Born: (Unknown)—Date of Death: 12 February 1851
Place: El Paso County
Event: Legal Execution/Hanged

Alexander Young, a white man who was the ringleader of the incident (see above) that took place on the evening of Wednesday, 29 January 1851, involving the murder of E. C. Clark, son of a Senator from Rhode Island, was eventually captured on February 10 and brought to Socorro for trial on the 11th.

Young made a full confession in writing. He was executed by hanging on the 12th, swinging from the same tree that his companions had decorated just two weeks previous.[84]

Wersdoerfer, Joseph Heinrich
Born: circa 1809—Date of Death: 3 July 1851
Place: Comal County
Event: Lynching/Shot

A white gentleman of German ancestry named Joseph Wersdoerfer was charged with horse theft at New Braunfels. Wersdoerfer had arrived in Texas in 1844 with his wife Anna Schmidt and their two young children.[85]

The accusations against Wersdoerfer stemmed from an incident that occurred on the Comal

River involving the animal's rightful owner, Mr. Perryman. Bound in chains, Wersdoerfer went to trial. Evidence was presented sufficient to all but two jurors to convict him. Infuriated at the court's inability to agree on a verdict the august body had no choice but to release the man.

Wersdoerfer, a locally known scoundrel, promptly traveled to the home of a woman whose husband was away and attacked her for some trifling cause, shooting her in the head with his pistol loaded with cut lead. This incident took place on 2 July 1851, about a mile from New Braunfels. Wersdoerfer was, once again, taken into custody and transported to town under the guard of six men. For want of a jail, he was chained and kept at the courthouse.

Much to the delight of townspeople, someone shot and killed Wersdoerfer through the open window of the courthouse on Thursday, 3 July 1851, thus saving them the trouble of another trial and a bothersome hanging.[86]

One Unidentified Black Man
Born: (Unknown)—Date of Death: 7 July 1851
Place: Washington County
Event: Lynching/Hanged

On Sunday, 6 July 1851, an overseer of Dr. Peebles was in the process of whipping a black servant girl belonging to Peebles when a black man from the crowd of onlookers sprang forth and stabbed him twice in the heart with a knife. The enraged black man then turned on Dr. Peebles who, had it not been for the interference of other slaves, would have killed him as well.

A jury of local citizens was quickly assembled and a trial of sorts was given to the black fellow. As the popular adage goes, "...he was given a fair trial and a speedy hanging" which was promptly administered bright and early on Monday morning, 7 July 1851.[87]

One Unidentified Black Man
Born: (Unknown)—Date of Death: August 1851
Place: Travis County
Event: Lynching/Hanged

A fugitive black slave lad who had earlier been seized by Mr. Baker and taken to his house decided to improve his situation and, once again, escape. To accomplish this he first needed to murder Mr. Baker and his wife.

Determined to win his freedom the youth carried out the double murder. Soon afterwards, he was captured while hiding in a corncrib near Austin. The lad was taken to the jail and housed for protection.

A committee of a dozen citizens was appointed to review his situation. The group traveled to the jail where they were refused entry. Thereupon they forced their way in, removed the young man, tried, convicted and lynched him.[88]

O'Connell, A. W.

Born: (Unknown)—Date of Death: August 1851
Place: Caldwell County
Event: Lynching/Hanged

A. W. O'Connell, a white man who had murdered John Euren at Huntsville some days' prior, was captured at Caldwell County for possessing a stole horse. O'Connell was immediately lynched. [89] Poor O'Connell's fate proves once again that "...one can get away with murder in Texas, but not with horse theft."

Ragsdale, Peter Hamilton

Born: circa 1818—Date of Death: December 1851
Place: Bastrop County
Event: Lynching/Hanged

A white man identified only as Ragsdale shot down a teamster named Smith while the man was sitting around a campfire. The wounds proved fatal as Smith expired the following morning. Two brothers of Smith pursued Ragsdale and captured him. He was taken before citizens of the area and found guilty of murder. A rope was fastened to a branch of a tree and to Ragsdale, then he was run up where he dangled until all signs of life had left his mortal body.

     Based on the newspaper article that related this story the incident is thought to have occurred on 15 or 16 December 1851.[90]

Eight Unidentified Mexican Men

Born: (Unknown)—Date of Death: April 1852
Place: Starr County
Event: Lynching/Hanged

A hapless fellow named Patton who was from the Brazos left Rio Grande City for the interior of Texas in pursuit of "Maverick" cattle. En route, he stopped to spend the night at a popular camping stop called "The Wells" where a gang of Mexican highwaymen waylaid and robbed him of his possessions, then murdered him.[91]

     The culprits were tracked down. One was captured. After a speedy trial at Rio Grande City the man was found guilty and hanged. At the occasion of his lynching he gave up the name of his accomplice. A party of men set out for Roma to apprehend the fellow, which they did. He was also quickly strung up.

     The work of the posse was not yet over, as they also managed to capture six additional Mexican men who had been regularly involved in bushwhacking travelers in the vicinity, robbing and murdering them for the possessions. Among their suspected victims was a Mr. Thomas H. Harris of Rome. The party also killed the six Mexican men, thus bringing the tally of dead outlaws in this particular incident to eight. Before they died, they confessed to having been a part of an organized gang from the other side of the river whose purpose was to murder American travelers.[92]

Sharkey, August
Born: (Unknown)—Date of Death: 4 April 1852
Place: Calhoun County
Event: Lynching/Hanged

August Sharkey, a white man and a recent immigrant from Mississippi, provoked and attacked on an innocent man at Lavaca in Calhoun County. Sheriff James Preston Fulkerson intervened and took Sharkey's weapon from him. Sharkey, infuriated by the officer's actions, demanded "it or him." Fulkerson would not relent, and ordered Sharkey to leave town at once.

Rather than complying with the sheriff, Sharkey went to Justice Maulding for a writ of replevin for his weapon. As soon as the gun was back in his possession he marched to Fulkerson's office and shot him in the head. The wound was fatal.

Sharkey was immediately arrested and placed in irons. At a town meeting that was quickly convened Starkey's record as a malefactor, as well as his guilt in the murder of Fulkerson, was revealed to all.

Starkey was returned to confinement, but during the course of the night a mob of vigilantes removed him from custody under force. The following morning his body was discovered hanging from a nearby tree.[93]

One Unidentified White Man
Born: (Unknown)—Date of Death: May 1852
Place: Houston County
Event:Lynching/Hanged

An unidentified white man of German ancestry was murdered by a fellow compatriot at the town of Crockett. Local citizens seized the fellow and did the same for him, hanging the man from a tree until he expired.[94]

Brown, James
Born: (Unknown)—Date of Death: 3 July 1852
Place: Houston County
Event: Lynching/Hanged

A man identified only as James Brown was hung for murder at Crockett, in Houston County, sometime around 3 July 1852.[95] It is possible that this is the same incident as the one described above titled "One Unidentified White Man" dated May 1852.

Surname Unknown, Daniel
Born: (Unknown)—Date of Death: 14 May 1853
Place: Fort Bend County
Event: Lynching/Hanged

Surname Unknown, Hector
Born: (Unknown)—Date of Death: 14 May 1853
Place: Fort Bend County
Event:Lynching/Hanged

Two black slaves identified as Hector and Jim Monroe, along with a black preacher named Daniel, conspired to murder their owner Mr. Lewis Lum. Their plan was to kill Lum by shooting him. Their involvement was ascertained by means of a powder horn belonging to Daniel that was discovered concealed in a pile of cottonseed. Once confirmed, Daniel and Hector were handed over to the sheriff who placed them in jail.

As might be expected, their stay there was a brief one. During the night a mob of fifty or sixty vigilantes, disguised so as to mask their identity, broke into the jail and lynched the pair from a convenient nearby tree.[96] Jim Monroe seems to have gotten away.

Elkins, Jane
Born: (Unknown)—Date of Death: 27 May 1853
Place: Dallas County
Event: Legal Execution/Hanged

Jane Elkins, a black slave woman from Dallas, had been hired to care for the children of Mr. Wisdom. Although her proficiency as a nanny was not mentioned, her prowess as a killer was sufficient to accomplish the murder of Mr. Wisdom. She was indicted on 10 May 1853, tried and convicted on the 16 May 1853, and sentenced to death on Thursday, 17 May 1853.

Elkins went to the gallows on Friday, 27 May 1853. She is believed to be the first woman to have been legally executed in Texas.[97]

Kennedy, Given Name Unknown
Born: (Unknown)—Date of Death: 21 June 1853
Place: Starr County
Event: Lynching/Hanged

On Tuesday, 21 June 1853, a white man identified only as Kennedy murdered a soldier identified only as Corporal Riley at Rio Grande City. Riley was attached to Lieutenant Tilford's company of Mounted Rifles. Immediately following the incident Kennedy fled to the Mexican side of the river to avoid capture. A reward of $100 was offered for his arrest and return. The sum was eminently sufficient to insured that someone would go over and fetch Kennedy. He was promptly returned, then lynched from a convenient tree thus settling the matter satisfactorily. [98]

One Unidentified Black Man
Born: (Unknown)—Date of Death: August 1853
Place: Smith County
Event: Lynching/Hanged

An unidentified black man outraged and murdered Mrs. John T. Hooper (Cooper) at Smith County. Hoping to prevent the lad from telling the story of his awful deeds, the villain also slit the throat of the woman's young son in the course of his attack. Fortunately for authorities the youth survived and was able to identify his mother's killer. The murderer was quickly apprehended by authorities, and even more quickly taken from their control and lynched on the spot as a crowd of about 500 looked on.[99]

One Unidentified Mexican Man
Born: (Unknown)—Date of Death: 20 August 1853
Place: Travis County
Event:Lynching/Beaten, Hanged and Shot

An unidentified Mexican man whose crime is not known was taken across the river from town, whipped most barbarously, hung until he was nearly dead then cut down and shot. He died of his wounds twenty-four hours later.[100]

Washington, Given Name Unknown
Born: (Unknown)—Date of Death: 24 August 1853
Place: Red River County
Event: Legal Execution/Hanged

Various accounts of this incident are conflicting so far as the date and details are concerned. What can be confirmed is that a black slave named Washington, who belonged to a white man named Epperson, had runaway and was subsequently captured at Fort Arbuckle. John Wilkins, of the firm of Epperson and Wilkins, brought Washington back to Clarksville where he took him to a blacksmith shop to have a set of leg irons fashioned for him. In what seems a foolish move, Washington was given a sledgehammer to act as the striker. While Wilkins bent over the anvil Washington hit him on the head. Epperson, who was Wilkins' brother-in-law, heard Wilkins scream and found him mortally wounded. He died about ninety minutes later from the results of the blow.

Washington fled, but was soon captured. It was reported that Washington had been caught stealing several weeks earlier, and had threatened to burn the town to the ground and kill the constable.

One source, the *Washington Reporter*, stated that "A negro [Negro] in Red River County, Texas, committed murder on Monday, Sept. [September] 20, was indicted on Tuesday, tried on Wednesday, and hung on Thursday." Actually, 20 September was a Tuesday and the murder occurred on or about 11 or 13 of August 1853.

The Clarkesville *Standard* reported that "...a special term of the District Court under the Statute of the Republic is to be held on Tuesday next for the trial of the Negro man Washington, whom murdered Mr. Wilkins." The *Nacogdoches Chronicle* had the definitive date. Washington was indicted on Tuesday, 21 August, tried on Thursday, 23 August and hanged on Friday, 24 August.[101]

Fitzgerald, Given Name Unknown
Born (Unknown)—Date of Death: circa September 1853
Place: Webb County
Event: Lynching/Hanged

A man named Fitzgerald reportedly murdered a man named Robinson at Laredo in the spring of 1853. Some time following that incident Fitzgerald was taken from the custody of lawmen and shot several times. On the morning following the incident, a rope was placed around his neck and he was positioned on a horse. The animal was driven from beneath him thus accomplishing the hanging. Sources noted that the citizens must have had little confidence in the law to deal full justice in the Fitzgerald case.

One source claimed that the hanging incident occurred at Saledo.[102]

One Unidentified Black Woman
Born (Unknown)—Date of Death: 23 December 1853
Place: Walker County
Event: Legal Execution/Hanged

On Tuesday, 13 December 1853, the sons of Mrs. Randolph left their aged mother at her home, located about five miles from Huntsville, to attend a fox hunt. About 11:00 pm an unidentified black woman described as the "family negro [Negro]" took an axe and went into Mrs. Randolph's bedroom where she was sleeping with her granddaughter. There she struck them in the head with the weapon, inflicting mortal wounds. The black woman, who was reported to have had fits of insanity, did not try to escape.

On Friday, 23 December 1853, a jury of citizens tried the unrepentant black woman, found her guilty and sentenced her to be hanged. That judgment was to be carried out the same evening.[103]

Jones, George
Born: (Unknown)—Date of Death: circa 1854
Place: Madison County
Event: Legal Execution/Hanged

Jones, Nancy
Born: (Unknown)—Date of Death: circa 1854
Place: Madison County
Event: Legal Execution/Hanged

Nancy Jones and her son George, both white, were tried and convicted of murdering Nancy's husband (also George's father). The pair was sentenced to a term in prison. Dissatisfied with the result of their judgment the two requested, and were granted, a new trial.

At the second trial they were, once again, found guilty. At that hearing, however, much to their shock and horror they were sentenced to hang.[104] That verdict was carried out sometime in 1854, thus proving the old adage that sometime it is best to leave well enough alone.

One Unidentified Mexican Man
Born: (Unknown)—Date of Death: 2 January 1854
Place: Nueces County
Event: Lynching/Shot

Two Unidentified White Men
Born: (Unknown)—Date of Death: 2 January 1854
Place: Nueces County
Event: Lynching/Shot

According to unverified sources, a Mexican man who had killed a United States soldier was himself shot and killed at Corpus Christi by another soldier who was angry over the death of his colleague. The name of the victim in this case was not given. It is likely that this report is a duplication of an incident involving a group of white teamsters who were engaged in an affray with a band of Mexicans. The outcome of that dustup, said to have taken place on or about 10 January, was the death of two whites and the injury of three more.[105]

Flores, Lino
Born: (Unknown)—Date of Death: 5 January 1854
Place: Bexar County
Event: Legal Execution/Hanged

Quiroz, Francisco
Born: (Unknown)—Date of Death: 5 January 1854
Place: Bexar County
Event: Legal Execution/Hanged

Lino Flores and Francisco Quiroz, both Mexican men, were tried and convicted of murder. Each received a death sentence. That judgment was subsequently carried out on Thursday, 5 January 1854.[106] Flores is buried at the now defunct Campos Santo Cemetery in San Antonio.

One Unidentified Black Man
Born: (Unknown)—Date of Death: 21 March 1854
Place: Upshur County
Event: Legal Execution/Hanged

One Unidentified Black Woman
Born: (Unknown)—Date of Death: 21 March 1854
Place: Upshur County
Event: Legal Execution/Hanged

Two black slaves who murdered their master, a man named James Gentry, were found guilty and hanged on Tuesday, 21 March 1854. The incident had taken place at Gentry's plantation in Upshur County. Gentry's killers, a man and a woman, were working with him at the time constructing a fence. The male black man knocked him to the ground and the woman finished the job. Afterwards, the couple built a pyre of logs whereupon Gentry was placed until the flames had consumed his body. [107]

It was said that the two blacks had, "...very bad countenances, their appearance is brutal and revolting."[108]

Gonzales, Manuel
Born: (Unknown)—Date of Death: June 1854
Place: Bexar County
Event: Lynching/Hanged

Unverified sources claim that Manuel Gonzales, a horse thief, was lynched at San Antonio in June 1854. It seems that Gonzales's fondness for other people's horses was the source of his undoing.[109]

Linton, Dr. Given Name Unknown
Born: (Unknown)—Date of Death: June 1854
Place: Webb County
Event: Lynching/Hanged

Dr. Linton, a white man whose given name is not known, apparently murdered two men at Laredo. For his crime, two soldiers lynched him in June 1854.[110]

Wilson, James
Born: (Unknown)—Date of Death: 2 June 1854
Place: Tyler County
Event: Legal Execution/Hanged

James Wilson, a white man, was tried and convicted of murder. He received a death sentence. That judgment was carried out on Saturday, 2 June 1854. Unfortunately no evidence has been located as yet to support the claim.[111] There was a man named James Wilson who was convicted of murdering a man named William Adams. He was executed on 2 June 1854. The location of that hanging was Charleston State Prison in Massachusetts. Either this is a remarkable coincidence or perhaps this incident was accidentally categorized as a Texas case by journalists anxious to pad the tally.[112]

Wells, J. H.
Born: (Unknown)—Date of Death: 22 October 1854
Place: Navarro County
Event: Lynching/Hanged

A white man named J.H. Wells was found guilty of "negro [Negro] stealing." His conviction was based largely on the confession of a man named Morgan. Two mulatto boys were his targets. Wells had also planned to murder Colonel Elliot, their owner.

Wells was quickly taken charge of by an angry mob and lynched. Afterwards his body was horribly mutilated for good measure. After Wells was quite dead, Morgan recanted his confession, claiming that the persons who had a noose around his neck forced him to make the confession.[113]

Surname Unknown, Bob
Born (Unknown)—Date of Death: 30 March 1855
Place: Fayette County
Event: Legal Execution/Hanged

On or about 30 March 1855, J. A. Fitz, the acting Sheriff of Fayette County, executed a slave named Bob at La Grange. The death sentence was carried out near the town's graveyard. Bob had been found guilty in a court of law of murdering his master, D. D. McSween.[114]

Four Unidentified Mexican Men
Born: (Unknown)—Date of Death: circa May1855
Place: El Paso County
Event: Lynching/Hanged

Sources report that four unidentified Mexican men were lynched at El Paso for having outraged an entire family. Reliable Confirmation of this rather ambitious incident has proven difficult to locate.[115]

Hill, Franklin "Frankie"
Born: (Unknown)—Date of Death: 18 May 1855
Place: Gonzales County
Event: Legal Execution/Hanged

Newspaper reports of the day claim that a white man named Franklin "Frankie" Hill, who had been tried and convicted of murdering a man named John Guy on Peach Creek in February 1852, was hanged at Gonzales on Friday, 18 May 1855.[116]

One Unidentified Mexican Man
Born: (Unknown)—Date of Death: 31 May 1855
Place: Webb County
Event: Lynching/Hanged

An unidentified Mexican man who was suspected of having murdered a woman was said to have been tried, convicted and hung at Laredo by "judge lynch."[117]

Cady, Lovett
Born: circa 1805—Date of Death: 29 June 1855
Place: Red River County
Event: Legal Execution/Hanged

Lovett Cady, a white saloon owner, was tried and convicted of the murder of a man named Sinclair. He was hanged at Clarksville on Friday, 29 June 1855.

Cady's wife screamed as the noose was adjusted around her husband's neck, and ran to him once the trap had been sprung. The distraught woman attempted to hold Lovett up and prevent him from strangling. So determined were her efforts that the sheriff had to restrain her. After dangling for a full thirty-five minutes Cady was cut down and found to still be clinging to life. Later in the evening his spirit flew from his mortal body and Cady was at last at rest.[118]

Schultz, John Henry

Born: circa 1811—Date of Death: 29 June 1855
Place: Galveston County
Event: Legal Execution/Hanged

Early in January 1845, Simeon Bateman, a planter, and Matthew Jett, a young man residing in San Antonio, left Gonzales for Galveston. The pair was on their way to New Orleans to buy slaves. Bateman had $6,000 and Jett $1,000, with which they intended to make their purchases. They left their horses near Virginia Point with a man named John Schultz. Schultz had once lived with Bateman. During the night, Schultz murdered both men and robbed them of their valuable, including the $7,000 in specie they were carrying.

The next morning Schultz made his way to Virginia Point and boarded a ferry bound for Galveston. From there he caught a steamer to New Orleans. Some sources record this incident as having occurred on 19 June 1855.[119]

On the day of his departure the bodies of Bateman and Jett were discovered. Suspicion was immediately directed at Schultz. Lawmen were dispatched to Louisiana in pursuit of Schultz, but the trail eventually went cold somewhere near Mobile, Alabama.

Almost a decade passed with no word of Schultz. Suddenly, in 1855, a man named Ballinger from Gonzales was traveling in South Carolina and recognized Schultz at a local hotel. Authorities were alerted. Schultz was arrested and returned to Galveston for trial.

Schultz's attorney pled insanity as a defense, but jurors did not buy the claim and Schultz was found guilty. He appealed the decision, but on 5 February 1855, a higher court upheld the ruling. Schultz's only problem with lucidity was thinking that his past would not overtake him in Alabama.

On Friday, 29 June 1855, Schultz rode to his hanging seated on a coffin in the back of a wagon. He attempted to leap from the conveyance but was prevented from doing so by a guard. While climbing the gallows he made a few remarks to onlookers. Schultz confessed to having been born in 1811, in Indiana, and to having lived in Tennessee, Kentucky and Alabama. He also admitted to having been a member of the Murrell Gang.[120] John A. Murrell and Daniel Crenshaw were generally regarded as rough thieves, robbers, horse-stealers, negro-runners, highwayman, burglars and counterfeiters who operated largely in Tennessee.[121] When the gang broke up Schultz joined a group bound for Natchez and, once in Texas, enlisted in the army. Schultz deserted from the army and repaired to Mississippi where he induced a cousin who had some money to return to Texas with him. Once back in Texas he murdered the cousin and stole the money. Schultz had been implicated in the robbery of the patent office at Washington in 1855 and had, by his own admission, slain no less than seven or eight men during his lifetime.

At the appropriate signal, Sheriff Grove pulled the lever and the trapdoor fell, propelling the unrepentant Schultz into eternity where, and in all likelihood the devil received one of his own.

Ainsworth, William
Born: circa 1834—Date of Death: 31 July 1855
Place: DeWitt County
Event: Lynching/Shot

A man named William Ainsworth had apparently killed a man named Clinton at a political gathering in DeWitt County on Monday, 30 July 1855. He was apprehended and lodged in the jail at Clinton.

On or about Tuesday, 31 July 1855, armed men entered the jail and dropped a flaming turpentine ball into Ainsworth's cell. Next, they fired four volleys of buckshot into the man, fatally killing him while he was still in his cell.[122]

Eleven Unidentified Mexican Men
Born: (Unknown)—Date of Death: August 1855
Place: Nueces County
Event: Lynching/Hanged

Newspaper reports of the day indicate that Mexicans were becoming a great problem in the area and that eleven Mexican men were found along the banks of the Nueces River "...in a hung up condition..."[123]

Phillips, (Given Name Unknown)
Born: circa 1811—Date of Death: 5 October 1855
Place: Cass County
Event: Legal Execution/Hanged

Uncorroborated reports indicate that a black slave named Phillips was tried and convicted of murder. He was hanged in Cass County on Friday, 5 October 1855.[124]

Surname Unknown, Nathan
Born: (Unknown)—Date of Death: 26 October 1855
Place: Walker County
Event: Legal Execution/Hanged

A black man identified only by his given name of Nathan was hanged for murder at Huntsville on Friday, 26 October 1855. Nathan had been found guilty of murdering a teamster in Walker County.[125]

Dunn, William J.
Born: (Unknown)—Date of Death: November 1855
Place: Webb County
Event: Legal Execution

Newspaper reports of the day indicate that William J. Dunn, a white man and a private in the army, was executed at Fort McIntosh for mutiny sometime in November 1855.[126] It is unclear from the account if Private Dunn's sentence was actually carried out however.

One Unidentified Mexican Man
Born: (Unknown)—Date of Death: 1 December 1855
Place: Nueces County
Event: Lynching/Hanged

At about dawn on Tuesday, 1 December 1855, screams and cries were heard coming from the "Mexican part of town." One Mexican man was found dead and two women wounded. All had been cut with a knife. The newspapers reported that the incident had been spawned by the jealous rage of an unidentified man. The knife wielding fellow was arrested and placed in jail at Corpus Christi.

At about noon a crowd gathered at the mayor's office and demanded that the man be tried immediately. At the insistence of the mob, a hearing took place at about 3:00 pm. The justice remanded the man into the custody of the sheriff to be held for trial at the next session of the regular court. That night a number of citizens entered the jail, removed the prisoner by force of arms, and led him a half a mile from town where they hung him from a tree. His lifeless body was discovered some time afterwards, handcuffed and dangling from a branch.[127]

Two Unidentified Men
Born (Unknown)—Date of Death: circa 1856
Place: Robertson County
Event: Legal Execution/Hanged

The not always reliable source *The Death Penalty Information Center* indicates that two unidentified men were legally executed in Robertson County in 1856. Although questions persist regarding the veracity of this sources claim, the case is being included in the interest of completeness.[128]

Four Unidentified White Men
Born: (Unknown)—Date of Death: circa 1856
Place: Jack County
Event: Lynching/Hanged

One source reports that vigilantes in Jack County hanged four unidentified white men sometime during 1856.[129]

One Unidentified Mexican Man
Born: (Unknown)—Date of Death: circa 1856
Place: Starr County
Event: Lynching/Hanged

Ryan, Tom
Born: (Unknown)—Date of Death: circa 1856
Place: Starr County
Event: Lynching/Shot

In a related incident, a Rifle Regiment apprehended one unidentified Mexican man, a fellow named Tom Ryan along with a man named Hines near Rio Grande City. They were suspected of stealing horses from the government and robbing the church at Guerrera. It is unclear which was the greater crime in the eyes of Texans.

The Mexican was lynched. Tom Ryan was shot while trying to escape. He died soon afterward at the Ringgold Barracks. The third culprit, Hines, made good his escape but was wounded in the process.[130] Although the precise date of this incident is uncertain, it occurred some time before 1 June 1856.

An additional newspaper account of this case claims that Ryan and the Mexican man were also responsible for the murder of a man named Todd at Corpus Christi.[131]

Welch, Anthony
Born: (Unknown)—Date of Death: circa 1856
Place: Kinney County
Event: Legal Execution/Hanged

Private Anthony Welch of Company I, First Artillery, a white man, was tried by court martial and found guilty of murdering Sergeant Dennis H. Moore of the same company. The incident took place on Monday, 31 May 1856.

Welch was ordered to hang. His sentence was to be carried out on the fourth Friday of the month following his conviction, which based on the date of the newspaper article would likely have been December 1856. The precise date has not been ascertained.[132]

Blasingame, Woodson Martin
Born: circa 1798—Date of Death: 19 April 1856
Place: Blanco County
Event: Lynching/Shot

Blasingame, Calvin
Born: circa 1831—Date of Death: 14 April 1856
Place: Blanco County
Event: Lynching/Shot

Two men, Captain Callahan and Captain Johnson, went to the Blasingame home at Blanco to settle some sort of difficulty. The visit did not work out to well for the pair, as they were killed by Woodson Blasingame and his son Calvin.

Blasingame, his son Calvin and his wife Mary "Polly" were all placed under arrest. Not long after, on Monday, 14 April 1856, fifty to one hundred vigilantes removed Woodson Blasingame from custody and shot him to death. His son Calvin attempted to flee and was also fatally shot.[133]

Alexander, Burwell
Born: (Unknown)—Date of Death: 14 June 1856
Place: Orange County
Event: Lynching/Shot

Baxter, Given Name Unknown
Born: (Unknown)—Date of Death: circa June 1856
Place: Orange County
Event: Lynching/Shot

Fielden, John
Born: (Unknown)—Date of Death: circa June 1856
Place: Orange County
Event: Lynching/Shot

Meers (Mages), Given Name Unknown Doctor
Born: (Unknown)—Date of Death: 14 June 1856
Place: Orange County
Event: Lynching/Shot

Sexton, Charles
Born: (Unknown)—Date of Death: circa June 1856
Place: Orange County
Event: Lynching/Shot

Five-Six Unidentified White Men
Born: (Unknown)—Date of Death: circa June 1856
Place: Orange County
Event: Lynching/Shot

Although their transgression was not mentioned in the newspaper accounts of the day, Doctor Meers and Burwell Alexander had been warned by Regulators to leave Orange County. The men failed to comply. Their decision proved fatal, as they were shot to death by a mob of twenty to thirty men at Green's Bluff on Saturday, 14 June 1856. During the same time period Regulators were reported to have killed Charles Sexton, John Fielden, a man named Mr. Baxter, and five to six unidentified persons.

Alexander was involved in the murder of a man named Deputy. That incident occurred on Thursday, 15 May 1856. The killing sparked what would later become known as the "Orange County War of 1856."

The episode began when Deputy Samuel Deputy accused a freed black man named Clark Ashworth of butchering hogs that did not belong to him. Clark's cousin, Sam Ashworth, threatened to kill Deputy. Ashworth was charged with "abusive language by a mulatto" and sentenced to thirty lashes. He was remanded to Sheriff E. C. Glover, who was friendly with the Ashworth clan. Glover allowed Sam to escape.

Ashworth and his eighteen-year-old friend Jackson Bunch ambushed Deputy and a companion on Cow Bayou while the two men were rowing their boat to Deputy's home. Ashworth and Bunch shot Deputy and beat him with the butts of their guns. Deputy died. His companion escaped and alerted authorities. The sheriff made a halfhearted search attempt.

Two factions, called the Moderators and Regulators, quickly formed after this incident. The Moderators declared the sheriff's office vacant. Sheriff Glover and his supporters organized as Regulators. The Moderators eventually captured the sheriff at a Regulator meeting and killed him.

Bunch was brought to trial for the murder of Samuel Deputy. During the trial, which took place in Beaumont, rumors spread that friends planned to rescue Bunch. Because of the threat, people carried guns and knives into the courthouse during the trial. Bunch was convicted on 12 November 1856, and hanged two weeks later on 21 November 1856. The scaffold was so crudely constructed that the condemned youth had to climb a ladder that was then twisted and pulled out from under him.

Sam Ashworth fared somewhat better. After a period in west Texas, he fled to the Indian Territory and lived with the Choctaw tribe for several years. It is claimed, although unverified, that when the Civil War began he enlisted in the Confederate army and was killed at the Battle of Shiloh in April 1862.

In a letter to the editor of the *Calcasieu Press* in Louisiana dated 1856, to someone in Orange County Texas the incident involving Burwell Alexander is described in some detail, and provides a clue into why the man had been asked to leave Houston County.

The letter indicates that good citizens of the county are under arms, trying to drive out a gang of gamblers, cow, hog and horse thieves, mail robbers, mail burners, counterfeiters, and murderers, who have been collecting in this county for many years. The outlaws have increased in boldness as they grew in numbers.

Among them is William Ashworth, mulatto, who possessed a handsome stock of cattle. Ashworth's sons Luke and Henderson are also a part of the outfit. Luke Ashworth and others penned eighteen head of cattle belonging to the neighbors and killed them at one time, for the hides. He also assisted in the murder of Samuel Deputy. Clark Ashworth, William Ashworth's third son was recently bound over the court for the hog stealing. Another family member, Sam Ashworth, seems to inherit all the most diabolical qualities of the clan and was the murderer of Samuel Deputy, a very useful and enterprising citizen.

Those considered to be direct accessories to the murder of Deputy are Jackson Bunch, Ned Glover, Bill Blake, Burwell Alexander, and Henderson Ashworth, the Cow Thief.[134]

Hyde, John
Born: (Unknown)—Date of Death: 11 July 1856
Place: Harris County
Event: Legal Execution/Hanged

John Hyde, a white man, was tried and convicted of the murder of Charles Butler and a man named Nelson.

The Butler murder occurred in 1853. Hyde fled, but was returned from Arkansas to Texas in June 1855. He was tried in Harris County in December 1855. Hyde appealed his case to the Texas Supreme Court. The original verdict was upheld in March 1856.

According to other sources, while on the gallows and facing his death Hyde did not confess to the crime for which he had been condemned, but he did own up to killing the aforementioned Charles Butler along the Sabine River some time earlier. He also confessed to murdering a fellow in Louisiana identified only by the surname of Nelson.

At about 11:00 am on Friday, 11 July 1856, the Light Guard took Hyde to his place of execution near the old graveyard. A vast crowd accompanied the procession, including Reverends Twichell and Brann. While the preachers dueled to see who could outperform the other in worship Hyde walked on with determined gate, head bowed, ready to meet his end.[135]

Three Unidentified Black Men
Born: (Unknown)—Date of Death: 5 September 1856
Place: Colorado County
Event: Lynching/Beating

In a newspaper report dated 23 September 1856, sources claim that racial strife was imminent at Columbus. Upwards of 400 blacks planned to take up arms against their masters, rob and murder them. Mass hysteria reigned, fueled by fears that the slave community, which generally outnumbered their keepers, would take over Texas.

Upon investigation, it was found that the blacks had in the possession a supply of guns, ammunition, Bowie knives and other assorted weaponry. Saturday, 6 September 1856, was the intended date for the implementation of their plan. However, the fiendish plot was divulged by one of their number, resulting in two unidentified black men who were the ringleaders of the plot being lynched. That hanging took place at about 2:00 pm on Friday, 5 September 1856. A third black man was said to have been beaten so severely that he failed to recover. Other newspaper accounts claim that three or more blacks were lynched in this incident. Pandemonium reigned.[136]

Blake, Bill

Born: (Unknown)—Date of Death: November 1856
Place: Orange County
Event: Lynching/Hanged

Bill Blake, a white man, was arrested in Angelina County and charged with assassinating the Moore family. Before he was lynched by a mob of vigilantes Blake confessed to the heinous deed, protesting that he had been compelled to do it by others.[137]

Apparently, Bill Blake was a well-known and accomplished horse thief, gambler and counterfeiter. Included on the list of persons who were considered direct accessories to the murder of Samuel Deputy were Jack Bunch (see below), Ned Glover, Bill Blake, Burwell Alexander, and Henderson Ashworth, the Cow Thief. Jack Bunch, cousin to Sam, assisted in killing Deputy and was guilty of killing a man named Terly who was the drunken keeper of his sister. That incident took place a few years earlier.[138]

Bunch, Jackson

Born: circa 1838—Date of Death: 21 November 1856
Place: Jefferson County
Event: Legal Execution/Hanged

Jackson Bunch, a man identified as being of French, Spanish and black ancestry, was involved in a murder that later lead to what is known as "The Orange County War of 1856."

The incident began when Samuel Deputy accused a freed black man named Clark Ashworth of butchering hogs that did not belong to him. Clark's cousin Sam Ashworth threatened to kill Deputy. Ashworth was charged with "abusive language by a mulatto" and sentenced to thirty lashes. He was remanded to Sheriff E. C. Glover, who was friendly with the Ashworth clan. Glover allowed Sam to escape.

Ashworth and his eighteen-year-old friend Jackson Bunch ambushed Deputy and a companion on Cow Bayou while the two men were rowing their boat to Deputy's home. Ashworth and Bunch shot Deputy and beat him with the butts of their guns. Deputy died. His companion escaped and alerted authorities. The sheriff made a halfhearted search attempt.

After this incident two opposing factions called the Moderators and Regulators were formed. The Moderators declared the sheriff's office vacant. Sheriff Glover and his supporters organized as Regulators. The Moderators eventually captured the sheriff at a Regulator meeting and killed him.

Bunch was brought to trial for the murder of Deputy. During the tribunal, which took place in Beaumont, rumors spread that friends planned to rescue him. As a result of that threat people carried guns and knives into the courthouse during the hearing. Bunch was convicted on 12 November 1856, and he was scheduled to hang two weeks later.

On 21 November 1856 (some sources claim 23 November) Bunch descended from the third floor of the courthouse where he had been held and, when seeing the guard in the room below exclaimed, "God damn it gentlemen, how do you do, all."[139] Bunch scaled the gallows structure, which had been so crudely constructed that the condemned youth had to negotiate a ladder, which was afterwards pulled out from under him. The guards struggled to remove his handcuffs. An exasperated Bunch declared, "Cut the hands off if you can not get them off any other way." The execution was carried out.

Granza, Marcus
Born: (Unknown)—Date of Death: circa 1857
Place: San Saba County
Event: Lynching/Hanged

Two Unidentified Indians
Born: (Unknown)—Date of Death: circa 1857
Place: San Saba County
Event: Lynching/Hanged

Newspaper accounts of the day speak of an Indian Chief named Marcus Granza and two of his braves being lynched at Hall's Ranch. The Hall place is located about six miles west of Richland Springs in San Saba County. It was surmised that Granza and his men had been a part of an aggregation of Lipan and Mescalero Indians who had recently attacked a patrol of eighteen U.S. Troops near the Devils' River.[140] John Mabin "Pony" Hall and a handful of other early settlers, including Frank Templeton, Bill Wicker, and Mr. Woolsey, founded the Hall Ranch and the little hamlet of Hall in 1855.[141]

Johnson, William Joseph "Bill"
Born: circa 1819—Date of Death: March 1857
Place: McLennan County
Event: Lynching/Hanged

A white man named Bill Johnson, who was arrested at Waco for suspicion of murder, was lynched by citizens thus saving the town the trouble of a trial.[142]

O'Connell, W. J.
Born: (Unknown)—Date of Death: 3 March 1857
Place: Calhoun County
Event: Legal Execution/Hanged

W. J. O'Connell, a white man, had been tried and found guilty of murdering a man named Vanzile at Port Lavaca. That incident took place two years earlier. O'Connell was subsequently hanged for his crime at Powder Horn, in Calhoun County, on Tuesday, 3 March 1857.[143] Some sources list the unfortunate man's surname as O'Conner.[144]

Eight Unidentified Mexican Men
Born: (Unknown)—Date of Death: April 1857
Place: Goliad County
Event: Lynching/Hanged

According to one often unreliable source, eight unidentified Mexican men who were all suspected of theft were taken out and lynched near Goliad in April 1857.[145]

Surname Unknown, Martin
Born: (Unknown)—Date of Death: 8 May 1857
Place: Unknown County
Event: Legal Execution/Hanged

Surname Unknown, David
Born: (Unknown)—Date of Death: 8 May 1857
Place: Unknown County
Event: Legal Execution/Hanged

A newspaper article dated 11 April 1857 indicates that a black slave identified as David, the property of William C. Mims, was sentenced to be hanged on 8 May 1857. David had killed a man named A. Abney. In the same article a slave named Martin, property of James Cellum, was also found guilty of murdering a man named Rufus Crenshaw. Martin was to be hanged on the same date, 8 May 1857. Verification of these two executions has proven difficult to produce. It is presumed that they were hanged on the date stipulated.[146]

Wall, David M.
Born: (Unknown)—Date of Death: 22 May 1857
Place: Liberty County
Event: Legal Execution/Hanged

The *Belton Weekly Independent* indicated that a man named David M. Wall was executed at Liberty on Friday, 22 May 1857. A reason, or details of his transgression, was not provided.[147]

Hart, Bill
Born (Unknown)—Date of Death: 29 May 1857
Place: Bexar County
Event: Lynching/Shot

A Mexican woman identified as Garza was robbed and murdered about twenty miles below San Antonio on the San Antonio River. Suspicion fell upon a desperado named Bill Hart and his two accomplices, Wood and Miller. A warrant was issued and given to Assistant City Marshal Frederick W. Fieldstrup who, with several others, went to Hart's home to arrest him. Wood answered the door and told the officer to go away. Fieldstrup insisted on making the arrest, and shot and killed Wood when he protested. When Miller tried to interfere, Fieldstrup shot and killed him. Hart then ran to the door and shot Fieldstrup, the bullet striking him just above the left eye. The wound was fatal.

Citizens took up arms, grabbing bowie knives, pistols and guns of every description as they surrounded the Hart residence. Captain James Taylor from Atascosa, along with several other men, rushed the house and broke down the door. Hart shot Taylor in the chest, inflicting a painful but not mortal wound. In turn, Taylor did the same for him, fatally wounding Hart. For good measure the crowd riddled Hart's corpse with bullets.[148]

One Unidentified Man
Born (Unknown)—Date of Death: circa June 1857
Place: DeWitt County
Event: Lynching/Hanged

An unidentified man was lynched as a horse thief in DeWitt County. The *Sunday Delta* newspaper noted, "Horse-thieves are said to be unusually active in the frontier counties of late."[149]

Craig, William
Born: (Unknown)—Date of Death: 11 June 1857
Place: Bexar County
Event: Lynching/Hanged

A notorious malefactor named William Craig, who also went by the name of William King, was apprehended at New Braunfels under suspicion of horse theft. Along with his fondness for other people's horses Craig, a white man, was suspected of having been involved in the recent murder of a man named Thompson.

Craig was sent to San Antonio to be jailed. He never arrived. Craig's body was discovered on Thursday, 11 June 1857, hanging from a pecan tree about a mile from the Alamo. Vigilantes had done the work, taking Craig from his captors by force of arms, holding their own private trial and execution, thereby saving Bexar County the trouble.[150]

Two Unidentified Black Men
Born: (Unknown)—Date of Death: July 1857
Place: Bexar County
Event: Lynching/Hanged

Newspaper accounts of the day tell of two unidentified black men who were suspected of having outraged a white girl being lynched at San Antonio. The incident took place during the week of 26 July 1857.[151]

One Unidentified Man
Born: (Unknown)—Date of Death: August 1857
Place: Karnes County
Event: Lynching/Hanged

A man, whose identity is not known, was suspected of killing a cow and was taken out and lynched along the banks of Escondido Creek for having done that deed. [152]

Seventeen Unidentified Men
Born: (Unknown)—Date of Death: September 1857
Place: Unknown County
Event: Lynching/Hanged

Accounts of the day, from an Indianola newspaper, indicate that one man returning to New Orleans had reported that he had seen a dozen men hanging from one tree and five more from another, all horse thieves and assorted malefactors. [153]

Delgado, Jose Antonio
Born: circa 1796—Date of Death: 12 September 1857
Place: Goliad and Karnes Counties
Event: Lynching/Shot

Reports of the day by an unverified source alleged that a Mexican man named Jose Antonio Delgado and perhaps as many as seventy-four other Mexican's were taken out and lynched during a wild mêlée that occurred in Goliad and Karnes Counties sometime around 12 September 1857. It seems that these persons only crime was that of competing for work with white men. Upon further examination of additional, more reliable sources, it appears as though Delgado was the only one killed and that the claims concerning the racial motivation of the attack are untrue. Several other Mexican men were injured, however, in the wonton and seemingly unprovoked attack on a band of men who were transporting goods peaceably along the public highway. Afterwards, a reward of $500 was offered for the arrest and delivery of the perpetrators to the sheriff of Karnes County.[154]

Amberson, William
Born: (Unknown)—Date of Death: 26 September 1857
Place: Liberty County
Event: Lynching/Hanged

The *Belton Weekly Independent* indicated that a man named William Amberson was lynched near the county line between Live Oak and Atascosa Counties on Saturday, 26 September 1857. Some eight or ten unidentified persons took him from his home in the middle of the night and did the deed. A reason was not provided.[155] It is possible that Amberson is the same man identified by family genealogists as hailing from Mississippi and meeting his end at Median, not Atascosa County.

One Unidentified Indian Man
Born: (Unknown)—Date of Death: January 1858
Place: Polk County
Event: Lynching/Hanged

Newspaper accounts of the day claim that an Indian man of the Alabama tribe, aged about eighteen or twenty years, was pretending to be ill to avoid work. The seven-year old son of his employer, Mr. Walker of Moscow, called the Indian man a racial expletive, one that is generally reserved for blacks. The Indian sprang forth angered, threatening to kill the lad as he left to get his gun. When he returned he attempted to shoot the boy, but his weapon misfired. He tried again, but the gun failed to discharge a second time. On the third attempt the pesky shooter finally went off, killing the young Walker boy instantly. After the incident the Indian lad fled into the woods.

When Mr. Walker returned home and learned the news he sent word to the chief that unless the guilty man was turned over he would kill the entire encampment. Believing Walker to be a man of his word, the chief complied. Once in custody the boy's killer was lynched.[156]

One Unidentified Mexican Man
Born: (Unknown)—Date of Death: 13 January 1858
Place: Cameron County
Event: Lynching/Hanged

Newspaper reports of the day indicate that Justice of the Peace E. J. McLane Esquire of Brownsville was stabbed and killed by a Mexican man.

McLane had the misfortune of walking past the man's home while the fellow was engaged in a heated argument with his spouse. He attempted to intervene on the woman's behalf and was stabbed repeatedly for his trouble. McLane died instantly.

Almost immediately citizens of Brownsville took the Mexican man into custody and lynched him from a tree in front of Young's Store on Liberty Street. McLane, who was known locally as a terror to evildoers, had lived on the Rio Grande for years and had recently killed a man named Robinson who had attacked him in his office while he was writing a warrant for the fellow's arrest.[157]

Mitchell, David C.
Born: (Unknown)—Date of Death: 13 January 1858
Place: Robertson County
Event: Lynching/Hanged

David C. Mitchell, a white man, had been accused of the murder of a man named John Brown. That crime had occurred in December 1857, at Owensville in Robertson County. Mitchell had fled to Louisiana, where he was arrested at Alexandria, jailed, and eventually returned to Robertson County for trial.

Mitchell was housed in the county jailed. On Wednesday night, of 13 January 1858, vigilantes broke into the building and removed him. Mitchell was lynched in the town square.[158]

Surname Unknown, Lucy
Born: circa 1818—Date of Death: 5 March 1858
Place: Galveston County
Event: Legal Execution/Hanged

Mrs. Maria Dougherty was the proprietor of the Columbian Hotel, which once stood at the corner of Strand and Twenty-Fourth Streets in Galveston. Dougherty owned a black slave woman named Lucy who she had purchased from Captain H. J. Starrett. Lucy was said to have been of poor character, giving evidence of that by having set fire to the hotel on at least one occasion. When caught in the act she swore to bring vengeance down on her master, Maria Dougherty.

On Sunday, 3 January 1858, Mrs. Doughtery went missing from the hotel. A search was conducted, which led to the discovery of her body in a brick cistern in the back yard. Blows from a heavy instrument had crushed Dougherty's head. When confronted, the unrepentant Lucy confessed to having killed her mistress, boldly saying "Yes, and I would do it again."

Lucy was brought to trial on Friday, 12 January 1858. Having no attorney of her own, the court appointed Major R. H. Howard to defend her. She was found guilty of the killing and returned to jail. On 23 January 1858, Lucy was brought before the court and sentenced to death. She was to be hanged on 5 March.

The evening prior to her execution a gallows was constructed on the second floor of the jail building. A few minutes after noon on Friday, 5 March 1858, Sheriff Westerlage tripped the latch and Lucy's sentence was carried out. She was the first, and last, woman to be executed in Galveston County.[159]

Two Unidentified Mexican Men
Born: (Unknown)—Date of Death: May 1858
Place: Gonzales County
Event: Lynching/Shot and Drown

Newspaper reports of the day reveal that two unidentified Mexican men had been forming a plot to aid several black slaves in their escape to Mexico. The plan was uncovered and the two Mexicans were said to have been "...entangled in the brushy bottoms of the Guadalupe [River]..." thus it was unlikely that they would be causing further trouble to local slaveholders.[160]

Huizan, Francisco
Born: (Unknown)—Date of Death: 29 May 1858
Place: Bexar County
Event: Lynching/Hanged

Longoria, Pablo
Born: (Unknown)—Date of Death: 29 May 1858
Place: Bexar County
Event: Lynching/Hanged

Lopez, Felipe
Born: (Unknown)—Date of Death: 29 May 1858
Place: Bexar County
Event: Lynching/Hanged

Urdiales, Nicanor
Born: (Unknown)—Date of Death: 29 May 1858
Place: Bexar County
Event: Lynching/Hanged

Four Mexican men, Francisco Huizan, Pablo Longoria, Felipe Lopez and Nicanor Urdiales, were seized by a band of thirty masked men from Mission San Jose and taken out and lynched near San Antonio. They were all said to have been thieves.[161]

Four Unidentified White Man
Born: (Unknown)—Date of Death: June 1858
Place: Bell County
Event: Lynching/Hanged

Four unidentified white men who were responsible for killing an entire family of seven persons were apprehended and lynched by a mob of furious neighbors. The men, who had disguised themselves as Indians to commit the heinous deed, were identified by one of three youths who had managed to survive the massacre.[162]

Incidents of this nature, where white men disguise themselves as Indians to perform robberies and murders, dot the pages of early Texas history. Groups of such ne're-do-wells, often comprised of German settlers, were known to roam Kerr, Gillespie and San Saba Counties.[163]

Jones, Given Name Unknown
Born: (Unknown)—Date of Death: June 1858
Place: Lampasas County
Event: Lynching/Hanged

Morris, Given Name Unknown
Born: (Unknown)—Date of Death: June 1858
Place: Lampasas County
Event: Lynching/Hanged

Tipton, Given Name Unknown
Born: (Unknown)—Date of Death: June 1858
Place: Lampasas County
Event: Lynching/Hanged

Willis, Given Name Unknown
Born: (Unknown)—Date of Death: June 1858
Place: Lampasas County
Event: Lynching/Hanged

Several white men identified only by their surnames as Jones, Willis, Tipton and Morris were lynched at Lampasas County. The men, together with several Indians, were believed to have been guilty of the murders of the James B. Cameron and Thomas Mason families in Jack County, seven killings in all. Another source, however, claimed that the foursome were not hung but were acquitted.[164]

Busby, John W.
Born: (Unknown)—Date of Death: 16 June 1858
Place: Ellis County
Event: Lynching/Shot

Donegan, John
Born: (Unknown)—Date of Death: 16 June 1858
Place: Ellis County
Event: Lynching/Shot

Newspaper accounts of the day indicate the John Donegan, a white preacher, was accused of arson at Waxahachie. Also on the list of offenses that Donegan is said to have committed was burglary, horse stealing and tampering with "Negroes". He received 100 lashes administered with a leather whip, doled out "...at the hands of a big Negro..." Afterwards Donegan was banished from the county.

Donegan swore to return and clear his name, which he did. This time he showed up well armed, and prepared to take on all comers, accompanied by his brother and a friend named John W. Busby. Citizens had other ideas, however. On Wednesday, 16 June 1858, a mob of about 100 mounted vigilantes left Waxahachie and rode to Donegan's place where they shot and killed him and John Busby. Their bodies were found punctured with numerous bullet holes.[165]

Six Unidentified Men
Born: (Unknown)—Date of Death: July 1858
Place: Navarro and Limestone Counties
Event: Lynching/Hanged

Newspaper reports indicate that at least four unidentified thieves, members of a larger group of ne're-do-wells, were caught in the process of robbing the home of Mr. Graves on the Corsicana to Waco road. Four were lynched. Before giving up the ghost, they indicated that the organization of highwaymen numbered as high as fifty or sixty persons. The report went on to claim that two other confederates of this mob were hung in Limestone County.[166]

One Unidentified Man

Born: (Unknown)—Date of Death: July 1858
Place: Marion and Harrison Counties
Event: Lynching/Hanged

Newspaper accounts of the day tell the tale of an unidentified man who was found lynched in the Black Cyprus Swamp, which is located in Marion and Harrison Counties.[167] Afterwards a local newspaper, the *Gilmer Democrat,* indicated that a coroner's inquest had been held into the incident but that the paper was not at liberty to disclose the findings.

One Unidentified Indian Man

Born: (Unknown)—Date of Death: July 1858
Place: Unknown County
Event: Lynching/Hanged

The esteemed tabloid the *Lowell Daily Citizen and News* of Lowell, Massachusetts, claimed that an unidentified Indian man had been recently lynched in Texas for the murder of a child. On the gallows, the fellow claimed that he was going to Arkansas, and wished that his colleagues would send his gun along to him when he arrived.[168]

One Unidentified Man

Born: (Unknown)—Date of Death: 11 July 1858
Place: Upshur County
Event: Lynching/Hanged

On Sunday, 11 July 1858, an unidentified white man was found hanged from a tree near the road to Little Cyprus Swamp in Upshur County. Judging by the degree of mortification of his remains the poor fellow appeared to have been dead for about two weeks. Although the head remained attached to the hangman's rope fastened to a tree, the body had since fallen to the ground. The man, who appeared to be about thirty-five or forty years of age, had dark brown hair and was dressed in a beaver hat, dove colored cashmere coat and dark trousers.[169]

One Unidentified Man

Born: (Unknown)—Date of Death: 15 July 1858

Place: Uvalde County

Event: Lynching/Hanged

An unidentified man had apparently stolen a fine, large mule from the United States Government at Fort Inge. Two citizens and two soldiers from the post overtook him somewhere in his flight at a point west of the Nueces River. He was returned to the post where, according to the newspaper account, he was turned loose for some reason. To the surprise of few, the following morning, Thursday 15 July 1858, the man was found hanged about a half mile from the fort.[170] It was correctly presumed that the mule had not done the lynching.

Wardick, Bryant

Born: (Unknown)—Date of Death: 15 July 1858

Place: Goliad County

Event: Lynching/Shot

Bryant Wardick, a white man from Navarro County who was an outlaw, horse thief and murderer, was shot and killed by vigilantes at Goliad. Wardick and his colleagues, listed below, were suspected of having been the group who had been killing Mexicans in the region.[171] In addition, they had operated a horse theft ring that covered a huge area, including Bexar, Limestone, Navarro, Hill, Ellis, Dallas, Freestone, Bosque, Milam, Falls, Robertson, Burleson and Washington Counties.[172]

Browning, Elisha

Born: (Unknown)—Date of Death: 17 July 1858

Place: Goliad County

Event: Lynching/Hanged

Goldman, J.

Born: (Unknown)—Date of Death: 17 July 1858

Place: Goliad County

Event: Lynching/Hanged

Wardick, John

Born: (Unknown)—Date of Death: 17 July 1858

Place: Goliad County

Event: Lynching/Hanged

Wardick, Michael
Born: (Unknown)—Date of Death: 17 July 1858
Place: Goliad County
Event: Lynching/Hanged

Elisha Browning, J. Goldman, along with John and Michael Wardick, all followed Bryant Wardick to the lynching tree just two days after his appointment. They were all strung up by vigilantes at Goliad, hung from a live oak tree in the town square. Together with Bryant, all of these men were outlaws, horse thieves and murderers and were suspected of having been the group who had been killing Mexicans in the region.[173] Murder was often overlooked at the time in Texas. Stealing horses or cattle was not.

Garner, Washington
Born: (Unknown)—Date of Death: 27 August 1858
Place: Polk County
Event: Legal Execution/Shot Trying to Escape

The citizens of Livingston were treated to a much grander show than had been anticipated at the hanging of Washington Garner, a white man, who had been tried and convicted of murdering a man named Grant in Polk County.

Garner was scheduled to hang for his crime on Friday, 27 August 1858. A gallows had been erected at Livingston for that purpose. Garner and a confederate named Drake were led by officers to the prescribed spot and were in the process of being prepared for their punishment when Garner requested a glass of ardent spirits. His hosts politely complied with the appeal. When Garner had consumed the glass full of whiskey he threw it to the ground and ran off, hollering back to his captors, "...they could shoot and be damned." The lawmen complied, opening fire and felling Garner, thus making it no longer necessary to hang him. Drake was returned to his cell.[174]

Vivian, Given Name Unknown
Born: (Unknown)—Date of Death: September 1858
Place: Gonzales County
Event: Lynching/Hanged

Newspaper reports of the day indicate that a white horse thief identified only as Vivian was lynched at a camp meeting at Gonzales. He had been arrested on 28 August 1858, two miles above Gonzales, and taken to jail there pending trial.[175]

Three Unidentified Black Men
Born: (Unknown)—Date of Death: 8 October 1858
Place: Jackson County
Event: Legal Execution/Hanged

Three unidentified black men were tried and found guilty of murdering their master, Mr. Homer Gilead Bostwick, at Texana. The threesome went to the gallows together on Friday, 8 October 1858.[176]

One Unidentified Man
Born: (Unknown)—Date of Death: 21 November 1858
Place: Brazos County
Event: Lynching/Hanged

On Sunday morning, 21 November 1858, the body of a stranger was discovered hanging from a tree in the town square at Boonsville. The man, whose race was not mentioned, was totally unknown to townspeople. He had been lynched in an unusual manner, with the rope strung under his armpits rather than around his neck, giving rise to the suspicion that he had been killed by some other means, elsewhere, and tied up to the tree for display.[177]

Middleton, Thomas Jefferson
Born: circa 1822—Date of Death: 17 December 1858
Place: Bastrop County
Event: Lynching/Hanged

Thomas Jefferson "Tom" Middleton, a notorious desperado, was lynched at Bastrop on Friday, 17 December 1858. Middleton had been confined in the jail pending legal action when a mob numbering about 100 strong overpowered jailers, removed Middleton, and lynched him from a convenient tree while most of the townspeople looked on. [178]

Although Middleton was no doubt guilty of some form of nefarious deed for which his neighbors felt lynching was a suitable punishment, journalists of the day saw fit to mention only the hanging itself, leaving no clue to the crime for which he met this fate.

Seven Unidentified Indians
Born: (Unknown)—Date of Death: 27 December 1858
Place: Young County
Event: Lynching/Shot

The Brazos Reservation originally consisted of almost 19,000 acres, and was located twelve miles south of Fort Belknap, where the Brazos River makes three big bends. The size was doubled when an adjacent tract of equal size, intended for the western Indians, was added to it. The main building there was three miles east of the site of Graham, where a few scattered stones mark the remains of the agency.

Seventeen Indians, men, women and children, were camped along the Brazos River grazing their horses at a spot about fifteen miles from the Brazos Agency. On Monday, 27 December 1858, a group of white men attacked the party, killing four men and three women. Most of the remaining Indians were wounded. The newspaper described the victims as a man and woman from the Caddo tribe, claiming that the rest were from the Anadarko tribe. One of the children wounded in the incident was expected to die. Two of the white men were reported to have been killed in the exchange.[179]

One Unidentified Black Man

Born: (Unknown)—Date of Death: circa 1859
Place: Tarrant or Navarro County
Event: Lynching/Hanged

Newspaper accounts of the day speak of an unidentified black man being taken out and lynched for having killed a white man. No specific detailed information was provided in this journalist's story. [180]

Bula, Given Name Unknown

Born: (Unknown)—Date of Death: circa 1859
Place: Grayson County
Event: Lynching/Hanged

Newspaper accounts of the day indicate that a Methodist Minister, identified only as Reverend Bula, was lynched for his views on religion.[181] Judging by the year of his death, and the pro-slavery sentiment in parts of Texas, one might well hypothesize that Pastor Bula was lynched because he was considered a Unionist, an Abolitionist, or some other form of undesirable "Yankee rabble."

Butcher, Given Name Unknown

Born: (Unknown)—Date of Death: circa 1859
Place: Comanche County
Event: Lynching/Hanged

Daley, Given Name Unknown

Born: (Unknown)—Date of Death: circa 1859
Place: Comanche County
Event: Lynching/Hanged

Down, Given Name Unknown
Born: (Unknown)—Date of Death: circa 1859
Place: Comanche County
Event: Lynching/Hanged

Three white men identified only as Butcher, Daley and Down were found out to be mule thieves. The men had used local mixed race Indians to do the dirty work of stealing the animals, and then they would take the beasts out of state and sell them at a great profit. After a disagreement with their partners over compensation, the Indians turned the three white men over to local regulators who promptly lynched them. Butcher and Daley were said to be local produce merchants.[182]

Johnson, Bill
Born: (Unknown)—Date of Death: circa 1859
Place: McLennan County
Event: Lynching/Hanged and Shot

In 1895, a partially buried body was discovered by a local man named George Renick protruding from the sand along the banks of the Brazos River at Waco. Upon examination the remarkably well preserved remains it was determined that they were those of Bill Johnson, notorious outlaw and murderer who, after an incident in 1859, had been shot and lynched.[183]

Surname Unknown, Peter
Born: circa 1843—Date of Death: 27 January 1859
Place: Red River County
Event: Legal Execution/Hanged

A black slave named Peter who was only sixteen years of age, was tried and convicted of murdering his mistress. The newspaper referred to him as "Peter Valentine" using his master's last name which was common at the time. Peter was executed by hanging on Thursday, 27 January 1859.[184]

Mask, Pleasant M.
Born: (Unknown)—Date of Death: 4 March 1859
Place: Wood County
Event: Legal Execution/Hanged

Pleasant M. Mask, a white man who had been tried and convicted of murdering a woman named Smith, was hanged for his crime at Holly Springs on Friday, 4 March 1859.[185] Upwards of 4,000 people turned out for his hanging.[186]

Mason, Given Name Unknown
Born: (Unknown)—Date of Death: 23 March 1859
Place: Karnes County
Event: Lynching/Hanged

On Wednesday, 23 March 1859, citizens of Helena in Karnes County captured and lynched a white man named Mason who was accused of being a horse thief. The same group of vigilantes who carried out the trial for Mason were said to be in pursuit of his associate, also accused of horse theft.[187]

Two Unidentified Indians
Born: (Unknown)—Date of Death: April 1859
Place: Young County
Event: Lynching/Shot and Scalped

An unidentified elderly Waco Indian man had a rope place around his neck and was dragged some distance before being shot and scalped. According to newspaper articles of the day an old Waco Indian woman who was tending her garden was also killed. This incident was the proud work of a detachment of 1st Infantry soldiers under the command of Captain John R. Baylor and Captain Plummer. The man's crime was noted as "resisting capture."[188]

Baylor, who was born in Paris, Kentucky, had moved to Texas at age of eighteen. He became a prominent citizen, state legislator, Indian Agent and publisher of a decidedly racist newspaper called *The White Man*.[189]

Jordan, R. B.
Born: (Unknown)—Date of Death: 17 April 1859
Place: Milam County
Event: Lynching/Shot

Mr. R. B. Jordan, a white man, was assassinated at Saint Andres in Milan County for living with a widow woman.

Citizens of the community had cautioned Jordan against his actions, but he foolishly paid them no heed. Although a magistrate ordered him to marry the woman or cease the cohabitation, he refused. Shortly after leaving his home on Sunday, 17 April 1859, Jordan was shot and killed. Neighbors heard the report of nine gunshots. Jordan's body was discovered, riddled with bullet holes.[190]

Family genealogists note his place of death as San Antonio.[191]

One Unidentified Black Man

Born: (Unknown)—Date of Death: 23 May 1859
Place: Cass County
Event: Lynching/Hanged

On Friday, 20 May 1859, an unidentified black slave who was the property of Mr. David Dixon from Lafayette County, Arkansas, became involved in an altercation with a Mr. Thomas Crabtree, Dixon's overseer. The black man struck Crabtree over the head with a hoe, killing him instantly. The attacker fled to the woods but was eventually found on Monday, 23 May 1859. He was placed on a mule, taken just over the Texas State Line, and lynched.[192]

White, George

Born: 15 February 1805—Date of Death: June 1859
Place: Harris County
Event: Lynching/Hanged

George White, a white man, committed an outrage on an eleven year old girl at Harrisonburg sometime in June 1859. White was arrested and taken into custody. He was held with great care and effort until after his hearing. Once the magistrate had declared his guilty White was returned to jail. En route, a mob of angry citizens took him by force, carried him a short distance and lynched him from a convenient tree.[193]

　　White's grave is located within the boundaries of Glenwood Cemetery at Houston in Harris County. The stone, which is obviously a newer replacement, indicates that his date of death was 16 September 1859. That error was no doubt made at the time the surrogate cenotaph was commissioned. [194]

One Unidentified White Man

Born: (Unknown)—Date of Death: July 1859
Place: Angelina County
Event: Lynching/Hanged

Newspaper reports of the day note that an unidentified white man was lynched at Huntington for having maliciously assaulted a little girl. Men of the community promptly lynched the individual from a tree.[195] One wonders if this newspaper account is a duplicate of the earlier Harris County entry from June 1859.

One Unidentified Black Man
Born: (Unknown)—Date of Death: 27 July 1859
Place: Hopkins County
Event: Lynching/Hanged

An unidentified black slave, the property of Mr. Wylie S. Ferrett of Tarrant, a community in Hopkins County, was taken from the jail at that town by a mob on Wednesday, 27 July 1859. Vigilantes broke down the door and, under force of arms, removed the man and lynched him from a tree.

The man had attempted to outrage a white woman named Morell on Saturday, 23 July 1859, beating her and choking her then leaving her for dead. The woman survived to identify her assailant. The black man confessed to the crime as he was being hanged.[196]

One Unidentified Black Man
Born: (Unknown)—Date of Death: 6 August 1859
Place: Tarrant County
Event: Lynching/Hanged

A black man, identified only as "...a Negro man of Col. [Colonel] Harton of Navarro County..." was judged, found guilty and hanged by the townspeople of Fort Worth for having robbed and murdered a twenty-two year old man named Joseph McFerron "Bud Joe" English of Fort Bend County.[197]

The twenty-two year old English was a clerk for Dick Kennedy and Captain Fields at their store in Ft. Worth. He had been sent by Kennedy and Fields to Houston with several wagonloads of cotton to be sold there. Along the route a black man saw English with the cotton then, several days later, observed him returning from Houston and looking very tired from the journey. The black man approached English and hit him over the head with a heavy stick, then robbed him of the money he was carrying from the sale. English's body was taken to a ranch nearby and covered with leaves and brush.[198]

Fike, Carroll
Born: (Unknown)—Date of Death: 26 August 1859
Place: Fort Bend County
Event: Legal Execution/Hanged

Carroll Fike, a white man, was executed at Richmond for murdering a fellow named Anthony Hauks. That crime had taken place at Walker's Station. The hanging was carried out at Richmond, in Fort Bend County, on Friday, 26 August 1859. Few spectators were present to witness Fike's final farewell.[199]

King, Finis Ewing Reverend
Born: 22 May 1819—Date of Death: 16 October 1859
Place: Ellis County
Event: Lynching/Hanged

Lieutenant John Salmon reported that Reverend Finis Ewing King, who was supposed to be investigating the killing of a man named Collins by another fellow named Johnson, was lynched at Waxahachie for being an abolitionist. [200] King is buried at the Shiloh Cemetery at Waxahachie.[201]

Two Unidentified Black Men
Born: (Unknown)—Date of Death: 28 October 1859
Place: Bowie County
Event: Lynching/Hanged

Two unidentified black male slaves, the property of Colonel S. A. Tickle, were lynched at Bowie for murdering their master. The incident took place on Friday, 28 October 1859.[202]

Cabrera, Tomas
Born: (Unknown)—Date of Death: 16 November 1859
Place: Cameron County
Event: Lynching/Hanged

Tomas Cabrera, a Mexican man who was said to have been second in command of Juan Cortina's gang, was lynched at Brownsville.[203] A *New York Tribune* account of 29 November 1859 claimed that the incident occurred shortly after the arrival of a detachment of Texas Rangers under the command of the famous John "RIP" Ford, sent o join forces with a local citizens group called the "Brownsville Tigers." The Tigers had been organized to resist Cortina.[204] Cabrera was captured after Cortina's men seized Brownsville on 28 September 1858. He killed Cameron County jailer Robert L. Johnson and Constable George Morris.[205]

Cortina, known as "The Red Robber of the Rio Grande," was a Mexican rancher, politician, military boss, outlaw and folk hero. He is famous for leading a paramilitary Mexican force in the Cortina Wars against the United States Army, the Texas Rangers and the local militia of Brownsville, Texas and Matamoros, Tamaulipas.

Cabrera's family seems to have been located at Goliad, although his father, already deceased by 1859, had lived at San Antonio.

Grundy, (Given Name Unknown)
Born: (Unknown)—Date of Death: circa late 1860s
Place: Falls County
Event: Lynched/Hanged

Unverified sources report that vigilantes lynched a man named Grundy for cattle theft. No other useful information was provided by the source.[206]

Heaton, (Given Name Unknown)
Born: (Unknown)—Date of Death: circa late 1860s
Place: Falls County
Event: Lynched/Hanged

Heaton, a white man whose given name is unknown, was involved in a disagreement over the sale of some cattle. The incident turned fatal for him when he was murdered by a group of vigilantes lead by Abner Walker.[207]

White, Riley
Born: (Unknown)—Date of Death: circa 1860
Place: Navarro County
Event: Lynched/Hanged

Local county historians report that the first hanging in Navarro County was that of black man named Riley White. Sources are vague with regard to the precise date, or the details. None-the-less, in the interest of completeness this entry is being listed.[208]

Witty, Cab
Born: (Unknown)—Date of Death: Early 1860s
Place: Fannin County
Event: Lynching/Hanged

A man named Cab Witty was being held on suspicion of horse theft sometime in the early 1860s. Two attempts were made on his life. The first failed. On the second occasion, Witty was removed from the jail by force and dragged through town, gagged. His muffled screams of "They are going to hang me" were so loud that citizens were alerted. On the second try, the vigilante mob was more cunning. A majority of the force hid while two men approached the jail and asked to interview Witty. Witty was told that they were in a position to assure his escape and freedom if only he would sign a pledge to be loyal to the Confederacy. The ruse worked and Witty agreed. As he left jail, however the remainder of the mob materialized, threw a rope around his neck and dragged him to the edge of town where he was strung up and lynched from an oak tree.[209]

Hinton, William
Born: (Unknown)—Date of Death: 25 March 1860
Place: Falls County
Event: Legal Execution/Hanged

William Hinton was tried and convicted of murder. He was hanged on Sunday, 25 March 1860.

Various sources, although not confirmed, indicate that William Hinton shot and killed his brother-in-law Pleasant Clark Whitaker during a dispute at a party. Whitaker, who some have claimed was the local sheriff, was killed on 27 December 1859. No records of Whitaker as a lawman have surfaced. He is listed as "Colonel" in several genealogical records. Hinton was tried, convicted and hanged for the crime in Falls County Texas.[210]

One Unidentified White Man
Born (Unknown)—Date of Death: 25 April 1860
Place: Johnson County
Event: Lynching/Burned

A letter dated Monday, 25 April 1860, indicates that a white peddler was discovered to have copies of maps, books and religious materials along with Abolitionist books. The incident took place at Buchanan. The man was unmercifully flogged and the contents of his wagon stolen. The fellow's bad luck continued when a runaway slave with forged papers was brought to the scene. The black man was whipped until he identified the peddler as having assisted him.

Whether the slave's confession was true or not seemed to have made little difference. The peddler's wagon was rolled under a tree by six men who filled the bed with dry twigs and tar. They stripped the man and placed him in the wagon. Next, a rope was fastened around the poor wretches' neck and draped over a convenient limb. The man was pulled up until his toes barely touched the top of the tinder pile. Next, the slave was ordered to light the pyre. He did...and the peddler was burned to death.[211]

Swaid, A.
Born: circa 1833—Date of Death: 30 April 1860
Place: Galveston County
Event: Legal Execution/Hanged

Mr. Swaid, a white male whose given name is not listed, was executed by legal hanging at Galveston on Monday, 30 April 1860. Swaid is buried at the City Cemetery.[212]

Surname Unknown, Emma
Born: (Unknown)—Date of Death: circa May 1860
Place: Fannin County
Event: Lynching/Hanged

Surname Unknown, Jesse
Born: (Unknown)—Date of Death: circa May 1860
Place: Fannin County
Event: Lynching/Hanged

Surname Unknown, Ruben
Born: (Unknown)—Date of Death: circa May 1860
Place: Fannin County
Event: Lynching/Hanged

According to reports, in May of 1860 three blacks who were identified only by their given names of Jess, Ruben, and Emma allegedly murdered their master and his family in Fannin County, north of Dallas. They reportedly confessed, and indicated that an insurrection of blacks was being planned and that the movement was led by a white man. The threesome was then hanged.[213]

Four Unidentified Black Men
Born: (Unknown)—Date of Death: 18 May 1860
Place: Grayson County
Event: Lynching/Hanged

The incident took place near Kentuckytown in Grayson County on Friday, 18 May 1860. A white man named Kincade whipped "his negro [Negro] boy." In retaliation for the beating, that night the youth murdered Kincade, his wife, an orphan boy and a baby while they were asleep. He chose an axe to do the work.

    The axe-wielding slave confessed to the crime and was promptly lynched. A few days after the killing three additional black men who had been implicated in the incident were also lynched. A diarist named C. B. Moore of Collin County recorded the same affair, but reported the location as Pilot Point in Denton County. He also claimed that three black men were lynched."[214]

McDaniel, Given Name Unknown
Born: (Unknown)—Date of Death: June 1860
Place: Jackson County
Event: Lynching/Hanged

Citizens of Navidad, fifteen miles above Texana, organized a lynch party. The group nominated a white man identified only as McDaniel to be the guest of honor. McDaniel, who had confessed to dealing in horses and Negroes, was taken to a post oak and strung up.[215] Some sources identify the specie of tree as Black Jack, and the spot as being along the Navidad River. That same source indicates that McDaniel had stolen the black man and the horse, which is subtly different from the earlier explanation, which claimed that he was simply "dealing in."

It is believed that the victim in this case was a man named Adam McDaniel (1828-1860) however, corroboration has been difficult to pin down.

Pitman, William
Born: 11 April 1828—Date of Death: 8 June 1860
Place: Cooke County
Event: Legal Execution/Hanged

William Pitman, a white man, had been tried and convicted of waylaying and murdering a man identified only as Dr. Rowe in Cooke County. Pitman was sentenced to hang. To the delight of a large throng of onlookers, that sentence was carried out at Gainesville on Friday, 8 June 1860. Such sentiment apparently reflecting the crowd's admiration for Dr. Rowe, or their disdain for Pitman.[216]

One Unidentified Black Man
Born: (Unknown)—Date of Death: 11 June 1860
Place: Fannin County
Event: Lynching/Hanged

Two Unidentified Black Men
Born: (Unknown)—Date of Death: 13 June 1860
Place: Fannin County
Event: Lynching/Hanged

Newspaper reports of the day describe the murder of a white slave owner, his mistress and two of the couple's children at Orangeville. The incident took place on the night of Monday, 11 June 1860. The killer, a slave whose name was not given, claimed that two other slaves had aided him in the commission of this heinous act.

A crowd of neighbors seized the man. Claiming that the justification for his actions was that "his master had not used him well of late" and was planning on selling him, the poor wretch faced a mob intent on burning him. Those favoring lynching prevailed, and the man was strung up from a nearby tree. He was not to be sent off to eternity alone however, as his two companions were also lynched two days later. All of their bodies were left hanging from the same tree, making a rather morbid adornment.[217]

Covington, Rolley Peter "Riley"
Born: circa 1827—Date of Death: July 1860
Place: Bosque County
Event: Lynching/Hanged

Rolley Peter "Riley" Covington, a white man who seemed to like other people's horses, was taken out and lynched for his penchant at Bosque County in July 1860.[218] He was strung up by a rather large band of vigilantes.[219] According to the newspaper account, the last anyone saw of Covington he was up a tree, dancing in mid air to the Blue Grass spiritual tune of "...Jordan am a hard road to travel, I believe."[220]

    Family genealogists claim that this lynching occurred at Dallas, in Dallas County.[221] Regardless of where he met his end Covington, an otherwise upstanding fellow, left behind a wife, Frances Elizabeth "Tennessee" Jones and three children.

Two Unidentified Black Men
Born: (Unknown)—Date of Death: July 1860
Place: Grimes County
Event: Lynching

Newspaper accounts of the day claimed that two abolitionist preachers were jailed for trying to hatch an insurrection plot. After admitting their guilt, the pair was lynched.[222]

One Unidentified Black Man
Born: (Unknown)—Date of Death: July 1860
Place: Tarrant County or Parker County
Event: Lynching/Hanged

Conflicting newspaper accounts of the day claimed that an abolitionist was lynched at Tarrant County or Parker County in July 1860.[223]

Two Unidentified White Men
Born: (Unknown)—Date of Death: July 1860
Place: Central Texas
Event: Lynching

Reports of the day claimed that persons unknown lynched two white abolitionists who were plotting a slave rebellion at an unspecified place somewhere in Central Texas.[224]

    It is highly probable that this incident, and the one reported above as having involved two black men, were one in the same. Over zealous revisionist historians occasionally rush to press, anxious to add a racial component to every lynching even when there is no credible evidence present to support that hypothesis. Their attempts to pad the count are unnecessary, considering the stunning number of legitimate lynchings and burnings of blacks in Texas. These attempts to overdramatize are demeaning to the memory of the legitimate victims.

Several Unidentified Black Men
Born: (Unknown)—Date of Death: July 1860
Place: Ellis County
Event: Lynching/Hanged

Newspaper accounts of the day speak to the reported lynching of "several" blacks at Waxahachie in Ellis County. No specifics are provided, thus the number of persons involved and the paucity of the information remain somewhat questionable. [225]

Crawford, William H.
Born: (Unknown)—Date of Death: 17 July 1860
Place: Ellis County
Event: Lynching/Hanged

The body of William H. Crawford, a bricklayer from Ft. Worth, was discovered hanging from a peach tree about three quarters of a mile from town. A large number of citizens visited the site during the day. At an evening meeting strong evidence was brought forth that Crawford had been an abolitionist. Those present endorsed the actions of whoever had lynched him.[226] Some sources claim that Crawford was a black man, although it has proven difficult to be certain of that fact. He was, however, an abolitionist who was swept up in the racial turmoil of the day.

Two Unidentified White Men
Born: (Unknown)—Date of Death: 21 July 1860
Place: Ellis County
Event: Lynching/Hanged

Newspaper accounts of the day claimed that two white men were lynched on Saturday, 21 July 1860, in connection with a plan that was said to have been hatched by blacks to murder citizens of the town of Waxahachie. The article goes on to indicate that an additional twenty or so blacks were to be hung that week, also involved in the evil scheme. Reports said that the two men had distributed fifty rifles and fifty six-shooters among the blacks.[227]

One Unidentified Black Man
Born: (Unknown)—Date of Death: 23 July 1860
Place: Ellis County
Event: Lynching/Hanged

Newspaper accounts of the day claimed that a black man, who was the leader of the insurrection to poison and kill citizens of Waxahachie, was captured on Red Oak Creek and lynched.[228]

Miller, Cato "Uncle Cato"
Born: (Unknown)—Date of Death: 24 July 1860
Place: Dallas County
Event: Lynching/Hanged

Jennings, Patrick "Pat"
Born: (Unknown)—Date of Death: 24 July 1860
Place: Dallas County
Event: Lynching/Hanged

Smith, Samuel "Sam"
Born: (Unknown)—Date of Death: 24 July 1860
Place: Dallas County
Event: Lynching/Hanged

Newspaper accounts of the day claimed that three black men identified as Sam Smith, Cato Miller and Patrick Jennings, were members of a reported insurrection. The group were discovered with poison in their possession. All three were lynched. Jennings was said to have been the most prominent in the plot, and the person who set the torch to the town. Smith, a "hardened old scoundrel," was a preacher. Miller was a well-known troublemaker.

There had been wholesale violence in Texas, with twenty-two or more building set afire at the capital city of Austin on 22 August 1860. The violence at Waxahachie was equally extreme.

At about 4:00 pm the threesome was removed from the jail and paraded through the once flourishing town as they surveyed the vestiges with composure. Jennings remained calm the entire day. The old preacher Sam Smith, so called for the surname of his master, had apparently come by his villainous ways from talking with two abolitionist preachers named Blunt and McKinney. The hanging took place on the banks of the river above town. All three men were buried near the gallows site.[229]

Twenty-Two to Twenty-Five Unidentified Black Men
Born: (Unknown)—Date of Death: 28 July 1860
Place: Ellis County
Event: Lynching/Hanged

Various East Coast newspapers claimed that twenty-two to twenty-five black men had been arrested and were scheduled to be lynched at Waxahachie that same day, Saturday 28 July 1860.[230] The men were suspected of being involved in the attempt to set fire to roughly two dozen prominent structures in the town.[231] According to reports, had a woman not been sitting up with a sick friend and witnessed the start of the blaze perhaps the entire town would have gone up in flames.

Emotions were running high in the area where abolitionists had stirred up strong sentiment in the black community. Numerous incidents of poisonings by use of strychnine had been reported. It is very likely that there are duplicate entries for lynchings connected with this incident fostered by journalists anxious to draw attention to the racial strife that preceded succession and the Civil War.

One Unidentified White Man
Born: (Unknown)—Date of Death: circa August 1860
Place: Colorado County
Event: Lynching/Hanged

One Unidentified Black Man
Born: (Unknown)—Date of Death: circa August 1860
Place: Colorado County
Event: Lynching/Hanged

A traveling map seller and a black man were reportedly hanged together near Columbus in Colorado County. Although their assassins probably had a reason for the lynching it was not mentioned in the newspaper article.[232]

Lemon, J. F.
Born: (Unknown)—Date of Death: circa August 1860
Place: Wood County
Event: Lynching/Hanged

J. F. Lemon, referred to as an "abolitionist," was lately hung in Wood County.[233]

One Unidentified Man
Born: (Unknown)—Date of Death: August 1860
Place: Smith County
Event: Lynching/Shot

According to sources, in Tyler a night patrolman shot and killed a man he thought was trying to set fire to the town.[234] At the time mobs of blacks were thought to be organizing to kill their masters.

One Unidentified Black Man
Born: (Unknown)—Date of Death: August 1860
Place: Tyler County
Event: Lynching/Beaten

According to one source, at Billums Creek in Tyler County four blacks were whipped severely, resulting in the death of one of them.[235]

One Unidentified White Man
Born: (Unknown)—Date of Death: August 1860
Place: Ellis County
Event: Lynching/Hanged

One unidentified white man who was employed at a store at Waxahachie was lynched for having given strychnine to slaves so that they might poison wells.[236]

Two Unidentified Black Men
Born: (Unknown)—Date of Death: August 1860
Place: Washington County
Event: Legal Execution/Hanged

Two unidentified black men were found guilty of murdering their master, Thomas Erwin, and were hanged at Brenham sometime before 7 August 1860. The men, employed by Erwin and his father, were building a structure at their direction at a place about seven miles from the elder Erwin's home.

On the night in question the two black men waited until the white employees had retired, then saddled a horse, stole a shotgun, and rode to the Erwin home. Once there one of the men decoyed the dogs away while the other tied rags on his feet and crept into the home and fatally shot Erwin.

The men were captured shortly afterwards and jailed at Brenham. Texas Rangers reported that Mrs. Erwin has been in convulsions since the incident.[237]

Two Unidentified White Men and Several Unidentified Black Men
Born: (Unknown)—Date of Death: August 1860
Place: Henderson County
Event: Lynching /Hanged

Several Unidentified Black Men
Born: (Unknown)—Date of Death: August 1860
Place: Henderson County
Event: Lynching /Hanged

Newspaper accounts of the day claim that two unidentified white man and "several" blacks were lynched at Athens for attempting to burn the town. The white men were no doubt abolitionists. Although no exact date was provided by the source, the incident occurred sometime just before 7 September.[238]

Two Unidentified White Men
Born: (Unknown)—Date of Death: August 1860
Place: Stephens County
Event: Lynching/Hanged

Two unidentified white men, both abolitionists, were lynched at Breckenridge in August 1860.[239]

Morrison, (Given Name Unknown)
Born: (Unknown)—Date of Death: August 1860
Place: Upshur County
Event: Lynching/Hanged

A white man identified only as Mr. Morrison was lynched at Upshur County for stealing a black woman and for inciting the black population to insurrection. Morrison was hung in the suburbs of Gilmer.[240] Although he was lynched without benefit of a trial, the citizens of Gilmer were satisfied with his guilt.

Kirk, (Given Name Unknown)
Born: (Unknown)—Date of Death: August 1860
Place: Cooke County
Event: Lynching/Hanged

Hensley, (Given Name Unknown)
Born: (Unknown)—Date of Death: August 1860
Place: Cooke County
Event: Lynching/Hanged

Templeton, (Given Name Unknown)
Born: (Unknown)—Date of Death: August 1860
Place: Cooke County
Event: Lynching/Hanged

Three white abolitionists identified only as Templeton, Kirk and Hensley were lynched at Gainesville. Some sources claim that the hanging took place at Clarksville. Before their death, the threesome implicated fifteen additional abolitionists.[241]

Butry, Charles
Born: (Unknown)—Date of Death: 4 August 1860
Place: Galveston County
Event: Legal Execution/Hanged

Although the authors have, thus far, been unable to verify this incident, reports of the day claim that a white man named Charles Butry was executed by hanging at Galveston. He is buried at the City Cemetery.[242]

Cable, Alfred
Born: 3 June 1838—Date of Death: 5 August 1860
Place: Anderson County
Event: Lynching/Hanged

Wyrick, Anthony
Born: 3 March 1833—Date of Death: 5 August 1860
Place: Anderson County
Event: Lynching/Hanged

Anthony Wyrick and his cousin Alford Cable were wagon makers and blacksmiths by trade, and had settled at Catfish Creek near the Tennessee Colony and Bethel. They were lynched for inciting insurrection among the black slaves at Anderson County. Blacks were found there in possession of firearms and strychnine poison. Wyrick had previously been charged with selling ardent spirits to blacks.[243]

After their so called "trial", the men were made to ride in a wagon, seated on their own coffins, as they traveled to the spot where the hanging was to take place.[244]

By 1860 the city had enacted a rigorous code that prohibited slaves from hiring their own kind, finding or owning their dwellings, buying or drinking ardent spirits, gambling, congregating in groups of five or more without permission, holding dances without permission, and going about on their own after sunset without a pass from their owners. The city council, at the urging of Galveston slaveholders, repeatedly increased the severity of punishments for slaves buying liquor or whites selling it to them.

One Unidentified Black Man
Born: (Unknown)—Date of Death: 5 August 1860
Place: Henderson County
Event: Lynching/Hanged

According to sources, an unidentified black man who was suspected of arson was lynched at Science Hill on 5 August 1860.[245] Were it not for the fact that this report was provided by the same source as the following case involving a man named Allen one might hypothesize that both involved the same person.

Surname Unknown, Allen
Born: (Unknown)—Date of Death: 10 August 1860
Place: Henderson County
Event: Legal Execution/Hanged

On Friday, 10 August 1860, a black man was legally hanged at Science Hill for committing arson on the residence of Dr. Renfro. When captured the man, identified only as Allen, and who had been the property of Colonel Dunn, was found to have in his possession pistols, knives, bullets, musket and a half full keg of powder.[246]

Tucker, Robert
Born: (Unknown)—Date of Death: 16 August 1860
Place: Johnson County
Event: Lynching/Hanged

On Friday, 16 August 1860, Robert Tucker, a white man, was lynched at Poluxy Springs. Tucker, a notorious horse thief, was apprehended by Mr. R. Brown of Robertson County. He confessed his crimes, and repented shortly before being hanged on orders from a vigilante committee. [247]

Boatwright, Willoughby
Born: circa 1815—Date of Death: 19 August 1860
Place: Robertson County
Event: Lynching/Hanged

Boatwright, Richard
Born: 20 June 1807—Date of Death: 19 August 1860
Place: Robertson County
Event: Lynching/Hanged

Newspaper accounts of the day indicate that two white men with the surname Boatwright were lynched at Robertson County for "tampering with slaves."[248] Willoughby and Richard Boatwright were cousins, both living at Robertson County.[249] They were brought before a vigilante committee where they were found guilty and sentenced to hang. The verdict was carried out, and the Boatwright cousins were swung into eternity.[250]

Two Unidentified White Men
Born: (Unknown)—Date of Death: Week of 19 August 1860
Place: Tarrant County
Event: Lynching/Hanged

Newspaper accounts of the day claim that while passing through Belton in his travels George M. Flournoy, then candidate for attorney general (an office that he would ultimately be elected to) reported the lynching of two abolitionists at Tarrant County.[251] Just like contemporary politicians, Flournoy failed to provide any useful information about the incident.

Hernden, Green
Born: (Unknown)—Date of Death: 25 August 1860
Place: Rusk County
Event: Lynching/Hanged

Unidentified Black Woman
Born: (Unknown)—Date of Death: 25 August 1860
Place: Rusk County
Event: Lynching/Hanged

On Saturday, 25 August 1860, Green Hernden and a black female referred to as his "slave girl" were lynched for having started a fire that nearly burned the town of Henderson to the ground.[252]
     The principal hotel and all but one of the businesses were destroyed in the blaze. The loss was

estimated to have totaled $175,000 to $250,000. $50,000 worth of damaged goods were burned in the street after removal from the stores. The entire supply of groceries and perishables for the town were ruined, leaving many families reduced to want. The slave girl belonging to Green Herndon, a tavern-keeper, confessed to having started the blaze. Herndon and his brother were placed under arrest for their involvement in the fire.

Herndon was already accused of having dealt with slaves for stolen goods. A citizen's committee was investigating that affair, and many blacks had confessed to having knowledge of a general plot involving the fire as well as murder.[253]

One newspaper, *The Tyler Reporter*, claimed that a report had just reached there that Belleview, in Rusk County, was burned on the night of 4 August 1860. The same paper said that Dangerfield, in Titus County, was burned. At Athens, Henderson County, a well was discovered to be poisoned on Sunday night, 5 August, and over 100 bottles of strychnine were found in possession of slaves.

One Unidentified White Man

Born: (Unknown)—Date of Death: September 1860
Place: Houston County
Event: Lynching/Hanged

An unidentified white man was lynched near Angel's Store in Valley, about twenty-two miles north of Sumpter.[254] One newspaper pundit opined that he knew practically everyone in the area, and that he was certain they would not have hung this man without sufficient grounds.

Staton, William R.

Born: circa 1829—Date of Death: September 1860
Place: Anderson County
Event: Lynching/Hanged

A man identified in newspaper accounts as William Staton, a white man and a long time resident of Anderson County, was lynched for having incited local blacks to riot. A vigilante committee reviewed the facts, found him guilty, and carried out the execution.[255] Staton, who was aged about thirty-one at the time, lived with his parents and six siblings near Pruitt's Tanning Yard.[256]

Garner, John T.

Born: (Unknown)—Date of Death: 6 September 1860
Place: McLennan County
Event: Lynching/Hanged

John Garner, a white man, was found lynched from the limb of a live oak tree near the town of Waco.

The work had been done by a local vigilante committee. Owing to the fact that Garner was a horse thief, his fate was predictable.[257] A coroner's inquest ruled that Garner had "...died for want of breath" and that "...there being no hope for his becoming a better man."[258]

Various accounts of Garner's death place the date anywhere from 6 September to 13 September, but 6 September is believed to be most accurate.

Bewley, Anthony

Born: 22 May 1804—Date of Death: 13 September 1860
Place: Tarrant County
Event: Lynching/Hanged

Anthony Bewley was a white abolitionist and a Methodist preacher. From 1829 to 1834, he served as a circuit-riding member of the Holston Conference of Virginia. In 1834, he married Jane Winton and by 1837 had moved to Polk County, Missouri. Six years later Bewley resumed his circuit-riding ministry and joined the Missouri Conference of the Methodist Episcopal Church.

When the church divided over the issue of slavery in 1845, he chose to remain in what was then considered to be the true Methodist Church, and by 1848, they had reorganized into the Missouri Conference of the Northern Church, still referring to themselves simply as members of the Methodist Episcopal Church.

By 1858, Bewley had moved his family to Johnson County and established a mission sixteen miles south of Fort Worth. Although he was considered to be weak on the slavery issue by some northern Methodists, his antislavery views were threatening to southerners. In the summer of 1860, there was a widespread abolitionist plot to burn Texas towns and murder citizens. Suspicion immediately fell upon Bewley and other outspoken critics of slavery. Bewley drew special attention to himself as a consequence of an incendiary letter, dated 3 July 1860, addressed to a Rev. William Bewley and supposedly written by a fellow abolitionist, William H. Bailey. Many argued that the letter, which urged Bewley to continue with his work in helping to free Texas from slavery, was a forgery.

Recognizing the danger, Bewley left for Kansas in mid July with part of his family. En route, he stopped for eleven days in Indian Territory to wait for the remainder of his family and later visited with his wife's relatives in Benton County, Arkansas. On 3 September 1860, a Texas posse caught up with him near Cassville, Missouri. His captors returned him to Fort Worth on 13 September. Late that night vigilantes seized Bewley and delivered him into the hands of a waiting lynch mob at Veals' Station.

His body was allowed to hang until the following day when his remains were buried in a shallow grave. In an especially gruesome turn of events, three weeks after his burial Bewley's bones were unearthed, stripped of their remaining flesh, and placed on top of Ephraim Daggett's storehouse where children made a habit of playing with them.

After Bewley's death the Northern Methodists ended their activities in Texas."[259]

Montgomery, Robert
Born: (Unknown)—Date of Death: 30 September 1860
Place: Bexar County
Event: Lynching/Hanged

Rivers, Frank
Born: (Unknown)—Date of Death: 30 September 1860
Place: Bexar County
Event: Lynching/Hanged

Two horse thieves, Colonel Bob Montgomery and Frank Rivers, who hailed from Fort Smith, Arkansas, were lynched for their nefarious trade at San Antonio on Sunday, 30 September 1860. Rivers had formerly been the proprietor of a saloon at Fort Smith before choosing this decidedly more risky profession.[260]
    Some sources list the lynching as having taken place on Saturday, 13 October 1860.

Foster, Given Name Unknown
Born: (Unknown)—Date of Death: 18 October 1860
Place: Unknown
Event: Lynching/Hanged

Shreeves, John P.
Born: (Unknown)—Date of Death: 18 October 1860
Place: Unknown
Event: Lynching/Hanged

According to newspaper reports of the day Dr. John Shreeves and Mrs. Foster were abolitionists who, after having been threatened for their beliefs, were on their way out of Texas with their families when they were overtaken and lynched. Mr. Foster and the remainder of the party made it out unscathed.[261]
    After a train ride home, Shreeves was buried at Monument Cemetery, Philadelphia, Pennsylvania on 24 October 1860.[262]

Four Unknown County Commissioners
Born: (Unknown)—Date of Death: 21 October 1860
Place: Navarro County
Event: Lynching/Hanged

On Tuesday Morning, 21 October 1860, four county commissioners were lynched at Navarro County. Newspapers claimed that they knew of no reason for this action to have been taken. The vigilantes who did the work must have thought otherwise.[263]

Wilburn, Given Name Unknown
Born: (Unknown)—Date of Death: 5 November 1860
Place: Hardin County
Event: Lynching/Hanged

Three Wilburn Sons
Born: (Unknown)—Date of Death: 5 November 1860
Place: Hardin County
Event: Lynching/Hanged

A feud of some sort had existed between the Mooney and Wilburn families. Both clans lived in the Nacogdoches area when the hostilities began. Mooney eventual removed from the region, setting up residence at Concord in Hardin County. On Sunday, 4 November 1860, Mr. Wilburn and his three sons murdered Mooney and outraged his wife. According to newspaper reports of the day, Mooney was generally well liked and was a man of good character.

     Wilburn and his sons were taken into custody and placed in confinement. The following day all four men were found hanging from a tree limb at Boggy Bayou, about a mile from Concord. Apparently local citizens did not want to wait for the formality of a trial.[264]

Jefferson, James
Born: (Unknown)—Date of Death: 8 November 1860
Place: Bosque County
Event: Lynching/Hanged

On Thursday, 8 November 1860, a man named Charles Bechtel was murdered at his own grocery store at Kimball. His killer, James Jefferson, shot Bechtel in the head one time, then concealed the body beneath the counter at the man's own store. Jefferson fled.

     Unwisely, Jefferson returned some time later to retrieve money that he had deposited with a firm in town. The visit led to his capture. Jefferson was confined to the local jail awaiting a hearing. The same evening he was forcibly removed by vigilantes and lynched from a tree at the outskirts of town.[265]

Three Unidentified White Men
Born: (Unknown)—Date of Death: December 1860
Place: Washington County
Event: Lynching/Hanged

According to newspaper reports of the day, three unidentified white men were lynched at Brenham for the "...greatest crimes against the peace of the community." The definition of the foregoing is unclear, but it was serious enough to warrant justice at the end of a vigilante's rope.[266]

Two Unidentified White Men

Born: (Unknown)—Date of Death: 7 December 1860
Place: Coryell County
Event: Lynching/Hanged

In a tale that sounds too remarkable to be true...even for Texas...one East Coast newspaper reported that two unidentified white men were lynched at Coryell County for voting for Abraham Lincoln in the presidential election.[267] Regardless of how far fetched it may sound this account is being included in the interest of completeness.

Five Unidentified Black Men

Born: (Unknown)—Date of Death: circa 1861
Place: Lamar County
Event: Lynching/Hanged and Beaten

In an unverified account, sources claim that three unidentified black men were lynched and two whipped to death for their participation in a plot to slay whites.[268]

In this case the source cited seems anxious to lay off the identification of their primary source on several secondary sources, leading one to the conclusion that perhaps they did not bother to check a source document themselves. On examining the resources claimed it was learned that they had no primary source either, leaving one to ponder the veracity of this case.

Frank, Given Name Unknown

Born: (Unknown)—Date of Death: circa 1861 - 1865
Place: Atascosa County
Event: Legal Execution/Hanged

Newspaper accounts of the day filed an extremely vague report of a man named Frank having been legally hanged at Jourdanton for murder. No details were provided, and the time period spans five years in total.[269]

One Unidentified Man

Born: (Unknown)—Date of Death: circa 1861
Place: Colorado County
Event: Lynching/Hanged

The killer of Colonel C. C. Hubbard, a prominent state congressional representative who had been gunned down on the streets of Columbus in 1861, was taken from jail a few days afterwards and lynched. The man's identity remains unknown.[270]

Bradley, Joseph
Born: (Unknown)—Date of Death: May 1861
Place: Harris County
Event: Lynching/Hanged

Joseph Bradley, a white man and a shoemaker, was lynched at Harris County for being a Unionist. A Mr. H. O. Ayers of Manchester, New Hampshire witnessed the incident. Ayers barely escaped considering he shared views with Bradley.[271]

Barron, James H.
Born: 17 February 1827—Date of Death: 19 July 1861
Place: Coryell County
Event: Lynching/Hanged

Barron, David
Born: circa 1840—Date of Death: 19 July 1861
Place: Coryell County
Event: Lynching/Hanged

Beck, William
Born: (Unknown)—Date of Death: 19 July 1861
Place: Coryell County
Event: Lynching/Hanged

Underwood, Given Name Unknown
Born: (Unknown)—Date of Death: 19 July 1861
Place: Coryell County
Event: Lynching/Hanged

Four Unidentified White Men
Born: (Unknown)—Date of Death: 19 July 1861
Place: Coryell County
Event: Lynching/Hanged

One newspaper source indicated that three unidentified men had been lynched for murder and cattle theft somewhere in central Texas in April 1861. A mob from Coryell, Hamilton, Bosque, Comanche and McLennan Counties did the work.[272] Another account claims that nine men were lynched on Thursday, 18 July 1861, at Neill's Creek in Coryell County. That source identified the victims as a man named Underwood, three to four men named Barnes, and other unnamed persons.[273]

Further accounts seem to reveal that the individuals involved were James Barron and his younger brother David, along with another man named Beck. They had murdered an old man named Gardner from Coryell County the preceding spring, and had developed a particular fondness for their neighbor's cattle. For that they were lynched by a group of stockmen and vigilantes from Coryell, Hamilton, Bosque, Comanche and McLennan Counties. According to the second and seemingly more reliable source, the lynching took place on 19 July 1861.[274] A host of family genealogists believe that the deaths occurred on 20 July 1861.[275]

Haygood, Thomas
Born: (Unknown)—Date of Death: 16 August 1861
Place: Grimes County
Event: Lynching/Hanged

Jones, Benaiah III
Born: 31 May 1795—Date of Death: 17 August 1861
Place: Grimes County
Event: Lynching/Hanged

It seems that Judge James H. Anderson of Grimes County was walking through a field belonging to a man named Benaiah Jones and, while doing so, shot several hogs. Thomas Haygood, who was in the employ of Jones, shot and killed Anderson, presumably for having killed the pigs.

Citizens of the county quickly assembled. They lynched Haygood the same day as the Anderson killing. Before he was hung, Haygood boasted that he had killed three men and had served ten years in the penitentiary. The following day the vigilantes caught up with Jones and did the same for him.[276]

Jones left behind a widow named Amanda Evans Hutchinson and six children. Interestingly, it seems that Mr. Jones never bothered to obtain a divorce from his first wife, Lois Olds, who he had wed in Ohio in 1818, before marrying Amanda in Texas circa 1848. Five of the couple's eight children were still living when Benaiah was lynched.[277]

One Unidentified Mexican Man
Born (Unknown)—Date of Death: circa September 1861
Place: Nueces County
Event: Lynching/ Hanged

Some time in September of 1861, an unidentified Mexican man attempted to poison the family of Mr. Egbart of Banquete. He did so by mixing strychnine with milk and coffee served at the family meal. The fellow was "...given an impartial trial by a committee of local citizens and hanged..."[278]

Augustine, Bob
Born (Unknown)—Date of Death: 9 or 18 September 1861
Place: Bexar County
Event: Lynching/Hanged

Bob Augustine was described as a dandy and a notorious desperado. In 1857, he was tried at San Antonio on a charge of assault with intent to kill. The outcome was that Augustine was sentenced to serve five years in the penitentiary.

Before completing his sentence he escaped from prison and joined a group of volunteers fighting in Nicaragua. After being wounded, he returned to New Orleans where he was arrested and returned to Texas to finish his sentence.

The governor issued him a pardon. Augustine went back to San Antonio to seek revenge against those whom he believed were instrumental in his conviction. He threatened to kill the jurors. Augustine rode through the market destroying the stands and creating a disturbance.[279] Accounts vary as to the exact date of that vendetta ride. On Monday, 9 September 1861, a city judge found Augustine not guilty and released him. A mob of citizens seized Augustine and promptly hanged him from a tree.[280] The *Houston Telegraph* cited the date as being Wednesday, 18 September 1861. Another source claims the incident took place on 9 September. It is unclear which is correct.[281]

Esry, Given Name Unknown
Born (Unknown)—Date of Death: circa November 1861
Place: North Texas
Event: Lynching/Hanging

The *Dallas Weekly Herald* of 13 November 1861, reported that the Sherman and Paris papers had noted the hanging of several men in Northern Texas. Their crime was unsoundness on the "southern question." The tabloid went on to say, "A Mr. Esry, of Captain Brinson's company was hung for another and different offense, but one as bad and as shocking to every sense of manliness. We suppose they were all served about right."[282]

Beal, James A.

Born: (Unknown)—Date of Death: 12 November 1861

Place: Grayson County

Event: Legal Execution/Firing Squad

The *Sherman Patriot* newspaper reported that James A. Beal, who had been acting as adjutant of one Red River Regiment camped at Grayson, was shot as a spy on Tuesday, 12 November 1861.[283]

Ensor, Eli

Born: (Unknown)—Date of Death: December 1861

Place: McLennan County

Event: Lynching/Hanged

In December 1861, Eli Ensor was lynched for having fornicated with a black person. A mob led by William Johnson did the vigilante work.[284]

Hays, Demetrius

Born: circa 1801—Date of Death: 21 December 1861

Place: McLennan County

Event: Lynching/Hanged

On Saturday, 21 December 1861, Demetrius Hays was lynched for harboring a fugitive slave. As in the case of Eli Ensor, a mob led by William Johnson did the vigilante work.[285] Hays was the brother of Judge Daniel Smith Hays. He came to Waco in the 1850s as a surveyor and helped George Erath in the platting of Waco. Hays is buried at the First Street Cemetery in Waco.[286]

Simon, Ferdinand

Born: (Unknown)—Date of Death: circa 1862

Place: Bexar County

Event: Legal Execution

Ferdinand Simon, a white Unionist was tried by courts martial at San Antonio, found guilty and sentenced to die. It is unclear if that verdict was carried out, however. Given that there are several men named Ferdinand Simon who were living in the area at the time it is difficult to pinpoint any of them as being the person referred to here. Based on genealogical information it appears that all of these men lived well past 1862, therefore this account may be in error.[287]

Turknett, Jacob
Born: circa 1787—Date of Death: circa 1862
Place: Gillespie County
Event: Lynching/Beaten

Turknett, John S.C.
Born: circa 1845—Date of Death: circa 1862
Place: Gillespie County
Event: Lynching/Beaten

Turknett, Philip Brandon
Born: circa 1822—Date of Death: circa 1862
Place: Gillespie County
Event: Lynching

In about 1862, a patrol of Confederate Frontier Regiment soldiers under Captain James W. Duff out of Camp Davis found young John S.C. Turknett and his grandfather Jacob Turknett just north of Mountain Home looking for lost livestock on the Peril ranch.[288] Separating the pair, troopers beat the seventy-five year old grandfather Jacob Turknett to death with a bullwhip while others alternately hung and questioned John in an effort to get information about his father, Philip Brandon Turknett. John, just fourteen at the time, died without revealing the location of his father, who subsequently fled to Mexico. Philip Turknett was also killed in a separate incident on Goat Creek in 1862, and is buried in the Rogers Pasture on the old Ed Peril Ranch. [289]

John and Jacob are buried at the Peril Cemetery in Gillespie County. Philip is buried at the Henderson Cemetery, located on the Lazy Hills Ranch property, in Kerr County.

Six Unidentified White Men
Born: (Unknown)—Date of Death: January 1862
Place: Cooke County
Event: Lynching/Hanged

According to a *Hudson Telegraph* newspaper, reports of the day claim that six men were lynched from one tree near Waco, "...most on account of horse theft."[290]

Bone, Given Name Unknown (Father)
Born: (Unknown)—Date of Death: 9 January 1862
Place: Cooke County
Event: Lynching/Hanged

Bone, Given Name Unknown (Son)

Born: (Unknown)—Date of Death: 9 January 1862

Place: Cooke County

Event: Lynching/Hanged

On Thursday, 9 January 1862, Mr. Bone and his son brutally murdered a young man named McCall at Gainesville. Father and son were taken into custody and housed in the jail. Under cover of darkness, a mob of angry citizens removed the pair and lynched them from a horse rack in the center of town.[291]

Wood, Given Name Unknown

Born: (Unknown)—Date of Death: 20 March 1862

Place: McLennan County

Event: Lynching/Hanged

Mr. Wood was hanged by a mob of eight men for being a Yankee Abolitionist.[292] The mob included Henry and John T. Russell and Calvin T. Tinsley, who were themselves dealt with for their actions not long after the lynching of Wood.

  Newspaper accounts of the day seem to indicate that this incident took place in May, not March. However, a convincing number of family genealogists present evidence that the deaths took place in March 1862.

Russell, Henry

Born: 4 June 1842—Date of Death: 23 March 1862

Place: McLennan County

Event: Lynching/Hanged

Russell, James T.

Born: 23 December 1816—Date of Death: 23 March 1862

Place: McLennan County

Event: Lynching/Hanged

Tinsley, Calvin Thomas

Born: 7 January 1830—Date of Death: 23 March 1862

Place: McLennan County

Event: Lynching/Hanged

James T. Russell, his son Henry, and Calvin T. Tinsley were responsible for the lynching of Mr. Wood. That incident took place on 20 March 1862. Wood's only crime was that of being a Yankee Abolitionist. It seems that was not always a sufficient transgression to warrant hanging in Texas, even in 1862. Thus, enraged citizens dealt harshly with the perpetrators and, in turn, lynched them for their treatment of Wood.[293] He is buried at the Liberty Grove Cemetery in McLennan County.

Newspaper accounts of the day seem to indicate that this incident took place in May. However, in this case as well a convincing number of family genealogists present evidence that the deaths took place in March 1862.

Baker, Charles
Born: (Unknown)—Date of Death: 10 April 1862
Place: Galveston County
Event: Lynching/Hanged

A man of German ancestry named Charles Baker kept a saloon and boarding house at the corner of Strand and Twenty-Sixth Street. Baker had chickens stolen from him and was trying to catch the thieves. As a group of soldiers from Captain Duprees' 26th Regiment of Texas Cavalry passed in the alley behind his house Baker opened fire, mortally wounding a solider named White.

Baker fled and hid out beneath one of the nearby wharfs. He was eventually apprehended and taken to the guardhouse. At about 9:00 am on the morning following the incident (Thursday, 10 April 1862) members of the slain soldiers outfit removed Baker from the guardhouse and hanged him from a signpost where his body remained for hours before being cut down. Baker is buried in the City Cemetery at Galveston.[294]

Thompson, Given Name Unknown #1
Born: (Unknown)—Date of Death: 1 May 1862
Place: McLennan County
Event: Lynching/Hanged

Thompson, Given Name Unknown #2
Born: (Unknown)—Date of Death: 1 May 1862
Place: McLennan County
Event: Lynching/Hanged

Parties unknown lynched two men with the surname Thompson for horse theft. The source in this case had nothing further to say about the matter.[295]

One Unidentified Black Man
Born (Unknown)—Date of Death: circa July 1862
Place: Guadalupe County
Event: Lynching/Hanged

Newspaper reported of the day indicate that a white slave owner attempted to outrage a black woman in the presence of her slave husband. The incident took place near Seguin. The woman's husband struck the master, which led to his being hanged for defending his wife's honor.[296]

Lount, Given Name Unknown
Born: (Unknown)—Date of Death: 25 July 1862
Place: Harris County
Event: Legal Execution/Hanged

Mr. Lount, a black slave, was convicted of robbery and murder. He was legally hanged in Harris County on Friday, 25 July 1862.[297]

Nelson, Hiram Louis
Born: 12 November 1797—Date of Death: 27 July 1862
Place: Gillespie County
Event: Lynching

Scott, Charles Franklin "Frank"
Born: circa 1836—Date of Death: 22 August 1862
Place: Gillespie County
Event: Lynching

Scott, Given Name Unknown
Born: (Unknown)—Date of Death: 22 August 1862
Place: Gillespie County
Event: Lynching

Scott, Given Name Unknown - Elder
Born: (Unknown)—Date of Death: 22 August 1862
Place: Gillespie County
Event: Lynching

Johnson, Parson
Born: (Unknown)—Date of Death: 22 August 1862
Place: Gillespie County
Event: Lynching

Henderson, Seabird
Born: circa 1805—Date of Death: 22 August 1862
Place: Gillespie County
Event: Lynching

Tegener, Guss
Born: (Unknown)—Date of Death: 22 August 1862
Place: Gillespie County
Event: Lynching

Tegener, William
Born: (Unknown)—Date of Death: August 1862
Place: Gillespie County
Event: Lynching

Henderson Schram
Born: (Unknown)—Date of Death: 22 August 1862
Place: Gillespie County
Event: Lynching

On Friday, 22 August 1862, a patrol of Confederate Frontier Regiment soldiers under the command of Captain James W. Duff, out of Camp Davis, massacred a group of Unionists at Spring Creek in Gillespie County. Duff's men tied rocks to the men's feet and threw them into Spring Creek. Their crime was refusing to pledge allegiance to the Confederacy within the three-day period they had been allowed.

Included on the list of victims were Gus Tegener, Schram Henderson, Sebird Henderson, Frank Scott, Unidentified Scott, Parson Johnson, and elder Unidentified Scott. Duff's men had killed Hiram Nelson a few days earlier, on 27 July 1862. They also killed William Tegener a few days after the Spring Creek incident.[298]

All of these men are believed to be buried at the Spring Creek Cemetery in Gillespie County, however only the graves of Charles Scott, Seabird Henderson, and Hiram Nelson are marked.

Throughout the course of the Civil War Captain James W. Duff (1828-1900) and his band of troops from Camp Davis, near Fredericksburg, were feared throughout the Hill Country region. Their brutal treatment of Union sympathizers was noteworthy. The number of lynching's, shooting, drowning and beating that his band was responsible for has never been accurately accounted for.

Thirty-Six Unionists - "Nueces Massacre"
Bauer, Leopold
Born: circa 1839—Date of Death: 10 August 1862
Place: Kinney County
Event: Lynching/Shot

Behrens, Frederick "Fritz"
Born: (Unknown)—Date of Death: 10 August 1862
Place: Kinney County
Event: Lynching/Shot

Beseler, Ernst
Born: circa 1842—Date of Death: 10 August 1862
Place: Kinney County
Event: Lynching/Shot

Boerner, Louis
Born: circa 1842—Date of Death: 10 August 1862
Place: Kinney County
Event: Lynching

Bruns, Albert
Born: circa 1838—Date of Death: 10 August 1862
Place: Kinney County
Event: Lynching/Shot

Degener, Hilmar
Born: circa 1840—Date of Death: 10 August 1862
Place: Kinney County
Event: Lynching

Degener, Hugo
Born: circa 1842—Date of Death: 10 August 1862
Place: Kinney County
Event: Lynching/Shot

Dias, Pablo
Born: (Unknown)—Date of Death: 10 August 1862
Place: Kinney County
Event: Lynching/Shot

Flick, Herman
Born: circa 1840—Date of Death: 10 August 1862
Place: Kinney County
Event: Lynching/Hanged

Kallenberg, Johann George
Born: 6 September 1842—Date of Death: 10 August 1862
Place: Kinney County
Event: Lynching/Shot

Luckenbach, Frederick August
Born: 7 March 1833—Date of Death: 10 August 1862
Place: Kinney County
Event: Lynching/Hanged

Markwardt, Heinrich Wilhelm "Henry"
Born: 30 June 1828—Date of Death: 10 August 1862
Place: Kinney County
Event: Lynching/Shot

Schaefer, Christian
Born: circa 1844—Date of Death: 10 August 1862
Place: Kinney County
Event: Lynching/Shot

Schierholz, Louis
Born: circa 1833—Date of Death: 10 August 1862
Place: Kinney County
Event: Lynching/Shot

Schreiner, Aime
Born: circa 1839—Date of Death: 10 August 1862
Place: Kinney County
Event: Lynching/Shot

Stevens, Heinrich
Born: (Unknown)—Date of Death: 10 August 1862
Place: Kinney County
Event: Lynching/Shot

Telgmann, Wilhelm
Born: circa 1830—Date of Death: 10 August 1862
Place: Kinney County
Event: Lynching/Shot

Vater, Adolph
Born: circa 1830—Date of Death: 10 August 1862
Place: Kinney County
Event: Lynching/Shot

Vater, Friedrich "Fritz"
Born: circa 1830—Date of Death: 10 August 1862
Place: Kinney County
Event: Lynching/Shot

Weirich, Michael
Born: circa 1839—Date of Death: 10 August 1862
Place: Kinney County
Event: Lynching/Shot

Weyerhausen, Heinrich
Born: 10 January 1830—Date of Death: 10 August 1862
Place: Kinney County
Event: Lynching/Shot

Lange, Frederick "Fritz"
Born: circa 1832—Date of Death: 18 August 1862
Place: Kinney County
Event: Lynching/

Boerner, Wilhelm F.
Born: circa 1830—Date of Death: 20 August 1862
Place: Kinney County
Event: Lynching/Hanged

Buckisch, Theodore
Born: (Unknown)—Date of Death: 20 August 1862
Place: Kinney County
Event: Lynching/Hanged

Ruebsamen, Louis
Born: circa 1843—Date of Death: 20 August 1862
Place: Kinney County
Event: Lynching/Hanged

Ruebseman, Adolph
Born: circa 1840—Date of Death: 20 August 1862
Place: Kinney County
Event: Lynching/Hanged

Bock, Conrad
Born: 9 December 1836—Date of Death: 24 August 1862
Place: Kinney County
Event: Lynching/Hanged

Stieler, Heinrich
Born: circa 1841—Date of Death: 24 August 1862
Place: Kinney County
Event: Lynching/ Hanged

Tays, Heinrich Frederich "Fritz"
Born: circa 1842—Date of Death: 24 August 1862
Place: Kinney County
Event: Lynching/Hanged

Bonnet, Johan Peter
Born: 9 February 1833—Date of Death: 18 October 1862
Place: Kinney County
Event: Lynching/Shot

Elstner, Joseph
Born: circa 1840—Date of Death: 18 October 1862
Place: Kinney County
Event: Lynching/Shot

Felsing, Ernst
Born: circa 1829—Date of Death: 18 October 1862
Place: Kinney County
Event: Lynching/Shot

Hermann, Henry
Born: circa 1841—Date of Death: 18 October 1862
Place: Kinney County
Event: Lynching/Shot

Hohmann, Valdin Valentine
Born: circa 1828—Date of Death: 18 October 1862
Place: Kinney County
Event: Lynching/Shot

Weiss, Franz
Born: circa 1843—Date of Death: 18 October 1862
Place: Kinney County
Event: Lynching/Shot

Weiss, Moritz
Born: circa 1836—Date of Death: 18 October 1862
Place: Kinney County
Event: Lynching/Shot

The Nueces Massacre, or the *Geh Mit Ins Texas* as the descendents of German settlers call it, involved the murder of Thirty-Five Unionists, largely from the German-American community of the Hill Country.

On 1 August 1862, sixty-eight men, sixty-three of whom were Germans, one Mexican, and four white men, gathered at Turtle Creek in Kerr County. The group was comprised mostly of older men. They were all from Mason, Kendall, Kerr, and Gillespie Counties. All of them were targeted conscripts of Captain James Duff's Confederate forces. The men elected a Fritz Tegener, sometimes called Major Tegener, as their commander. Serving as Tegener's second-in-command was his Fredericksburg neighbor, Henry Joseph Schwethelm, who later documented the account of this gruesome episode. Jacob Kuechler also joined the company. Some sources argue that the band's aim was just to get to Mexico, in order to avoid conscription.

Back at Fredericksburg, Duff received word of the mass flight and burst into a rage. To Duff, the Germans were deserters. He sent word to Lieutenant C.D. McRae in San Antonio and instructed him to intercept the Germans, by forced march, at any cost. McRae raised of force of ninety-four men a headed out to cut off the Unionists.

McRae's out riders discovered the Germans camped near a cedar brake on the West Fork of the Nueces River, in Kinney County, not far from the Rio Grande. McRae devised a plan to attack the Germans at first light and, just before midnight on 10 August 1862, sent his men quietly forward in single file to take up positions around the German encampment. The Germans were taken completely by surprise. About twenty-six of them were killed while still in their bedrolls in the first volley. A large number died under the hooves of the charging Confederate soldiers. The remaining few were shot as they tried to surrender. All but seven of the survivors were hauled back to White Oak Creek in Gillespie County and hanged.

According to the article covering this incident in the *Handbook of Texas*, nineteen unionists were killed and nine wounded during the initial battle. The nine wounded were later hanged. Thirty-seven escaped. Six more unionists were killed while trying to cross the Rio Grande. Only eleven reached home safely. Twenty reached Mexico.

The most widely held opinion of the event, particularly among today's Hill Country descendants of those who perished, is that it was an out-and-out massacre of politically innocent Germans who were loyal to the Union. German immigration to the Hill Country region began in earnest in the 1830s. Those settlers came here to be a part of the United States, and had left a homeland where slavery had just been outlawed, in 1807.[299]

Killed in the Battle at Nueces on 10 August 1862:

Leopold Bauer, F. Behrens, Louis and Ernst Boerner, Albert Bruns, Hugo Degener, Fritz Vater, Hilmar Degener, Pablo Dias, Adolph Vater, Johann Geo. Kallenberg, Heinrich Markwart, Christian Schaefer, Louis Schierholz, Heinrich Stevens, Aime Schreiner, Wilhelm Telgmann, Michael Weirich, Heinrich Weyerhausen.

Captured, Taken Prisoner and Lynched:

Wilheim Boerner, Theodore Buckisch, Conrad Bock, F. Tays, Heinrich Stieler, Herman Flick, August Luckenbach, Louis Ruebsamen, Adolph Ruebseman.

Killed at Rio Grande on 18 October 1862
Joseph Elstner, Ernst Felsing, Peter Bonnet, H. Hermann, Valentine Hohmann, Fritz Lange, Franz and Moritz Weiss.[300]

Cottrell, John
Born (Unknown)—Died - October 1862
Place: Cooke County
Event: Legal Execution/Hanged

Johnson, A. N.
Born (Unknown)—Died - October 1862
Place: Cooke County
Event: Legal Execution/Hanged

McCool, William
Born: circa 1838—Died - October 1862
Place: Cooke County
Event: Legal Execution/Hanged

John Cottrell, A. N. Johnson and William McCool were tried by courts martial for treason and executed by the Confederate military during the Gainesville incident.[301] They are all buried at the Great Hanging burial site in Cooke County.

Kilborn, Hiram
Born: circa 1803—Died - 1 October 1862
Place: Cooke County
Event: Lynching/Shot

Hiram Kilborn was shot while trying to evade arrest during the "Great Hanging at Gainesville incident. He was not claimed as one of the Citizen's Court victims. He is buried at the Great Hanging burial site in Cooke County.

The Great Hanging at Gainesville

Forty suspected Unionists in Confederate Texas were hanged at Gainesville in October 1862. Two others were shot as they tried to escape. Although the affair reached a climax in Cooke County, men were killed in neighboring Grayson, Wise, and Denton counties. Most were accused of treason or insurrection, but evidently few had actually conspired against the Confederacy and many were innocent of the abolitionist sentiments for which they were tried.

The Great Hanging was the result of several years of building tension. The completion of the Butterfield Overland Mail route from St. Louis through Gainesville brought many new people from the upper South and Midwest into Cooke County. By 1860, fewer than ten percent of the heads of households owned slaves. The slaveholders increasingly feared the influence of Kansas abolitionists. During the summer of 1860 several slaves, and a northern Methodist minister, were lynched in North Texas. Cooke and the surrounding counties voted against secession, thus forcing the fears of planters on the non-slaveholders in the region. Rumors of Unionist alliances with Kansas Jayhawkers and Indians along the Red River, together with the petition of E. Junius Foster, editor of the Sherman Patriot, to separate North Texas as a new Free State, brought emotions to a fever pitch.

Actual opposition to the Confederacy in Cooke County began with the Conscription Acts of April 1862. Thirty men signed a petition protesting the exemption of large slaveholders from the draft and sent it to the Congress at Richmond. Brigadier General William Hudson, commander of the militia district around Gainesville, exiled their leader, but others who remained used the petition to enlist a nucleus for a Union League in Cooke and nearby counties. The members were not highly unified, and their purposes differed within each faction. Most joined to resist the draft and provide common defense against roving Indians and renegades. Rumors began to circulate, however, of a membership of over 1,700 and of plans for an assault when the group had recruited enough men. Fearing that the stories of Unionist plots to storm the militia arsenals at Gainesville and Sherman might prove to be true, Hudson activated the state troops in North Texas in late September 1862 and ordered the arrest of all able-bodied men who did not report for duty.

Texas state troops led by Colonel James G. Bourland arrested more than 150 men on the morning of 1 October 1862. In Gainesville he and Colonel William C. Young of the Eleventh Texas Cavalry, who at the time was home on sick leave, supervised the collection of a "citizen's court" of twelve jurors. Bourland and Young together owned nearly a fourth of the slaves in Cooke County, and seven of the jurors chosen were slaveholders. Their decision to convict on a majority vote was a bad omen for the prisoners, all of whom were accused of insurrection or treason and none of whom owned slaves. The military achieved its goal of eliminating the leadership of the Union League in Cooke County when the jury condemned seven influential Unionists, but an angry mob took matters into its own hands and lynched fourteen more before the jurors recessed. Violence in Gainesville peaked the next week when unknown assassins killed Young and James Dickson. The decision already made to release the rest of the prisoners was reversed, and many were tried again. Nineteen more men were convicted and hanged. Captain Jim Young, Colonel Young's son, supervised their execution. Brigadier General James W. Throckmorton prevented the execution of all but five men in Sherman, but in Decatur, Captain John Hale supervised a committee that hanged five suspects. A Southern partisan shot a prisoner in Denton.

Texas newspapers generally applauded the hangings, disparaged the Unionists as traitors and common thieves, and insisted they had material support from Kansas abolitionists and the Lincoln administration. The state government condoned the affair. Governor Francis Richard Lubbock, an ardent Confederate, praised Hudson for his actions, and the legislature paid the expenses of the troops in Gainesville. Articles from the Texas press were reprinted across the South. President Jefferson Davis, embarrassed, abandoned his demand for an inquiry into a similar incident involving northern troops in Palmyra, Missouri, and dismissed Gen. Paul Octave Hébert as military commander of Texas for his improper use of martial law in several instances, including the hangings. The northern press heralded the story as another example of Rebel barbarism. Andrew Jackson Hamilton, a former congressional representative from Texas and a Unionist, had been speaking in the North warning of the danger to loyal citizens in Texas. Reports of the Great Hanging and other incidents lent support to his campaign and led to his appointment as military governor of Texas and the disastrous Red River campaign of 1864.

The unrest did not end with the hangings in North Texas. Albert Pike, Confederate brigadier general in charge of Indian Territory, was implicated in testimony and arrested. Although later released, Pike continued to be regarded with suspicion and served the rest of the war in civilian offices. Captain Jim Young killed E. Junius Foster for applauding the death of his father. He also tracked down Dan Welch, the man he believed to be his father's assassin, then returned with him to Cooke County and had him lynched by some of the family slaves. The Union League was powerless to exact revenge. Many members fled along with the families of the slain prisoners, leaving bodies unclaimed for burial in a mass grave. A North Texas company of Confederate soldiers in Arkansas learned of the executions and almost mutinied, but Brigadier General Joseph O. Shelby, their commander, successfully defused the situation. Several men later deserted to return home, but Shelby prevented a mass assault on Gainesville. The half-hearted prosecution of those responsible for the hangings after the war, resulting in the conviction of only one man in Denton, increased resentment among the remaining Unionists in North Texas, but the failure of a Union League march on Decatur indicated the futility of further attempts at retaliation.[302]

Chiles, Ephraim
Born: 23 February 1826—Died - 4 October 1862

Chiles was survived by his wife Margaret "Peggy" Kendrick and three of the couple's four children. He is buried at the Great Hanging burial site in Cooke County.

Chiles, Henry Dr.
Born 21 November 1825—Died - 4 October 1862

Chiles was survived by his wife Dicey Ann Kennedy and eight children. He is buried at the Great Hanging burial site in Cooke County.

Fields, Henry S.
Born (Unknown)—Died - 4 October 1862

Nothing further is known about Fields. He is buried at the Great Hanging burial site in Cooke County.

Harper, Manadier D.
Born: circa 1821—Died - 4 October 1862

Harper was survived by his wife Eliza Dougherty and six children. He is buried at the Great Hanging burial site in Cooke County.

Morris, William Washington
Born: circa 1839—Died - 4 October 1862

Morris was survived by his wife Josephine Hornbuckle and four children. He is buried at the Great Hanging burial site in Cooke County.

Lock, Jacob W. P.
Born: circa 1822—Died - 7 October 1862

Lock was survived by his second wife Evaline Dale and five children. He is buried at the Great Hanging burial site in Cooke County.

Floyd, Thomas B.
Born: circa 1833—Died - 10 October 1862

Floyd was shot and killed while trying to escape. He was survived by his wife Cloe Carter and three children. He is buried at the Great Hanging burial site in Cooke County.

Foster, James F. Doctor
Born: circa 1823—Died - 10 October 1862

Foster was shot and killed while trying to escape. Nothing further is known about Foster. He is buried at the Great Hanging burial site in Cooke County.

Hampton, Edward D.
Born (Unknown)—Died - 10 October 1862

Nothing further is known about Hampton. He is buried at the Great Hanging burial site in Cooke County.

Anderson, Edward Frost (C.F.)
Born: circa 1810—Died - 13 October 1862

Anderson was survived by his wife Nancy Matilda Farris and four children. Two of Anderson's children were killed during the same incident (William and George). He is buried at the Great Hanging burial site in Cooke County.

Anderson, George W.
Born: circa 1835—Died - 13 October 1862

Anderson was not married. He is buried at the Great Hanging burial site in Cooke County.

Baker, Thomas O.
Born: circa 1840—Died - 13 October 1862

Baker was survived by his wife Ann Tinney. He is buried at the Great Hanging burial site in Cooke County.

Barnes, Bennett C.
Born: circa 1824—Died - 13 October 1862

Barnes was survived by his Sarah Ann Rodgers and five children. He is buried at the Great Hanging burial site in Cooke County.

Carmichael, Samuel
Born: circa 1821—Died - 13 October 1862

Carmichael was survived by his wife Anna. He is buried at the Great Hanging burial site in Cooke County.

Clark, Nathaniel M.
Born: 26 June 1816—Died - 13 October 1862

Clark was survived by his wife Mahulda Maron Lutisha Hicklin and eight children. He is buried at the Clark Family Cemetery outside Gainesville.

Cockrum, William Henry
Born: Circa 1831—Died - 13 October 1862

Cockrum was survived by his wife Elizabeth Lackey and six children. He is buried at the Great Hanging burial site in Cooke County.

Dye, Rama
Born: circa 1818—Died - 13 October 1862

Dye is buried at the Great Hanging burial site in Cooke County.

Jones, Charles (C.A.)
Born: circa 1842—Died - 13 October 1862

Nothing further is known about Jones. He is buried at the Great Hanging burial site in Cooke County.

McNeese, Abraham B.
Born: circa 1830—Died - 13 October 1862

McNeese is buried at the Great Hanging burial site in Cooke County. McNeese's surname is also seen spelled McNice or McNeice.

Morris, John W.
Born: circa 1828—Died - 13 October 1862

Morris is buried at the Great Hanging burial site in Cooke County. Some sources show his date of hanging as 19 October.

Powers, James A.
Born: circa 1833—Died - 13 October 1862

Powers was survived by his wife Priscilla Moriah Barnett and three children. He is buried at the Great Hanging burial site in Cooke County.

Rhodes, William R.
Born: circa 1818—Died - 13 October 1862

Rhodes was survived by his wife Amanda Lindsey and nine children. He is buried at the Great Hanging burial site in Cooke County.

Scott, Elliot "Eli" M.
Born: circa 1811—Died - 13 October 1862

Scott was survived by his second wife Maria and three children from that marriage along with three children from an earlier marriage to Sarah Ervin. He is buried at the Great Hanging burial site in Cooke County.[303]

Wornell, William Wilson
Born: circa 1814—Died - 13 October 1862

Wornell was survived by his wife Elizabeth Wilkerson and nine children. He is buried at the Great Hanging burial site in Cooke County. Some family genealogists list Wornell' birth year as 1814, 1815 or 1816.

Anderson, Richard J.
Born: circa 1832—Died 19 October 1862

Anderson was survived by his wife Lucinda and three children. He is buried at the Great Hanging burial site in Cooke County.

Anderson, William B.
Born: circa 1831—Died - 19 October 1862

Anderson was survived by his wife Lucinda Davis and one child. He is buried at the Great Hanging burial site in Cooke County.

Birch, Barnabas
Born circa 1798—Died - 19 October 1862

Birch was survived by his second wife Mary Tennyson and six of his seven children. He is buried at the Great Hanging burial site in Cooke County.

Crisp, John Mansil
Born: 23 June 1824—Died - 19 October 1862

Crisp was survived by his wife Alice Hawkins Stevens and six of the couple's seven children. He is buried at the Great Hanging burial site in Cooke County.

Dawson, Arfaxton R.
Born: circa 1805—Died - 19 October 1862

Dawson was survived by his third wife America Jane and seven of his twelve children by his first wife Mary Horn along with three children by his second wife Jane Caroline Stalcup. He is buried at the Great Hanging burial site in Cooke County.[304]

Esman, Hudson John
Born (Unknown)—Died - 19 October 1862

Nothing further is known about Eastman. He is buried at the Great Hanging burial site in Cooke County.

Goss, Carl Curd
Born: 9 March 1819—Died - 19 October 1862

Goss was survived by his wife Mary Evelyn "Polly" Alexander and one child. He is buried at the Great Hanging burial site in Cooke County.

Johnson, William W.
Born (Unknown)—Died - 19 October 1862

Nothing further is known about Johnson. He is buried at the Great Hanging burial site in Cooke County.

Leffel, David Miller
Born 20 January 1816—Died - 19 October 1862

Leffel had married Susan Emeline West in 1837. The couple had eight of their children were all born in Ohio. His place of burial is unknown.

Martin, Richard N.
Born: circa 1838—Died - 19 October 1862

Martin was survived by his wife His wife Cynthia Jane Neely and two children. He is buried at the Great Hanging burial site in Cooke County.

Miller, John M.
Born: circa 1821—Died - 19 October 1862

Miller was survived by his wife His wife Mary Eubanks and three children from his earlier marriage to Martha Jane Sandusky. He is buried at the Great Hanging burial site in Cooke County.

Morris, John A.
Born: circa 1820—Died - 19 October 1862

Morris was survived by his wife His wife Marguerite. He is buried at the Great Hanging burial site in Cooke County.

Morris, Michael Wesley
Born: circa 1828—Died - 19 October 1862

Morris was survived by his wife His wife Mary Carter and two children. He is buried at the Great Hanging burial site in Cooke County.

Scott, Alexander Dudley
Born: circa 1821—Died - 19 October 1862

Scott was survived by his wife His wife Mary Ann Woolsey and two children. He is buried at the Great Hanging burial site in Cooke County.

Smith, Gilbert
Born: circa 1838—Died - 19 October 1862

Nothing further is known about Smith. He is buried at the Great Hanging burial site in Cooke County.

Taylor, William B.
Born: circa 1828—Died - 19 October 1862

William Taylor was survived by his wife His wife Martha Ann Welch and one child. He is buried at the Great Hanging burial site in Cooke County.

Thomas, Eli Sigler Doctor
Born: 17 August 1822—Died - 19 October 1862

Eli Thomas was survived by his wife His wife Susan Mary Hedenberg and two children. He is buried at the Great Hanging burial site in Cooke County. Some family genealogists list Thomas' given name as Elliott. He was a medical doctor in Rutledge, Ohio.[305]

Ward, James Andrew
Born: circa 1802—Died - 19 October 1862

James Ward was survived by thirteen children. His wife Nancy Muirhead preceded him in death. Ward is buried at the Great Hanging burial site in Cooke County.

Burdick, Ira
Born: circa 1832—Date of Death: 18 October 1862
Place: Wise County
Event: Legal Execution/Hanged

Conn, John M.
Born: (Unknown)—Date of Death: 18 October 1862
Place: Wise County
Event: Legal Execution/Hanged

Maples, Parson
Born: (Unknown)—Date of Death: 18 October 1862
Place: Wise County
Event: Legal Execution/Hanged

McKinn, Jim
Born: (Unknown)—Date of Death: 18 October 1862
Place: Wise County
Event: Legal Execution/Hanged

Ward, Given Name Unknown
Born: (Unknown)—Date of Death: 18 October 1862
Place: Wise County
Event: Legal Execution/Hanged

A citizen's court convicted Ira Burdick, John Conn, Parson Maples, Jim McKinn and a man named Ward of treason to the Confederacy. All were legally hanged at Wise County in 1862. Ward's case remains unverified however.

Fifty Unknown Union Sympathizers
Born: (Unknown)—Date of Death: December 1862
Place: Cooke County
Event: Lynching

According to newspaper reports of the day, a total of about fifty Union sympathizers and traitors to the Confederacy were lynched in December 1862.[306] It is highly probable that this entry is a duplicate of the lynchings highlighted in the Great Hanging incident, above.

A group had been formed that supported reinstating Texas to the Union. The factions, acting in secret, had developed their own code, handshake and password. When discovered a spy who had given them up took about seventy persons under control. Described by the elitist east coast tabloid as being men of, "...low character, with here and there a man of limited influence" about twenty-five of them went before some form of tribunal then were executed.

The newspaper account of this story is high on emotion and short on detail, leaving one to wonder if this incident actually happened, or if it had already been covered in another, more accurate accounts of the hangings and lynching's of the day.

White, Pess
Born: circa 1833—Date of Death: circa 1863
Place: Collin County
Event: Legal Execution/Shot

Pess White, a thirty-year old black man, was charged with attempted outrage. He was shot by a firing squad.[307]

One Unidentified White Man
Born: (Unknown)—Date of Death: circa 1863
Place: Bexar County
Event: Lynching/Hanged

Newspaper accounts of the day indicate that two unidentified persons lynched an unidentified white man near San Antonio. His crime was an unwillingness to accept Confederate specie as payment for a cow. The unfortunate man's body was discovered hanging from a tree by his children who, after his absence of two days, had been sent out to searching for him.[308]

One Unidentified White Man
Born: (Unknown)—Date of Death: circa 1863
Place: Galveston County
Event: Lynching/Hanged

Newspaper reports of the day claim that an unidentified Unionist was lynched for his beliefs by a mob at Galveston sometime during 1863.[309]

Eight Unidentified Unionists
Born: (Unknown)—Date of Death: circa 1863
Place: Kerr County
Event: Lynching/Seven Hanged and One Shot

Unionist sentiment continues to be a problem for the Confederate government in some regions of Texas. In a single day, eight unionists were lynched at Camp Verde in Kerr County.

Newspaper reports seem to confuse this incident with the Spring Creek Massacre, which took place in 1862, where stones were tied to the feet of the poor souls and they were tossed into a body of water called Spring Creek.[310] In this case, which took place while Confederate Captain John Lawhorn's Company C of the Frontier Regiment were stationed at Camp Verde, rumor was received that a group of Unionists consisting of eight men and one boy, all well armed and well mounted, were traveling from Florence in Williamson County through the Camp Verde patrol area. A group of twenty-five men under the command of Major Duff, Company D of the Texas Rangers intercepted the party about ten miles from Hondo. Alexander's men took the group into custody and started a march back to Camp Verde with the prisoners. Since they were civilians, they were actually free to travel as they wished.

Along the route Duff's troops robbed the Williamson County men of roughly $1,000 in cash. Next, they constructed horsehair nooses and lynched all but one of the eight men. The eighth man begged to be shot. They accommodate his wish, firing a musket ball with the ramrod still in the barrel into the poor fellow. He was discovered the following day pinned to the ground next to his seven dead companions. The boy somehow survived.

One Unidentified White Man
Born: (Unknown)—Date of Death: circa January1863
Place: Zapata County
Event: Lynching/Hanged

According to newspaper accounts of the day raiding Mexican bandits who had been busy stealing horses and cattle on the Texas side of the Rio Grande River took time out from their work to lynch the county judge (or chief justice) of Zapata County. The incident was first reported on 2 February 1863, thus likely occurred in January.[311]

Smith, Thomas "Nicaragua"
Born: (Unknown)—Date of Death: 8 January 1863
Place: Galveston County
Event: Legal Execution/Shot

Smith was a notorious character around Galveston. He had served under General William Walker's expeditionary force in Nicaragua, thus explaining the source of his pet name.

Smith had a checkered past, including an enlistment in the military where he was stationed at Pelican Point from whence he deserted to the enemy. After being captured in January 1863, he was brought ashore on the steamship *Cambria*. Courts martial tried Smith on 5 January 1863, for deserting to the enemy and convicted. He was executed by firing squad on the open plains near the city cemetery. Smith's body was placed in an unmarked grave in the Potter's Field at Galveston.

Some sources indicate the execution took place on 6 January 1863, not 8 January 1863.[312]

Nelson, Given Name Unknown
Born: (Unknown)—Date of Death: February 1863
Place: Unknown
Event: Lynching/Hanged

A well respected gray haired old unionist identified only as Mr. Nelson was hung in the presence of his wife and had his home burned to the ground for discrediting Confederate script.[313]

Montgomery, William W.
Born: circa 1814—Date of Death: 15 March 1863
Place: Cameron County
Event: Lynching/Hanged

U.S. Army Colonel Edward Jackson Davis and the 1st Texas saw extensive service during the Civil War. They were at Galveston on 3 January 1863, and barely escaped capture when Confederates took the city back from Union hands.

On Sunday, 15 March 1863, Confederate forces and off-duty soldiers seized Davis, along with Captain William W. Montgomery and a handful of troops, at Matamoros where he was attempting to take his family out of Texas and recruit men for their unit. Diplomatic trouble between the Confederacy and Mexico soon followed, and continued until General Hamilton P. Bee released Davis to appease Mexican governor Albino López. Montgomery was not as fortunate. He was lynched.[314]

Grundy, Felix E.
Born: circa 1821—Date of Death: 8 August 1863
Place: Falls County
Event: Lynching/Hanged

A white man named Felix Grundy of Marlin became intoxicated and was taken to jail by the sheriff for his own protection against. It seems that certain citizens had been threatening him. Grundy's wife was sent for, but she refused to aid her man, telling authorities that they could keep her drunken and wayward spouse, hastening to add that she would prefer to see him hang. Some local vigilantes aided Mrs. Susan Grundy in fulfilling her wish. While the sheriff was relocating the unpopular Grundy to a place of better security a mob took control of him and lynched him without benefit of trial. Be careful what you wish for, it just might come true.[315]

Riddel, Given Name Unknown
Born: (Unknown)—Date of Death: 13 September 1863
Place: De Witt County
Event: Lynching/Shot

Mr. Riddle, the owner of a steamer at De Witt County, was shot to death by some Confederate troops for refusing to accept Confederate currency.[316]

Thirty-Three Unidentified White Men
Born: (Unknown)—Date of Death: October 1863
Place: Fayette and Bastrop Counties
Event: Lynching/Hanged

Greemeyer, W.
Born: (Unknown)—Date of Death: October 1863
Place: Fayette and Bastrop Counties
Event: Lynching/Hanged

Newspaper accounts of the day claim that thirty-four white men, thirty of whom were identified as "Germans" (including a seventy year old gentleman named W. Greemeyer of La Grange) and the remaining four "Americans," were lynched for being Unionists at Bastrop and Fayette Counties in early October 1863.[317]

Boyles, William C.
Born: circa 1826—Died - November 1863
Place: Cooke County
Event: Lynching/Shot

William Boyles was shot during the Gainesville incident, escaped, and later died of his wounds at Collinsville, Grayson County in November 1863. See "Gainsville Hangings" for details.

Boyles was survived by his wife Elizabeth T. West and four children. He is buried at the Great Hanging burial site in Cooke County. [318]

Rodríguez, Chipita (Josefa)
Born: (Unknown)—Date of Death: 11 November 1863
Place: San Patricio County
Event: Legal Execution/Hanged

Chipita Rodríguez's given name was probably Josefa. Facts surrounding her arrest, trial, and execution are limited. Much cannot be verified. Not unlike the legendary Billy the Kid, Chipita's story has become popular folklore. Chipita is believed to have been the daughter of Pedro Rodríguez, who is said to have fled from Antonio Lopez de Santa Anna.

Chipita moved San Patricio de Hibernia with her father while she was a youth. For many years she provided travelers with meals and a cot on the porch of her shack on the Aransas River. One such traveler named John Savage, who was carrying $600 in gold, was discovered murdered with an ax. Chipita was accused of robbery and murder. The subsequent recovery of the gold from the Aransas River north of San Patricio, where Savage's body was found in a burlap bag, raised substantial doubt about the motive for the crime. Nevertheless, Chipita and Juan Silvera, who some claim was her illegitimate son, were indicted on circumstantial evidence. The pair was tried before Fourteenth District Court judge Benjamin F. Neal at San Patricio. Chipita pleaded not guilty. The jury recommended mercy, but Neal ordered her executed, which was to take place on 13 November 1863.

Chipita was held at Sheriff William Means's home in Meansville, where two attempts by a lynching mob were thwarted. According to legend, Chipita was kept in leg irons and chained to a wall in the courthouse. At the time, she was described as being "very old" or "about ninety," but was probably in her sixties.

The court records, except for a week of transcripts, were burned in a courthouse fire or lost in a flood. There are many discrepancies in trial accounts. From these it has been determined that no list of qualified jurors existed, but the sheriff, instructed as jury foreman to produce "at least twenty qualified men," produced closer to thirty. Chipita's sole defense was the words "not guilty." According to folklore, resident Kate McCumber drove off hangman John Gilpin when he came for her wagon to transport Chipita to the hanging tree. Afterward, at least one witness to the hanging claimed he heard Chipita moan from the coffin, which was placed in an unmarked grave.

Many tales have arisen as a result of the trial and the hanging. Her ghost is said to haunt the area, especially when a woman is sentenced to be executed. She is pictured as a specter with a noose around her neck. Chipita has been the subject of two operas, numerous books, newspaper articles, and magazine accounts.

Over a century later, in 1985, Corpus Christi businessman and Democratic State Senator Carlos F. Truan asked the Texas legislature to absolve Chipita Rodríguez of murder. The Sixty-ninth Legislature passed the resolution, and it was signed by Governor Mark White on 13 June 1985.[320]

Three Unidentified Black Men

Born: (Unknown)—Date of Death: circa 1864
Place: Galveston County
Event: Legal Execution/Hanged

Seven black men were tried at Galveston for the murder of the Neff Family. The crime occurred near Port Hudson in January 1864. Three of the men were sentenced to be hanged. Thus far, verification of the execution has proven elusive. This incident is being included in the interest of completeness.[321]

One Unidentified White Man

Born: (Unknown)—Date of Death: circa 1864
Place: Galveston County
Event: Legal Execution/Shot

An unidentified Confederate deserter was shot and killed by a firing squad at Galveston.[322]

One Unidentified Black Man

Born: (Unknown)—Date of Death: circa 1864
Place: Unknown County
Event: Lynched/Beaten

According to unverified sources, three railroad workers in late 1864 took all day to beat an unidentified black man to death for having stolen three yards of homespun cloth.[323]

One Unidentified Black Man

Born: (Unknown)—Date of Death: circa 1864
Place: Smith County
Event: Lynched/Hanged and Burned

According to unverified sources, in late 1864, an unidentified black man was lynched and his body burned at Tyler for having killed his master.[324]

One Unidentified White Man

Born: (Unknown)—Date of Death: circa 1864
Place: Collin County
Event: Lynched/Hanged

According to unverified sources, in early 1864 an unidentified white man was lynched at Collin County. His only crime was that his son had joined the Union army.[325]

Armstrong, James
Born: (Unknown)—Date of Death: January 1864
Place: Fannin County
Event: Legal Execution/Shot

Benson, Given Name Unknown
Born: (Unknown)—Date of Death: January 1864
Place: Fannin County
Event: Legal Execution/Shot

On or about Sunday, 10 January 1864, Colonel George Baylor held courts martial at Camp Irene, presumed to be near the present day town of Irene in Fannin County. Four men were tried and found guilty of treason, two of whom were youths. The older two, James Armstrong and a man named Benson, were marched to the edge of the prairie near the North Fork of the Clear Fork and executed by firing squad.[326]

Hall, C. C.
Born: (Unknown)—Date of Death: January 1864
Place: Montgomery County
Event: Lynching/Shot

C. C. Hall, a twenty-three year old white man, was arraigned on charges of murder at the City of Montgomery. Discovering that the crime had been committed in Walker County, the magistrate ordered that county's sheriff, Arthur Mearsfelder, and a twenty-man posse to take Hall to that place for trial. Not far from town, 100 to 200 armed and determined mobsters waylaid the lawmen and took Hall from their custody, forcing a confession from him.

Hall spilled his story, admitting to murdering Colonel Wait S. Hart and Mr. Boone of Cherokee County. He robbed the men of their valuables, along with some black slaves that belonged to Boone. That formality out of the way, Hall was lynched.[327]

Gonsolas, J. J.
Born: (Unknown)—Date of Death: 25 April 1864
Place: Cooke or Fannin County
Event: Lynching/Shot

J. J. Gonsolas, a Mexican man, was shot and killed by border troops on Monday, 25 April 1864. Gonsolas was a private serving under First Lieutenant Thomas Smith's company from Jack County, First Frontier District. The ranger muster roll indicates Gonsolas was "[t]aken by Col. Bourland's men and killed April 25th." Colonel James Bourland was the commanded of Bourland's Texas Cavalry Regiment [also known as "Border Battalion" and "Border regiment]". There was no mention made of his crime.[328].

Still, Washington
Born: (Unknown)—Date of Death: 28 April 1864
Place: Wise County
Event: Legal Execution/Hanged

Washington Still, a white man, was hanged at Wise County on Thursday, 28 April 1864. He was a private serving in Captain J. M. Hanks' Company B of the First Frontier District. There was no mention made of his crime[329].

Hempel, E.
Born: (Unknown)—Date of Death: 30 April 1864
Place: Colorado County
Event: Legal Execution/Hanged

E. Hempel, a white soldier, was convicted of murder. He was hanged for his crime on Saturday, 30 April 1864. Hempel was a Private in the 5th Light Field Artillery Battery and had enlisted in 1863.[330]

Holcomb, Joseph E.
Born: (Unknown)—Date of Death: 18 May 1864
Place: Smith County
Event: Lynching/Hanged

McReynolds, James Monroe
Born: circa 1820—Date of Death: 18 May 1864
Place: Smith County
Event: Lynching/Hanged

Read, James Lawrence
Born: 28 May 1828—Date of Death: 18 May 1864
Place: Smith County
Event: Lynching/Hanged

Joseph E. Holcomb, James McReynolds and James Read, all white men, were lynched at Tyler on Wednesday, 18 May 1864.

By 1864, the woods were alive with army deserters and, aided by this unrest, a gang called Quantrill's Raiders robbed towns and farms at will while the Confederate Army looked the other way. After some nasty incidents that began at McKinney some citizens insisted that their sheriff, James Read, take a stand against the outlaws. In a gun battle with the raiders that lasted all day, where they were greatly outnumbered, Read and his cousin Judge James McReynolds from Kaufman County escaped under cover of darkness. They fled to the home of Read's mother-in-law. She offered sanctuary on her place in the Lovejoy Survey, adjacent to the Warenskjold farm.

In May of 1864, a gang of men described as the "home guards" decided to show these Union men a thing or two. Not only were Sheriff Read, Judge McReynolds, and Read's brother-in-law Joe Holcomb arrested, but Wilhelm and three Norwegians were also rounded up. They took the three first to Tyler and from there to Shreveport. The men were William Warenskjold, A. Knudson, K. Knudson and G. Shafstad. As reported in the Fitzgerald newspaper, "it was that time when they hung Holcomb, Reed [Read] and McRunnell [McReynolds] in Tyler."

An angry mob gathered in the courthouse square, out for blood. Their wrath was principally directed at Read, McReynolds, Joe Holcomb, and Jeff Davis. All were locked up for their own protection. Thomas H. Thornton, enrolling office clerk, describes the prisoners thusly, "Read was a low, heavy set man, about thirty years of age. I think that his hair was long and tolerably light color. McReynolds was tall, about six feet two inches high. He was a man about forty years of age . . . of florid complexion. Think he would weigh about one hundred and seventy-five pounds. Holcomb was a young man, about twenty or twenty-one years of age. He was five feet ten or eleven inches high, and [I] think that his hair was of a light color." Another clerk, John D. Dorough, said Captain Tilley, enrolling officer from Henderson County and one of the soldiers bringing them in, appealed to the gang leaders, saying the prisoners should be released. Another man replied, "Captain, if you don't wish to have anything to do with this, get out of the way and let us act."

The condemned men were marched toward the road leading back to Canton, taken into the tall, dark pines, where a bystander from Tyler describes how the men were executed. "Holcomb was bound, placed upon a horse, a rope around his neck . . . the horse was led under a hickory tree, and Mr. Holcomb was hung to a limb . . . a portion of the crowd took another man, Read . . . and carried him some hundred and fifty yards, where he was also bound and placed upon a horse in the same manner. After Read ceased to show any signs of life, I passed the tree where Holcomb had been hung, and a third man, McReynolds, was placed under . . . and hung upon the very same limb."

After dark, Corporal Collier returned, and made the following statement, "That about 5 o'clock this evening, an armed mob of at least eighty men demanded the prisoners, and of course, they were given up . . . the prisoners were then carried out of town, and three of them hung on one tree.' "

The fate of Jeff Davis, the fourth "jayhawker" brought in, is described in an article in the *Galveston Daily News*, "Just as they were fixing to execute Davis, a gentleman came up who recognized him as being a member of his command, and said that he had always made a good soldier. He was, of course, released and sent to Camp Ford. McReynolds has a son out at camp who is now offering any price for a wagon to carry his father's body home to Rockwall, Kaufman County."[331]

Read was survived by his wife Nancy Catherine Holcomb and three children. McReynold's wife had preceded him in death.

Garcia, Pedro
Born (Unknown)—Date of Death: 22 June 1864
Place: Cameron County
Event: Legal Execution/Firing Squad

On Wednesday, 22 June 1864, Pedro Garcia, a private in the First Texas Cavalry, was shot by a firing squad at Brownsville. Garcia had been convicted at courts martial of deserting his picket duty and firing on the guard who had arrested him.[332]

Allen, E. P.
Born: (Unknown)—Date of Death: August 1864
Place: Jefferson County
Event: Legal Execution/Firing Squad

E. P. Allen, a Confederate deserter, was executed by firing squad in August 1864.[333]

Jackson, Given Name Unknown
Born: (Unknown)—Date of Death: October 1864
Place: Galveston County
Event: Lynched/Shot

Although reconstructing the details of the killing of a boy named Jackson is a bit convoluted, it seems that Jackson, who was a young black man, was taken from his mother's house and shot to death for aiding his brother who was a deserter.[334]

Nail, Clark B.
Born: (Unknown)—Date of Death: circa 1865
Place: Bell County
Event: Lynched/Hanged

Nail, B.
Born: (Unknown)—Date of Death: circa 1865
Place: Bell County
Event: Lynched/Hanged

Taylor, Edwin
Born: (Unknown)—Date of Death: circa 1865
Place: Bell County
Event: Lynched/Hanged

According to one source, unknown members of the home guard in Bell County hanged three unidentified Confederate deserters.[335] Another source identified the men as B. Nail, Clark Nail and Edwin Taylor, all of Bosque County. The National Park Services Database of Civil War Soldiers and Sailors has entries for all three men.

Slimp, John Floyd
Born: circa 1847—Date of Death: circa 1865
Place: Bell County
Event: Lynched/Hanged

According to unverified sources, John Slimp (Slemp) is reported to have been lynched by vigilantes at Bell County for horse theft "just after the Civil War." No documentation has been found to support this allegation.

Slimp is an unusual surname, and there have been few with that moniker in Texas. There seems to be ample proof that the subject gentleman, John Slimp, lived a long life, finally surrendering his spirit at Wilbarger County on 8 December 1915. He and his wife Susan Carrol Chronister produced thirteen children.[336] The source for this incident is Carrigan's book, *The Making of a Lynching Culture*. The authors have elected to include it anyway on the chance that the claim may be accurate.[337]

One Unidentified Black Man
Born: (Unknown)—Date of Death: circa 1865
Place: Galveston County
Event: Lynching/Hanged

In the early part of 1865, a black man was charged with assaulting a white woman near the Central Market at Galveston. He was captured and taken to the rear of a home at Twentieth and Winnie Street where he was hanged from a sign projecting from an outbuilding. The body was left to dangle there from 9:00 am until nightfall as a warning to others of his race.[338]

Two Unidentified White Men
Born: (Unknown)—Date of Death: circa 1865
Place: McLennan County
Event: Lynched/Hanged

According to unverified sources, two white men were lynched at McLennan County. Their crime, or the time period during which this incident occurred, was not mentioned. However vague, it is being included in the interest of completeness.[339]

Richers, Antone
Born: (Unknown)—Date of Death: 3 March 1865
Place: Galveston County
Event: Legal Execution/Firing Squad

Antone Richers, a white man and a soldier of the Confederate Army, was executed by firing squad for desertion at Galveston on Friday, 3 March 1865. He had stolen a boat and attempted to row out to the Union blockade when his purloined vessel capsized and he was fished from the bay. Richers attempted to bribe the Confederate officer who had rescued him but the man, loyal to his oath, refused to accept the inducement thus sealing Richer's fate.

The night preceding Richers's execution his friend, Reverend Father Ansteadt, had traveled by handcar to Houston to secure a pardon using document that proved that Richers was not of sound mind. Unfortunately, the telegraph line between Houston and Galveston malfunctioned, and remained inoperable until fifteen minutes before the time of the execution. Word did not reach authorities at Galveston until after Richers's body had been pierced by a score of musket balls and he lay dead.

Richers was the second, and final, military execution at Galveston following that of "Nicaragua" Smith.[340]

Yorick, Given Name Unknown
Born: (Unknown)—Date of Death: April 1865
Place: Fayette County
Event: Lynched/Hanged

According to unverified sources, a black man who had been a slave committed outrage on a German girl at La Grange, afterwards attempting to escape his pursuers. He was captured and promptly lynched. [341] According to the source, the black man was found "endeavoring to accomplish a purpose too horrid to mention upon a German girl."

Barney, R. J.
Born: (Unknown)—Date of Death: 8 May 1865
Place: Cameron County
Event: Legal Execution/Firing Squad

George F. Anders of the Giddings Battalion Cavalry was gunned down in the vicinity of the market house at Brownsville. R. J. Barney was charged with the murder, tried and convicted. He was sentenced to death by firing squad.

On Sunday, 7 May 1865, Barney attempted an escape but failed. On Monday, 8 May 1865, the troops of the Brownsville post were assembled. Barney marched into the center of the group and took up his position alongside his coffin. Chaplin Cox administered to him. Barney declined a blindfold and sternly looked back at his executioners as muskets were leveled and a volley fired.[342]

It is thought that Barney was actually R. A. Barney who enlisted as a Private in 1863 in the Twenty-fifth Cavalry (Gillespie's Regiment, Third Lancers, Third Regiment, Carter's Brigade).[343]

Two Unidentified Men
Born: (Unknown)—Date of Death: 28 May 1865
Place: Starr County
Event: Lynched/Hanged

On Sunday, 28 May 1865, a group traveling from Rio Grande City to San Antonio encountered about forty Jayhawkers who stopped their coach, rifled through their luggage and searched for items of value.[344] The wagon was eventually allowed to proceed. Not far distant two men were found hanging from a tree alongside the road, about forty miles north of town.[345]

Several Unidentified Black Men
Born: (Unknown)—Date of Death: December 1865
Place: Marion County
Event: Lynched/Shot/Attacked

In yet another vague and unconfirmed report of white on black violence after the Civil War, some sources claim that "several" black men were set upon and killed by white planters at Marion County sometime during December 1865.[346]

Four Unidentified Indian Men
Born: (Unknown)—Date of Death: circa 1866
Place: Coryell County
Event: Lynching/Shot

Four unidentified Indian men who were suspected of attempted murder were shot and scalped by a mob of thirty to forty white vigilantes.[347] Some sources report that there were six victims in this incident.

Four Unidentified Black Men
Born: (Unknown)—Date of Death: circa 1866
Place: Bell County
Event: Lynching/Hanged

Newspaper accounts of the day claim that four unidentified black men were lynched at Salado in Bell County. No further details were provided.[348]

One Unidentified Black Man
Born: (Unknown)—Date of Death: circa 1866
Place: Bell County
Event: Lynching/Hanged

Newspapers reported that one unidentified black man was hung at the fork of the Lampasas and Leon Rivers in Bell County.[349]

Two Unidentified Black Men
Born: (Unknown)—Date of Death: circa 1866
Place: Bell County
Event: Lynching/Shot and Drown

Newspapers reported that two unidentified black men were found killed, floating in the Little River at Bell County.[350]

Jackson, Given Name Unknown
Born: (Unknown)—Date of Death: circa 1866
Place: Bell County
Event: Lynching

A black man identified only as Jackson was killed at Owl Creek in Bell County.[351]

Adams, Luke
Born: (Unknown)—Date of Death: circa 1866
Place: Bosque County
Event: Lynching/ Whipped to Death

Harding, Henry
Born: (Unknown)—Date of Death: circa 1866
Place: Bosque County
Event: Lynching/ Whipped to Death

Luke Adams and Henry Harding, both black men, where whipped to death at Bosque County.[352] No reason for the killings was mentioned, other than that the men were black.

Hampton, Wade
Born: (Unknown)—Date of Death: circa 1866
Place: Unknown County
Event: Lynching/ Whipped to Death

Unverified sources claim that a black man named Wade Hampton was whipped to death for having stolen a knife. The county where this alleged incident took place is not mentioned.[353]

White, George Washington
Born: 3 February 1840—Date of Death: circa 1866
Place: Bell County
Event: Lynching

Newspaper reports of the day claim that George Washington White, a white man, was assassinated in the streets of Belton for being a Unionist.

    White had been born at Lauderdale, Alabama, and served the Confederacy during the Civil War, making the newspaper's allegation that he was affiliated with the Unionist movement somewhat dubious.[354] Even then, facts rarely got in the way of a good news story. It is more likely that Yankee Carpetbaggers killed him for opposing reconstruction policies or local government control.

    White was survived by his wife Zilpha Elizabeth Thigpen.[355]

Burmistier, Herman
Born: (Unknown)—Date of Death: 4 February 1866
Place: Cameron County
Event: Lynching/Hanged

Windsor, Nathaniel

Born: circa 1845—Date of Death: 4 February 1866
Place: Cameron County
Event: Lynching/Hanged

Nathaniel Windsor, a white man and a dispatch carrier for the 4th Wisconsin Cavalry along with an attorney named Herman Burmistier of the firm Droeya, Octling and Company of Matamoros were lost sight of while traveling along the road between Brownsville and Brazos. They disappeared at a point about twenty-five miles from the former. On Sunday, 4 February 1866, the bodies of both were found. Windsor had been lynched from a mesquite tree no more than thirty paces from the road, and a distance of about seven miles from Brownsville. Burmistier's remains were found about two miles further. He too had been lynched. Both men's belongings had been taken, along with their horses and tack. [356]

Windsor, who hailed from Cheboygan, Wisconsin, had enlisted in Company C, 4th Wisconsin Cavalry Regiment on 19 February 1864. He had just mustered out on 4 February 1866, at Brownsville, Texas, the day he disappeared.[357]

Shackelford, John C.

Born: circa 1827—Date of Death: March 1866
Place: Bell County
Event: Lynching

John C. Shackelford, an otherwise respectable man from Missouri, was found out to be a horse thief. He was killed by unknown members of a vigilante group at Bell County.[358]

Shackelford was survived by his wife Ann Abbott and one son.[359]

Park, Given Name Unknown

Born: (Unknown)—Date of Death: 7 April 1866
Place: Bell County
Event: Lynching/Hanged

Unknown members of a vigilante group lynched Mr. Park, yet another Bell County horse thief.[360]

Garner, James "Jim"

Born (Unknown) - - Date of Death: circa May 1866
Place: Nueces County
Event: Lynching/ Hanged

In mid-May 1866 a man named James Garner, who was described as a murderous pest to the public, assassinated a local Corpus Christi merchant named M. Schuer (also identified Scheuer). Schuer's brother was reportedly murdered earlier near the Rio Grande River. Schuer was standing in the doorway of his store when Garner rode up and shot him through the heart with a revolver.

A crowd seized Garner and hanged him from a tree limb. The Schuer killing was Garner's third or fourth known murder. Regardless of the tally, it was his last.[361]

Hill, Benjamin Franklin
Born: circa 1815—Date of Death: 24 May 1866
Place: Victoria County
Event: Lynching/Axed to Death

Benjamin Franklin Hill was a white man who was charged with killing a black soldier. He was taken from the custody of the sheriff at Victoria by a mob of United States soldiers and brutally murdered.[362]

Little is known of Hill's Civil War activities, but by 1864, he was serving the Confederacy as a procuring agent. Although newspapers of the day reported his rank as that of Colonel, which is the title he was best known by, Hill served for a time as Adjutant General. During the Union occupation after the war he lived in Victoria. There he was a candidate for county clerk in June 1866, when he quarreled with a discharged Union soldier in the Smile Saloon and killed him, apparently in self-defense. The post commander, Captain Spaulding, arrested Hill. Troops of the 3rd Michigan Infantry, a black regiment, and the 18th New York Cavalry, both encamped at Victoria, became outraged at the death of their comrade. Although Spaulding tried to preserve order, he was, "...ineffective against the hundreds of drunken, infuriated wretches, running riot, and thirsting for human blood," as characterized by the *Victoria Advocate*. Union troops broke into Hill's cell and hacked him to death with an ax. Next, they hung his mutilated body from the jail banisters.

Hill was survived by his wife Mary Hubert and five children. His wife and family moved to Cuero, though she returned to aid fellow Victorians during the 1867 yellow fever epidemic.[363]

Hill's murder was only one of a number of similar clashes that occurred with Union occupation forces in Texas, contributing greatly to the general bitterness Texan's associate with Reconstruction.[364]

Bingham, Oliver Harris
Born: circa 1815—Date of Death: 12 June 1866
Place: Bell County
Event: Lynching/Shot

Lindley, Jasper
Born: circa 1846—Date of Death: 12 June 1866
Place: Bell County
Event: Lynching/Shot

Miller, Samuel Cornelius

Born: circa 1847—Date of Death: 12 June 1866

Place: Bell County

Event: Lynching/Shot

Jasper Lindley, Oliver Bingham and Sam Miller learned first hand that Bell County citizens have a low tolerance for horse thieves. All three were shot and killed by unknown members of a vigilante group at that place. Their bodies were found along the Little River on Tuesday, 12 June 1866.[365] According to one rumor, vigilantes had shot them for horse theft. What role their support for the Union played in their deaths is unknown, but it could only have helped convince the lynch mob to carry out their work.

There is some question concerning the involvement of Oliver Bingham in this incident however. A host of family genealogists indicate that he died at Bell County on 21 November 1865, marking his passing seven months before the earliest newspaper coverage of the death.[366]

Garcia, Vincente

Born: (Unknown)—Date of Death: 22 June 1866

Place: Cameron County

Event: Legal Execution/Hanged

Garza, Florencio

Born: (Unknown)—Date of Death: 22 June 1866

Place: Cameron County

Event: Legal Execution/Hanged

Vela, Juan

Born: (Unknown)—Date of Death: 22 June 1866

Place: Cameron County

Event: Legal Execution/Hanged

Juan Veal, Florencio Garza and Vincente Garcia, members of Juan Cortina's earlier raiding party in this area, were all found guilty of murder and sentenced to be hanged.

On Friday, 22 June 1866, the prisoners left the jail seated on the coffins and riding in the back of a wagon. Sheriff Dye, City Marshal John Price and about one hundred black troops with fixed bayonet's accompanied the men forming a rather magnificent procession. The gallows structure, stout and fresh, had been erected on a prairie east of the city.

All three condemned men scaled the gallows at Brownsville with a swagger. White caps were pulled down over their heads and a priest led the men in prayer. The latch was pulled and all three dropped about six feet through the floor. Two swung deadly quite, with broken necks. Garza hit his head on the floor of the structure on his way through the opening. Stunned but not dead he raised both hands and pulled himself up by his own hangman's rope. Seeing this, the executioner laid down on the platform and twisted Garza's hands from the rope, adjusted the noose and let him swing once again. The scene was horrific. Although their irons had been removed at the jail, their hands and feet had not been bound in the conventional way for hanging. Garza eventually expired, but not without a grand and horrific spectacle.[367]

Duncan, Thomas C.
Born: 12 February 1821—Date of Death: 12 July 1866
Place: Bell County
Event: Lynching/Shot

Daw, Given Name Unknown
Born: (Unknown)—Date of Death: 12 July 1866
Place: Bell County
Event: Lynching/Shot

Mr. Daw and his colleague Thomas Duncan, malefactors wanted for murder, were overtaken by a posse of seventeen men and shot for their crime. Their verdict and instant implementation was in lieu of a bothersome trial.[368]

Some sources refer to Duncan as a Unionist, claiming that he was lynched at Belton for so being. That seems odd, since Duncan served as a Private in Company G, Baylor's Texas Cavalry and was clearly on the Confederate side of the fight between North and South.

Duncan was survived by his wife Mary Ann Griffin and three daughters.[369] Some family genealogists list Mrs. Duncan's maiden name as Lauderdale, not Griffin. Duncan's tombstone has the date 11 July 1866, which is incorrect. He is buried at the South Belton Cemetery.

Lindley, Jonathan "Doc"
Born: circa 1824—Date of Death: 14 July 1866
Place: Bell County
Event: Lynching/Shot

Lindley, Newton
Born: circa 1848—Date of Death: 14 July 1866
Place: Bell County
Event: Lynching/Shot

The Lindley family was enraged at the murder of Jasper Lindley and Sam Martin, which had occurred on 12 June 1866. On 14 July 1866, Jonathan and Newton Lindley, Jasper's father and brother, set off with fifteen U.S. soldiers to arrest the men they believed to have been involved in the killings. They eventually overtook the killers, pulled them from their homes and shot them to death.

After considerable protest, Jonathan and Newton Lindley were placed in the Belton jail. Soon thereafter a mob broke in and shot them in their cells.[370]

Two Unidentified Black Men
Born: (Unknown)—Date of Death: 22 August 1866
Place: Bosque County
Event: Lynching/Hanged

According to an often unreliable source, parties unknown lynched two unidentified black men at Bosque County. Their transgressions were not mentioned.[371]

Matthews, Marshall
Born (Unknown)—Date of Death: 26 December 1866
Place: Lavaca County
Event: Lynching

Blackly, Levi
Born (Unknown)—Date of Death: 26 December 1866
Place: Lavaca County
Event: Lynching

On the night of 26 December 1866, assassins entered to home of John Newman at Hackberry, slashing the throats of Newman, his wife, an infant child, and a twelve year old black girl. The killers then set fire to the house. Suspicion fell on two black men, Marshall Matthews and Levi Blackly. They were arrested and ordered to be jail. Sources claimed that while being transferred to the jail at Halletsville they tried to escape custody and were killed.[372]

Byron, Given Name Unknown
Born: (Unknown)—Date of Death: circa 1867
Place: Unknown County
Event: Lynching/Shot

Flake's Bulletin of 23 June 1868, lists a black man identified only as Mr. Byron as having been found dead tied to a tree and shot to death. The precise date and location are not given.[373]

Chamy, John
Born: (Unknown)—Date of Death: circa 1867
Place: Bell County
Event: Lynching/Shot

John Chamy, a black man, was assassinated at Bell County in 1867.[374]

Gillespie, Given Name Unknown
Born: (Unknown)—Date of Death: circa 1867
Place: Bell County
Event: Lynching/Shot

Mr. Gillespie, said to have been a German man and perhaps a Unionist, was assassinated at Bell County sometime in 1867.[375]

Jacobs, S.
Born: (Unknown)—Date of Death: circa 1867
Place: Unknown County
Event: Lynching/Hanged

Flake's Bulletin of 23 June 1868, lists a black man identified only as S. Jacobs as having been found lynched to a tree. The precise date and location were not provided.[376]

Jones, Green
Born: (Unknown)—Date of Death: circa 1867
Place: Unknown County
Event: Lynching/Hanged

Flake's Bulletin of 23 June 1868, lists a black youth named Green Jones as having been hung in the woods by a mob of white men. The precise date and location is not given.[377]

Surname Unknown, Tom
Born: (Unknown)—Date of Death: circa 1867
Place: Unknown County
Event: Lynching/Shot

Flake's Bulletin of 23 June 1868, lists one unidentified black youth with the given name of Tom as having been hung by a group of four white men who formed a court, convicted the young man and executed him. The precise date and location is not given.[378]

One Unidentified Black Man
Born: (Unknown)—Date of Death: circa 1867
Place: Unknown County
Event: Lynching/Shot

Flake's Bulletin of 23 June 1868, lists one unidentified black man as having been murdered by whites. The precise date and location is not given.[379]

One Unidentified Black Man
Born: (Unknown)—Date of Death: circa 1867
Place: Unknown County
Event: Lynching/Shot

Flake's Bulletin of 23 June 1868, lists one unidentified black man charged with horse theft as having been hung by a mob. The precise date and location is not given.[380]

One Unidentified Black Man
Born: (Unknown)—Date of Death: circa 1867
Place: Unknown County
Event: Lynching/Shot

Much like the foregoing case, *Flake's Bulletin* of 23 June 1868 lists one unidentified black man charged with horse theft as having been hung by a mob. The precise date and location is not given.[381]

One Unidentified Black Man
Born: (Unknown)—Date of Death: circa 1867
Place: Rusk County
Event: Lynching/Shot

Flake's Bulletin of 23 June 1868, lists one unidentified black man as having been taken out by four white men and found near Angelina Creek the following morning with his hands tied behind his back, shot in the head. The precise date and location is not given.[382] The Angelina River is formed by the junction of Barnhardt and Shawnee creeks, three miles northwest of Laneville in southwest central Rusk County, consequently it is presumed that this was the location of this incident.

Three Unidentified Black Men
Born: (Unknown)—Date of Death: circa 1867
Place: Unknown County
Event: Lynching/Hanged

Flake's Bulletin of 23 June 1868, lists three unidentified black men as having been found lynched. The precise date and location are not given.[383]

Three Unidentified Black Men
Born: (Unknown)—Date of Death: circa 1867
Place: Unknown County
Event: Lynching/Shot

Flake's Bulletin of 23 June 1868, lists three unidentified freedmen as having been found shot to death. The precise date and location are not given.[384]

Three Unidentified Black Men
Born: (Unknown)—Date of Death: circa 1867
Place: Unknown County
Event: Lynching/Shot and Drown

Flake's Bulletin of 23 June 1868, lists three unidentified black men as having been found dead, tied up in bed sacks and floating in the river. The precise date and location are not given.[385]

Two Unidentified Black Men
Born: (Unknown)—Date of Death: circa 1867
Place: Unknown County
Event: Lynching/Shot

Flake's Bulletin of 23 June 1868, lists two unidentified black men as having been taken from their beds and shot to death. The precise date and location are not given.[386]

White, Warner
Born: (Unknown)—Date of Death: circa 1867
Place: Bexar County
Event: Lynching/Hanged

Flake's Bulletin of 23 June 1868, lists a black man identified as Warner White as having been lynched three miles from San Antonio.[387]

Johnson, (Given Name Unknown)
Born: (Unknown)—Date of Death: circa 1867
Place: Harris County
Event: Legal Execution/Hanged

A black man identified only as Johnson was accused of murder and allegedly executed by hanging at Harris County in 1867. No separate verification of this incident has been located.[388]

Lyons, Given Name Unknown
Born: (Unknown)—Date of Death: circa 1867
Place: Unknown County
Event: Lynching/Hanged

Flake's Bulletin of 23 June 1868, lists a white doctor named Lyons as having been hung in the woods. The precise date and location is not given.[389]

Tinley, Given Name Unknown
Born: (Unknown)—Date of Death: circa 1867
Place: Unknown County
Event: Lynching/Shot

Flake's Bulletin of 23 June 1868, lists a black man identified only as Tinley as having been hung for expressing Union sentiments. The precise date and location is not given.[390]

Wade, Given Name Unknown
Born: (Unknown)—Date of Death: circa 1867
Place: Lamar County
Event: Lynching/Shot

Seven Unidentified Men
Born: (Unknown)—Date of Death: circa 1867
Place: Lamar County
Event: Lynching/Shot

Newspaper reports of the day claim that a man identified only as Mr. Wade, along with seven of his colleagues who were all Unionists, were executed in Lamar County in 1867.[391] No further details were provided by the source.

One Unidentified Black Man
Born: (Unknown)—Date of Death: January 1867
Place: Burleson County
Event: Lynched/Hanged

An unidentified black man is said to have been lynched near Cameron for killing a German.[392]

Fore, Augustus
Born: circa 1816—Date of Death: 2 January 1867
Place: Bell County
Event: Lynched

Augustus Fore, a white man from Coryell County, was lynched at Bell County. Newspaper reports of the day claim that the job was botched, and that Fore lived for days before giving up the ghost.[393] Although no reason for his lynching was given, evidence pointed to the fact that Unionists killed him for having served the Confederacy. Fore was a veteran of the 28th Regiment of Texas Mounted Rangers.[394]

Fore was survived by his wife Elizabeth Montgomery and one of the couple's four children. He is buried at the Odd Fellows Cemetery at Gatesville, in Coryell County.[395]

Three Unidentified Mexican Men
Born: (Unknown)—Date of Death: 10 January 1867
Place: Frio County
Event: Lynching/Shot

Unverified sources claim that three Mexican men were executed at Arroyo De San Miguel. There is no mention of their transgression.[396]

San Miguel was a farm and ranch community on San Miguel Creek, located about ten miles northeast of Pearsall in northeastern Frio County. A post office called Music was established near the site in 1880. [397]

One Unidentified Black Man
Born: (Unknown)—Date of Death: March 1867
Place: McLennan County
Event: Lynching/Hanged

According to an unverified and oft dubious source, an unidentified black man was brutally lynched by Tuck Decker and others at McLennan County.[398]

Ten Unidentified Men
Born: (Unknown)—Date of Death: March 1867
Place: Grayson County
Event: Lynching

Newspaper accounts of the day claim that ten men were lynched at Grayson County for robbery. Five had stolen from an old gentleman near Sherman. The other five had robbed Mr. Boern's store at Farmersville. The race of the victims was not identified.[399]

Three Unidentified Black Men
Born: (Unknown)—Date of Death: 20 March 1867
Place: Brazos County
Event: Lynching

A group of black men attempted to rescue a freedman from jail at Bryan Station on Wednesday, 20 March 1867. Their jailbreak escapade proved unsuccessful, however, and led to three of the men being lynched for their trouble.[400]

Libby, George
Born: (Unknown)—Date of Death: circa April 1867
Place: Unknown County
Event: Lynching/Hanged

A day or two before 25 April 1867, George Libby, who was confined in the jail at Centerville for killing Phillip Kenser (or Carrey) at D'hanis, was forcibly removed from the jail by a mob and lynched. A local newspaper opined that, "[w]hile everybody regrets the violent means used to punish the criminal, nobody seems to regret his fate."[401]

Abby, Lewis
Born: (Unknown)—Date of Death: June 1867
Place: Bosque County
Event: Lynching/Shot

Lewis Abby, a black man, was forcible removed from his home by a group of four men led by E. J. Tally. The vigilante group shot Abby to death for having filed a lawsuit against a white woman.[402]

Alexander, M. H.
Born: (Unknown)—Date of Death: June 1867
Place: Hill County
Event: Lynching/Hanged

Matlock, Samuel M. "Sam"
Born: (Unknown)—Date of Death: June 1867
Place: Hill County
Event: Lynching/Hanged

Two white men identified as Sam Matlock and M. H. Alexander were lynched from a tree near the Doyle place in Hill County. The pair had murdered a freedman, and was also thought to have been the culprits who had killed Judge Doyle and his son in 1866. In a fitting gesture, the men were lynched a few hundred yards from the graves of their victims.[403]

Gray, George Washington
Born: 24 November 1824—Date of Death: 3 August 1867
Place: Falls County
Event: Lynching/Shot

According to Carrigan's *The Making of a Lynching Culture,* persons unknown shot George Gray to death in a thicket.[404] But alas, in the words of Mark Twain, "The reports of my [his] death are greatly exaggerated." Family genealogists tell a different story, documenting that Gray lived until 2 August 1902, and is buried at the Theo Cemetery in Falls County. Facts are pesky things, but often run afoul of an otherwise good story.[405]

1868

Alexander, Given Name Unknown
Born: (Unknown)—Date of Death: circa 1868
Place: Bell County
Event: Lynching/Hanged

A black man identified only as Alexander, which means that Alexander may have been either his given name or his surname, was lynched at Bell County sometime in 1868. No further clues as to the identity of this man were provided.[406]

Jackson, Ed
Born: (Unknown)—Date of Death: circa 1868
Place: Bell County
Event: Lynching/Hanged

A white man identified as Ed Jackson was lynched at Bell County sometime in 1868. No mention of his crime was made.[407]

Jornigan, Given Name Unknown
Born: (Unknown)—Date of Death: circa 1868
Place: Bell County
Event: Lynching/Hanged

A white man identified only as Jornigan was lynched at Bell County sometime in 1868. No mention of his crime was made.[408]

McKougn, Given Name Unknown
Born: (Unknown)—Date of Death: circa 1868
Place: Bell County
Event: Lynching/Hanged

A white man identified only as McKougn was lynched at Bell County sometime in 1868. No mention of his crime was made.[409] Based on the spelling of the surname, the authors are quite confident that the newspaper journalist made an error in his or her report.

Culver, Given Name Unknown
Born: (Unknown)—Date of Death: circa 1868
Place: Limestone County
Event: Lynching/Shot

One Unidentified Man
Born: (Unknown)—Date of Death: circa 1868
Place: Limestone County
Event: Lynching/Shot

Newspaper accounts of the day tell of a Captain Culver and his orderly being assassinated at Limestone County for attempting to form a Loyalty League. Loyalty Leagues were popular at the time, and were intended to foster support for and allegiance to the Union.[410]

Four Unidentified Men
Born: (Unknown)—Date of Death: circa 1868
Place: Hunt County
Event: Lynching/Shot

Newspaper accounts of the day claim that four unidentified men, probably white, were murdered in Hunt County for being Unionists. No further details were provided.[411]

Six Unidentified Men
Born: (Unknown)—Date of Death: circa 1868
Place: Bell County
Event: Lynching/Shot

Newspaper accounts of the day claim that six unidentified men, probably white, were murdered in Bell County for being Unionists. No further details were provided.[412]

Surname Unknown, Anthony
Born: (Unknown)—Date of Death: circa 1868
Place: Bell County
Event: Lynching

Surname Unknown, Sam
Born: (Unknown)—Date of Death: circa 1868
Place: Bell County
Event: Lynching

Newspaper accounts of the day tell of two black men identified only by their given names of Anthony and Sam as being killed by some unknown means at Bell County in 1868.[413]

Miller, Given Name Unknown
Born: (Unknown)—Date of Death: circa 1868
Place: Bell County
Event: Lynching/Hanged

Newspaper accounts of the day tell of a white man named Miller being lynched for some undefined crime at Bell County in 1868.[414]

Surname Unknown, Tom
Born: (Unknown)—Date of Death: circa 1868
Place: Kaufman County
Event: Lynching/Shot

In Kaufman County John Love, L. T. Nash, Joe Hardin and A. J. Hardin were tried and convicted of lynching a black man named Tom.[415]

One Unidentified Black Man
Born: (Unknown)—Date of Death: February 1868
Place: McLennan County
Event: Lynching/Shot

A vigilante group thought to have been led by E. J. Tally shot an unidentified black man.[416] The man's transgression is unknown. Tally was also responsible for the killing of Lewis Abby in June 1867.

McKinney, George Washington James
Born: circa 1824—Date of Death: 13 February 1868
Place: Grimes County
Event: Lynching

George McKinney, a white man and a noted desperado, murdered a man named Clay Searcy. Texas Rangers had McKinney in custody and were transporting him from Anderson for trial when six armed men ambushed them in a strip of woods outside of town. The lawmen were forced to hand McKinney over to the vigilantes at gunpoint. All were disguised, and spoke broken English to hide their identity. McKinney was lynched from a convenient tree, however, the rope broke during the process. A fresh rope was secured and the process began anew. The second time McKinney was hoisted over ten feet in the air, which resulted in a successful outcome (for the hangmen that is).[417]

McKinney's given name is not mentioned in the newspaper article that reported this incident, only the initial "D," which is thought to be an error.

Scoby, Bill
Born: (Unknown)—Date of Death: March 1868
Place: Bastrop County
Event: Lynching/Shot

Weaver, Jim
Born: (Unknown)—Date of Death: March 1868
Place: Bastrop County
Event: Lynching/Shot

Sometime in March 1868, two black men, Bill Scoby and Jim Weaver, were shot down on the streets of Bastrop. Newspaper accounts of the day were unclear as to the reason for their execution.[418] Scoby was described as "a youth."

Two Unidentified Black Men
Born: (Unknown)—Date of Death: March 1868
Place: Panola County
Event: Lynching/Shot

Newspaper accounts of the day speak of two unidentified black men being lynched at Elysian Fields in March 1868.[419] This case may be a duplicate of the story that follows on 14 March 1868.

Three Unidentified Black Men
Born: (Unknown)—Date of Death: 14 March 1868
Place: Panola County
Event: Lynching/Shot

One Unidentified Black Woman
Born: (Unknown)—Date of Death: 14 March 1868
Place: Panola County
Event: Lynching/Shot

In one shooting incident that occurred at a dance that was taking place at the plantation of Major Spearman Holland at Panola a crowd of white men crept up on the home and opened fire through open windows, killing three black men and one black woman. Three other blacks attending the affair were wounded.[420]

The same newspaper that reported this incident also mentioned it two months later, but by then had misplaced the exact date as well as the circumstances of the killing.

Taylor, Given Name Unknown
Born: (Unknown)—Date of Death: 22 March 1868
Place: Bastrop County
Event: Lynching/Shot

Two Unidentified Black Men
Born: (Unknown)—Date of Death: 22 March 1868
Place: Bastrop County
Event: Lynching/Shot

During the week of 22 March 1868, two freedmen were killed and a stranger named Taylor who was passing through town was shot and killed at Bastrop.[421] No other details were provided by the source.

Hirsh, William
Born: (Unknown)—Date of Death: 28 March 1868
Place: Coryell County
Event: Lynching

Ivey, Given Name Unknown
Born: (Unknown)—Date of Death: 28 March 1868
Place: Coryell County
Event: Lynching

On Saturday, 28 March 1868, William Hirsh and Ivey (given name unknown) who had been confined in the jail at Gatesville were taken out by a mob of drunken vigilantes and strung up from a tree limb repeatedly, in order to encourage the pair to confess to their crimes. Unfortunately the prescription, which might have worked had it not been administered one too many times, proved a failure. Both men expired during the interrogation.[422] Ivey had been held on a charge of suspected horse theft. Hirsh was a known thief.

Genealogists list a Marcus Lafayette Ivey as having died on 20 March 1868, but at Rusk County. It is possible that this person and the man referred to in the article are the same man.[423]

Pitts, Joe
Born: (Unknown)—Date of Death: 4 April 1868
Place: Falls County
Event: Lynching/Shot

Joe Pitts, a black man, was shot in the head and killed by persons unknown.[424]

Fry, Given Name Unknown
Born (Unknown)—Date of Death: 18 April 1868
Place: Hopkins County
Event: Lynching/Hanged

Green, Given Name Unknown
Born (Unknown)—Date of Death: 18 April 1868
Place: Hopkins County
Event: Lynching/Hanged

On Saturday, 18 April 1868, two people, a brother and sister, were in Hopkins County en route from Mount Pleasant to Sulphur Springs traveling in a buggy. Two white men named Fry and Green overtook the hack and "offered the young lady indignities of the most shocking character." Her brother protested, and stated he was unarmed, whereupon one of the pair shot him fatally. The young woman escaped with her dignity. A posse was quickly formed and gave chase, eventually overtaking the pair and lynching them.[425]

One Unidentified Black Man
Born: (Unknown)—Date of Death: 27 April 1868
Place: Upshur County
Event: Lynching/Hanged

A young black man, approximately fifteen or sixteen years of age, worked for a man named Mr. Jeter. One night Mr. Jeter's son saw the youth in the barn with a rope. The following morning the younger Jeter and his brother-in-law, identified as Mr. Barlow, arrested the black youth for horse theft and took him before a justice of the peace. The judge released the lad due to the lack of evidence. Apparently Mr. Barlow and young Jeter were not satisfied. In any case, they left for Gilmer with the black lad in tow. Several hours later they returned, claiming the youth had escaped. This incident occurred sometime between 1 and 10 March 1868.

On Monday, 27 April 1868, a young man out turkey hunting discovered the black youth hanging from a dogwood limb, his knees on the ground. The body showed evidence of having been killed elsewhere, then hung from the tree on display. It is not known if Jeter and Barlow were ever prosecuted.

Flake's Bulletin had a slightly different account, claiming that an unidentified black man was found dead, floating in the bayou near Gilmer. It is believed that he was a suspected thief. The newspaper reported, "...he is only a Negro, who cares," thus providing insight into the prevailing racial sentiment of the day.[426]

Lee, William H.
Born: (Unknown)—Date of Death: 30 April 1868
Place: Coryell County
Event: Lynching/Shot

William H. Lee, a white man, was shot and killed near the Leon River. Owing to the fact that his hat, saddle, pantaloons and shoes were all splattered with blood thus it was presumed that he had been shot while mounted.[427]

Hudson, James W.
Born: (Unknown)—Date of Death: May 1868
Place: Rusk County
Event: Lynching

According to reports, a white man named James W. Hudson was lynched at Henderson in Rusk County for having committed a murder. The precise date in May is unclear from the story.[428]

Dial, Hardy H.
Born: circa 1845—Date of Death: 5 May 1868
Place: Coryell County
Event: Lynching/Hanged

According to accounts of the day, a white man named Hardy Dial was taken from the jail where he had been confined and lynched by a vigilante mob.[429]

Dial is connected to the Lee-Peacock Feud, which took place in northeast Texas. After the Civil War area residents resented the intrusion of Reconstruction ideals and new Carpetbagger governance. When Bob Lee returned home he was seen as a natural leader, given that for many the Civil War was still being fought in northeast Texas. At the helm of the Union contingent was Lewis Peacock, who had arrived in Texas in 1856 and lived just south of Pilot Grove. To Peacock, Lee was a threat to his cause and to reconstruction itself. In order to skirt this, the Union League of which Peacock was the head hatched a plan to extort money from Lee.

Peacock and his cohorts arrived at Lee's house one night and "arrested" him, allegedly for crimes that he had committed during the war. Lee would later say that he recognized the men as Lewis Peacock, James Maddox, Bill Smith, Sam Bier, Hardy Dial, Doc Wilson, and Israel Boren. Stating to Lee that he was to be taken into Sherman, they instead stopped in Choctaw Creek bottoms where they took Lee's watch, a $20 gold coin, and forced him to sign a promissory note for $2,000. Later, Lee refused to pay the note, and brought suit at Bonham. This incident started what became known as the Lee-Peacock Feud, of which Dial was a casualty.

Ellington, Isaac
Born: (Unknown)—Date of Death: 5 May 1868
Place: Corner of McLennan, Coryell and Bell Counties
Event: Lynching/Shot

May, Bernard
Born: (Unknown)—Date of Death: 5 May 1868
Place: Corner of McLennan, Coryell and Bell Counties
Event: Lynching/Shot

Schoonover, Benjamin
Born: circa 1801—Date of Death: 5 May 1868
Place: Corner of McLennan, Coryell and Bell Counties
Event: Lynching/Shot

Schoonover, George
Born: (Unknown)—Date of Death: 5 May 1868
Place: Corner of McLennan, Coryell and Bell Counties
Event: Lynching/Shot

Schoonover, Given Name Unknown #3
Born: (Unknown)—Date of Death: 5 May 1868
Place: Corner of McLennan, Coryell and Bell Counties
Event: Lynching/Shot

Shackelford, George
Born: (Unknown)—Date of Death: 5 May 1868
Place: Corner of McLennan, Coryell and Bell Counties
Event: Lynching/Shot

Sessions, Daniel
Born: (Unknown)—Date of Death: 5 May 1868
Place: Corner of McLennan, Coryell and Bell Counties
Event: Lynching/Shot

Unidentified "Union Boy"
Born: (Unknown)—Date of Death: 5 May 1868
Place: Corner of McLennan, Coryell and Bell Counties
Event: Lynching

Sixty-seven year old Benjamin Schoonover, his crippled son George Schoonover, George Shaddeford,

Isaac Ellington, Daniel Sessions, Bernard May and an unidentified boy, all Unionists, were killed by a mob thought to be members of the Ku Klux Klan.[430] One source lists the Schoonover incident as being separate, and having taken place on Thursday, 23 April 1868, not 5 May 1868, as was claimed by Carrigan in his book *The Making of a Lynching Culture*. The same source lists Isaac Ellington's death as 23 April 1868 as well, and places George Shackelford's passing on 21 April.

Bowles, C.
Born: circa 1844—Date of Death: 21 May 1868
Place: Rusk County
Event: Lynching/Hanged

Lee, J. F.
Born: (Unknown)—Date of Death: 21 May 1868
Place: Rusk County
Event: Lynching/Hanged

Miller, George
Born: (Unknown)—Date of Death: 21 May 1868
Place: Rusk County
Event: Lynching/Hanged

C. Bowles, J. F. Lee and George Miller, all white men, were suspected of having murdered R. J. Masters along the road between Palestine and Crockett on Thursday, 21 May 1868. Not long after that date, but before 2 June 1868, the threesome were overtaken and lynched for the crime. Before meeting their end Lee confessed that the three men had come together to watch the road and rob passersby of their money and valuables. Miller died defiantly. Bowles died calmly. Lee wanted to climb the tree and fasten his own lynching rope to a limb so as to hang himself, making sure the thing was done properly.[431]

One Unidentified Black Man
Born (Unknown)—Date of Death: 23 May 1868
Place: Brazos County
Event: Lynching/Hanged

On Friday, 22 May 1868, a black man allegedly killed his employer, a man named Gray. Gray was a well-known citizen of Robertson County. The suspect fled but was caught and executed by a number of citizens in nearby Bryan in Brazos County on Saturday, 23 May 1868.[432]

Hatch, Henry
Born: (Unknown)—Date of Death: 27 May 1868
Place: Falls County
Event: Lynching/Shot

A newspaper account of the day reported that Henry Hatch was shot and killed near the Crugar Cedar Break. It is unclear if Hatch was white or black, or if he was a part of the general race rioting taking place in the region at the time.[433]

Burgess, George L.
Born: (Unknown)—Date of Death: 28 May 1868
Place: Rusk County
Event: Lynching/Hanged

Hudson, James W.
Born: (Unknown)—Date of Death: 28 May 1868
Place: Rusk County
Event: Lynching/Hanged

On Thursday, 28 May 1868, Doctor J. H. Caldwell was murdered about fifteen miles south of Henderson. The killing was the work of two men, George Burgess and James Hudson. Both were captured and, while being transported to Henderson, were taken by force from posse men and lynched along the roadside.[434]

Proctor, David
Born: (Unknown)—Date of Death: 30 May 1868
Place: Bell County
Event: Lynching/Shot

Shanklin, Dennis
Born: (Unknown)—Date of Death: 30 May 1868
Place: Falls County
Event: Lynching/Shot

Shanklin, Sol
Born: (Unknown)—Date of Death: 30 May 1868
Place: Falls County
Event: Lynching/Shot

Two freedmen identified as Dennis and Sol Shanklin were killed on Saturday, 30 May 1868, at Falls County. It is surmised that their death was associated with the general race rioting taking place in the region at the time.[435] In the same article the journalist makes mention of another black man, David Proctor, who was also lynched at Bell County.

Hall, Given Name Unknown
Born: (Unknown)—Date of Death: June 1868
Place: Robertson County
Event: Lynching/Hanged

Horton, Given Name Unknown
Born: (Unknown)—Date of Death: June 1868
Place: Robertson County
Event: Lynching/Hanged

One 9 June 1868, the *Waco Examiner* reported that a man named Scott from Sterling was found murdered on the highway. Two black men whose names were given only as Messer's Hall and Horton had held him up. Scott had been robbed of a suite of linen clothing and $5 in cash. The merchant who had sold Scott the clothing that was found in the possession of Hall and Horton identified both items. Since that provided sufficient evidence of wrongdoing, the men were lynched.[436]

Four Unidentified White Men
Born: (Unknown)—Date of Death: 3 June 1868
Place: Bosque County
Event: Lynching/Hanged

Four unidentified white men, presumed to have been Unionists, were lynched in Bosque County.[437]

Two Unidentified Black Men
Born: (Unknown)—Date of Death: 6 June 1868
Place: Falls County
Event: Lynching/Shot

Newspaper reports of the day claim that two unidentified freedmen were shot down at Doelson's Plantation in Falls County on 6 June 1868.[438] No other details were provided.

Howard, Jesse Howard
Born: circa 1810—Date of Death: 6 June 1868
Place: Falls County
Event: Lynching/Shot

Howard, Samuel Green "Sam"
Born: circa 1826—Date of Death: 6 June 1868
Place: Falls County
Event: Lynching/Shot

On Saturday, 6 June 1868, Clark Jones and Belton Dodd rode up to the home of Jesse and Sam Howard and shot them down without ever speaking a word. Some sources claim that the Howards were Unionists, while others indicate that the men were horse thieves.

Howard family lore, written by the daughter of Mary Elizabeth Howard, Samuel's daughter, asserts that the brothers were blacksmiths. Apparently a neighbor had come to their residence and a disagreement occurred during which a fistfight took place. The men separated friends. Not long after, however, the neighbors and several of their colleagues returned and killed two Howard men.[439]

Samuel was born at Wood County, Texas. His brother, Jesse, was born in Georgia. It seems unlikely that the Howard family were Unionists, as claimed by one East Coast newspaper. Thus, it remains unclear if the men were just law-abiding blacksmiths who had become involved in an altercation with a neighbor or if they had a love for pinching other people's horses.[440]

Two Unidentified Men
Born: (Unknown)—Date of Death: 26 June 1868
Place: Unknown County
Event: Lynching/Hanged

On 26 June 1868, two unidentified men murdered a white man named J. H. Caldwell from Sandusky, Ohio somewhere in Texas. The culprits were apprehended and placed in the jail. Soon afterward vigilantes removed them by force and lynched them.[441]

Bowen, John H.
Born: (Unknown)—Date of Death: 29 June 1868
Place: Colorado County
Event: Lynching/Hanged

Columbus City Marshal Robert Goode was shot and killed while responding to a report of a disturbance involving three men. While attempting to separate the men one of them named John H. Bowen shot Goode in the heart. The wound proved fatal. Goode expired several minutes later.

In another episode of Texas vigilante justice "swiftly administered," at about 4:00 am on Saturday, 29 June 1868, a mob of twenty-five masked men removed Bowen by force of arms from the jail, carried him about 500 yards distant, and lynched him from a convenient tree.[442]

Upton, Wheelock Horace
Born: circa 1843—Date of Death: 3 July1868
Place: Brazos County
Event: Lynching/Hanged

Newspaper accounts of the day claimed that Wheelock Upton, a Unionist from Virginia, was lynched for his political leanings. Another source, however, claimed that his sentence, administered by "Judge Lynch," had come as a result of his affinity for other people's cattle. Upton allegedly was selling stolen cattle in Navasota a few days before he was lynched. On Friday, 3 July 1868, a mob of citizens in Brazos County hung him.[443] Either one could lead to a quick lynching in Texas.

Twenty-Five to Sixty Unidentified Black Men
Born: (Unknown)—Date of Death: 4 July 1868
Place: Marion County
Event: Lynching

Independence Day is observed in a variety of way across the United States. However, in the post Civil War south it was not widely celebrated for many years after the cessation of hostilities. Apparently in Marion County, in 1868, some citizens decided to memorialize the event by lynching between twenty-five and sixty blacks. One East Coast newspaper set the count at sixty, while references that are more reasonable claim twenty-five.[444]

One Unidentified Black Man
Born: (Unknown)—Date of Death: 8 July 1868
Place: Marion County
Event: Lynching/Hanged and Shot

According to newspaper accounts of the day, one black man was lynched and shot by Ku Klux Klan nightriders at Marion on Wednesday, 8 July 1868.[445]

One Unidentified White Man
Born: (Unknown)—Date of Death: 9 July 1868
Place: Marion County
Event: Lynching/Hanged and Shot

In a related incident that followed the lynching of a black man on the preceding night, one white man, presumed to have been a Unionist, was lynched and shot by Ku Klux Klan nightriders at Marion on Thursday, 9 July 1868.[446]

One Unidentified Black Man
Born: (Unknown)—Date of Death: 10 July 1868
Place: Falls County
Event: Lynching/Shot

According to some reports, in a newspaper account of the day one black man was robbed and shot by white men at Falls County on Friday, 10 July 1868.[447]

One Unidentified Black Man
Born: (Unknown)—Date of Death: 11 July 1868
Place: Smith County
Event: Lynching/Shot

According to newspaper reports of the day, six unidentified masked white men shot and killed a freedman about four miles from Tyler.[448]

Surname Unknown, Robert
Born: (Unknown)—Date of Death: 15 July 1868
Place: Brazos County
Event: Lynching/Shot

Thomas, Harry
Born: (Unknown)—Date of Death: 15 July 1868
Place: Brazos County
Event: Lynching/Shot

Zenber, Dan
Born: (Unknown)—Date of Death: 15 July 1868
Place: Brazos County
Event: Lynching/Shot

Hardy, Moses
Born: (Unknown)—Date of Death: 16 July 1868
Place: Brazos County
Event: Lynching/Shot

Holiday, King
Born: (Unknown)—Date of Death: 17 July 1868
Place: Brazos County
Event: Lynching/Shot

Brooks, George E.
Born: (Unknown)—Date of Death: 17 July 1868
Place: Brazos County
Event: Lynching/Shot

Federal troops arrived at Millican in June 1865, signaling the start of eight years of racial strife in Brazos County. Blacks and white landowners struggled to work out the economic and social relations brought about by Reconstruction. Freedmen's Bureau agents, backed by federal soldiers, attempted to mediate between the groups. Whites and blacks quarreled constantly over labor contracts, leading to interracial violence. This strife reached its peak in the Millican race riot of 1868.

The Ku Klux Klan had made its first appearance in the county in June when a group of masked men paraded through the black neighborhood in Millican. Armed blacks fired at the Klan members, drove them off, and organized a militia company under the leadership of a black clergyman named George Brooks. Brooks had been active in registering black voters and was much hated by white county residents. In July, false rumors spread among the black community of Millican that whites had lynched a local black leader named Miles Brown.

Escalating tensions on both sides eventually led to several armed confrontations between groups of whites and blacks that left at least six blacks dead, including Brooks. Newspaper accounts of the day add to the confusion surrounding this unfortunate event, listing scores of victims and a plethora of convoluted storylines making the events difficult to unravel. The victims, all of whom were black men, were, Harry Thomas, Dan Zenber, Moses Hardy, King Holiday, Reverend George Brooks, and one unidentified black man.[449]

Caleb (Cobb), Given Name Unknown
Born: (Unknown)—Date of Death: 28 July 1868
Place: McLennan County
Event: Lynching/Shot

On Tuesday, 28 July 1868, a black man identified only as Caleb who was returning home from purchasing some medicine for his sick wife was lynched at McLennan County by person or persons unknown.[450] Carrigan's *The Making of a Lynching Culture* incorrectly lists this incident as having occurred on 1 August 1868. *Flake's Bulletin* claimed that the man's name was Cobb, and that he had been killed along Tehuacana Creek on the Brazos River. The article went on to claim that Cobb had been charged with horse theft, a crime for which there was no question of his guilt. It is a bit difficult nailing down exactly what happened to Caleb.

Seven Unidentified Mexican Man
Born: (Unknown)—Date of Death: August 1868
Place: Kendall County
Event: Lynching

According to one Texas newspaper, as many as seven unidentified Mexican men may have been lynched at Boerne in Kendall County for their suspected role in a murder.[451]

One Unidentified Black Man
Born: (Unknown)—Date of Death: 14 August 1868
Place: Hopkins County
Event: Lynching/Shot

Crary, Edward
Born: circa 1846—Date of Death: 14 August 1868
Place: Hopkins County
Event: Lynching/Shot

Miller, John B.
Born: 8 January 1843—Date of Death: 14 August 1868
Place: Hopkins County
Event: Lynching/Shot

On Friday, 14 August 1868, Lieutenant C. F. Morse reported that his party of nine soldiers had been ambushed and fired upon from the brush near Sulphur Springs. First Sergeant Edward Crary and Private John Miller, both white men from Pennsylvania, were killed, as was one unidentified black man who was serving as a scout.[452] The group had been sent out to investigate an incident involving the severe beating of a black woman by a white man.

One Unidentified Black Man
Born: (Unknown)—Date of Death: 27 August 1868
Place: Hopkins County
Event: Lynching/Shot

On Thursday, 27 August 1868, an unidentified black man who had sought refuge at the military post at Sulphur Springs was shot and killed by a desperado who was traveling through town.[453] The name of the killer was not revealed.

Three Unidentified Black Men
Born: (Unknown)—Date of Death: 31 August 1868
Place: Falls County
Event: Lynching/Hanged

Three unidentified black men were found hanging in the woods at Falls County. Clearly, they had not gotten themselves into that fix on their own. Their apparent lynching had been at the hands of a person or persons unknown.[454]

One Unidentified Black Man
Born: (Unknown)—Date of Death: 5 September 1868
Place: Bell County
Event: Lynching/Shot

Surname Unknown, Dennis
Born: (Unknown)—Date of Death: 5 September 1868
Place: Bell County
Event: Lynching/Shot

At about 8:00 am on Saturday, 5 September 1868, an unidentified masked rider trotted up to the cabin of a black youth named Dennis, drug him out and shot him to death. Next the rider made his way to town, loped past an older black man leading his horse and shot him dead. Two killings under his belt, the mysterious masked assassin galloped out of town and was not seen or heard from again.[455]

One Unidentified Black Man
Born: (Unknown)—Date of Death: 5 September 1868
Place: McLennan County
Event: Lynching

According to unverified and sometimes questionable sources, an unidentified black man was killed for disobeying a white man's orders while he was looking for work at McLennan County.[456]

Turner, Norwood
Born: (Unknown)—Date of Death: 5 September 1868
Place: McLennan County
Event: Lynching/Shot

A person or persons unknown shot Norwood Turner to death while he was standing at the threshold of his own home. Turner was a black man. [457]

Bridges, John
Born (Unknown)—Date of Death: 21 September 1868
Place: Grayson County
Event: Lynching

Estes, William
Born (Unknown)—Date of Death: 21 September 1868
Place: Grayson County
Event: Lynching

Morgan, Given Name Unknown
Born (Unknown)—Date of Death: 21 September 1868
Place: Grayson County
Event: Lynching

On Sunday, 21 September 1868, a report circulated at Paris in Grayson County that a dead man had been found lying on the prairie eight or nine miles from Mormon Grove. The next day a detachment of soldiers was sent to search for the body. Instead, they discovered the bodies of two white men and one black man.

It was learned that some weeks earlier a party of citizens from Montague County captured three alleged horse thieves near Mormon Grove. Two of the thieves were white and one black. A citizen's posse had started back to Montague County with the stolen horses and the three men. Apparently the group decided to kill the three criminals and leave their bodies on the prairie. A young man who assisted in the arrest gave the names of the dead men as John Bridges, age twenty-six or twenty-eight, William Estes age twenty-four, and a black man identified only as Morgan. One local newspaper opined "[w]e give the facts as we receive them and leave the reader to make his own comments, but that there are three thieves less is beyond question."[458]

Addams, William H.
Born: (Unknown)—Date of Death: 30 September 1868
Place: McLennan County
Event: Lynching

William Addams, an avowed Unionist, was killed for that belief and for not leaving the county when told to do so by parties unknown.[459]

One Unidentified Black Man
Born: (Unknown)—Date of Death: October 1868
Place: Waller County
Event: Lynching/Hanged

An unidentified black man outraged a German woman named Wentz near Waller's Store at Hempstead. Local citizens took the matter into their own hands, finding the man guilty by "lynch law" and hanging him at a convenient spot. The exact date of the incident was not reported.[460]

Smith, George Webster
Born: 2 December 1841—Date of Death: 4 October 1868
Place: Marion County
Event: Lynching/Shot

Two Unidentified Black Men
Born: (Unknown)—Date of Death: 4 October 1868
Place: Marion County
Event: Lynching/Shot

On Sunday, 4 October 1868, George W. Smith, a white man, and two unidentified black men were taken by force and shot to pieces at Jefferson.

Smith was an ardent Reconstructionist who had fought on the side of the Union during the Civil War. He had "locked horns" as it was with local Confederate veteran Colonel R. P. Crump and his cohorts over political and reconstruction matters. Smith had just returned from a trip. His valise was being transported to his home by a group of black men when they were met on the road and robbed. Learning of the incident Smith went to town in search of the culprits. A little after dark he was accosted in the streets and, claiming to have been fired upon drew his own weapons and wounded ten of his attackers.

Fearing for his safety Smith fled to the military headquarters of Major Curtis, commander of the local outpost. Curtis placed him in the jail for protection. Between nine and ten o'clock a group of seventy-five to one hundred men, disguised with painted faces and armed with shotguns and pistols, stormed the building and took Smith and several black men from protective custody. Smith's attackers were members of the recently formed *Knights of the Rising Sun*, a Ku Klux organization that had come to prominence after the war. Smith was literally shot to pieces. Two of the black men were fatally shot and two others wounded.[461]

Twenty-three men were brought to trial in 1869 for the killing of Smith. Three were convicted and sentenced to life in prison.

Seven Unidentified Black Men

Born: (Unknown)—Date of Death: 15 October 1868
Place: Marion County
Event: Lynching/Shot

At about sunrise on Thursday, 15 October 1868, a mob of fifty armed men made their way to the Whitaker Plantation, located about fifteen miles above Jefferson in Marion County. There they shot and killed seven blacks, wounded three others and burned the gin to the ground. That building contained forty bails of cotton and 2,000 bushels of corn. One of the black men was lynched.[462]

Bennett, Aleck (Albert)

Born: (Unknown)—Date of Death: 31 October 1868
Place: McLennan County
Event: Lynching/Shot

Killum, Henry

Born: (Unknown)—Date of Death: 31 October 1868
Place: McLennan County
Event: Lynching/Shot

Aleck Bennett and Henry Killum, both black men, were shot and killed by a mob of about thirty masked men.[463] There was no mention of their transgression.

One Unidentified Black Man
Born: (Unknown)—Date of Death: 3 November 1868
Place: Falls County
Event: Lynching/Shot

An unidentified black man was shot and killed while trying to escape from a posse of five men. His offense is not known.[464]

One Unidentified Black Man
Born: (Unknown)—Date of Death: 7 November 1868
Place: Brazos County
Event: Lynching/Shot

On Saturday, 7 November 1868, four armed men went to the home of Mr. S. B. Farrar at Fair Oak Creek and demanded that a black man, believed to be the employer of Mr. Farrar, be turned over. When the subject presented himself he was taken a short distance from the house and killed.[465]

One Unidentified Black Man
Born: (Unknown)—Date of Death: 22 November 1868
Place: McLennan County
Event: Lynching/Shot

According to sources of the day, specifically the *Waco Register,* three men, armed and well mounted, called on a home about two and one half miles from Mastersville in McLennan County and killed one unidentified black man. The riders claimed that the fellow had robbed an apple wagon near Bryan and killed a man.[466]

Miller, James
Born: (Unknown)—Date of Death: 25 November 1868
Place: Falls County
Event: Lynching/Shot

On Wednesday, 25 November 1868, a traveler named James Miller was ambushed and killed by a group of five or six men near a place called Dog Town in Falls County. Miller's assassins were followed on their route to Bryan the next day by eight men from the area, captured and taken into custody. The disposition of any charges against them are not known.[467]

Williams, Joe
Born: (Unknown)—Date of Death: 18 December 1868
Place: Parker County
Event: Legal Execution/Hanged

Joe Williams, a black man who had been convicted of murder and robbery, was hanged at Weatherford on 18 December 1868.[468]

Six Unidentified Indian Men
Born: (Unknown)—Date of Death: circa 1869
Place: Bosque County
Event: Lynching

A crowd of citizens killed six unidentified Indian men for trespassing and marauding.[469]

George, John Washington
Born: circa 1846—Date of Death: circa 1869
Place: Denton County
Event: Lynching/Hanged

John George, a white man, was hanged by a band of at least seven desperate characters from the Hill Country.[470]

One Unidentified White Man
Born: (Unknown)—Date of Death: February 1869
Place: Cherokee County
Event: Lynching/Shot

Grant, Given Name Unknown
Born: (Unknown)—Date of Death: February 1869
Place: Cherokee County
Event: Lynching/Shot

A merchant named Grant from the lower edge of Cherokee County was among those who protested the then popular initiative to force all of the freedmen in the county to leave. A fight followed when blacks remonstrated, resulting in the death of one of the movement's leaders. A week or two after the mêlée mob members called at the home of Mr. Grant. The knock at the door was answered by a schoolteacher who was a boarder there. The vigilantes, in a state of excitement, mistook the poor fellow for Grant and shot him. When they realized their mistake, they sought out Grant and finished him off as well. Afterwards the mob rifled through Grant's possessions and looted his home of valuables.[471]

Calvin, John
Born: (Unknown)—Date of Death: 4 February 1869
Place: McLennan County
Event: Lynching/Hanged

A black man named John Calvin was lynched by parties unknown for some unidentified transgression. Confirmation of this incident, reported in Carrigan's *The Making of a Lynching Culture*, has proven difficult to ascertain. [472]

Brown, Henry
Born: (Unknown)—Date of Death: 10 March 1869
Place: Matagorda County
Event: Lynching/Shot

On Wednesday, 10 March 1869, Henry Brown, a black man and formerly the property of Colonel R. H. Williams, was shot and killed by a mob of black men at Matagorda. Brown was in the custody of lawmen at the time, confined and restrained in heavy irons. He had been accused of shooting and seriously wounding a black man named Bob Houston.[473]

Two Unidentified Black Men
Born: (Unknown)—Date of Death: 15 March 1869
Place: McLennan County
Event: Lynching

Two unidentified black men were murdered by a group of white men using some unlawful means. Their crime or transgression is not known.[474]

Crawford, George
Born: (Unknown)—Date of Death: 17 March 1869
Place: Denton County
Event: Lynching/Shot

George Crawford, a freed black man, had been accused of outraging Mrs. Sarah Newland, a highly respected local citizen of Denton. Once Newland, who was knocked insensible from the excitement, managed to recover she returned home and sounded the alarm. Crawford was soon tracked to his cabin where he was captured and brought before Newland for identification. That accomplished, most voted to lynch him on the spot. Calmer heads prevailed however, fearing reprisal from the military government yet in place.

Crawford was taken before lawyer John McCombs and given a trial. He was found guilty and placed under strong guard. The following morning, while being escorted to the home of Mrs. Lauderdal for breakfast, he managed to overpower guards and escape under a hail of fire.

Crawford was tracked to the Elm Bottoms but managed to evade his pursuers. It is unclear if he was recovered, escaped, or died from wounds received in his flight.[475]

One newspaper account of the day claimed that Crawford was eventually captured, and that he was shot and killed by the woman he had outraged, Mrs. Newland. In this journalist's account Newland, who upon firing the fatal shot, excitedly exclaimed, "Vengeance is mine saith the Lord."[476] The veracity of this claim, no matter how appealing it may sound to some, seems dubious. The journalist also took the scriptural passage, which is from Romans 12:19, somewhat out of context. The verse actually reads, "Dearly beloved, avenge not yourselves, but rather give place unto wrath: for it is written, Vengeance is mine; I will repay, saith the Lord."

Spears, Given Name Unknown
Born: (Unknown)—Date of Death: 22 March 1869
Place: Limestone County
Event: Lynching/Shot

In Carrigan's *The Making of a Lynching Culture,* the author claimed that a black man named Spears was killed by a group of blacks for having robbed a black man at Springfield. *Flake's Bulletin* of 3 April 1869, relates a much different version of the story, and does not identify the race of the two men who rode up to a freedman's house to commit a robbery, demanding all of the firearms that were contained therein. In *Flake's* version, as the group rode away with the weapons a lone black man fired a shot from the bushes striking one of the robbers in the breast and face. His friend took the wounded man to the cabin where he called for a physician and a lawman to place the fellow under arrest. The wounded thief identified himself as Spears, and claimed that he was from Cherokee County. On Monday, 22 March 1869, newspapers reported that Spears was still alive but was not expected to live.[477]

Baker, Joe
Born: (Unknown)—Date of Death: 26 March 1869
Place: Brenham County
Event: Lynching/Hanged

Barfield, Holly
Born: (Unknown)—Date of Death: 26 March 1869
Place: Brenham County
Event: Lynching/Hanged

On the night of Friday, 26 March 1869, Joe Baker, a black man, and Holly Barfield, a white man, were lynched on a little side road about two miles from Brenham by a mob of twenty-five blacks. The pair had been accused of harming a black woman.[478]

Blackmore, William O.
Born: (Unknown)—Date of Death: 26 March 1869
Place: Grayson County
Event: Legal Execution/Hanged

Thompson, John
Born: circa 1822—Date of Death: 26 March 1869
Place: Grayson County
Event: Legal Execution/Hanged

John Thompson and William O. Blackmore, both white men, had robbed, shot and killed a man named Bill Wilson who was from Missouri. The incident took place at Mantua. Both were tried, convicted, and subsequently hung for their crime on Friday, 26 March 1869.[479]

Bickerstaff, Benjamin F.
Born: circa 1840—Date of Death: 5 April 1869
Place: Johnson County
Event: Lynching/Shot

Thompson, Josiah
Born: circa 1834—Date of Death: 5 April 1869
Place: Johnson County
Event: Lynching/Shot

Sometime in the fall of 1868, the notorious Ben Bickerstaff first made his appearance in Johnson County, at the time giving his name as Thomas. A former Confederate veteran and prisoner of war, Bickerstaff was wanted for the murder of a black man in Louisiana. That incident had taken place shortly after the Civil War. Bickerstaff and others had been accused of holding up a United States supply wagon near Sulphur Springs. The men allegedly stole the mules and set fire to the wagons and their contents. He headed for Alvarado to hide out at the invitation of an old friend, Robert Moore, who owned a general store in town. Bickerstaff, the North Texas outlaw and master associate of late Cullen Baker, joined Alvarado business owner Josiah Thompson, who was also a Confederate veteran. Thompson ran a saddle and tack shop while, at the same time, peddling bootlegged whiskey out the back door.

Given their individual reputations the smart move would have been to maintain a low profile. Instead, they ran afoul of the law, performing egregious breeches of etiquette, harassing recently freed slaves and terrorizing citizens by firing six shooters into the air in the town square. Locals were not amused.

By April, townspeople had grown weary of their antics but lacked the resolve to end the harassment. Ultimately, shop owners decided to arm themselves and deal with the matter. The plan was that when the duo rode into town they would ambush them. The maneuver was set to be executed on Monday, 5 April 1869. Anticipating their arrival, residents positioned themselves on rooftops and other strategic locations. When Thompson and Bickerstaff rode up, stopped at the town square and dismounted, a fuselage of bullets showered the streets. Thompson died immediately. Bickerstaff received at least twenty-six wounds, but stubbornly lingered for about forty minutes before dying, long enough to request water, whiskey and morphine. Before he expired, Bickerstaff said of himself, "...they had killed one of the bravest men of the South."[480]

Their bodies were left on the street where they fell until the following morning. Christian burial calls for an east-facing placement, based on the belief that Jesus on the judgment day, will return from the east. According to folklore, Bickerstaff and Thompson had so angered the townspeople that they made a point of burying them north to south.

Both men are buried at Balch, in the Old Alvarado Cemetery.

Green, Given Name Unknown
Born: (Unknown)—Date of Death: 3 April 1869
Place: Rusk County
Event: Lynching/Beaten, Hanged and Buried Alive

Jones, Julius
Born: (Unknown)—Date of Death: 6 April 1869
Place: Rusk County
Event: Lynching

Four Unidentified Black Men
Born: (Unknown)—Date of Death: 6 April 1869
Place: Rusk County
Event: Lynching

A young man identified as Colonel Green, who was a new settler in the county, had left Henderson on Saturday evening, 3 April 1869, to return to his home. About seven miles from town he stopped at the home of the widow Griffin for supper. Green was apparently in a seriously intoxicated state when he arrived. While Green was eating supper with the widow Griffin, five black men who had been working in the fields seized him, hauled him to the woods where they beat him insensible, hanged him, and then placed him in a shallow trench, finally rolling a log over him and leaving him there to die. Two of the blacks that attacked Green were preachers in a nearby town, one named Julius Jones.[481]

All five black men were arrested and jailed pending trial. At about 11:00 pm on Tuesday, 6 April 1869 a mob of about fifty armed men, all disguised, overpowered the guards and took the men by force from the jail with ropes tied around their necks. Accounts of this incident vary, depending upon which newspaper one wished to favor. Some claim that all five men were hung on the town square with the two preachers being strung up from the same tree. Other accounts indicate that three men were found hanged to shade trees outside the Baptist Church and the fate of the remaining two was not mentioned.[482]

Green's brother admitted to leading the mob. He was arrested and jailed at Jefferson. A jury of inquest was organized under direction of attorney Whitley. Newspapers reported that, "The verdict was death by strangulation caused by hanging done by some parties to us unknown on the night of 6 April, 1869."[483]

Johnson, Daniel
Born: (Unknown)—Date of Death: 27 April 1869
Place: Waller County
Event: Lynching/Hanged

Daniel Johnson, a black man, was lynched near Hempstead on Tuesday, 27 April 1869. The incident took place at the home of Charles Thompson, another black man. Apparently Johnson had a good reputation locally, thus the cause of his lynching was something of a mystery.[484]

Two Unidentified Black Men
Born: (Unknown)—Date of Death: May 1869
Place: Navarro County
Event: Lynching/Hanged

In what seems to be a rather convoluted story, as well as a bizarre miscarriage of justice, a mob of black persons lynched a black man who had killed another black man in a disagreement over a gun.

The principal man involved was taken to the town of Dresden, near where the incident occurred, to be handed over to authorities. Upon arrival the vigilantes found no county officials present, and were told to take the man to Waco and hand him over to lawmen there. En route members of the mob became concerned that after turning the man over to officers he would be forced into the military, and later return and take out his vengeance on his captors. Thus, when the procession was a mile or so from town the idea was brought forth that they should just lynch the man and get it over with. Most agreed, and the suggestion was promptly carried out. One member of the mob protested violently, however. For his trouble he was lynched alongside the first man.[485]

Poe, Willis H.
Born: (Unknown)—Date of Death: 11 June 1869
Place: Rusk County
Event: Legal Execution/Hanged

Robinson, Harris B. "Pad"
Born: 6 November 1832—Date of Death: 11 June 1869
Place: Rusk County
Event: Legal Execution/Hanged

Willis Poe and H. B. Robinson were tried and found guilty of the murder of Colonel Ely and Colonel Ward. Both were sentenced to death. The victims had been carrying a large amount of money and were going towards Mount Enterprise to purchase cotton when the killing took place. Poe admitted later to shooting both men, but claimed that he was inebriated at the time and therefore was not responsible for his actions. A jury saw it differently.

On Friday, 11 June 1869, an eager crowd assembled to witness the execution. They came "two to the mule" as the expression goes. An aggregation numbering 6,000 strong, intent on seeing Robinson and Poe swing from the hangman's rope.

Robinson and Poe were taken to the newly erected gallows at the fairgrounds. The prisoners were given an opportunity to speak. Poe took advantage of the offer, holding forth for about ten minutes. During his talk he remained calm, confessed to his crime and asked forgiveness from the relatives of his victim. After a brief silence for prayer, the latch was sprung and the pair dropped through the floor of the gallows. Robinson's neck was broken and he died almost instantly. Poe's was not, and he remained hanging for a time until he finally suffocated.[486]

One Unidentified White Man
Born: (Unknown)—Date of Death: July 1869
Place: Tarrant County
Event: Lynching/Hanged

Sometime during the week of 11 July 1869, an unidentified white man, who was a teacher at a local black school, was lynched by a mob of blacks. The unfortunate fellow had obtained a license to marry one of his pupils, a black girl. The lynch party, which was comprised of black people, expressed concern that miscegenation of this sort would result in the white men making off "...with all of the best looking wenches." The man's marriage license was tacked to the tree from which he was lynched, thus serving fair warning to all others who might be harboring similar intentions.[487]

Wilson, Jake
Born: (Unknown)—Date of Death: August 1869
Place: McLennan County
Event: Legal Execution/Hanged

Jake Wilson, a black man, was executed by hanging at Waco for the murder of a man named John Colive. About 2,500 persons witnessed Wilson go to his death. Newspaper accounts of the day fail to mention the precise date of the execution.[488]

Jones, Clark (Clarke)
Born: circa 1844—Date of Death: 13 August 1869
Place: Falls County
Event: Legal Execution/Hanged

Nelson, Dennis
Born: circa 1834—Date of Death: 13 August 1869
Place: Falls County
Event: Legal Execution/Hanged

Clark Jones, who was about twenty-five, was convicted at the spring term of district court of the murder of the Howard brothers, Jesse and Sam. That crime took place on 6 June 1868.[489] Jones appealed, but the verdict was upheld and a sentence of death was set in July.

Dennis Nelson, who was about thirty-five, was convicted of the murder of a man named Walker. That incident had taken place in Falls County in February. Nelson, reported to have been "...an exemplary member of the Methodist Church," had shot and killed Walker while the man was riding in a buggy with his wife. Presumably, Nelson, the stalwart Methodist, had some reason for shooting the fellow.

At about 9:00 am on Thursday Morning, 12 August 1869, a procession of lawmen and soldiers left Waco en route to Marlin with Jones and Nelson in tow. From the description in the newspaper story one would have thought that this murderous pair had assassinated a sitting president. Sherriff Morris, deputies Moore and R. B. Smith, jailer Gates, thirty mounted troops from the 6th Cavalry as well as a citizen guard numbering about twenty persons accompanied the two doomed souls. Not surprisingly, the procession arrived safely at Marlin at about 4:00 pm.

During the night of the 12 August the prisoners remained in the courthouse under heavy guard. At around noon on the 13 August the solemn procession towards the gallows commenced. The gibbet structure had been constructed by Mr. Gates, and stood about one half mile north of town in a small mesquite patch. Jones scaled the edifice first, and at his request, Reverend Mattison read the twenty-third chapter of Luke. Nelson, the Methodist, followed, muttering, "Oh, did I ever think it would come to this." When asked if they wished to speak Jones stepped forth, announcing to the crowd that he was innocent of the crime he was charged with and that he had never killed anyone in Falls County. He did, however, confess to having taken a shot at a man named Rice, and left speculation open to murders he might have committed outside Falls County. Jones claimed that he was being hanged because people were afraid of him.

Neslon kept his speech brief, simply saying that, "I thought I was justified in doing what I did." After the black caps had been placed over the pair's respective heads Jones turned to Sheriff Morris and asked that he check the ropes, making certain that they were correct so that, "...an honest man can die easy." Morris complied, and at exactly 1:00 pm the latch was sprung and both men fell to their death. After about twenty minutes the attending physician pronounced both men dead.

Mendoza, Bartolo
Born: (Unknown)—Date of Death: 13 August 1869
Place: El Paso
Event: Legal Execution/Hanged

Bartolo Mendoza was tried and convicted of murdering his stepdaughter, Merced Avalos.

Mendoza had tried repeatedly to seduce the young woman, but she rebuffed his advances. Avalos was engaged to be married. On the day of her murder she was en route to El Paso, Old Mexico (Juarez) to be wed. Mendoza followed the girl and confronted her. When she refused to agree not to marry, he pulled a revolver and shot her through the heart. Mendoza re-cocked his pistol and fired a second time at the girl's younger sister who happened to be accompanying Avalos to the nuptials. Both shots proved fatal. Mendoza would likely have fired at the women again had his pistol not gone off by accident, sending a bullet through his own cheek and nose.

At the time of the killing Mendoza was already wanted by authorities for having killed man in Chihuahua some months earlier.

On the day of his hanging, Sheriff Caleb B. Miller brought Mendoza the typical black shroud, or cap, which is placed on a victim's head during the hanging. Mendoza was displeased with the color, asking that one of maroon or purple be made for him. The sheriff explained that there was not enough time for that to be done. At about 3:00 pm the sheriff and Father Borrago accompanied Mendoza to the gallows. He was firm and resolute during his walk, and remained silent as the charges were read. At about 3:30 pm the sheriff sprung the trap and Mendoza swung into eternity.[490]

Six Unidentified Men
Born: (Unknown)—Date of Death: 2 October 1869
Place: Denton County
Event: Lynching/Hanged

"A Good Deal of Such Fruit Is Raised in Texas" was the comment that appeared in the *Washington Reporter* on 27 October 1869, apparently the journalist's half hearted attempt at humor while telling the tale of the lynching of five men and a boy in Denton County.

It is presumed that the collection of unfortunates referenced were horse thieves, a breed that are customarily dealt with most harshly in Texas. Two were found hanged from a tree. The others, including the boy, were strung up from a pole, extending from the crotch of a tree and supported on the other end by a stake. This incident gave further weight to the adage that "...one can get away with murder in Texas, but not horse theft."[491]

Surname Unknown, Elijah
Born: (Unknown)—Date of Death: 27 December 1869
Place: Limestone County
Event: Lynching/Shot

Puckett, Jeff
Born: (Unknown)—Date of Death: 27 December 1869
Place: Limestone County
Event: Lynching/Shot

Jeff Puckett and a man identified only as Elijah, both black men, were murdered by a band of three white men at Limestone County.[492]

One Unidentified White Man
Born: (Unknown)—Date of Death: circa late 1870s
Place: Bell County
Event: Lynching/Hanged

One Unidentified Black Man
Born: (Unknown)—Date of Death: circa late 1870
Place: Bell County
Event: Lynching/Hanged

Sometime in late 1870s two unidentified men, one black and the other white, were forcibly removed from their jail cells and lynched. Their respective crimes are unknown.[493]

Frank, Given Name Unknown
Born: (Unknown)—Date of Death: 29 January 1870
Place: McLennan County
Event: Lynching/Shot

Thornton, Given Name Unknown
Born: (Unknown)—Date of Death: 29 January 1870
Place: McLennan County
Event: Lynching/Shot

Sources identified two black men known only as Thornton and Frank as having been killed by unknown means at McLennan County on 29 January 1870.[494]

Two Unidentified Mexican Men
Born: (Unknown)—Date of Death: 6 March 1870
Place: Hays County
Event: Lynching/Hanging

Newspaper accounts of the day tell of the discovery of two unidentified Mexican men hanging from a tree within plain sight of the stage route between San Marcos and Austin. It was alleged that the pair were horse thieves.[495]

Young, Henry
Born: circa 1832—Date of Death: 8 April 1870
Place: Uvalde County
Event: Lynching/Shot

Henry Young, a white man, shot and killed a man named Asbury at Uvalde on Friday, 15 April 1870. The killing was without provocation. Young was taken into custody and placed in the jail. At about midnight that same day a person or persons unknown shot Young to death through the open window of his cell.[496]

Young was survived by his wife, Mary Elizabeth Rose and one child. His occupation was stated a "gambler" on his death records and the cause was "homicide." Some disagreement exists regarding the correct date of Young's murder.[497]

Washington, John

Born: (Unknown)—Date of Death: May 1870
Place: Sutton County
Event: Lynching/Shot

In May 1870, a black man named John Washington had been confined in jail under suspicion of committing some crime, the nature of which the newspaper articles of the day neglected to mention. The fellow was released under the care of Judge Eckles, who took the man four or five miles from town and shot him.

Eckles, aided by two companions, tried to conceal Washington's body in a mud hole. As it turned out, however, Washington had not fully expired. He crawled from his intended burial place and made it as far as a nearby home where he was able to tell his story before expiring. As of the date of the article Eckles had not yet been captured.[498]

Anderson, Ike

Born: (Unknown)—Date of Death: 3 May 1870
Place: Bell County
Event: Lynching/Shot

According to newspaper sources of the day a man identified as Ike Anderson was killed by a mob on the Lampasas River near Belton in Bell County on Tuesday, 3 May 1870. The reason for the murder or the means of death was not mentioned by the source, the *Belton Intelligencer* of 14 May 1870.[499] Other sources claim that Anderson was staying at the residence of J. C. Burris and was called out during the evening by a man identified as Alfred Polk. At about sunrise the following day Anderson's body was discovered, shot to pieces and severely mangled, laying along the roadside not far from the Burris home.[500]

Lunn, (Given Name Unknown) - Brother #1

Born: (Unknown)—Date of Death: June 1870
Place: Matagorda County
Event: Lynching/Hanged

Lunn, (Given Name Unknown) - Brother #2

Born: (Unknown)—Date of Death: June 1870
Place: Matagorda County
Event: Lynching/Hanged

Smith, John
Born: (Unknown)—Date of Death: June 1870
Place: Matagorda County
Event: Lynching/Hanged

Unidentified Black Man
Born: (Unknown)—Date of Death: June 1870
Place: Matagorda County
Event: Lynching/Shot

A gang of outlaws had made the district along Tres Palacious near Matagorda their hideout. These malefactors stole horses and cattle, robbed travelers and murdering them. So bold was their defiance of the law that they threatened the sheriff, in writing no less. The gang had stolen so many cattle that they found the need to construct a large pen to hold the beasts. Animals were slaughtered and their hides shipped off by boat to Indianola. It was said, with some degree of certitude, that the ne're-do-wells had murdered at least two freedmen and two whites. It was estimated that this bunch had purloined no less than 10,000 head of cattle.

Some time in June 1870, a posse of about ten men was assembled to deal with this gang. They caught up with the bandits near their own cattle pen and lynched three of them from the gate. The unlucky outlaws included two Lunn Brothers and a man named John Smith. Smith was thought to be an alias for some other surname.

Once the nasty business of the Lunn Brothers and John Smith had been attended to, the posse rode to nearby Elliott's Ferry on the Colorado where they came upon the cabin of a desperate black man who was a member of the same league of freebooters. As the posse approached the shack the black man came to the door, fired, and killed young Edward Anderson of Wharton. The remainder of the posse did the same for the black man.[501]

Lindsay, Jerry
Born: (Unknown)—Date of Death: 10 July 1870
Place: McLennan County
Event: Lynching/Shot

Jerry Lindsay, a cattle thief, was shot and killed by a large group of disguised and otherwise unidentified men.[502]

Lindsay, Tom
Born: (Unknown)—Date of Death: 12 July 1870
Place: McLennan County
Event: Lynching/Shot

Not unlike his brother Jerry, Tom Lindsay was apparently a cattle thief. He too was shot and killed on 12 July 1870, by a large group of disguised and otherwise unidentified men. His final episode came just two days after his brother.[503]

Johnson, Jake
Born: (Unknown)—Date of Death: 5 August 1870
Place: Harris County
Event: Legal Execution/Hanged

In the afternoon of 1 December 1869, a report reached townspeople that B. W. Loveland, who ran a grocery store on Fannin Street, had been found murdered in his own shop. Loveland had apparently just cut off a slab of bacon and was bending down to draw some molasses when he was struck over the head with a round iron bar. The blow was fatal. Suspicion was raised when the store had remained closed all day. A black woman and her children, seeing the door ajar, stepped in and discovered the scene. Mr. Loveland, a good Presbyterian and well liked by the community, lived at the rear of the store and had no family.

Four black men were eventually arrested and tried for the murder. John Jamison, Doc Wheeler, Jake Johnson and Jules Mitchel. Mitchel was indicted but discharged as a principal witness. Jamison, although implicated, was also discharged. Wheeler was never tried. Johnson did have his day in court, and was found guilty. After an appeal failed, Judge Dodge handed down a sentence of death for the first-degree murder of Loveland.

On Wednesday, 27 July 1870, reporters interviewed Johnson. During that session he confessed to having singlehandedly done the killing of Loveland, admitting that along with Wheeler and Jamison the three had hatched the plan to do the murder and robbery. He was the one who struck Loveland twice, inflicting the fatal blows.

At precisely noon on Friday, 5 August 1870, Johnson emerged from the jail with the sheriff and guards. He was loaded into a hack and rapidly transported to the gallows at Hangman's Grove in the southwest suburbs of the city, near the cemetery. Once there, Johnson hurriedly ascended the steps in the company of a black preacher, eyed the crowd and inquired if his brother was there. Johnson addressed the gathering, essentially repeating what he had told the reporter earlier and imploring the youth in attendance not to follow his wicked path. Reverend Sandy Parker read a hymn. The black preacher prayed, after which Johnson knelt and joined in worship. Hands and feet bound and black cap pulled over is head Johnson dropped from the gallows and, with hardly a quiver, passed into the hereafter.[504]

Clark, Oscar

Born: (Unknown)—Date of Death: circa 1871

Place: Cooke County

Event: Legal Execution/Hanged

Oscar Clark, a black freedman, was tried and convicted of having murdered W. A. Jones of Gatesville. His sentence was death. Sometime between January and the end of April 1871, Clark was executed by hanging for his crime.[505]

Miller, Henry

Born: (Unknown)—Date of Death: 28 July 1871

Place: Washington County

Event: Legal Execution/Hanged

Henry Miller, a black man, was found guilty of murdering a man named Dehay. The incident took place in April 1871. Miller's death sentence was handed down by an all black jury.

At about 1:00 pm on Friday, 28 July 1871, Miller kept his appointment on the gallows. In front of about 5,000 citizens who had gathered to witness the event, Miller was hanged at Brenham. The process went off without incident.[506]

Haynes, Meredith

Born: circa 1844—Date of Death: 15 December 1871

Place: Travis County

Event: Legal Execution/Hanged

Meredith Haynes, a black man and a tenant farmer, was tried and convicted of murder. He was hanged at Austin on Thursday, 15 December 1871.[507]

Guerra, Bartolo

Born: (Unknown)—Date of Death: 22 December 1871

Place: Bee County

Event: Legal Execution/Hanged

Numerous sources have reported the legal execution of Guerra Bartolo at Bee County, which took place on Friday, 22 December 1871. Unfortunately, no documentation has been located to support this claim. Even so, it is being included in the interest of completeness.[508]

One Unidentified Man
Born: (Unknown)—Date of Death: 12 January 1872
Place: Nueces County
Event: Lynching/Hanged

In Carrigan's book, *Forgotten Dead* the author claims that an unidentified man was lynched for being a thief at Banquette, in Nueces County. The *Galveston Tri-Weekly News* account is somewhat different, claiming, "The citizens of Banquette read a long communication to the *Nueces Valley*, in which they describe the outrages committed by a Mexican at the houses of Mrs. Hunter and Mrs. Elliff, and justify the punishment of the criminal."[509]

Dove, Jesse
Born: (Unknown)—Date of Death: 10 April 1872
Place: Freestone County
Event: Lynching

Early on Saturday, 30 March 1872, three men, the first identified only as "Garrett," the second as George Storey, and the third as Jesse Dove arrived in Fairfield in Freestone County. Sheriff James Rogers suspected that they were horse thieves and went to speak with them at the Planter's Hotel. A man identified by some sources as Wood, but who was more likely Deputy Blood Noland, accompanied the sheriff.

The three suspected rustlers were sitting in front of the establishment having a conversation. Rogers asked the three men to go inside the hotel with him. When they refused, he told them to consider themselves under arrest. At that point, Storey drew his Colt Army six-shooter and shot Rogers. The bullet entered through his back and came out under his left breast. Deputy Noland, who had either accompanied the sheriff or joined the group in the meantime, drew his revolver and shot Storey, killing him instantly. Dove and Garrett fled the scene.

Rogers lingered until 3 April 1872 when he finally died from his wounds. Dove was quickly apprehended near Thornton Depot. On Wednesday, 10 April 1872, a group of unknown persons overpowered the guards and removed Dove from jail. Neither Dove nor the group of jail breakers was ever located. The third man, the man named Garrett, escaped and was never found. [510]

Bellew, Stephen M.
Born: circa 1844—Date of Death: 24 May 1872
Place: Collin County
Event: Legal Execution/Hanged

The first legal hanging in McKinney took place on Friday, 24 May 1872. Stephen M. Bellew, sometimes called Ballew, was a horse trader from Illinois. He was executed for the murder of James P. Golden.

Golden was also from Illinois. The murder took place in Collin County, in early October 1870, while they were on a trading expedition. Bellew had struck Golden in the head with an ax and killed him, then buried the body alongside the trail.

Bellew's execution took place about a quarter of a mile from the jail, in a valley surrounded by hills upon which an estimated 5,000 persons had gathered to witness the spectacle. Bellew rode in a wagon with the sheriff to the place then scaled the gallows stairs looking to witnesses to be in good health, a bit heavier perhaps than when he had been captured in Quincy, Illinois. Sheriff Bush asked the condemned man if he had anything to say. He replied, "No." When everything had been made ready, the signal was given to spring the latch and Bellew dropped through the trapdoor. Owing to some imperfection with the knot, the condemned man's neck was not broken. He hung there for fully sixteen minutes without expiring before being raised to the platform. The rope was adjusted and Bellew was dropped a second time. On his second trip through the gallows floor he remained dangling at the end of the rope until he ultimately suffocated. In total, the gruesome ordeal lasted a punishing thirty-nine minutes.[511]

Four-Five Unidentified Mexican Men

Born: (Unknown)—Date of Death: 21 August 1872
Place: Cameron County
Event: Lynching/Hanged and Shot

On Tuesday, 20 August 1872, Cameron County Sheriff William Scanlon left Brownsville with a cavalry escort in quest of Francisco Flores, alias Chicou, who had murdered Charles Alexander. On or about Wednesday 21 August 1872, the sheriff and his military escorts surrounded five Mexicans about thirty miles above the city. Four escaped into Old Mexico where they were captured and hanged by a group of Mexican cavalry who were cooperating with the sheriff. The fifth man attempted to swim across the Rio Grande into Mexico. He was shot and killed by the sheriff's men in the process.

The *Auburn Daily Bulletin* reported that "Floores, alias Chican, the most desperate outlaw on the frontier, and the murdered of Charles Alexander, has gathered together number of fellow desperadoes and expresses his intention of crossing into Texas to avenge the death of his two brothers who were killed a short time ago since, one by a sheriff's party, and the other by the Mexican cavalry."

In Carrigan's book *Forgotten Dead* the author claimed that there were only three Mexicans who were hanged by the Mexican cavalry and one shot by the sheriff.[512]

One Unidentified Mexican Man

Born: (Unknown)—Date of Death: October 1872
Place: McLennan County
Event: Lynching/Hanged

An incident took place about six miles from Waco along the Tehuacana Creek that involved the lynching of a Mexican man for an unknown crime.

At about midnight a group of eight or nine white men came upon a cabin along the creek that was occupied by a Mexican man and his wife. A spokesman from the group approached the dwelling and found the Mexican man and his wife in bed asleep, which was understandably considering the time of day. Under the ruse of looking for a rifle that he said had been left in the building, the intruder searched the cabin then announced that he was the Sheriff of Limestone County. Next, he took the Mexican man from his bed and dragged him out into the night. The following morning the woman found her husband hanging from a tree about 400 yards from the house. The riders were long gone. Their identity was never discovered.[513]

Barclay, John

Born: (Unknown)—Date of Death: 4 October 1872
Place: Colorado County
Event: Legal Execution/Hanged

John Barclay, a white man, was found guilty of the murder of Charles F. Garner. The incident had taken place one year earlier, in October 1871.

On Friday, 4 October 1872, Barclay scaled the gallows stairs at Columbus and, before a large crowd, confessed his guilt in the matter. Barclay went on to warn of the evils of consuming ardent spirits, and how such excessive libation had brought him to this place on the hangman's scaffold. When he had concluded his talk his arms and legs were tied, a black cap pulled down over his head, and the trap door was sprung. Barclay dropped a few feet to his death.[514]

Unidentified Mexican Man

Born: (Unknown)—Date of Death: 2 October 1872
Place: Limestone County
Event: Lynching/Hanged

A party of eight or nine men lynched an unidentified Mexican man who was labeled as a thief.[515]

Shelby, Arthur

Born: (Unknown)—Date of Death: 15 January 1873
Place: Burnet County
Event: Legal Execution/Hanged

Shelby, Benjamin

Born: (Unknown)—Date of Death: 15 January 1873
Place: Burnet County
Event: Legal Execution/Hanged

Smith, William
Born: (Unknown)—Date of Death: 15 January 1873
Place: Burnet County
Event: Legal Execution/Hanged

Woods, Ball
Born: (Unknown)—Date of Death: 15 January 1873
Place: Burnet County
Event: Legal Execution/Hanged

Arthur Shelby, Benjamin Shelby, William Smith and Ball Woods, all white men, were tried and convicted of the murder of Benjamin McKeever. McKeever had been shot while riding a horse at night, near the Shelby residence. His throat was then cut, and his body carried off a distance of three miles where it was thrown into a cave.

On Wednesday, 15 January 1873, all four men went to the gallows together. It must have been quite a show.[516]

Eleven Unidentified White Men
Born: (Unknown)—Date of Death: February 1873
Place: Western Counties
Event: Lynching/Hanged

One Unidentified Indian
Born: (Unknown)—Date of Death: February 1873
Place: Western Counties
Event: Lynching/Hanged

Twelve cattle thieves who all appeared to be Indians were caught in the western counties of Texas and hanged from a tree. Suspecting from the group's appearance that their outfit might be a disguise, their captors scrubbed their faces and discovered that eleven of the dozen were white orphans from Kansas. That fact did not, however, cause the vigilante party to alter their plans for the bunch. All dozen were still hanged for their crime.[517]

Brothers, Milton
Born: 3 May 1846—Date of Death: 21 February 1873
Place: McLennan County
Event: Lynching/Hanged

Milton Brothers, a white man, was lynched by a mob of vigilantes for having purloined some cattle.[518]

Brothers' family genealogists list his place of death as Blue Ridge, in Falls County, which is where he is buried. His grave is marked with a period tombstone, correctly inscribed.

The original source for the McLennan County reference is Carrigan's *The Making of a Lynching Culture*. That reference claimed, incorrectly, that this incident occurred in 1870. On balance the family sources are thought to be most accurate in this case.

Brothers was survived by his wife Laura Mitchell.[519]

Barnes, George W.
Born: circa 1847—Date of Death: 14 April 1873
Place: Travis County
Event: Legal Execution/Hanged

Kimball, Lawson J.
Born: circa 1842—Date of Death: 14 April 1873
Place: Travis County
Event: Legal Execution/Hanged

George Barnes and Lawson Kimball, both white men, had been tried, convicted, and sentenced to death for highway robbery and the murder of a man named Philpot.

On Monday, 14 April 1873, the pair scaled the gallows stairs at Austin. They had been scheduled to hang on Friday, 11 April 1873, but owing to the fact that that day was Good Friday, the Christians of Travis County postponed the event until the 14th. Kimball, upon reaching the platform, executed a dance step in an apparent effort to draw a reaction from the crowd. Barnes was dressed in a pair of spotted, short grey trousers and a blue jacket buttoned over his chest. Kimball had on a striped shirt, a pair of coarse yellowish trousers and dark woolen jacket. Deputy Sheriff Stokes read the death warrant. Neither man really addressed the crowd. Kimball did comment that, "You are hanging an innocent man." Barnes had nothing at all to say.

At 12:51 pm the trap was sprung. Barnes met a speedy death. Kimball's rope slipped. He had to be hoisted to a standing position and hung a second time. The gruesome ordeal took seven minutes while the crowd waited breathlessly for the hangman to correct his error. On the second try the procedure was effective, snapping Barnes's neck at the end of the drop.[520] Barnes is buried in an unmarked grave at the Oakwood Cemetery at Austin. He was survived by his wife Palee Williams and one son.

Unidentified Black Man
Born: (Unknown)—Date of Death: 1-10 May 1873
Place: Marion County
Event: Lynching/Shot

Sometime between 1 and 10 May 1873, a group of about a dozen men visited a work camp on the Texas and Pacific Railroad located around twenty miles north of Jefferson. The riders were clearly intoxicated. Their leader, a man named Porter from Cass County, began to antagonize a black man identified as a "peaceable and unoffending fellow." The black pushed Porter off him and made every effort to keep out of his way. Porter took great offense. Based on the number of railroad workers Porter apparently considered himself under armed for appropriate retaliation, and returned home for reinforcements. A couple of days later he returned, this time with a larger band of compatriots. The work camp had moved, but Porter tracked down the unfortunate black man at his new jobsite.

Taking him into his custody Porter and his crowd bound the fellow and spit tobacco juice in his eyes. Now partially blind, they fastened a rope around the man, tied the other end to a horse, and set out at a fast pace compelling the black man to keep up or be dragged. Once the attackers had reached a place among a grove of trees they secured the unfortunate black man so that he could only move his head, then carved a cross in his forehead and scalped him. When they had suitably tortured the wretch they shot him several times and tossed his body into a nearby creek. [521]

Wallace, Mat A.
Born: (Unknown)—Date of Death: 29 June 1873
Place: McLennan County
Event: Lynching/Hanged

Mat Wallace, brother-in-law of the noted horse thief Bill Posey, was lynched near the north limits of Waco in July 1873. Newspaper reports of the day seem to accuse Wallace of sharing his sibling's fondness for other people's horses, but are somewhat unclear as to the crime he was lynched for. What the tabloids do express, in a rather poignant way, is their distain for "midnight murderers," claiming that Wallace, based on the outcome of this incident, apparently had a greater right to fear his neighbors than they him.[522]

DeGraffenreid, George
Born: (Unknown)—Date of Death: 29 July 1873
Place: Kerr County
Event: Lynching/Hanged

Eastwood, Frank
Born: circa 1842—Date of Death: 29 July 1873
Place: Kerr County
Event: Lynching/Shot

Jamison, John
Born: (Unknown)—Date of Death: 29 July 1873
Place: Kerr County
Event: Lynching/Shot

Ratliff, James
Born: (Unknown)—Date of Death: 29 July 1873
Place: Kerr County
Event: Lynching/Hanged

Frank Eastwood began a life of crime almost immediately after the Civil War. By 1872, his gang had drawn new outlaws from all over the state to the Kerr County area. Feeling pressure from local law enforcement the gang moved to Kendall County near the end of 1871 or the beginning of 1872. In 1872 a posse under the command of Nimrod J. Miller located gang member Bill Bell. Bell was wanted for murder in another county. Miller ultimately shot and killed Bell, but his death did not deter the likes of Bill Longley and the Ake brothers (Jesse and Bill) from filling the vacancy and joining Eastwood's crowd.

On 14 July 1873, the band traveled through Kerrville while being pursued by Sheriff James J. Finney of Mason County and a collection of posse men. Kerr County Sheriff John M. Tedford joined Sheriff Finney, and together they caught up with the Eastwood Gang about thirteen miles from Kerrville. The posse approached the gang at dusk, and wisely decided to hide out in the brush and wait until daylight at which time they plotted to descend upon the bunch. On the morning of 24 July 1873, they descended on the encampment at dawn and arrested Frank Eastwood, Bill Longley, John Jamison, George DeGraffenreid, James Ratliff and the Jeff Ake and Bill Ake. Miraculously they managed to do this without incident.

The entire covey of outlaws was escorted to the jail in Kerrville where they remained for less than a week. On 29 July 1873, in the early hours of the morning, a mob of angry citizens overpowered the sheriff and his deputies and took all of the men except Bill Longley from jail. Prisoner John Jamison was shot and killed during the struggle inside the jail. Frank Eastwood's body was found the next day. He had been shot seven times and left near the mouth of Goat Creek at the Guadalupe River. The Ake brothers, Jeff and Bill, were set free. Two other gang members, George DeGraffenreid and James Ratliff, were lynched from an oak tree by the mob of vigilantes.[523]

Hill, Nancy
Born (Unknown)—Date of Death circa September 1873
Place: Montague County
Event: Lynching/Hanged

Nancy Hill was taken from the jail at Montague by a vigilante committee and hung from a tree. Local newspapers reported that "She had carried off a halter belonging to a neighbor, neglecting to take out the horse's head which was in it at the time of the theft."[524]

One Unidentified Man
Born (Unknown)—Date of Death: 16 September 1873
Place: Nueces County
Event: Lynching/Hanged

An unidentified man was hanged at Nuecestown for theft on Tuesday, 16 September 1873.[525]

Two Unidentified Black Men
Born: (Unknown)—Date of Death: 14 October 1873
Place: Colorado County
Event: Lynching/

Newspaper reports of the day stated that the arrest of a freedman at Eagle Lake for theft of a beef had caused quite a disturbance in the town. Another freedman attempted to break the first man from jail, but his effort was thwarted when a deputy struck him over the head with his six-shooter, rendering him insensible. The deputy's actions spawned even greater unrest among the blacks, resulting in a crowd of three or four hundred to form, threatening to destroy the town. A mob of armed black men numbering roughly seventy-five loitered about the town posing a threat. Aid was sought from Columbus.

On 12 October 1873, two black men went missing. Their bodies were discovered two days later, on 14 October 1873, hanging from trees not far from Eagle Lake. That finding resulted in a resurgence of turmoil. By 18 October 1873, a deputy U.S. Marshal was dispatched to the town to help maintain order. Newspaper reports of the day stated the painfully obvious, which was that whites were suspected of being responsible for the lynching. The County Sheriff, J. R. Brooks, wisely hypothesizing that the two fellows had not lynched themselves, and issued the manifestly foolish declaration that "...they had come to their death by foul means, at the hands of unknown parties."[526]

Garcia, Vincente
Born: (Unknown)—Date of Death: 28 November 1873
Place: Duval County
Event: Lynching/Hanged

Garza, Leonardo
Born: (Unknown)—Date of Death: 28 November 1873
Place: Duval County
Event: Lynching/Hanged

Mata, Blas
Born: (Unknown)—Date of Death: 28 November 1873
Place: Duval County
Event: Lynching/Hanged

Reinas, Jose M.
Born: (Unknown)—Date of Death: 28 November 1873
Place: Duval County
Event: Lynching/Hanged

Rios, Epifanio
Born: (Unknown)—Date of Death: 28 November 1873
Place: Duval County
Event: Lynching/Hanged

Rios, Filomeno
Born: (Unknown)—Date of Death: 28 November 1873
Place: Duval County
Event: Lynching/Hanged

Rodriguez, Jorge
Born: (Unknown)—Date of Death: 28 November 1873
Place: Duval County
Event: Lynching/Hanged

According to a sworn affidavit, Vincente Garcia, Leonardo Garza, Blas Mata, Jose Reinas, Epifanio Rios, Filomeno Rios and Jorge Rodguez who were shepherds in the employ of Don Toribio Lozano, of Aguafrio, Nuevo Leon, Mexico were all lynched for theft at the Rancho Las Chuza in Duval County. The bodies were found hanged from a tree, in a creek bed, about one mile from the sheep pens at the ranch.[527]

One Unidentified Black Man
Born: (Unknown)—Date of Death: December 1873
Place: Rusk County
Event: Lynching/Hanged

In what was billed by the *Jackson Citizen Patriot* newspaper of Jackson, Michigan as a real down home Texas celebration, residents of Henderson made a bonfire of the black school house, mobbed the "Yankee" teacher and finished off the day by lynching a black man who was suspected of being a "radical." The facts of this matter remain undiscovered.[528]

Goff, Ed
Born: circa 1862—Date of Death: circa 1874
Place: Hunt County
Event: Lynching/Hanged

Hunt County Deputy William Mason was reportedly shot and killed by a known horse thief named Ed Goff (or Ed Gee) sometime in about 1874. A posse tracked Goff down and hung him from a tree not far from the location where he had shot Mason. The body was left adorning the tree for a week as a warning to other horse thieves and criminals that similar actions would be dealt with harshly.

Mason's exact date of death is unknown, but believed to have been after 1 January 1874. He was survived by his wife Margaret Kelly and is buried at the East Mount Cemetery in an unmarked grave.[529]

There was a man named Edward Goff, born circa 1862, who appears on the 1870 census. He had disappeared by 1880, however. There is also a man named Edmund Goff who appears to have been a black slave. He is absent from the census by 1880 as well. It is unclear which person was the subject of the guest of honor at this particular hanging party.[530]

Three Unidentified Mexican Men
Born: (Unknown)—Date of Death: circa 1874
Place: Cameron County
Event: Lynching/Hanged

According to the *New York Herald*, a newspaper that was notoriously short on details in such matters, three unidentified Mexican men were lynched at Cameron County for being bandits sometime during 1874. Neither followers of that profession, nor lynchings of Mexican men, were at all rare during the period.[531]

One Unidentified Man
Born: (Unknown)—Date of Death: circa January 1874
Place: Grayson County
Event: Lynching/Hanged

An unidentified man who sources claimed to have been a horse thief was lynched at Grayson County sometime before 20 January 1874.[532]

Four Brothers Named Brooks

Born (Unknown)—Date of Death: March 1874

Place: Wharton County

Event: Lynching/Shot

In March of 1874, Gray Franks, a former state senator, led a group of white men to the Brooks plantation near Wharton. The men arrived near midnight. They took four brothers named Brooks from the house and shot them dead in front of their families. The brothers were prominent black Republicans. No indictments or arrests were ever made in spite of the fact that the men were well known.

Franks was clearly a violent man. In late 1873, he shot and seriously wounded Isaac Baughman, the former Wharton County sheriff who was also a Republican. On 11 June 1874, Franks met his match when he ordered a young white Republican named Lee Lacey to leave town, then attempted to kill him. Lacey shot first, killing Franks.[533]

One Unidentified Man

Born: (Unknown)—Date of Death: 14 April 1874

Place: Hill County

Event: Lynching/Dragged to Death

On Tuesday, 14 April 1874, a gang of cowboys broke into the jail at Hillsboro and removed a man who was being held there under charges of horse theft. The unfortunate fellow was dragged into the street by means of a lariat looped around his neck. There he was eventually strangled to death. The accused horse thief did not go down without a fight. Before he finally succumbed he took up a wooden bar and thrashed several of his attackers, rendering them ineffectual.[534]

Seven Unidentified Men

Born: (Unknown)—Date of Death: 26 April 1874

Place: Williamson County

Event: Lynching/Hanged

After hearing rumors of a planned jailbreak, vigilantes removed nine prisoners from the lockup at Georgetown on Sunday, 26 April 1874. The assortment of malefactors included two or three horse thieves and one murderer. No indication was given as to the race of any of these men. All were shot and killed to prevent the possibility of their escape.[535] The citizen's plan was effective. None of the men, now quite dead, had managed to get away.

Seven Unidentified Black Men
Born: (Unknown)—Date of Death: 30 April 1874
Place: Brazos County
Event: Lynching/Hanged

Newspaper accounts of the day claim that seven black men assaulted a Mr. Leak at Bryan in Brazos County, leaving him dead. Afterwards the group outraged Mrs. Leak. The men were was captured and confined to the jail. Not long after, a mob removed them by force and lynched them. Some accounts of this story claim that there were only four or five black men involved in the lynching.[536]

Bragg, Sol
Born: circa 1842—Date of Death: 1 May 1874
Place: Tarrant County
Event: Legal Execution/Hanged

One particular newspaper, apparently bent on denigrating Texans, printed the headline, "The Last Moments of Sol Bragg - How the Thing is Celebrated in the Western Wild."

Sol Bragg, a black man, had had a long and illustrious career as a criminal. Bragg had logged quite an impressive resume that included a murder conviction. All of these facts went not mentioned by the scribe of the newspaper article. Rather, he chose to level his criticism at the Texas judicial system, and at the "motley crowd" that gathered at Fort Worth to see the convicted murder Sol Bragg hang for the murder of Matthew Green.

Shortly after 2:00 pm a wagon transported Bragg to the gallows site. Bracketed by lawmen, the condemned man ascended the platform stairs and addressed the crowd, professing his innocence of the murder charge to the end. Once he had concluded his oration, he stepped forward on to the trap where the customary black cap was pulled over his head. With a final, "God have mercy on my soul" the device was tripped and Bragg dropped six feet, hanging for some time while he suffocated as his neck was not broken by the fall.[537] That is, "...How the Thing is Celebrated in the Western Wild."

Three Unidentified Mexican Men
Born: (Unknown)—Date of Death: 16 May 1874
Place: San Patricio County
Event: Lynching/Hanged

On Saturday, 16 May 1874, three unidentified Mexican men were found hanging from a tree near Cayman Lake, about thirty miles northwest of Corpus Christi. According to the newspaper report, "it is not supposed they hanged themselves." The unfortunate threesome is thought to have been involved in the robbery of two American men that had occurred two days earlier, on Thursday, 14 May 1874.[538]

Alexander, John
Born: (Unknown)—Date of Death: 24 May 1874
Place: Bell County
Event: Lynching/Shot

Buckneal, Winfield
Born: (Unknown)—Date of Death: 24 May 1874
Place: Bell County
Event: Lynching/Shot

Coleman, William Lloyd
Born: (Unknown)—Date of Death: 24 May 1874
Place: Bell County
Event: Lynching/Shot

Cowen, William
Born: (Unknown)—Date of Death: 24 May 1874
Place: Bell County
Event: Lynching/-Shot

Crow, Given Name Unknown
Born: (Unknown)—Date of Death: 24 May 1874
Place: Bell County
Event: Lynching/Shot

Grumbles, William Henry
Born: circa 1851 [539]— Date of Death: 24 May 1874
Place: Bell County
Event: Lynching/Shot

McDonald, Francis Marion
Born: 8 November 1854—Date of Death: 24 May 1874
Place: Bell County
Event: Lynching/Shot

McDonald, Thomas James
Born: 27 December 1815[540]—Date of Death: 24 May 1874
Place: Bell County
Event: Lynching/Shot

Smith, William S.
Born: (Unknown)—Date of Death: 24 May 1874
Place: Bell County
Event: Lynching/Shot

Wingfield, Given Name Unknown
Born: (Unknown)—Date of Death: 24 May 1874
Place: Bell County
Event: Lynching/Shot

The hilly cedar brakes that extended along the western border of Bell and Coryell counties offered a secure hideout for outlaws. Captain Robert B. Halley and his deputies managed to corral ten of these desperate fellows at one time, and transport them to the jail of Bell County. The charges against the men included murder, robbery, and horse-theft. There was little question of their guilt it seemed.

The jail itself was a notoriously insecure prison. On Sunday night, 24 May 1874, while the Sheriff was away, the sound of horses' hooves pounding the hard packed streets of Belton was heard, thundering over the night sounds of an otherwise tranquil summer evening.[541] Suddenly mobs of vigilantes began to appear, coming by groups of ten or twenty, from all directions, and converging on the jail. The poor fellow serving as the jailer that Sabbath evening was practically defenseless against this horde, which in the span of only a few minutes battered down the doors and shot nine of the ten prisoners to death.

Falling victim to the vigilante gunmen were John Alexander (alias Daily), William Henry Grumbles, William S. Smith, Thomas James McDonald and his son Francis Marion McDonald, Wingfield, Buckneal, Crow, and William Loyd Coleman. All had been charged with stealing horses, except Coleman who was accused of having murdered his wife. The lucky tenth man, Tyre Thompson, had fallen ill and had been placed on a cot in an adjoining room. He was overlooked by the mob and thus escaped the grim reaper.

The incident struck fear in the hearts of the remaining, organized outlaws throughout the region who, henceforth, gave Bell County a wide berth.[542]

Thomas James McDonald's second wife Martha Ann Newton, and nine of his ten children by an earlier marriage survived him. All of the murdered men are buried at the South Belton Cemetery.

Surname Unknown, Juan
Born: (Unknown)—Date of Death: 8 June 1874
Place: Refugio County
Event: Lynching/Hanged

Surname Unknown, Antonio
Born: (Unknown)—Date of Death: 8 June 1874
Place: Refugio County
Event: Lynching/Hanged

Surname Unknown, Marcelo

Born: (Unknown)—Date of Death: 8 June 1874
Place: Refugio County
Event: Lynching/Hanged

On Monday morning, 8 June 1874, the bodies of Mr. and Mrs. Thad Swift were discovered at their home near Rockport. Thad's brother Frank made the find. The couple's three children, the eldest of whom was only five years old, had walked to Frank's home at an early hour that morning asking for breakfast. They said they were unable to wake their parents. When Frank went to investigate he discovered the awful scene. Mrs. Swift was laying in the yard near the house, one bullet wound to the head and her throat cut. Her body was mangled, and had at least two-dozen dagger wounds. Upon entering the house, Frank found the body of his brother, his head practically severed from having had his throat cut so unreservedly.

A party was immediately organized and a search began. Mexicans were suspected of having done the dirty work. Each ranch in the surrounding area was scoured. An unfortunate young man named Dan Holland was shot to death by the posse, his only crime being that of wearing a sombrero, which made the searchers believe that perhaps he was one of the Mexican men who had murdered the Swift family.

When the party of perpetrators was finally located, secreted in a hut nearby, reinforcements were summoned. Upon their arrival a rush on the building was made. Three Mexican men were arrested. They were identified as Juan and his two sons, Antonio and Marcello. One newspaper reported that one Mexican received a broken arm during the ensuing struggle. Two others escaped into Old Mexico, one of whom was the notorious Juan Flores.[543]

Now in custody, the Sheriff headed for Goliad with the prisoners in tow. He never made it. Vigilantes took the three suspected murderers One was hanged and two were shot to death.[544]

Two Unidentified Black Men

Born: (Unknown)—Date of Death: 15 June 1874
Place: Coryell County
Event: Lynching

A person or persons unknown shot and killed two unidentified black men believed to be horse thieves.[545]

Dixon, Thomas K. "Tom"

Born: (Unknown)—Date of Death: 23 June 1874
Place: Comanche County
Event: Lynching/Hanged

Dixon, William A. "Bill"
Born: (Unknown)—Date of Death: 23 June 1874
Place: Comanche County
Event: Lynching/Hanged

Hardin, Joseph Gibson "Joe"
Born: (Unknown)—Date of Death: 23 June 1874
Place: Comanche County
Event: Lynching/Hanged

On 26 May 1874, Brown County Deputy Webb was shot and killed by the notorious outlaw John Wesley Hardin. At the time of the shooting Hardin was wanted for murder, robbery, and cattle rustling.

Webb encountered Hardin outside a local saloon. Hardin confronted him, and asked if Webb had papers for his arrest. Webb reportedly said that he did not. The psychopathic Hardin, in his classic style, became verbally aggressive. It is claimed that both Webb and Hardin went for their guns at the same time. In any case, a gunfight took place. Webb was able to shoot Hardin in the side before being shot in the left cheek. As Webb fell to the ground two of Hardin's accomplices, Jim Taylor and Bud Dixon, opened fire on Webb and finished the job. After the incident John Wesley Hardin and some of his associates made good their escape.

Joseph G. Hardin, Tom Dixon and Bill Dixon were arrested as accomplices and held in the Comanche Jail. On Tuesday, 23 June 1874, a body of armed men rode into the town under cover of darkness and, under force of arms, removed the three prisoners from the jail. The men were taken about two miles west of town and lynched from trees, each having their own respective impromptu gallows all to themselves. Afterwards the mob of vigilantes quietly dispersed.[546]

Webster, Jeremiah G. "Jerry"
Born: circa 1841[547]—Date of Death: 23 June 1874
Place: Guadalupe County
Event: Lynching/Hanged

West Texas Methodist Preacher Reverend Jeremiah G. Webster, a black man, was lynched at Guadalupe County on Tuesday, 23 June 1874. His attackers were the same crowd that had scourged Reverends Washburn and Marmot and driven the Gesner family out of Texas. Webster was stationed at San Antonio.[548]

Webster was born in Virginia. He was survived by his wife and one child who later followed in his father's footsteps and became a preacher.

Robles, Mateo
Born: (Unknown)—Date of Death: 25 June 1874
Place: Austin County
Event: Lynching/Disappeared

Unverified accounts from Carrigan's *Forgotten Dead* claim that Robles, a Mexican man, was taken from his home at San Felipe and never seen again. It is presumed that he was murdered.[549]

Levya, Gabriel
Born: (Unknown)—Date of Death: 30 June 1874
Place: Austin County
Event: Lynching

Unverified accounts of the day claim that Gabriel Levya, like Mateo Robles, was taken from his home at San Felipe then killed. His dead body was thrown into the Brazos River.[550]

Burges, Nathaniel
Born: (Unknown)—Date of Death: July 1874
Place: Limestone County
Event: Lynching

Burges, Given Name Unknown
Born: (Unknown)—Date of Death: July 1874
Place: Limestone County
Event: Lynching

Nathaniel Burges and his wife, both black, were murdered by a mob of five people. There was no provocation mentioned for this incident.[551]

Bairfield, Given Name Unknown
Born: (Unknown)—Date of Death: August 1874
Place: Camp County
Event: Lynching/Hanged

Sometime in later August or during the first few days of September 1874, a white man identified only as Mr. Bairfield was lynched at Pittsburgh. Bairfield had been accused of horse theft.

For want of a proper jail, Bairfield was kept under watch in a room at the Pittsburg Hotel.

From there he was taken by a band of masked men and spirited off in the darkness to a spot about two miles north of the town where vigilantes strung him up from a convenient tree. His body was discovered the following morning.[552]

Bly, Ely
Born: (Unknown)—Date of Death: 7 August 1874
Place: Jack County
Event: Legal Execution/Hanged

On Tuesday, 16 June 1874, Ely Bly, a stalwart black man, murdered Thomas Carmichael Jr. at Jacksboro. Carmichael was a trader from Parker County who frequently traveled the area. He had set out from Fort Griffin on Thursday, 11 June 1874, bound for Jacksboro. Bly, a discharged soldier, was seen with him. The men were observed at Emmett Hackett's, twenty-three miles from Fort Griffin and were once again spotted fourteen miles from the salt works.

Carmichael and Bly camped about three miles from Rock Creek. The following morning two passersby discovered the body of Carmichael lying in the water with his head beaten in. A heavy bludgeon covered with hair and blood was found nearby. One of the horses from Carmichael's team was missing as well as his gun. The day after the incident Bly sold Carmichael's gun at Jacksboro and boarded a stage for Fort Worth. He was apprehended, tried and found guilty of the murder based entirely on circumstantial evidence. Bly was sentenced to death.

On Friday, 7 August 1874, Bly met his fate. When the trap fell Carmichael's father, who was in attendance at the event, grasped his rifle tightly hoping for a botched hanging, which might require its use. None came, and Bly passed quietly. The grieving old man lingered for a time, and then finally asked the executioner for the black cap that Bly had worn on the gallows. He then returned to his wagon, cap in hand giving it to his wife to hold while he drove off.[553]

Davila, Andres
Born: (Unknown)—Date of Death: 7 August 1874
Place: Nueces County
Event: Legal Execution/Hanged

Tapia, Hypolita
Born: (Unknown)—Date of Death: 7 August 1874
Place: Nueces County
Event: Legal Execution/Hanged

Four men were brutally slain at a store in Peñascal, on Baffin Bay. Locals claimed that they had seen sheepherders looking for work who were staying in an old jacal in the area. A posse found the hut empty, but came across a lone rider who remembered seeing a group of armed men camped in a sheep pen a few miles away. They soon located the site and arrested two men, Hypolita Tapia and Andres Davila.

The prisoners were taken to Mean's village and placed in a vacant room under guard. Hypolita was interrogated first, then Davila. Both confessed. Tapia said he was a vaquero and sheepherder, and that a Corpus Christi policeman named Tomas Basquez had been in Buckley's store one morning and overheard men talking about a large consignment of goods and money going to Peñascal that evening. Basquez wanted to raise ten men (some report eleven) and go down there to steal the goods.[554] Tapia said he agreed to do it, and enlisted ten men to go with him, including Davila, a white man named Joe, Teodoro Aguillar, Pancho Luna, Antonio Martinez, Amador Lerma, a man called Octaviano and another called Chimito. When they arrived, they discovered that the boat that was carrying the merchandise was anchored some distance from shore. Seeing this, they incorrectly assumed that the boat had already offloaded the money and goods. It had not. The bungling prospective bandits found only $12 or $13 in the store's cash drawer.

Four men were killed during the incident. One of the foursome, Michael Morton, had been shot in the head four times (some report six times) and once in the chest while he was kneeling in prayer. Next the killers had tied up a customer named F. M. Coakley and executed him. They shot the storeowner, John Morton, in both arms and forced him to carry out the merchandise they were stealing from the store. Afterwards, they shot him six more times. His body was found behind the counter, one leg bent under him and a prayer book by his side. All the merchandise nearby was covered with blood.

The killers remained at the store all night, drinking whisky and donning the new clothes they had helped themselves to from the store's larder.

Tapia and Davila were tied up and delivered to Sheriff John McClane. During the trial, the pair changed their stories and said they were with the gang but had arrived at Peñascal after the shootings had taken place. Both men were found guilty and their hangings set for Friday, 7 August 1874.

The week the hangings were to take place Tapia asked that he be allowed to marry Trinidad Bayestero, who had lived with him for several years. His request was granted. On the day before the hanging both prisoners were allowed to shave and dress in white shirts and black trousers. Tapia's friends and relatives were allowed to attend the ceremony. The bride wore a calico dress and black shawl. Father Claude Jaillet, who returned the following morning to escort the two men to the scaffold, performed the nuptial ceremony.

Theirs was not a public hanging. A list of official observers were granted access to the event by permit from the sheriff. The gallows were constructed as an extension off the balcony on the side of the old county courthouse. While being led to the scaffold Tapia spoke to the modest aggregation of witnesses, saying, "My friends, I am here today to die by hanging. I have killed no person nor helped kill anyone. The people forced the party that was guilty to swear against me but it is all right. Goodbye." Davila stood with his eyes downcast and said nothing. Screams were heard outside as the prisoners dropped the seven feet through the trapdoor to their deaths.[555] There is no record of what happened to the policeman, Tomas Basquez.

Jenkins, Edward
Born: (Unknown)—Date of Death: 17 August 1874
Place: Bexar County
Event: Legal Execution/Hanged

Sources report that a black man named Edward Jenkins was hanged at Bexar County for murder. Evidence of this execution has proven difficult to produce. The Jenkins hanging is being included in the interest of completeness.[556]

Romirez, Francisco
Born: (Unknown)—Date of Death: 27 August 1874
Place: Cameron County
Event: Lynching/Hanged

Unverified reports indicate the Francisco Romirez, one of Juan Cortina's bandits, was lynched near Brownsville on 27 August 1874.[557]

Gallagher, Dan
Born: (Unknown)—Date of Death: 8 November 1874
Place: Robertson County
Event: Lynching/Hanged

On Sunday, 8 November 1874, the notorious outlaw Dan Gallagher was involved in an altercation with a man named Lehey at Hearne. Gallagher thrust a large knife into Lehey's chest, entering near his heart. While withdrawing the instrument Gallagher said, "now we are even."

    Gallagher was arrested, but while being transported to the jail by ten officers a gang of about forty masked men overpowered the lawmen, took control of Gallagher and lynched him from a convenient tree just at the outskirts of the town.[558] At that point Gallagher and Lehey were truly "even."

Seven Unidentified Mexican Men
Born: (Unknown)—Date of Death: 8 November 1874
Place: Duval County
Event: Lynching

Newspaper accounts of the day published a report by Captain Charles Hood of the 24th Infantry stationed at Fort McIntosh. In Hood's statement he claimed that seven Mexican shepherds had been lynched at San Diego. An additional twenty-two persons in the vicinity had also been killed. All of this murderous work was said to have been accomplished by a band of Comanche Indians operating in the area. As the savages proceeded on their homicidal hunt they threw two men down a well at Boryas Rancho, one of whom broke his neck and died. On the Salado River they killed a shepherd and wounded another.[559]

The account of this particular Indian raid is extensive, with much detail given concerning the number of horses, saddles, tack and cattle taken. Deaths associated with Indian raids are not, for the most part, considered to be a part of this account of lynchings and hanging in Texas. However, to the extent that these seven individuals were specifically listed as having been lynched they are included for purposes of completeness.

Smith, Bob
Born: (Unknown)—Date of Death: December 1874
Place: Anderson County
Event: Lynching/Hanged

Sheriff Ed Davis of Anderson County had deputized James Godley, a man who was a physician by profession. The sheriff ordered Godley and J. F. Henderson to arrest a fellow named Bob Smith. Smith was wanted on a charge of bigamy. When the two deputies tried to take Smith under their control, he shot Godley with a shotgun, mortally wounding him. Godley died the following day. Bob Smith managed to escape in a hail of gunfire.

Smith was arrested several weeks later. According to some reports, Smith was lynched in his jail cell at Fosterville during December 1874. The veracity of that claim has not been verified. [560]

One Unidentified Mexican Man
Born: (Unknown)—Date of Death: 1 December 1874
Place: Cameron County
Event: Lynching/Hanged

A large party of Mexican cattle thieves made their camp near the ranch of Carlos Danache, about fourteen miles from Brownsville. The following morning, after the men had left the site, the body of one unidentified Mexican man was noted as having been found, lynched and badly mutilated. It was hypothesized that the unfortunate fellow had been an honest man who had accidentally fallen in among the band of thieves.[561]

Johnson, Reuben
Born: (Unknown)—Date of Death: 20 December 1874
Place: Dallas County
Event: Lynching/Hanged

At about 10:00 pm on Sunday night, 20 December 1874, Mr. Dill left his home, telling his wife that he was checking on a corn wagon. He met up with Mr. Bell and Mr. Rice, and together the men traveled to the home of Clemency Reed where they asked if a black man named Reuben Johnson, who was living at Dill's place, was there. When Johnson appeared three white men grabbed him, dragged him a mile or so to the bottoms where Rice tied a rope around his neck. One of the threesome climbed a tree and looped the rope over a limb, whereupon the men hoisted Johnson up and lynched him. Wishing to make certain that they had done the job thoroughly, Dill slashed Johnson's throat with a knife, thereby insuring that they had freed the man's spirit from its mortal host.

The lynching had apparently been the result of Johnson, who was a black man, having had carnal intercourse with Rice's sister, a white woman. [562]

Twenty-Five Unidentified Blacks
Born: (Unknown)—Date of Death: circa 1875
Place: Harris County
Event: Lynching

Unverified stories claim that as many as twenty-five black persons were murdered at a church in Houston sometime during 1875.[563]

Three Unidentified Mexican Men
Born: (Unknown)—Date of Death: circa 1875
Place: Cameron County
Event: Lynching/Hanged

Three men, one white and two Mexicans, allegedly lynched three Mexican men at the King Ranch. No verification of this incident has been located, however, the details of the killing were published in the *New York Herald*. That, in itself, by no means guarantees the veracity of the claim.[564]

Sneed, William John
Born: (Unknown)—Date of Death: circa 1875
Place: Lampasas County
Event: Lynching/Hanged

William John Sneed, a white man, was allegedly lynched for stealing a horse. The exact location and date have not been located. What is known is that Sneed's brothers later killed John W. Pennell. That incident took place at Burnet County in 1875. The Sneed family believes that Pennell had been one of the men involved in the lynching of William John Sneed.

According to family lore, Sneed was hanged in front of his own home while his children looked on.[565]

Garza, Pedro
Born: (Unknown)—Date of Death: 5 January 1875
Place: Cameron County
Event: Lynching/Hanged

Guerra, Antonio
Born: (Unknown)—Date of Death: 5 January 1875
Place: Cameron County
Event: Lynching/Hanged

On Tuesday morning, 5 January 1875, the bodies of Pedro Garza and Antonio Guerra, both Mexican men, were found hanging from an elm tree about five miles from Brownsville in the direction of Port Isabella. Both men were still dressed and their pockets had not been emptied. From one man the sum of $ .37 ½ cents was recovered.[566] The other man had only a flint and a steel in the pocket of his trouser pants. Their saddles and tack were under their respective trees with them. The pair of unfortunate men had been suspected of cattle theft in the area. "Judge Lynch" had caught up with them before the law had a chance to do so.[567]

White, Billy
Born: (Unknown)—Date of Death: 22 January 1875
Place: Navarro County
Event: Legal Execution/Hanged

Billy White, a black man, was charged wit the murder of Thomas Thomason. He was convicted and sentenced to death.

On Thursday, 22 January 1875, White was executed by hanging at Corsicana. He confessed to the murder of Thomason on the gallows. It was estimated that 6,000 people watched the hanging.[568]

Baccus, Elijah
Born: circa 1849—Date of Death: 18 February 1875
Place: Mason County
Event: Lynching/Hanged

Baccus, L. Peter "Pete"
Born: circa 1856—Date of Death: 18 February 1875
Place: Mason County
Event: Lynching/Hanged

Wiggins, Abe
Born: (Unknown)—Date of Death: 18 February 1875
Place: Mason County
Event: Lynching/Shot

On Friday, 12 February 1875, Sheriff John Clark arrested nine men and a boy who were driving a herd of cattle north along Brady Creek in McCulloch County. Clark had no legal authority there. He abandoned the herd but hustled the men back to Mason.

Among those arrested were Elijah and Peter Baccus, Abe Wiggins, Tom Turley and Charley Johnson. All were charged with illegally driving a herd of cattle beyond the county line without having had them inspected. This was not the first time Clark had overstepped his authority and managed to blunder an arrest. All of the cattlemen made bond and were released. Four immediately left town. The rest remained, but were promptly arrested for a second time.

On Thursday, 18 February 1875, a mob stormed Mason's jail and seized the prisoners. Both of the Baccus cousins, and Turley, were hung. When a posse interrupted the vigilante work, the mob members began shooting the remaining prisoners. Abe Wiggins was hit in the head and died the following day. Johnson escaped. Turley, who had been strung up, was cut down in time to save his life.

The following day another man, a teenager named Allen Bolt, was found murdered by the mob just west of Mason. Sheriff Clark and powerful German ranchers controlled the mob's actions. The law failed, for obvious reasons, to seriously investigate the murders of these nonresident cattleman.

Infused with success, three months later the vigilantes proceeded to kill a man named Tim Williamson. Williamson turned out to be innocent of the crime for which he was charged. While the law did not investigate the killings, a former Texas Ranger named William Scott Cooley did. Williamson had been Cooley's foster father.

On 13 May 1875, Tim Williamson had been falsely arrested in Mason County for cattle rustling by Deputy Sheriff John Wohrle. While Wohrle was escorting Williamson to jail, a mob of angry German cattle ranchers jerked Williamson aside and shot him to death. That event marked the beginning of what would be called the Mason County War, also known as the "Hoodoo War". Cooley swore revenge. He patiently waited for indictments to be passed down from the court against those responsible. When none came, he took matters into his own hands. Cooley went to Wohrle's home and found him working on his well with a helper. He shot and killed Wohrle on sight. Next, he scalped him then tossed his body down the well.

Soon after the Wohrle incident Cooley killed German cattleman Carl Bader. By that time gunman John Peters Ringo and several other supporters had joined with Cooley in the fight. Following the Bader slaying two of Ringo's friends, Moses Baird and George Gladden, were ambushed by a posse led by Sheriff John Clark. During the ambush Baird was killed and Gladden seriously wounded. That posse included Peter Bader, brother to Cooley's second victim, Carl Bader.

Cooley hid out at the Nimitz Hotel at Fredericksburg. After eating supper one afternoon he felt sick and returned to his room. He died a short time afterward, presumably of what was then referred to as "brain fever".[569]

Cooley is buried at Miller Creek Cemetery near Blanco, in Blanco County. Elijah Baccus was survived by his wife Josie Bigelow.[570]

Two Unidentified White Men
Born (Unknown)—Date of Death 26 March 1875
Place: Jim Wells County
Event: Lynching/Hanging

Two Unidentified Mexican Men
Born (Unknown)—Date of Death 26 March 1875
Place: Jim Wells County
Event: Lynching/Hanging

Newspaper reports of the day claimed that on or about Friday, 26 March 1875, a man and his wife who were traveling with teamsters from Laredo found two white men dead at San Fernando Creek, about thirty-five miles from Corpus Christi. The dead persons had been stabbed several times. Their horses and arms were still at the site of the incident. The group proceeded on their way. About twenty miles from the city they discovered the bodies of two Mexican men hanged from a tree. All in all that was a rather gruesome journey for the couple. [571]

Godines, Felix
Born: (Unknown)—Date of Death: 27 March 1875
Place: Nueces County
Event: Lynching/Hanged

The postmaster of Nueces, who was also a storekeeper there, reported that at about 4:00 pm on Friday, 26 March 1875, he was conversing with a man named Smith when a band of Mexican robbers approached his store. The shopkeeper dashed to the sitting room to retrieve his Winchester. When he returned he saw Smith being chased by one of the robbers. He prepared to fire, but thought better of it when he saw that the outlaws numbered upwards of fifty strong. At that point he and his wife, along with Smith, took shelter in a secret subterranean room he had constructed for such eventualities.

The thieves sacked the store, loading everything of value on a wagon. After torching the building, they left. Before doing so, however, they mistreated several whites who were present, stripping them and making them walk barefoot in the cactus. One man who fainted from exhaustion was beaten and left on the roadside.

One of the gang's leaders, Felix Godines, was apprehended sometime later. On Saturday, 27 March 1975, a brief hearing was held during which he was identified as one of the men involved in the incident. Godines was found guilty and sentenced to hang. That verdict was carried out immediately.[572]

One Unidentified Man

Born (Unknown)—Date of Death: circa April 1875
Place: Nueces County
Event: Lynching

In Carrigan's book, *Forgotten Dead* the author claims that in April of 1875, an unidentified man was accused of horse theft at Nuecestown. A vigilante committee killed him and fed his body to hogs. Although the author's claim of the victim being fed to hogs makes for a gripping tale, no confirmation of that detail has been found.[573]

Two Unidentified Mexican Men

Born (Unknown)—Date of Death: 1 April 1875
Place: Calhoun County
Event: Lynching

In Carrigan's book, *Forgotten Dead* the author claims that on or about Thursday, 1 April 1875, two unidentified Mexican men were hanged for unknown reasons at Chocolate. No other confirmation of this incident has been found.[574]

Two Unidentified Mexican Men

Born (Unknown)—Date of Death: 27 April 1875
Place: Nueces County
Event: Lynching

In Carrigan's book, *Forgotten Dead* the author claims that on Tuesday, 27 April 1875, two unidentified Mexican men were hanged for murder near Corpus Christi. [575]

Cooper, James

Born: (Unknown)—Date of Death: 30 April 1875
Place: Washington County
Event: Legal Execution/Hanged

Williams, Griffin

Born: (Unknown)—Date of Death: 30 April 1875

Place: Washington County

Event: Legal Execution/Hanged

Sources claim that two black men, James Cooper and Griffin Williams, were legally executed by hanging on Friday, 30 April 1875. Cooper's crime was murder, and Williams' crime was outrage. Thus far, independent confirmation of this incident has not been found.[576]

Land, David

Born: (Unknown)—Date of Death: 1 May 1875

Place: Houston County

Event: Lynching/Shot

On the evening of 27 April 1875, a white man named David Land stole a horse from M.C. Depuy at Colonel Tharps' place, located about eighteen miles from Crockett. Mr. Depuy and Houston Precinct 3 Constable T. C. Craig pursued Land, eventually overtaking him after a chase of about seven miles.

It was already dark by the time the men reached Land. He concealed himself in the bushes and fired several shots at Craig and Depuy. One bullet struck Craig, killing him instantly. Another hit Depuy, seriously wounding him. One horse fell victim during the exchange of gunfire. Land emerged unscathed from the encounter and escaped.

On 1 May 1875, Land was captured. He was asleep at a friend's house when the apprehension occurred. Land was bound to a horse by his feet and neck and taken ten miles away. His captors said they offered Land the ominous choice of "jail or death?" To a man, they claim that Land chose death. Thus, the impromptu posse obliged and shot him. His body was found riddled with buckshot and left in the woods where Land's portentous choice had been made.

A related and unfortunate incident occurred on 1 May 1875, at Phelps Station. Several citizens arrested a man who matched the general description of Land. When a deputy sheriff and constable arrived to investigate they discovered that the man, whose name was Tobe Morris, had been at Land's house the morning after the murder and saw Constable Craig's friends loading his body in a buggy. The lawmen decided to arrest Morris, but a horde of now intoxicated citizens demanded the $500 reward. A scuffle took place during which a man named Arthur Davis shot and killed another citizen named J. H. Patrick.[577]

One Unidentified Black Man

Born: (Unknown)—Date of Death: 22 May 1875

Place: Limestone County

Event: Lynching/Shot

An unidentified black man was removed from the jail where he had been confined and was executed by shooting. A mob of unknown size did the work. The man's crime was not mentioned.[578]

Smith, Frank

Born: (Unknown)—Date of Death: June 1875

Place: Montague County

Event: Legal Execution/Hanged

Frank Smith, a black man, was hanged at Montague County in June 1875. Newspaper article of the day fail to identify his crime, or anything about the trial. Rather, the majority of the prose written by period journalists centers on the events of the hanging itself.

Smith mounted the gallows before a large crowd of onlookers, addressed the masses with great patience and in a deliberate manner as he bade them his last farewell. Some in the audience began to rush the gallows, intent on setting him free. The sheriff and his deputies, with cocked pistols at the ready, held off the crowd. Their efforts would have failed had it not been for Smith himself who called for order, yelling out to his supporters saying, "Let the law take its course," this amidst their shouts of "shoot the rope." Smith said, "I am a man and can die like a man. This is no time for a row; let us not disgrace ourselves in this manner."

Smith wore a smile as he faced his executioner, standing straight and proud as he met his end.[579]

One Unidentified Man

Born: (Unknown)—Date of Death: June 1875

Place: Leon County

Event: Lynching/Hanged

A most interesting lynching occurred at the town of Marques Station in June 1875. A man was observed hanging from a tree branch, apparently lynched, but no one seemed to know anything about it. Nearby there was horse tied to a tree. When discovered the man was exceedingly dead, and probably had been swinging from that limb for several hours.

The unidentified man was eventually taken down from his perch. When his pockets were examined for identification a letter was discovered from a Mr. L. W. Hardin compelling the fellow to meet him at a certain place and time and to make sure and show up, even if it required him to have to steal a horse. It was generally the opinion of all in observance that the man had probably complied with the "even if you have to steal one" aspect of Mr. Hardin's letter, thus winding up in the condition in which he was found. Apparently the horse's owner did not hold the animal in much regard as he left it behind, lashed to a tree.[580] With no clue as to the poor man's identity, he was buried without a headstone.

Pitts, Jerry
Born: (Unknown)—Date of Death: 6 June 1875
Place: Unknown County
Event: Lynching/Shot

On Sunday, 4 June 1875, a party of men consisting of Justice of the Peace W. A. Price, Robert Treadway, Constable Kelly, a clergymen's son, a Scott, and a black man named Rom Stevens forced their way into the home of an elderly black man named Jerry Pitts. The vigilantes were all in "black face" to disguise their identity. After an attempt at ransacking the Pitts home Mr. Pitts took up a shotgun and tried to halt the gang of ruffians. He was shot to death for his trouble. It remains unclear what Pitts was suspect of that would have warranted such treatment.[581]

Flores, Juan
Born: (Unknown)—Date of Death: 26 June 1875
Place: Refugio County
Event: Legal Execution/Hanged

Reports of the day claim that Juan Flores, a Mexican man who had been convicted of murder, was hanged at Refugio County on Saturday, 26 June 1875. Thus far, no independent confirmation of this event has been located.[582]

Surname Unknown, Alf
Born: (Unknown)—Date of Death: 26 July 1875
Place: Bosque County
Event: Lynching/Hanged

Ledwell, John
Born: (Unknown)—Date of Death: 26 July 1875
Place: Bosque County
Event: Lynching/Hanged

Wood, Marcus
Born: (Unknown)—Date of Death: 26 July 1875
Place: Bosque County
Event: Lynching/Hanged

Samantha and Amos Smith lived near Iredell. While Amos, a gambler, was away from home Samantha apparently became intimate with one or both of Amos' gambling buddies, Marcus Wood and John Ledwell. The culprit apparently hired a black man named Alf to kill Amos. After the deed was done,

Alf was apprehended. He told authorities of Wood and Ledwell's plan, and that he had killed Amos Smith precisely as he had been contracted, and paid to do.

On Monday, 26 July 1875, a vigilante mob numbering roughly thirty strong removed Alf, Ledwell and Wood from the Bosque County jail and lynched all three. According to newspaper reports, the well deserving men were "hanged at the same time and to the same limb."[583]

All three are buried at Riverside Cemetery in Iredell. As an interesting aside, Marcus and John are buried in the conventional way, east to west. The black man, Alf, is buried north to south. Headstones were placed as markers for the three graves almost 100 years after the hangings. Sometime about 2010 the headstones were stolen.[584]

Mitchell, Nelson A. "Cooney"
Born: 16 November 1796—Date of Death: 8 October 1875
Place: Hood County
Event: Legal Execution/Hanged

Nelson "Cooney" Mitchell was born in Granville County, North Carolina in 1796. After his first wife died, he remarried and had several children. Mitchell moved his family to Texas in the 1860s, later moving to Hood County in the 1870s where they purchased land along the Brazos River at a place later to become known as Mitchell Bend, located about seven miles south of Granbury.

While living in Mitchell Bend they met a neighboring family named Truitt. Mitchell came to the aid of his new neighbor by carrying the note on their property. Eventually a dispute developed, which turned into a full-fledged feud. The matter went to court.

The lawsuit created ill feelings between the families, which came to a head on Saturday, 28 March 1874, when Bill Mitchell and Mit Graves met up with three of the Truitt boys (James, Sam, and Isaac) who were in en route to their home. Although the details are unclear, it seems that the Mitchell boys gunned down Sam and Isaac and wounded James Truitt. Reportedly, Nelson "Cooney" Mitchell and a man named William J. Owens had lagged behind the group and were not present at the shooting.

The following morning "Cooney" Mitchell, William Owens, and others were arrested. Although "Cooney" appears to have been innocent of the crime he was facing an inflamed jury and an outraged community. He was found guilty and sentenced to hang.

William Owens was sentenced to life in prison. "Cooney's son Jeff, age twenty-one, was killed while attempting to smuggle "Cooney" a gun to be used for an escape attempt and some poison to be used on himself if the attempt failed. At the time young Jeff was armed with a double barrel shotgun and had a brace of Colt pistols in his belt. Young Jeff also had a vial of laudanum in his coat, intended for his father. When an armed guard at the jail saw a man crawling towards the building he shot him, blowing the top of Jeff's head completely off.

On Friday, 8 October 1875, "Cooney" was taken to the hanging tree, located on Reunion Street in the northeast portion of the city. He was given a moment to speak. Mitchell reiterated his innocence, charging his son Bill with the task of avenging his death against the "liars" that had placed him in this predicament.

Years later, Bill Mitchell calmly walked into the East Texas house of James Truitt, and in front of the preacher's family, shot the former Mitchell family friend through the head.

"Cooney" Mitchell was eighty years old at the time of his hanging, and the only man ever legally hanged in Hood County. Both "Cooney" and his son Jeff were buried in Mitchell Cemetery at the bend. William Owens was pardoned after serving five years.

Bill Mitchell fled to New Mexico where he lived under the alias of Bill Russell, more commonly known as Baldy Russell. After seventeen years he returned to Texas, found James Truitt, and gunned him down in cold blood in front of his family. Afterwards Mitchell again removed to New Mexico where he remained for several more years. He was eventually apprehended and sent to prison in Texas. After a brief stay he escaped and fled back to New Mexico where he remained until his death.

Mitchell is buried at the Mitchell Bend Cemetery in Hood County. There remains some discrepancy as to his date of hanging. Some records reflect 8 October while other record 9 October. His tombstone is inscribed 1 October.

Holt, Given Name Unknown
Born: (Unknown)—Date of Death: November 1875
Place: Unknown County
Event: Legal Execution/Hanged

A man who was condemned to die by execution, identified only as Holt, attempted to hang himself in his cell and cheat the executioner. Jailers discovered him in time and revived him, only to escort the poor fellow to the gallows where, according to newspaper reports of the day, it turned out that he had been wise to attempt to administer his own punishment. The sheriff botched the job completely. After the rope broke twice the executioners finally accomplished the task on the third go-around. The fellow was hanged four times in one day before finally succumbing.[586]

Campbell, Given Name Unknown
Born: (Unknown)—Date of Death: circa 1876
Place: Unknown County
Event: Lynching/Hanged

Campbell, Stuart
Born: (Unknown)—Date of Death: circa 1876
Place: Unknown County
Event: Lynching/Hanged

McElroy, Given Name Unknown
Born: (Unknown)—Date of Death: circa 1876
Place: Unknown County
Event: Lynching/Hanged

Newspaper accounts of the day covering the lynching of two Campbell brothers and a man named McElroy focus almost entirely on the fact that the men were strung up by vigilantes, failing to identify their given names, location, or the nature of their transgression. Unfortunately the journalist who wrote the article telling of this incident failed to give his readers any more than a teaspoon full of facts.[587]

Love, Bat
Born: (Unknown)—Date of Death: 10 January 1876
Place: Bastrop County
Event: Lynching/Hanged

Waddle, Given Name Unknown
Born: (Unknown)—Date of Death: 10 January 1876
Place: Bastrop County
Event: Lynching/Hanged

On the morning of 10 January 1876, Bat Love and a man identified only as Waddle, both white men, were found lynched and dangling from a tree at Elgin. According to newspaper reports, the pair seemed to have difficulty discerning between "mine and thine." In other words, they were thieves. Reading further it appears that the pair had first been locked up in the jail, then were removed by force and lynched.[588]

Williams, Tom
Born: (Unknown)—Date of Death: 20 January 1876
Place: Milam County
Event: Lynching/Shot and Burned to Death

Tom Williams, a black man identified by some newspaper accounts as Anthony Smith, had been charged with the murder of a young white farmer named J. M. Baker. The incident occurred at Cameron, in Milam County. Williams shot and killed Baker while the two were riding in a wagon, returning from the sale of a bale of cotton and three or four hides. Williams robbed Baker of the approximately $35 in specie that he had on his person.

The trial drew a great crowd. After being found guilty Williams was led to the blacksmith shop to be fitted with irons for his confinement while he awaited execution. The angry mob, some murmuring that hanging was too good for him, swarmed around Williams as he was escorted to the new jail, a double thick brick building with secure iron bars.

At about 12:05 am on Thursday, 20 January 1876, a small group of young men, some quite young, approached the jail and knocked on the door asking to be admitted. The jailer, who was startled awake, declined to grant entrance. The mob backing up the smaller contingent then threatened to tear down the jail. Ultimately the vigilantes were granted access and given the key to Williams' cell. He was removed by the mob of about seventy-five mounted men and boys who headed out along the Bell County road about two miles to the site of the crime. There they bent mesquite saplings together and attached Williams' chains to them then built a fire beneath the doomed man. When the fire had consumed Williams, burning off his legs, scalp, face and hands, the crowd fired a volley of bullets into him for good measure. The sound of those gunshots was heard in the town at about 6:00 am. No one came to investigate.[589]

Gonzales, Emilio
Born: (Unknown)—Date of Death: 28 January 1876
Place: Duval County
Event: Lynching/Hanged

Lerma, Ponciano
Born: (Unknown)—Date of Death: 28 January 1876
Place: Duval County
Event: Lynching/Hanged

Perez, Anastacio
Born: (Unknown)—Date of Death: 28 January 1876
Place: Duval County
Event: Lynching/Hanged

According to unverified reports, three Mexican men who were murder suspects were taken from the jail at San Diego and lynched on Friday, 28 January 1876. The victims were Emilio Gonzales, Ponciano Lerma and Anastacio Perez.[590]

McCaslin, A.
Born: (Unknown)—Date of Death: 30 January 1876
Place: Gonzales County
Event: Lynching/Shot

A. McCaslin, who had recently killed Columbus Carroll and seriously wounded "Old Man" Carroll at Gonzales County, was found dead on Peach Creek with two bullet holes to the head. His horse was found grazing nearby. It is presumed that he fell victim to foul play as it is difficult to commit suicide by firing two shots into ones own head.[591]

Burleson, Steve

Born: (Unknown)—Date of Death: February 1876
Place: Live Oak County
Event: Lynching/Hanged

Two Unidentified Men

Born: (Unknown)—Date of Death: February 1876
Place: Live Oak County
Event: Lynching/Hanged

Newspaper reports of the day claim that the bodies of Steve Burleson, along with two unidentified men, were discovered hanged to a tree near Oakville.[592]

Lee, Sam

Born: (Unknown)—Date of Death: February 1876
Place: Jasper County
Event: Legal Execution/Hanged

Neil, Thomas Jefferson

Born: (Unknown)—Date of Death: February 1876
Place: Jasper County
Event: Legal Execution/Hanged

Sam Lee and Thomas Jefferson Neil, both freedmen, went to the gallows at Jasper together for the murder of another freedman. Both were reported to have met their fate calmly, expressing a hope for blessing and faith in the hereafter.[593]

Eight Unidentified Mexican Men

Born: (Unknown)—Date of Death: 2 February 1876
Place: Hidalgo County
Event: Lynching/Hanged

According to unverified reports, eight unidentified Mexican men were lynched at Edinburg on Tuesday, 2 February 1876. They men were all suspected of murder.[594]

Three Unidentified Mexican Men
Born: (Unknown)—Date of Death: 5 February 1876
Place: Lavaca County
Event: Lynching/Hanged

According to unverified reports, three unidentified Mexican men were lynched at Hallettsville on Friday, 5 February 1876. They men were all suspected of murder. This incident was reported by the same source as the case listed above, on 2 February 1876. It is thought that perhaps they are one in the same.[595]

Irwin, (Given Name Unknown)
Born: (Unknown)—Date of Death: 29 February 1876
Place: Lee County
Event: Lynching

Irwin, (Given Name Unknown)
Born: (Unknown)—Date of Death: 29 February 1876
Place: Lee County
Event: Lynching

Shaw, Pat
Born: (Unknown)—Date of Death: 29 February 1876
Place: Lee County
Event: Lynching

On Tuesday morning, 29 February 1876, a band of unidentified vigilantes broke into the jail at Giddings and removed Pat Shaw and two Irwin boys, all white men, and murdered the entire bunch. The prisoners had been accused of horse theft. The band of vigilantes shot one of the men full of holes in the street and lynched the other two.[596]

Two Unidentified Black Men
Born (Unknown)—Date of Death: 29 July 1876
Place: Colorado County
Event: Lynching/Shot

Two Unidentified Black Men
Born (Unknown)—Date of Death: 7 August 1876
Place: Colorado County
Event: Lynching/Shot

Baughman, Isaac N.
Born: circa 1841—Date of Death: 28 August 1876
Place: Colorado County
Event: Lynching/Shot

On Saturday, 29 July 1876, two unidentified black men stopped at a store belonging to two brothers named Frazer. The business was located a short distance from Eagle Lake. The men made some purchases and started home. That night their horses returned home without them. About three days later the bodies of the two men were discovered on the prairie about six miles from the store. The newspaper empathically stated, "[t]here is no doubt but that they were killed by stockmen - killed because they were notorious cattle thieves." The newspaper went out to claim that they were a part of a gang of whites and blacks that slaughtered cattle for their hides.

A great many blacks were incensed at the murders, and threatened to kill the Frazer's and destroy their store. Allegedly a former sheriff of Wharton County, Isaac N. Baughman, provided ammunition to the black citizens and encouraged them to burn down Eagle Lake. Whites turned out under arms to protect the city. Persons unknown murdered two unidentified black men on Monday, 7 August 1876. Groups of armed whites and blacks continued to menace each other for several more days. One newspaper reported that a reliable source claimed thirteen blacks were murdered, and in a later edition reported a total nine black men had been killed.

Baughman had served in the union army prior to being appointed sheriff of Wharton County during Reconstruction on 3 April 1869. He was well liked by the black population and elected sheriff on 3 December 1869. He served until 3 December 1873. After leaving office he ran a small store near the Wharton-Colorado county line. On Monday, 28 August 1876, a group of white men removed him from his sick bed, tied him to a tree and shot him eighteen times. It seems that the local white population was less fond of Bauhman than the blacks' were.[597]

Dickson, Given Name Unknown
Born: (Unknown)—Date of Death: August 1876
Place: Brazos River
Event: Lynching/Hanged

Mr. Dickson, thought to have been a white man, was tortured and lynched for inappropriate behavior with a white woman.[598]

Dickson was courting a young woman who, at the same time, was being paid attention to by another young man. Dickson became jealous and apparently unleashed a barrage of uncomplimentary epithets in the woman's direction. After telling her father of the incident the woman's dad assembled a posse, gave chase and overtook the young fellow in Comanche County. In the process of returning him to Bosque County they thrashed and lynched Dickson at a spot somewhere along the banks of the Brazos River in either Comanche or Bosque County. His decomposed and mutilated body was discovered a few days later. The father and his colleagues were arrested.[599]

Jones, Wesley
Born: (Unknown)—Date of Death: 11 August 1876
Place: Dallas County
Event: Legal Execution/Hanged

On Friday morning, 11 August 1876, Wesley Jones, a black man, went to the gallows at Dallas for having outraged a white woman.

A crowd of over 10,000 persons gathered to witness the event, among them Jones's wife and child. On the platform he made a farewell speech, claiming that he had complete confidence in a full pardon by his creator. When the rope was cut and the trap sprung there was a brief cheer that rose from some members of the crowd, but the inappropriate outburst soon subsided. The Lamar Rifles were present, just in case a disorder developed.[600]

Sims, William Henry
Born: 8 October 1828—Date of Death: 31 August 1876
Place: Burnet County
Event: Legal Execution/Hanged

According to unverified reports William H. Sims was a Texas Ranger Captain, and the commanding officer of Rangers Company "O" at Burnet County in 1873.

According to an oral history provided by a long time area resident, on the night of 31 August 1876, Sims's wife awoke to find a man standing about fifteen feet from her bed. She aroused her husband, who grabbed for a gun. Six or more intruders materialized, and dragged Mr. Sims out of the shelter. The men were masked and had their faces painted. The younger children, thinking the men to be Indians, hid in the thick woods until the next morning. Sims and his wife begged for mercy. Their teenage daughter joined in, pleading with captors but to no avail.

Somehow news of this incident reached neighbors. When help finally arrived they found Sims' body about three-quarters of a mile from his camp at Morgan Creek hanging from a tree.

The Texas State Archives do not have any data to support the claim that Sims was a Ranger Captain. It is possible that he was part of a Minute Man company, for which records are frequently scarce.[601]

Sims was survived by his wife Emily L. Harris and eleven children. An infant son had preceded Sims in death one year earlier.[602]

Brazzell, Sr., George
Born (Unknown)—Date of Death: 19 September 1876
Place: DeWitt County
Event: Lynching/Shot

Brazzell, Jr., George

Born (Unknown)—Date of Death: 19 September 1876
Place: DeWitt County
Event: Lynching/Shot

During the night of Tuesday, 19 September 1876, Dr. George Brazzell and his son George were in their home at Shilo Mill near Yorktown when a group of armed men seized them. The pair were taken a few hundred yards away and shot to death. Newspapers of the day opined that Dr. Brazzell was a good and peaceful citizen, but his son did not bear a good name in the community. Strangely, the newspaper stated, "his death is not regretted, but the killing of the old man is looked upon as a cold-blooded murder."[603]

McCann, James

Born: (Unknown)—Date of Death: 31 September 1876
Place: McLennan County
Event: Lynching/Hanged

An oft inaccurate source claimed that James McCann, a black man, was apprehended for threatening to murder someone. He was tortured and lynched by a group of vigilantes.[604]

Allen, Dick

Born: (Unknown)—Date of Death: 21 October 1876
Place: Caldwell County
Event: Lynching/Hanged

On Friday, 7 July 1876, Deputy Sheriff Blackstone B. Sullivan was shot and killed at a local store while attempting to arrest a white man named Dick Allen. As Sullivan struggled to handcuff Allen he pulled a revolver from his boot and shot Sullivan. Allen was later arrested by the Hays County sheriff and convicted of Sullivan's murder. He was sentenced to hang.

     When citizens learned that his conviction might be overturned on appeal they stormed the county jail at Lockhart on Saturday, 21 October 1876, and lynched him.[605]

Catchings, Eugene

Born: circa 1856—Date of Death: 3 November 1876
Place: Kaufman County
Event: Legal Execution/Hanged

Payne, Bill
Born: circa 1851—Date of Death: 3 November 1876
Place: Kaufman County
Event: Legal Execution/Hanged

Eugene Catchings and Bill Payne, both black men, were hanged at Kaufman on Friday, 3 November 1876. Both men had been convicted of murder. Both met their death within eleven minutes of one another. One admitted that he would not receive forgiveness for his deeds. The other gave his body over to a doctor for the sake of science.[606]

Wood, Convich
Born: (Unknown)—Date of Death: 10 November 1876
Place: Falls County
Event: Legal Execution/Hanged

Unconfirmed records of legal executions in Texas indicate that a man named Convich Wood was hanged for murder on Friday, 10 November 1876. Documentation to support this claim has proven difficult to uncover.[607]

Black, John
Born: (Unknown)—Date of Death: 23 December 1876
Place: Bastrop County
Event: Lynching/Hanged

The incident took place on 23 December 1876. A son of Henry Owens had disappeared. A voodooist named Sam Squirrelhunter was called in to perform incantations on the lost lad's behalf. The whole party, consisting of Smith Jackson and Pryor Jones along with Thomas Robinson, Sol Ridge, Henry Owens, William Peterson, Steve Robinson, Burrell Jackson and George Veal went to the home of John Black and placed a rope around his neck, attached it to the pommel of a horses saddle and drug him about a mile, ending up in a nearby woods. Black was practically dead from the dragging. The rope was disconnected from the saddle horn and thrown over a tree limb. Black was hauled up and interrogated. He firmly denied having any knowledge of the boy's disappearance. Squirrelhunter, however, insisted that he did because he himself had see it, "...written in the coffee grounds." Black was repeatedly hauled up the tree until almost dead, then dropped to the ground and revived. He maintained his innocence. On the final hoisting they left him up too long and he succumbed.

Sometime afterwards, the missing boy returned home, saying that he had been taken by a stockman, and that Black had nothing to do with the abduction. The boy went home. Squirrelhunter was arrested.[608]

Singleton, John Edward
Born: (Unknown)—Date of Death: 27 April 1877
Place: Bee County
Event: Legal Execution/Hanged

John Singleton went to the gallows at Beeville on Friday, 27 April 1877, tried and convicted of the murder of John Dwyer. Newspaper accounts claimed that the killing had been, "...without parallel for diabolic atrocity..." Singleton's mother used every means available to plead for her son's pardon, including circulating a petition as well as imploring the governor for a pardon or stay. In the end her efforts were in vain.

For his last supper Singleton, ordered one baked chicken, one dish of ham and eggs, one apple pie, one peach pie, one egg custard, one fruit pudding, one large pound cake and two bottles of wine. Singleton was obviously quite fond of his groceries, especially deserts.

On the gallows Singleton confessed to the crime, saying that he had done the thing over a trivial matter and deserved the sentence he had received. He emphasized that he had not planned the killing. It was a spontaneous act, conceived seconds before he took the action.[609]

Five Unidentified Mexican Men
Born: (Unknown)—Date of Death: 14 June 1877
Place: Fannin County
Event: Lynching/Hanged

Unverified sources claim that five unidentified Mexican men were lynched near Bonham for murder and outrage.[610]

Forty Unidentified Mexican Men
Born: (Unknown)—Date of Death: July 1877
Place: Nueces County
Event: Lynching/Hanged and Shot

Unverified sources claim that roughly forty unidentified Mexican men suspected of murder were lynched and shot.[611]

Two Unidentified Mexican Men
Born: (Unknown)—Date of Death: 7 July 1877
Place: Nueces County
Event: Lynching/Shot

Unverified sources claim that two unidentified Mexican men were captured and killed by a posse near Banquette. The men were suspected of murder.[612]

Bowen, Allen (Allan)
Born: (Unknown)—Date of Death: 20 July 1877
Place: Coryell County
Event: Lynching/Hanged

Allen Bowen was found hanging from a tree near Eagle Springs. He had been a witness for the defense in the trial of a man named Bill Green recently. It is unclear what role that testimony might have played in his untimely death.[613]

Monte, Given Name Unknown
Born: (Unknown)—Date of Death: August 1877
Place: Brown County
Event: Lynching/Hanged

A man identified only as Monte was taken from officers who were transporting him from Fort Griffin to Brownwood and lynched. When his body was discovered a placard reading, "Beware of Horse Thieves" had been fastened to his chest, thus it seems reasonable to hypothesize that Monte was a horse thief.[614]

Wadsworth, Walter L.
Born: 20 August 1854—Date of Death: 18 August 1877
Place: Llano County
Event: Lynching/Shot

In August 1877, a posse of lawmen was organized to run down a herd of stolen cattle near the town of Brady and, hopefully, the men who had spirited them off. The group included Sheriff J. J. Bozarth of Llano, Sheriff Jesse Leslie of Mason, and Sheriff H. T. Eubank of McCulloch County. Also in the posse was a man named Miles Barler who chronicled the event in him memoirs some years later, albeit somewhat inaccurately. In Barler's account, the posse was met by Sheriff W. R. Doran at San Saba. Ben Beeson, Bob Rowntree, Dan Trent and Francis Taylor were also in the group when the struck out to collar the outlaws. In due course one of the suspected thieves, a known malefactor named Henry Hoy, was shot and killed by Beeson and Barler. A member of the outlaw band identified only as Scott was captured. Another one of the suspects, a man named Walter Wadsworth, was also apprehended and taken to the jail at Llano on 18 August 1877. During the night, persons unknown tossed a turpentine soaked ball of some sort through the window bars and into the cell where Wadsworth was sleeping, then shot him in the side and back with shotguns, resulting in his death. According to newspaper reports of the day, a band of about 300 Llano citizens, convinced of Wadsworth's innocence, were determined to find his killers. The *San Saba News* denounced the slaying as "...a high handed outrage."[615] The *Galveston Weekly News* added that the deed had been "...a most dastardly act."

Some newspapers report this incident as taking place at 1:00 am on 30 August 1877.[616] It would appear as though Walter Wadsworth was the son of Martin Harwick Wadsworth (1804-1877) and his second wife, Frances C.D. Henderson (1830-1913). The family lived in San Saba. Martin Wadsworth had come to Texas from South Carolina and settled at San Saba in about 1860. Wadsworth had fourteen children in total.[617]

Davis, Perry
Born: (Unknown)—Date of Death: 30 August 1877
Place: McLennan County
Event: Legal Execution/Hanged

On Wednesday, 6 February 1877 Officer Alpheus D. Neill of the Waco Police Department was shot and killed by Perry Davis. The incident occurred when Neill was responding to a disturbance in which Davis had been threatening to kill his wife and father-in-law. As Neill came on the property Davis shot him.[618]

At 2:00 pm on Thursday, 30 August 1877, Davis was put in a wagon with the sheriff, a deputy, and Reverend Stephen Cobb and transported to the gallows. The site for the hanging was in East Waco. A large crowd, estimated at 7,000 persons, swarmed the streets and blocked traffic as they rushed to witness the show. Deputy Moore read the death sentence. Davis acknowledged that the verdict was just. Reverend Cobb offered a short prayer and requested that the hymn "On Jordan's Stormy Banks I Stand" be sung for him. Davis himself led the hymn while a thousand voices from the crowd obliged by joining in.

As the black cap was placed on his head Davis whispered, "Lord save me." The trap was sprung and the condemned man dropped to his death, dangling there for thirty minutes before being declared dead.[619]

Three Unidentified Men
Born: (Unknown)—Date of Death: September 1877
Place: Red River County
Event: Lynching/Hanged

Newspapers of the day reported that three unfortunates were discovered hanging from a tree near Sulphur Springs in Red River County. One of the men had a placard fastened to him that read, "They stole horses; here is where we found them and here is where we left them."[620]

Unidentified Mexican Man
Born: (Unknown)—Date of Death: 2 November 1877
Place: Bexar County
Event: Lynching/Hanged

Unidentified White Man
Born: (Unknown)—Date of Death: 2 November 1877
Place: Bexar County
Event: Lynching/Hanged

Two lads came upon the corpses of two men, one Mexican and one white. The pair was hanging from an oak tree near Leon in Bexar County, about six miles southwest of San Antonio. Both were wearing white hats. The white man appeared to be young and the Mexican much older. Both had been lynched with the same rope.

Understandably the youths were quite shaken by the find and rush back to tell authorities. When a group went out to view the scene the young lads were unable to guide them to the spot, owing perhaps to the size and density of the mot of oaks where they had discovered the corpses. Nevertheless, authorities seemed willing to believe the boy's yarn.[621]

Ellis, Charles E.
Born: (Unknown)—Date of Death: 12 December 1877
Place: El Paso County
Event: Lynching/Shot

Atkinson, John George
Born: circa 1838—Date of Death: 17 December 1877
Place: El Paso County
Event: Lynching/Shot/Shot

Howard, Charles Henry
Born: 3 February 1842—Date of Death: 17 December 1877
Place: El Paso County
Event: Lynching/Shot

McBride, John E.
Born: circa 1845—Date of Death: 17 December 1877
Place: El Paso County
Event: Lynching/Shot

The El Paso Salt War began in the late 1860s. It was a political struggle between White entrepreneurs desiring to acquire title to the salt deposits at the foot of Guadalupe Peak (100 miles east of El Paso) and citizens of Mexican origin wanting the salt flats to remain open to the public. Feelings between the two groups erupted into open warfare in 1870. In 1872 Charles Howard tried to claim ownership of the salt flats, an act that outraged local citizens who seized Howard and released him on bond only if he would leave the state.

On 10 October 1877, Howard returned and killed a rival political leader. On 11 November 1877, Lieutenant John B. Tays took command of newly organized Detachment of Company "C." Howard was arraigned for the murder and freed pending trial.

Howard was guarded at an adobe house the rangers used as quarters in San Elizario. The Mexicans gathered, roped Howard's associate and former El Paso County Sheriff Charles Ellis and dragged him through the streets slashing him to death with knives and mutilating his corpse.

On 13 December 1877, John Atkinson, a former El Paso police lieutenant and San Elizario businessman, managed to get through the citizen militia and into the ranger quarters with a trunk containing about $11,000. Second Sergeant Mortimer was walking between the buildings when a single shot from a sniper's rifle struck him and passed through his body. Mortimer staggered a few steps then collapsed in the middle of the road. Tays ran into the street and carried Mortimer inside. Mortimer died just before sundown that day. The rioters charged the building several times, but were beaten back.

On 17 December 1877, Tays met with the Mexican junta leaders who advised the rangers to surrender Howard or they would blow up the ranger quarters. Howard was not fooled by guarantees of his safety, and against Tays' advice agreed to surrender to save the rangers. Atkinson offered the mob the $11,000 to save Howard and First Sergeant McBride who continued acting as Howard's agent in San Elizario after his enlistment. The junta agreed and swore to uphold their end of the agreement. Atkinson returned to the ranger quarters with a flag of truce and told the rangers that Tays had ordered them to surrender. They agreed. This is the only time in the history of the Texas Rangers that they were forced to surrender.

Tays was not aware of the surrender agreement, and when he saw the rangers file out and be disarmed he was furious. The junta decided to execute Howard, Atkinson and McBride despite guarantees not to harm them. Each man was shot by a firing squad. Their bodies were stripped, mutilated and thrown in a well. A mob among the insurgents then wanted to kill the twenty or so rangers, but the junta military commander regained control and the rangers were released on 18 December. Four days later rangers and a sheriff's posse (actually New Mexican mercenaries) descended on San Elizario killing four or five men and wounding several others until the US Army put a stop to the rampage. The leaders of the insurgents and many of their followers fled to Mexico.

Some of the participants were arrested and later escaped. Some were indicted, but none were ever brought to trial.

More recently, one historian has suggested that it would be incorrect to call the local citizenry involved in this affray a "mob."[622] The source claimd that the citizens were highly organized into a junta, or town councils, and were an armed force with leaders and sub-leaders that had a long history of local self-rule and military self-defense. But, the group's lawless actions and flagrant murder of

Texas lawmen hardly warrants the use of any terminology less powerful than "mob."[623]

Howard is buried at the Oakwood Cemetery at Austin, in Travis County.[624]

Dening, (Given Name Unknown)

Born: (Unknown)—Date of Death: 9 April 1878

Place: Walker County

Event: Lynching/Shot

In 1878 Texas an amorous relationship between a black man and a white woman was an unspeakable taboo. Such "mongrelizations of the races" were frequently met with fatal interventions. Such is the case with young Mr. Dening, a black man, who became involved with the daughter of his employer, a rich white farmer.

In 1875, Mr. McGuire hired Dening to work on his farm. McGuire had three daughters, one of whom was named Fannie. Fannie was an attractive looking seventeen-year old girl who stood well in society. Fannie became attracted to Dening. The couple eloped from the father's home, taking a wagon and fleeing to the railroad station where they boarded transport to Houston. Once there, they took up residence in a shack in the black section of town. As one might expect, Fannie's brother mounted a search party and found the lovebirds in their hut, locked in conjugal endearment.

Dening was arrested on a charge of carrying a concealed weapon. He was taken to the jail then transferred to Riverside where the McGuire family resided. Once there, Dening was placed in an unoccupied house and chained around his neck to the floor. Towards midnight on Tuesday, 9 April 1878, a mob of about twenty masked riders stormed the building, overpowering Deputy Sheriff Morris and Operator Johnson and taking their keys. The vigilante horde entered the house where Dening slept, awakened him and opened fire with shotguns, filling his body with lead. Afterwards they calmly remounted and rode off.[625] That is the way they "...do things up..." in Texas.

Bowen, Joshua Robert "Brown"

Born: 27 September 1849—Date of Death: 17 May 1878

Place: Gonzales County

Event: Legal Execution/Hanged

Joshua Robert "Brown" Bowen, the eldest child of Neill and Mary Weston Bowen was born in Milton, Santa Rosa County, Florida. The family settled in Texas at least by 1850, landing first in Bastrop County then moving on to Karnes and Gonzales Counties. On 17 October 1868, Bowen married Margaret Reese. In the late 1860s and into the 1870s the Sutton-Taylor feud cost numerous lives, and it was on this conflict that Bowen blamed his ultimate fate.

On 17 December 1872, Thomas J. Haldeman was shot to death. A number of men were drinking and carousing at a store in rural Gonzales County. Haldeman imbibed freely, to the point of lying down and leaning against a tree where he fell into a drunken sleep. While napping someone shot him in the head. His killer remains a mystery, although some suspect that John Wesley Hardin had done the job. At trial, however, the jury believed Bowen was the murderer.

Bowen was arrested, but he quickly broke jail and fled to Florida where he was arrested in 1877. Ironically, that occurred shortly after brother-in-law Hardin was also arrested. Bowen's defense was that Hardin had shot Haldeman because he thought he (Haldeman) was a spy for Captain Joe Tumlinson, one of the leaders of the Sutton forces. However, the storeowner claimed that Bowen had done the killing. Hardin also reportedly informed David Haldeman, Tom's father, that Bowen had done the evil deed.

Although Bowen accused Hardin of the murder, Hardin denied it, stating that he could not and would not kill a sleeping man. Each man was charged with murder: Hardin for the 1874 killing of a deputy sheriff, Bowen for the 1872 killing of Haldeman. Hardin was convicted of murder in the second degree. Bowen was convicted of murder in the first degree. Hardin was sentenced to twenty-five years in the penitentiary while Bowen was sentenced to the gallows. Bowen was scheduled to die by hanging on 17 May 1878, at Gonzales.

Sheriff Alonzo T. Bass was in charge of the execution. To assist he had two deputies - G. H. Bruton and John R. Lewis. In addition, Texas Ranger Captain J. L. Hall was on hand with a detachment of Rangers incase the crowd became disorderly and to assure that the sentence of the court was carried out.

Moments before the trap was sprung Bowen called Tom's brother John Haldeman forward to answer questions. That exchange was not recorded in full. Haldeman did state that he believed Bowen had killed his brother. To that statement Bowen was recorded as saying: "You believe a doggone lie." Before the trap was sprung Bowen implored the crowd to avoid bad company. The noose was adjusted around his neck as the condemned man gazed sternly at the crowd showing "no sign of fear or weakness in this supreme moment. He was Brown Bowen the defiant" as the Gonzales newspaper, reported. At 2:55 p.m. Sheriff Bass sprang the trap. Bowen fell perfectly straight. He expired after only four minutes.

Estimates of the size of the crowd ranged from 4,000 to 5,000. Bowen was buried at the Bowen home place. Through the years the headstone was broken in many pieces. A number of years ago Gonzales County author and historian Chuck Parsons visited the site, gathered the fragments of the headstone and placed them in the Gonzales "Old Jail" Museum where they remain today.[626]

Robertson, Fred
Born: (Unknown)—Date of Death: 31 May 1878
Place: Limestone County
Event: Legal Execution/Hanged

Fred Robertson, a black man, was found guilty of outraging a white woman named Miss Oatley. Robertson confessed to his crime on the gallows and admitted that his sentence was just.[627]

Larn, John M.
Born: 1 March 1849—Date of Death: 24 June 1878
Place: Shackelford County
Event: Lynching/Shot

John Larn, a white man, had reportedly killed a fellow in Colorado and a sheriff in New Mexico before he arrived at Fort Griffin in Shackelford County in 1871. He was also said to have killed three men while on a trail drive.

By 1873, Larn was rumored to be rustling cattle while at the same time serving as a vigilante, killing and lynching suspected cattle thieves. His reputation for bringing law and order to the county was instrumental in his election as sheriff on 15 February 1876. After his election the vigilante killings continued.

Larn obtained a contract with the army to deliver cattle to Fort Griffin. He deputized his friend, John Selman, to assist him in stealing enough livestock to fill the order. Area ranchers soon grew suspicious of Larn and Selman. Larn resigned as sheriff on 20 March 1877, and became a deputy county hide inspector with Selman.

The Larn gang increased the level of violence and cattle rustling in the area until, in February of 1878, a band of citizens obtained a warrant and arrested Larn. Unfortunately he was soon released. Larn later shot and wounded a local rancher who had been behind his arrest. Sheriff W.R. "Bill" Cruger arrested Larn on 23 June 1878. He shackled him in a cell. The following night vigilantes stormed the jail and shot Larn to death.

He is buried at the Camp Cooper Ranch next to his infant son who preceded him in death.[628]

Parras, Paolo
Born: (Unknown)—Date of Death: 28 June 1878
Place: Nueces County
Event: Legal Execution/Hanged

Paolo Parras, a well-experienced Mexican outlaw, finally met his just end at Corpus Christi on Friday, 28 June 1878. Fridays seem to be a popular day for hangings in Texas.

Included on the long list of Parras' nefarious deeds was the murder of Dr. Newman at Gatesville on 2 December 1870. Considering that Parras' purpose was to rob the doctor, dragging the man at the end of a lasso and butchering him with a knife seems a bit extreme. Parras was also charged with complicity in an assault on the jail at Rio Grande City where a man named Noah Cox was killed.

Parras was transported from Rio Grande City to Corpus Christi under heavy guard. Twenty-nine men and three officers of the Star Rifles, as well as nine state police officers, made up the heavily armed contingent.

On the gallows Parras was asked if he wanted to brace himself with a drink. He took advantage of the proposal. The condemned man then began to address the crowd, admitting that he was an unprincipled and contemptible person, but yet professed his innocence. Moments later, with a hearty

"Viva Mexico" Parras uttered his last words and the latch was sprung. Considering his weight of 180 pounds the fall of five feet should have snapped his neck as had been planned. The calculations were faulty. Parras struggled for about eleven minutes before expiring.

Parras left behind a will, bequeathing his Colt's improved pistol and a black horse to his father so that the elder Parras might sell the items and use the proceeds to raise his children.[629]

Solomon, George
Born: circa 1853—Date of Death: 28 June 1878
Place: Freestone County
Event: Legal Execution/Hanged

George Solomon, a black man, was found guilty of the murder of his wife and stepchild. The incident took place in 1877. He was also suspected of having committed other murders.

At 1:40 pm on Friday, 28 June 1878, Solomon climbed the gallows at Fairfield. When asked if he wished to speak he did so, claiming that he was innocent of committing the crime for which he had been charged. At 2:25 pm the rope was cut, the trapdoor sprung, and Solomon's worldly troubles came to an end.[630]

Jones, James E.
Born: (Unknown)—Date of Death: 6 July 1878
Place: Fayette County
Event: Legal Execution/Hanged

On Christmas Eve 1875, James Jones, a black man, murdered another black man named High Hill at a dance he was attending in Fayette County. The two men quarreled about their place in a dance, both claiming rights to the same position. Jones settled the matter by fatally shooting Hill, then fled to Gonzalez County where he was eventually captured in the spring of 1877.

The hanging took place on the banks of the Colorado River. Jones, who had denied his guilt all along, finally confessed before he went to the gallows. Reverend William Calhoun and Sheriff Rabb accompanied Jones as he scaled the stairs to the hanging platform in plain view of about 2,000 spectators. The time was about 2:00 pm. Jones delivered a speech during which he cautioned the crowd to take fair warning from witnessing his fate. He added that he saw the chariot of heaven coming to take his soul to glory. The preacher prayed while the sheriff adjusted the noose. The hangman pulled the trap and Jones fell, presumably to meet the aforementioned heavenly conveyance.[631]

Hadley, Amos
Born: (Unknown)—Date of Death: 30 August 1878
Place: Gregg County
Event: Legal Execution/Hanged

Powell, Diamed
Born: (Unknown)—Date of Death: 30 August 1878
Place: Gregg County
Event: Legal Execution/Hanged

Amos Hadley, an Indian man, and Diamed Powell, a black man, went to the gallows together at Longview for the murder of August Reinke. Although both appeared very penitent, they professed their innocence and forgave their enemies.[632]

Speer, John
Born: circa 1856—Date of Death: 23 September 1878
Place: McLennan County
Event: Legal Execution/Hanged

On Wednesday, 14 July 1875, John Speer shot and killed Johnson Simmon Pledger. He did the job with a double barrel shot gun loaded with buckshot. Pledger was plowing in his field in northern McLennan County when the incident took place. Speer was arrested the night of the shooting in nearby Mudtown (present day Aquilla) where Pledger was a pastor.

On Monday, 23 September 1878, Speer was hung in the Waco Jail Yard. Pledger's wife Mary, son Robert, a daughter Mrs. Gawdy, along with their young child, all died within a ten days after the Speer hanging. Records show that they where buried side by side in a neighboring churchyard.

Some sources list this hanging as taking place on 20 September 1878.

Longley, William Preston "Bill"
Born: 6 October 1851—Date of Death: 11 October 1878
Place: Lee County
Event: Legal Execution/Hanged

Tales of Bill Longley's criminal career are an amalgam of facts, augmented by Longley's own boastful and fictional commentary of his life of crime. What is known for certain is that at the end of the Civil War a rebellious Bill Longley took up with other likeminded young men and terrorized newly freed slaves.

On 20 December 1868, Longley and his confederates intercepted three former slaves from Bell County. They shot and killed one man named Green Evans. Although the two surviving black men reported the incident to local law enforcement authorities no formal charges for the killing of Evans were ever brought against Longley or his associates.

Fact and legend become hopelessly snarled at this point. Longley later claimed that after the Bell County incident he worked as a cowboy in Karnes County where he killed a soldier as he rode through Yorktown. There is no corroboration for either of these claims. Longley also asserted that he rode with the notorious bandit Cullen M. Baker in northeast Texas. That declaration is also unlikely, and no substantial evidence has surfaced to support the claim.

In 1869-70 Longley surfaced in south central Texas. There he and his brother-in-law John W. Wilson were busy terrorizing residents. It is alleged that in February 1870 they killed a black man named Paul Brice in Bastrop County. The pair was also accused of killing a black woman, but no evidence to support that allegation has ever surfaced.

In 1874 Longley traveled north. He claiming that he killed a trail driver named Rector, fought Indians, killed a horse thief named McClelland, and killed a soldier at Leavenworth, Kansas for impugning the virtue of a Texas woman. None of these claims have been validated either. He joined the army and tolerated the structured life in the mountains of Wyoming for a time. In June 1872, he deserted and eventually turned up in Texas in February 1873.

During the cool, crisp evening of 13 November 1875, Longley was part of a drunken foxhunt during which he managed to get into an argument with a young man named George Thomas. The quarrel soon led to a fistfight, and that escalated into a gunplay. Longley managed to acquire a six-shooter from someone in the group and proceeded to shoot Thomas three times. The wounds were fatal. He was indicted for the shooting, but promptly stole a horse and left the county.

Longley next surfaced in Uvalde County, in the Dry Frio Canyon, sometime late in 1875 or early January 1876. He had now chosen a new alias...Jim Webb. In the Dry Frio Canyon country he met William "Lou" Shroyer, a Pennsylvania native and former Union soldier who also had a reputation as a bad hombre. Shroyer suspected Webb's true identity, and is said to have conspired to capture or kill Longley for the reward. When Longley learned of the plot he somehow managed to get himself deputized by the town of Uvalde to arrest Shroyer in connection with the scheme. Accompanied by a deputy named William Hayes, Longley returned to formulate a plan for dealing with Shroyer.

In January 1876 Longley launched his plan and killed Shroyer in what was probably the only legitimate gun battle Longley was ever involved in.

On the move again Longley fled Uvalde County. There he became involved in an altercation over a love interest. He wound up in jail, this time using the name of William Black. On 6 June 1876, he was jailed at Cooper, the Delta County seat. Six days later he burned a hole in the jail door and escaped. Blaming a man of the cloth named Lay for his predicament, Longley armed himself with a shotgun and ambushed the preacher. As dawn broke Longley crept up on his victim who at the time was calmly milking a cow and shot him without warning.

In the spring of 1877, Longley adopted a new alias, Bill Jackson. One cannot help but note that most of the time when Longley selected a new pseudonym he choose the given name Bill or William. Not terribly imaginative. Longley took a job working for a farmer named W. T. Gamble near Keatchie in De Soto Parish, Louisiana. Eventually the local constable named June Courtney knew his identity. Courtney notified authorities in Texas and, on 6 June 1877, Nacogdoches County Sheriff Milt Mast, his Deputy Bill Burrows, and Constable June Courtney apprehended Longley.

Longley's trial was set for 3 September 1877, and was to take place in a temporary courthouse in Giddings. It took only one day for the prosecution to present its case, and the jury took just an hour and a half to return a verdict of guilty of murder in the first degree. The sentence was death by hanging.

Longley was soon transferred to the Galveston County jail pending the outcome of the appeal of his death sentence. There he made a feeble and unsuccessful attempt at escape in early March 1878. On 13 March the court of appeals affirmed Longley's conviction, finding that his trial had been just and fair. In July, while waiting for court to convene in Giddings so that he finally could be sentenced, he converted to Catholicism. A petition effort was mounted in Nacogdoches asking that the governor commute his sentence to life. On 6 September 1878, he was sentenced by District Judge E. B. Turner to be executed on 11 October.

Friday, 11 October 1878, promised to be a gray, gloomy day. There was a threat of rain in the air. Thousands of people traveled to the small community of Giddings to see Bill Longley's hanging. He dressed in a black suit, with a white shirt, black tie and a broad-brimmed low-crown hat. On his lapel he wore a blue rosette arrangement, and beneath his shirt hung a small Catholic medal on a thin cord. Only one family member, a ten-year-old niece, visited him. When he kissed her goodbye even the strongest hearts in the jail were touched.

At 2:15 pm Longley mounted the scaffold. He stood as Sheriff Brown read the death warrant then briefly addressed the crowd, atoning for his evil deeds and asking forgiveness. The crowd watched as the hangman performed the deed. Longley dropped through the trap door and hit the ground, neck sore but not dead. The hangman had used the wrong length rope for the job. To the crowds, and Longley's astonishment he would have to be hanged twice. Again the latch was released and Bill Longley dropped from the execution platform. This time his death sentence was carried out.

Between 1992 and 1994 an effort was made to find his body in the Giddings Cemetery. The undertakings were to no avail. Finally, in July 1998, using a computer to match up the old photo of his burial with new photos of the cemetery the spot was located where the older photograph must have been taken. An excavation of that site revealed the skeleton of a white man fitting Longley's physical description. Forensic science revealed that the man had suffered from periodontal disease as well as a broken leg, which was perhaps the result of the fall from the scaffold. The most eerie evidence yielded up by the examination was a Catholic medal that had been worn around the man's neck on a thin cord. Also found was a small piece of artificial material with the design of a leaf that could have been from the rosette Longley wore.

The remains were taken to the Smithsonian Institution in Washington, D.C., for DNA testing, skull reconstruction and identification. In June 2001 it was announced that the remains were indeed those of Bill Longley. His bones were subsequently reinterred in Texas, providing an end to his story at long last.[633]

One Unidentified Man
Born: (Unknown)—Date of Death: November 1878
Place: Duval County
Event: Lynching/Hanged

An unidentified man was allegedly lynched at San Diego for suspicion of murder. He was captured in Mexico and brought to Texas where he was hanged in front of a hundred people.[634]

Hernandez, Juan Antonio

Born: (Unknown)—Date of Death: 21 November 1878
Place: Refugio County
Event: Legal Execution/Hanged

Juan Antonio Hernandez, a Mexican man, was hanged at Refugio for the murder of two men named Walder and Maton.[635]

Stull, John

Born (Unknown)—Date of Death: 8 December 1878
Place: Coryell County
Event: Lynching/Shot

Smith, Rufus

Born (Unknown)—Date of Death: 8 December 1878
Place: Coryell County
Event: Lynching/Shot

A merchant named J. T. Vaughn was shot to death at Hog Creek, six miles west of Valley Mills in Bosque County on 28 May 1878. A group of four men did the killing. Suspicion fell on Vaughn's former business partner, Bill Babb. John Stull, who by one account was said to have been a deputy US Marshal but in another version of the story an ordinary citizen, swore out a warrant and arrested Babb and several others. The prisoners were placed in the Bosque County jail. Babb was never tried for the murder.

On Sunday, 8 December 1878, John Stull and his wife invited Rufus Smith and his wife to spend the night at their home at Turnersville. Around 11:00 pm they smelled fumes from burning kerosene. One report claimed that the odor was coming from a torpedo bomb and not a stove. Mr. Smith grabbed his baby and, together with his wife, ran outside. Once free of the burning structure Smith was killed. In some accounts so was his wife. When Mr. Stull exited the building he was also shot and killed. According to reports, the killers examined each body and when they came to John Stull they riddled his body with bullets.

Next the masked men then went to the home of John's brother, Anthony Stull. He was able to drive them off, shooting one of the men in the process. The date of this incident was also reported as 7 and 9 December 1878.[636]

Jackson, Smith

Born: (Unknown)—Date of Death: 14 December 1878
Place: Bastrop County
Event: Legal Execution/Hanged

Jones, Pryor
Born: (Unknown)—Date of Death: 14 December 1878
Place: Bastrop County
Event: Legal Execution/Hanged

In a rare "two for the price of one" execution Smith Jackson and Pryor Jones, both black men, went to the gallows together at Bastrop. They had been found guilty of the murder of another black man named John Black.

The incident had taken place on 23 December 1876. A son of Henry Owens had disappeared. A voodooist named Sam Squirrelhunter was called in to perform incantations on the lost lad's behalf. The whole party, consisting of the aforementioned along with Jackson, Jones, Thomas Robinson, Sol Ridge, Henry Owens, William Peterson, Steve Robinson, Burrell Jackson and George Veal went to the home of John Black and placed a rope around his neck, attached it to the pommel of a horses saddle and drug him about a mile, ending up in a nearby woods. Black was practically dead from the dragging. The rope was disconnected from the saddle horn and thrown over a tree limb. Black was hauled up and interrogated. He firmly denied having any knowledge of the boy's disappearance. Squirrelhunter, however, insisted that he did because he himself had see it, "...written in the coffee grounds." Black was repeatedly hauled up the tree until almost dead, then dropped to the ground and revived. He maintained his innocence. On the final hoisting they left him up too long. Black succumbed to the ordeal.

Sometime afterwards the missing boy returned home, saying that a stockman had taken him, and that Black had nothing to do with the abduction. The boy went home. Squirrelhunter was arrested.

Thus, after a trial during which the pair were convicted of Black's murder, Smith Jackson and Pryor Jones kept their appointment with the hangman on Saturday, 14 December 1878. Burrell Jackson, another participant, had his sentence commuted just days earlier or the good folks of Bastrop County might have see the most rare triple execution.

Sheriff Jenkins and a posse of forty men formed a line and marched the condemned men the 100 yard distance from the jail to the gallows. Both scaled the structure's stairs with cigars in their mouths, imitating the notorious Bill Longley's last walk. Both made a brief address to the crowd bidding them farewell. At 2:20 pm the sheriff sprung the trap. Jackson and Jones dropped to their death, breaking their necks in the fall.

Newspapers reported that, "The vast crowd that had gathered, many of whom were darkies [blacks], sang and chanted as if at a camp meeting."[637] Sam Squirrelhunter, the voodoo chief, had escaped from jail and was a fugitive. [638]

Horrell, James Martin "Mart"
Born: circa 1846—Date of Death: 15 December 1878
Place: Bosque County
Event: Lynching/Shot

Horrell, Thomas L. "Tom"
Born: circa 1848—Date of Death: 15 December 1878
Place: Bosque County
Event: Lynching/Shot

Sympathetic locals in Lampasas, Texas regarded brothers Sam, Mart, Merritt, Tom, and Ben as "fun-loving cowboys".[639] However, all did not share that opinion of the family. Late author and columnist Claude Douglas wrote that no family played a more prominent role in the lawlessness in Lampasas than did the Horrells. They often shot up the town, and were counted among the worst of ruffians. Mart Horrell, as described by neighbor John Nichols was as "a round shouldered troublemaker." More recently, however, authors have painted a far more balanced view of the Horrell clan, uncovering evidence to reveal that much of the earlier reports of the family being little more than a band of malefactors has been flawed.[640]

On 22 January 1877 Pink Higgins and a group of his colleagues shot and killed Merritt Horrell at Scott's Tavern at Lampasas. Merritt Horrell was in the back room, seated on one side of the fireplace. Opposite Horrell was Old Bow Legged Saunders.[641] Some contend that Higgins stepped through the back door and pumped four shots into an unarmed Merritt Horrell with his Winchester as he announced, "Mr. Horrell, this is to settle some cow business...."[642] Others have asserted that Higgins shot Merritt Horrell for no reason. Regardless, the deed was done. It ignited a feud between the two factions that lasted for years. A complete accounting of the Horrell Family would require scores of pages of text. A number of books have been written on the topic, and interested parties should consult one for the complete story.[643]

In 1878, Mart and Tom Horrell were arrested for robbing and killing merchant J. F. Vaughn at a place called Rock School House on Hog Creek in Bosque County. They were jailed at Meridian, Texas. On 15 December 1878, at around 8:30 pm, James and his brother Tom were murdered by an armed mob. According to official stories, the number of men involved ranged from between 100 to 300 men, although only fifty were actually seen. The men simply knocked on the jailhouse door, identified himself as a deputy sheriff. The jailor admitted the man and was speedily covered by drawn pistols. Once inside the mob moved the cells and riddled the Horrell brothers with bullets. Evidence suggests that neither of the brothers may have been guilty of the crime. Some speculated that John Higgins, Horrell Family foe from the Lampasas incident, may have instigated the murders.[644]

Both are buried at the Oak Hill Cemetery at Lampasas.

Johnson, Green
Born: (Unknown)—Date of Death: 20 December 1878
Place: Menard County
Event: Legal Execution/Hanged

Green Johnson, a black man and former soldier, was tried and convicted of murdering his wife. He was sentenced to death. That judgment was carried out on Friday, 20 December 1878, at Menardville where Johnson hung for his crime.[645] The fall did not break his neck, and he struggled for about ten minutes while he suffocated.[646]

Collier, James "Jim"
Born (Unknown)—Date of Death: 3 April 1879
Place: Lampasas County
Event: Lynching/Hanged

Van Winkle, William "Bill"
Born (Unknown)—Date of Death: 7 April 1879
Place: Lampasas County
Event: Lynching/Hanged

The Mason County War, commonly known as the Hoodoo War, was one of a number of feuds that developed during this period of Texas history. Fueled in part by accusations of cattle theft, the confrontation lasted from about 1874 to 1902. Two victims of the feud were Jim Collier and Bill Van Winkle.

On Thursday, 3 April 1879, Collier was called out of his house near Lampasas by a mob of masked men. The vigilante group hanged him and attached a note to his body that read, "This will be the fate of all who harbor horse thieves." Collier was related to the Horrell brothers.

On Monday, 7 April 1879, Bill Van Winkle was camped out in Lampasas County with his two brothers when four men rode up and told him he was wanted by the sheriff. Van Winkle, who had been arrested earlier by Texas Rangers for his involvement in a jail escape, went along peacefully. The men traveled about two miles then shot Van Winkle to death.[647]

Bradley, Ezekiel
Born: circa 1854—Date of Death: 2 May 1879
Place: Brazos County
Event: Legal Execution/Hanged

On Christmas Day 1878, Ezekiel Bradley, a black man, shot and killed John Pollock in cold blood and with no apparent cause. Pollock was a middle aged well to do farmer. The killing took place at a crossroads grogshop and tenpins alley in the Brazos Bottoms.[648] Pollock had gone there with his nephew who had been shooting Chinese firecrackers with Bradley's cousin. An altercation of an unknown cause ensued. Ezekiel Bradley stepped in and without a word opened fire on Pollock. One bullet entered Pollock's mouth, breaking his neck as it exited and killing him instantly. As he fired Bradley was heard to say, "God damn you, take that."

Bradley was arrested, tried and convicted of the murder. He offered no evidence to the contrary or in his defense. The death sentence was prescribed.

Before leaving the jail Bradley received communion from Father Victor. He was accompanied to the gallows by the sheriff, a host of deputies and a contingent of the Bryan Rifles. Upon the platform Bradley was cool and composed, addressing the crowd and beseeching them to leave ardent spirits and revolvers alone. The sheriff read his death warrant, pinned his hands and feet and placed the black cap over Bradley's head as he adjusted the noose. The trap was sprung and Bradley was shot into eternity. Newspaper reporters of the day commented that Bradley, "...like all other Negro's hanged, said he was going straight to Jesus while the crowd said Amen."

Bradley's widow was present for her husband's going away party, seated about ten feet from the drop.[649]

Cordova Jr., Jose

Born: circa 1853—Date of Death: 7 July 1879
Place: Bexar County
Event: Legal Execution/Hanged

On Thursday, 5 July 1877, Robert Trimble, a young farmer from Atascosa County, started from home with a load of corn he intended to sell at San Antonio. He also had with him a money draft for $400. Arriving safely he sold the corn and made several purchases of necessary items for his family then headed home. Trimble was last seen alive about five miles from town. When he did not return a search part was sent out. About nine miles from San Antonio, at Indian Creek, they discovered a place where his wagon had left the trial and proceeded about a mile or two through the brush. At that spot his body was discovered. Attached to his left leg was a rope about thirty feet in length. Apparently Trimble had been dragged some distance through the underbrush. His body showed the evidence of same, along with two deep stab wounds to his heart that had caused his death.

A search was conducted for the murderers. On Thursday, 12 July 1877, four days after the murder, Texas Ranger Captain Dolan and his men overtook a group of Mexicans traveling near Uvalde. One of the wagons in their parts was Trimble's, and contained the provisions that he had purchased at San Antonio just days earlier.

Rangers placed the group under arrest. One ranger was guarding the wagon while the other was looking after two mounted men when one of the young men, Jose Cordova Jr., produced a Winchester from the wagon and began firing. He hit the first ranger in the back, knocking him from his horse and inflicting a serious and painful wound. Next Cordova sprung from the vehicle and opened fire on the second ranger, killing his horse from under him. Cordova and his younger brother Feliciano, accompanied by two colleagues named Salcedo and Diaz, seized the opportunity created by the confusion to make good their escape.

After some difficulty, further complicated by the fact that Cordova and his associates had fled to Mexico, Texas Rangers crossed the Rio Grande to make the collar on Tuesday, 1 January 1878. All were brought to San Antonio for trial. Jose Cordova was found guilty. His only comment was, "bueno."

Cordova maintained his innocence all the way to the gallows. On Monday, 7 July 1879,

Cordova kept his date with the hangman at San Antonio. Over 5,000 persons gathered to witness the event, excited by the prospect of a daring and bold attempt at a recovery of the doomed man orchestrated by Mexican outlaws and led by his family. The expected liberation attempt never took place, and the hanging went off without incident.[650]

Garcia, Antonio
Born: (Unknown)—Date of Death: 11 July 1879
Place: Nueces County
Event: Legal Execution/Hanged

On Thursday, 23 January 1879, a court of appeals affirmed the death sentence for Antonio Garcia, a Mexican man, who had been tried and found guilty of the murder of Augustin Amallo. His hanging date was set for 11 July 1879, at Corpus Christi.[651]

Amallo and Garcia were both shepherds. Amallo's wife and two children had deserted him and taken up with Garcia. Amallo had gone to Garcia's home to visit his children. Garcia lured him away and crushed his head with a rock.

At 11:25 am the drop fell and Garcia descended to his death. His neck was broken by the fall and he died instantly.[652]

Hainline, Ennes Jacob
Born: circa 1847—Date of Death: 8 August 1879
Place: Bexar County
Event: Legal Execution/Hanged

Jacob Hainline, a white man, was executed at San Antonio for the murder of Peter Maddox. That incident had occurred in February 1878, when Hanline had gone with Maddox, an older man, to Fort Concho in an ox wagon. They had left Atascosa on 1 October 1877, and entered a partnership in produce, but soon abandoned that pursuit for buffalo hunting. After killing enough of the beasts to fill their wagon with cured meat and hides they headed back towards Atascosa. Along their route they encountered William Patterson and Messer's McChesney and Crompton, with whom they were acquainted. They all camped together along the Johnson Fork of the Guadalupe River, near Kerrville. After a stop on 21 February 1878, near Leon Spring the pair arrived at San Antonio. Maddox began to make contacts to sell the buffalo meat.

On 24 February two boys rambling along a creek discovered Maddox's body floating face up in the water, quite dead. Hanline was arrested, tried and found guilty of the murder. He was sentenced to death.

On the night preceding his date with the executioner Hanline rested well. Although he protested his innocence right to the end, he chose to be baptized by Catholic Priests Johnson and Neraz...just in case. Only fifty persons witnessed the private execution, which took place on the same site as Cordova's just one month earlier. Unlike Cordova's going away party, Hanline's hanging attracted little interest, drawing a meager 300 Mexicans and blacks who ringed the jailhouse straining for a peak at the condemned man. To their delight Hanline appeared, wearing a pair of white pantaloons, a black alpaca coat, white shirt and polished shoes. At 11:15 am the sheriff sprung the trap and Hanline dropped six and one half feet to his death.[653]

Hanline was the first white man to be executed by hanging in Bexar County.

Ake, Taylor
Born: circa 1861—Date of Death: 22 August 1879
Place: Travis County
Event: Legal Execution/Hanged

Taylor Ake, a black man, was found guilty of the assault and outrage of a German girl in July 1878. On Thursday, 22 August 1878, Ake scaled the gallows at Austin, denying his guilt to his final breath. When the trap was sprung Ake fell, his neck snapped, and all discussion on the matter was settled for eternity.[654]

Harris, Charley
Born: circa 1858—Date of Death: 29 August 1879
Place: Montague County
Event: Legal Execution/Hanged

Charley and John Harris lived together with their father, Charley Harris, Sr., on a farm fifteen miles east of Montague. For some reason the father had been telling Charley that his brother John wished to run him off and take his share of the farm and belongings. John was constantly deprecating Charley, making the father's story all the more believable. It is not known for certain if that was, in fact, John's plan but throughout the evidence presented in the newspaper accounts of the day it seems doubtful. In any case, the father convinced Charley to go to town and purchase some poison and put in John's milk. He did as the old man had suggested, but John did not drink the potion, thus avoiding death on that occasion.

Next, the father convinced Charley to get the shotgun and shoot John while he was feeding the horses. That plan failed as well, since there were visitors at the house that evening. The following morning, however, Charley did manage to shoot his brother, with the aforementioned shotgun, inflicting a wound in the man's chest near the heart. The wound was fatal.

The newspaper commentary claimed that Charley was a "weak minded" individual, or developmentally impaired as would be the politically correct contemporary equivalent. He had been used by his father to dispose of John. Either the father or John owned forty head of cattle, eight horses, and a great deal of land. From newspaper accounts it appears as though John was the true owner, and that the father wished to have him out of the way so as to take control of the inheritance and consummate a marriage with a local widow named Straum who had refused him, and refused to share her property with him. The elder Harris did in fact approach the widow Straum with a proposal of marriage shortly after John's murder.

Based in part on his own confession to the crime, the unfortunate fellow was tried and found guilty. Charley Harris was sentenced to hang.

The twenty-one year old Charley Harris was a slight built fellow, standing about six feet in height with delicate features apart from a coarse mouth. He had a "darling little wife" as he called her named Jessie Sims, who he lived with near Pilot Point. She died while he was incarcerated and before his execution.

Fully 5,000 persons assembled to witness the hanging. Harris appeared, festooned in a new black suit and vest, white shirt and black hat. He walked steadily up the gallows stairs with Sheriff Perryman. Once on the platform Harris delivered a brief speech to the crowd, acknowledging that he had not expected to see such an aggregation of men, women and children. At his request the hymn "In The Sweet Bye and Bye" was sung. Harris expressed his grief for his crime. The quintessential black cap was fitted, his hands and feet bound. In an instant Charley Harris Jr. dropped through the trap and was catapulted into eternity.

Pocket, Given Name Unknown
Born: (Unknown)—Date of Death: 12 September 1879
Place: Lavaca County
Event: Legal Execution/Hanged

According to one newspaper source, on Friday, 12 September 1879, a Sioux Indian named Pocket was hanged at Hallettsville for the murder of a black man named Frank Edwards. That crime had occurred in February 1878.[655] A crowd of several thousand men and women witnessed the event, which took place at the Shooting Match Grounds, now a city recreation park.

A more reliable source, however, claims that Pocket was hanged for murdering an Englishman named Leonard Hyde. Hyde was a white man who was born at Surrey, England on 28 December 1857, and had recently arrived in Texas.[656]

Lew B. Allen, an early cattleman from nearby Sweet Home, took a liking to Pocket, who he had met while driving cattle through the Indian Territory (Oklahoma). He persuaded the youth to return with him to his Lavaca County ranch where Pocket grew to manhood.

On 14 February 1878, while under the influence of ardent spirits, Pocket went on a rampage in Hallettsville, hollering and racing his horse through town. He went to the home of Frank Edwards, a former slave, and began to terrorize the Edwards women. Ultimately, Edwards knocked him off his feet and halted his advances. Pocket got up and left, but swore to return and kill Edwards.

After borrowing a pistol on his first stop he galloped to the L. D. Peterson ranch, about five miles west of town, where he asked for the loan of a shotgun, claiming that it was to "kill some turkeys he had seen near the road." Hyde, who was helping Peterson shuck corn, said he would go with Pocket and help him shoot the turkeys. Pocket got the shotgun, but instructed Hyde not to follow. When Hyde persisted, Pocket shot him in the head with the pistol, killing him instantly.

Pocket was arrested later and returned to Hallettsville to stand trial. A jury found him guilty and condemned him to death by hanging. After an appeal, based on two technicalities the original judgment was upheld.[657]

Surname Unknown, Esther
Born (Unknown)—Date of Death: 11 October 1879
Place: Dallas County
Event: Lynching/Shot

Surname Unknown, Charley
Born (Unknown)—Date of Death: 11 October 1879
Place: Dallas County
Event: Lynching/Shot

On Saturday, 11 October 1879, a band of forty disguised men went to the cabin of a black woman identified as Esther. The home was located on the Aldridge's Plantation. They demanded her son Charley. When she refused the men opened fire, shooting through the cabin door. An unidentified girl inside was wounded. Some freedmen inside returned fire and wounded one of the attackers. Eventually the door was forced open and Esther's family, along with a black man from a neighboring cabin, were seized. Several people managed to escape. Esther and her son Charley were shot to death. The newspaper reported several arrests were made.[658]

Davis, William "Bill"
Born: (Unknown)—Date of Death: 6 November 1879
Place: Caldwell County
Event: Legal Execution/Hanged

On Sunday, 20 October 1878, Bill Davis murdered Dolly Hudspeth. Davis was tried and convicted of the crime and sentenced to death. At about 2:00 pm on Thursday, 6 November 1879, that verdict was carried out. From his perch on the gallows Davis confessed to having committed the murder, thus setting his conscience straight for the hereafter.[659]

Toetel (Toettel), Julius
Born: circa 1847—Date of Death: 14 November 1879
Place: Grayson County
Event: Legal Execution/Hanged

Julius Toetel murdered Joseph A. Brenner. The incident took place at Brenner's own saloon in Denison at about midnight on Wednesday, 15 January 1879.

Toetel had been living in Denison for a few months and had been running up a whiskey bill at Brenner's saloon. Brenner presented the bill to Toetel. He refused to pay. Brenner became angry, and ordered Toetel to leave and to never return. On Tuesday, 15 January Toetel ignored Brenner's decree and returned. Brenner ordered him out. When he did not leave he was put out. At about 10:00 pm Toetel went to his boarding house, announcing that he was going to his room to sharpen his butcher knife and that he intended to "cut a man's heart out". True to his pledge, he went to his quarters, found a whetstone, sharpened his knife and went out onto the street looking for a fight. The time was about 11:00 pm. Toetel found a butcher shop still open. Fearing his weapon might not be in order he asked the butcher to sharpen it for him. When the blade was returned he told the butcher "If there was a dead man found next morning he might tell the people that Toetel killed him."

It was near midnight when Toetel returned to Brenner's saloon. Brenner was near the bar. Another man was seated at a table some distance across the room. Toetel went directly towards Brenner and a struggle began immediately. After a few moments Toetel dashed from the building. Brenner said he had been stabbed. Sure enough, he had, and he died soon afterward. Toetel was captured in the Indian Territory (Oklahoma) three days later.

Toetel was a Frenchman who had entered the country through New York. Soon after his arrival he had enlisted in the regular army and served six years. On discharged, he came to Texas. Toetel had been in Denison for seven years.

Julius Toetel was hanged in the jail yard. He made no confession. On the gallows he simply said, "I am ready." He was strangled to death.[660]

Brown, Andrew J.
Born: 13 June 1854—Date of Death: 21 November 1879
Place: Denton County
Event: Legal Execution/Hanged

Brown Jr., George W.
Born: 26 January 1852—Date of Death: 21 November 1879
Place: Denton County
Event: Legal Execution/Hanged

Andrew J. Brown is believed to have been a member of a secret organization known as "The Law and Order League." This group is thought to have been responsible for a number of mysterious slay, including the murder of Robert S. Morrow for which Brown was tried and convicted. Members of the "Law and Order League" pledged to aid officers in enforcing the laws, especially local lawmen, and to clean up their town and county of crime. In many instances their vigilante efforts wound up stepping afoul of the law.

Morrow had settled on a pre-emption claim in the neighborhood of the Browns, on Farmers creek, in Montague County. He lived on good terms with the Browns. The brothers allegedly killed Dr. McClain on Sunday, 10 May 1876, at Farmer's Creek in Montague County. On the day McClain was killed George Brown, Jr., Andrew Brown, a man named Sampson and another named John Barrass were seen coming towards and passing out of sight into a ravine near the banks of which the deceased was killed. A witness saw McClain walking ahead of him on a bridle-path, heading toward the ford of the creek at about the same time that he noticed George Brown and his companions enter the ravine. McClain walked about one hundred yards further when, according to the witness, Brown's group rose up from behind the bank and shot McClain. McClain immediately fell and commenced struggling as though he was in agony. A minute later a witness saw George Brown, Jr., run out of the ambush and shoot McClain with a pistol.

A change of venue from Montague to Denton County was obtained. Andrew and George Brown, Jr., were convicted and sentenced to death. On Thursday, 21 November 1879, the execution took place outside and immediately north of the jail at Denton. The sheriff read the death warrant and the governor's refusal to commute the sentence to imprisonment for life. When the sheriff had finished Andrew Brown refused to speak. George Brown addressed the crowd. In a five minutes speech during which he said that he had made a statement for publication which would show that he was not guiltier than others who are at large.

Reverend Dr. Grafton of the Cumberland Presbyterian Church read the fourteenth chapter of Job (Job 14:14, "If a man dies, shall he live again"). Two hymns were sung. The assembled masses joined in.

Andrew's father, who was the only family member present, left the gallows before the trap was sprung. Handshaking was indulged in for several minutes. At 2:10 pm the ropes were adjusted and the black caps put on. At 2:18 pm Sheriff R. H. Hopkins cut the rope and the trapdoor was sprung. Andrew died of strangulations eleven minutes afterwards. George died in only nine minutes. His neck had been broken in the fall. The execution was witnessed by seven thousand people.[661] Once the festivities had ended, "...a knife fight broke out between the blacks and whites..." [662]

Andrew Brown was survived by his wife Elizabeth J. Bettie Hart and three children. He is buried at the Oakwood Cemetery in Denton. George Brown was survived by his wife Nancy Elizabeth Gibson. He is buried at the Oakwood Cemetery in Denton.

Uvalte, Cresencio

Born: (Unknown)—Date of Death: 28 November 1879
Place: Webb County
Event: Legal Execution/Hanged

Cresencio Uvalte, a Mexican man, was hanged at Laredo on Friday, 28 November 1879. He dropped from the gallows nine feet, breaking his neck and expiring in seven minutes.

Uvalte, a shepherd, had murdered his wife after suspecting her of infidelity. One day while she was washing clothes at a pool he hit her over the head with a stick, knocking her into the water where he held her head under until she expired. Next Uvalte mutilated her body with a knife in a "fearsome manner."[663]

Myers Jr., Samuel Houston "Sam"
Born: circa 1859—Date of Death: 19 March 1880
Place: Johnson County
Event: Legal Execution/Hanged

Samuel Houston Myers Sr. and his first wife Martha "Patsy" Wallace Myers came to Texas with their six children in 1851. Patsy died in 1853. Myers Sr. married Cynthia Ann Bales in 1854.

When Myers Sr. passed he left Mary two tracts of land totaling 183 acres with the proviso that the land be return to his estate should Mary remarry. In due course Mary wed a man named Hester on 4 January 1877, but continued to occupy the property. That spawned a great deal of anger among the many Myers descendents who, on balance, believed that they had not received their fair share of their father's estate.

The situation came to a head on the evening of Wednesday, 21 February 1877. Mary Hester was sitting at the supper table, surrounded by her family, when an assassin slipped up to the open window and shot her. The 2 March 1877, edition of the *Daily Fort Worth Standard,* added the gruesome commentary"...blowing off her head and spattering her brains in her husband's face." The following day a man named John Bailes found tracks leading from Hester's house to the home of James Bowden. Bowden was married to one of the Myers daughters. Bowden was arrested and indicted for murder.

While in prison Bowden was taken from his cell and placed on a horse with a rope around his neck, presumably to encourage speed and truthfulness, while being questioned by Sheriff John C. Brown. He confessed that Sam Houston Myers Jr. had actually fired the shot that killed Mary, and that he and Thomas Jefferson Myers had helped him plan to murder Mary.

Subsequently, Thomas Jefferson Myers was imprisoned in Cleburne on 13 July 1877. When he went to trial, Judge W. H. Wood said, "There is no question but that this affiant is guilty." Myers was sentenced to death by hanging in June 1878. His attorney appealed, claiming that Judge Wood and a Judge Leavitt inappropriately discussed the trial outside of the courtroom. The attorney's venue-change request was denied. Myers was re-tried, and once again found guilty. This time he received a sentence of life in prison with hard labor. Myers' attorney's second venue-change request proved successful and Myers was tried a third time, this time in Hood County. During that trial, Myers was allowed to call witnesses who vouched for his activities and those of Sam Myers, Jr. the night of the murder, testimony that had been quashed in the Johnson County trials. After three years in prison and as many trials, jurors found Thomas Jefferson Myers not guilty and set him free. It is not clear if he was innocent or if he simply had the better lawyer.

Sam Myers, Jr. was not so lucky. Bowden's wife Mollie initially testified that Bowden fired the shot that killed Mary Hester. Bowden called her into his cell and convinced her to change her story and say Sam fired the fatal shot. Based on his sister's testimony, Sam, eighteen at the time, was indicted for the murder of his stepmother.

Sam's trial was set for 13 July 1877, but was postponed four times until 1880. He was found guilty and sentenced to be hanged. That verdict was carried out on Friday, 19 March 1880, at

Cleburne.[664] A black cap pulled over his head, rope adjusted and the word "all ready" given the trap was sprung at 2:45 pm and Myers dropped about five feet to his death.

On his deathbed James Bowden confessed to the murder of Mary Myers Hester.

Sam Myers, Jr. is buried at the Myers Cemetery at Alvarado.

Henry, John
Born: (Unknown)—Date of Death: 26 March 1880
Place: Navarro County
Event: Legal Execution/Hanged

John Henry, a black man, was hanged at Corsicana for the murder of his friend, Alonzo Whitman. That incident had taken place on 8 January 1879. On that day Henry, along with Jim Young and several other black men were amusing themselves with an ox whip at Young's home. Whitman came up to the fence and engaged in an argument of some sort with Young. Young tried to hit Whitman with an ax, but was prevented from doing so. Whitman then tried to cut Young with a knife, but Young ran from him down the road about fifty yards and stopped, picking up a stick and facing off with Whitman. Friends tried to intervene and separate the pair of combatants. Meanwhile, Henry had run to the house and got a gun. He dashed to the fence, leaned over and announced, "Clear the track God damn it, I'll settle that fuss." The crowd parted like the Red Sea as Henry fired. Whitman took a few steps and dropped over dead, whereupon Henry proudly announced, "I told you God damn it, I would fix it." Yes indeed, he truly had.

Hoping to expiate his crime in the eyes of the Lord, on the Sunday preceding his hanging Henry was publically baptized in front of a large crowd of both black and white spectators. His execution, on Friday 26 March 1880, was private. Rather than the conventional gallows structure the apparatus for Henry's date with the executioner consisted of only a rope and pulleys, designed to simplify the procedure. Although a large crowd gathered outside the jail only a handful of persons were allowed access to the actual event. At about 3:00 pm Henry was brought forth, wearing a new black broadcloth suite. When asked if he wished to speak he said, "no, I have nothing to say and am ready to take my portion." After a short pause Henry completed the thought by adding, "I am willing to go." When asked by Reverend Z. Pardee if he wished to make a clean breast he replied, "I've nothing to confess."

At about 3:50 pm Deputy Sheriff Mallery cut the rope that operated the devise which instantly jerked the rope around Henry's neck tight and thrust him skyward with a start, hoisting him about four and one half feet in the air. Henry was pronounced dead several minutes later.[665]

Towles, Allen
Born: (Unknown)—Date of Death: 26 March 1880
Place: Freestone County
Event: Legal Execution/Hanged

On Sunday night, 21 December 1879, Allen Towles, a black man, had been out on the town drinking heavily. When he returned home to his wife and two children she had already retired, thus she was not awake to greet him. Towles was enraged. At the same time, however, his wife was righteously indignant at his inebriated condition. The couple began to quarrel. That led to Towles pulling his large caliber pistol and firing five shots at point blank range into his wife's body, so close that the powder burns set her clothing on fire. Afterwards he went to the home of his neighbors and made some excuse as to the gunfire, then returned home and went to bed, sleeping until well into the morning. Neighbors alerted officers who visited the Towles' home the following morning. Towles offered no excuse other than that he had been too drunk to be held accountable for his actions.

Not surprisingly, a jury found Towles guilty of the brutal murder and sentenced him to death. On Friday, 26 March 1880, a large crowd assembled outside the jail in hopes of catching a glimpse of the hanging of Towles. The event was to be private, held within the confines of the jail building. The condemned man had been spending his time while awaiting his execution reading Thomas Paine's *Age Of Reason*, rejecting the Bible as "...no better authority than an old almanac." Friends and relatives compelled him to accept Jesus, but he refused, claiming that, "If there is a hell I may have to go there." Towles added, "I will be sure to meet my jury if I do."[666]

At 2:14 pm the drop fell and Towles was propelled directly to the life beyond, presumably to hell as he had foretold.

Knight, Richard
Born: (Unknown)—Date of Death: 16 April 1880
Place: Robertson County
Event: Legal Execution/Hanged

Richard Knight, a black man who also went by the alias Bill Walker, was a most fearsome criminal, drunkard and thief.[667] His victim, whose name is never mentioned in newspaper reports, was black man, married with seven or eight children. The man had labored hard in the fields and saved enough to purchase some land to erect a cabin on the property for his family.

On Friday, 16 April 1880, Knight scaled the gallows at Calvert, along with the sheriff, a handful of deputies and ministers. He was dressed neatly in a long black gown and black cap. Knight turned to the crowd and bid farewell. A 2:20 pm the trap was sprung and Knight dropped to his death. His neck was broken. Knight hung for twenty-six minutes then was cut down and handed over for burial.[668]

Noftsinger, Lucius
Born: circa 1850—Date of Death: 30 April 1880
Place: Cooke County
Event: Legal Execution/Hanged

Lucius Noftsinger, a thirty-year old store clerk, was tried and convicted of murder.

At 4:00 pm on Friday, 30 April 1880, Noftsinger ascended the gallows stairs at Janesville amid ever increasing murmurs of sympathy on the part of the crowd. An estimated 10,000 souls were in attendance for the highly contested hanging. As the sheriff fastened the hangman's rope to the beam an ineffectual attempt was made to cut it in two. Once repairs were made the procedure continued. Members of the crowd rushed the gallows in an attempt to free Noftsinger, but their effort was halted by the sheriff and his deputies, all of whom were brandishing pistols and shotguns. Women and children were trampled as the aggressing men were turned and dashed to the rear of the horde.

Once quiet had been restored Noftsinger spoke, claiming innocence. At that, a second unsuccessful attempt was made to free him by the gathering throng. At about 4:25 pm, black cap pulled down over his head, hands and feet bound, the latch was sprung and Noftsinger dropped to his death. He was declared dead after about nine minutes.

Noftsingers remains were shipped to Virginia for burial.[669]

Ramirez, Maria Inez
Born: (Unknown)—Date of Death: 1 May 1880
Place: Collin County
Event: Lynched/Burned to Death

Ramirez, Refugio
Born: (Unknown)—Date of Death: 1 May 1880
Place: Collin County
Event: Lynched/Burned to Death

Ramirez, Silvestre Garcia
Born: (Unknown)—Date of Death: 1 May 1880
Place: Collin County
Event: Lynched/Burned to Death

Refugio Ramirez, his wife Silvester and daughter Maria were all burned to death for witchcraft at Collin County.[670]

Capps, Isham
Born: circa 1850—Date of Death: 7 May 1880
Place: Tarrant County
Event: Legal Execution/Hanged

Isham Capps, a black soldier, was tried and convicted of the outrage of a white woman named

Thornton. The assault took place in February. Two other black men, Ben Mosely and Nathan House had been arrested and jailed along with Capps, but in a confession made at the occasion of his hanging Capps admitted that he was the evildoer, and that the other men had no part in it. Capps also confessed that on earlier occasions he had fantasized about, and planned to have his way with, Mrs. Thornton.

A scaffold was erected about a mile from town on the river bottom. Thousands of spectators turned out for the hanging. Farmers came in out of their fields, shops were closed and families came in wagons decked out in their best attire. Capps rode to his execution in the back of a wagon, seated on his own coffin. In a seemingly fitting gesture, a hangman's noose that had been fashioned by the victim's father was placed around his neck.

At about 2:00 pm Capps, the sheriff and deputies, along with two black clergymen ascended the scaffold. There was perfect stillness while Capps addressed the crowd and atoned to his maker for his crimes, saying that he was perfectly satisfied and willing to die for his crime. At 2:20 pm the latch was sprung and Capps dropped ten feet to his death. His neck had been broken.[671] Capps swung into eternity without incident.[672]

Capps is buried in the Potters Field.

Quarles, Henry
Born: circa 1850—Date of Death: 11 June 1880
Place: Harris County
Event: Legal Execution/Hanged

Henry Quarles, a black barber, was tried and convicted of murdering his wife. He was sentenced to be executed by hanging.

On the morning of his impending execution, Friday, 11 June 1880, Reverend J. J. Clements held services in Quarles' cell. At about noon Quarles emerged from the jail and mounted the gallows. He made a brief statement bequeathing his belongings to his illegitimate child when the lad turned eighteen. Both the child and his/her mother were with Quarles that morning. At 1:50 pm a black cap was pulled down over his head and adjusted. The trap was sprung and Quarles dropped seven feet. The fall had not broken his neck, and he died of strangulation while in a fit of contortions.[673]

Quarles was buried next to his murdered wife. The location is unknown.

Howard, Samuel S.
Born: (Unknown)—Date of Death: 18 June 1880
Place: Bastrop County
Event: Legal Execution/Hanged

Samuel Howard was tried and convicted of the murder of Aleck Farmer. That killing had taken place seven years earlier, in 1873.

After consuming a meal of primarily vegetables at half past noon on Friday, 18 June 1880, a staunchly unrepentant Howard dressed in a neat black suit and made his way to the gallows. The walk began at about 1:00 pm, and covered a distance of about fifty yards from the courthouse to the structure where he ascended the steps, all the time chewing tobacco with avidity. The death sentence was read. Aleck Farmer's brother addressed Howard, compelling him to tell the truth in his last few minutes of life before meeting his maker. Howard simply replied, "I did not do it." At a quarter past the hour the black cap was pulled down over his head, his hands and feet bound and the hangman's noose place around his neck. The latch was sprung and Howard dropped from the platform. His neck was broken. Howard was declared dead twenty minutes after the hanging.[674]

Carter, English
Born: circa 1858—Date of Death: 2 July 1880
Place: Walker County
Event: Legal Execution/Hanged

English Carter, also known as L. B. Jones, was tried and found guilty of the murder of W. K. Spaulding. That incident took place near the town of Dodge on 24 July 1879. According to newspaper reports Carter, a sawmill worker, rode up to Spaulding's house professing friendship then shot him at the front gate as he departed. He was sentenced to be executed by hanging for his crime.

Shortly after 2:00 pm on Friday, 2 July 1880, Carter was hung at Huntsville. A large crowd had gathered to witness the event.[675]

Doran, George
Born: circa 1858—Date of Death: 20 August 1880
Place: Navarro County
Event: Legal Execution/Hanged

George Doran, a twenty-year old white man from Indiana, was executed on Friday, 20 August 1880, at Corsicana for the murder of William Fitzsimmons. That killing occurred on Sunday, 1 June 1879.

Both Doran and Fitzsimmons were in the home of a black woman of easy virtue named Josie Cash. Apparently the two were vying for her attention, with Fitzsimmons making the better progress at the matter. On that evening Miss Cash was feeling poorly. Doran suggested that she pull the sheet over her head and remain in bed. When she awoke she discovered Doran straddling Fitzsimmons, stabbing him repeatedly with a knife. Cash fled, screaming "murderer." She sought protection at a neighbor's house where Doran found her, declaring, "Well, I have settled him," meaning poor Fitzsimmons.

Officer Congers arrested Doran soon after. Fitzsimmons, who was found lying in the street near the St. Charles Restaurant clinging to life, in a pool of blood with his bowels protruding from the gaping gash in his abdomen, died a painful death soon after.

Doran was tried and found guilty. He struggled desperately to secure a pardon or acquittal, claiming that the only evidence against him had come from an old black "sporting woman." At 2:50 pm the jail yard was cleared and Doran brought forth to the gallows by Sheriff Dunn, who said, "This is the saddest duty I have ever had to perform, and God grant it may be the last of the kind ever required at my hands." Father Chandy prayed a short supplication as the noose was affixed around Doran's neck. The trap was sprung, and after a few convulsive shudders Doran was declared dead at 3:12 pm. His body was given over to members of the Catholic Church for burial. [676]

Burks, J. Lynesfield
Born: circa 1839—Date of Death: 27 August 1880
Place: McLennan County
Event: Legal Execution/Hanged

Lynesfield Burks, a forty-one year old white man, had moved to Waco from Tennessee. His wife had passed and he had hired Mrs. Mary McBee as his housekeeper. Burks lived at Robinson, about six miles from town. On the night of 20 August 1870, Mrs. McBee's nine-year old daughter Sarah was outraged and handled roughly in the doing by Burks. Mrs. McBee, who by this time was also Burks's paramour, became suspicious and called in a doctor who informed her of the cause of the young girl's and the young woman's serious condition.

Both Mrs. McBee and Burks were arrested and charged with the crime. McBee was released when her daughter refused to testify against her. Burks was found guilty and sentenced to death. That verdict was carried out on 27 August 1880, when Burks kept his appointment with the executioner at Waco.[677]

Wright, Allen
Born: circa 1858—Date of Death: 27 August 1880
Place: Dallas County
Event: Legal Execution/Hanged

Allen Wright, a black rail-splitter, was charged and convicted of murder. He was sentenced to death by hanging.

Wright's sentence was to be carried out at Dallas on 20 August 1880. Governor Oran M. Roberts granted him a one week reprieve, delaying the inevitable until Friday, 27 August 1880, when Wright's luck finally ran out.[678]

Sheppard, Warren
Born: circa 1858—Date of Death: 12 November 1880
Place: Montgomery County
Event: Legal Execution/Hanged

According to the testimony of two witnesses, on Friday, 22 March 1878, Levy Comer and two black men named Sam Jones and Claiborne Chaney were chopping wood about a mile from Winkler's sawmill which was located between Montgomery and Willis. Sheppard, a black man, approached Comer. He was armed with a double barrel shotgun, and announced, "let us compromise this matter." Almost without pause Sheppard shot Comer twice, killing him.

So far as a motive for Sheppard's actions, the evidence was less clear than the murder itself. On one occasion Sheppard had apparently pulled Comer out of bed and beat him. There was also a rumor held forth that Comer and Sheppard had a difficulty over an intimacy with white women near the railroad. It was claimed that Sheppard had made advances toward the female and Comer knew of it, thus he was a dangerous witness against Sheppard.

A gallows was erected in a field about a quarter of a mile east of Montgomery so as to facilitate a private hanging, constructed so as to shield the view of the body of the hanged man once he had fallen through the trapdoor. At about 2:00 pm Sheriff Ashe and Deputy Simonton escorted Sheppard from the jail. He mounted the gallows by means of a ladder. When allowed to speak Sheppard said that he had surely gone wrong, but believed that he had been saved and forgiven. Reverend Lewis Hunter then read a hymn that was then loudly sung by most in attendance. Hunter followed with several verses of scripture, then knelt and prayed with Sheppard. At 2:27 pm the sheriff placed the black cap on Sheppard's head and adjusted the noose, while all the time the condemned man continued to mutter supplications. At half past two the latch was pulled and Sheppard dropped eight feet, breaking his neck. He was pronounced dead after ten minutes. At 3:10 pm the body was cut down and turned over for burial.[679]

Williams, Albert
Born (Unknown)—Date of Death: 31 January 1881
Place: Colorado County
Event: Lynching/Shot

On Monday, 31 January 1881, Albert Williams, a black man, was arrested for horse theft at Columbus. Soon afterward, Williams was taken from the constable by person's unknown and shot to death.[680]

One Unidentified Man
Born: (Unknown)—Date of Death: February 1881
Place: El Paso County
Event: Lynching/Hanged

According to a claim made in Carrigan's book *Forgotten Dead* an unidentified man who was suspected of having committed a murder was lynched at El Paso. No corroboration of this incident has been located.[681]

Janrequez, Given Name Unknown
Born: (Unknown)—Date of Death: 13 April 1881
Place: El Paso County
Event: Lynching/Murdered

Sanchez, Given Name Unknown
Born: (Unknown)—Date of Death: 13 April 1881
Place: El Paso County
Event: Lynching/Murdered

In an apparently related but unverified incident, two Mexican men named Sanchez and Janrequez were murdered in a conflict over land.[682]

Wood, Dick
Born (Unknown)—Date of Death: 26 June 1881
Place: Dimmit County
Event: Lynching/Shot

On Sunday, 26 June 1881, the Dimmit County sheriff arrested the notorious desperado Dick Wood near Carrizo Springs. Vigilantes soon took Wood from the sheriff's custody and shot him to death. According to newspaper sources of the day Wood's killing was "in consequence of cattle transactions." Some sources claim that Wood was shot while others indicate that he was hanged. In either case he met his end on 26 June 1881.[683]

Thompson, Adam
Born: circa 1855—Date of Death: 1 July 1881
Place: Dallas County
Event: Legal Execution/Hanged

On Saturday, 1 July 1876, West Pollard and Adam Thompson, both black men, broke into the grocery store of an old German man named Shumaker. The business was located on the highway about six miles west of Dallas. Shumaker, who was not married, lived at the store and was startled awake by the sound of breaking glass as the pair of robbers burst into the building. The old German man was treated cruelly by the pair of able bodied young men, who battered him about at will as he put up his last and perhaps most intense battle for life. Using the same rock that they had used to break the door glass and gain entry to the store the men savagely battered Shumaker, leaving his mutilated corpse lying in the backyard of his own enterprise. The walls and furniture inside the store were spattered with his blood from the fierce battle for life that had taken place.

Pollard and Thompson ransacked the shop, taking a small box in which Shumaker had kept his meager earnings. Their tracks led to a cotton field about a mile away where that container was discovered. Suspicion immediately fell on Thompson, and his confederate Pollard, who had been seen in the area the same day. When arrested Thompson had in his possession a door key and a counterfeit half dollar known to have belonged to the murdered man.

Thompson was tried and convicted of the murder, but owing to the fact that the case was handed over to the jury on a Saturday night and the verdict returned on Sunday his lawyer filed an exception and was granted a new trial. The verdict in that adjudication, as predicted, came out the same. Thompson was sentenced to death for his crime, but had bartered for a few more years of life with his lawyer's trickery.

Although the gallows was erected within the confines of the jail yard to restrict viewing, hundreds managed to secure elevated positions around the perimeter to see the event. Thompson could see the structure from his cell window, and asked the jailers to show him how it worked. When they humored him, and demonstrated the trap being sprung, he fainted dead away his curiosity having been fully satisfied. When he awakened he admitted for the first time that he understood the gravity of his situation.

At about 1:30 pm on Friday, 1 July 1881, Thompson left his cell, bidding farewell to the "boys" as he passed on his approach to the gallows. He was decked out in a black suit, lacing gaiters and white gloves. Thompson appeared calm as he professed to the last having made his peace with God and appeared quite moved by the singing and prayer of the black preacher and the women who led the group in "Savior Hear My Humble Prayer." When asked to speak he said nothing more than goodbye, "I want everybody to be good. Farewell vain world." At 1:58 pm Sheriff Jones sprung the trap, this time with Thompson standing on the door. He was dead in six minutes.[684]

Walker, Isaiah
Born: (Unknown)—Date of Death: 28 July 1881
Place: Gonzales County
Event: Legal Execution/Hanged

Isaiah Walker, a black man, was hanged at Gonzales for the murder of his wife. That incident had taken place a few months earlier.[685]

Delno, Charles

Born: (Unknown)—Date of Death: August 1881

Place: Orange County

Event: Lynching/Shot

Delno, O. L.

Born: (Unknown)—Date of Death: August 1881

Place: Orange County

Event: Lynching/Hanged

Garsom (Garcon), Robert

Born: (Unknown)—Date of Death: August 1881

Place: Orange County

Event: Lynching/Hanged

Saxon, Samuel

Born: circa 1861—Date of Death: August 1881

Place: Orange County

Event: Lynching/Shot

Four Unidentified Black Men

Born: (Unknown)—Date of Death: August 1881

Place: Orange County

Event: Lynching/Shot

The incident leading up to the lynching of these eight black men began sometime around 1 August 1881, when O. L. Delno, a notorious outlaw, escaped from jail at Orange. Detective Wood, who gave chase and came upon Delno in the woods, discovered his absence. Wood ordered Delno to stop, which he did not do, so Wood shot him. The wound was not fatal and Delno was returned to the jail. Delno was a member of a gang, some of who were also in the jail.

An angry mob demanded that Sheriff George W. Michael hand over Wood to them for punishment. Obviously Sheriff Michael declined, stating that Wood was simply doing his duty and claiming that Wood had anticipated the repudiation and had fled. Actually Michael had aided in hiding Wood until the event blew over. The plan was a success and Wood escaped harm. However, the following day gang members swore that they would get even with Michael for his actions in aiding Wood.

Expecting trouble Sheriff Michael recruited a group of temporary deputies from the amble supply of plainsmen in town. His plan thwarted their plot for a time, but the mob staged a fight at a saloon near the edge of town to draw Michael's attention. The gang succeeded in drawing out Sheriff Michael by breaking practically everything that was fragile and setting the structure on fire. As Sheriff Michael and his posse approached, a man named Sam Saxon leaped from cover and distracted Michael's attention. Michael gave chase. Saxon led him into an ambush involving Charles Delno, Dug Harris, Bob Saxon and a number of black members of the gang. A volley of shots was fired, striking Michael several times. He was returned to the jail, sporting multiple bullet wounds and bleeding profusely.

A public meeting was immediately held to discuss the attempted assassination of Michael. A resolution was adopted to lynch every member of the gang. A group of 150 citizens was appointed to carry out the plan. Soon after four black members of the outfit were caught, taken to a public place and shot to death. Next to meet his fate was Robert Garsom (Garcon). He was captured, questioned, and with hands and feet bound hung from the limb of a tree. When he had just about suffocated he was cut down and questioned again. When no information was obtained Garsom was, once again, hoisted into the tree. This process was repeated no less than five times over the course of an hour or more. Finally the man relented and gave up the names of his confederates. After doing so he was strung up a 6th time, and perhaps much to his surprise left dangling until the last breath of life had left his body.

On the information obtained from Garsom, Charles Delno and Sam Saxon were captured and jailed. Citizens decided almost unanimously to lynch them. Charles Delno and Saxon taken into the street for the proceedings where they wept and pled for that their lives be spared. While the vigilante posse waited for ropes to be prepared Delno and Saxon decided to take their chances and make a run for it. Rather than attempt to stop the fleeing men the crowd opened up like Moses parting the Red Sea, forming a path for the pair to escape down. As they did the onlookers opened fire and cut the escaping prisoners down. Their bullet pierced bodies were left where they fell and the crow dispersed.

The last of the group, O. L. Delno was arraigned and asked if he could provide any reason why he too should not be immediately dispatched to join his recently departed companions. He was unable to do so. With a hangman's noose around his neck Delno was dragged down the street and lynched from a nearby telegraph pole.

Their business now concluded the vigilante committee congratulated themselves on a job well done and quietly disbanded. A general celebration then began, the scope of which might lead an uninformed passerby to believe that there was a jubilee of some sort taking place. It seems that several additional "suspicious characters" also disappeared during the excitement.[686]

The only member of the group for which personal information has been located is Samuel Saxon. Saxon, a mulatto sawmill worker, who was survived by his mother Nancy.[687]

Williams, Tom
Born: circa 1860—Date of Death: 23 September 1881
Place: Rusk County
Event: Legal Execution/Hanged

Tom Williams, a black man, was hanged at Rusk on Friday, 23 September 1881, for the murder of Mr. Tinkle. The killing had taken place during the fall of 1880. Williams had made several unsuccessful appeals, culminating with his trip to the hangman...late but no less fatal.[688]

Lightfoot, John
Born (Unknown)—Date of Death: 8 October 1881
Place: Coryell County
Event: Lynching/Hanged

On Thursday, 6 October 1881, the constable of the Sugar Loaf precinct arrested John Lightfoot for entering the home of a man named Williamson and stealing some personal articles. The justice of the peace ordered him remanded to the county jail at Gatesville. Heavy rains on Saturday, 8 October 1881, kept the constable from transporting Lightfoot to the county jail, so Lightfoot was taken to his home under guard and kept there. At about 10:00 pm an armed mob removed Lightfoot and spirited him off to places unknown.

On Sunday, 9 October 1881, travelers observed Lightfoot hanging by a rope from a tree along side the road. An inquest was conducted, after which the lifeless body of Lightfoot was cut down and buried near the tree on which he had met his end.[689]

Post, Jack
Born: 27 October 1852—Date of Death: 28 October 1881
Place: Young County
Event: Legal Execution/Hanged

G. B. McDermot was a farmer, living a quiet life about sixteen miles southwest of Graham. In October 1879 he suddenly disappeared. The two Post boys, Jack and Nelson, reported that McDermot had left the country after selling his belongings to them. Mrs. McDermot was away visiting at the time and knew nothing of any such plan on her husband's part. When she returned things looked suspicious to her. She had the Post boys arrested, along with a cohort named Smith who was a renter at the Post place.

In November 1879 the body of Mr. McDermot was discovered in a shallow grave located not far from the farmhouse where hogs had been mutilating it.

The Post boys went to trial. Jack was tried and convicted of the murder. In spite of the fact that all of the evidence against him was purely circumstantial he drew the death sentence. At his trial he acted as if insane, gesticulating wildly while being held down in his chair by officers. Once the sentence had been read and he was removed from the courtroom he attempted an escape, which failed.

When it came time for his hanging Jack was calm, walking quietly with the guards to the gallows at about 1:00 pm on Friday, 28 October 1881. His mother and sister, both frantic with grief, were in attendance to see their boy off. At about 2:00 pm a wagon carrying his coffin transported Post to the gallows. Seeing the casket he commented, "I guess this is my box." When his time came to speak he said little, reinforcing his view that they were hanging the wrong man, but adding that it would do little good to protest at that point.

At the prescribed moment the trap was sprung. Post's noose slipped around in front of his head as he fell, requiring the hangman and the sheriff to hoist him up and try again, all to the horror of onlookers. The latch was reloaded and tripped once again. This time the drop was a success. Post was left to hang for forty minutes to be certain of his death. Fortunately his mother and sister had bid him farewell at the jail, thus being spared the gruesome spectacle of his protracted death.[690]

Post is buried at the Old Eastside Cemetery at Graham. [691]

Surname Unknown, "Russian Bill"
Born (Unknown)—Date of Death: circa November 1881
Place: Unknown
Event: Lynching/Hanged

According to newspaper reports of the day a man identified only as "Russian Bill" was hanged for being a cattle rustler. The incident took place in about November of 1881.[692] It is possible that the person identified by this source was actually William Rogers "Russian Bill" Tattenbaum who claimed to be Russian nobility. Bill, who turned to the outlaw way, was eventually hanged in the barroom of the Shakespeare Hotel in Tombstone, Arizona.

Unidentified White Man
Born: (Unknown)—Date of Death: circa 1882
Place: McLennan County
Event: Lynched/Hanged

According to this unverified source, an unidentified white man is said to have been lynched for horse theft by parties unknown.[693]

White, D.C.
Born: circa 1845—Date of Death: 2 February 1882
Place: Van Zandt County
Event: Legal Execution/Hanged

D.C. White, a white man, was executed at Willis Point on Thursday, 2 February 1882, for the murder of a peddler named George Conquest.

Hundreds of people flocked to see the event. White protested his innocence to the end.[694] In a bizarre twist of events, on 11 February 1882, the *Times Picayune* of New Orleans published an article claiming that White had made a complete confession, in writing, and given it to his attorney with the provision that it was not to be released until after his death.

White is buried at the Hillcrest Cemetery at Canton.[695] His tombstone is dated 3 February.

Thompson, Miles
Born: (Unknown)—Date of Death: 18 February 1882
Place: Austin County
Event: Legal Execution/Hanged

Miles Thompson, "...an ignorant and brutal Negro..." as described in an article by the *Standard* of Clarksville, Texas in their 24 February 1882, was hanged at Belleville on Saturday, 18 February 1882, for the outrage of Mrs. Johnson and the murder of her father who was trying to prevent Thompson's escape.[696]

Gaitan, Quirius
Born: (Unknown)—Date of Death: 9 June 1882
Place: Cameron County
Event: Legal Execution/Hanged

On the night of Saturday, 13 August 1881, Quirius Gaitan attended a fandango put on by Ramon Villareal. The part was near Brownsville. Gaitan, along with two companions, swaggered about the ballroom and, at one point stepped on the foot of a man named Lux Contreras. Contreras, annoyed by Gaitan's clumsiness and breach of decorum commented, "Are you driving a cart sir?" Gaitan, angered by the statement replied, "Don't you like it?" Contreras responded, "Why, how should I like it sir?" Rather than let the matter lie Gaitan replied, "Take that then and see how you like it" as he thrust a knife into Contreras' back. Contreras staggered a few feet, collapsed and died. Obviously he did not "like it."[697]

Gaitan fled but was soon captured, seriously wounding the police officer who arrested him. He was charged, tried and convicted of the murder. The sentenced was death.

On Friday, 9 June 1882, Gaitan was hanged at Brownsville. The scaffold, located in the open lot in front of the courthouse, was guarded by at least forty deputy sheriffs. An immense crowd that was comprised largely of Mexicans was gathered to witness the hanging. Gaitan died game. He stepped to the fore and addressed the crowd in Spanish. At the prescribed moment the hangman, concealed in a box so as to mask his identity, sprung the trap and Gaitan dropped five feet to his death.[698]

Aguilar, Pablo
Born: (Unknown)—Date of Death: 28 July 1882
Place: Webb County
Event: Lynching/Shot

Gomez, Pedro
Born: (Unknown)—Date of Death: 28 July 1882
Place: Webb County
Event: Lynching/Shot

On or about Friday, 28 July 1882, a fight broke out amongst a group of Mexicans at Mount Fernadez near Laredo. Gomez was shot dead by the crowd. Aguilar protested the lack of fair play in the brawl. As a reward, he was shot and killed for registering his grouse. One report claimed that whites had killed Gomez. The same crowd killed Aguilar when he tried to defend Gomez.[699]

Larque, Frank "Mexican Frank"
Born: (Unknown)—Date of Death: 28 July 1882
Place: Oldham County
Event: Lynching/

C. B. "Cape" Willingham was the first sheriff of Oldham County. He was elected on 12 January 1881. Sheriff Willingham appointed Henry W. McCullough as Constable of Precinct One. On 1 June 1882, Willingham asked and received permission to appoint McCullough as a deputy sheriff and as city marshal of Tascosa. He was paid $25 per month.

On 17 July 1882, McCullough attempted to arrest Frank "Mexican Frank" Larque (name also reported as Larqus, Larques and Largus) for a gambling violation. The incident took place at the Jenkins and Donnelly Saloon and Dance Hall in Tascosa. Because Larque was not going to be taken to jail so he was not ordered to remove his pistol from his holster. In an unanticipated and "trick" move, Larque fired the revolver at McCullough while the weapon was still holstered, hitting the lawman in the stomach and killing him.

Larque fled towards New Mexico Territory but was quickly captured. Newspaper of the day reported the posse lynched him.

He was convicted on 12 September 1882, and sentenced to twenty-two years in the state prison. According to unverified sources, however, Larque is said to have been murdered at Tascosa by person or persons unknown.[700]

Porter, George

Born (Unknown)—Date of Death: 2 August 1882
Place: Lampasas County
Event: Lynching/Shot

On Wednesday, 2 August 1882, a mob of twenty-five men went to the camp of J. P. Higgins, a cattleman in the county, and took a man named George Porter under their control. They shot him several times, resulting in his death. Newspaper accounts claimed that he was mobbed for horse theft, and to his discredit had the stolen animals in him possession at the time of the incident.[701]

Agirer, Augustine

Born: (Unknown)—Date of Death: 8 August 1882
Place: Travis County
Event: Lynching/Shot

According to unverified sources, Augustine Agirer is said to have been shot to death at Oatmanville for attempting to take a white man to court.[702]

Thomas, Chess

Born: (Unknown)—Date of Death: 11 August 1882
Place: Anderson County
Event: Legal Execution/Hanged

Chess Thomas and another man named Henry Micheaux had sworn out an affidavit against a fellow named Houston McMeans for unlawful gaming. McMeans went to trial and was found guilty. The court slapped him with a heavy fine. Soon after and in a drunker state McMeans swore an oath that he would get even with the pair for lying, even if he had to die for it.

On Saturday night, 5 March 1881, McMeans confronted Thomas. A fight ensued, which resulted in Thomas ejecting McMeans from the house that they were at. On Sunday morning, 6 March 1881, McMeans, who was still in an intoxicated condition, went to the bar at which Thomas was an employee. McMeans approached Thomas in a friendly way and asked him to have a drink. Afterwards, he implored Thomas to accompany him to the stable and assist him in hitching up a team so that he could do some hauling. Thomas ordered him out of the establishment, emphasizing that he had better comply in a hurry. McMeans exited with Thomas on his heals. When the pair hit the street Thomas pulled a pistol and, as described in one newspaper of the day, got the drop on McMeans and "with Texas promptitude fired instantly."[703]

Thomas' first shot hit McMeans in the back. The latter fled, with Thomas on his heels. Thomas fired twice more, felling McMeans. At that moment the city marshal appeared, disarming Thomas and taking him into custody. Bleeding from a soon to be fatal wound McMeans ran from Spring

Street to Main through an alley where he collapsed. McMeans was taken to a nearby home, pleading that his wife be brought to him so that he might have a final word with her before he died. McMeans passed at about 3:00 pm. It is unclear if his spouse arrived at the deathbed before his spirit flew from its mortal host.

Thomas' trial took place at the November term of court. He was found guilty and sentenced to death. He appealed his case, making a lengthy speech to the court. His efforts failed. After an unsuccessful attempt at having his sentence commuted by Governor Oran M. Roberts.

According to New York newspapers that seemed to harbor a low opinion of Texans in general, Thomas displayed "Texas Characteristics" and was frequently in trouble. He had shot and killed three men, but "...managed to prove all of them cases of justification." The piece went on to state, "a bad man was disposed of in the hanging of Chess Thomas."[704]

At 1:45 pm on Friday, 11 August 1882, Chess Thomas' death sentence was carried out. The trap was sprung and Thomas swung into eternity. His neck broken by the fall he was pronounced dead in fifteen minutes. Friends took charge of his body for burial.

Caldwell, Shack
Born: circa 1862—Date of Death: 18 August 1882
Place: Collin County
Event: Legal Execution/Hanged

Shack Caldwell, a twenty-year old black man, was hanged at McKinney for the murder of W. R. Norville. That incident had taken place in November 1881.[705]

All trains into the town that day were packed with spectators, having come from miles around to witness the event. Thousands attended, watching Caldwell deliver his speech, which he had memorized. The condemned man confessed his guilt and placed his fate in the hands of God. The execution venue was about a mile and a half from town. Photographs of Caldwell sold out quickly, having been prepared for the financial benefit of his mother. Fully sixty mounted men guarded the doomed man as he left the confines of the jail and headed to the gallows singing "As I passed By The Wicked Crowd I Heard A Woman Cry."

After Caldwell's oration Reverend Griggs from Dallas conducted the service. Caldwell said, "Goodbye friends, I am going home." At 2:17 pm the trap was sprung and Caldwell was hurled into eternity.[706]

Ward, Charles
Born: circa 1847—Date of Death: 21 August 1882
Place: Bexar County
Event: Legal Execution/Hanged

Charles Ward, a thirty-five year old black man, was hanged at San Antonio on Monday, 21 August

1882. Ward had criminally assaulted and outraged an eleven-year old white girl named Dorah Ellerman. That incident had taken place almost a year earlier.

Since then Ward had lost a leg, thus he mounted the gallows on crutches and stood before his executioner propped up by the devices. There were no religious services, hymns or bible readings at Ward's going away party. He denied his guilt to the end. A handful of persons were allowed to witness the event. A crowd of over 500 gathered outside the jailhouse.[707]

Fraley, George W.
Born (Unknown)—Date of Death: 26 November 1882
Place: Comanche County
Event: Lynching/Hanged

Fraley, James "Jim"
Born (Unknown)—Date of Death: 26 November 1882
Place: Comanche County
Event: Lynching/Hanged

Terry, Given Name Unknown
Born (Unknown)—Date of Death: 2 December 1882
Place: Comanche County
Event: Lynching/Hanged

Terry, Given Name Unknown
Born (Unknown)—Date of Death: 2 December 1882
Place: Comanche County
Event: Lynching/Hanged

Brothers George W. and Jim Fraley were arrested on charges of stealing cotton. A constable made the arrest and placed the men in jail at Hazel Dell under armed guard. About 10:00 pm a mob, armed with shotguns, induced the guards to release the prisoners. The following morning the men were found suspended from the same tree, both at the end of a rope and both quite dead from the experience.

The brothers are buried in the Hazel Dell Cemetery. Their tombstone indicates their date of death as Sunday, 26 November 1882. The inscription reads, "Killed by an outlaw mob that was active in the area from the late 1860s to mid 1880s. These men were near the last of more than 20 [twenty] victims that perished in this period of terror."[708]

Newspapers reported that a gang of desperadoes was stealing cattle in Comanche County. Allegedly one gang member was caught and hanged near Coleman and another was caught and hanged at Sipe Springs. On Friday, 2 December 1882, two men named Terry were forcibly taken from lawmen at Hazel Dell and hanged. It is possible that the lynching of the Fraley brothers and two men named Terry are the same incident.[709]

Scott, Isham
Born: (Unknown)—Date of Death: 5 January 1883
Place: Lamar County
Event: Legal Execution/Hanged

Joseph Speer, a respectable white man, was found waylaid, shot and robbed just a few miles outside Paris. A chain of circumstantial evidence pointed towards Isham Scott, a black man, who had disappeared from Lamar County a few weeks earlier. Scott and three accomplices had done the work. He was captured and held in jail, but was indicted for horse theft since the connection to the Speer killing had not yet been made.

Clever thinking on his part caused him to enter a guilty plea in his trial for purloining the horses, which resulted in him drawing a thirty year sentence at Huntsville and thus avoiding the gallows for the Scott killing, should he be discovered as the murderer. His ruse did not work. Scott was removed from the penitentiary and returned to the Paris jail where he stood trial for the Scott incident. He was tried in the fall 1881 session of court and found guilty. After a failed appeal he was scheduled to pay for his crime on the gallows, with that sentence to be carried out on 5 January 1883.

Although Texas law required that the hanging be done in private with only a handful of witnesses being allowed to attend by special pass only, Sheriff Cook had the gallows erected on the site of the Speer murder just outside town. He justified his actions as being necessary due to the ongoing construction at the jail building preventing the event from taking place there. Thus on Friday, 5 January 1883, Isham Scott kept his appointment with the hangman, in full view of thousands of curious onlookers.[710] One newspaper account of the day claimed that at his going away event Scott had, "...indulged in the normal amount of Glory Hallelujah's."

Jackson, Andrew
Born (Unknown)—Date of Death: 7 January 1883
Place: Rusk County
Event: Lynching/Hanged

On Sunday, 7 January 1883, a black man named Andrew Jackson was taken from the jail at Henderson and hanged from a tree in front of a hotel. Jackson had been arrested for the attempted assault of a young woman.[711]

One Unidentified Black Man
Born: (Unknown)—Date of Death: 27 February 1883
Place: Bastrop County
Event: Lynching/Hanged

According to newspaper sources of the day an unidentified black man was lynched near Elgin for attempting to outrage a white girl.[712]

Waite, Fred E.
Born: circa 1861—Date of Death: 23 March 1883
Place: Robertson County
Event: Legal Execution/Hanged

At about 9:00 am on Sunday, 28 May 1882, Deputy Addison "Ad" Wyser was the jailer on duty at the county lockup in the town of Franklin. Three prisoners who were in the process of making an escape beat Wyser to death. All three men were successful in getting away.

The prisoners had been locked up for an odd assortment of crimes. Prisoner Fred E. Waite had been charged with the theft of a drummer's valise at the Junction House in Hearne. Prisoner Watts Banks had been charged with the theft of a horse and default of payment of a gambling fine. Prisoner Daniel Compton was charged with the most salacious of the crimes, incest, and for running off with his fifteen year old stepdaughter. Banks was also recovering in the jail after having been shot while attempting to escape from contract labor at a local farm.

Waite asked for a severance and was convicted. He was sentenced to death. That verdict was carried out on Friday, 23 March 1883, when Waite was executed by hanging at a spot about a half-mile outside of Franklin. Practically 2,000 people turned out for the show, which took place at about 1:05 pm. Waite met his fate. He refused to allow the presence of any preacher or the recital of any prayer. When the black cap was pulled down over his head he simply said, "Goodbye boys." [713]

Waite is buried at Franklin Cemetery. Compton was convicted of murder and sentenced to life in prison. Banks was also convicted and sentenced to death.

Chaney, Given Name Unknown
Born: (Unknown)—Date of Death: 15 April 1883
Place: Coryell County
Event: Lynching/Shot

O'Connor, John
Born: (Unknown)—Date of Death: 15 April 1883
Place: Coryell County
Event: Lynching/Shot

John O'Connor and a man identified only as Chaney were shot to death by a mob on Sunday, 15 April 1883. Given that their names appear in the *Tuskegee Lynching Files* it is presumed that they met their end at the hands of vigilantes.[714]

Banks, Wyatt
Born: circa 1858—Date of Death: 23 April 1883
Place: Robertson County
Event: Legal Execution/Hanged

Wyatt Banks, a black man, was found guilty of the murder of Deputy Addison "Ad" Wyser at Franklin. See above - Fred Waite.

A somewhat more generously proportioned Banks was executed by hanging on Monday, 23 April 1883. He had sold his body to a medical doctor and had smoked, drank and eaten up the proceeds from that sale while he languished in the jail.[715]

Two Unidentified Mexican Men
Born: (Unknown)—Date of Death: 26 April 1883
Place: Nueces County
Event: Lynched/Hanged

In Carrigan's book *Forgotten Dead* the author claims that two unidentified Mexican men were taken from officers by force and lynched near Collins. The men were suspected of theft. No corroboration of this incident has been found.[716]

Quintinilla, Pedro
Born: (Unknown)—Date of Death: May 1883
Place: Duval County
Event: Lynched/Hanged

In Carrigan's book *Forgotten Dead* the author claims that Pedro Quintinilla was lynched near Rosita Creek. Quintinilla was suspected of theft. No corroboration of this incident has been found.[717]

McCracken, Given Name Unknown
Born: (Unknown)—Date of Death: June 1883
Place: Gonzales County
Event: Lynched/Hanged

Mr. McCracken, a white man whose given name is unknown, was lynched by a mob of angry stockmen in Gonzales County sometime in early June. McCracken, along with John House, three of the Trammell brothers and one of the White brothers were involved in cattle rustling. The latter were arraigned on 4 June. McCracken, on the other hand, was not as fortunate. His trial was by "judge lynch."[718]

Austin, Gabe

Born: (Unknown)—Date of Death: 2 June 1883
Place: McLennan County
Event: Lynched/Hanged

Alex and William Harris, both black men, accidentally strangled Gabe Austin, another black man. Austin was accused of having had criminal intimacy with his own niece. Alex, William Harris and four other black men had intended to give Austin a sound whipping. They placed a rope with a slipknot around his neck and dragged him to the place where they intended to administer the punishment. When they removed the rope they discovered that Austin was dead.

Although some sources list Austin's death as a lynching, from the explanation provided in other newspaper accounts of the day his punishers intended to dispense chastisement for his transgression, not to kill him. Accidental homicide might be a more appropriate classification. However, not being certain of his killer's intentions Austin is being included on this roster in the interest of completeness. Seven men were indicted for the murder.[719]

Two Unidentified Mexican Man

Born: (Unknown)—Date of Death: 7 June 1883
Place: Galveston County
Event: Lynched/Hanged

While being transported by lawmen from Galveston to San Diego in Duval County, two unidentified Mexican men who were charged with horse theft were removed by force from their escorts by a band of approximately twenty-five men and lynched somewhere en route.[720]

Anderson, Joe

Born: (Unknown)—Date of Death: 14 June 1883
Place: LaSalle County
Event: Lynched/Hanged

One Unidentified Mexican Man

Born: (Unknown)—Date of Death: 14 June 1883
Place: LaSalle County
Event: Lynched/Hanged

According to accounts of the day, the bodies of a black man named Joe Anderson and an unidentified Mexican man were discovered hanging in LaSalle County on 14 June 1883. Anderson's corpse, although missing the head and lower limbs, could still be identified. Both men were suspected of theft. The newspaper report mentioned that some of the "Star Route Gang" had ranches in the area, and surmised that it might be best for all concerned if they moved on.[721]

Douglas, Jasper
Born: (Unknown)—Date of Death: 28 June 1883
Place: Marion County
Event: Lynched/Hanged

Lacy, Alexander
Born: (Unknown)—Date of Death: 28 June 1883
Place: Marion County
Event: Lynched/Hanged and Shot

On Thursday morning, 28 June 1883, Alexander Lacy, a black man, was lynched near Lacy's Bridge at Jefferson in Marion County for committing an outrage on a white woman named Rogers. Later the same day a band of about 150 armed horsemen surrounded the jail at Jefferson where Lacy's companion and co-conspirator was being held. The vigilantes quickly overpowered guards and removed Jasper Douglas. The mob disappeared just as mysteriously as they had arrived. Lacy's body was found on Wednesday, 4 July 1883, dangling from a tree with four bullet holes in his head. [722]

Brewster, Joseph
Born: (Unknown)—Date of Death: 5 July 1883
Place: El Paso County
Event: Legal Execution/Hanged

Joseph Brewster, a white soldier who was tried and convicted of the outraging of Mrs. Davis, was sentenced to death for his crime. The incident occurred at Fort Davis, the naming of which had no connection to the victim.

On Thursday, 5 July 1883, Brewster scaled the gallows stairs at Ysleta to begin what newspaper reports would describe as "...another disgraceful display," giving evidence to the need for a public hangman who could carry out executions in a merciful and expeditious manner. Brewster delivered a lengthy oration, pausing twice to take a big slug of whiskey. On one occasion his spiritual advisor endeavored to take the bottle away from him. At the culmination of Brewster's oration the trap was sprung. The poor man strangled to death in a horrific manner. Brewster's hanging was said to have been "...a barbarous display," witnessed by over 800 persons. The hangman's noose had been adjusted in a bungling manner.[723]

Cone, John
Born: circa 1855—Date of Death: 6 July 1883
Place: Harris County
Event: Legal Execution/Hanged

John Cone, a twenty-eight year old a black man, had come to Texas from Mobile, Alabama with his family when he was five years old. Family members were formerly slaves, and became the property of Colonel Horace Cone, prominent local farmer.

John Cone was a well-built, light-skinned colored black man who, according to accounts of the day, facially did not appear to be very intelligent. At about 11:00 am on Monday, 16 January 1882, Cone approached the home of Mrs. Scott, who was living near the ten mile tank on the Galveston-Harrisburg-San Antonio road. Mr. Scott was away at the time. Cone asked for food and inquired about the distance to Galveston. He also asked the time. When Mrs. Scott turned to look at the clock he grabbed her by the arm and placed his hand over mouth to prevent her from calling out. Cone picked up a bootjack from the floor and struck Mrs. Scott over the head with it, telling her that if she screamed again he would kill her. Next he outraged the woman. Once finished, he fled in the direction of Bray's Bayou.

Cone was soon arrested. He and thirteen other black prisoners were paraded in front of Mrs. Scott for identification. Mrs. Scott instantly and without hesitation picked Cone out of the makeshift lineup. In spite of an alibi offered, Cone was convicted and sentenced to death. No attempt was made to secure a reprieve or pardon.

On the day of the execution as many as 100 visitors were admitted to witness the hanging. Cone, dressed in a sharp new black suit of clothes and sporting a pair of white gloves, abandoned his half consumed breakfast at the foot of his cot and greeted Reverend S. H. Werlein, a Methodist preacher, and Reverend Scott, a black minister as they entered his cell. Cone's half brother, John White, was present with him as a string of visitors paraded through his cell offering their last farewells.

At 11:30 am Sheriff Fant led Cone to the gallows. The platform was crowded as he and the sheriff ascended, with members of the press, Deputies Rutherford, Burroughs and McDonald as well as three men of the cloth. When asked if he wished to speak Cone once again professed his innocence. He requested a glass of water, which was provided to him by Deputy Glasscock. Moments before noon the black cap was placed on his head and the sheriff affixed and adjusted the noose. The trap was pulled almost immediately and Cone dropped to his death. It was a full thirty minutes before Dr. Rutherford declared Cone dead. His neck had not been broken by the fall, thus he dangled there for practically a half hour.[724]

Weaver, Thomas

Born: (Unknown)—Date of Death: 28 July 1883
Place: Coryell County
Event: Lynching/Shot

Thomas Weaver, a white man who by some sources was identified as Woods, was murdered near Gatesville for horse theft early on Saturday morning, 28 July 1883, (or perhaps in the late evening hours of Friday, 27 July). The perpetrators entered the home of John Vaught, where Weaver was staying, and shot him to death in his bed.

Sources thought to be most reliable report this incident as having occurred on 28 July, which is when word of the killing was made known.[725]

Allen, Given Name Unknown
Born: (Unknown)—Date of Death: circa July-August 1883
Place: Erath County
Event: Lynching/Shot

Very little information about this incident has been uncovered. Sometime in July-August of 1883, an elderly black man named Allen was beaten and shot by a mob at Alexander.[726]

Bradley, Martin
Born: (Unknown)—Date of Death: 17 August 1883
Place: Terrell County
Event: Lynching/Hanged

After having been arraigned for the outrage of a local white woman, Martin Bradley, a black man, was taken from jail by a gang of angry citizens and lynched on the grounds of the asylum east of the city on Friday, 17 August 1883.

Although citizens claim to deprecate mob law, the Bradley case had been the second attempted outrage of a white woman in about two weeks. In the other incident, which occurred near town, it was the quick action of the woman's daughter who fired at the intruder while in the act that saved the day by causing the attacker to flee. Otherwise, there might have been a pair of hangings to report in Terrell County this week.[727]

Johnson, Silas
Born: (Unknown)—Date of Death: 24 September 1883
Place: Harrison County
Event: Lynching/Hanged and Shot

On the night of Monday, 24 September 1883, the body of Silas Johnson, a black man, was found lynched and pierced with three bullets, hanging along a roadside half a mile from Marshall. Johnson's wife reported that a mob of sixteen men had come calling at their home and had removed Mr. Johnson by force. Johnson was suspected of having been involved in some recent "race troubles." [728]

Foster, Lewis (Louis)
Born (Unknown)—Date of Death: 18 October 1883
Place: Lavaca County
Event: Lynching/Hanged and Shot

On or about 18 October 1883, Louis Foster, a black man, was found hanging from a tree near the South Union Church in Lavaca County. He had been shot in the neck with a charge of buckshot. To finish the job someone had shot him in the head with a pistol. Newspapers reported that "Foster... bore a bad reputation for years."[729]

Stanley, James
Born: (Unknown)—Date of Death: 19 October 1883
Place: Colorado County
Event: Legal Execution/Hanged

James Stanley, a black man, was tried and convicted of the murder of Robert Strickland a white youth age sixteen. The incident took place in November 1882. Stanley was married, but was infatuated with a black woman named Sarah Walker. He killed Stickland to obtain money in order to run away with Walker to Mexico.

Stanley's sentence was carried out at Columbus, at about 2:58 pm on Friday, 19 October 1883 before a crowd of 4,000 people. At his hanging Stanley left a full written confession. He made a speech urging the crowd to abandon whiskey and cards. After some hymns, and as the cap was being placed over his head, Stanley asked to see Sarah Walker. She was brought to the foot of the gallows. He told her, "Oh! Sarah, see what you have brought me to. You did not tell me to commit this crime, but I did it for you. Pray, Sarah; farewell. I'll see you again in heaven."[730]

Bailey, Dee
Born: (Unknown)—Date of Death: 20 November 1883
Place: Comanche County
Event: Lynching/Hanging

Bailey, James
Born: (Unknown)—Date of Death: 20 November 1883
Place: Comanche County
Event: Lynching/Hanging

Maston Reynolds "Boss" Greene was the city marshal at Comanche, and had been a Texas Ranger captain before being appointed a deputy U.S. Marshal under Thomas Purnell of the Western District of Texas.

On Saturday, 12 May 1877, Greene and a man named Hill left Comanche in pursuit of two brothers, Dee and James Bailey, who were counterfeiters "pushing the queer" around the town. Greene caught up with the Bailey brothers and arrested them. Dee Bailey tossed over the saddlebags containing about ten dollars worth of counterfeit money. Jim Bailey, still mounted, gave his pistol to Mr. Hill. Greene had failed to notice the Winchester rifle belonging to Dee Bailey that was still in Dee's saddle scabbard.

Greene's horse flared, a trait for which the animal was well known. Dee Bailey pulled the Winchester rifle from the scabbard. Greene fired once from his Colt revolver, grazing Dee Bailey in the head and dislodging a lock of hair and hide. Dee Bailey fired twice from his Winchester, hitting Greene in the lower jaw on his second shot. The first shot had gone wild and missed its mark. The .44 caliber bullet travelled upwards into Greene's cheekbone. As Greene fell from the horse Dee Bailey shot him again, this time in the foot. The Bailey brothers made good their escape.

Mr. Hill fled without making any attempt to aid Marshal Greene. Greene crawled to a nearby house and died at 7:30 pm that evening. He is buried in Oakwood Cemetery in Comanche.

The Bailey brothers were eventually captured and incarcerated. On 19 September 1883 they appeared in the District Court of Comanche and were granted bail. On Tuesday, 20 November 1883, a mob of angry citizens, fearing that the Bailey brothers might be released, took the pair from jail and lynched them from a post oak tree.

On Thursday, 6 March 1884, the State of Texas finally dismissed the case against the Bailey brothers, citing that the two men were already "deceased."[731]

Garcia, Silvestre
Born: (Unknown)—Date of Death: 3 December 1883
Place: Cameron County
Event: Lynching/Hanged

According to unverified sources, Silvester Garcia was lynched near Ranchito on 3 December 1883. His crime is not known.[732]

Four Unidentified Mexican Men
Born: (Unknown)—Date of Death: 7 December 1883
Place: Jeff Davis County
Event: Lynching/Hanged

Four unidentified Mexican men who were suspected of the murder of a man named Domingo Paloma four weeks earlier were taken into custody at Fort Davis. Soon after a mob took control of the foursome, by force of arms, and hanged them all. [733]

Duran, Juan
Born: (Unknown)—Date of Death: 14 December 1883
Place: Presidio County
Event: Legal Execution/Hanged

Juan Duran, a Mexican man who was tried and convicted of killing a "Chinaman" [Asian] about a year earlier, was hanged on Friday, 14 December 1883. It is a bit unclear as to the location of the execution. Some sources cite Presidio County while others mention only "Davis," perhaps meaning Fort Davis that is in Jefferson Davis County.[734]

Taylor, James
Born: circa 1862—Date of Death: 21 December 1883
Place: Lee County
Event: Legal Execution/Hanged

On Friday, 21 December 1883, James Taylor, a twenty-one year old black man, went to the gallows at Giddings for the outrage and murder of Sarah Chappell. The details are shocking.

The incident had taken place on Sunday, 26 August 1883. Taylor was employed, and lived at the home of Mrs. Chappell. That morning he and Mrs. Chappell started out to the pea patch, located a short distance from the house, to pick the vegetables for supper. When Mr. Chappell returned home he found his wife missing. Taylor could offer no good explanation as to her whereabouts. A search party was quickly organized. They discovered Sarah's violated and mutilated remains in a home along Yegua Creek. She had been stripped naked and was lying beside her two infants of premature birth.

Taylor was immediately suspected of being the perpetrator and was arrested. When pressed he confessed that once he and Mrs. Chappell had cleared hearing distance from the house he had made a lewd proposition which she had refused. Taylor pushed the point, but Mrs. Chappell remained adamant in her rejection. At that point Taylor threw her down to the ground and outraged her. Afterwards he cut her throat and made her walk to the creek where he stuffed her dress in a hole under a tree then killed her.

Taylor walked the distance of about two thirds of a mile to the gallows showing no evidence of concern. Reverends Jones and Haggett were present. Jones read Luke 23, where Jesus says, "...Father forgive them; for they know not what they do. And they parted his raiment, and cast lots."[735] Sheriff Brown, on the other hand, read the death warrant, noting that unlike Jesus, the State of Texas does not forgive. Taylor declared, "Farewell to all. I hope to meet you in heaven." At 2:25 pm the trap was sprung and Taylor dropped six feet, snapped his neck and was thrust into eternity.[736]

McLemore, Thaddeus Koesko
Born: 8 November 1846—Date of Death: 24 December 1883
Place: Bastrop County
Event: Lynching/Hanged

McLemore, Wright Keaton
Born: 10 November 1837—Date of Death: 24 December 1883
Place: Bastrop County
Event: Lynching/Hanged

Pfeiffer, Henry
Born: (Unknown)—Date of Death: 24 December 1883
Place: Bastrop County
Event: Lynching/Hanged

Thirty seven year old Lee County Sheriff's Deputy Isaac "Bosse" Heffington was shot and killed on 3 December 1883. The incident occurred while he was in pursuit of a man who was wanted for robbery and murder. While he was searching a building an unidentified man stepped out from behind some boxes, said something to him, and then shot him. Heffington signed a statement while on his deathbed implicating a man in the shooting, but that fellow was found not guilty and the case was never solved. Henry Pfeiffer, Thad McLemore and Wright McLemore were suspected of being involved in the killing, however. As it turns out the threesome would swing at the end of a rope, but not for the Heffington killing.[737]

The headlines on Christmas Day of 1883 read, "Three Men Hung, Three Shot and Several Others Wounded."

The wild affray began at about half past seven in the evening on Monday, 24 December 1883. Henry Pfeiffer, Wright McLemore and Thad McLemore, all white men, were taken out of the saloon at McDade by masked men, under force of arms, and carried about a mile into the brush where they were lynched to a tree. Thad McLemore had been arrested late in the evening on a charge of burglary made by S. E Walker of McDade. He was under arrest at the time the masked men took him. The other two parties happened to be present. Pfeiffer was charged with horse theft in Bastrop County. The group who did the hanging was comprised of about forty or fifty well armed citizens.

On Christmas day a party of six men, all friends and relatives of the men who had been lynched, came to town looking for justice. They picked a fight with Tom Bishop and George Milton. That soon escalated into gunplay. Shotguns and pistols blazed as John "Jack" Wisdom Batey and his brother Jerry Asbury "Az" Batey were killed. Nathan Haywood Batey, another sibling, was badly wounded but managed to escape. William Gamble "Willie" Griffon, a very estimable young man of the town, was shot though the head and mortally wounded by Nathan Haywood Batey. Griffin was assisting Milton and Bishop in defending themselves.

The five dead bodies of the two McLemore men, two Batey brothers and Henry Pfeiffer were left lying in the Market house.[738]

McLemore was survived by his wife Texana Baker and seven children. He is buried at the Baker Hill Cemetery at McDade.

Although some family genealogists cite Wright McLemore's birth date as January 1835, several others list it as being 10 November 1837, and reference source documents to substantiate that assertion. Wright was survived by his wife Rebecca Ransom and one daughter. He is buried at the Baker Hill Cemetery at McDade.

Batey was survived by his wife Martha Blanche Nash. Both Batey boys are buried at the Jefferies Cemetery at McDade.

William Gamble "Willie" Griffon is buried at the Piney Creek Cemetery at Smithville.

Brown, Tom (Sam)
Born: (Unknown)—Date of Death: 20 January 1884
Place: Caldwell County
Event: Lynching/Hanged

According to newspaper reports of the day, a man named Tom or Sam Brown was lynched near Lockhart in Caldwell County. He was suspected of murder. [739]

Walker, Anthony
Born: circa 1848—Date of Death: 23 January 1884
Place: Harrison County
Event: Legal Execution/Hanged

Anthony Walker, a black man, was tried and convicted of murdering a wealthy white planter named William Henry near Marshall. Walker ultimately confessed to the crime, claiming that he had shot Henry from ambush, and that he had been compelled to do it by Mrs. Henry, who promised him 150 acres of land and $100 in specie. Walker indicated to the judge that two other black men were aware of the bargain he had made with the murdered man's wife.

Mrs. Henry was subsequently arrested. Walker was hanged for his role in the evil covenant.[740]

Robinson, Sandy
Born: (Unknown)—Date of Death: 3 February 1884
Place: Houston County
Event: Lynching/Hanged

On Wednesday night, 9 January 1884, Houston County Sheriff F. H. Payne organized a posse to arrest a desperado named Sandy Robinson. Robinson, a black man, was found hiding in a cabin at the Bannerman plantation on the Trinity River in Leon County. As twenty-nine year old Posseman

James W. Lathrop entered the cabin through the door Robinson shot and killed him. Robinson then grabbed Lathrop's weapon and fled. He was later arrested and placed in the Houston County Jail in Crockett.

Sheriff Payne received information concerning a possible lynching attempt involving Robinson. He summoned a guard of ten or more men to stay at the jail and protect the prisoner. Only about six men and the sheriff were present when the expected mob, numbering between seventy-five and one hundred masked citizens on horseback, arrived at 1:00 am on Sunday, 3 February 1884. The sheriff begged the vigilantes not to take Robinson, but he and his small contingent of guards were quickly overpowered. The sheriff succeeded in drawing his pistol but was unable to defend the prisoner when the gun discharged by accident during the scuffle.

Mobsters took the sheriff's keys and entered the jail. Of the ten or so prisoners in the building at the time none were molested except Robinson, who was taken away and lynched near the graveyard.[741]

Williams, Harrison
Born: (Unknown)—Date of Death: 7 March 1884
Place: Navarro County
Event: Legal Execution/Hanged

Harrison Williams, a black man, was hanged at Corsicana on Friday, 7 March 1884. Williams had been tried and found guilty of the murder of his sister-in-law who had complained to authorities that he had been treating his wife in a harsh manner. The incident took place in June.[742]

Burleson, Bill
Born: (Unknown)—Date of Death: 25 March 1884
Place: Gonzales County
Event: Lynching/Hanged

On Tuesday, 25 March 1884, Bill Burleson, a black man, was tried at Gonzales for the attempted outraging of a German woman. He was placed under a $1,000 bond. On the way to the jail officers escorting Burleson were stopped by a mob of about seventy-five white men. After some discussion the lawmen managed to prevail, and Burleson was taken to the jail and locked up.

All day citizens remonstrated. By dark the vigilantes had managed to break down all opposition, removing Burleson and dragging him about a half mile from town to a Negro graveyard and lynching him from a convenient tree. Many of the town's best citizens were involved, claiming that their wives and daughters were not safe as long as men like Burleson roamed free.[743]

Garrison, W. B.

Born: (Unknown)—Date of Death: 8 April 1884

Place: Coryell County

Event: Lynching/Hanged

In the early morning hours of Tuesday, 8 April 1884, a man named W. B. Garrison was taken by force from the jail at Gatesville and lynched. Garrison was being held on a charge of horse theft. A mob of masked men surrounded the building and removed Garrison, stringing him up from a nearby tree. Although mob actions such as this are generally looked down upon, it was thought that their harsh dealings with Garrison would have some moderating effect on criminals with similar plans.[744]

Surprisingly, the hypothesis that lynching Garrison might have a moderating effect on local crime proved to be an accurate one. There is only one more hanging on the register for Coryell County. A man named Sim Woods was lynched a year later on 16 July 1885, for resisting arrest.[745]

Gomez, Refugio

Born: circa 1856—Date of Death: 6 June 1884

Place: Duval County

Event: Legal Execution/Hanged

Refugio Gomez, a twenty-eight year old Mexican man who was tried and convicted of murder, was hanged at San Diego on Friday, 6 June 1884.[746]

Berge, Given Name Unknown

Born: (Unknown)—Date of Death: 8 June 1884

Place: Karnes County

Event: Lynching/Hanged

A man identified only as Berge who had been accused of murdering a man named McAda was forcibly taken by an angry mob of about 100 persons and lynched at Helena.[747]

Lady, Isaac "Zeke"

Born: (Unknown)—Date of Death: 24 June 1884

Place: Hill County

Event: Lynching/Hanged

Isaac Lady, a black man, was charged with the attempted outrage of three white women. Newspaper accounts were not clear as to whether the multiple molestations occurred during one wild affray or if they happened individually, over a period of time. Lady was captured near Hubbard City and jailed at Galveston.

Just after midnight on Tuesday, 24 June 1884, seventy-five horsemen entered the city and broke down the door to the jail, removing Lady and lynching him from a nearby tree. The vigilante mob cut off Lady's ears and left a written statement pinned to his body defending their actions.[748]

Three Unidentified Men
Born: (Unknown)—Date of Death: 8 August 1884
Place: Chambers County
Event: Lynching/Hanged

"Phases of Texas Life Often Shortened by Bullets" was the tagline of a particular East Coast newspaper piece on Friday, 8 August 1884.

A man named Ben Dick, who at the time was under the protection of Chambers County Sheriff Davis, was shot and killed at Lone Oak Bayou in Chambers County on Monday, 4 August 1884. The sheriff and a posse were searching Dick's place, under warrant, looking for evidence of Dick having killed stolen cattle for hides.

At a coroner's inquest held at Galveston on Friday, 8 August 1884, a man named Charles Wilburn was identified as the killer. Dick's surviving six brothers, angry about the killing of their kin, ran down three of the posse men and lynched them then peppered their bodies with bullets.[749]

McCullough, Green or George
Born (Unknown)—Date of Death: 13 August 1884
Place: La Salle County
Event: Lynching/Hanged

Green McCullough was a noted desperado who was reportedly involved in eight murders. In 1883 he became engaged in an altercation with Charles Bragg, a young and prominent citizen of Cotulla. The dust up was over politics. Bragg shot McCullough in the hand, resulting in the loss of three of his fingers. McCullough returned fire, and accidentally killed County Judge Williams. On Wednesday night, 13 August 1884, Bragg was seated in a room at the rear of O'Meara's saloon with his back to the window. Someone fired a Winchester rifle through the window from outside the building, hitting Bragg in the heart and inflicting a mortal wound. The crowd identified the fleeing assassin as McCullough. He was arrested and placed in jail.

At about 9:30 am practically the entire population of the town proceeded to the jail and demanded the keys. The jailer refused, but he was overwhelmed by the mob and relented. McCullough's cell was unlocked and the crowd called him out. He emerged with a jaunty step, showed no fear or excitement. A rope was placed around his neck and he was marched to a mesquite tree. When asked if he had anything to say, he replied "No, I don't want to say anything, talking wouldn't do any good;

but I am not afraid." A signal was given by someone and McCullough was hoisted slowly from the ground. His body jerked violently as he strangeled to death.

At the time of his death McCullough was under several indictments for murder and theft. In 1885 his widow sued several Cotulla citizens for $200,000 in damages for lynching her husband. The results of that litigation are not known.[750]

Howard, John William
Born: 17 October 1838—Date of Death: 18 August 1884
Place: Coryell County
Event: Lynching/Shot

According to some sources, John Howard was an elderly white man who had been charged with arson. He was murdered while en route to the Lampasas jail where he was being sent for safekeeping. The incident took place near Langford's Cave. A mob overpowered officers who were transporting Howard and shot him to death.[751]

In Carrigan's *The Making of a Lynching Culture* this incident is said to have taken place on 23 August 1884, which is no doubt the date of the newspaper account. Other, more reliable sources, which include numerous family genealogists, indicate 18 August as the correct date.[752]

Howard is buried at the Murphree Cemetery, one mile north of Evant in Coryell County.

Fleishing, Richard
Born: circa 1863—Date of Death: 20 August 1884
Place: Galveston County
Event: Legal Execution/Hanged

On Wednesday, 20 August 1884, the body of a young German named Richard Fleishing who had been in the employ of Charles Junemann, a dairyman, was discovered hanging from a tree in a grove of salt cedars near the fairground. Fleishing had been accused of assaulting Junemann's wife.

An inquest was held which concluded that Fleishing had been lynched by a group of residents who suspected him of the alleged assault of the Junemann woman.[753] Five years later, on 29 May 1889, Judge Henry Weyer, Mr. W. T. Allen and Charles Junemann were arrested at Galveston and confined to the jail, charged with the lynching of Fleishing. The indictment also included Fred Koehler, former constable, and Cliff Porter who left Galveston suddenly, just after the Fleishing lynching.[754]

Hawes, George
Born: (Unknown)—Date of Death: 24 August 1884
Place: Refugio County
Event: Lynching/Shot

Riley, Robert
Born: (Unknown)—Date of Death: 24 August 1884
Place: Refugio County
Event: Lynching/Shot

On Tuesday, 19 August 1884, someone attempted to outrage the daughter of the Refugio County Treasurer. The next day a black man named Robert Riley, who was suspected of committing the crime, was arrested by the sheriff and placed in the county jail. The sheriff put an increased guard on Riley in anticipation of the citizen's reaction to the crime. It was believed by some that Riley had been involved in two other similar assaults during the course of the preceding two months.

On Sunday, 24 August 1884, a group of unidentified men went to the jail, drove away the guards, and attempted to break down the door. The mob threw lighted turpentine balls into the cell and shot Riley to death. A mob of black citizens had also gathered, threatening to seek retaliation if Riley was injured. During the assault on the jail a black man named George Hawes tried to browbeat the mob into halting their attack. For that Hawes was shot "beyond recovery." Jailer Cornelius Sweeney was shot in the leg as he retreated from the jail. Local newspaper claimed that members of the black mob were responsible. Regardless of the culprit, Sweeney died from his wound on 3 December 1884. Riley died on the spot.[755]

Taylor, William Allen
Born: (Unknown)—Date of Death:12 September 1884
Place: Dallas County
Event: Lynching/Hanged

William Allen Taylor, a black man, had been positively identified as the person who had brutally murdered Mrs. W. H. Flippin of Dallas. Thinking he was not safe in that town, Sheriff Smith had him moved to the jail at Waxahachie for safekeeping.

On Thursday night, 11 September 1884, a party of officers set out from there to return Taylor to Dallas. A mob got word of the plan and positioned riders along all roads out of Waxahachie, intent on intercepting the posse. Just after daylight on Friday, 12 September 1884, the group of lawmen who were traveling the Midlothian road ducked into the brush and awaited the arrival of Sheriff Smith and Constable Miller. They soon arrived in a surrey and took Taylor with them to finish the journey to Dallas. About half a mile west of Dallas Taylor his escorts were met by a mob of about 500 masked riders who took Taylor from their custody and lynched him from a convenient tree.[756]

Green, Jesse
Born (Unknown)—Date of Death: 26 September 1884
Place: Coryell County
Event: Lynching/Hanged

Jesse Green was a nephew of Bill Bass, and an active member of the Bass party that had terrorized Coryell County for years. Green retired to the backwoods where he attracted little notice. On Wednesday, 24 September 1884, Tom Lopland, who was a well-to-do black man, and his family were poisoned at supper. The incident resulted in the death of their daughter. Suspicion fell on a twelve year old black youth who was subsequently arrested and confessed to the poisoning. He implicated Jesse Green.

In light of Green's unsavory reputation the youth's story was believed. A party was organized to "wind up Green's affairs." On Friday, 26 September 1884, Green was surprised at his home and strung up.[757]

Dunlap, Given Name Unknown
Born (Unknown)—Date of Death: 6 October 1884
Place: McLennan County
Event: Lynching/Shot

Hayes, Given Name Unknown
Born (Unknown)—Date of Death: 6 October 1884
Place: McLennan County
Event: Lynching/Shot

A farmer named Hayes lived at Sipe Springs. He had been warned by a citizen's committee to leave the county because they believed one of his sons was stealing horses. Mr. Hayes refused to comply. On Monday, 6 October 1884, a mob went to his residence. Mr. Hayes's son-in-law, a man named Dunlap, and a young son of the elder Hayes (not the one alleged to be stealing horses) went to meet the mob head on. Both were shot to death. A posse of citizens went in pursuit of the assassins, several of whom Mr. Hayes recognized as the vigilantes who had done the killing. The outcome is not known.[758]

Bass, Bill
Born: circa 1859—Date of Death: 31 October 1884
Place: Lamar County
Event: Legal Execution/Hanged

Bill Bass, a twenty-five year old black man, was hanged at Paris for having outraged a white woman named Lou Williams. Williams was a paralytic and was living at the poor farm. At 4:25 pm on Friday, 31 October 1884, Bass was brought to the gallows before a crowd of 1,200 people. He spoke to the crowd briefly. At 4:45 pm the trap was sprung and Bass dropped through the floor to meet his fate. He expired in about ten minutes, protesting his innocence to the bitter end.[759]

Russell, Clara

Born (Unknown)—Date of Death: 2 November 1884
Place: Bell County
Event: Lynching/Shot

Before daylight on Sunday, 2 November 1884, a man mysteriously entered the jail at Temple. He went into the cell of a black woman prisoner named Clara Russell (also identified as Clara Wilson). Russell had been charged with carrying a concealed weapon. A brief scuffle ensued which was followed by the sound of several gunshots. Guards rushed to the cell and found Russell dead. The man somehow managed to escape. A black man named Cleveland Clark was a suspect of being the killer.[760]

Three Unidentified Mexican Men

Born: (Unknown)—Date of Death: 30 November 1884
Place: Live Oak County
Event: Lynching/Shot

According to unverified sources, a posse in Live Oak County shot three Mexican men who were suspected of murder. The incident occurred on Sunday, 30 November 1884.[761]

Walker, Anthony

Born (Unknown)—Date of Death: 23 January 1885
Place: Harrison County
Event: Legal Execution/Hanged

On Friday 23 January 1885, a black preacher named Anthony Walker was hanged at Marshall in the presence of several thousand spectators. His crime was the murder of William Henry, a wealthy white planter. That killing had taken place in November 1883. Walker confessed to the crime but implicated Henry's wife, whom he said instigated the deed. His neck was broken from the fall and he died in nine minutes.

Walker was an educated black man who was expelled from the Baptist ministry when he became a Campbellite preacher.[762]

Hawkins, Ben

Born (Unknown)—Date of Death: 4 February 1885
Place: Robertson County
Event: Lynching/Hanged

On Wednesday, 4 February 1885, a mob of 200 men visited the county jail at Franklin and demanded the keys. Not surprisingly, the jailer refused to surrender. The mob then forced their way through an entrance and seized Ben Hawkins, a black man. Hawkins, who had murdered an old peddler a week earlier, was hanged from a tree. Judges Collared and Crawford tried unsuccessfully to get the mob to break up. When they were eventually placed under armed guard the rabble disperses quietly.[763]

Flores, Manuel
Born (Unknown)—Date of Death: 28 February 1885
Place: Dimmit County
Event: Lynching/Hanged

Two or Three Unidentified Mexican Men
Born (Unknown)—Date of Death: 28 February 1885
Place: Dimmit County
Event: Lynching/Shot

The sheep ranch of Ryan and Level in Dimmit County allegedly "...bore a bad reputation for a long time, being regarded as headquarters for cattle thieves and Mexicans..." On Saturday, 28 February 1885, a group of men raided the ranch and hanged the overseer, Manuel Flores. Two or three sheepherders were shot and killed, and sheep were scattered in all directions. The newspaper reported that no effort was made to arrest the guilty parties.[764]

Pryor, John
Born (Unknown)—Date of Death: 24 April 1885
Place: Anderson County
Event: Lynching/Shot

On Friday, 24 April 1885, a black man allegedly assaulted a married white woman near Palestine. Friends and family suspected John Pryor, who with another black man had been digging a well on the neighboring property. Tracks in the yard were made by a person with a boot that had a half sole and were well worn. Pryor had similar footgear. On Saturday, 25 April 1885, the lifeless body of Pryor was found near Gull Springs with four bullet holes in his breast.[765]

Dyer, Eli P.
Born: circa 1862—Date of Death: 8 May 1885
Place: Fannin County
Event: Lynching/Hanged

Dyer, Samuel B.
Born: March 1860—Date of Death: 8 May 1885
Place: Fannin County
Event: Lynching/Hanged

Fannin County Sheriff Thomas A. Ragsdale and Deputy Buchanan were shot and killed as they attempted to serve warrants on a pair of suspected horse thieves. As the officers approached the home of the two horse thieves, brothers named Samuel and Eli Dyer, the men opened fire on them killing the sheriff and mortally wounding the deputy. Deputy Buchanan died the next day.

The Dyer brothers fled, and hid under a corncrib. They were arrested, but an irate group of local citizens decided not to wait for a trial. Vigilantes saved the county the time and expense of a trial by lynching the pair. At about 2:30 am on 8 June 1885, a mob of disguised men removed the Dyer brothers from the jail at Bonham and lynched them from a tree, not 300 yards from the jailhouse building. According to the jailer, who stood helpless against the superior force, the vigilantes numbered 100 or more. Never, it is said, was a lynching carried out in a more quiet and organized manner.[766]

Rhodes, Jasper
Born: circa 1863—Date of Death: 22 May 1885
Place: Galveston County
Event: Legal Execution/Hanged

In April 1884, a black man named Jasper Rhodes was married to a mulatto woman named Mary May who, at the time, was employed as a servant by Richard Tiernan. They were allowed to live at the Tiernan residence, conditioned upon Jasper's good behavior. Such condition was soon violated, and the Rhodes family was compelled to leave. Not long after, Jasper committed an assault with intent to murder on a man named Ramson Bridgely. Jasper became a fugitive from justice and Mary returned to the Tiernan residence where she continued as a servant, this time conditioned upon Jasper's absence.

On Tuesday, 21 October 1884 Jasper Rhodes returned to the Tiernam residence. On this occasion he was in the company of a confederate named Sam Wilson. After a brief argument he shot Mary through the brain, then cut her throat from ear to ear. He was captured and confined in jail on Saturday, 25 October 1884, and went to trial in January 1885. On 20 March 1885, Rhodes was found guilty and sentenced to be hanged. That sentence was to be carried out on 22 May 1885.

At about noon on the prescribed day, Friday, 22 May 1885, Sheriff Owens and Deputy Ed Giebel escorted Rhodes to the foot of the gallows that had been erected on the second story of the court building. He bid farewell to his father and requested that a ring on his finger be removed and given to his mother. Once this had been done the trap was sprung, at precisely 12:25 pm, and Rhodes swung motionless for about fifteen minutes before he was cut down and placed in a coffin. Rhodes, who had earlier tried to cheat the gallows by committing suicide while in jail, had now gone to atone to his maker.[767]

Gibson, Archie
Born: circa 1850—Date of Death: 29 May 1885
Place: Fort Bend County
Event: Legal Execution/Hanged

Archie Gibson, a thirty five year old black man, went to the gallows at Richmond on Friday, 29 May 1885, for the murder of his wife. The incident had occurred in September 1884 when, in a fit of jealousy, Gibson had slit his wife Clara's throat with a knife while the couple worked in a cotton field. The wound had been so serious that the woman's head was practically severed.

Gibson confessed, professed faith, and claiming that he was going straight to glory. He asked that his coffin be brought to his jail cell where he examined it closely, brushed it off with a handkerchief and remarked that it would be, "...a nice place to rest in."[768]

Lumkins, Henry
Born: (Unknown)—Date of Death: 4 June 1885
Place: Robertson County
Event: Lynching/Shot

The newspaper coverage of the lynching of Henry Lumkins was short and to the point. Lumkins, a black man, was accused of murder. Apart from mentioning the particulars, including the fact that the execution occurred at Hearne on Thursday night, 4 June 1885, his passing went largely without notice.[769]

Morgan, Frank
Born: (Unknown)—Date of Death: 21 June 1885
Place: Cooke County
Event: Lynching/Hanged

Williams, Bill
Born: (Unknown)—Date of Death: 21 June 1885
Place: Cooke County
Event: Lynching/Hanged

Moore, Given Name Unknown
Born: (Unknown)—Date of Death: 21 June 1885
Place: Cooke County
Event: Lynching/Hanged

Bill Williams, a farmer living near Mud Creek, was suspected of being a horse thief. On Sunday, 21

June 1885, a posse of thirty-two determined men who had been hunting stock thieves along the Red River suddenly appeared at Williams' home. Expecting his fate, Williams bade his family farewell and rode off in the custody of the posse.

The armed men led Williams to a stand of tree where they were met by another group of riders who had in their custody two additional horse thieves, Frank Morgan and a boy named Moore. After some deliberation concerning the advisability of hanging the youth, it was decided that all three should be lynched, thereby avoiding having to hang the boy at some future date should he continue his lawless ways. According to reports, all three were strung up from the same tree. Posse members clambered up and placed their feet on the dying men's shoulders, adding their weight to speed up the job of dying so they could get out of the blazing hot Texas summer sun.

Newspaper reports of the day claimed that this lynching occurred near Healdtown, which is actually located north of the Red River in the Indian Territory, north of Gainesville. After having dealt with the aforementioned threesome of horse thieves the posse continued up the Wichita River and is claimed to have captured and lynched nine additional ne're-do-wells who were involved in stock rustling. There is no corroboration available for that incident however.[770]

Hayes, Frank
Born: (Unknown)—Date of Death: 23 June 1885
Place: Anderson County
Event: Lynching/Hanged

Jackson, Andy
Born: (Unknown)—Date of Death: 23 June 1885
Place: Anderson County
Event: Lynching/Hanged

Jackson, Lizzie
Born: (Unknown)—Date of Death: 23 June 1885
Place: Anderson County
Event: Lynching/Hanged

Norman, Joe
Born: (Unknown)—Date of Death: 23 June 1885
Place: Anderson County
Event: Lynching/Hanged

Rogers, William
Born: (Unknown)—Date of Death: 23 June 1885
Place: Anderson County
Event: Lynching/Hanged

Two Unidentified Black Man
Born: (Unknown)—Date of Death: 24 June 1885
Place: Houston County
Event: Lynching/Hanged

Martin, John
Born: (Unknown)—Date of Death: 26 June 1885
Place: Grayson County
Event: Lynching/Hanged

On Saturday night, 20 June 1885, a young white woman named Mattie Hazell, wife of ex-constable Randolph Hazell, was taken from her home near Elkhart and brutally outraged by a gang of black men comprised of Frank Hayes, Andy Jackson, Joe Norman, and William Rogers. A black woman named Lizzie Jackson, daughter of Andy Jackson, was also a member of the group. Hazell's naked body was discovered by her husband when he returned home and found her missing. Nearby the body was a pair of men's drawers. About 300 yards distant a men's undershirt was found. She had been spirited off to a nearby field where the evil deeds were done. Andy Jackson had held a pistol to the poor woman's head while the other three men violated her. Afterwards Mrs. Hazell was strangled and had her throat cut from ear to ear. Her jugular vein was cut with a common knife and her face bore evidence of great gashes having been cut from her flesh. She was buried on Sunday evening, 21 June 1885.

Hazell ran to town and sounded the alert. A posse with dogs was quickly organized. The group of perpetrators was arrested and charged with the crime. A jury of inquest rendered a guilty verdict. Throughout the course of the day the accused maintained a stolid indifference, laughing and smiling all the while.

The now convicted murderers were held under heavy guard in an empty store building Houston Center. Their overseers were armed with shotguns and six-shooters. As darkness fell the prisoners became rightfully concerned for their safety. On Tuesday, 23 June 1885, a large group of heavily armed men breached the security of the building and took the five prisoners to a nearby Negro church where they lynched them all from the same limbs of a large tree. There the bodies remained there, adorning the tree limbs for quite some time. Although the vigilantes expressed their contempt for mob law they claimed that they were certain that they had punished the right parties.[771] One newspaper commented that, "...it seemed that the mob could not get them hanged quick enough."

On Wednesday, 24 June 1885, two black men who were reportedly companions of the five black men lynched at Elkhart were seized and lynched in Houston County.[772] It appears that this report may be inaccurate, and the result of hysteria on the part of certain newspapers.

John Martin, a black man who was wanted for being involved in the murder of Mrs. Hazell, was arrested at Bells in Grayson County. Sheriff Davis of Anderson County was notified. He confirmed the description of Martin as a suspect. On receipt of the description a mob broke into the jail, seized Martin and took him a short distance and strung him up. On 26 November 1885, a farmer found the decomposed body of a black man who had been hanged by a mob at Bells. The newspaper identified the corpse as that of Andrew Jackson. That was yet another error by journalists since Andrew Jackson and his four confederates had been hanged on June 23 1885.[773] What is certain is that at least six black men were lynched for the outrage and murder of Mrs. Hazell.

Hall, Bob
Born: (Unknown)—Date of Death: July 1885
Place: McLennan County
Event: Lynching/Shot

Bob Hall, a black man was reported to have been shot and killed while trying to escape. His body was never found.[774]

Hathorne, Joel
Born (Unknown)—Date of Death: 5 July 1885
Place: Houston County
Event: Lynching/Hanged

On Friday, 3 July 1885, a black man identified as Joel Hathorne was alleged to have criminally assaulted the four-year old daughter of a prominent citizen at Trinity. The sheriff captured Hathorne on Sunday, 5 July 1885, near Lovelady in Houston County. Fearing a lynch mob, officers decided to secret Hathorne in the woods and tie him to a tree. While they were gone for water the prisoner's location was discovered and he was taken by the mob. Hathorne was hanged within 300 yards of the county jail. His name was also reported as James Hatherton and Jason Hathorn.[775]

Woods, Sim
Born: (Unknown)—Date of Death: 16 July 1885
Place: Coryell/McLennan County
Event: Lynching/Shot

According to newspaper reports, Sim Woods, a black man, was shot by a posse of three men while resisting arrest for committing an unknown crime. No corroboration for the cited source's report of this incident has been uncovered.[776]

Aldava, Christino
Born: circa 1859—Date of Death: 14 August 1885
Place: Webb County
Event: Legal Execution/Hanged

Chivarria, Caledonio
Born: circa 1862—Date of Death: 14 August 1885
Place: Webb County
Event: Legal Execution/Hanged

Christino Aldava and Caledonio Chivarria, both Mexican men and both convicted of murder, were executed at Laredo on Friday, 14 August 1885. Both convicted men claimed to their death that they were innocent, professing that they had done the thing in self-defense.

On the gallows Chivarria jokingly implored the hangman to adjust the knot so it would do the job properly. Apparently the executioner ignored his request, since when the trap fell and Chivarria dropped the ten foot length of his tether his neck was not broken. He died slowly of strangulation. Aldava suffered a more humane fate. His neck snapped as planned, sapping the life from his mortal host almost at once. Witnesses had crowded the rooftops surrounding the site of the execution to get a better view. On this day they got their money's worth.[777]

Lackey, Albert Newton "Al"
Born: circa 1838—Date of Death: 26 August 1885
Place: Hays County
Event: Lynching/Hanged

Dark rumors persisted about the character of Albert Lackey and the nature of his relationship with his daughter Martha "Mattie," and possibly the stepdaughter Mary as well. According to local newspaper reports, Lackey, who was an elderly citizen and well connected in the area, had at some point seduced and had carnal relations with both his daughter and stepdaughter.

On Tuesday, 25 August 1885, Albert Lackey murdered six persons. Included in that tally was his own fourteen year old daughter Martha, who said she had been despoiled by her own father. She was the sixth and final victim.

Albert Lackey, Winchester in hand, mounted his horse and rode to the home of his brother Nathanial Greenberry "Berry" Lackey who immediately fled but was pursued by Alfred. When Berry had covered a distance of about 100 yards he stumbled. Albert ran up to him and shot him in the head, killing him instantly. Next Albert Lackey mounted up and rode a short distance to the home of J. C. Stokes. A neighbor named John Nicholson, who had heard the gunfire, approached Lackey and rode with him for a while trying to talk him out of what he was doing. Nicholson was unsuccessful. Lackey finished his ride and killed Stokes as well.

Not yet completed with the day's blood bath, Lackey returned home and killed Fannie Stokes

Lackey, wife of his stepson Charles. He also put a bullet in the body of his daughter Martha. She died later from the wound. Now out of ammunition, he went after his wife Aley Jane Pruitt with a knife. Had she not fled speedily her fate would have been sealed. Lackey drew the knife across his own throat in an attempt to take his life. Unfortunately he was not successful.[778] A man by the name of Tom Burdick rode up to the house at just the right moment. Lackey approached him, holding his neck with one hand and the knife in the other. He extended his left hand to Burdick in a gesture of greeting then began cutting him with the knife he held in his right hand.

Sheriff Jackson proceeded to Johnson City, where the killer had fled after the incident. He took Lackey into custody and returned him to the jail at Blanco. The unrepentant Lackey later commented that he, "...would have killed three or four other families if his cartridges had not given out."[779]

After sundown, at about 7:30 pm, on 26 August 1886, a mob of about sixty citizens who were understandably unwilling to wait for the often-shaky hand of justice to take its course stormed the Blanco lock up and overpowered Sheriff Jackson, removing Lackey from his custody. The crowd demanded to know if he had committed the unspeakable act of outraging his own daughters. Lackey coyly replied that he did not remember. At that the disgusted mob lynched the wretch from a tree and walked away, leaving him dangling. According to reports, his body remained in situ until lunchtime the following day. Lackey was buried in an unmarked plot northwest of Blanco. His victims were laid to rest at Sandy Cemetery.

Anderson, Dave
Born (Unknown)—Date of Death: 26 September 1885
Place: Orange County
Event: Lynching/Hanged and Shot

On 16 August 1885, Dave Anderson, a black man, fled Nashville, Tennessee to Orange, Texas after murdering a railroad brakeman who tried to stop him from stealing a ride on the train. Orange County Sheriff J. C. Fennel attempted to arrest Anderson on a murder warrant on 25 September 1885. Anderson shot the sheriff to death.

On the night of 26 September 1885, a torchlight mob of masked men marched to the jail and forcibly removed Anderson. He was quickly carried to an oak tree on First Street and hanged. After the lynching, the mob dispersed leaving Anderson's bullet-pierced body on display.[780]

Little, Benjamin
Born: (Unknown)—Date of Death: 9 October 1885
Place: Titus County
Event: Lynching/Hanged

On 7 October 1885, two black men named Benjamin Little and Charley Young robbed a rancher named John M. C. Avery living near Mount Pleasant. The men were taken before Justice of the

Peace Benjamin Johnson on Friday, 9 October 1885. Bond was fixed at $400 each and the men were released.

At about 4:00 pm Little traveled to the house of Mr. A. C. Austin, who lived in the northern suburbs, to work for the man. At about 8:30 pm that same evening he was removed by force by a body of unknown men from a shed on the Austin property where he had been sleeping. Little was taken to a nearby wooded area and lynched.

A crude note found at the scene indicated that Little had not been lynched for the robbery, but rather for making disparaging comments about a white family nearby that had been deemed unacceptable by the mob. The note went on to add that the vigilantes believed they had, "...not committed sin in the eyes of God and furthermore feel that we have done a great and noble act for our country and as gentlemen, etc. Speak to the dead for further information." The document was signed "Citizens of Mount Pleasant, Total Amount 68 [sixty-eight]."[781]

Charley Young remained locked up in the jail, safe for the moment. The sheriff vowed to, "... see the color of the man's hair who gets him out."

Johnson, Henry
Born: circa 1845—Date of Death: 13 November 1885
Place: Houston County
Event: Legal Execution/Hanging

On 27 December 1883, a forty-year old black man named Henry Jackson murdered a twenty-year old mulatto woman named Mattie Murchiso at Crockett. Jackson denied having killed the woman, claiming that two white men had come upon them while walking along the road and carried Mattie off into the woods and outraged her. Afterwards he heard her screams and discovered her lifeless body.

An investigation discovered Mattie lying about 150 yards from the road with her throat cut from ear to ear. There were other knife wounds on her body. Tracks were found leading to the water's edge where a blood soaked handkerchief was found. A man named Newton Owens, who she had last been seen with, was arrested under suspicion. Owens was convicted, but on appeal the case was reversed. During the course of the trials, however, evidence and testimony seemed to point to Johnson. He was eventually arrested, tried and convicted of Mattie's murder.

On 13 November 1885, Johnson, dressed in a nice black suit, marched past the Crockett Rifles who were guarding the event, appearing to be practically emotionless as he made his way to the gallows just 100 yards distant. As the condemned man, bracketed by two preachers named Rotfield Cotton and James Jackson, was made ready to pay for his deeds Johnson delivered a rambling talk, professing his innocence to the end and citing scripture, Exodus 23:7, "Keep far from a false charge, and do not kill the innocent and righteous, for I will not acquit the wicked." He accused Newton Owens of making up the entire story. At the conclusion of his speech a prayer was made, then the assembled mass joined in singing the hymn, "That Awful Day Shall Surely Come."

A man named B. E. Hail, who together with many others had come to the conclusion that

Johnson was truly innocent, drew near the gallows and asked the sheriff that the thing be postponed until a telegram could be sent to the governor. Hail claimed that he could get a thousand names to sign a petition. Hail was reminded by the sheriff that he had a writ in hand dictating that Johnson be hanged between 11:00 am and 3:00 pm on that day, and that he intended to carry it out. Accordingly, at 12:30 pm the noose was adjusted around Johnson's neck, the black cap pulled down. At 12:40 pm the trap sprung. Johnson dropped about eight feet and hung there about fifteen minutes before being declared dead. A crowd of over 5,000 spectators looked on that day.[782]

Jackson, Andrew
Born: (Unknown)—Date of Death: 19 December 1885
Place: Montgomery County
Event: Lynching/Hanged

On Friday night, 11 December 1885, a black man named Andrew Jackson robbed and brutally murdered the Robert Smith family at Mink Prairie in Montgomery County. Jackson fled. A posse, ably assisted by a pack of bloodhound dogs, trailed him for fifteen miles as he covered ground and tried to conceal his path by repeated stream crossings in an effort to confound and throw off the dogs. Unfortunately for Jackson, a dog's brain is specialized for identifying scents, with a unique segment of that organ dedicated to analyzing smells. It is estimated that a bloodhound can identify an aroma somewhere between 1,000 to 10,000 times better than a human can. Thus, Jackson was defeated before his flight began. He was soon run to ground, legs arms and face bearing the evidence of his dash through thick cover.[783]

Jackson was transported to the jail at Montgomery. Fearing a lynch mob, the sheriff decided to spirit Jackson off to a more secure holding cell at Houston. At about midnight on Friday, 18 December 1885, the sheriff's posse left Montgomery with Jackson in tow. They had barely cleared the city limits when a band of vigilantes surrounded the party and took Jackson from their custody, dragging him off into the woods and hiding him until an appropriate time. In the morning it was announced that the lynching would occur at a crossroads, near town. Jackson was brought forth and confessed his crime, adding that he deserved to be hanged. The crowd obliged him, and promptly lynching him from a high tree limb that had been the scene of two earlier vigilante executions.[784]

Madison, William "Bill"
Born: circa 1862—Date of Death: 15 January 1886
Place: Jefferson County
Event: Legal Execution/Hanged

William Madison, a black man, was hanged at Beaumont on Friday, 15 January 1886, for the murder of Albert Smith. Madison had killed Smith, who was also a black man, the preceding summer for reasons of jealousy.[785]

Mendiola, Jose Maria
Born: circa 1856—Date of Death: 15 January 1886
Place: LaSalle County
Event: Legal Execution/Hanged

Jose Maria Mendiola, a thirty-year old Mexican man, was hanged at Cotulla at 2:00 pm on Friday, 15 January 1886. Mendiola had been tried and convicted of the murder of L. M. Hodges, a Southern Pacific Railroad agent. The incident had taken place near Cotulla eight months earlier. The condemned man displayed great composure and bravery, professing penitence before meeting his maker.[786]

Brown, Sidney
Born: (Unknown)—Date of Death: 21 January 1886
Place: Milam County
Event: Lynching/Hanged

On Wednesday, 20 January 1886, Samuel Ford, a farmer, was returning home in his wagon when he was set upon by Sidney Brown, a black man. Brown robbed him and beat him insensible with a heavy iron pole. Brown thought that he had killed Ford, so he dragged the body to the International and Great Western railroad tracks and left him there in hopes that a passing train would run over him and mutilate the corps so the murder would go undetected. The plan fell apart, largely because Ford was not dead. When he regained conciseness he managed to drag himself home, a distance of two miles. Ford had undergone a most savage thrashing. One of his eyes was knocked from the socket and his skull was fractured. Once he reached safety he sounded the alarm for help.

Brown was captured the following day with Ford's belongings in his possession. He was lodged in the jail at Rockdale. His stay there was a brief one. On the evening of Thursday, 21 January 1886, Brown was forcibly removed from his cell and taken about two miles from town where he was lynched from a hickory tree. [787]

Garrett, R. T.
Born: (Unknown)—Date of Death: 8 February 1886
Place: Lamar County
Event: Lynching/Hanged

R. T. Garrett had been arrested by Deputy Clay Davis for disturbing the peace at a Christmas tree festival at Shockey's Prairie. He asked to be allowed to stop at his home on the way to jail. Deputy Davis relented. While at the residence Garrett grabbed a rifle and killed Davis, then fled into the nearby woods. He was captured, but not until after sustaining serious gunshot wounds to his person.

In a very well planned and executed attack, at about 2:00 am on Monday, 8 February 1886, a mob of roughly one hundred masked riders approached the jail at Paris. Lookouts had been positioned about the town by the rabble so that their scheme would go undetected. About a dozen of the vigilantes dismounted and pounded on the door of the jail, looking to be admitted. Jailor Baldwin resisted the mob, pulling his pistol and firing. His bullet failed to find a mark and his gun was taken from him, tossed out into the crowd beyond his reach. The intruders who had strangled Baldwin until he was practically lifeless quickly overwhelmed him and made his way into the building. Deputies Hamp Sanders and Jim Booth, who occupy a room in the jailhouse, were held at gunpoint as were several other parties. Next the mob rushed the cell of Garrett, who was still recovering from his gunshot wounds. They dragged him to a nearby wagon on North Main Street and hustled him to an appropriate tree, about three quarters of a mile distant. There they lynched him with a small rope that looked to have been used as a plow line or a horse halter.

Garrett's body was not discovered until the following day. The only clue to the identity of the vigilantes was the presence of a hat that had been left in the jail cell.[788] Garrett's body was shipped to Arkansas for burial.

Polk, Thomas Oscar
Born: circa 1864—Date of Death: 15 March 1886
Place: Coryell/Lampasas County
Event: Lynching/Hanged

Thomas Polk was lynched near Copperas Cove, just over the line in Lampasas County. The incident occurred sometime around 1:00 am on Monday, 15 March 1886, and was done by persons unknown. Polk answered a knock at the door and found a party of masked men asking for a fellow named Tom Walters. When he granted them admission they grabbed him, dragged him into the yard and beat him insensible with a heavy club. Afterward his limp body was transported about a half mile and lynched from a tree limb. His neighbors suspected him of being a horse thief. If the neighbors had proof of his wrongdoing it was not mentioned by the source.[789]

Some reports claim the date of this incident was 14 March 1886.[790]

Lane, Ben
Born: circa 1860—Date of Death: 19 March 1886
Place: San Augustine County
Event: Legal Execution/Hanged

After his appeal for clemency failed, Ben Lane, a twenty-six year old black man, was hanged on Friday, 19 March 1886, for committing murder.[791]

Washington, Wash
Born: circa 1856—Date of Death: 31 March 1886
Place: Falls County
Event: Legal Execution/Hanged

Wash Washington was a thirty-year old black man who was tried and convicted of murder. He was sentenced to be executed by hanging.

On Wednesday morning, 31 March 1886, Washington climbed aboard the wagon that was to carry him to his execution and took a seat on his own coffin. After mounting the gallows stairs he proceeded to pass a hat for a collection to defray his funeral expenses. The crowd, apparently willing to pay the star actor in this show for his performance, anteed up $22. As a pundit for one Midwest newspaper who obviously had a low opinion of the Lone Star State put it, "the whole scene was characteristic of Texas." [792]

Gonzales, Camillo
Born: (Unknown)—Date of Death: 17 April 1886
Place: Kinney County
Event: Legal Execution/Hanging

At about 2:30 pm on Saturday, 17 April 1886, the notorious outlaw Camillo Gonzales went to the gallows at Brackettville. Gonzales made a short talk before his fall, protesting his conviction for murder and robbery to the bitter end. The killing of Peter Johnson, which had occurred on 1 November 1884, had finally caught up with Gonzales.[793]

Throngs of bystanders watched the last minutes of Gonzales's life, a cold and heartless outlaw they called a "caged beast." He jeered at the spectators and reporters, defiant to the last breath.

Cadena, Mateo
Born: (Unknown)—Date of Death: 18 April 1886
Place: Duval County
Event: Lynching/Hanged

Pena, Pedro
Born: (Unknown)—Date of Death: 18 April 1886
Place: Duval County
Event: Lynching/Hanged

Several rancheros residing along Los Alamos Creek, which is forty miles from Corpus Christi, in Duval County, were suffering heavy losses of horses at the hands of thieves. On Sunday, 18 April 1886, the stockmen rounded up two Mexicans thieves and promptly hanged them to nearest tree.

The sheriff is said to have investigated the lynching but there is no information as to the outcome of that inquiry. In Carrigan's book *Forgotten Dead* the author identifies the victims are as Mateo Cadena and Pedro Pena.[794]

Cardena, Jose Maria
Born: (Unknown)—Date of Death: 18 April 1886
Place: Nueces County
Event: Lynching/Shot

Martinez, Andres
Born: (Unknown)—Date of Death:18 April 1886
Place: Nueces County
Event: Lynching/Shot

On Sunday, 18 April 1886, a posse under the command of Nueces County deputy sheriff P. M. Coy captured two Mexican outlaws and horse thieves identified as Jose Maria Cardena (or Cadena) and Andres Martinez. Once in custody the men were housed at the residence of Constable Johnson at Collins. During the night a body of masked men surrounded the constable's home forcing their way in and disarming the officer. The manacled prisoners were pierced with bullets while pleading for mercy.

On Monday, 26 April 1886, the town of Collins was surrounded by a band of armed Mexicans who searched every house looking for Deputy Coy. Coy was, however, out of town and in another part of the county. Unsuccessful in their attempt at vengeance, the mob rode away. Suspicion as to the identity of the armed mob seemed to point to the father of Andres Martinez, who was a wealthy man. Afterwards Martinez's father offered a $1,000 reward for the murderers of his son.

The sheriff took a posse to Collins to sort out the affair and arrest the leaders of the raid. Newspapers of the day praised Deputy Coy for ferreting out horse thieves and other lawless desperadoes.[795]

One Unidentified Mexican Man
Born (Unknown)—Date of Death: 25 April 1886
Place: Howard County
Event: Lynching/Hanged

On Sunday, 25 April 1886, a Mexican herder shot and killed his partner, William Mack, while the latter was asleep near Big Springs. No cause for the shooting was provided by reporting sources, although it seems logical that he would have one. A posse caught up with the killer and hung him from a tree.[796]

Telles, Juan

Born: (Unknown)—Date of Death: 26 April 1886
Place: Lubbock County
Event: Lynching/Shot

Unverified reports of the day claim that a Mexican man named Juan Telles, suspected of having committed a murder, was dragged behind a horse and shot to death.[797]

Two Unknown Men

Born: (Unknown)—Date of Death: 4 May 1886
Place: Galveston County
Event: Lynching/Hanged

Newspaper reports of the day indicate that the bodies of two unidentified men were discovered hanging from a tree on the morning of Tuesday, 4 May 1886. Henry Weyer, a Justice of the Peace, made the unpleasant find.[798]

Young, George

Born: circa 1855—Date of Death: 8 May 1886
Place: Ellis County
Event: Legal Execution/Hanged

George Young, a black man about thirty-one years old who was from Palmer, was tried and found guilty of murdering his wife, Fannie.

Young was a freedman who had come to Texas from Caloway County, Missouri in 1855. According to newspaper reports, George and Fannie were not legally married but had been living together for some time. On Sunday, 5 April 1885, Young left the house to get a bag of coal. When he returned he quietly slipped around the building and shot Fannie through a window with his six-shooter. After the incident he fled the scene and remained at large for about a week, vowing to "die game." He was eventually captured, tried, convicted and sentenced to hang.

According to newspaper reports of the day six thousand people witnessed the execution of Young. The gibbet had been constructed on a vacant plot of land near the creek known as the Circus Lot. At 1:11 pm on Saturday, 8 May 1886, Sheriff Ryburn accompanied Young to the gallows. Once they had mounted the stairs Young was given the opportunity to speak, which he accepted. At 1:54 pm the trap was sprung and Young dropped about seven feet. When he had come to rest his neck was broken. Eleven minutes afterwards he was pronounced dead.[799]

Pruitt, William
Born: (Unknown)—Date of Death: 14 June 1886
Place: Eastland County
Event: Lynching/Hanged

William Pruitt was accused of robbing and murdering an elderly man named Hosetter.

On Monday, 14 June 1886, a mob of four men lynched Pruitt at a location about ten miles south of Carbon, near Sipe Springs. According to reports his body was discovered the following day.[800]

Williams, Ed
Born: (Unknown)—Date of Death: 29 June 1886
Place: Cooke County
Event: Lynching/Hanged

On Sunday, 20 June 1886 an attempt was made by an individual identified as Ed Williams to outrage a Gainesville woman named Cook. When Cook screamed a neighbor came to her rescue and scared off the intruder. Later the same night Williams returned, this time grabbing Mrs. Cook by the throat. Her struggle caused her infant to cry. Williams attempted to strike the child, but Mrs. Cook's grown daughter who had been awakened by the commotion came into the room to investigate.

Williams severely abused the elder Cook. She had cuts and bruises all over her body and her neck was swollen from the strangulation. The daughter had also been beaten extensively. As Williams was trying to retreat, with the daughter close at his heals and now sporting an ax, a neighbor woman named Collins spotted him.

After a spirited chase by hounds Williams was apprehended later the same day. He was rushed to the jail for his own protection. On the night of Monday, 28 June 1886, a group of disguised men estimated to be one hundred strong surrounded the jail. After overpowering the guard the mob removed Williams and took him to Pecan Creek where he was lynched from a willow tree.[801]

On 1 October 1886, a man named Redman who was sought in the lynching surrendered to authorities. T. J. Parrish, one of the men accused in the lynching, boarded an eastbound train at Paris on 17 November 1886, but was captured at Belton and returned. Another alleged member of the lynch party, a man named Smith, tried to commit suicide by cutting his own throat on 20 November 1886. He failed in his attempt when his groans were heard, the doctor summoned, and a needle and thread employed to repairing the damage.

Davis, Sidney "Sid"
Born: (Unknown)—Date of Death: 10 July 1886
Place: Bosque County
Event: Lynching/Hanged

Sidney Davis, a black man, was lynched on Saturday, 10 July 1886. Davis was accused of outraging a white woman. After being convicted he confessed his guilt in four other cases of outrage. A mob of six hundred citizens removed Davis from the jail at Meridian and hanged him.[802]

Davis was an acquaintance of another black man named Bill Harris who would also be lynched at Whitehall for outrage not long after.

Surname Unknown, Tom
Born: (Unknown)—Date of Death: 26 July 1886
Place: Comanche County
Event: Lynching/Hanged

On Monday, 26 July 1886 a black youth identified only as Tom was lynched for having shot and killed Sallie Sarah (Hulsey) Stephens. The murder had occurred on Saturday, 24 July 1886, at Downing in Comanche County.

Benjamin Stephens, who was a horse trader, was in the habit of picking up young black boys from an orphanage in Kentucky during his travels and bringing them to Texas to work for him. Tom was such a lad.[803] Newspaper reports of the day claim that just prior to the lynching young Tom had confessed to the crime, indicating that he had come out of the fields and taken a gun down to shoot a hawk. The killing of Mrs. Stephens had not been planned. Why he suddenly decided that it was a good idea was not disclosed.

At about 1:30 pm Tom was placed in a hack and driven to a nearby tree. A rope was thrown around his neck and looped over a limb. Mr. Hulsey, the father of Sallie Stephens, asked Tom why he had killed his daughter. The boy replied "meanness." At about 2:00 pm Tom was pulled up by the rope and hung. He remained there for only about a minute before the limb broke and he fell to the ground. Undaunted, the lynching party restrung the rope and hauled Tom up another limb of the same tree. This time the branch they had selected held up under the load. Those in attendance pondered shooting Tom while he hung there. Some members of the agitated mob wanted to burn the body. In the end calmer heads prevailed when the mother of the murdered woman intervened.[804]

Harris, Bill
Born: (Unknown)—Date of Death: 4 August 1886
Place: McLennan County
Event: Lynching/Hanged

Bill Harris, a black man, was charged with the outrage of Mrs. Frederick Hittmiller, a white woman from Waco. Another black man named Alex Greggs had been taken into custody under suspicion, but when Mrs. Hittmiller was unable to positively identify him the man was released. Harris and two other black men had been held at the jail Whitehall. Mrs. Hittmiller was called to identify Harris. She asked that he be stripped down and placed in the position that she had seen him in last. Once done, she burst into tears and exclaimed that she was quite certain that Harris was her molester.

Harris never made it to trial. He was taken off by a mob of about thirty men to a clump of trees along the South Bosque and lynched from a convenient tree. Once the deed had been done the lynch mob returned to town, all this in the span of just ten minutes. The vigilantes traveled in groups of twos and threes so as not to call attention to themselves.[805]

Smith, John
Born: (Unknown)—Date of Death: 1 September 1886
Place: Hunt County
Event: Lynching/Hanged

Jack County Sheriff's Deputy John William Benjamin Adair was stabbed to death while escorting six escapees back to the Hunt County Jail.

As Adair was traveling back to the jail on Saturday, 28 August 1886, one of the inmates attempted to escape. Adair gave his pistol to a passing citizen and told him to go after the fleeing man. While Adair was guarding the remaining prisoners they attacked him. One of the black captive, a man named John Smith, cut Adair's throat and wrist then slashed him from his shoulder to his waist. He died of his injuries four days later on Wednesday, 1 September 1886.

Seeing no need to wait for the bothersome formality of a trial, as soon as word was out on the street that Adair had died a mob was on its way to the jail to remove Smith from custody. He was taken some distance from Greenville and lynched.[806]

Murray, Irvin
Born: (Unknown)—Date of Death: 10 September 1886
Place: Williamson County
Event: Legal Execution/Hanged

Irvin Murray, a black man, was hanged at Georgetown on Friday, 10 September 1886, for murdering his wife Molly. That incident had occurred at Taylor, on 19 December 1885, when Murray struck the woman in the head several times with an ax and slashed her throat from ear to ear with a razor. After the verdict had been read at his trial on 21 January 1886, Murray passed by his eleven year old son who had been the principal witness against him and gave the boy a small book and a silver dollar. He also told the lad to be a good boy.

On the morning of 10 September 1886, the town of Georgetown was a beehive of activity as thousands of people poured in to witness the upcoming hanging. They came "two to the mule." All manner of conveyance crowded the streets as prospective spectators vied for the best viewing spot. In the jailhouse, Murray professed his innocence to the end, claiming that Molly had a paramour and that he must have done the thing. As with most condemned men, he had found religion and claimed to be ready to meet his maker. Sheriff John T. Olive brought him a new suit of clothes that he donned prior to the arrival of reporters.

The site that had been selected for the hanging was in an open field of about ten acres near the Granger road, one mile from town. A large campfire had been set as wagons circled. Ice cream and lemonade stands were erected, and all for the enjoyment set up for the attendees. At about 11:45 am Sheriff Olive brought Murray to the site. Their route to the gallows was lined with people, wagons and men on horseback. Some galloped alongside straining to get a glimpse of the condemned man.

Methodist Parson J. C. Williams asked the crowd to join in the singing of "And was I born to die" followed by "And lay the body down." Just before the black cap was pulled down over his head Murray said to Deputy Sheriff Lockhart, "Lock, be a better man. Come up and shake hands with me." Lockhart complied, and was followed by a string of black men, women and children who filed past Murray offering their last farewell. The procession went on for ten minutes or more.

At 1:53 pm the trap was sprung and Murray dropped seven and one half feet, breaking his neck. With the exception of a slight shrug of the shoulders there was no sign of movement. He was declared dead a few minutes afterwards.[807]

Farrar, Tom
Born: (Unknown)—Date of Death: 3 October 1886
Place: Throckmorton County
Event: Lynching/Hanged

Tom Farrar, a black man, had confessed to the outrage and murder of Miss Lizzie Urney (Urry), "... according to newspaper sources the most brutal crime yet committed in Throckmorton County." After doing the evil deed and attempting to flee the Urney ranch on horseback, Farrar encountered Mr. Urney. Not wishing to be found out for his evil deed he lassoed Urney and dragged him to his death to avoid discovery.

Farrar was held in the jail at Albany. At about 1:00 am on Sunday morning, 3 October 1886, a mob of about thirty-two armed, masked and mounted vigilantes overpowered the guard, threw a rope around Farrar's neck and drug him about a quarter of a mile from the jail to a spot where they hung him from a tree limb.[808]

Two Unidentified Mexican Men
Born: (Unknown)—Date of Death: 14 October 1886
Place: Webb County
Event: Lynching/Hanged

Two unidentified Mexican men were lynched near Laredo on Thursday, 14 October 1886. The pair had been found guilty of being among the gang of outlaws who had held up the Mexican National Railroad three years earlier. Officers left Laredo with these two prisoners in custody and had planned on transporting them to Monterey, Mexico. En route vigilantes decided to carry out a death sentence a bit sooner than had been anticipated.[809]

Petland, Jim
Born: (Unknown)—Date of Death: 29 October 1886
Place: Cass County
Event: Lynching/Hanged

Miss Sallie Evans, a white girl, was returning from school at Kildare when Jim Petland, a black man, burst upon the scene and assaulted her. The girl's screams alerted her mother, who came to her rescue and frightened the attacker. Miss Evans was the daughter of the wealthiest man in Kildare.

Petland fled, but was captured the following day at Atlanta. He was taken to the depot building where United States Marshals held him under guard. About forty masked and armed men took him by force to a place about a mile from town where they lynched him from the limb of a prominent oak tree located just alongside the road. It was claimed that the unfortunate fellow confessed to his crime before his end.[810]

Hughey, Given Name Unknown
Born (Unknown)—Date of Death: 31 October 1886
Place: San Jacinto County
Event: Lynching/Hanged

On Sunday, 31 October 1886, a mob overpowered the guard and took custody of a man named Hughey who was accused of killing Sam Day about ten days earlier. Hughey was transported a short distance from Cold Spring and hung him from a tree.[811]

Four Unidentified Black Men
Born: (Unknown)—Date of Death: 29 November 1886
Place: Bowie County
Event: Lynching/Hanged

Newspaper reports of the day claimed that four unidentified black men were lynched near DeKalb for the murder of a farmer named George Taufo. The murder had taken place in Indian Territory (Oklahoma).[812]

Felder (Feldner), Shed
Born: circa 1841—Date of Death: 2 December 1886
Place: Washington County
Event: Lynching/Hanged

Jones, Alfred
Born: circa 1826—Date of Death: 2 December 1886
Place: Washington County
Event: Lynching/Hanged

Jones, Ephraim (T.H.)
Born: circa 1841—Date of Death: 2 December 1886
Place: Washington County
Event: Lynching/Hanged

Three black men...Shea Felder, Alfred Jones and Ephraim Jones...were implicated in the murder of Dewees Bolton at Howellen's Store on election night of 1886. Local citizens were fuming. Sheriff Devere had the men moved to a jail in Houston for safekeeping. Once feelings had subsided the men were returned to the jail at Brenham.

On Wednesday, 1 December 1886 a crowd of citizens formed outside the jail. Jailer James Estes answered their knock at the door. The mob rushed the building, throwing a slicker over Estes and pushing him aside. Estes dropped his keys, which were promptly picked up and used to gain entry to the cell containing Felder and the two men named Jones. The threesome was quietly removed and taken about a mile from town, up the Independence road, where they were lynched. A crowd of twenty to sixty men had done the work. They were said to have all been orderly and sober during the undertaking.

The hanging went undetected until the following morning when the bodies were discovered and cut down from their perch.[813]

Howard, James
Born: circa 1851—Date of Death: 15 December 1886
Place: Bowie County
Event: Lynching/Hanged

Thirty-five year old James Howard was arrested on a warrant sworn out by his mother-in-law, Mrs. Winchew. She charged him with maltreating his wife. Ms. Howard, who was barely fourteen years old at the time, testified that her husband had frequently beat her, and had often tied her feet together while she was in a state of nudity and hung her upside down while he beat her. In one last act of perverse behavior, taking spousal abuse to a new level, he had marked her in two places with a hot branding iron in the form of an "H".

At about midnight on Wednesday, 15 December 1886, Howard was removed from his jail cell by a mob of masked men and taken a short distance from town where he was lynched. Vigilante justice had been swiftly administered. It is doubtful that there were many in the community who mourned his passing.[814] This may be one situation where the expression, "...he just needed killing" is appropriate.

Two Unidentified Mexican Men
Born: (Unknown)—Date of Death: 1 January 1887
Place: Guadalupe County
Event: Lynching/Shot and Burned

On New Year's Day 1887, three black men, identified as Coly Thompson, Andy Williams and Warren Wilson, attacked the camp of four Mexican men. They shot two of the men to death and burned their bodies. Two managed to escape. According to reports the Mexicans had filed a legal action against one of the black men prior to the incident, probably the motive of the violent attack.

Another source reported that three Mexicans had been killed.[815]

Thompson, Cody
Born: (Unknown)—Date of Death: 2 February 1887
Place: Guadalupe County
Event: Lynching/Hanged

Williams, Andy
Born: (Unknown)—Date of Death: 2 February 1887
Place: Guadalupe County
Event: Lynching/Hanged

Wilson, Warren
Born: (Unknown)—Date of Death: 2 February 1887
Place: Guadalupe County
Event: Lynching/Hanged

At about 10:00 am on Wednesday, 2 February 1887, a party of roughly thirty masked and heavily armed riders converged on the jail at Seguin. They overpowered the jailers, took the keys, and removed Cody Thompson, Andy Williams and Warren Wilson, all black men, from their cells. The last townspeople saw of the mob was their dust as they lit out with their captors up the Gonzales road. The bodies of the three men were found about three miles from town, hanged from a tree with a note pinned to the shirt of one man that said they had been lynched for murder, outrage and house burning.

The three victims had been locked up in the jail for about three weeks, accused of attacking a group of Mexicans camping along the San Marcos River. After robbing the party of about $40 they murdered two of four Mexicans seated around the fire. The two who managed to escape did survive, but were peppered with bullet holes. The three black men then butchered the two unfortunate fellows they had killed and burned the portions in the campfire in an effort to conceal their deeds. [816]

Richards, Jim

Born: (Unknown)—Date of Death: 14 February 1887
Place: Grimes County
Event: Lynching/Hanged

On Sunday, 13 February 1887, a black man named Jim Richards stole a trunk from J. F. MacDonald, a man for whom he had been working at Bedias. The next day Deputy Sheriff Milton Upchurch arrested Richards, but stopped at his residence to have dinner before making the trip to the jail in Anderson. Richards snatched Upchurch's pistol and shot him in the abdomen. The wound was considered fatal, but Upchurch survived until his death many years later in 1934. At about sundown that same day a mob of around seventy-five heavily armed men took Richards from guards and lynched him from a convenient tree.[817] The newspaper reported that Richards "had a bad reputation, while Upchurch is one of the best citizens of the county."

Blocker, Tim

Born: (Unknown)—Date of Death: 4 March 1887
Place: Hays County
Event: Lynching/Hanged

Tim Blocker, described by the newspapers as a "colored youth," was lynched on 4 March 1887.[818] Blocker had been jailed on 1 March 1887, for the attempted outrage of Mrs. William Patterson. A mob of approximately 250 angry vigilantes stormed the jail and removed Blocker, took him to the San Marcos River and lynched him from a tree.

Jones, James "Jim"

Born: circa 1860—Date of Death: 13 May 1887
Place: Bowie County
Event: Legal Execution/Hanged

According to reports of the day, Jim Jones, a black man, was a tough character and a successful gambler. He had been the terror of a railroad camp near Bassett, fleecing workers out of their hard earned dollar until a white commissary cook named Cate Hicks ordered him out. Jones responded by killing the cook. He was tried and convicted of the slaying. The sentence was death.

Jones wanted to be baptized by Reverend Booth of the Baptist Church before he was hanged, apparently believing that last minute salvation was better than the rigors of a lifelong walk without Christ. The sheriff refused to allow him to be released for the procedure, so a tank was erected in the jail for the purpose and clergy admitted to perform the rite.

A large contingent of the Bowie Rifles had been stationed around the town to keep the peace on the day of the hanging. At half past noon on Friday, 13 May 1887, the condemned man addressed the crowd, professing his salvation. At 12:45 pm the trap door dropped and Jones was propelled downward to his death in full view of about 5,000 spectators. The body was cut down and placed in a coffin at 1:10 pm. Jones's hanging marked the first legal execution in Bowie County since the end of the Civil War.[819]

Benson, Crawford
Born: circa 1869—Date of Death: 24 July 1887
Place: Kaufman County
Event: Lynching/Hanged

At about 11:00 pm on 24 July 1887, an angry throng removed Crawford Benson, an eighteen-year old black man, from the jail at Kaufman and lynched him from a nearby tree. After the hanging Benson's body was shot full of bullets to make certain that the strangulation had taken effect.

Benson had outraged the nine-year old white girl, the daughter of J. N. Ludom. The crime had occurred about two miles south of time, in the farm country. For some unknown reason the child's mother had sent her to where Benson was working. Benson sprang upon her, threatening her with a knife and saying if she screamed he would kill her. Somehow the resilient little girl managed to break free and alert her mother. [820]

Adams, Joe
Born: (Unknown)—Date of Death: 3 October 1887
Place: Nacogdoches County
Event: Lynching/Hanged

On Friday, 23 September 1887 J. F. Looney, a merchant and postmaster at Douglass, was nearly decapitated while walking to his store from his home. Twenty black men were arrested. One of them implicated a black man named Joe Adams. Bloody clothes were found when Adams was arrested. Adams confessed that he was trying to burglarize Looney's store when he was caught, and had no choice but cut Looney's throat.

On Monday, 3 October 1887, a mob of about 100 masked men battered down the door of the jail at Nacogdoches and removed Joe Adams. Under duress from the vigilantes Adams confessed to the crime, which probably satisfied the collective conscience of the mob. After coming clean they quickly lynched him.[821]

Nine Unidentified Mexican Men

Born: (Unknown)—Date of Death: 12 October 1887
Place: Starr County
Event: Lynching/Shot

According to unverified reports, nine unidentified Mexican men were executed by a posse at Starr County for kidnapping.[822]

"Unconfirmed" reports, or tales told in oral histories, are generally transcribed from interviews done more than a century or more after the event. Some tales have been passed down over multiple generations and have become folklore, having little or no basis in fact. On balance, such oral histories are generally 10% to 90% accurate, thus that they are also 10% and 90% incorrect. One is always best served by the discovery of empirical evidence before claiming that a thing is true rather than relying solely on an oral history.

Giles, Robert

Born: (Unknown)—Date of Death: 14 October 1887
Place: Henderson County
Event: Legal Execution/Hanged

On Friday, 14 October 1887 Robert Giles, a black man, walked to the gallows at Athens for the murder of another black man Albert Williams. About 1:00 pm Sheriff Osborne and Deputy Sheriff McRea emerged from the jail with Giles and entered an open hack containing his coffin. Twenty armed men guarded the one-mile route to the gallows. Giles's speech was rambling. He urged the young black people to avoid gambling and craps. He did not feel a jury could give justice to white and black alike. At 1:55 pm the trap was sprung and Giles swung into eternity.

Glies was a former slave. He had been sentenced to two years in prison for shooting a black man at Ferris. After release he moved to Henderson County. Adams and Williams were chopping wood ties near Malakoff when they became engaged in a quarrel. Giles claimed Williams tried to hit him with an ax. Giles grabbed the tool, then struck Williams with it. [823]

Wade, Hamp

Born: (Unknown)—Date of Death: 15 October 1887
Place: Walker County
Event: Legal Execution/Hanged

Hamp Wade, a black man, had been hired by a chap named Jones to kill a black man named "Smutty My Darling." Wade's fee for killing Mr. Smutty was to be a yoke of oxen and a bale of cotton. Wade executed his agreement promptly and thoroughly, extinguishing "Smutty My Darling" around Christmas time 1886. Afterwards he fled successfully and managed to stay on the lam for about four months before being captured, tried and convicted.

After a failed attempt to have his sentence commuted, made on his behalf to the governor by prominent citizens of Huntsville who apparently thought that Mr. "Smutty My Darling" needed to be killed. Wade was hanged on Saturday, 15 October 1887.[824] The *Dallas Morning News* of 25 October 1887 cited a quote from Byron on the occasion of Wade's hanging:

> *Wounds by Christian sabers given are the surest pass to the Turkish heaven, but the direct road to everlasting bliss is over the scaffold, so far as negro [Negro] murderers are concerned. They invariably proclaim from the gallows that their sins have been forgiven, and that they will drop into Paradise when the drop falls.*

Diaz, Vivian
Born: (Unknown)—Date of Death: 7 December 1887
Place: Starr County
Event: Lynching/Hanged

Ybarra, Cicilio
Born: (Unknown)—Date of Death: 7 December 1887
Place: Starr County
Event: Lynching/Hanged

On Wednesday, 7 December 1887, the Starr County sheriff arrested Vivian Diaz and Cicilio Ybarra at Gruela Ranch. The lawman started for Rio Grande City with the pair in tow when at a place about eight miles from Rio Grande City the party was overwhelmed by a group of fifteen to twenty Mexicans. According to reports, the kidnappers lynched Ybarra and Diaz from a nearby tree. Afterwards the raiders rode off towards Rio Grande City and probably into Old Mexico.

Ybarra and Diaz were part of the group that aided Juan Garcia in the "Berrera robbery" two months earlier. It is thought that their lynching was directly tied to that incident.

Some sources spell Ybarra's given name as Cecilio and Diaz's as Viviano. It is unclear which is correct.[825]

Rodriguez, Cruz
Born: (Unknown)—Date of Death: 9 December 1887
Place: Uvalde County
Event: Legal Execution/Hanged

Cruz Rodriguez, a Mexican man, was tried and convicted of murder. On 1 April 1887, he was sentenced to hang for his crime. That verdict was carried out on Friday, 9 December 1887, when Rodriguez climbed the steps of a Uvalde gallows to keep his appointment with the hangman. At precisely 2:03 pm the trap was sprung and the condemned man dropped through the floor, breaking his neck when he reached the end of the fetter. His only request was that the traditional black cap not be placed over his head. Authorities complied. Rodriguez had nothing to say before meeting his fate.[826]

Casas, Jose Maria
Born: (Unknown)—Date of Death: 10 December 1887
Place: Starr County
Event: Lynching/Hanged

Contreras, Gerardo
Born: (Unknown)—Date of Death: 10 December 1887
Place: Starr County
Event: Lynching/Hanged

In Carrigan's book *Forgotten Dead* the author claimed that two Mexican men named Gerardo Contreras and Jose Maria Casas were taken from the jail and lynched near Rio Grande City in Starr County for theft.

A newspaper reported that the men were found hanged near Ringgold Barracks. They had been captured in Mexico by government troops, placed in jail, and then released. It was hypothesized that vigilantes from Texas, or Mexican troops, hanged the men.[827]

Kelley, Mr. (Given Name Unknown)
Born: (Unknown)—Date of Death: 30 December 1887
Place: Unidentified County
Event: Lynching/Shot

Kelley, Mrs. (Given Name Unknown)
Born: (Unknown)—Date of Death: 30 December 1887
Place: Unidentified County
Event: Lynching/Shot

Kelley, Bill
Born: (Unknown)—Date of Death: 30 December 1887
Place: Unidentified County
Event: Lynching/Hanged

Kelley, Miss (Given Name Unknown)

Born: (Unknown)—Date of Death: 30 December 1887
Place: Unidentified County
Event: Lynching/Shot

In spite of overwhelming evidence to the contrary, some nonbelievers question the existence of the devil, Lucifer or Satan as he is often called. Most agree, however, that there are evil forces at work, calling us to surrender our souls and step over to the dark side. On occasion we hear of wicked deeds like the numerous man burnings listed in this book. Regardless of our personal position on capital punishment, or on Christianity, it causes one to wonder how civilized people could visit such evil on their fellow man. The Kelley story is more sinister than most and makes for the stuff of reoccurring nightmares.

The Kelley Family was, for all intents, a clan of folks who had marched straight out of the fires of Hell. Their farm was located alongside a well-traveled path about fifty miles from a place called Oak City. No record exists of an Oak City, Texas. Not even in the log of Texas ghost towns. Based on the reports given in newspapers of the day it would seem that the Kelley's house of horrors was located somewhere in the Panhandle Region. One of the men relating the Kelley's sage was a cattle dealer named Charles Graham (also called Green/Greene) who had arrived at that place and told the story from his eyewitness account.

It seems that the Kelley's served meals to travelers who happened along the road. Although uneducated, the family appeared clean, well attired and neatly groomed. Civilized by all outward accounts one might say. Supper guests would be positioned at the table so that they were seated over a trap door. At the appropriate signal the latch would be sprung and the unsuspecting dinner guest would tumble through the floor into the cellar, generally breaking his or her neck in the process. If the drop did not kill them the Kelley clan would finish the job.

When the Bender Family visited the Kelley home and afterwards disappeared suspicions were raised. Investigators discovered the clever trap door apparatus, and the decaying remains of three persons in the cellar beneath. A more thorough search of the ground revealed a number of bodies buried at various locations around the home and outbuildings. Most were men. At least one was a woman. Rumors were pervasive that the Kelly Clan would occasionally eat the flesh of their victims, however, no forensic evidence of such deeds was uncovered.

A posse went to the Kelley's camp to arrest them. According to accounts of the day they "fought like tigers" and refused to be taken in. Mrs. Kelley and the daughter were shot down and killed. The father escaped, but was soon shot and killed as well. The son, Bill, was captured and lynched from a suitable tree. It is doubtful that many mourned their passing.[828] The surname Kelley is sometimes spelled Kelly in certain accounts of this incident.

Peters, Albert
Born: (Unknown)—Date of Death: 30 December 1887
Place: Polk County
Event: Legal Execution/Hanged

Albert Peters, a white man, was hanged at Marianna for the 1885 murder of William Johnson. His trip to the gallows on Friday, 30 December 1887, was uneventful for everyone apart from Peters.[829]

Bolo, William "Bill"
Born: (Unknown)—Date of Death: 3 January 1888
Place: Madison County
Event: Lynching/Shot

Page, "Red"
Born: (Unknown)—Date of Death: 4 3 January 1888
Place: Madison County
Event: Lynching/Hanged

Whitten, Alf
Born: (Unknown)—Date of Death: 3 January 1888
Place: Madison County
Event: Lynching/Hanged

As reconstruction came to a close in the 1870s the second wave of the temperance movement took hold in Texas. Various organizations emerged, some growing from assorted religious denominations that supported abstinence. The movement took root in a few Texas towns, although it was tough sledding for the teetotalers practically everywhere in the Lone Star State. For many, their ethnic heritage, culture and folkways involved the consumption of wine or beer. Ardent spirits were widely partaken of. Then, as today, progressive do-gooders occasionally managed to exert heavy influence in favor or prohibition.

On Tuesday, 3 January 1888, reformers at Madisonville shot and killed "Bill" Bolo, then hanged "Red" Page and Alf Whitten. All of these men were guilty of wanting to maintain saloons in the town. Then as now, "peaceful social reengineering" is rarely that.[830]

In another newspaper account "Red" Page was identified as a horse thief, not a saloon proponent. Whitten was shot and not hanged. Some reports indicate that five men were killed. It is unclear which is correct. The temperance story is far more salacious, and thus more appealing.[831]

Pettis, Mat
Born: (Unknown)—Date of Death: 15 January 1888
Place: Caldwell County
Event: Lynching/Shot

Reto, Given Name Unknown
Born: (Unknown)—Date of Death: 15 January 1888
Place: Caldwell County
Event: Lynching/Shot

A mob gained entrance to the jail at Lockhart on Sunday, 15 January 1888. Their intended mission was that of lynching four Mexicans who were incarcerated there and had been charged with the murder of a planter named Alfred. That killing had occurred several days earlier. One of prisoners (identified as Pettis and Pazo) had confessed. The mob found the men in a cell with a black man. They ordered the black man to throw the Mexicans out one at a time. Accordingly, Pettis (Pazo) and another man (identified as Reto) were dutifully tossed out. After a terrible struggle both were shot to death and the mob retired, satisfied that they had done what they intended to do.

There is some confusion as to the correct date of this incident. Some claim 15 January and other 14 January.[832]

Salazar, Santos
Born: (Unknown)—Date of Death: 22 January 1888
Place: Nueces County
Event: Lynching/Hanged

On Sunday, 22 January 1888, the bullet riddled body of Jacob Stafford was found behind his home. Tracks found at the scene of the crime matched those of the horse of Santos Salazar. He was hunted down and hanged by ranchers and cowboys. [833]

Battle, William
Born: (Unknown)—Date of Death: 26 February 1888
Place: Wharton County
Event: Lynching/Hanged

Seven Unidentified Blacks
Born: (Unknown)—Date of Death: 26 February 1888
Place: Wharton County
Event: Lynching/Shot and Burned

On Sunday Morning, 26 February 1888, a cabin occupied by blacks was set afire. The structure was located near Spanish Camp, about sixty miles west of Houston. Five black people were brutally shot down as they fled from the inferno. Two more perished inside the building, falling victim of the blaze. The newspaper article was not specific with regard to gender. One additional black man, William Battle, was found lynched in the same neighborhood, hanging from a nearby tree. It was presumed that his death was associated with the same event that triggered the killing of the seven other blacks in the blaze.

The entire bloody affair is said to have originated over a legal dispute involving the title to a parcel of land.[834]

Forsythe, William Thomas "Tom"
Born: 7 October 1867—Date of Death: 29 February 1888
Place: Panola County
Event: Lynching

Tom Forsythe was lynched at Carthage on Wednesday, 29 February 1888.[835] He was hanged for the robbery and murder of Panola County Treasurer D. C. Hill, a crime to which he had confessed.

After supper on Friday, 10 February 1888, Hill had gone downtown. He did not return to his home that evening. Although that fact did not alarm his family as he had been sitting up with a sick friend several nights during that week, not being seen the next morning did cause some uneasiness.

Judge Long went to the county treasurer's office to investigate. He found the door locked. Long adjusted the blinds so that he could look in. What he saw was horrifying. Hill was lying dead on the floor with a fearful gash in his throat. The door was broken down and it was found that Hill had been struck twice on the head with an ax and his throat cut. The doors of the iron safe were open and $5,000 in cash was gone.

Forsythe, a deputy sheriff and the son of the Panola County sheriff James Pickney Forsythe, was taken from the jail to a nearby red oak tree. With the help of about 500 to 600 of his friends and neighbors Forsythe scaled the tree and, after the son of the victim adjusted the rope, voluntarily jumped from the limb and affected his own lynching.

Forsyth's body was taken to Carthage City Cemetery for burial.[836]

Banks, Chillers
Born: circa 1860—Date of Death: 13 April 1888
Place: Chambers County
Event: Legal Execution/Hanged

On Tuesday, 19 June 1888, Chillers Banks, a black man, got word that a black woman named Martha Penderson had slandered him. Banks went to her home, called her out and shot her dead.

He was tried and convicted of the killing and sentenced to be hanged for the deed. On Friday,

13 April 1888, Banks went to the gallows at Wallisville. He had little to say, and maintained his innocence in the matter until the bitter end.[837]

Roe, William H.
Born: circa 1857—Date of Death: 26 May 1888
Place: Grimes County
Event: Legal Execution/Hanged

William H. Roe served as a deputy sheriff and jailer for Walker County Sheriff W. D. Adair. He had previously been a convict camp guard in Falls County for two years and a camp guard at Huntsville where he killed an escaping prisoner. Roe was tried and acquitted of that murder. In 1882 he married. Roe was elected Town Marshal of Huntsville, but was defeated in his 1886 reelection attempt after being accused of "pandering to coloreds." Next he went into the saloon business, then back to serving as a prison guard.

On 7 April 1886, Roe murdered his wife Jennie by lacing her coffee with strychnine. He was convicted of the crime and sentenced to death. Although many vigilantes wanted to lynch him, Roe was legally hanged two years later at the town of Anderson in Grimes County on Saturday, 26 May 1888. His killing by legal sentence marked the only execution in Grimes County history. Historians also claim that Roe was the first lawman to be legally executed in Texas.

Roe is buried at the Odd Fellows Cemetery at Anderson in Grimes County. Conflicting years of birth for Roe range from 1856 to 1858.[838]

Foster, Given Name Unknown
Born: (Unknown)—Date of Death:7 June 1888
Place: Harrison County
Event: Lynching/Hanged

Mr. Foster, a black man who used the alias Taldeger, was lynched for having outraged three white women near Longview. It is unclear if the three incidents took place at one time or were separate crimes.

A search party came upon Foster at Lansing Switch, about six miles from Longview. He was sitting on the tracks with a shotgun across his lap. Foster was surprised, and disarmed. He was taken to the nearby woods and lynched. The following morning at about 8:00 am a group of black that lived nearby discovered his body, still hanging from the tree. Later in the day the corpse remained there, bloated and covered with flies. No one seemed compelled to notify authorities and no one seemed disposed to touch the corpse and bury the poor fellow.[839]

Jackson, Charles

Born (Unknown)—Date of Death: 9 July 1888
Place: Cass County
Event: Lynched/Hanged

On Sunday, 8 July 1888, a black man named Charles Jackson who was living at Cussota, twenty miles west of Atlanta, visited the bedchambers of three different women at three different houses. At each stop he attempted to get into bed with them. In each instance he was frightened away by their screams. Citizens turned out en masse to hunt for him. Jackson was captured on Monday, 9 July 1888. Not long afterwards he was taken from guards by a mob of masked men and, after making a full confession, hanged from a tree. Jackson's body was left dangling from the makeshift gallows until the following day. Newspapers claimed that Jackson had two brothers who had been hung for the same offense some years ago.

Other newspapers claimed that a black man named Ham Staples was lynched on Monday, 9 July 1888, at Custer, fourteen miles from Atlanta. Staples had assaulted a seventeen-year old girl named McCoy who was the daughter of a well-to-do family. It appears that this report may be that of the same incident, except of course for the confusion regarding the victim's name.[840]

Jackson, Conrad

Born: (Unknown)—Date of Death: 16 July 1888
Place: McLennan County
Event: Legal Execution/Hanged

Conrad Jackson, a black man, was hanged at Waco on Monday, 16 July 1888, for the murder of a local white farmer. The killing had occurred one year earlier.[841]

Walker, Jack

Born: (Unknown)—Date of Death: 22 July 1888
Place: Washington County
Event: Lynching/Hanged

Sources claim that a man named Jack Walker was lynched at Brenham on Sunday, 22 July 1888.[842] It seems that all the newspapers of the day could find nothing at all to say about the passing of Walker, apart from this brief comment, "Negro Found Hanged. Six men were arrested on suspicion."[843]

One Unidentified Black Man
Born (Unknown)—Date of Death: circa August 1888
Place: Fort Bend County
Event: Lynching

In Joe H. Mitchell book *The Strangest Fruit: Forgotten Black-on-Black Lynchings 1835-1935* the author claimed that the *Colorado Citizen* (Columbus, Texas) dated 23 August 1888, contained an article with the headline, "Colored Rapist Lynched by Blacks." Mitchell went on to note that "In Fort Bend County, Texas, the negroes lynched a colored rapist." No other verification of this incident has been located.[844]

Seventeen Unidentified Men
Born: (Unknown)—Date of Death: 27 August 1888
Place: Armstrong County
Event: Lynching/Shot

"Texas Vigilantes Exterminate a Band of Daring Outlaws" was the headline of an article that graced page one of the Rockford, Illinois newspapers, the *Morning Star*, on 4 September 1888. City slickers who live their lives vicariously through the deeds of Wild West outlaws and lawmen scrambled to pick up a copy of this edition of the *Morning Star*, a local rag that had just been founded that same year.

In an incident that occurred near the breaks of Sand Creek, at Palo Duro Canyon in Armstrong County, seventeen unidentified outlaws and three members of the vigilante group that were pursuing them met their end in a desperate gunfight worthy of being memorialized on stage and screen. Events that have drawn greater popular interest over the years, like the shootout at the OK Corral, which left only three men dead (Bill Clanton, Frank McLaury and Tom McLaury) pale in comparison to this wild and wooly gun battle on the open plains of the Texas Panhandle.

The outlaw band, notorious in the Colorado, New Mexico, Kansas, Texas and No Man's Land area had stolen a number of horses that they were holding at picket in their camp on Sand Creek. The vigilante group that had tracked them overtook the bunch on Monday, 27 August 1888. A strict watch was kept over the camp. When the posse felt the time was right they placed a cordon around the camp and sent in a contingent of six riders to attempt to arrest the gang and take them peaceably.

Their demand to surrender was met with a volley of gunfire, wounding James Aldrich, one of the half dozen vigilantes. The outlaw's intentions now certain, the posse opened fire from their superior position above, raining lead down on to the unsuspecting band of ne're-do-wells. After the wild battle had ranged for what seemed like an hour, the gunfire from the camp ceased. A cloud of acrid smoke was slowly carried away from the spot where the fight had occurred by the seemingly ever-present breeze, revealing the deadly evidence of the affray. There were sixteen dead outlaws on the ground and one more mortally wounded and still clinging to life. Three posse members had been killed in the exchange. In only a handful of old west gunfights ever recorded have there been so many fatalities in a single shootout, yet apart from this one source this incident has gone unreported.

The only outlaw mentioned to have been extinguished in this battle was "Thompson's Kid." Unfortunately that is not enough information with which to identify him. The names of the remaining sixteen, nor the three posse men, were cited by the source.[845]

Mitchell, Burke
Born: circa 1852—Date of Death: 31 August 1888
Place: Harris County
Event: Legal Execution/Hanged

Burke Mitchell, a thirty-eighty year old black man and wife killer, went to the gallows at Houston on Friday, 31 August 1888. His crime is said to have been among the most brutal ever recorded in the county.[846]

Spencer, Harrison
Born: (Unknown)—Date of Death: 31 August 1888
Place: Harrison County
Event: Lynching/Hanged and Shot

Deputy Sheriff Walter discovered the body of Harrison Spencer, a black man, hanging from a tree at Longview on or about Friday, 31 August 1888. Spencer, who was a local politician and recent deserter from the Union Labor Party, is thought to have been lynched by black Ku Klux Klansmen for withdrawing support for their cause. Spencer had been shot behind the ear and in the side, then hauled fifteen feet up a tree using a heavy, three inch diameter rope. His hands were tightly bound and his shirt had been ripped off, revealing where he had been severely thrashed before the lynching.[847]

Williams, Wesley
Born: circa 1848—Date of Death: 29 September 1888
Place: Falls County
Event: Legal Execution/Hanged

Wesley Williams, a forty-year old black man, was hanged at Marlin on Saturday, 29 September 1888, for murdering his wife. The incident had taken place on 5 March 1887.[848]

Beene, Aaron
Born: (Unknown)—Date of Death: 3 October 1888
Place: Jasper County
Event: Lynching/Shot

The young daughter of John Lee, a prominent farmer at Magnolia Springs, was out horseback riding when a black man later identified as Aaron Beene rode up to her. She whipped her horse and attempted to escape but he overtook her and dragged her from the saddle.

A party of white men came along at that juncture, opening fire on Beene. After wounding the attacker they arrested him and turned him over to the sheriff. When the sheriff started out in the direction of the jail with the prisoner a mob that had formed seized Beene from authorities and shot him full of holes.[849]

Johnson, Lamar
Born: (Unknown)—Date of Death: 13 October 1888
Place: Fort Bend County
Event: Lynching/Shot

On Saturday, 13 October 1888, a crowd of white men rode up to a black church at Pittsville and called out the people gathered therein. Once the congregants had filed outside the mob opened fire on them, killing one black man named Lamar Johnson and wounded another black man named Taylor Randon. After the shooting Randon fled the county.

The sheriff arrested six white youths who were members of the Jaybird Club. Their names were Dick Preston, Walter Sims, Theophilus Simington, Seth Miller, Fred Fuller and George Lass. Between 1888-1889, two political factions, the Jaybirds and the Woodpeckers, were feuding for control of Fort Bend County. The Jaybirds were predominately white and were trying to oust blacks from the county.[850]

Joiner, Joe
Born: (Unknown)—Date of Death: 16 October 1888
Place: Williamson County
Event: Lynching/ Hanged

On Sunday, 14 October 1888, a black man named Joe Joiner attempted to assault and outrage S. W. Wolsey's twelve-year old daughter near Hutto. The girl and her little sister began screaming, causing Joiner to flee on horseback. A posse pursued Joiner and shot him in the shoulder during his capture.

Joiner was returned to Hutto. At about 11:00 pm a person or persons unknown seized him and hanged him from a nearby tree.[851]

Nathaniel, Nat

Born: (Unknown)—Date of Death: 17 October 1888

Place: Brazoria County

Event: Lynching/Hanged

On Monday, 15 October 1888, Nat Nathaniel and two or three other black men confronted a man named Isaac Van Dorn who was an engineer on a plantation. The black men wanted to whip a "negro boy." Van Dorn objected, and ordered the men to leave. They issued threats as they departed. That night Van Dorn was shot in the face and throat. The wounds were fatal. On Tuesday, 16 October 1888, a posse was formed and commenced a search for Nathaniel. He was eventually captured at Wharton. On Wednesday, 17 October 1888, citizens seized the prisoner and hanged him while the posse was en route to the Brazoria jail.[852]

Washington, William

Born: (Unknown)—Date of Death: 20 October 1888

Place: Caldwell County

Event: Legal Execution/Hanged

William Washington, a black man, was convicted of outraging and murdering a white woman. Washington was sentenced to hang for his crime. That judgment was carried out on Saturday, 20 October 1888, at Columbus. A crowd of about 3,000 people assembled three miles west of town to witness the event. Washington, like so many other condemned men, found salvation in the Lord two days before his death sentence was carried out.[853]

Smith, Sam

Born: (Unknown)—Date of Death: 25 October 1888

Place: Kaufman County

Event: Lynching/Hanged

Sam Smith, a black man, was lynched near Forney on Thursday, 25 October 1888.[854] Smith had attempted to outrage Mrs. Boyd, the wife of a section hand foreman for the Texas and Pacific Railroad. Apparently Smith had assembled quite a record for himself as a malefactor.

Smith had been brought to Forney and taken before Justice of the Peace Wood for a hearing, during which he wilted and confessed to the act. He was placed in a hack with a strong guard of determined men surrounding him and sent on his way towards the county seat at Kaufman to be locked up in that jail for safe keeping. No more than a mile along the way the transport was set upon by a mob of armed men who sprung forth from the bushes and trees alongside the road, overpowered the guards and took Smith under their control. Several shots were exchanged in a feckless attempt to retain custody of the prisoner. Fortunately no one was wounded. Smith was lynched from a nearby tree, never uttering a syllable throughout the process.

Although Smith's body was cut down from the hanging tree and returned to Forney for burial, townspeople refused to allow him to be interred within the boundaries of their local cemetery.[855]

Levar, Casimiro
Born: (Unknown)—Date of Death: 7 December 1888
Place: Hidalgo County
Event: Legal Execution/Hanged

On Saturday, 10 December 1887, Theodore Marks, a storekeeper who ran a general merchandise business at the Agua Negra located about twenty-five miles from Hidalgo, left the shop and rode by horseback to a ranch about two miles distant. He never returned. The following day his horse walked home, absent the rider. A search part was sent out, with suspicion immediately focused on three Mexican families...Casimiro Levar, Ruis and Leon. All three were arrested.

After some aggressive interrogation, Ruis gave up the story. On Sunday, 11 December 1888, the three men had encountered Marks on his return trip. They rode close alongside him and Levar jumped onto Marks's horse, diligently holding him while the others bound him with a rope. Next they took him to a clump of Chapperell where they quietly discussed the best way to kill him. Marks had had Levar indicted for theft at some point in the past, thus a grudge existed.

Eventually the threesome formed their plan for Marks' fate. They shot him full of holes and killed him, then cut his body into small pieces and cremated the remains over a campfire. The process took several days. Investigators later discovered parts of the skull in the ashes of the fire along with some brass buttons that his brother was able to identify.

On Friday, 7 December 1888, Casimiro Levar went to the gallows at Rio Grande City. He remained cheerful and optimistic to the end, believing that his friends on the south side of the border would rescue him from the hangman. Unfortunately for Levar, his colleagues failed to come through for him when he was at his hour of greatest need. At half past four in the afternoon the trap was sprung and Levar was launched into eternity. [856]

Johnson, John Andrew
Born: circa 1871—Date of Death: 21 December 1888
Place: Houston County
Event: Legal Execution/Hanged

Friday is traditionally "hanging day" in Texas, although any day seems to have been a good day for a lynching. The Friday before Christmas weekend was no excuse for not having a good necktie party, especially when it involved a black man who had outraged a little white girl. Thus, John Andrew Johnson, a seventeen-year old black man, went to the gallows at Crockett on Friday, 21 December

1888. The fact that he had not been lynched during the several months he was on the run, or locked up in two different jails, is in itself remarkable.

Johnson professed his innocence to the end, claiming that it was Coke Gunnels who had done the deed. He slept well, had a hearty breakfast, and at 11:00 am was led by the sheriff to the gallows structure within the jail. Asked if he had anything to say he replied that he did not. All together not three words were spoken on the platform that day. At 11:30 am the lever was thrown and an uncharacteristically quiet John Johnson dropped through the trap. He was declared dead at 11:40 am.

Johnson's trouble began when he had been working on a farm in Houston County. Living next door to the farm where he was employed was the young daughter of a prominent white man in the area. Johnson had been plowing the field all day and at about 8:00 pm lay down in the grass to rest and to wait in hiding for the girl to walk past. The girl had led one of her father's horses out into the meadow near where Johnson was hiding. As she did so he burst forth from his nest and outraged her. Another black man named Coke Gunnels was sitting on a fence nearby and witnessed the entire torrid scene.

The girl sounded the alarm and a posse was immediately formed to search for Johnson. He managed to evade his pursuers for several days until captured by members of an International and Great Northern Railroad section gang who spotted him walking along the tracks.

A mob of about 500 citizens gathered in town waiting for the chance to take Johnson from the jail and lynch him. They went as far as to plant sledgehammers at strategic points about the circumference of the building to facilitate their work. While the mob took a break from their labor to prepare for the upcoming lynching party Sheriff Holcomb and several deputies, waiting until the cover of darkness, took Johnson, mounted up and high tailed it for the jail at Huntsville. The word of their flight got out, and the mob took to the trail, chasing the sheriff and his prisoner. Unbeknownst to the crowd of vigilantes, Holcomb took a fork in the trail and headed for a railroad station, boarded the midnight express and landed Johnson safely in the Harris County jail.

An effort was made to have Johnson returned to Crockett for trial, the purpose being to create another opportunity to take the man from officers and lynch him. Their plan was foiled when Sheriff Holcomb, once again, safely transported Johnson back to the Houston County jail at Crockett. While he was incarcerated there two unsuccessful attempts were made to break him out and lynch him. Johnson finally went to trial on 18 October 1888, and was found guilty. He was sentenced to death by hanging. That sentence was carried out, as scheduled and as outlined above, on 21 December 1888.[857] Some sources list Johnson's middle name as Anderson.[858]

Rather, Joe

Born: (Unknown)—Date of Death: 28 December 1888
Place: Shelby County
Event: Legal Execution/Hanged

Joe Rather, a black man, paid the price for murdering his wife when he went to the gallows at Center on Friday, 28 December 1888. The crime had taken place in early January 1888, near Shelbyville.

Rather and his wife lived in a cabin on the farm of Mr. James Armourn. He and his wife had attended a party on the farm given by another black couple. There had been a disagreement and Rather sent his wife home. When he returned he took a shotgun loaded with squirrel shot, placed it against her forehead and fired. The blast practically blew her head from the torso. Afterwards Rather calmly walked away.

Sheriff Sims had the necessary structure completed in good order, well in advance of when needed. Rather walked to the gallows with firm stride, smoking a cigar. Once on the platform he held forth a lengthy speech, adding that he knew he was going straight to heaven.[859]

Marlow, Alfred "Alf"
Born: 1 June 1862—Date of Death: 19 January 1889
Place: Young County
Event: Lynching/Shot

Marlow, Lewellyn
Born: (Unknown)—Date of Death: 19 January 1889
Place: Young County
Event: Lynching/Shot

Alfred "Alf" Marlow and his brother Lewellyn were shot to death in Young County on 19 January 1889.[860]

Four of the Marlow brothers were arrested when Boone Marlow shot Young County Sheriff Marion D. Wallace. Wallace was attempting to serve an arrest warrant. The US Marshal in Dallas ordered the four Marlow brothers to be transported to Weatherford. Several attempts were made by citizens and law enforcement officials to lynch them. On Saturday night, 19 January 1889, the brothers were shackled in pairs for the trip to Weatherford. When the group reached Dry Creek, outside of Graham, a signal was given and a hidden mob opened fire on the defenseless gang. The guards ran to join the mob while the brothers leaped from the wagon and armed themselves with guns taken from guards. In the vicious gunfight that followed, Lewellyn and Alfred were killed. The other two brothers, George and Charlie, were seriously wounded.

McGill, Charles
Born: circa 1854—Date of Death: 25 January 1889
Place: Milam County
Event: Legal Execution/Hanged

Charles McGill, a black man, was hanged at Cameron on Friday, 25 January 1889, for the murder of Willie Leonard.[861]

Alkins, Nick
Born (Unknown)—Date of Death: circa February 1889
Place: Gregg County
Event: Lynching

A black man named Nick Alkins was reported to have been killed by a mob whose members had disguised themselves as women.[862]

Smith, Charles Wilson "Charlie"
Born: 22 November 1842—Date of Death: 15 February 1889
Place: San Saba County
Event: Lynching/Hanged

Brown, Asa Robertson
Born: 16 September 1840—Date of Death: 15 February 1889
Place: San Saba County
Event: Lynching/Hanged

Two white men, Charles W. "Charlie" Smith and Asa Robertson Brown, were hanged near the Colorado River in the northern part of San Saba County. Smith had last been seen on Monday evening, 11 February 1889. Asa Brown left home on Friday, 15 February 1889, on a summons from Sheriff Cunningham to aid in the search for Smith. Brown's body was discovered on Sunday, 17 February 1889, hanging from a low limb of a tree, his hands bound with his own pigging string and hung with his own rope. His horse had walked home. Other hoof prints were observed in the area of the lynching.[863] Brown had been robbed of his money, but his gun and cartridges were found nearby.

The body of Smith had not yet been found, though the party in search of him discovered unmistakable evidence of his having been hung. Smith's gun, rope, watch and other personal effects were uncovered at the site of the hanging.

There are many different theories as to the manner of the death. Family genealogists place Smith's date of death as 11 February 1889, which is entirely possible given the circumstances and lack of evidence.[864]

Brown was known locally as a hard man. He had killed his sister Rebecca's husband, Andrew Smart, in a barroom brawl on 30 July 1883, at San Saba. The event was reported in *The Daily Banner* of Brenham on 11 August 1883. Brown was survived by his wife Mary Sophia Kirkpatrick and eight children. Family genealogists indicate that he is buried at the J. H. "Shorty" Brown cemetery at San Saba, not the Odd Fellows Cemetery as was reported by the local newspapers.[865]

Two Unidentified Black Men
Born: (Unknown)—Date of Death: 19 February 1889
Place: Liberty County
Event: Lynching/Hanged

According to some sources, two black men were lynched at Liberty County on 19 February 1889. Although this incident appears on the popular reference source *The Lynching Calendar* it remains unverified. In all likelihood it is a duplicate of, or in some way connected to, the following entry covering George Walker's legal execution.[866]

Walker, George
Born: (Unknown)—Date of Death: 5 April 1889
Place: Liberty County
Event: Legal Execution/Hanged

On Friday, 5 April 1889, a black man named George Walker was hanged at Liberty for the murder of Charles Lecour. The crime had taken place in January 1888. After killing Lecour, Walker threw his body into the Trinity River to conceal his crime.[867]

Diggs, George
Born: (Unknown)—Date of Death: 14 April 1889
Place: Waller County
Event: Lynching/Hanged

George Diggs, a black man, was removed from the jail by persons unknown and lynched in the city park at Hempstead in Waller County on Sunday, 14 April 1889.

During the preceding week Diggs had gone to the farm of Mr. Horn and asked Horn's wife for food. She generously complied, and fed him. As gratitude for her benevolence Diggs produced a pistol and attempted to outrage the woman. She grabbed the gun and struggled with Diggs. The pistol discharged accidentally, alerting Mr. Horn who came to the rescue of his wife. Vigilantes dealt with Diggs in the expected manner shortly after his capture. [868]

One Unidentified Black Man
Born: (Unknown)—Date of Death: 17 May 1889
Place: Brazos County
Event: Lynching/Hanged

On Friday, 17 May 1889, sources claimed that an unidentified black man was lynched at Millican for outraging a woman. No confirmation of this incident has been uncovered.[869]

Newton, Roma
Born: (Unknown)—Date of Death: July 1889
Place: Fannin County
Event: Lynching/Hanged

The body of a little girl, Roma Newton age unknown, was discovered hanging in a tree near Bonham. She had been lynched. The person or persons responsible were never found nor was a motive ever uncovered. The girl's father was prostrate with grief and the neighbors quite upset over the tragedy.[870]

Davis, William "Henry"
Born: (Unknown)—Date of Death: 13 July 1889
Place: McLennan County
Event: Lynching/Hanged

William "Henry" Davis, a black man, was lynched near Waco by a mob of 150 men for the attempted outrage of a white woman.[871]

The site of the lynching was about three quarters of a mile from the town of Robinson and about seven miles south of Waco. Davis's lifeless body was discovered hanging from the limb of a hackberry tree, not far from a church. One source claimed that the corpse was pierced with .45 caliber bullet holes. Pinned to the lapel of his coat was a note saying, "Take warning; executed by 150 men for seven attempts to outrage white women."

According to testimony taken the following day by Justice Harrison at the scene of the lynching, Davis, clothed only in a shirt, had crept into the sleeping quarters of an esteemed lady and laid down beside her. He placed his hands upon her until her screams for help drove him off. The alarm was sounded, and Deputy Burke led a posse, giving chase. Henry was overtaken in the Little River country and was being returned to Waco when the lynching occurred. A number of men all mounted on white horses and wearing red handkerchiefs to cover their faces surrounded Burke's posse and took Davis to a mott of trees where they strung him up. The group must have presented a striking image.

Before he died it is claimed that Davis confessed to having outraged a white woman some years ago at Cedar Grove and another on the South Bosque. The latter woman was the wife of a settler. Davis caught her alone while her husband had gone to town for supplies. He abused her in front of her small children. Afterwards Davis fled to Louisiana where he hid out for two years.[872]

Some sources report this incident as having occurred on 11 July 1889.

Swinney, Charles
Born (Unknown)—Date of Death: 15 July 1889
Place: Bell County
Event: Lynching/Shot

On Monday, 15 July 1889, an unidentified number of white men went to the home of a black man named Charles Swinney and called him out. When Swinney responded the mob opened fire on him. Swinney called for his wife to bring him his gun. He fired once from a double barrel shotgun, hitting Bud Ellison in the left side and killing him. The effect of his second shot is not known. Swinney was shot through the heel and thigh, near the hipbone, resulting in bones being shattered. He was not expected to recover. The newspaper reported that no cause was known for the mob attack as Swinney bore good character in the neighborhood. No arrest of the attackers was made.[873]

Lewis, George

Born: (Unknown)—Date of Death: 21 July 1889
Place: Bell County
Event: Lynching/Hanged

George Lewis, a black man, was lynched near Belton on Wednesday, 21 July 1889. He was accused of having poisoned the well of William Shaw.[874] The vigilantes involved in the killing were not identified. Soon after, Shaw, his wife Minnie and their two children moved to Waco.[875]

Lindley, George

Born: (Unknown)—Date of Death: 28 July 1889
Place: Hunt County
Event: Lynching/Shot

According to sources, a black man named George Lindley was executed at Wolfe City in Hunt County on 28 July 1889.

Blacks had displaced white workers at the brickyard at Wolfe City, causing great unrest between the two groups. Angry whites bent on teaching the blacks a "lesson" sought to grab a few of the leaders and whip them, thus making their point that blacks ought not try to compete with whites for lucrative employment. Lindley was one of the victims of this scheme. Things got a bit out of hand, however. The white mob decided to castrate their captors, making the experience an especially memorable one for all involved. Lindley managed to break loose before the thing was done though. He was fired upon and wounded by one of the ruffians named W. P. Mills. Next a vigilante named Lorance finished the job by shooting Lindley in the head, inflicting a fatal wound.[876]

Brooks, James

Born: (Unknown)—Date of Death: 14 August 1889
Place: Orange County
Event: Lynching/Hanged and Shot

James Brooks, a black man and an escaped convict from the Louisiana State Penitentiary, was arrested near Orange for attempting to outrage an old woman. A mob captured him from his guard at about 1:00 am, lynched him then shot him full of holes for good measure.[877]

McCoy, James E. "Jim"

Born: 14 May 1858 [878]—Date of Death: 23 August 1889
Place: Bexar County
Event: Legal Execution/Hanged

Charles Brown "Charlie" McKinney had served for ten years as a Texas Ranger, and was sheriff of La Salle County when he was killed.

McKinney was assassinated at Twobig Station on Sunday, 26 December 1886, shot and killed by Bud Crenshaw. McKinney had beaten Crenshaw in the recent election for sheriff and Crenshaw had planned the killing for several years. He had a woman make a false report that her daughter's virtue had been violated. When McKinney arrived to investigate he spoke with Crenshaw and James E. "Jim" McCoy. Suddenly Crenshaw shot McKinney in the head with a Winchester rifle. Crenshaw and McCoy also shot at Deputy Pete Edwards, wounding him in the shoulder. Edwards' horse became frightened and flared, so the assailant's bullets missed their mark and Edwards was only slightly wounded.[879]

Texas Rangers tracked down Crenshaw and McCoy. Crenshaw was shot and killed in an exchange of gunfire. McCoy escaped, but later surrendered. His exploits as an outlaw spanned more than a decade. No one but McCoy himself knows how many men he had killed. One newspaper claimed nineteen. McCoy had lost an eye in a shooting affray in the streets of Cotulla some years earlier.

McCoy was tried and convicted of the murder and subsequently sentenced to death. He received the verdict with calmness and coolness, commenting that, "I am glad of it, I had rather be hanged now than be in jail another month."

At 11:15 McCoy mounted that gallows unassisted. The drop fell at 11:33 am on Friday, 23 August 1889, and the notorious Jim McCoy fell through the gallows floor at San Antonio and into history.

McCoy is buried at the Brummett Cemetery at Bigfoot in Frio County.[880]

One Unidentified White Man

Born: (Unknown)—Date of Death: circa September 1889
Place: Atascosa County
Event: Lynching/Hanged

The 28 September 1889, edition of the *Elkhart Daily Review* from Elkhart, Indiana claimed that a man had been hanged at Pleasanton, in Atascosa County. The paper went on to add that to celebrate the event the townspeople had thrown a barbecue that was largely attended.[881]

The tagline of the article reads, "In the southwest they do things differently from most every other part of the country." Unfortunately the scribe of this *Elkhart Daily Review* piece was in a bigger hurry to print his quip than he was to identifying the victim's name, or to specify if the event was a legal hanging or a lynching. The journalist also failed to mention the victim's race. It is presumed that he was white, since had he been otherwise there is little doubt that that fact would have been emphasized for its dramatic effect. The article went on to comment about how, in a neighboring county, a white man who was on trial for killing a "Chinaman [Asian]" had been set free, owing to the fact that the judge could find no law providing for "the murder of a Chinaman [Asian]." One is left speechless.

Harrell, Given Name Unknown
Born (Unknown)—Date of Death: 24 October 1889
Place: Colorado County
Event: Lynching/Hanged

On Thursday, 24 October 1889, a black man named Harrell was lynched near Columbus for attempting a heinous crime upon a young woman.[882] No other information was provided by this source.

Fierro, Demeiro
Born: (Unknown)—Date of Death: 1 November 1889
Place: Presidio County
Event: Legal Execution/Hanged

Demeiro Fierro, a Mexican man who had been tried and convicted of murdering William Nations and Jacob Simpson, was hanged at Marfa on Friday, 1 November 1889. The incident took place a few months earlier, just over the border from Mexico, along the Texas side of the Rio Grande River near Marfa. Three Mexican men had been involved in the killing. Two escaped back into old Mexico. Fierro was less fortunate. Mexican authorities had refused to allow extradition of the other two killers.

Fierro's hanging was held in public. Newspaper reports of the day claimed that "most" of the people from Alpine and Marfa attended, and that hopefully, "...this would teach the Mexicans a lesson."[883]

Keys, J. H.
Born: (Unknown)—Date of Death: 18 November 1889
Place: Lamar County
Event: Lynching/Hanged

On Monday, 18 November 1889, J. H. Keys, a black man, was lynched near Paris for horse theft. The vigilante party consisted of Henry Wandom, Bill Isabell, Nick and Dick Everhart, Tony Webber, John Stephens and John Blackburn. All were arraigned on 30 January 1891, and much to their surprise were remanded over to the sheriff to be confined in jail without bond. Such stern treatment of white men connected with white on black crime in Lamar County was truly extraordinary for the era.[884]

Two Unidentified White Men
Born: (Unknown)—Date of Death: 14 December 1889
Place: Hill County
Event: Lynching/Hanged

Unverified sources report that two unidentified white men were lynched for robbery and murder in Hill County.[885]

Anderson, Paul
Born (Unknown)—Date of Death: 20 December 1889
Place: Waller County
Event: Lynching/Shot

One source claimed that on Friday, 20 December 1889, Paul Anderson, a black man, was assassinated at Hempstead.[886] No confirmation of this incident has been located.

O'Dell, W M.
Born (Unknown)—Date of Death: 28 December 1886
Place: Uvalde County
Event: Lynching

O'Dell, Given Name Unknown
Born (Unknown)—Date of Death: 28 December 1886
Place: Uvalde County
Event: Lynching

According to one, unverified and uncorroborated source, two outlaws were lynched at Uvalde on Saturday, 28 December 1886. No confirmation of this incident has been located.[887]

Cade, Bedford
Born: (Unknown)—Date of Death: 4 January 1890
Place: Rusk County
Event: Lynching/Hanging

Bedford Cabe, "A negro of bad repute", was lynched on Saturday, 4 January 1890, at New Salem by a mob of angry citizens. The nature of his crime is not known.[888]

Heyward, W.W.
Born: (Unknown)—Date of Death: March 1890
Place: Grayson County
Event: Lynching/Hanging

W. W. Heyward was lynched in March 1890. The nature of his crime is unknown. Heyward was found hanging from a tree on the Red River, near Blue Bluff, about five miles northeast of Denison. Though he was blindfolded, his hands tied behind his back and his feet tied together. Remarkable, authorities ruled his death a suicide.[889]

Clark, "Bill"
Born: (Unknown)—Date of Death: 26 March 1890
Place: Limestone County
Event: Lynching/Hanged

A black man referred to as "Bill" Clark escaped from the county convict farm. After he was arrested at Headsville, he confessed that he had assaulted and murdered Mrs. Belle McLennan, the bride of a farmer. As officers were about to transfer him to the county jail a group of citizens interfered and hanged him from a tree. As he swung in the air struggling for his last breath the mob shot him full of holes.[890]

Williams, William
Born: (Unknown)—Date of Death: 3 April 1890
Place: Limestone County
Event: Lynching/Hanged

A black man named William Williams was charged with committing an outrage on the eight-year old daughter of Charles Griffin, a white man, at Kosso. Griffin noticed that the young girl was ill, and acting strangely. A doctor was called who examined her and announced that she had been wronged, and dealt with most harshly in the doing.

Williams was confined in the jail at Kosso. It was determined that it would be best to transport him to Groesbeck for safekeeping. While doing so officers were set upon by an angry mob of about 125 citizens who lynched Williams near Headsville. After stringing him up the crowd filled Williams's body with bullets, just to be sure he was dead.[891]

Jacobson, Stephen
Born: (Unknown)—Date of Death: 20 April 1890
Place: Unknown County
Event: Lynching

According to unverified sources, a black man named Stephen Jacobson was lynched somewhere in Texas on 20 April 1890. This account comes from the reference source, *The Lynching Calendar*, and thus far has not been verified.[892]

Garrett, Simon
Born: (Unknown)—Date of Death: 20 April 1890
Place: San Augustine County
Event: Lynching/Hanged

Teel, Jerry
Born: (Unknown)—Date of Death: 20 April 1890
Place: San Augustine County
Event: Lynching/Hanged

On Sunday night, 20 April 1890, the jail at San Augustine was broken into and two black prisoners, Simon Garrett and Jerry Teel, removed and lynched. Although the newspaper accounts of the day are vague as to the charges under which the pair had been held, it appears that Colonel John H. Brooks and his family had somehow been threatened with poisoning by the pair.[893]

One Unidentified Man
Born (Unknown)—Date of Death: 24 April 1890
Place: Milam County
Event: Lynching

One source has claimed that an unidentified man was lynched at Cameron Station in Milam County for outrage. The incident occurred on Thursday, 24 April 1890. Thus far no verification of this claim has been located.[894]

Bennett, Edward "Ed"
Born: (Unknown)—Date of Death: 10 May 1890
Place: Robertson County
Event: Lynching/Hanged

On Saturday, 10 May 1890, Edward Bennett, a black trustee convict, was taken by force by persons unknown and lynched. The incident took place while he was working on the farm of H. K. Hearne. Bennett was being held on a charge of having outraged a white woman.[895]

Brown, Thomas "Tom"
Born: (Unknown)—Date of Death: 1 June 1890
Place: Unidentified County
Event: Lynching/Hanged

On or about Sunday, 1 June 1890, parties unknown assassinated a noted black desperado named Tom Brown. Brown was killed from ambush, at Hook's Ferry near Paris. Three bullets from a Winchester rifle pierced his body and did the job.[896]

Holden, Fletcher
Born: (Unknown)—Date of Death: 6 June 1890
Place: Cass County
Event: Legal Execution/Hanged

Holden, Henry
Born: (Unknown)—Date of Death: 6 June 1890
Place: Cass County
Event: Legal Execution/Hanged

Miller, Tom
Born: (Unknown)—Date of Death: 6 June 1890
Place: Cass County
Event: Legal Execution/Hanged

Tom Miller along with Henry and Fletcher Holden, all black men, went to the gallows at Linden on Friday, 6 June 1890. All three had confessed to murdering James McGear. That crime occurred on 7 December 1889.[897]

Jones, Bell
Born (Unknown)—Date of Death: 7 June 1890
Place: Polk County
Event: Lynching

Little information regarding this incident was offered by the source. According to reports, a black man named Bell Jones was lynched at Corrigan On Saturday, 7 June 1890. No confirmation has been located.[898]

One Unidentified Black Man
Born: (Unknown)—Date of Death: 12 June 1890
Place: Williamson County
Event: Lynching/Hanged

A man who was suspected of having committed an outrage was removed from the custody of lawmen by a mob of citizens and lynched at Taylor.[899]

One Unidentified Black Man
Born: (Unknown)—Date of Death: 16 June 1890
Place: Polk County
Event: Lynching/Hanged

Two Unidentified White Men
Born: (Unknown)—Date of Death: 16 June 1890
Place: Polk County
Event: Lynching/Shot

On Friday, 20 June 1890, the front page headlines of the notoriously bias *Philadelphia Inquirer* newspaper read, "A Texas Race War Feared." Reading further, calmer heads could discern that although they were presented in an intentionally salacious manner there had been a lynching in Texas.

A black man, whose name was not mentioned, had slit the throat of a white man named Morris. That incident occurred near Livingston, in Polk County. Obsessed with the prospect of a "race war," the journalist did not take the time to discover the victim's name. In retaliation, whites had taken the knife-wielding fellow out and lynched him. Not a particularly unusual outcome in such a case, even in 1890s Pennsylvania.

The vigilante action against the black man set off another riot, this time with local blacks killing two of the white men alleged to have been involved in the lynching of the black man. The Houston Light Guards under General King went under alert, waiting to be called to Polk County should Sheriff Hammond determine that the apocalypse was near and their services would be required.[900]

One Unidentified Black Man

Born: (Unknown)—Date of Death: 28 June 1890
Place: Unidentified County
Event: Lynching

According to unverified sources, a black man was lynched near a place called Antlers on 28 June 1890. Neither the location nor the source, which is in *The Lynching Calendar*, can be confirmed.[901]

Henry, Patrick

Born: (Unknown)—Date of Death: 29 June 1890
Place: Anderson County
Event: Lynching/Beaten and Drown

On Sunday evening, 29 June 1890, the body of a black man named Patrick Henry was discovered at the bottom of an old well near the Gaston Plantation at Palestine. A rope was fastened around his waist and the back of his head had been stove in with an ax.

     It seems that Henry had turned up in the area about three months earlier. Over time he had managed to win at the local card games with local black, taking their razors, pistols, watches and other valuables as collateral. A local black man named John Wilson was seen disappearing into the woods near the well with Henry. When he returned he had Henry's watch and money, and claimed that he had won them from him in a card game. Afterwards Henry had quickly packed up and left. Ten days later Wilson also quit the country. He was suspected of having visited the foul play on Henry. This case was included since it was reported as a lynching.[902]

Young, Andy

Born: (Unknown)—Date of Death: 19 July 1890
Place: Red River County
Event: Lynching/Shot

At about 2:00 am on Saturday morning, 19 July 1890, a party of six white men went to the home of Andy Young, a black man, living about twelve miles southeast of Paris at the farm of Nathan Grant. They called him outside. When Young appeared the men produced pistols and Winchesters, firing more than twenty-five shots into Young. One bullet severed his tongue. In spite of his serious wounds Young managed to survive a short time before expiring. Due to the loss of his tongue, however, the illiterate man was unable to speak and thus was not able to identify his attackers.

No reason for the shooting was given, other than that Young had had a difficulty with some white boys.[903]

Melena, Vitolo
Born: (Unknown)—Date of Death: 21 July 1890
Place: Williamson County
Event: Lynching/Shot

Melena, Mrs. (Given Name Unknown)
Born: (Unknown)—Date of Death: 21 July 1890
Place: Williamson County
Event: Lynching/Shot

Melena, Unidentified Given Name - Daughter of Vitolo
Born: circa 1885—Date of Death: 21 July 1890
Place: Williamson County
Event: Lynching/Shot

According to sources, the home of Vitolo Melena, his wife, two daughters and one son was invaded just after midnight on Monday, 21 July 1890. The culprits, J. P. Gibbs, John Gibbs and Andrew Sutton fatally shot Mr. and Mrs. Melena and their five-year old daughter. The other two children escaped and fled to a neighbor's home where they reported the incident.

Newspaper sources of the day reported that the crime was a revenge killing of some sort, but failed to elaborate. Andrew Sutton, J. P. Gibbs and his son John had been taken into custody.

One source claimed that the motivation for the crime had been the fact that Melena was encouraging racial mixing.[904]

Hawkins, William
Born: (Unknown)—Date of Death: 30 July 1890
Place: Harris County
Event: Lynching

Unverified sources claim that a black man named William Hawkins was lynched at Cypress in Harris County on Wednesday, 30 July 1890. No confirmation of this incident has been uncovered.[905]

Brown, John
Born: (Unknown)—Date of Death: 5 August 1890
Place: Grimes County
Event: Lynching/Hanged and Shot

John Brown, a black man, was accused of outraging a young white girl. He was confined in the jail awaiting arraignment when a mob of citizens removed him from the custody of lawmen and lynched him from a nearby tree. Afterwards, they shot him full of holes to make certain he was dead. Brown confessed to having done the act before he died.[906]

Two Unidentified Black Men
Born: (Unknown)—Date of Death: 14 August 1890
Place: Limestone County
Event: Lynching/Hanged

According to unverified sources, once again *The Lynching Calendar*, two unnamed black men were lynched near Mexia in Limestone County on 14 August 1890.

It is thought that this incident is the same case reported by the *Dallas Morning News* of 9 August 1890, involving Tobe Garnett, a black man, and his wife whose given name was not listed. Garnett fatally stabbed his wife at the crossing of the Texas Central Railway at Hull Street then walked away. No other killings of blacks can be located during this time period.[907]

Kriner, Jim
Born: (Unknown)—Date of Death: 12 September 1890
Place: McLennan County
Event: Lynching/Shot

Jim Kriner, a black man and a tenant farmer, was shot and killed for threatening a white man during a dispute with his landowner and the landlord's son.[908]

Baugh, Andrew Tyler
Born: circa 1842—Date of Death: circa December 1890
Place: Unknown County
Event: Lynching/Hanged and Shot

Andrew T. Baugh, a white man who had served meritoriously as a Captain in Cobb's Legion Cavalry for the Confederate army and who hailed from Fulton County, Georgia, was shot and lynched for cattle rustling somewhere along the Texas/Mexico border in late November or early December 1890.

Baugh had been wanted in two counties in Georgia for purloining livestock. He fled to Texas, where he apparently stuck with the same profession. Unfortunately for Baugh, a group of cowboys spotted him and his coconspirators while they were in the process of driving stolen beeves across the Rio Grande into Mexico. Baugh's gang tried to make a run for it. Two got away but Baugh was shot and wounded, making his further flight impossible. Without delay the cowboys strung him up from the closest suitable shrub.[909]

Gillard, Charles
Born: (Unknown)—Date of Death: 13 December 1890
Place: Bastrop County
Event: Lynching/Shot

Charles Gillard, a black man who was a county commissioner of Bastrop County, was waylaid and shot to death on Saturday, 13 December 1890. Gillard made a dying statement implicating seven white men from the neighborhood as having been his attackers. Gillard had recently defeated J. S. Shomer, a white man, in the last election race for commissioner. It is thought that hard feeling over the defeat were at the root of the murder.[910]

Beale, Charles
Born: circa 1870—Date of Death: 1 January 1891
Place: Falls County
Event: Lynching/Hanged

Charles Beale, a black man accused of murder, was lynched by a mob of about 200 vigilantes.

On Tuesday, 31 December 1890, Beale entered the home of James Burwell Fisher, a farmer living near Lang in Falls County. Finding Mrs. Martha Faye (Clark) Fisher alone he outraged and terribly abused her, finally hitting her in the head with a hammer. When he had completed his beastly deed he robbed the woman of a small sum of money.

Beale was pursued by a small posse and captured on Thursday, 1 January 1891. He was positively identified by Mrs. Fisher, then taken to a grove of trees and hoisted up one of them by the neck. According to newspaper reports of the day, the severely injured and traumatized Mrs. Fisher was not expected to survive the ordeal.[911]

Some sources report this incident as having taken place on 2 January 1891.[912]

Taylor, George
Born: (Unknown)—Date of Death: 4 January 1891
Place: Falls County
Event: Lynching/Shot

George Taylor, a young white farmer at Chilton, was shot to death on Sunday, 4 January 1891. Intruders entered his home and shot him full of buckshot. The local black community believed that Taylor had led the lynching of Charles Beall on Thursday, 1 January 1891. Three black men were identified as suspects and were pursued by the sheriff and a posse. No outcome of that endeavor was noted by this source.[913]

Murphy, Jack
Born: (Unknown)—Date of Death: 9 January 1891
Place: Burleson County
Event: Legal Execution/Hanged

Jack Murphy (also identified as Jace Murphy), a black man who had murdered his wife, was hanged at Caldwell in Burleson County on Friday, 9 January 1891. The execution took place inside the jail building. Only a handful of spectators turned out to witness the event. Murphy was left dangling for twenty-two minutes after the trap had been sprung.

Murphy was convicted at the spring term of 1890 and sentenced to be hanged in June 1890. As he was about to be taken to his place of execution a telegram was received from the governor ordering a respite until a hearing concerning his sanity could be held. That inquiry took place, and a local jury determined that he was quite lucid. Murphy was sentenced to be hanged a second time. On that occasion the governor refused to commute his sentence and the thing was done as scheduled. [914]

Salcido, Jesus
Born: (Unknown)—Date of Death: 6 February 1891
Place: Tom Green County
Event: Lynching/Hanged

On Friday, 6 February 1891, a Mexican man named Jesus Salcido was found hanging from a tree near Knickerbocker, twelve miles south of San Angelo. Salcido, who was from Fort Stockton, had been visiting friends near there on Wednesday when three mounted white men came to the door and asked him to accompany them down the road a bit. That was the last anyone saw of Salcido until his corpse was discovered ornamenting a tree.[915]

Rollin, Henry
Born: (Unknown)—Date of Death: 14 February 1891
Place: Nacogdoches County
Event: Lynching/Hanged

According to the *Dallas Morning News,* on Saturday, 14 February 1891, three masked vigilantes hanged a black man who was identified as Henry Rollin. Rollins had attempted to assault a white woman at Douglass, in the western part of the county. The *Lynching Calendar* identified the man as Thomas Rowland, who they claimed was lynched on 24 February 1891. The same source cited a man named Thomas Rebin as being lynched on 17 February 1891.

     The *Fresno Morning Republican* identified the man as Tom Robin, and claimed that he was not guilty of any special crime. The newspapers did indicate that the man was a notorious criminal, and that the people wanted him hanged on general principles.[916]

Two Unidentified White Men
Born: (Unknown)—Date of Death: 27 February 1891
Place: Coryell County
Event: Lynching

Williams, Jasper
Born: (Unknown)—Date of Death: 27 February 1891
Place: Coryell County
Event: Lynching/Shot

Jasper Williams, a white man, and the father of Calvin Williams who had just recently been convicted of murdering a Bohemian man (white man of German ancestry), was assassinated at his own store in Leon Junction on Friday, 27 February 1891. At about 8:00 pm Williams left the building to get something to eat. As he exited he was cut down by a blast from a shotgun fired from concealment. Wounded in the side, Williams ran to a house about thirty yards away where he expired.

     Two other white men whose names are not mentioned were also executed at Leon Junction during the weeks leading up to the Williams killing.[917]

Blackwell, William "Will"
Born: circa 1870—Date of Death: 6 March 1891
Place: Gonzales County
Event: Legal Execution/Hanged

Will Blackwell, a twenty-one year old black man, was tried and convicted of the murder of a white man named Jump (or Lump) Rainey. Accordingly, Blackwell was hanged for that crime at Gonzales on Friday, 6 March 1891.[918]

Lewis, Joe
Born: circa 1854—Date of Death: 27 March 1891
Place: Bell County
Event: Legal Execution/Hanged

Joe Lewis, a black man aged about thirty-seven years, was found guilty of murdering his mother-in-law. The killing had occurred in August 1889. Lewis was hanged at Belton on Friday, 27 March 1891. His neck was broken by the fall.[919]

One Unidentified Black Youth
Born (Unknown)—Date of Death: circa April 1891
Place: Red River County
Event: Lynching/Hanged

Sometime about April 1891, a black youth was taken from the jail at Clarksville and lynched. No information to corroborate this story has been located.[920]

Field, William
Born (Unknown)—Date of Death: 1 April 1891
Place: Wood County
Event: Lynching

On Wednesday, 1 April 1891, a man named William Field was lynched for the attempted outrage on a woman at Mineola. No confirmation of this incident has been found. Based on the source of this report it is presumed that the man was black.[921]

Three Unidentified Black Men
Born (Unknown)—Date of Death: circa May-June 1891
Place: Unknown County
Event: Lynching/Hanged

In his book *The Strangest Fruit: Forgotten Black-on-Black Lynchings 1835-1935* the author, Joe H. Mitchell, claimed that the *San Antonio Light* ran a headline announcing that "Three Negro Crapshooters Lynched by Negroes. Negro killed on Grand View plantation over game of craps. Negroes hang the murderer and his two accomplices" in their 4 June 1891, edition. [922]

There are several Grandview communities in Texas as well as a Grand View plantation in Mississippi. The exact location of this incident has not been conclusively established. No records exist for the *San Antonio Light* newspaper for the years 1885 to 1894, thus the veracity of this claim cannot be verified.

Johnson, Henry A.
Born: circa 1866—Date of Death: 8 June 1891
Place: Rains County
Event: Legal Execution/Hanged

Henry Johnson, a twenty-five year old white man, went to the gallows at Emory on Monday, 8 June 1891. His crime was murder. It was said to have been one of the most brutal and heinous ever seen in the area.

On Sunday night, 27 April 1890, Johnson crept up on William Shumate, an old man well into his sixties who was napping quietly by a fire. Johnson drove a hatchet into his head, and afterwards beat his brains out with the ax. When the corpse had become cold and rigid he loaded it on horseback with the aid of his wife. He then carried the body about 400 yards from the scene of the killing and dropped it off. Afterwards, Johnson occupied Shumate's home and helped himself to the man's possessions.

On the night of 28 April 1890, Johnson attempted to quit the country and flee to the Indian Territory. He would have made good on his plan had it not been for the swollen condition of the Red River at the time. His flight blocked, the Rains County sheriff was able to pick up his trail and overtake him.

Church Elder J. J. Lockhart of Greenville entered Johnson's cell the morning of his execution and never left his side until the thing was done. At 1:30 pm Sheriff Montgomery escorted him to the gallows, Lockhart leading and Johnson bracketed by deputies Moore and McMahon. Asked if he had anything to say, Johnson declined. Lockhart sung "Jesus, Lover of My Soul" while Johnson's feet and legs were bound. Sheriff Montgomery cut the rope and sprung the trap. He died without a struggle.[923]

Sheppard, Monroe
Born: (Unknown)—Date of Death: 16 June 1891
Place: Bell County
Event: Lynching/Shot

Monroe Sheppard, a white man, was executed near Belton on Tuesday night, 16 June 1891. Sheppard was called to the door and shot repeatedly by a party of unidentified men.[924] Some sources report that this incident took place on Thursday, 28 May 1891. That source also claims that two other white men, whose identity is not indicated, were killed either in the same or in a related incident.

Note that the following entry is believed to be of the same incident.

Hartfield, William
Born: (Unknown)—Date of Death: 26 June 1891
Place: Cass County
Event: Lynching/Shot

Sheppard, Monroe "Mun"
Born: (Unknown)—Date of Death: 26 June 1891
Place: Cass County
Event: Lynching/Shot

Two black men, Mun Sheppard and William Hartfield, were taken out and shot to death by a group of unknown persons at a place about ten miles east of Daingerfield. Sheppard had a notoriously bad reputation, and that was supposed to have been the cause of the trouble.[925]

Johnson, William
Born: (Unknown)—Date of Death: 22 July 1891
Place: Rusk County
Event: Lynching/Hanged

William Johnson, a black man, was lynched at Henderson for suspicion of having committed a criminal assault.[926]

Caldwell, William
Born: circa 1865—Date of Death: 31 July 1891
Place: Harris County
Event: Legal Execution/Hanged

On Tuesday night, 31 July 1888, Dr. J. M. Shamblen was shot and killed while seated at his dinner table. He was leading the family blessing at the time. A blast from a shotgun fired through a nearby window knocked him from his chair and killed him more or less instantly. Shamblen was a Democrat, and a prominent Jaybird. He was also the leader of those who opposed the persons in control of the politics, and thus the destiny of Fort Bend County. Shamblen's killer, a black man named William Caldwell, was a member of the rival Woodpecker faction and a Republican.

Caldwell went to the gallows at half past eleven in the morning on Friday, 31 July 1891, at Houston. He entered the life hereafter without making a statement. In a procedure that spanned but a few minutes, Caldwell scaled the platform and dropped through the trap to his death in eight minutes.

The "Reconstruction Period" in the South may have officially ended in 1877, but the Republican Party had gained a stronghold in many counties with the support of freed black voters. Congress removed the civilian governments in the South in 1867, and put the former Confederacy under the rule of the U.S. Army. The army now conducted all elections. Freed slaves could vote while white men who had held leading positions under the Confederacy were denied that right. Whites were also banned from running for public office.

In ten states, including Texas, coalitions of Freedmen, recent arrivals from the North (Carpetbaggers), and white Southerners who supported Reconstruction (Scalawags) cooperated to form the Republican state governments that introduced various reconstruction programs that were often marred by widespread corruption. Violent opposition emerged in numerous localities. Democrats calling themselves "Redeemers" regained control state by state, sometimes using fraud and violence to control state elections.

A feud broke out in Fort Bend County in 1888 between wealthy white Democrats called the "Jaybirds," and Republicans called the "Woodpeckers." The Woodpeckers had held power since Reconstruction. The dispute crossed racial, social and politics lines. Assassination and violence became commonplace. Sheriff Garvey was a leader of Woodpeckers and opposed the efforts of the Jaybirds to return to power through violence. The town was an armed camp. The governor sent Texas Rangers to maintain order.

On Friday, 16 August 1889, members of the Jaybird faction faced off against the Woodpeckers in front of the courthouse. Sheriff Garvey and a crowd of armed men warned the Texas Rangers to get out of the way, claiming that the fight was none of their business. Ranger Sergeant Ira Aten and four privates on horseback tried to block the two sides from clashing. Nonetheless, a gun battle ultimately erupted during which Sheriff Garvey was killed. Two Jaybird leaders, Garvey's uncle and former Sheriff J. W. Blakey and H. H. Frost were also casualties, as well as an innocent bystander. Numerous participants were wounded. Ranger Private Frank Schmid Jr. was critically wounded and later died from his injuries on 17 June 1893.[927]

Two Unidentified Black Men

Born: (Unknown)—Date of Death: 14 August 1891
Place: Limestone County
Event: Lynching

Two unidentified black men, charged with the outrage of a woman, were executed by some means outside the law on Friday, 14 August 1891.[928]

Duncan, Richard H. "Dick"

Born: 6 December 1864—Date of Death: 18 September 1891
Place: Maverick County
Event: Legal Execution/Hanged

In February 1889, the body of a woman was discovered in the Rio Grande River. The corpse was weighted down with a heavy rock. Two days later a deputy found the bodies of a young man and young woman further upstream, also tied up and beaten to death. A fourth body, that of a young girl, was also found nearby.

Texas Rangers were called in to help with the identification of the remains and apprehension of the murderer. Completely by chance rangers recalled seeing a stranger at a camp in Nueces Canyon a week or two earlier. They also remembered seeing the same stranger and another man some time later, on the Nueces River, with a wagon carrying three females and a male. The men identified themselves as Richard H. "Dick" Duncan and Walter Landers. One ranger recalled that Mitchel made the wagon, and that there was a sign on the back indicating that the vehicle had been "Sold by Joe Clark, San Saba, Texas."

In March, the rangers tracked the two men and questioned them, but having no evidence was not able to arrest them. One of the rangers went to San Saba and spoke with the wagon maker, and the sheriff. He discovering that that a family named Williamson had left San Saba recently, bound for old Mexico. Duncan had agreed to buy the Williamson place before they moved and to guide them to their new home south of the border. The ranger returned to town where the learned that Duncan was locked up in the jail on an unrelated charge.

Duncan was charged with murder and sent to Eagle Pass for trial. His brother George Taplin "Tap" Duncan and their father both swore that Dick was in Mexico at the time of the murders. Walter Landers was never seen or heard from again, thus causing lawmen to conclude that Duncan had murdered him to insure his silence.

Duncan was tried, convicted and sentenced by District Court Judge Winchester Kelso's Court in Maverick County to hang on Friday, 18 September 1891. The gallows were constructed inside the jail building. On the morning of the execution Duncan, dressed in a new black suit and black boots ate his breakfast calmly. At 11:07 am Sheriff Cooke escorted him to the gallows. Duncan was totally indifferent to his fate.[929]

Tap Duncan and his father claimed the body from the mortuary and took it back to San Saba for burial.

Leeper, James "Jim"
Born: circa 1866—Date of Death: 29 September 1891
Place: Coryell County
Event: Legal Execution/Hanged

Powell, Edward "Ed"
Born: (Unknown)—Date of Death: 29 September 1891
Place: Coryell County
Event: Legal Execution/Hanged

"Laughed on the Scaffold" was the tag line of the article in the *Daily Inter Ocean* from Chicago, Illinois announcing the hangings of Jim Leeper and Ed Powell, both white men, who went to the gallows at Gatesville at 2:00 pm on Friday, 29 September 1891. When the governor's message was read that there would be no interference in the hanging Leeper was heard to say, "Let her go!"

In December 1889, Leeper and Powell stopped a wagon driver named John T. Mathison and tried to rob him and take his horses. Mathison put up a fight and was shot by either Leeper or Powell.

The driver lived long enough to identify the men. They were arrested, tried and found guilty. Both spent a year in the Coryell County jail while appeals went to the governor.

On Tuesday, 29 September 1891, Powell and Leeper were both hanged in the first double execution ever to take place at Gatesville. Leeper broke into a hearty laugh when he took his seat on the gallows platform. Both protested their innocence to the end, between intermissions for smoking. Upon learning that the governor would not intervene on her son's behalf Powell's mother told the pair to die like men and to pay no attention to religion, claiming that if there was a God he was unjust.

Albert Leeper, James' older brother, was convicted of trying to bribe a jurist, possibly in another trial. At any rate Albert spent two years in the state penitentiary at Huntsville. After he was released the family moved to the Indian Territory. [930]

Felder, John
Born: (Unknown)—Date of Death: 9 October 1891
Place: Cherokee County
Event: Legal Execution/Hanged

Felder, Wade
Born: (Unknown)—Date of Death: 9 October 1891
Place: Cherokee County
Event: Legal Execution/Hanged

On Monday night, 17 August 1891, while Yance Thompson and Mack Beasley were asleep in their beds at Thompson's house, Wade and John Felder crept up on the residence, armed with shotguns, and fired into the building. The blast instantly killed Yance Thompson. The Felder brothers, both black men, had been angry with Thompson and Beasley for some reason that was not disclosed.

The Felder brothers remained together until the bitter end, taking their walk to the gallows in unison on Friday, 9 October 1891. At about 1:00 pm they scaled the stairs and took up their assigned positions. Confident of their forthcoming redemption in heaven right to the end, the trap was sprung and they learned if their faith was sufficient to sustain them.[931]

Mooney, Martin
Born: (Unknown)—Date of Death: 18 October 1891
Place: Tarrant County
Event: Lynching/Hanged

Martin Mooney, a white man who used the alias John Martin, was found hanging from a tree along the banks of the river on Wednesday, 18 October 1891. Considering that Mooney had probably not gotten himself into that condition on his own, it was presumed that he had been lynched by person or persons unknown.

Threats against Mooney's life were said to have been made in recent weeks. The same source claimed that Mooney had been put in his own wagon and driven to the spot of the lynching where he was hanged with his own lead rope. Mooney had arrived at Fort Worth just a few weeks earlier with several good wagons and teams. He also had a family. Mysteriously, the teams and wagons disappeared. He was buried in the public plot, at the cities expense, and no one came to the burial. One newspaper source, an obvious romantic, mused that there was a woman at the bottom of it all.[932]

Green, Leo
Born: (Unknown)—Date of Death: 26 October 1891
Place: Cass County
Event: Lynching/Burning

On Saturday, 24 October 1891, Leo Green, a black man, murdered Mary Alice Sorrell Lowe, wife of John Henry Lowe, along with the couple's daughter Estelle Lowe. The incident took place seven miles west of Queen City. Green was arrested near Kildare the same night as the killing.

A crowd began to gather at the jail at Queen City around 5:00 am on Monday, 26 October 1891, demanding the keys to Green's cell from the wife of the sheriff. The woman put up a feckless defense, then relented. Determined mobsters took Green from his cell and returned the keys. Next they took him to the scene of the crime where the grieving husband, John Lowe, confronted him. Green confessed to the deed, claiming that he had done it all for the $60 that he was owed by Lowe.

Throughout the course of the day citizens from surrounding towns and counties began to congregate at the Lowe farm. Over time between 500 and 1,000 persons had amassed...both black and white. At about 2:30 pm a trace chain was placed around Green's neck and he was secured to a tree. Forty-six members of the mob piled firewood beneath him. To a person all of their numbers were black. An elderly black man lit the pyre. Once the flames had done their work the crowd quietly disbursed.[933]

Mary Alice and her daughter Estelle are both buried in the same grave at Douglassville Cemetery in Cass County.[934] There was very little of Green remaining after the fire.

Hughes, Lee
Born: circa 1867—Date of Death: 30 October 1891
Place: Washington County
Event: Legal Execution/Hanged

Lee Hughes, a twenty-four year old black man, was tried and convicted of murdering his wife Charlotte of about six years. The incident took place on Friday, 30 January 1890. Hughes had had hit her in the head repeatedly with an ax, practically severing her head, then left her body on the cabin floor where the couple lived.

Hughes went to the gallows at Brenham on Friday, 30 October 1891. He was dressed in a brand new dark broadcloth suit, new hat and shoes and was sporting a pair of gleaming white gloves. Every available square inch of ground was packed with the nearly 8,000 excited spectators. Accompanied by Sheriff Teague, Deputy W. H. Salles, Constable C. C. Boyd, County Attorney Ben S. Rogers and his spiritual advisors Elders Dickerson and Martin Johnson, Hughes made his way to the scaffold shortly after 2:50 pm. He was unshaken in his profession of innocence, right to the end, summing up his last speech with the statement, "Well, I am about to retire from you all. Good Bye, prepare to meet me in heaven."

Hughes's hands and feet were bound, the customary black cap pulled down over his head. Sheriff Teague took a brand new hand ax and prepared to cut the rope, asking, "Are you ready Lee?" Hughes replied, "Ready" to wit the sheriff plunged the blade of the shiny new cutting tool into the rope and Hughes's body shot through the trap at 3:08 pm. As he dropped a cry went up from the crowd, "Good Bye Lee."

Hughes hung for about twenty minutes before being pronounced dead.[935] He is buried at Chappell Hill Cemetery.

Two Unidentified Black Men
Born: (Unknown)—Date of Death: 9 November 1891
Place: Washington County
Event: Lynching/Hanged

On Sunday evening, 9 November 1891, there was a general row at a black dance held at the residence of Jim Hartley near Gay Hill. On the Monday following the gruesome discovery of the double lynching of two black men near Blake's Crossing on the Yegus River was made. Both had been hung with the same rope, clutched in an embrace. They had been strung up on Monday night. It is though that the two events were linked.[936]

Salinas, Felice
Born: (Unknown)—Date of Death: 11 November 1891
Place: Starr County
Event: Lynching/Hanged

Pedraza, Bandino
Born: (Unknown)—Date of Death: 11 November 1891
Place: Starr County
Event: Lynching/Hanged

Felice Salinas and Bandino Pedraza, both Mexican men, were found hanged from a tree near Rio Grande City on Wednesday, 11 November 1891. The pair was suspected of being revolutionists. Their bodies were cut down and buried in shallow graves, which the coyotes soon unearthed.[937]

Frizzell, William Henry
Born: 29 January 1864 —Date of Death: 20 November 1891
Place: Taylor County
Event: Legal Execution/Hanged

William Frizzell, a white man, went to the gallows at Abilene on Friday, 20 November 1891, for the murder of his wife.

The incident took place at Comanche, on Saturday, 24 January 1891. Frizzell and his wife Annie Brown had recently been divorced at Granbury. She and her mother moved to Comanche and set up at tent near the railroad station, doing laundry for the workers and making a good living at it. She had divorced Frizzell for lack of support. He had been utterly useless in terms of being a breadwinner, and relied entirely on the fruits of her industrious nature for his support. Frizzell had traveled to Comanche with the intent of killing Annie. He approached her, pistol in hand, saying. "If you won't live with me, you shan't live at all." Annie fled. Although he only had four cartridges in his gun Frizzell emptied the weapon's content into his former wife's back, killing her almost instantly. He then put the revolver in his pocket and calmly walked to town. Several men who were nearby and had witnessed the shooting took him into custody and handed him over to the sheriff.[938]

At about 2:20 pm the cowardly, deadbeat back shooter and wife killer Frizzell was led from his cell to the gallows. Reverends J. C. Wingo and R. S. Stuart both conducted services in the jail and on the gallows. Frizzell had requested that the pastors lead the group in the popular hymn, "What a Friend We Have in Jesus."[939] They complied with his wishes. The death warrant was read at 2:23 pm. Shortly after, the trap was sprung and another sinner was sent on his way.[940]

Black, William "Billy"
Born: (Unknown)—Date of Death: 22 November 1891
Place: Polk County
Event: Lynching/Hanged

The "Whitecaps" paid the town of Moscow a visit on Sunday night, 22 November 1891. The body of Billy Black was discovered the following morning, lynched from a large beam erected in the middle of an elevated spot in the street.

Billy Black, a black man, had only been in town a few days but had managed to offend and infuriate many decent folks. His insults and foul language around women and children caused one poor girl to sprain her ankle trying to escape from the rascal. Apparently lawmen had been too slow in dealing with this nuisance.[941]

Perez, Lorenzo
Born: (Unknown) —Date of Death: 27 November 1891
Place: Jackson County
Event: Legal Execution/Hanged

Lorenzo Perez, a Mexican man, went to the gallows at Midland on Friday, 27 November 1891, for the murder of Sam Murphy. He confessed to the killing, and stated that although his friend Juan Benevides had accompanied he was innocent of the shooting. Perez also stated that Murphy, who had followed them for a distance before overtaking them, had fired at them first.

The train carrying Father Albert Wagner of Marionfield had been delayed, thus explaining the late afternoon execution. Sending one to his maker without benefit of a clergyman was unthinkable. At 8:15 pm the trap was sprung. Perez broke his neck in the fall and died quickly. There was a large crowd present to witness his hanging.[942]

Mendez, Jose Maria
Born: (Unknown)—Date of Death: 10 December 1891
Place: Val Verde County
Event: Legal Execution/Hanged

On 18 December 1890, a group of riders discovered the bodies of Frank Wilkins and Si Walton on the Wilkins Brothers Ranch, along the Pecos River, in Crockett County. Jose Mendez, who had murdered the pair, was arrested in Mexico and brought back to Texas for trial. He was subsequently tried, convicted, and sentenced to death by hanging.[943]

At about 10:00 am on Thursday, 10 December 1891, the father of Jose Mendez entered his son's jail cell at Del Rio and bade him farewell. At 11:00 am the sheriff led Mendez out of his cell and down the hall to the execution chamber. As he passed a series of windows Mendez asked to speak to the crowd that had gathered outside to witness the event. He confessed his guilt, and expressed sadness for having committed such an act, but reaffirmed that his victim was a bad man who treated Mexicans poorly. For that he had no regrets. Mendez spoke for about five minutes, then ascended the steps to the gallows and took his place on a chair where he was asked to sit. Once there he lit a cigarette. When he had finished smoking he stepped to the trap where his hands and feet were bound and the noose was placed around his neck. When finished he drew up his hands and remarked, "How nicely it [the noose] fits." At 11:30 am the trap was sprung and Mendez shot into eternity.

Shields, Joe
Born: (Unknown)—Date of Death: 28 January 1892
Place: Fort Bend County
Event: Lynching/Hanged

On Thursday night, 28 January 1892, a young black man named Joe Shields, living about eight miles from Thompson, was putting his horse in the lot when he was knocked over the head and dragged off by four men. His attackers lynched him from a tree. No cause was mentioned for the hanging.[944]

One Unidentified Mexican Man
Born: (Unknown)—Date of Death: 7 March 1892
Place: Encinal County
Event: Lynching/Hanged

A man from Encinal County reported finding the body of an unidentified Mexican man hanging from a tree at the El Pato Ranch. A number of spent Winchester rifle cartridges were found near the site. It was thought that Garza sympathizers killed the man for having aided troops who were seeking them out during the recent campaign.[945]

      Encinal County was established on 1 February 1856, and was to consist of the eastern portion of present-day Webb County. The town of Encinal was selected as the county seat. However, Encinal County was never organized, and its territory was ultimately absorbed into Webb County on 12 March 1899.

One Unidentified Mexican Man
Born: (Unknown)—Date of Death: 13 March 1892
Place: Encinal County
Event: Lynching/Hanged

In a similar incident to the one reported on 7 March 1892, another body of an unidentified Mexican man was discovered hanging from a tree at the El Pato Ranch. As in the first instance, a number of spent Winchester rifle cartridges were found near the site. Again, it was thought that Garza sympathizers killed the man for having aided troops who were seeking them out during the recent campaign.[946]

One Unidentified Black Men
Born: (Unknown)—Date of Death: 22 April 1892
Place: McLennan County
Event: Lynching/Hanged

On Tuesday, 19 April 1892, postmaster Eugene Kaufman was robbed and murdered at Reisel by two unidentified black men. A neighbor came to investigate the disturbance and one of the men fired at him. Unfortunately he missed. The robbers got away with $3.00. A posse soon commenced a search for two black men named John Lee and Dobbs Williams. One of the killers was found near the Limestone County line and lynched. The fate of the other is not known.[947]

Fisher, James
Born: circa 1859—Date of Death: 27 May 1892
Place: Delta County
Event: Legal Execution/Hanged

James Fisher, a thirty-three year old white man, went to the gallows at Cooper on Friday, 27 May 1892. It was about 2:00 pm when the trap was sprung and Fisher was finished. The event took place in full view of 5,000 approving witnesses who had come to see justice done.

Fisher had brutally murdered Austin Hardy on Sunday, 5 July 1891. Many believed that Fisher's father was an accessory to the crime. However, James Fisher confessed to Sheriff Acker that he had acted alone. Whether a noble deed or an affirmation of fact, readers will never know. In either case, Fisher alone paid the penalty of the crime.[948]

Scott, George
Born: circa 1869—Date of Death: 27 May 1892
Place: Rusk County
Event: Legal Execution/Hanged

George Scott, a twenty-three year old black man, was tried and convicted of having outraged and murdered his own sister. Such an unspeakable act immediately drew the death penalty.

At half past two in the afternoon on Friday, 27 May 1892, the gallows trap fell at Henderson and Scott began his trip to the hereafter. Several hundred persons turned out to see him off.[949]

Cook, Tobe
Born: circa 1855—Date of Death: 10 June 1892
Place: Bastrop County
Event: Legal Execution/Hanged

On Friday, 10 June 1892, Tobe Cook, a thirty-seven year old black man who was convicted of murder and outrage, was executed by hanging at the Bastrop County jail.[950]

White, Alf
Born: circa 1842—Date of Death: 11 June 1892
Place: Walker County
Event: Legal Execution/Hanged

Alf White, a fifty-year old black man, was tried and convicted of having murdered Russ Bassford, another black man. White went to the gallows at Huntsville game, smoking a cigar as he walked and chatted with friends on his way to scale the platform stairs.[951]

Sims, King
Born: circa 1872—Date of Death: 24 June 1892
Place: McLennan County
Event: Legal Execution/Hanged

The headlines read "Died Game and Pious" on the morning following the execution of King Sims, a twenty year old black man who had been convicted of murder.

Record crowds mobbed Waco to see the hanging. Every door, window and house surrounding the jail yard was crowded with spectators, eager to catch a glimpse of the event.

On Monday, 11 May 1891, Sims had been hired to chop cotton for Edmond Brandon, and old bachelor who lived at Robinsonville, seven miles south of Waco. After working for Brandon only three days Sims learned that the old fellow had a great deal of money. Sims returned to Waco to visit a woman friend, Melisa Brown, who was locked up in jail at the time. During their conversation he promised to bail her out. He returned to Brandon's place and vowed to rob him. Seeing the other hands in the field he became convinced that he would not be able to pull off a robbery by daylight, so he concealed himself in the bushes and waited until dusk.

Near the spot where he concealed himself was a woodpile. Sims took the ax that was lying nearby and broke the handle off and made a club for himself. He then approached Brandon and demanded all of his money. When the man refused, Sims struck him over the head knocking him insensible. Sim's rifled through the house, stealing a quantity of clothing as well as $19.15 in specie that he found in the pocket of Brandon's trouser pants. Next, Sims beat Brandon to death with the ax handle so that he would not be able to identify him as the thief.

Predictably, Sims was captured, tried and convicted of murder and robbery. At 1:47 pm on Friday, 24 June 1892, he mounted the gallows at Waco in the company of Sheriff Ford. A prayer was offered on his behalf. Sims confessed his crime, then offered "Well, Good-by boys. I hope you will all lead a better life." The trap was sprung. Sims was pronounced dead at 2:09 pm.[952]

Gaines, Henry
Born: (Unknown)—Date of Death: 28 June 1892
Place: Tyler County
Event: Lynching/Shot

Smith, Thomas
Born: (Unknown)—Date of Death: 28 June 1892
Place: Tyler County
Event: Lynching/Shot

Wood, Prince

Born: (Unknown)—Date of Death: 28 June 1892

Place: Tyler County

Event: Lynching/Shot

On Tuesday, 28 June 1892, three black men were lynched at Spurger for outraging Mrs. Beasley and her daughter. The threesome, all blacks, were Prince Wood, Thomas Smith and Henry Gaines.[953]

Smith, George William

Born: 2 January 1889—Date of Death: 8 July 1892

Place: Grayson County

Event: Legal Execution/Hanged

At about 10:00 pm on Wednesday, 14 January 1891, a holdup took place at the town of Bells. A man named George Smith walked into Sam Risenberg's Saloon and demanded that the crowd "shell out." Jim Isbell, the thirty year old city marshal, was tending bar at Risenberg's Saloon the time. Isbell placed the money from the till on the billiard table. Smith took it. He then ordered a bar patron to take all of the money from the remaining customers. As Smith's attention was diverted, Isbell grabbed his own pistol and fired once at the robber. Smith calmly returned fire, hurling one shot from his .45 caliber revolver at Isbell. The bullet struck him in the face and exited through his neck. A bystander quickly grabbed Smith, causing the crowd to join in and disarmed him. The patrons considered lynching Smith, but decided to place him under guard.

George Smith, a white farmer from Grayson County, admitted that he had bought the pistol the day before in anticipation of the holdup. City Marshal Isbell succumbed to his wound on 17 January 1891. Although not certain, it is believed that he is buried in an unmarked grave in the Old Bells North Cemetery.

Farmer come pistoleer Smith was convicted of murder. The Grayson County sheriff hanged him at Sherman on Friday, 8 July 1892. Smith rose that day and was shaved at about 8:30 am. Prior to his execution he had quizzed his captors, wanting to know why that black cap was placed on the condemned man's head. Was it so that he could not see the executioner? Smith was told that it was for the benefit of the audience, since often the executed man's face becomes morbidly contorted during his struggle to hold on to precious life. Several times he asked if he might see his coffin. When finally allowed his eyes lit up with excitement and joy. When asked if he had anything to say Smith replied, "There is nothing I wish to say. It would do no one any good."

For his going away clothing Smith selected a blue suit with white shirt and turned down collar. He was, to be certain, a handsome looking man in his very finest livery that day. At noon he ate a hearty meal, and at about 2:08 pm was administered a dose of morphine to buoy him up for his upcoming ordeal. At 2:23 pm, accompanied by the sheriff, Smith began his walk to the gallows.

As the hangman placed the black hood over his head Smith uttered, "A fellow can't breathe much in this." Next he offered, "That is pretty tight." Smith commented about the rope securing his hands behind his back as well, saying "Wouldn't you just as soon tie them in front of me?" [954]

Smith is buried at Choctaw. Numerous family genealogy files list Smith's date of execution as 6 July 1892, not 8 July 1892, which several newspapers have also claimed. Smith's tombstone is inscribed with the date 6 July 1892.[955]

Parks, Cal
Born: circa 1871—Date of Death: 15 July 1892
Place: Burleson County
Event: Legal Execution/Hanged

Cal Parks, a black man, was tried and convicted of having outraged a woman named Mrs. Jessie McDonough. After violating her, Parks murdered the woman as well as her seven-year old stepson. The incident took place at a section house on the Santa Fe Railroad track near Caldwell.

Parks went to the gallows at Caldwell on Friday, 15 July 1892. A crowd of 3,000 persons witnessed the murderer drop to his death, breaking his neck and passing in seven and one half minutes.[956]

Washington, Archie
Born: circa 1871—Date of Death: 26 July 1892
Place: Orange County
Event: Legal Execution/Hanged

Clark Washington was appointed an Orange special policeman, which was customary at the time for black men in law enforcement.

On Saturday night, 4 April 1891, there was a public gathering attended primarily by blacks at a hall known as the "colored schoolhouse." A group of citizens had turned out to hear from candidates who were running for city offices. After the speeches concluded all of the white citizens left and the hall was converted into an ice cream bazaar. A black man named Archie Washington, who was not related to Clark Washington, was seen with a pistol in his hands. He reportedly told someone that he would empty his gun into anyone who interfered with him.

Officer Washington attempted to take the pistol away from Archie. A scuffle took place and the participants left the hall. About thirty minutes later Archie and the officer were seen conversing in a low tone, apparently in a cordial manner. Officer Washington was then heard to say, "If you don't quit making so much noise I will arrest you and put you in jail." Archie, who was in the process of leaving, answered, "I guess you are a God damned liar." Officer Washington then grabbed Archie and attempted to arrest him. Archie jumped back a few feet and shot him twice with his pistol. When Archie fired the second time, Washington turned and ran. Archie called out after him, "Now die, you [racial expletive], die."

Washington ran a short distance then staggered. He composed himself, called for a doctor, and then ran into the hall. When he reached the door he fell mortally wounded on the floor. Washington died twenty minutes later, having suffered a wound to the abdomen and a flesh wound through the left forearm.

Archie Washington was sentenced to life in prison but his case was overturned on appeal. He was sentenced to death at his second trial. Archie appealed again, but while waiting for the outcome escaped from jail for a few days. The court once again dismissed his appeal, this time owing to the recent escape episode. Archie was sentenced to death. Accordingly, he went to the gallows at Orange on Tuesday, 26 July 1892.[957]

McGee, Henry
Born: (Unknown)—Date of Death: 12 August 1892
Place: Harris County
Event: Legal Execution/Hanged

Thirty-three year old Houston Police Officer James E. Fenn was assigned to work at a black dance hall. He saw a man there named Henry McGee who was known to carry a gun. As Fenn approached to question him, McGee shot him in the stomach with a .44-caliber Bulldog revolver, inflicting a mortal wound. Fenn died at 1:30 am the following day.

McGee was identified as the killer. He had made threats against Fenn stemming from prior arrests. McGee was arrested, and after two trials was ultimately convicted. He was sentenced to death.

McGee scaled the gallows stairs at Houston on Friday, 12 August 1892, and kept his date with the executioner.[958]

Armor, William "Bill"
Born: (Unknown)—Date of Death: 6 September 1892
Place: Lamar County
Event: Lynching/Hanged

Ransom, John
Born: (Unknown)—Date of Death: 6 September 1892
Place: Lamar County
Event: Lynching/Hanged

Walker, John "Jack"
Born: (Unknown)—Date of Death: 6 September 1892
Place: Lamar County
Event: Lynching/Hanged

Lynching blacks at Paris, although not routine, was far from uncommon. A triple lynching, however, was a very special event...even by Lamar County standards.

Early in the morning on Wednesday, 7 September 1892, a messenger arrived at Paris announcing that three black men had been hanged by the roadside about nine miles southeast of town. The lynching had taken place the preceding evening. The bodies were those of William Armor, John Ransom, and John Walker. All were well known in the area. Officers learned that a mob of about thirty armed men, disguised with masks, had gone to the home of Gilbert Daniels at about midnight and dragged Ransom out of the house with a rope around his neck. The vigilantes claimed that they wanted to put other blacks that had been doing mischief in the area on notice. Next they went to the homes of Armor and Walker, doing the same to them. All three men, pulled along by their rope leashes, were taken to a nearby tree and hanged.

Racial strife in the area had boiled over not long before when a white man named John Ashley killed a notorious black ne'er-do-well named Jarred Burns. That incident had taken place on Friday, 29 July. Ashley had sold Burns a horse, which he had not paid for. The horse took to breaking into Ashley's field. Although warned, Burns would not keep the animal out. In desperation, Ashley kept the beast and would not give him back until Burns had paid him. Burns, angered by Ashley's actions, went to his home to retrieve the animal by force. An argument ensued, during which Ashley shot Burns to death.[959]

Various newspapers reported rumors of as many as three other lynching of blacks in the area, probably connected with this incident. However, thus far none can be verified.

Sullivan, William "Buck"
Born: circa 1874—Date of Death: 7 September 1892
Place: Grimes County
Event: Lynching

William Sullivan, an eighteen-year old black man, was employed as a cotton picker by a white farmer at Plantersville. The same farmer also had under his direction a white couple that had tried on several occasions to have Sullivan discharged. On Saturday, 17 September 1892, the white man left the field leaving his wife alone with Sullivan, apparently so she could file a charge of attempted outrage afterwards. It is unclear if the two may have had an ongoing amorous relationship that the husband was not aware of or if the incident was actually an attempted outrage.

Some newspapers went so far as to claim that the husband had caught the pair in the act of conjugal endearment. Others imply that the charge was a ruse. The husband gave his wife a chance to accuse Sullivan of outrage, which she did. Once the white woman's grievance was lodged Sullivan was marched to town at gunpoint by the husband and delivered to the sheriff.

Word spread, and a mob quickly formed. With minimal effort the vigilantes managed to remove Sullivan from custody. They fastened a rope around his neck and drug him about 500 yards, then lynched him from a tree. Just to make certain that he was dead, they pumped bullet after bullet into his corpse.[960]

It is worth mentioning that this account was published in the *Freeman* newspaper, Indianapolis, Indiana. The *Freeman,* published between 1884 and 1927, was a black newspaper that largely reported news of interest to their target readership. The publisher at the time was George L. Knox, a man who had been born into slavery, a fact that had not stopped him from becoming one of Indiana's most prominent black residents in the 1890s.

One Unidentified Black Man
Born: (Unknown)—Date of Death: 19 September 1892
Place: Lamar County
Event: Lynching

Perhaps linked to the foregoing case, unverified sources claim that a black man whose identity is unknown was lynched at Paris in Lamar County on 19 September 1892.[961]

Wilkerson, Buck
Born: circa 1868—Date of Death: 14 October 1892
Place: Bell County
Event: Legal Execution/Hanged

In about 1887 Buck Wilkerson, a black man, had married Susan Harrison, a black woman who was several years his senior. Miss Harrison had four children by previous relationships.

By all accounts, their marriage was not a happy one. In May 1891 Wilkerson took Harrison's eldest child, a thirteen or fourteen-year old girl named Jenny Lind Harrison, and eloped with her. They went to Cedar Creek, about ten miles north of Belton. In a short time they were arrested. Wilkerson was taken to jail and Jenny Lind returned to her mother.

Several days into his confinement Wilkerson posted bond and was released. He worked odd jobs around the town and, during his stay, made several attempts to get Jenny Lind away from her mother. At about 8:00 or 9:00 pm on Tuesday night, 21 July 1891, Susan Harrison was sitting on the porch of her home at Dangerfield with her children, enjoying the evening. Wilkerson crept up upon her and fired one shot from concealment, using his double barrel shotgun. The blast was devastating, taking off part of the woman's face and head. Death was instantaneous. Jenny Lind ran to her mother's side as Wilkerson took her by the arm and led her away. As he did so a neighbor, Ike Chaney, was alerted by the sound of gunfire and attempted to stop Wilkerson's flight. Although accompanied by other neighbors he was unable to stop the man's decampment when Wilkerson menaced him with the shotgun.

There was a black church nearby where an event had been planned for that night. Hearing the commotion a group of congregants rushed to the scene to investigate. A young man named Will Hamilton was in the lead of the bunch. As he approached Wilkerson he was hit full on in the chest with a blast of shot from Wilkerson's gun, killing him dead in his tracks.

Wilkerson had released his grip on Jenny Lind. She escaped his clutches and fled to the home of her grandmother where she hid out. Wilkerson took advantage of the confusion and fled the scene. Some claim that he was in the Dangerfield area for several days, trying to coerce Jenny Lind to elope with him once again. A liberal reward was offered and, after seeking shelter in Mexico, Wilkerson was eventually arrested at Laredo and returned to Belton.

On Friday, 14 October 1892, a defiant Buck Wilkerson went to the gallows. He told newspaper reporters that it made little difference to him if he was dead or alive. He inquired as to when Reverend Felix Washington of the Methodist Episcopal Church would be arriving and was told about noon. He commented that that would be too late. At about 1:00 pm Reverend Washington and two other black preachers arrived at the jail and were admitted. At 1:30 pm Sheriff S.A. Sparks read the death sentence, and at 1:55 pm escorted Wilkerson to the gallows as the pastors led the crowd in the song "I am so glad that Jesus loves me."

Wilkerson's last words were that he "...did not kill Will Hamilton on purpose. It was accidental. But I did kill the other [his wife Susan Harrison] on purpose." Dressed in a navy blue suit, Wilkerson displayed great nerve and poise as he stepped onto the trapdoor, knelt and prayed. At 2:12 pm the trap was sprung and Wilkerson dropped to his death.[962]

Castillo, Rosalio
Born: (Unknown)—Date of Death: 25 November 1892
Place: El Paso County
Event: Legal Execution/Hanged

On Sunday, 11 September 1892, Rosalio Castillo, a Mexican man, attacked and outraged a little girl named Luse Romero, daughter of Jesus Romero. Romero was less than twelve years old. The girl had been returning from visiting a friend when Castillo, described by her as a tall man with an ugly scar followed her. She paid him little attention until they reached a lonely spot along their path where Castillo dashed up to her, placed his hand over her mouth and dragged her into the bushes to perform the ghastly act.

Once the atrocity was over the girl fled, telling her story to her mother who raised the alarm. Castillo was soon arrested, tried and convicted of the atrocity.

On Friday, 25 November 1892, Castillo went to the gallows at El Paso.[963] Surprisingly, his hanging was only the second legal execution in the history of El Paso County.

Freeny, George
Born: circa 1842—Date of Death: 25 November 1892
Place: Robertson County
Event: Legal Execution/Hanged

George Freeny, a fifty-year old black man, was tried and convicted of murdering his twelve-year old stepson, John Robertson.

Freeny was too poor to hire a lawyer. The court appointed barrister suggested that he should have pled guilty in exchange for a life sentence. To everyone's surprise Freeny pled innocent. The court sentenced him to hang for his crime. For a change the lawyer was correct.

Freeny's judgment was carried out at Galveston on Friday, 25 November 1892, when he was hanged by the neck until dead.[964]

Farrell, Jack
Born: (Unknown)—Date of Death: 2 December 1892
Place: Wharton County
Event: Legal Execution/Hanged

Jack Farrell was tried, convicted and sentenced to hang for the murder of a man named Henry Kearby and his wife. Farrell had not acted alone. George Mitchell, Percy Paul and Willis Lawson lent a hand in the killings that grew out of a gambling game where Kearby had been the winner. Farrell, who was apparently a sore loser, murdered Kearby and his wife, robbed them of the winnings and set the house on fire to cover his crime.

On the prescribed day, Friday 2 December 1892, Jack Farrell scaled the gallows at Wharton. At the appointed time the latch was sprung and Farrell's 200 pound body dropped from the gallows, falling eight feet until the length of rope allotted by the executioner had been exhausted. Regrettably, the length of the rope and the weight of Farrell were a combination destined for disaster. In an incident reminiscent of the Thomas E. "Black Jack" Ketchum hanging, Farrell's head pulled free from his corpse with a loud snap. The noose flew up with the poor man's head still attached, this in full view of the horrified spectators. The body, liberated from the head and lying below quivered as the last bits of life abandoned the man's mortal host. [965]

For the benefit of the readers who have been patiently thumbing through scores of pages diligently searching for that single case that you just knew would be there...the one where the poor man's head pops off...well, this is it! The simple Newtonian physics involved in a hanging deals with mass, gravity and height (or length of the rope in this instance). Executioners were not always skilled in advanced physics, thus miscalculations involving length of rope versus the weight of the individual to be hanged were made occasionally. To err on the short side (rope that is) resulted in a painful and sometimes protracted strangulation. To err on the long side produced the result that poor Jack Ferrell experienced.

Farrell's execution was the first in Wharton County. The fact that it did not come off too well may help explain why there were only three more legal hangings in Wharton and only a handful of lynching's that followed Ferrell's performance.

Smith, Henry
Born: (Unknown)—Date of Death: 31 January 1893
Place: Lamar County
Event: Lynching/Burned to Death

On Friday, 27 January 1893, Henry Smith, a black man, attacked and murdered a four-year old white girl named Myrtle Vance, the daughter of Henry Vance.

At about 2:00 pm that same day a meeting was held and parties were sent out to search for the child. Her mangled body was discovered not far from her home, covered with leaves and branches. A search was undertaken for Smith, who was suspected of being the girls' killer. He was captured at Hope, Arkansas.

When a posse of deputy sheriffs and armed local citizens tried to return Smith by railroad for trial at Paris they were met at the station by a mob of agitated residents. The roads to Paris had been alive with a swarm of frenzied humanity in wagons, hacks, carriages, on foot and by horseback making their way to the depot to meet Smith's train. Whisky shops were closed, schools dismissed by a proclamation of the mayor and all prepared for vengeance.

With drawn and cocked pistols, lawmen resisted. Their remarkably valiant efforts were no match for the mob, as a superior force estimated to have numbered 20,000 soon overpowered them. Smith was placed on a carnival float and taken through town, mocked like a king on his throne. He was removed to a prairie about 300 yards from the Texas and Pacific depot and placed on a platform six feet square and ten feet high where he was secured with ropes and other fastenings. For fifteen minutes he was tortured with hot branding irons that were applied over practically every square inch of his body. Unconscious and perhaps already dead, Smith was doused with kerosene. Cottonseed hulls were place beneath him and he was set afire.[966]

From his screams, Smith's anguish must have been excruciating. Afterwards, curiosity seekers carried away pieces of charcoal from the pier. Onlookers tore off bits of his clothing for keepsakes. The scene was horrifying beyond belief. To imagine that civilized persons could do such a thing is unthinkable.

Smith's killing of the Vance girl was, according to reports, retaliation for the actions of her father, Henry Vance, while he was a police officer. Vance had arrested Smith for drunk and disorderly. He had been forced to use his club in the process. Unwisely, Smith swore to get even with him for having done so.

Butler, Will
Born: (Unknown)—Date of Death: 7 February 1893
Place: Lamar County
Event: Lynching/Hanged

Will Butler, a black man and the stepson of Henry Smith who was lynched and burned on 31 January 1893, for murdering a four year old white girl named Myrtle Vance was found hanging from a tree, his body riddled with bullet holes. The awful discovery was made near Paris on Tuesday, 7 February 1893. Butler had sealed his fate when he foolishly boasted that he knew the whereabouts of Smith but would not reveal it. [967]

Holland, Frank
Born: circa 1868—Date of Death: 23 February 1893
Place: Brazoria County
Event: Legal Execution/Hanged

Frank Holland and Jerome Baker, both white men, were employed by three wealthy stockmen to guide them through wild country near Brazoria in search of a site to establish a ranch. The pair murdered the stockmen, stole their money and buried their remains in the mud where they thought they would not be discovered. As is generally the case with criminals, they were wrong.

At the trial both were found guilty. Holland received the death sentence and Baker drew life in prison. Holland kept his appointment with the executioner 11:30 am on Thursday, 23 February 1893.[968]

Scott, Charles
Born: circa 1850—Date of Death: 15 April 1893
Place: Smith County
Event: Legal Execution/Hanged

Charles Scott, a black man, was hung at Tyler on Saturday, 15 April 1893, for the murder of B. H. Curtis. That incident had taken place on 12 July 1893.[969]

Burke, Jim
Born: circa 1873—Date of Death: 28 April 1893
Place: Fannin County
Event: Legal Execution/Hanged

Massey, Sam
Born: circa 1861—Date of Death: 28 April 1893
Place: Fannin County
Event: Legal Execution/Hanged

There was a rare double hanging at Bonham on Friday, 28 April 1893. Two black men, Jim Burke and Sam Massey were the guests of honor. Newspaper accounts of the day claim that 10,000 persons, men, women and children of all races turned out for the affair.

Burke had been tried and convicted of outraging a white woman near Ambia. Massey had been tried and convicted of a vicious assault on the Smith family, during which he outraged and killed Mrs. Smith and permanently crippled Mr. Smith.[970]

Davis, Zedolph
Born: circa 1872—Date of Death: 28 April 1893
Place: Lavaca County
Event: Legal Execution/Hanged

Zedolph (or Seedolph) Davis, a twenty-one year old black man, was hanged at Halletsville on Friday, 28 April 1893. On the night of 24 April 1893, Davis had outraged a widow woman, Mrs. William Ballard. His execution was swift and trouble free. Davis died within twelve minutes.[971]

Carlisle, John Thomas
Born: circa 1850—Date of Death: 12 May 1893
Place: Grayson County
Event: Legal Execution/Hanged

Luttrell, Charles
Born: circa 1861—Date of Death: 12 May 1893
Place: Grayson County
Event: Legal Execution/Hanged

Two white men named John Carlisle and Charles Luttrell went to the gallows at Sherman to expiate their crimes on Friday, 12 May 1893. To the dismay of all, the execution was private. Undaunted by that fact however, thousands ringed the jail looking for a glimpse and listening for a sound of the happening.

Mr. W. T. Sharman had been brutally murdered at Denison on 28 April 1892, while he lay asleep in his bed with his wife and baby by his side. His chest was filled with buckshot that had been fired through a nearby window from a double barrel shotgun. Luttrell had done the killing but had been paid to do the job Carlisle. The latter feared Sharman's testimony in the murder trial of Colonel Brown.

Colonel Jim Brown was killed in Chicago in 1892, during police raids on a racecourse in that city that had following the murder of two officers. Brown was the sheriff of Lee County at the time of Sharman's killing. Brown had a disagreement with a man named Sam Sparks over a racehorse. The man who fired the fatal shot in the Brown killing was one of Sparks' deputies named Meyers. He had been sent to prison for twenty years. One of his accomplices was Carlisle. After Meyers was sent up Carlisle had disappeared for a time, but was arrested at Fort Worth. Just before his trial Carlisle shipped a shotgun to Luttrell at Giddings. A few nights later Sharman was assassinated in his bed. Without Sharman's testimony Carlisle was acquitted of the Brown killing.

In spite of both these men's best efforts, and their cleverly executed plot, justice prevailed in the end and they were both convicted of murder. Both were sentenced to hang. Both men had a good breakfast on their final morning and were shaved at about 9:00 am. Religious services were held at 11:00 am, and when it was time to take their dinner neither man had the appetite for it. At 1:00 pm Carlisle was baptized in his cell.

Mrs. Sharman and W. T. Sharman's brother were both admitted to the hanging. Both had to have morphine injected into their arms to buoy them up for the affair. At 1:50 pm Carlisle and Luttrell were escorted to the gallows, both holding roses in their hands. At 2:04 pm the men were placed in their respective positions on the platform. Both smoked cigarettes while the ropes were being fitted. The drop was between seven and eight feet, resulting in the quick death of both condemned men. No gruesome scene here to add to the scheming plot of these doomed men.[972]

Graham, Henry "Harry"
Born: (Unknown)—Date of Death: 9 June 1893
Place: Fannin County
Event: Legal Execution/Hanging

Henry "Harry" Graham, a black man, had shot and killed a man in neighboring Titus County. He crossed into Morris County and made threats that "no little officer could arrest him."

Graham went to the town of Omaha, where Precinct 3 Constable F. M. Ledbetter and Deputy Sheriff Curlee attempted to defy the challenge and take him into custody. After a chase that covered several miles, thirty-seven year old Ledbetter cornered Graham inside a house and ordered him to surrender. Graham pulled a pistol and shot Ledbetter. The bullet struck him in the neck. He died within a few hours.

Graham was shot and wounded before he was eventually taken into custody at Commerce. He was convicted by a jury and sentenced to be executed at Dangerfield. On 26 May 1893, the governor granted him a two-week respite while he reviewed a request filed to commute the sentence of Graham. On 7 June 1893, Governor Hogg informed Sheriff J. W. High of Morris County that he was not going to interfere with the jury's decision and that the execution could precede.

Accordingly, on Friday, 9 June 1893, Graham kept his date with the executioner at Pittsburg. In front of several thousand onlookers the braggadocios outlaw, who had once claimed "no little officer could arrest him" was so weak from fright that he had to be held up by two lawmen while the noose was fitted. Graham made a rambling, unintelligible speech that carried on for more than a half hour. He wanted more time, but the sheriff gave the signal and sprung the trap, thus cutting short Graham's final oration.[973]

Jazo, Given Name Unknown
Born: (Unknown)—Date of Death: 15 July 1893
Place: El Paso County
Event: Lynching/Hanged

The body of a Mexican man known only as Jazo was discovered lynched to a tree, on the lower island near El Paso. This was the same island where Texas Ranger Captain Frank Jones had been killed on 30 June 1893, known locally as Pirates Island. The body had been hanging a day or two when discovered. Locals claimed that the unfortunate man was a Mexican citizen and Texans had hanged him.[974]

Brown, Alexander
Born: (Unknown)—Date of Death: 28 July 1893
Place: Bastrop County
Event: Legal Execution/Hanged

Alexander Brown, a black man, was hanged at Bastrop for murdering his wife. His execution took place on Friday, 28 July 1893.[975]

Brown's case had been appealed, but on Tuesday, 25 July the governor's office notified the sheriff that although the evidence in the case was almost entirely circumstantial, he could see no reason to interfere in the due course of the law. The day following the governor's determination Brown tried to cheat the hangman by committing suicide by attempting to slit his throat from ear to ear. He failed.[976]

Miller, Henry
Born: circa 1860—Date of Death: 28 July 1893
Place: Dallas County
Event: Legal Execution/Hanged

At 1:45 pm on Friday, 28 July 1893, Henry Miller, a thirty three year old black man, was hanged at the Dallas jail for the murder of Dallas Police Officer C.O. Brewer.[977]

The killing occurred on 24 May 1892. Miller was a "drinking Negro," and never failed to get into trouble with the law when he was in his cups.[978] Brewer was shot and killed at the Union Depot station while attempting to arrest Miller for slander. While Brewer was talking to the man, Miller pulled out a large-caliber handgun and began firing, fatally w o u n d i n g Brewer. He was convicted of the crime, and sentenced to death.

On the day of the hanging a crowd of men, women and children began to form at the jail at a very early hour, intent on seeing the hanging. Miller arose to a hearty breakfast of ham and eggs, chicken, bread and coffee. At noon he ate another large meal comprised of chicken and fish, then put on the handsome new black suite, dark striped shirt and black necktie. A threesome of black preachers led a prayer service, followed by the hymn "I'll Meet You In The City of The New Jerusalem." Miller greeted newspaper reports that had come to interview him, saying "Come in, ise [I am] powerful glad to see you." Asked how he was feeling he replied, "Fine," and added that he had already smoked five cigars that morning.

At about half past one in the afternoon Sheriff Ben E. Cabell escorted the doomed man to the gallows. As the black cap was being pulled down over his head he was heard to say, "Yes Jesus, yes Jesus, I am coming to you." Shortly after, the trap was sprung and Miller dropped through the floor, breaking his neck in the fall. A great crowd of blacks who had come to witness the execution took his body to the Macedonian Baptist Church afterwards.

Reynolds, Henry
Born: (Unknown)—Date of Death: 30 July 1893
Place: Montgomery County
Event: Lynching/Hanged and Shot

On the evening of Saturday, 29 July 1893, Henry Reynolds, a black man, waited until the Marsh family had retired and crept into their home, which was located about nine miles north of Montgomery. Mr. and Mrs. Marsh, along with their son and young baby, were asleep at the time. Reynolds assaulted the twenty-one year old Mr. Hira Marsh, then outraged his wife.[979] When Mrs. Marsh regained consciousness the following morning she discovered her husband, and young baby, both lying dead next to her in the bed. Her seven-year old son was in another room and had a broken leg from the brutal attack by Reynolds.

Mrs. Marsh gave the alarm and a posse was quickly organized to pursue Reynolds. The crime scene and evidence of the attack was shocking. Mrs. Marsh's eyes were both swollen closed, and Reynolds's brutal blows to her face had knocked all of her front teeth out. The twelve-month old infant had been violently thrown into the yard and lay there with a crushed skull. Mr. Marsh's own cranium had been split open by a blow from a heavy object.

The neighborhood was thoroughly aroused. A mob quickly gathered, bent on revenge. Reynolds was captured soon after. Cries of "Burn Him, Burn Him" were heard as some members of the throng began to gather wood for a fire. Others could not wait, and strung Reynolds up a tree, then filled his body with lead.[980]

One newspaper source reported that there were three black men involved in this incident. They also claimed that the boy who survived had his leg broken his tongue cut out.[981]

Shaw, Walter
Born: circa 1854—Date of Death: 4 August 1893
Place: Harris County
Event: Legal Execution/Hanged

Walter Shaw, a thirty-nine year old white man, was hanged at Houston on Friday, 4 August 1893. Shaw's case had been appealed, but on 25 July 1893, the governor's office notified county officials that there would be not interference with the course of the execution.[982]

One Unidentified Black Man
Born: (Unknown)—Date of Death: 31 August 1893
Place: Kenedy County
Event: Lynching

According to unverified reports, an unidentified black man was lynched at Yarborough on 31 August 1893. No mention was made of his grievance and no record of this incident has been uncovered.[983]

McDonald, Alfred
Born: circa 1872—Date of Death: 17 November 1893
Place: Walker County
Event: Legal Execution/Hanged

Alfred McDonald, a black man, was hanged at Huntsville for murdering his father and mother.[984] Much like the youth of today who ask their parents for the loan of the family automobile, McDonald's folks had refused to lend Alfred a horse so that he might attend a party.

      Prior to keeping his date with the executioner McDonald was baptized inside the prison by Elder Harris of the Baptist faith. McDonald maintained his innocence to the end, claiming that he had only confessed to avoid a mob.

Watson, Alf
Born: (Unknown)—Date of Death: 8 December 1893
Place: San Jacinto County
Event: Legal Execution/Hanged

Alf Watson, a black man, went to the gallows at Cold Springs on Friday, 8-December 1893. He did not sleep well the night before, and was unable to eat much in the way of a breakfast. When asked what he wanted for supper he replied that he would like a can of salmon and some crackers. He did not care for any whiskey or cigars.

      At about 10:00 am Reverend W. T. McDonald, baptized Watson. At noon the dinner he had requested was prepared by Mrs. Carnes and brought up to him. Included was a piece of candy, which he divided and shared with the other inmates. He dressed, and at 2:00 pm and headed to the gallows with the sheriff. After scaling the stairs Watson made a short speech to the crowd of about 3,000 onlookers. Two hymns were rendered, and at 2:25 pm Watson took his place over the trap. The black cap was pulled down over his head. Five minutes later the trigger was pulled and Watson dropped to his death. His neck was broken by the fall and he never moved a muscle.

Watson had brutally murdered his sweetheart, Elvira Miller. He had quit seeing Miller, but had been induced to return by the girl's mother. When he visited the two began to quarrel. Watson drew his pistol and tried to get her to stop yelling by waving it about. The gun discharged accidentally, hitting Miss Miller in the hand. She continued screaming, so Watson hit her over the head with the revolver, knocking her insensible.

At that point Miller's two younger sisters, eight and twelve years of age, ran up and asked what he was killing her for. Watson quickly deuced that it would be better to kill the children so that they could not testify against him, so he chased them down the road trying to shoot them both. He would have succeeded were it not for the fact that they reached the home of Ephraim Douglas before he was able to overtake the pair. Watson returned to the house and found Miller still alive, unable to raise her head. He determined that it would be best to finish the job of murdering her, thinking that no one would believe that he had done the deed. He grabbed an ax to split her head with. Thinking better of that he decided to cut her throat, but after several failed attempts found his knife to be too dull for the task. Watson then returned to the earlier plan, involving the ax, and finished the job.

Watson's remains were taken to the Snowfield Graveyard, about seven miles from Cold Spring, for burial. The location of that burial site seems to have been lost to the ages.[985]

Nichols, Ed
Born: (Unknown)—Date of Death: 12 January 1894
Place: Travis County
Event: Legal Execution/Hanged

On Thursday, 12 January 1893, Ed Nichols, a twenty-one year old black man, paid the ultimate price for his hideous crime on the gallows at Austin.

Between 5:00 and 6:00 pm on Friday, 31 March 1893, a Bohemian girl named Anna Strake, age eleven, was returning from her uncle's home to her own. She passed a particularly lonely spot alongside the road where it was already quite dark, since the sun was hidden by the hills. There she encountered Nichols. He spoke to her, but not understanding English Anna was unable to comprehend what he said. Thinking that he was interested in the parcel she was carrying Anna began to unwrap it and show it to him. At that point Nichols dragged the little girl into the nearby field and brutally outraged her, beating and lacerating her flesh so badly that she was not able to crawl back to the road for loss of blood.

Her father, missing her, began a search and discovered her in the field. Officers were called out and Nichols was an immediate suspect. His blood stained clothes and the path he had made to a nearby pool of water to wash the fluid from his hands gave him away.

Crowds began to gather early, ringing the jail and covering the roof of nearby buildings, straining for a glimpse at the villain through an open window. It was 3:00 pm when those permitted to witness the hanging were allowed to enter the confined area. Reporters crowded the stone cell, interviewing Nichols and asking demeaning questions of the obviously uneducated and backward youth. Their pointless dialogue filled the pages of several newspapers the following day, occupying more space than important news.

Reverend L.L. Campbell, a black Baptist preacher, came in and read Psalms 31, then Psalm 32, which begins, "Blessed is he whose transgression is forgiven, whose sin is covered...." When it was time, the doors of the jail swung open and the one hundred who were lucky enough to have tickets swarmed in. Nichols delivered a nice talk, denying his guilt in the matter right to the end. Reverend Campbell led those attending in the hymn "Nearer My God to Thee" as the ropes were fitted and the black cap pulled down over Nichols' head. At 3:55 pm Sheriff White sprung the trap and the condemned man dropped to his death.[986]

Dillingham, Jessie
Born: (Unknown)—Date of Death: 10 February 1894
Place: Harris County
Event: Lynching/Hanged

Newspaper reports of the day claim that a black woman named Jessie Dillingham was taken from the jail at Smokeville and lynched by an angry mob.

Dillingham was charged with wrecking the Missouri, Kansas and Texas passenger train at the White Oak Bayou Bridge. She was lynched from a cross member of the very same bridge where this incident is said to have occurred. A black man named Johnson is claimed to have been arrested.[987]

Davis, Mannon
Born: 16 November 1863—Date of Death: 30 March 1894
Place: Lamar County
Event: Legal Execution/Hanged

Gonzales, Eduardo R.
Born: circa 1868—Date of Death: 30 March 1894
Place: Lamar County
Event: Legal Execution/Hanged

Upkins, James
Born: circa 1868—Date of Death: 30 March 1894
Place: Lamar County
Event: Legal Execution/Hanged

Lamar County spectators were treated to a rare triple hanging. In this case there was one condemned person from each racial group: white, black and Mexican. No one could possibly go away disappointed.

Mannon Davis, a thirty-year old white man, was tried and convicted of killing John Rhoden. His crime took place in the Indian Territory on 26 December 1891. Davis entered Rhoden's house and accused him of insulting his wife, Celia L. Tatum. Rhoden denied the claim, but Davis drew a large knife and stabbed him to death in the presence of Mrs. Rhoden. Davis fled, but was captured in Arkansas two months later.

John Upkins, described as a twenty-six year old heavy built ginger colored black man, was convicted of outrage. The incident took place at Ardmore, in the Indian Territory, on 6 September 1893. Upkins outraged his own six year old stepdaughter Mary Warden, tearing the clothing from her body and lacerating her in a frightening manner. At his examining trial a group of blacks from the town organized a mob and attempted to take Upkins from officers and lynch him. Judge Gibbons stepped between the mob and the condemned man, saying that they would have to take him over his dead body. The ploy was effective, and Upkins lived to keep his appointment with the executioner.

Last but by no means was least Eduardo R. Gonzales, a twenty-six year old Mexican man, who murdered a singing schoolteacher named John Daniels. The killing took place in Blue County, in the Choctaw Nation, on 16 May 1893. Daniels had expelled Gonzales from the class due to his race. Gonzales took offense, and killed Daniels for revenge. [988]

Cash, Edward Barney
Born: 9 October 1873—Date of Death: 9 April 1894
Place: Coryell County
Event: Lynching/Hanged

Edward Cash, a twenty-one year old fence cutter, was lynched by a gang of ten men at Gatesville, Coryell County on Monday, 9 April 1894.[989] His body was found hung to a tree about fifty yards from his home. Cash had been tending the sick bed of his wife, along with Doctor Smith, when the incident occurred.

Cash was not married. He is buried at the Flint Creek Cemetery, The Grove, Coryell County.[990]

In the summer and fall of 1883 hostility had broken out between the free grazers, who wanted to retain the practices of open range feeding, and those who had bought land and sectioned it off with barbed wire to establish a perimeter for their ranches. The "Wire War" had been declared in Texas. Its scope and impact would be wide ranging. By the end of this decade long struggle dozens would be killed and the days of the free grazer would come to an end. The sunset of the majestic cattle drives up the ever-popular Western Trail, Goodnight-Loving Trail, Sedalia Trail, and Chisholm Trail followed in the wake.[991]

Bren, Alfred
Born: 9 October 1873—Date of Death: 14 April 1894
Place: Coryell County
Event: Lynching

Alfred Bren, a black man, was executed in some form that was outside the law for an unidentified transgression.[992]

One Unidentified Black Man
Born: (Unknown)—Date of Death: 9 May 1894
Place: McLennan County
Event: Lynching

According to uncorroborated reports of the day, an unidentified black man was lynched at West in McLennan County on Wednesday, 9 May 1894. There was no mention of his crime.[993]

Scott, Henry
Born: (Unknown)—Date of Death: 15 May 1894
Place: Marion County
Event: Lynching/Hanged

Henry Scott, a black man, claimed that the cause of his frequent quarrels with his wife was their six-year old stepdaughter. To remedy the problem he decided to kill the young girl. Although his course of action may have remedied his marital strife, killing one's children is generally frowned upon in civilized cultures.

On Tuesday, 15 May 1894 while three deputy sheriffs were escorting Scott to the magistrate's office for arraignment a mob of about 100 blacks took him from the officers and lynched him from a post oak tree in a nearby swamp. He remained there in that condition until found by the sheriff later that evening.[994]

Brown, Austin
Born: circa 1862—Date of Death: 25 May 1894
Place: Bexar County
Event: Legal Execution/Hanged

Austin Brown, a black man, was executed by hanging at San Antonio on Friday, 25 May 1894. The hanging took place in the county jail yard. Brown had stalked, ambushed and assassinated a black former a police officer named Anderson Harris on 6 February 1893.[995]

Guiles, Joe
Born: circa 1872—Date of Death: 25 May 1894
Place: Karnes County
Event: Legal Execution/Hanged

Joe Guiles, a twenty-two year old white man who used the alias John D. May, was fond of railroad trains. He enjoyed robbing them. In the process of doing so he managed to kill a fireman named Frank Martin. For that a jury found him guilty of murder and sentenced him to death.

      Guiles went to the gallows at Karnes City, forty miles south of San Antonio, on Friday, 25 May 1894. The trap was sprung at 4:10 pm. The scene beneath the gallows platform could not be described as anything other than horrendous. The fall did not break Guiles's neck. To the horror of onlookers he writhed in anguish for twenty-three minutes. A number of spectators fainted dead away.[996]

Hall, Lon
Born: (Unknown)—Date of Death: 11 June 1894
Place: Lavaca County
Event: Lynching/Hanged

Cook, Bascom
Born: (Unknown)—Date of Death: 11 June 1894
Place: Lavaca County
Event: Lynching/Hanged

Lon Hall and Bascom Cook, both black men, are reported to have attacked Albert McElroy and Walter Hogden, both white men. The incident occurred at Sweet Home. Eighteen-year old McElroy is said to have had his skull crushed and was not expected to live.

      What followed on Monday, 11 June 1894 was the swift lynching of the two black men. Both were taken from officers and strung up in short order.[997]

Williams, John
Born: (Unknown)—Date of Death: 29 June 1894
Place: Hopkins County
Event: Lynching/Hanged

On Wednesday, 27 June 1894, Albert Watts and his wife were walking near their home at Sulphur Springs, thirty miles east of Greenville, when John Williams, a black man, fired a gun at them. Mrs. Watts was killed instantly. Mr. Watts died a few hours later.

      Williams had been in the couple's employ, but had been discharged for stealing. A posse caught up with the killer near Weaver. He was returned to Sulphur Springs and placed on the upper floor of the Henderson Building for safekeeping. Not safe enough, apparently, since a mob rushed up the stairway and overpowered the guards on Friday, 29 June 1894. The vigilantes placed a rope around Williams's neck and dragging him down to the street some distance to a spot where he was lynched from a utility pole.[998]

Griffith, William
Born: circa 1877—Date of Death: 20 July 1894
Place: Tyler County
Event: Lynching/Hanged

On Friday, 20 July 1894, William Griffith, a seventeen-year old black man, was removed from the jail at Woodville by a party of armed men and lynched from a nearby tree.

Griffith was charged with the outrage of a "half-witted" eight-year old girl named Pink Forsdens.[999] The girl's father had whipped him severely for the act and swore that if anyone found out he would likely be lynched. He was right.

Griffith, who seems to have been an evil character, had earlier been convicted of beating his own elderly father.

Fulks, Eugene
Born: circa 1875—Date of Death: 28 September 1894
Place: Lamar County
Event: Legal Execution/Hanged

Moore, Tom
Born: circa 1861—Date of Death: 28 September 1894
Place: Lamar County
Event: Legal Execution/Hanged

"Nervy to the Last" was the newspaper headline announcing this rare and exciting double hanging at Paris. Tom Moore and Eugene Fulks paid the penalty for the murder they had committed on the gallows at Paris on Friday, 28 September 1894.

One day previous, the pair was taken from their cell in the upper story of the jail to the guardroom on the lower level where a barber shaved them and cut their hair. They were given a bath. Both were furnished with a new livery, consisting of a smart looking new black suit, shirt, cravat and underwear. Shortly before 9:00 am on Friday, 28 September 1894, Marshal Williams read the death warrant to Moore and Fulks. Fulks' replied in a surly fashion, "Suit yourself about that, Mr. Williams; I don't care anything about it."

There was no preacher present for the hanging. Neither man desired one. At 9:30 each condemned man was given a drink of whiskey. Fulks insisted on Moore drinking first, saying

"Tom I want to get you hoxey [haksi]," which a journalist claimed is Choctaw for drunk.[1000]

At 11:30 am an elegant meal was given, but the condemned men ate modestly. The pair was led up to the scaffold by deputy marshals. They were asked if they had anything to say. Moore's voice was inaudible to those below. He told Marshal Williams that he could tell him many things but it would do no good. After thanking the marshal and attendants he asked that he be given a decent burial.

Fulks spoke clearly and distinctly. He said, "I was jobbed into this. Misstatements were made and I must die for them." Turning to Moore he said, "Tom old boy, I don't know what country we are going to meet in next, but if we get separated, you'll know my tracks; I'll be barefoot."

After the black cap was on and the knot adjusted Fulks remarked to Deputy Oglesby, "This damned thing is choking me; don't let it do that till I drop." The pair was placed in position and the trap sprung by Deputy Marshal Oglesby. About fifteen minutes later they were pronounced dead. Four minutes after that they were cut down. Both their necks were broken by the fall.

Moore was buried in the potter's field. Fulks gave his body to Dr. S. S. Robinson of Arthur City, who had it embalmed and will dissect it.[1001]

Gibson, Henry

Born: (Unknown)—Date of Death: 6 October 1894
Place: Freestone County
Event: Lynching/Shot

Henry Gibson, a black man, attempted to outrage Miss Mary Mitchell near the town of Mills on Friday evening, 5 October 1894. His attempt was foiled by Mitchell's screams, which brought help. During the scuffle Mitchell was cut several times.

Gibson was arraigned and taken to a store at Milles. Before he could be transported to the jail someone shot him through the window, killing him.[1002]

Some confusion remains regarding the exact date of the incident. One newspaper claims 8 October 1894, while another seems to be indicating that Gibson was shot on 6 October 1894. That newspaper is dated 6 October 1894. Another report, also dated 6 October 1894, claimed that 5 October 1894, was the correct date. The widely referenced *Lynching Calendar* has the shooting taking place on 8 October 1894, which is most emphatically incorrect.

Allen, James

Born: (Unknown)—Date of Death: 20 December 1894
Place: Cameron County
Event: Lynching/Shot

James Allen, a black man, was shot to death at Brownsville for barn burning.[1003]

Wilcox, Ed
Born: (Unknown)—Date of Death: 11-January 1895
Place: Guadalupe County
Event: Legal Execution/Hanged

Ed Wilcox, a young black man, was executed by hanging at the poor farm a few miles from Seguin on Friday, 11 January 1895. He went to the gallows in good spirits, his optimism never fagging in the two plus years he was confined or during his several appeals. Wilcox was accused of outraging a French woman. Prior to his execution it was proven that he did not disturb her, which she herself testified to. Even so, Wilcox's sentence was carried out.[1004] I suppose, in the infamous words of Arnaud Amalric, "Kill them All. For the Lord knows those that are His own."

Jackson, Andrew
Born: (Unknown)—Date of Death: 18 January 1895
Place: Red River County
Event: Legal Execution/Hanged

Andrew Jackson, a black man, was hanged at Clarksville on Friday, 18 January 1895, for the murder of Henry Dyke. In October 1894 Jackson had gone to the home of Dyke and set it on fire. Jackson shot and killed Dyke when he came rushing out in his nightclothes. No motive was given for Jackson's actions by newspaper accounts of the day.[1005]

Miguel, San Juan
Born: (Unknown)—Date of Death: 18 February 1895
Place: Maverick County
Event: Lynching

According to unverified reports, a Mexican man named San Juan Miguel was lynched at Eagle Pass on 18 February 1895. There was no mention of his crime.[1006]

Manion, Isaac
Born: (Unknown)—Date of Death: 11 March 1895
Place: Henderson County
Event: Lynching

According to *The Lynching Calendar*, a black man named Isaac Manion was lynched at Athens in Henderson County on 11 March 1895.[1007]

Burleson, Richard

Born: circa 1874—Date of Death: 12 April 1895
Place: Limestone County
Event: Legal Execution/Hanged

Richard Burleson, a twenty one year old black man, went to the gallows at Groesbeck on Friday, 12 April 1895.

On Wednesday, 2 May 1894, Burleson followed a venerable old man named Mr. J. G. McKinnon out of Mexia and asked if he could have a ride. McKinnon agreed, and Burleson climbed aboard. Once in the wagon Burleson picked up a heavy object and beat the old gentleman to death with it, robbed him and fled to Texarkana where he had been living. A few hours later he was arrested and shipped off to Corsicana where he could receive a fair trial. Burleson was convicted, and sentenced to death.

In spite of the best efforts of his spiritual advisers, L. H. Linn of Mexia and J. Beckham and J. M. Jackson of Groesbeck, Burleson went to the gallows an unrepentant man, refusing to be baptized or to accept Jesus Christ as his savior. At 2:00 pm he bade farewell to his brother, who was incarcerated in an adjacent cell, and began his short walk to the gallows. The trapdoor malfunctioned, and as a result the hanging was delayed several minutes. Frustrated with the impediment, Burleson angrily commented, "...I could hang three or four N_____ in this amount of time myself." At 2:05 pm and in front of a crowd of about 4,000 onlookers, he shot through the trap, breaking his neck at the end of the fall.[1008]

Calhoun, Nelson

Born: (Unknown)—Date of Death: 12 April 1895
Place: Navarro County
Event: Lynching/Shot

On Wednesday, 10 April 1895, a black man named Nelson Calhoun criminally outraged Mrs. Hughes. The incident took place at Corsicana. Reports were made at once and hundreds of men and bloodhounds rushed to the scene to search for the violator. Calhoun was captured at about 11:00 am and taken to the residence of Mrs. Hughes. The city marshal demanded that he be turned over to him so that Calhoun could be held for identification and arraignment. The captors ultimately relented.

On Friday, 12 April 1895, Calhoun was taken before Mrs. Hughes and was positively identified as her assailant. He was placed in a carriage and, accompanied by fifty men, was driven to the scene of the crime. Before the hack arrived Calhoun broke free from the four men who were holding him and ran through a barbed wire fence, receiving considerable lacerations for his efforts. The fugitive made it about 100 yards before being riddled with bullets fired from the well-armed posse's numerous firearms.

Clothed only in his trousers, the dead man was taken back to Corsicana where he was proudly paraded through the town.[1009]

Crocker, John
Born (Unknown)—Date of Death: 25 May 1895
Place: Wharton County
Event: Lynching/Shot

Crocker, Given Name Unknown (wife)
Born (Unknown)—Date of Death: 25 May 1895
Place: Wharton County
Event: Lynching/Shot

Crocker, Given Name Unknown (son)
Born (Unknown)—Date of Death: 25 May 1895
Place: Wharton County
Event: Lynching/Shot

On Saturday, 25 May 1895, the bodies of the Crocker family were found on the prairie about two miles from Wharton. They were shot full of holes. Ten men were arrested for the murders. The Crocker family had been feuding with the neighbors for several years. Their home had been burned to the ground two years earlier. Last winter Mrs. Crocker killed a man. On the afternoon of the Crocker's killing a member of the mob had fired on John Crocker. He, in turn, killed the man. An adult son of the Crocker's also killed a member of the mob that same day.[1010]

Johnson, William
Born: (Unknown)—Date of Death: 11 June 1895
Place: Angelina County
Event: Lynching/Hanged

At about noon on Tuesday, 11 June 1895, William Johnson, a black man, was lynched at Lufkin. Johnson, identified as Walter Johnson not William in some newspaper accounts, had been positively identified as the person who had outraged the seven-year old daughter of Mr. Robert Schaffer.

    Once a mob numbering about 500 strong was certain of his identity, Johnson was forcibly taken from the custody of the sheriff and lynched in the public square at the center of town.[1011]

Cherry, John
Born: (Unknown)—Date of Death: 11 June 1895
Place: Liberty County
Event: Lynching/Hanged

White, Alexander "Alex"
Born: (Unknown)—Date of Death: 11 June 1895
Place: Liberty County
Event: Lynching/Hanged

Newspaper accounts of the day speak of the murder of an elderly pauper named William Johnson, a black man. The crime occurred near Keno. The countryside was wildly excited by this incident, and a search was begun for the suspected perpetrators. In due course two black men, Alex White and John Cherry were taken out and hanged. One of them had Johnson's watch in his possession.[1012]
    The veracity of this account is questionable, however. In the previous incident William Johnson seems to have been lynched for having outraged the Schaffer girl. Readers of these conflicting accounts might hypothesize, as have the authors, that Cherry and White may have been colleagues of Johnson, and therefore involved somehow in the outrage.

One Unidentified Black Man
Born: circa 1875—Date of Death: 12 June 1895
Place: McLennan County
Event: Unknown

A twenty-year old black man was found dead near the Missouri, Kansas and Texas railroad depot. The means of death, or his transgression were not mentioned. Although no corroboration of this incident has been found it is being included because the dubious source *The Lynching Culture* lists it as an unconfirmed lynching.[1013]

Phillips, Willie
Born: (Unknown)—Date of Death: 20 July 1895
Place: Falls County
Event: Lynching/Bombing

Phillips, Edward
Born: (Unknown)—Date of Death: 20 July 1895
Place: Falls County
Event: Lynching/Bombing

Phillips, Hannah
Born: (Unknown)—Date of Death: 20 July 1895
Place: Falls County
Event: Lynching/Bombing

Phillips, Mary
Born: (Unknown)—Date of Death: 20 July 1895
Place: Falls County
Event: Lynching/Bombing

Phillips Jr., Abe
Born: (Unknown)—Date of Death: 20 July 1895
Place: Falls County
Event: Lynching/Bombing

Johnson, Benjamin
Born: (Unknown)—Date of Death: 20 July 1895
Place: Falls County
Event: Lynching/Bombing

Taylor, K. D. "Kid"
Born: (Unknown)—Date of Death: 20 July 1895
Place: Falls County
Event: Lynching/Bombing

Benjamin Johnson, K. D. "Kid" Taylor and four members of the Phillips family, all of who were black and who were suspected of murder, were executed by a group of vigilantes who bombed the house that they were hiding out in. [1014]

The headlines read, "Blown to Eternity." That, more or less, sums up the events of Saturday, 20 July 1895. It happened twenty miles northeast of Waco, near the town of Mart. Mary Phillips, one of the victims, was the wife of Absalom Phillips who had been slain in a disagreement with white farmers, the Arnold brothers. That dust up had occurred about six weeks ago. The explosion, which was probably caused by a colossal charge of dynamite tossed into the building through an open window while the occupants slept, sent the cabin sky high. The damage was frightful, and the sound was heard four miles away. Bodies were torn and mangled.[1015]

Unidentified Black Woman
Born: (Unknown)—Date of Death: 23 July 1895
Place: Washington County
Event: Lynching/Hanged

Several undocumented sources report that an unknown black woman was lynched near Brenham. The reason for the hanging is also unrecorded. The authors have not been able to locate any verification of this incident, which is also referenced in the source *The Lynching Calendar*.[1016]

Loftin, Squire

Born: (Unknown)—Date of Death: 26 July 1895

Place: Lee County

Event: Lynching/Hanged

Squire Loftin, a black man, was accused of outraging a white woman at Lexington. A mob took him from officers by force of arms and lynched him.[1017]

Thomas, Lee

Born: circa 1871—Date of Death: 2 August 1895

Place: Navarro County

Event: Legal Execution/Hanged

Lee Thomas, a twenty-one year old white man, was hanged at Corsicana on Friday, 2 August 1895, for the murder of J. M. Farley. That killing had occurred in September of 1894.

Farley was a stranger around Corsicana, and had worked for Thomas. The two men lived together. After killing Farley, Thomas buried him near the house. The remains were discovered a month after the murder.[1018]

Mason, James

Born: (Unknown)—Date of Death: 2 August 1895

Place: Morris County

Event: Lynching/Shot

Mason, Mrs. James

Born: (Unknown)—Date of Death: 2 August 1895

Place: Morris County

Event: Lynching/Shot

On Thursday night, 1 August 1895, seven men called a black man named James Mason out of his home and shot him dead. Mason's wife was present at the time. She escaped into the house and jumped in bed with the children. Unfortunately her place of concealment proved insufficient, as she too was shot and wounded by the gang who fired at her through a crack in the wall of the home. One of the children was wounded as well. Mrs. Mason was expected to die. Newspaper accounts of the day gave no reason for the shooting, nor did they indicate if the assailants were black or white.[1019]

Stephens, William
Born: (Unknown)—Date of Death: 12 August 1895
Place: Delta County
Event: Lynching/Shot

Newspaper accounts of the day tell the story of William Stephens, a black man, being taken out and shot by White Cappers near Pacio at about 4:00 pm on Monday, 12 August 1895. The man had been warned, as had all blacks, to clear out of the area in ten days' time. Stephens had been unable to comply with the White Cappers order since he had crops in the field and a wife and two children to feed. [1020] Stephens' mother reported the incident to authorities.

Cole, Jefferson "Jeff"
Born: (Unknown)—Date of Death: 22 August 1895
Place: Lamar County
Event: Lynching/Shot

On Thursday night, 22 August 1895, Jeff Cole, an elderly and by all accounts "inoffensive" black man, was called out of his house and shot down at Paris. A mob of sixty or so Whitecappers armed with Winchesters and shotguns had been roaming the region, menacing blacks who would not sell their crops or land. Cole was one of their victims.[1021]

Stormer, John
Born: (Unknown)—Date of Death: 22 August 1895
Place: Wharton County
Event: Lynching/Hanged

On Thursday, 15 August 1895, Wharton County sheriff Rabb A. Rich received notice that six convicts had escaped from the state prison farm at Matagorda County. On Saturday, 18 August, Deputy Frank Brown arrested one of the escapees, a black man named John Stormer, who was hiding out at a local ranch. He placed a handcuff on Stormer and attached a rope to the saddle horn of his horse. Brown then started toward Wharton, with Stromer walking behind. Later that day, Brown was found dead alongside the road. He had been shot in the back with a pistol and hit with a blast from his own shotgun. Since Brown only carried a shotgun it appeared that he had failed to search Stormer thoroughly prior to cuffing him. Stormer escaped on the deputy's horse.

Stormer was captured by citizens near Kemp's store and was left chained to the building all night. When the sheriff reached the community where he was being held he was told that the prisoner had escaped. Brown's horse was recovered.

On Thursday morning, 22 August 1895, the lifeless body of John Stormer was discovered hanging from a tree near Grigg's Church at Wharton. Pinned to the corpse was a notice saying, "This

Negro Killed a White Man." The body was identified by an elderly black man named Reuben Kemp as that of John Stormer.[1022]

Key, Charles [1023]

Born: circa 1857—Date of Death: 13 September 1895
Place: Lamar County
Event: Legal Execution/Hanged

In June 1895, Charles Key, a white man, went to Gainesville representing himself as a stockman and looking to hire help to drive some cattle. He met Smith L. McLaughlin, who had a wagon and team and agreed to accompany him. On 1 July they left Gainesville headed for Sherman, but on 2 July diverted to Dennison and headed north to the Indian Territory. Key apparently murdered McLaughlin sometime during the trip, or once they had arrived at a bridge over the Red River. Sounds in the night had awakened the bridge keeper but all he heard was the thud of something heavy hitting the water. At about 8:00 am the following day the body of McLaughlin was found tucked into the bushes alongside the river.

The day after the murder Key sold the team and horses at Denison and was arrested. When questioned, Key appeared quite insane, rolling his eyes and speaking gibberish about steamboats and cannons.

On Friday, 13 September 1895, Key scaled the stairs of the gallows at Paris to meet his maker. Newspaper reports of the day claimed, "He was running over with whiskey and religion and was in love with everybody. Of course he went straight up [to heaven]."[1024]

Robinson, Kit

Born: circa 1875—Date of Death: 11 October 1895
Place: Liberty County
Event: Legal Execution/Hanged

Kit Robinson, a twenty-year old black man, was tried and convicted of killing John R. "Dowdy" Johnson. He was found guilty and sentenced to death.

Johnson was employed as a pumper on the Houston, East and West Texas Railroad. Robinson robbed him of $55 in specie then murdered him and burned the body.

Robinson was hung on the morning of Friday, 11 October 1895. The incident took place without fanfare. Robinson was cut down after twelve minutes and pronounced dead.[1025]

Suaste, Florentino or Florentina
Born: (Unknown)—Date of Death: 11 October 1895
Place: LaSalle County
Event: Lynching/Hanged and Shot

A Mexican named Florentino or Florentina Suaste who was being held on a murder charge was taken from jail by ten masked men shot and lynched for murder at Cotulla on 11 October 1895.

Suaste had been jailed, and charged with the murder of stockman U. T. Saul on Monday, 7 October 1895. Saul (also reported as Shaw) had lost a yearling steer and asked La Salle County deputy sheriff Swink to assist him in recovering it. The men came upon a cart driven by a Mexican woman with a child as a passenger. The wagon was carrying meat, believed to have been from the steer. Accounts vary, but as Saul was searching the cart a gunfight erupted that led to the death of Saul, two Mexicans (unknown if male or female) and the child. One Mexican female was wounded. Newspaper accounts report the lynched Mexican was a male. One author has reported that a Mexican female (Florentina Suarro) who was wounded in the gunfight was the lynching victim.

The surname of the individual killed was also reported as Suarro, Sulato, and Suarto. The given name was reported as both Florentino and Florentina.

On 9 April 1901, the San Jose, California *Evening News* reported that a payment of $2,000 had been made to the heirs of Florentino Suaste who had been lynched in La Salle County in 1895.[1026]

Crews, John Quincy Adams
Born: circa 1851—Date of Death: 14 October 1895
Place: Denton County
Event: Legal Execution/Hanged

John Quincy Adams Crews, a forty-four year old white man, went to the gallows at Denton for a triple murder of Thomas Murrell family members. The killing had occurred near Callisburg in Cooke County on 12 April 1894.

Prior to the incident Crews and Murrell had a misunderstanding. Murrell fired Crews and asked him to leave, which he did in the company of his wife. He returned under cover of darkness soon after, secreting himself under a pile of hay, lying in wait for Murrell. When the man appeared Crews burst forth with Winchester in hand and shot Murrell twice, killing him. Mrs. Murrell, hearing the gunfire, dashed to the barn and was also cut down by Crews, falling dead on the body of her husband. Crews rifled the pockets of Murrell and robbed him, then sought out the son, Morgan Murrell, who was working in a nearby field. Crews sent a rifle bullet into the young man's head, killing him instantly as well. When interviewed by authorities Crews claimed that he had killed Murrell because of an indignity the man had uttered against his wife.

The killings, labeled "an atrocity," came close to drawing an impromptu lynching for Crews. He narrowly escaped, only to wind up at the same end of the same rope...but under slightly different circumstance...and no less dead.[1027]

McKee, Alamo

Born: circa 1876—Date of Death: 25 October 1895
Place: Cass County
Event: Legal Execution/Hanged

According to uncorroborated reports, a nineteen-year old black man named Alamo McKee was legally executed at Cass County on 25 October 1895. McKee went to the gallows on a death sentence he received for committing a murder.[1028]

Spearman, D. L.

Born: (Unknown)—Date of Death: 25 October 1895
Place: Harrison County
Event: Legal Execution/Hanged

A crowd of 8,000 persons turned out at Marshall to witness the hanging of D. L. Spearman, a black man, on Friday, 25 October 1895. The trap was sprung at 2:30 pm. Nothing unusual was reported by the pundits of the day, thus it is presumed that Mr. Spearman was catapulted into eternity without incident. Spearman had been found guilty of murdering Horace Stevens. That crime took place in June 1894.[1029]

Hilliard, Henry

Born: (Unknown)—Date of Death: 29 October 1895
Place: Smith County
Event: Lynching/Burned on the Gallows

Henry Hilliard, a black man, murdered Mrs. "Becky" Bell. Soon after, Sheriff "Wig" Smith and Mr. Tarbutton captured Hilliard at Kilgore.

The sheriff and his men loaded Hilliard into a wagon and proceeded to transport him back to Tyler for confinement at the jail pending arraignment and trial. Along their route the procession stopped at the scene of the crime so that a photographer could memorialize the event with an image. Before the picture taker had a chance to do his work a band of vigilantes overpowered the lawmen, jerked the officer's pistols from their belts rendering them defenseless, and removed Hilliard from their control. In a convoy comprised of men on horseback, wagons, cotton trucks, carriages, hacks, ponies, mules, burrows and virtually every form of conveyance imaginable the crowd made their way to Tyler.

By the time they arrived the parade had reached about 5,000 strong. The procession made two loops around the town square to witness the gallows, which was already under construction in excited anticipation of Hillard's hanging. The scaffold portion at least complete, Hilliard was hoisted onto the structure and lashed firmly to the "T" post while protesting, "Don't hurry me." Hilliard was angrily tied with a chain while pleading for his life. In the background, only the echo of derisive laughter could be heard.

It was about dusk and a light drizzle had begun to fall when the husband of the slain woman, Mr. Bell, struck the match and the gallows structure was ignited.[1030] By the time the blaze had fully consumed the structure night had fallen, and the federation of citizenry watched Hilliard burn to death by the glow of the firelight and the final glimpses of the evening sun. The ghastly wail of mortal anguish must have been haunting to hear as the doomed man surrendered his last breath and his spirit flew from its mortal host. How truly proud of their handiwork these Christian folks of Tyler must have been that evening, having fully ignored the laws of God, "...avenge not yourselves, but rather give place unto wrath: for it is written, Vengeance is mine; I will repay."[1031]

One Unidentified Black Man
Born: (Unknown)—Date of Death: 20 November 1895
Place: Madison County
Event: Lynching/Hanged

One knows that the story is never a good one when the headlines read, "Lynched the Wrong Man."

On 21 November 1895, Reverend J. F. Horne of Madison County reported that a black man had been lynched in a remote part of the county for riding a horse over a white girl in the middle of the road, inflicting serious injuries on her. Later developments showed that the lynch mob got the wrong black man. The culprit escaped into the countryside.[1032]

Hennegan, Oscar
Born: circa 1874—Date of Death: 17 December 1895
Place: Lee County
Event: Legal Execution/Hanged

Oscar Hennegan, a twenty one year old black man, went to the gallows at Giddings one week before Christmas for committing murder, on Tuesday, 17 December 1895.

One newspaper reported that "He died game." Sheriff Scarborough took the condemned man to the photographer, then, with irons removed, transported him to his date with the executioner by wagon. At 1:15 pm Hennegan walked, bookended by two lawmen, up the stairs and took a seat on the platform. Two black preachers accompanied him. Hennegan held forth an eloquent oration, equal some mused to that of Bill Longley who had preceded Hennegan on the platform in 1878. Once concluded, the black cap was pulled over his head and the trap sprung as one of the black preachers offered a prayer. The pastor's plea apparently did not reach heaven in time, as Hennegan's neck was not snapped by the fall. He dangled there suffocating, before 4,000 spectators, until cut down twenty-two minutes later.

Hennegan had murdered Martha Bradley, a fourteen-year old girl from Lee County. Some sources report Miss Bradley's age as twenty-one. He had been seeing the woman, and everything was going well until she caught the attention of another man, to whom she was paying more attention than Hennegan. Enraged, Hennegan went into the field where Miss Bradley and her mother were working and asked the mother if she would attend his hanging. The young woman did not take him seriously until, at about 11:00 am on 14 September 1895, he placed an old shotgun to her head as she lay on a pallet in her home and blew the girl's head off. Hennegan then tried to kill the girl's cousin who was also in the house. He would have succeeded were it not for the fact that the gun misfired. He fled, but was soon captured. Hennegan was tried and convicted in the November term of the court.[1033]

One Unidentified Black Man
Born: circa 1881—Date of Death: 21 January 1896
Place: McLennan County
Event: Unknown

A fifteen-year old black youth was found dead near the Missouri, Kansas and Texas railroad tracks. His means of death or his wrongdoing were not mentioned. It is unclear if he was executed or fell victim to a violent crime. In the event that it was the former, he is being included on this roster in the interest of completeness.[1034]

Castello, Aureliano
Born: (Unknown)—Date of Death: 29 January 1896
Place: Bexar County
Event: Lynching/Shot and Burned

On Wednesday, 29 January 1896, Aureliano Castello, a Mexican man, was shot to death on the banks of the Median River. Hugh and Watson Stanfield, brothers and well to do farmers, did the work. The killing took place about fifteen miles west of San Antonio. After murdering Castello the pair saturated his clothing with coal oil and set him on fire.

The Stanfields had employed Castello. It was discovered that he had outraged the Stanfield's sister, a sixteen-year old girl who was of unsound mind.[1035]

Crawford, Foster "Bill"
Born: (Unknown)—Date of Death: 26 February 1896
Place: Wichita County
Event: Lynching/Hanged

Lewis, Elmer "The Kid"
Born: March 1876—Date of Death: 26 February 1896
Place: Wichita County
Event: Lynching/Hanged

On Tuesday, 25 February 1896, Foster "Bill" Crawford and Elmer Lewis, known as "The Kid," held up the City National Bank at Wichita Falls. In the process they shot and killed cashier Frank Dorsey and wounded bookkeeper P.P. Langford. "The Kid" claimed that $10,000 in species had been taken which he hid in a dugout near by the town. Crawford and Lewis fled, but were surrounded by a posse in a gully about nine miles from town less than two hours after the robbery. With no hope of escaping, they surrendered to state rangers and were transported to the jail at Wichita Falls.

At about 8:30 pm on Wednesday, 26 February 1896, a mob of several thousand persons attacked the jail at Wichita Falls and removed both Crawford and Lewis by force of arms. The doomed men were taken to the City National Bank, where their troubles had begun. "The Kid," wearing high heel boots, black trousers and a red flannel shirt was an eerie sight in the dim light of the kerosene lamps that illuminated the room. He was the first to be coaxed to confess by having the hangman's noose drawn tight around his neck. At first he refused to speak, sawing "That's alright. If you are impatient swing me up now. I ain't afraid to die, not a damn bit of it, pull the rope." He soon softened, confessing his real name, age, place of birth and the hiding place of the loot that had been purloined from the bank. When asked if he had any final words for his father he said, "Well, tell my father I was not scared a bit, that I died like a nervy man." "Times up..." said one of the mob, as Lewis was hauled up the rest of the way on the lynching rope. All present freely admitted that no gamer man ever died than "The Kid" Lewis.

Crawford, a small man who was poorly clothed and had a close trimmed black moustache, asked for Ranger Captain Burnett. Burnett was present in the mob and stepped forward. He had worked for the ranger for years and had stolen stock from him. Crawford confessed to the robbery but claimed that he had no part in the gunplay. He asked for whiskey, which he was given, and which he quickly consumed in great quantities while the vigilante mob waited for a second rope with which to hang him. Once that oversight had been remedied, Crawford was hauled up alongside Lewis. Both were still swinging in the air the following morning.[1036]

Foster "Bill" Crawford is buried at the Riverside Cemetery at Wichita Falls. Elmer "The Kid" Lewis is also buried at the Riverside Cemetery in Wichita Falls.[1037] Although the lynchings took place on 26 February 1896, their tombstones are inscribed 27 February 1896, which is probably the date that the undertaker received their remains.

Chappell, Buck
Born: circa 1878—Date of Death: 18 March 1896
Place: Austin County
Event: Legal Execution/Hanged

Strawther, Clem
Born: circa 1873—Date of Death: 18 March 1896
Place: Austin County
Event: Legal Execution/Hanged

On Wednesday, 18 March 1896, two black men went to the gallows together at Bellville. Both were tried and convicted of murder. Although their destinies converged on the gallows platform that day their crimes were totally unrelated.

On the evening of 18 December 1895, Buck Chappell had robbed and brutally murdered Mrs. Dora Emshoff on the road from Breenham to the neighborhood of Rocky, near Bellville. He did this crime in the presence of Mrs. Emshoff's ten-year old daughter after the poor woman had already handed over what money she had. The young girl positively identified Chappell afterwards.

Clem Strawther received his death sentence for killing Alvis Peter at Wallis. That incident took place on the night of 10 November 1895. Apparently Peter had whipped Strawther's brother and he wanted to get even with the man. He had crept up on Peter's while at home and shot him to death through an open window as the victim slept in his bed.

On the morning they were to keep their appointment with the hangman Chappell had no appetite for breakfast. Strawther, on the other hand, ordered up bread, biscuits, chicken, ham, cakes and pie. Wine was also served. The feast was presented on a white tablecloth and on a server. At 9:40 am Sheriff Glenn entered the cell and removed the shackles from the two men so that Reverend C. W. McCowan and his colleagues could baptize them. Both men dressed in dark suits and white ties, with a small bouquet of flowers on their coats.

Precisely at noon Chappell and Strawther were loaded into a hack and driven to the gallows. Both men scaled the steps to meet their fate and addressed the crowd briefly. At 1:10 pm Sheriff Glenn asked the pair, "Are you ready?" They replied, "Yes; goodbye." As quick as the words were spoken the trap was sprung and the pair dropped to their death.[1038]

Rolly, Albert
Born: circa 1876—Date of Death: 20 March 1896
Place: Williamson County
Event: Legal Execution/Hanged

Mootry, Mat
Born: (Unknown)—Date of Death: 27 March 1896
Place: Williamson County
Event: Legal Execution/Hanged

A repentant Mat Mootry stepped to the gallows at Georgetown on Friday, 27 March 1896. Mootry, a black man, confessed during his final minutes that he had killed Andrew Pickell, a Bohemian farmer, last May.

In the presence of 4,000 onlookers the condemned man sang a hymn and addressed the crowd at length, warning everyone against gambling and horseracing. Although he owned up to his misdeeds Mootry did not feel that the murder he had done justified death by hanging. Clearly the people of Williamson County did not agree. Mootry's confederate in crime, twenty-year old Albert Rolly, was hanged one week earlier for his part in the Pickell killing.[1039] The trap was sprung at noon and Mootry was dead in twelve minutes.

Bendy, William "Will"
Born: (Unknown)—Date of Death: 3 May 1896
Place: Jefferson County
Event: Lynching/Hanged and Shot

Reports of the day seem to be a bit unclear as to the precise nature of William Bendy's crime. Bendy, a black man, appears to have been involved in a shooting scrape that resulted in the death of Phil Haines and the wounding of Constable Bibb, E. B. Rone, and Rexy Wall.

A posse cornered Bendy in a thicket near Buda. He managed to escape and fled to his brother-in-law's home where he was once again surrounded. Told to surrender, Bendy was not quick enough to comply. A shot rang out as Benby fled from the residence. Once he had covered a distance of about fifty yards he gave up the race and surrendered. His captors led him to a suitable tree nearby where a rope was quickly adjusted and he was hauled up. Just to make certain that the noose had done its job about thirty gunshots were heard to ring, sealing the matter in perpetuity. "A Shortened Career" was the headline that memorialized Bendy's passing.[1040]

Goodson, Joseph "Joe"
Born: circa 1865—Date of Death: 20 May 1896
Place: Washington County
Event: Legal Execution/Hanged

Rutherford, Brady
Born: circa 1878—Date of Death: 20 May 1896
Place: Washington County
Event: Legal Execution/Hanged

Rutherford, John
Born: circa 1857—Date of Death: 20 May 1896
Place: Washington County
Event: Legal Execution/Hanged

The town of Brenham saw a rare triple hanging on Wednesday, 20 May 1896, when Joseph Goodson,

John Rutherford and Brady Rutherford, all black men, kept their assigned appointment with the hangman. All had been tried and convicted of the murder of Thomas Dwyer. All protested their innocence to the end, when the trap fell at 2:10 pm.[1041]

Johnson, George L.
Born: (Unknown)—Date of Death: 10 June 1896
Place: Brazos County
Event: Lynching/Hanged

Whitehead, Louis
Born: (Unknown)—Date of Death: 10 June 1896
Place: Brazos County
Event: Lynching/Hanged

Reddick, Jim
Born: (Unknown)—Date of Death: 10 June 1896
Place: Brazos County
Event: Lynching/Hanged

The headlines read, "Hanged by Bonfire Light." At about 9:45 pm on Wednesday evening, 10 June 1896, the sound of 200 to 250 horsemen thundering down the main street at Bryan broke the still of the summer evening. The troop halted in front of the jail, forming a half circle while some of the men dismounted and approached the building. Jailer Gee was not prepared for the confrontation. Although he had expected vigilantes to challenge the security of his lock up sometime that night he was without a posse when the mob arrived. The vigilantes quickly overpowered the poor sentry, broke the latch on the key box and removed three black men, Jim Reddick, Louis Whitehead and George Johnson from their cells. This trifecta of malefactors were all confined for having outraged white women, Reddick for molesting an Italian woman and Johnson and Whitehead for attempting to violate Dr. R. H. Wilson's twelve year old daughter. That incident had taken place on Sunday night, 7 June 1896.

Seldom is the crime of outrage met with anything short of instant vengeance, especially when committed by a black against a white, and particularly when the victim is a young girl.

The mob took the three black men in the direction of Boonville, to Carter's Creek bottom, where they were lynched...all from the same tree but each from a separate branch. A huge bonfire illuminated the scene, casting a morbid light on the three doomed men as they swung from that limbs in the flickering firelight. Mounted men patrolled the area to assure that their work went undisturbed. It was not until the following morning that the truth of it all could be discerned from the forensic evidence at the site. [1042]

In the opinion of many at the time, which was voiced in a *Dallas Morning News* column of 12 June 1896, the Bryan lynching was primarily attributable to the abject failure of the court system to hold criminals accountable for their evil deeds. It seems that the fair and speedy punishment of wrongdoers, in this case Reddick, has been giving way to the mistakes, tricks, traps and technicalities of the law. Criminals were being outrageously acquitted. Jurors had been lax in many instances, with frequent slips of technical matters that weigh nothing with the ordinary man and his idea of common sense. Citizens were encouraged to take stock, and tune up their consciousness in this matter. The remedy for mob law is the fair and speedy trial, and punishment, of criminals. When such demands are fairly and promptly met then lynching will no longer be necessary.

Afterwards, Sheriff Nunn, who had left the area just in time to avoid, being caught up in the incident, wrote a public letter of apology, attempting to justify his curious absence.[1043]

Wilkins, John
Born: circa 1875—Date of Death: 26 June 1896
Place: Johnson County
Event: Legal Execution/Hanged

On Thursday, 31 October 1895, Price Taylor was murdered at his home, eight miles northeast of Grandview. His body was not found until Saturday when the blood stained corpse was discovered lying near his dining table, his unconsumed meal of bread and honey awaiting his arrival.

Taylor was a well-to-do bachelor who lived the life of a hermit. Although well liked, he mixed little with the citizens of Grandview. His body had three bullet holes, one in the temple, one behind the ear and one in the throat. Someone who was obviously in search of money and valuables had ransacked the home. John Wilkins, a twenty one year old white man, had been hired by Taylor to do some work around the place and had stayed in the house during his employment. By the time the body of Taylor was discovered Wilkins had already vanished.

Wilkins was apprehended. Taylor's brother identified the horse he had been mounted on as having belonged to his deceased brother. A razor and watch also belonging to Taylor were found in Wilkins's possession. Throughout the trial Wilkins maintained his innocence. He was convicted of the Taylor murder, and sentenced to be executed by hanging.

On Friday, 26 June 1896, Wilkins was hanged in the presence of between 10,000 and 15,000 eager spectators. They flocked to Cleburne to see the show. Onlookers began to arrive at noon the day preceding the event, at first trickling in and then flooding the roads with wagons, hacks and carriages, all packed to the boards with picnic lunches, children and babies. Thousands camped on the banks of the Nolan River, four miles southeast of town. By noon on the 26th the mob had assembled around the jail and on the bluff overlooking the building.

At 1:10 pm Sheriff Stewart escorted the condemned man from the jail. Wilkins, clean- shaven, was decked out in a dark blue suit, patent leather pumps and a white shirt. He was sporting a red rose pinned to the left lapel of his coat. Wilkins was loaded into a carriage with the sheriff, a brace of reverends, and a few assorted lawmen. Together they made the short trip to the gallows. At 1:15 pm he scaled the stairs and took a seat in a chair that had been provided for him while Reverend F. E. Leach, pastor of the Cumberland Presbyterian Church, lead a prayer. Wilkins declined his opportunity to address the crowd, saying only that his lawyer had his statement. Next, Reverend A. R. Shaw of the Main Street Presbyterian Church spelled Pastor Leach with the ministerial duties. At 1:31 pm the black cap was pulled down over the condemned man's head and one half minute later the trap was sprung. Wilkins dropped only six and a half feet. His neck was not broken and he writhed in agony for some time before expiring.[1044]

Stanford, Given Name Unknown
Born: (Unknown)—Date of Death: 27 June 1896
Place: Delta County
Event: Lynching/Hanged

Professor Stanford of Paris, Texas, lost his only child on Saturday, 27 June 1896. The incident took place at Cooper in Delta County when a contractor jumped on the younger Stanford and beat him severely. Stanford ran to his home, retrieved a Winchester, and shot his assailant dead. In turn, a mob chased down Stanford and lynched him.[1045]

Hill, Jim
Born (Unknown)—Date of Death: 3 July 1896
Place: Polk County
Event: Legal Execution/Hanged

An oft unreliable source reported that Jim Hill was legally executed in Polk County on Friday, 3 July 1896. No confirmation of this incident was located.[1046]

Gay, Benjamin
Born (Unknown)—Date of Death: 13 August 1896
Place: Hopkins County
Event: Lynching/Hanged

One unconfirmed source claimed that on Thursday, 13 August 1896, a black man named Benjamin Gay was hanged for allegedly committing arson. No other information has been located.[1047]

Vaughn, Anderson
Born: (Unknown)—Date of Death:19 August 1896
Place: McLennan County
Event: Lynching/Shot

On Wednesday night 19 August 1896, Anderson Vaughn, a black man, was lynched in an episode of Whitecapping that occurred at the Kendrick's place at Hillside.

Vaughn, along with Hayward and Shade Robinson, Evan Sandler and Morris Davis occupied a house at Hillside. The men had finished their day's work in the cotton fields, eaten supper and had retired to their beds for the day when a flaming cotton ball soaked in turpentine was thrown through the window and into the home. Vaughn ran out of the building first and was shot to death by a mob of whites and Mexicans who all wore masks. Their purpose was to chase off the blacks so they could monopolize the cotton-picking market. In another, somewhat more salacious version, reporters claimed that Vaughn, who failed to respond quickly enough to the mob's demand for him to put his hands up, was kicked to death, not shot, and that his companions were "...frightfully beaten."

On 30 September 1896, a grand jury returned an indictment against the alleged White Cappers, Bruce Kendrick, Lee Kelly, Robert Hobbs, Will Rogers, Will Brimm, Charles Stephenson, Henry Douney and Mr. Evans.[1048]

Freeman, Hickman
Born: (Unknown)—Date of Death: 4 September 1896
Place: Lamar County
Event: Legal Execution/Hanged

Lee, Silas
Born: (Unknown)—Date of Death: 4 September 1896
Place: Lamar County
Event: Legal Execution/Hanged

Wheeler, George
Born: circa 1859—Date of Death: 4 September 1896
Place: Lamar County
Event: Legal Execution/Hanged

George L. Wheeler, a white man, along with Silas Lee and Hickman Freeman, both black men, were convicted in the United States District Court for the Eastern District of Texas for robbery and murder that they had committed in the Indian Territory (Oklahoma). Wheeler had killed Robert McCabe in the Chickasaw Nation on 12 June 1895. He laid in wait for McCabe, and shot him in the presence of his five-year old son. Silas Lee and Hickman Freeland had murdered Ed T. Canady, Jeff Maddox, Paul Applegate and an unknown man on the shanty boat at the Hear River on 14 November 1894. At about 11:00 am on Friday, 4 September 1896, Wheeler, who had requested that he not be hung with the black men, mounted the gallows at Paris first. His step and pace was strident. The trap was sprung at 11:16 am and he was pronounced dead at 11:38 am.

Lee and Freeman followed at 12:05 pm. The trap was sprung at 12:12 pm, and they were cut down fifteen minutes late. All three necks were broken. Freeman was remarkably cool, while Lee nearly broke down.[1049]

Two Unidentified Mexican Men
Born: (Unknown)—Date of Death: 22 September 1896
Place: Jeff Davis County
Event: Lynching/Shot

According to one unverified and dubious source, two unidentified Mexican men who were suspected of having committed a robbery were shot to death by a pursuing posse near Fort Davis.

Had these men been fleeing from lawmen their case would not meet the author's criteria. On the other hand, if the posse executed the men then the case should be included. Thus this incident is being counted in the interest of possible completeness.[1050]

Dove, John T.
Born: circa 1874—Date of Death: 27 November 1896
Place: Palo Pinto County
Event: Legal Execution/Hanged

John Dove, a twenty two year old white man, was hanged at Palo Pinto on Friday, 27 November 1896. He had been tried and convicted of outraging a woman. Dove's case was appealed, but that process failed to yield his desired result.[1051]

Washington, Eugene
Born: (Unknown)—Date of Death: 23 January 1897
Place: Brazos County
Event: Lynching/Hanged

Eugene Washington, a black man, forcibly entered the Brooks Wright home and made his way to the bedchamber of Miss DeHart, sister-in-law of Wright. There he outraged her at the point of a loaded pistol then fled. Washington was captured not long after and lynched from the limb of a cottonwood tree on Main Street at Bryan. His corpse remained there until the following day.[1052]

One Unidentified Black Man
Born: (Unknown)—Date of Death: 4 March 1897
Place: Bastrop County
Event: Lynching/Shot

Eternity at the End of a Rope

Newspapers of the day reported that a black man who was under arrest for burglary was being held at Christian's Saloon at Elgin when he was attacked. The two masked vigilantes peppered his body with bullets. The dead man's identity was not given.[1053]

Terrell, Alexander
Born: circa 1867—Date of Death: 2 April 1897
Place: Harris County
Event: Legal Execution/Hanging

At about 1:00 pm Tuesday, on 22 December 1896, Alexander Terrell, a black man, approached the home of Mrs. Millie Jackson and asked for a drink of water. The Jackson home was located in the Fifth Ward, a little way from Montgomery Road near the old cordage factory. Mr. Jackson was away at the time. Mrs. Jackson answered Terrell's knock, handed him a glass and told him to go to the cistern and help himself. Not satisfied with just water, Terrell asked if she might have something for him to eat. Mrs. Jackson quickly prepared a plate with what little she had around the house and returned to the door to hand it to Terrell. When she did so he grabbed her by the arm and placed his other hand around her throat, choking her as he forced her onto the bed. When he had finished outraging her he grabbed a small rifle that was near the bed and shot her dead, then fled into the nearby woods. He was eventually captured, tried and convicted. A death sentence was prescribed.

Terrell had little to say before his hanging. There was an expression of distress on his face, but not fear. "I ain't got much to say. My wrong deeds I acknowledge and ask for the mercy of God..." As the noose was placed around his neck he uttered, "Lord, this is the last of it. Jesus be with me." Sheriff Erickson pulled the lever and sprung the trap at 11:37 am on Friday, 2 April 1897. Terrell dropped through the floor without incident and his death was instantaneous. [1054]

Brown, Robert
Born: (Unknown)—Date of Death: 27 April 1897
Place: Harrison County
Event: Lynching/Shot

Wright, Hal
Born: (Unknown)—Date of Death: 27 April 1897
Place: Harrison County
Event: Lynching/Shot

Wright, Russell
Born: (Unknown)—Date of Death: 27 April 1897
Place: Harrison County
Event: Lynching/Shot

In what can only be described as a peculiar episode, Hal Wright and his son Russell were found dead and Robert Brown seriously wounded near Harleton on Tuesday, 27 April 1897.

Reports indicate that these three black men were all on their way to attend court at Harleton when five masked men opened fired on them. The incident occurred between 9:00 and 10:00 am, near the railway bridge about two miles from town. Russell was killed instantly. Justice Jones came to the site to hold an inquiry, during which a man walked up near the crowd of about seventy-five onlookers and fired a pistol into the air twice, warning them to "look out." He then pocketed the pistol and produced a Winchester, which he fired three times in the direction of Hal Wright, killing him. That done, the fellow turned and calmly walked away. Although the shooting took place in view of dozens of onlookers no one could identify the gunman.[1055]

Roane, Fayette
Born: circa 1876—Date of Death: 30 April 1897
Place: Castro County
Event: Lynching/Hanged

Gates, Will
Born: circa 1862—Date of Death: 30 April 1897
Place: Castro County
Event: Lynching/Hanged

Thomas, Lewis
Born: circa 1877—Date of Death: 30 April 1897
Place: Castro County
Event: Lynching/Hanged

Thomas, Aaron
Born: circa 1884—Date of Death: 30 April 1897
Place: Castro County
Event: Lynching/Hanged

Thomas, Jim
Born: circa 1883—Date of Death: 30 April 1897
Place: Castro County
Event: Lynching/Hanged

Thomas, Benny
Born: circa 1882—Date of Death: 30 April 1897
Place: Castro County
Event: Lynching/Hanged

Williams, Will
Born: (Unknown)—Date of Death: 30 April 1897
Place: Castro County
Event: Lynching/Hanged

On Thursday night, 29 April 1897, seven black men murdered three black men, assaulted two black girls, and then burned down the humble home of the victims at Sunnyside. The killers, Fayette Roane, Will Gates, Lewis Thomas, Aaron Thomas, Jim Thomas, Benny Thomas, and Will Williams were all taken into custody and locked in a room at Sunnyside. The group was tracked from the scene of the crime straight to their homes by bloodhounds. Blood stained shirts were discovered inside the men's home.

The group confessed to having killed Henry Daniels, one of the old men, and his seven year old stepdaughter Marie. They had burned the bodies of their victims in the house fire and thrown the corpse of the youngest child down the well. It seems that Daniels had the proceeds from a robbery that the Thomas boys had committed and refused to give it up. Adding to the despicable nature of this crime, the two oldest girls were outraged before being killed and burned.

Shortly after midnight a mob of angry black and white men forced entry to the building and removed all seven men, took them to a lot north of Sunnyside and lynched them from an oak tree. Forty or fifty gunshots rang out in the night, an added measure to make certain that the spirits of the seven culprits had flown from their mortal bodies. The corpses of six remained until morning. The body of the seventh man, Will Williams, was cut down and removed sometime during the night.[1056] The prevailing public opinion was that so long as the right perpetrators had been lynched, then no harm had been done.

One Unidentified Man
Born: (Unknown)—Date of Death: May 1897
Place: Milam County
Event: Lynching/Hanged

According to one unverified report, a man was lynched at Milam County in early May 1897.[1057]

Cotton, Dave
Born: (Unknown)—Date of Death: 14 May 1897
Place: Falls County
Event: Lynching/Hanged

Stewart, Sabe
Born: (Unknown)—Date of Death: 14 May 1897
Place: Falls County
Event: Lynching/Hanged

Williams, Henry "Berry"
Born: (Unknown)—Date of Death: 14 May 1897
Place: Falls County
Event: Lynching/Hanged

Dave Cotton, Sabe Stewart and Henry Williams, all black men, were charged with the outrage of a white woman. The victim was the daughter of William Coats. The three were arrested and taken into custody pending arraignment at Rosebud.

Anticipating that there might be trouble, the sheriff posted a heavy guard around the jail. At about midnight on Friday, 14 May 1897, a force of more than 1,000 men, some of whom were masked, tried to remove the threesome from custody but were repelled by officers. Undaunted, the mob swore to return and blow up the jail with dynamite if necessary. Lawmen immediately set out to transport the three prisoners to Marlin for their safety. About three miles from town the procession was overtaken by the mob that had been alerted to the relocation plan. Dave Cotton, Sabe Stewart and Henry Williams were all lynched from a nearby tree. Afterwards, the mob quietly retreated.[1058]

Nobles, Theodore
Born: (Unknown)—Date of Death: 14 May 1897
Place: St. Augustine County
Event: Lynching/Shot

The Lynching Calendar reported that three black men were killed on 18 May 1897, in St. Augustine County. The incident actually occurred on Friday, 14 May 1897, and involved two black men who went to the residence of George and Felix Johnson, white framers, to renew a quarrel. Other members of the Johnson family joined in. When the smoke cleared Theodore Nobles, presumed to have been one of the two black men, lay dead from gunshot wounds. George Johnson had been struck over the head with a gun and was insensible. Aaron Johnson was wounded in three places, and Felix Johnson had been shot in the arm and leg. The other black man, William White, had his skull fractured and was shot through the body. Afterwards, a posse searched for White's son, who was also a participant in the melee.

Jones, Will

Born: (Unknown)—Date of Death: 23 May 1897
Place: Smith County
Event: Lynching/Shot

Will Jones, a white man, murdered a local merchant named R. W. Stewart at Houston. On a tip from a black man named Effie Jones, Will Jones was arrested and confined to the jail.

Shortly after 1:00 am a mob broke into the jail, rushed Jones's cell and shot him to death where he stood, thus saving themselves the bothersome task of dragging the man into the street and lynching him.[1059]

Walker, Dan

Born: circa 1866—Date of Death: 28 May 1897
Place: Fannin County
Event: Legal Execution/Hanged

Dan Walker, a black man, was tried and convicted of murder at Bonham. He was to have hanged for his crime on Friday, 30 April 1897, were it not for an extremely unpopular stay of execution issued by Governor Charles A. Culberson. Former Sheriff Chaney and over 200 of the town's leading citizens protesting the governor's decision and submitted a petition. In due course, however, Walker's streak of luck ran out when he was made to pay the price for his deeds on Friday, 28 May 1897.[1060]

Williamson, Jim

Born: (Unknown)—Date of Death: 25 June 1897
Place: Wharton County
Event: Legal Execution/Hanged

On Sunday night, 19 May 1895, E. C. Crocker, his wife Nancy, and their fifteen-year old son were all murdered.

The killings occurred at the home of Emmett Colburn, at the settlement of Sandies near Wharton. The incident stemmed from some land troubles that Crocker had had with a fellow named Day. The day prior to the killings Crocker had been threatened by Jim Williamson and had taken refuge in the Colburn home, later being joined by his family and fortifying themselves in the residence. Williamson sought the aid of Frank Martin, Jim Martin, George Williamson and two other men to surround the house. Williamson's group attacked, shooting Crocker and the boy. Later, Mrs. Crocker was gunned down as she attempted to flee. When the siege ended and the bodies were gathered it was discovered that Mrs. Crocker was still breathing. Frank Martin took care of that pesky technicality by dispatching her with a bullet to the head.

All four men were tried and convicted. Jim Williamson and Frank Martin received the death sentence. The other two got to spend the remainder of their lives making new friends in the penitentiary.

Williamson's nerve finally failed him when it was his time to go to the gallows. He was given several injections of strychnine to enable him to scale the stairs unaided. Williamson's date with the executioner was on Friday, 25 June 1897, but it should have been a Friday the 13th given his perils. Owing to the condemned man's agitated state, and the fact that he practically fainted when the hangman's noose was placed around his neck, the process was done in a rush. When the trap was sprung he dropped several feet, then swung for about ten minutes until cut down. A check of his pulse revealed that Williamson was still alive. The poor man was hoisted up onto the platform and dropped again, this time left to dangle for twenty-two minutes. The second time the prescription was effective.

The same gallows that had been constructed for the purpose of hanging Williamson was later used for the Martin execution.[1061]

Deon, Prean
Born: circa 1870—Date of Death: 9 July 1897
Place: Orange County
Event: Legal Execution/Hanged

Prean Deon, a black man and a wife killer, was legally executed at Orange on Friday, 9 July 1897.[1062]

Deon had been born and raised at nearby Cow Bayou. He was reared at the Aaron Ashworth place. On 4 June Deon, in an intoxicated state, had lured his wife Maggie into a buggy and taken her to a place along the road where he murdered her, dragged her from the conveyance, beat her with an ax handle and shot her to death. Deon later confessed that his wife had screamed so loud he had to shoot her. The incident was grotesque beyond comprehension.

Although Deon denied wrongdoing at the onset, he proved an enigma to all. After receiving religion and being baptized in the jail he confessed his crime to Reverend C. H. Hays. Later, when pressed to confess completely, he tried to implicate others in the killing and would not take the final steps of profession. After religious services the sheriff asked if he had anything to say. Deon rose and declared that he made his peace with God.

Fully 3,000 persons turned out to see the event. At the last minute Deon asked for forgiveness from all, and called out to the father of his wife, Eli Boykin. Boykin scaled the stairs and listened attentively to Deon's ramblings about how his murdered spouse had come to him in his dreams and forgiven him. Finally he cried out, "Goodbye to everyone." The black cap was pulled down over his head as he, once again, addressed the gathered throng in a last minute effort to dodge complete responsibility for his evil deeds he said, "I want all you boys and young men to never allow yourselves to be talked into doing anything that you know to be wrong." The trap was sprung at 1:03 pm and thirteen minutes later Deon was declared dead. At least one source has incorrectly reported Deon as having been a Mexican man.

Martinez, Maximo

Born: (Unknown)—Date of Death: 30 July 1897

Place: Wilson County

Event: Legal Execution/Hanged

On 6 June 1897, Maximo Martinez murdered Mr. Plutocro and Mrs. Jesus Carillo. At the same time he outraged, then murdered, their granddaughter Miss Juanita Acosta. Miss Acosta was eighteen at the time and Martinez had romantic designs on her to begin with.

Martinez was a hard looking Mexican who was employed on a ranch nearby. On the night of the killing he went to the bedchamber of Miss Acosta. When she refused him he picked up an ax and split her head open with it. The girl's screams awakened he grandparents. Before they could flee Martinez pounced upon them, armed with a knife and an ax, and butchered the pair. The mortal incident had been ignited some time earlier when Martinez tried to convince Miss Acosta to elope with him. She had declined, largely because Martinez was already married, a bothersome detail that he had hoped she would overlook.

Martinez was tried and convicted of the triple slaying. He drew the death sentence for his hideous work. Not surprisingly, there was an attempt to lynch him, which proved unsuccessful.

Martinez went to the gallows at Floresville on Friday, 30 July 1897.[1063] A brass band attended at the condemned man's request, playing rousing tunes for the entertainment of those gathered, winding up with the fitting song "There'll be a Hot Time in the Old Town Tonight."

White, Esseck

Born: (Unknown)—Date of Death: 6 August 1897

Place: Nacogdoches County

Event: Lynching/Hanged

Esseck White and Armae Phillips, both black men, had attempted to outrage two white women at Nacogdoches on Wednesday, 4 August 1897. They were arrested and confined to the jail pending trial.

At about 10:00 pm on Friday, 6 August 1897, an impromptu army of about 500 men broke into the jail and removed the pair under force of arms and lynched White from an improvised scaffold constructed in the form of a teepee. It seems that during the melee Phillips managed to escape. Newspaper reports of the day claim that he would be lynched just as soon as the mob could locate him. Lacking confirmation, however, his name has not been included on this roster of victims.

White had boasted about the crime, and the fact that he had a lock of hair from the head of one of the victims.[1064]

Bembry, Will (Alias Will Bonner)
Born: (Unknown)—Date of Death: 26 August 1897
Place: Austin County
Event: Lynching/Hanged

Will Bembry, a black man who used the alias Will Bonner, had attacked four women at Bellville. The first victim, a seventy-two year old woman named Mrs. Anna M. Kunna, expired on 29 May 1897, not long after the incident. She is buried at the Schlapota Cemetery at Cat Spring in Austin County.[1065] The second victim, Mrs. Suhr, was cruelly molested and bitten on the cheek and arm. Two other women were frightened by Bembry but not physically harmed.

Bembry was confined to the jail for safekeeping. Once night fell, and throughout the course of the evening, small groups of men formed, gathering by threes and fours, assembling on the street as they spoke quietly of the matter. It was evident that some plot was afoot. Many of the townspeople went to sleep not believing that the jail would be violated. It soon became known that the Santa Fe night train would be bringing reinforcements for the gathering mob. When the train arrived sixty to seventy men from the lower part of the county disembarked.

At around 11:25 pm a prearranged and whispered signal was given and the horde moved almost in unison, approaching the side entrance of the jail. There they attempted to remove a set of iron bars from a window to gain access. Judge Blake addressed the mass, beseeching them to allow justice to take its course. But the judge's plea was muffled by the sound of the hammers attacking the jail window bars. Sheriff Palm was powerless to resist the vigilantes once they had gained entrance.

After great effort cutting bolts and breaching doors Bembry's cell was finally entered. He was bound, hand and foot, then carried downstairs and handed through the open window to the mob waiting outside. Once in the clear, Bembry was taken to a suitable tree where a new rope that had been brought for the purpose was found to be too short.

A large fire had been built, made from dried limbs and moss. It cast a morbid light on the affair. Some suggested that Bembry should be tortured for his deeds. Calmer heads prevailed however, not wishing to stoop to that depth of conduct. Some commented that they had come to send a brute on his way, not to be brutes themselves.

A well-worn lariat was pressed into service and placed around Bembry's neck. The unfortunate man was hauled up until his feet were fully six feet above the ground and left to hang until the last breath of life had left his body. As the dead man's corpse swayed in the summer breeze the crowd quietly walked away and disbanded as if nothing at all had happened.[1066]

Johnson, Wesley
Born: (Unknown)—Date of Death: 27 August 1897
Place: Falls County
Event: Lynching/Hanged

Wesley Johnson, a black man, was lynched by an angry mob outside Rosebud on Friday, 27 August

1897. Johnson was suspected of outraging Mrs. Clunley, who was the cook for the family of Captain McCulloch.[1067]

Carter, Robert "Bob"

Born: (Unknown)—Date of Death: 10 October 1897
Place: Washington County
Event: Lynching/Shot

Washington County operated a convict farm where prisoners worked off misdemeanor convictions. Jim Burch was a convict guard and the assistant superintendent. Burch had some trouble with a black convict and repeat offender named Robert "Bob" Carter.

About 7:15 pm on Sunday, 10 October 1897, Burch was standing under an awning in downtown Brenham when Carter came around the corner armed with a shotgun. When Carter got within feet of Burch he shot him in the face, killing him. Burch drew his pistol and fired at Carter. His shot was ineffective

At about 10:00 pm officers received word that Carter would surrender to R. S. Farmer. As Farmer was escorting Carter to the county jail, Burch's brother, Constable R. H. Burch, confronted him. Carter jumped from his horse to flee. Burch shot him two times with a shotgun. Constable Burch was arrested but never went to trial for the killing.[1068]

Sweat, Thomas "Tom"

Born: (Unknown)—Date of Death: 18 November 1897
Place: Brazos County
Event: Lynching/Hanged

On the night of 18 November 1897, George Cheatham, a black man, was stabbed twice while gambling near Allen Farm. Tom Sweat, another black man, was arrested for having done the work.

While being transported to Millican, Sweat was taken by force from his captors and lynched from a tree. The newspaper accounts of the day claimed that it was a crowd of black men who did the hanging.[1069]

Henry, George

Born: circa 1880—Date of Death: 18 February 1898
Place: Wise County
Event: Legal Execution/Hanged

Denton County Sheriff's Office Jailer Floyd Coberly was making his rounds when an inmate named George Henry attacked him. Henry, a black man, was in the process of trying to escape at the time. Henry beat Coberly with a blunt object so severely that it resulted in the jailer's death.

Henry was charged and convicted of the murder. On Friday, 18 February 1898, he was hanged at Decatur. Sheriff Sam Hawkins of Denton, Sheriff Sterling P. Clark of Tarrant, Assistant Chief of Police Mard Gunnels of Fort Worth and Constable W. A. Stevens of Alvord all came on the gallows platform and aided in preparing the paraphernalia for the event. A crowd of thousands began to assemble for the show that was to take place about a half mile south of town. Stevens tied the hangman's knot as the growing mass began to surge and become impatient. Finally, at 2:40 pm, the carriage with Henry in tow arrived and the condemned man began to make his way through the crowd. The Henry was neatly dressed in a black suite of clothes.

It was after 3:00 pm by the time the trap door had been sprung and Henry dropped those few precious feet to the end of the hangman's rope.[1070]

Gullien, Carlos
Born: (Unknown)—Date of Death: 5 April 1898
Place: Cameron County
Event: Lynching/Shot

Elections in South Texas often turned violent as the political parties vied for power. On Election Day in 1898 Deputy Sheriff Sam Cobb heard about a disturbance at a voting booth. He went on horseback to investigate. His brother, Cameron County Precinct 2 Constable Felipe "Philip" Cobb and a Brownsville city policeman followed on foot. Carlos Gullien stepped from an alley and grabbed the horse's bridle. Gullien shot Sam Cobb. The deputy fired back wounding Gullien. Both men fell to the ground. As Philip Cobb arrived Gullien rose up and shot him twice, killing him instantly. Gullien's brother appeared and shot Sam Cobb again. He died three hours after being shot.

Both of the Gullien brothers fled. Carlos Gullien was arrested and taken into custody. On Tuesday, 5 April 1898, a mob gathered and broke into the jail. Gunfire erupted and Gullien was shot to death. A mob dragged his body into the street. They were going to burn it, but the corpse was eventually returned to the jail cell. Gullien had been in numerous shooting scrapes and disliked the Cobb family. Carlos Gullien's brother whose given name is not known was convicted of assault to murder and the case was on appeal.[1071]

Burt, William Eugene
Born: 5 September 1869[1072]—Date of Death: 27 May 1898
Place: Travis County
Event: Legal Execution/Hanged

At 10:00 am on the morning of 30 July 1896, the bodies of Mrs. Burt and her two young children were found in the cistern at their home on North Street in Austin. Burt claimed that his wife and children had gone to San Antonio as he was packing up the house in preparation for their upcoming move to Dallas.

Burt jumped the northbound train to that city, which is where he was eventually arrested and charged with the murder of his family. He was subsequently returned to Austin for trial.

Burt was found guilty. He was given the death sentence for his crime. At 11:19 am on Friday morning, 27 May 1898, an unrepentant Burt paid the price for his deeds. The only statement he made on the gallows was, "excepting the disgrace, the present was the happiest moment of my life."[1073]

Washington, George
Born: (Unknown)—Date of Death: 6 June 1898
Place: Colorado County
Event: Lynching/Hanged

On Monday, 6 June 1898, Colorado County Precinct 4 constable Lee Wall was shot and killed while arresting a black man named George Washington for fighting at a local saloon.

Wall had made the arrest of Washington and was walking him to the jail. Washington pulled a pistol that he had concealed in his belt and shot Wall twice, once in the head and once in the chest. Washington still had four rounds left in his revolver. He menaced witnesses as he fled the scene. A crowd of about forty citizens, many of whom were armed, followed Washington. A running gun battle broke out that continued until the killer had exhausted his ammunition. The city marshal took custody of Washington, but was soon met by a mob of about 500 citizens when he tried to take the man to the jail. The vigilante horde overpowered authorities, seized Washington and lynched him from an electric utility pole. Sheriff Reese arrived afterward, just in time to cut Washington's body down from the makeshift gallows.[1074]

Watkins, Dee
Born (Unknown)—Date of Death: 9 June 1898
Place: Nacogdoches County
Event: Lynching/Shot

Dee Watkins was a young black man with a family who lived fourteen miles from Nacogdoches. Around midnight on Thursday, 9 June 1898, Watkins was at his home when he was shot twice and killed. The sheriff and other officers went to investigate. One newspaper claimed that several white men had done the killing. Another source blamed Whitecappers.[1075]

Martin, Frank
Born: (Unknown)—Date of Death: 10 June 1898
Place: Wharton County
Event: Legal Execution/Hanged

On Sunday night, 19 May 1895, E. C. Crocker, his wife Nancy and their fifteen-year old son were all murdered. The incident occurred at the home of Emmett Colburn at the settlement of Sandies near Wharton. The killing stemmed from some land troubles that Crocker had had with a man named Day.

The day prior to the incident Crocker had been threatened by Jim Williamson and had taken refuge in the Colburn home, later being joined by his family and fortifying themselves in the residence. Williamson sought the aid of Frank Martin, Jim Martin, George Williamson and two other men to surround the house. Williamson's group attacked, shooting Crocker and the boy. Later, Mrs. Crocker was gunned down as she attempted to flee. When the siege had ended and the bodies were gathered it was discovered that Mrs. Crocker was still breathing. Frank Martin took care of the pesky technicality by dispatching her straightaway.

All four men were tried and convicted. Jim Williamson and Frank Martin received the death sentence. The other two got life in the penitentiary.

Williamson had already been hanged for his part in the crime a year earlier, on 25 June 1897. The same gallows that had been constructed for that purpose was refitted to accommodate Martin, who was a taller and heavier man. Accordingly, a pit two feet deep was dug beneath the structure to allow for the added length and bulk of the intended victim.

At 11:30 am on Friday, 10 June 1898, the trap was sprung. Martin presented a striking image on the gallows, neatly dressed in a well pressed black suit of clothes, jet black hair and beard streaming down over his broad shoulders highlighting his white skin which had been made all the more so from his months in confinement. Standing erect with head poised he seemed to present more of an image of dignity than defiance. This picture of composure and calmness lasted only minutes however. Soon enough Martin dropped through the floor of the gallows and reached the end of his tether. At that point his head practically popped free from his torso, due to a fatal miscalculation in physics. Never the less, he quickly expired.[1076]

Cebron, Laura

Born (Unknown)—Date of Death: 14 June 1898
Place: Collin County
Event: Lynching/Shot

Whitecappers were busy visiting the homes of black residents at Plano, telling them that they had but four to ten days to leave town. At about 1:30 am on Tuesday, 14 June 1898, a party of between five and twenty Whitecappers were observed by Jake Cebron to be visiting the cabins of blacks on Main Street, south of the Cotton belt depot. When they got to his house he stepped outside holding a Winchester rifle. Cebron told the mob that there was no one in his home who had harmed anyone. As white men entered through the gate Cebron told them to approach no further. The men began to retreat, but as they did so one of them yelled out that Cebron had a gun. At that point the white men opened fire on the home. Cebron's wife Laura was asleep when she was shot twice. She died in about an hour. Cebron fired three times at the attackers but missed. He was slightly wounded in the hand.

Newspapers reported that the trouble had begun when wet weather prevented farm laborers from working. A group of thirty to forty black men had congregated in town. Notices had been posted in conspicuous place saying, "Mr. Negro, don't let the sun go down on you."

Two white men, Charley Gunter and Bob Cummings, were arrested and charged with murder. The city marshal tracked down several other mob members and was said to have been seeking their arrest. Mayor McFarlin called a citizen's meeting and condemned the violence. Five officers were appointed to patrol at night and protect the blacks living in the city.[1077]

Ogg, Dan
Born: (Unknown)—Date of Death: 8 August 1898
Place: Anderson County
Event: Lynching/Hanged

The wife of a railroad man and a young woman were visiting at Palestine. They were interrupted in their sleep by a black man who was trying to chloroform them, presumably to quiet the pair while he outraged the woman. They were awakened, and their screams frightened the man away. Soon after, Dan Ogg was arrested and positively identified as the night stalker by the terrified women.

Around midnight Ogg was removed by force from the jail at Palestine by about 200 men and hanged from a tree.[1078]

Malone, Joe
Born: circa 1875—Date of Death: 2 September 1898
Place: Dallas County
Event: Legal Execution/Hanged

Joe Malone, a twenty three year old black man, was tried and convicted of assaulting Mrs. Frederick Stein, a seventy five year old white woman from Dallas. He received the death penalty for his crime. Just before he was to be hanged Malone confessed to having assaulted another woman named Mrs. Ward. That incident had taken place near the Dallas city waterworks in 1894.

Malone had been baptized in a bathtub in the jail cell by a group of black preachers just prior to the confession. Perhaps washing away his sins aided him in admitting his wrongs publically. Apparently he received a thorough cleansing that day, as he also confessed to having killed one white man, one black man, and to having been involved in a great number of lesser offenses.

It was said that practically 10,000 persons gathered to witness Malone's execution. He displayed no concern for his fate. At 12:20 pm the trap was sprung and Malone dropped to his death. His neck was broken by the fall. Death came quickly.[1079]

Barber, Jim
Born: (Unknown)—Date of Death: 7 October 1898
Place: Gonzales County
Event: Legal Execution/Hanged

The headlines of the *San Antonio Express News* on 8 October 1898 read, "Negro Hanged for Uxorcide [sic]." The scribe of this piece was obviously referring to the little used term "uxoricide" which comes from Latin, meaning to kill one's wife. Matricide might have been a better choice, or at least one the journalist could have spelled correctly. The power of a clever phrase is often lost when it is flung carelessly.

In any case, Jim Barber, a black man, dropped through the trap door of the gallows at Gonzales at 2:30 pm on Wednesday, 7 October 1898. "The body shot down like an arrow," the newspaper claimed. Outfitted in a neat black suit, white shirt and tie Barber had scaled the stairs with a smile on his face, accompanied by Sheriff Glover, Deputy Fry, Newt Hampton and his spiritual advisor M. C. Smith. While on the platform he sung "Somebody Is Going To Miss me When I'm Gone."

Barber's troubles began at about 5:00 pm on 20 March 1897. He had come home to drop off some meat for supper with his wife, Patsy. Soon after, two shots were heard. The two daughters of Mrs. Scheske, a neighbor, ran to the window of the Barber residence and found that the curtains had been drawn. From within they could hear Patsy Barber begging for help. One of the girls ran to the Moore home for assistance. Mr. Moore returned and tried to gain entry to the Barber place but found that the door was bolted. Moore pled with Barber to open the door. When he finally did emerge he said that he had killed his wife. He said that he had to do it since she cut him with a knife, displaying the wound across his neck as evidence.

Barber fled. He went to the butcher shop of a friend where he tried to cut his own throat, but was prevented from doing so. When the body of Patsy Barber was examined she was found to have two gunshot wounds along with the knife slash to her throat that ran from ear to ear.[1080]

Kugadt, Charles A.
Born: 19 October 1853—Date of Death: 20 October 1898
Place: Washington County
Event: Legal Execution/Hanged

Charles Kugdat has the distinction of having been the first white man legally executed in Washington County. He murdered his half-sister Johanna Kugadt on Monday, 19 October 1896, stealing between $400 to $700 from her. After the killing he burned her body to cover up his crime. The remains were discovered a few days later.

Kugadt fled, but on Monday, 22 February 1897, was captured at Napa, California and brought back to Texas for trial. He was found guilty and received a death sentence on 31 March 1898. A stay of execution was granted on 25 May 1898, when his wife Marie pleaded that he was insane. The death sentence was eventually carried out on Thursday, 20 October 1898.

Kugadt is buried in Potters Field at Prairie Lea Cemetery at Brenham.[1081]

Autrey, Pete
Born: (Unknown)—Date of Death: 27 October 1898
Place: Fort Bend County
Event: Legal Execution/Hanged

Morris, Emanuel
Born: circa 1858—Date of Death: 27 October 1898
Place: Fort Bend County
Event: Legal Execution/Hanged

In a double hanging venue at Houston, Pete Autrey and Emanuel Morris, both black men, went to the gallows at the same time and on the same day. Morris's crime was perhaps the most hideous in that he had outraged a six-year old blind girl. Afterwards he murdered her. Autrey murdered his mistress when she tried to spurn him. The newspaper makes no mention of who dropped through the trap first, or if the thing was done in unison.[1082]

Shaw, John B.
Born: circa 1839—Date of Death: 25 November 1898
Place: Johnson County
Event: Legal Execution/Hanged

John Shaw was a white farmhand who was convicted of murdering Tom Crane, a well-to-do farmer. The incident took place on Wednesday, 3 November 1897. It seems that Crane's wife was quite fetching. Shaw had designs on the woman, and to ease the complication of taking another man's wife he decided it was simpler to murder Crane and get him out of the way. After the crime he fled, but was apprehended and confined to the jail pending trial. He had been sentenced to hang on 12 August, but on 8 August he escaped from the jail, triggering a massive manhunt. Shaw was re-captured on 21 August at Malakoff.

Shaw's defense attorney pled a case of insanity, which on its face sounded somewhat believable given his foolish conduct. On 18 November 1898, County Judge Hall saw otherwise, returning a guilty verdict. At 11:46 am on Friday, 25 November 1898, Sheriff Stewart cut the rope and Shaw, dressed in a neat fitting black suit, turned down collar and black gloves, was "...ushered into the presence of his God."[1083]

King, Jim

Born: (Unknown)—Date of Death: 2 December 1898
Place: Wharton County
Event: Legal Execution/Hanged

Jim King, a black man, went to the gallows at Wharton on Friday, 2 December 1898, for the murder of his mistress, Lucinda Wade.

Little more was offered in the way of facts by newspapers of the day, other than to mention that King had delivered a short speech from the platform urging others to live right. He claimed that he had received forgiveness and was not afraid to die. King's passing did not come with great ease, however. His neck was not broken by the fall, thus he strangled to death in full view of scores of witnesses.[1084]

Sawyer, Fred

Born: (Unknown)—Date of Death: 13 January 1899
Place: Ellis County
Event: Legal Execution/Hanged

Fred Sawyer, a black man, was legally hanged at Waxahachie on Friday, 13 January 1899. Sawyer had been convicted of committing and outrage on a white woman named Fannie Fuller of Ennis. That incident took place about one year earlier, on 5 June 1898, while Fuller was an employee at the Bardwell House. Not long after the incident Sawyer boarded a train for Dallas but was soon captured. He received a speedy trial and a quick hanging.

At about 11:00 am the condemned man was brought from his cell and dress for his execution. At noon he found religion and confessed his evil deeds to Reverend J. R. Swancey. At 12:24 pm Sheriff Sweatt escorted Sawyer to the carriage, bound to take him to the gallows. Several hundred spectators had gathered, some taking a perch in nearby trees to witness the event. As a slow cold rain soaked the site the mud soon became ankle deep. None were deterred by the weather, however. A good hanging practically always drew a large crowd in Texas.

At 12:28 pm Sawyer mounted the platform and took up his place, saying, "I am as cold as I can be." In an act of remarkable kindness, Deputy Sheriff Minnick removed his own Mackinaw and draped it about the condemned man's shoulders to warm him. At 12:36 pm Reverend Swancey led the prayers, which was followed by the hymn, "Where He Leads I Will Follow."

Sawyer was asked if he wished to speak. He stepped forward, claiming that he had been a participant in an affair with Miss Fuller but that it had not been an outrage as claimed. Their union was consensual. At 12:48 pm Sawyer's hands were bound and the black cap was pulled down over his head. The trap was sprung three minutes later and Sawyer fell to his death.[1085]

Harris, Caesar

Born: circa 1876—Date of Death: 16 March 1899
Place: Brazoria County
Event: Legal Execution/Hanged

Caesar Harris was known locally as a rather "queer" individual. Some believed that he had mysterious powers. Perhaps that interpretation of him came from the fact that Harris was an albino black man, as white as any white man, with pink eyes that darted about continuously.

Although Harris was only twenty-three at the time of his hanging his hair was as white as the driven snow. He had attended school for only a brief time, but was as smart as if he had studied for years and was by all accounts a scholar. Harris had accumulated a fine library of books including many on history, theology, astronomy and economics. His writing was as neat and precise as if it had been printed, his spelling correct and his grammar precise.

Harris loved his wife dearly and, in his own words, would have given anything had her affections not been alienated from him by another man. He was found guilty of her murder and sentenced to death. On Thursday, 16 March 1899, that judgment was carried out when Harris was hung by the neck until dead at Angleton, in Brazoria County. Or was he?

After the hanging, once the doctor had declared Harris dead, his body was placed in a pine coffin and he was loaded onto a wagon. An old man started out for Columbia with the casket, which was the planned burial location of his remains. Along their route, near Oyster Creek, the elderly gentleman heard a tapping on the pine box. The drumming continued. Over time the elderly fellow became practically paralyzed with fear. All at once and with a thunderous crash one of Caesar Harris's feet broke through the coffin lid. Seeing this, the old man leapt from the wagon and dashed for cover in the nearby woods, running as if the devil himself were chasing him. Late that night he reached Columbia, telling the mysterious story in a terror stricken tone. [1086]

The following day a party of men set out to recover the wagon and Harris' casket. When they found the cart they approached with care. As the old man had claimed, one of Harris' feet was protruding from the box. Harris' body was inside. He was still alive but his heart was beating faintly. Harris was taken to Columbia where he eventually expired. His funeral took place two days later. Harris is buried at Columbia.

Burton, Pate

Born: circa 1871—Date of Death: 24 March 1899
Place: Harris County
Event: Legal Execution/Hanged

Pate Burton was a twenty eight year old mulatto Indian, described by the newspaper pundit of the day as a "half breed." He was, by any definition, a notorious malefactor, guilty by his own admission of scores of heinous crimes including murder.

Burton admitted as much to Sheriff Anderson, and went on to add that he was guilty of crimes for which others had paid the price. Burton confessed to killing a white man in Polk County using a Winchester rifle. He and a black man named Kit Robinson had also murdered an elderly white man who was the tender of a water tank near Keno, located alongside the tracks of the Houston, East and West Railroad. They took $41 from the gent, killed him and burned his body. Burton claimed that Robinson had legally hanged for the crime and that two of his kinsmen had been lynched. Burton went on to add that he and another black man named Fisher had murdered another old white man at Cold Springs in San Jacinto County, taking $700 from his person. Burton also relayed a tale of having shot a companion in cold blood in Arkansas when the man fell and broke his leg as the pair fled from the law. Not wishing to be caught, Burton delivered the Coup de grâce.[1087]

Burton went to the gallows at Houston for killing Henry Meyer, along with Myer's wife and their child. No one mourned his passing. His hang up occurred on Friday, 24 March 1899.

Jekins, Granville
Born: (Unknown)—Date of Death: 24 March 1899
Place: Robertson County
Event: Legal Execution/Hanged

Granville Jekins, a black man, was found guilty of the murder of Peter Odom. He was hanged at Franklin on Friday, 24 March 1899.[1088]

Swan, Elisha
Born: circa 1880—Date of Death: 31 March 1899
Place: Bastrop County
Event: Legal Execution/Hanged

On Thursday, 23 June 1898, Elisha Swan killed his father. He did so because the elder Swan would not give him permission to use a horse and buggy.

Swan, a nineteen-year old black man, was tried and convicted of the murder. On Friday, 31 March 1899, Swan was executed by hanging at Bastrop. The fall from the gallows was not sufficient to break his neck. Swan died of strangulation.[1089]

Robinson, Tom
Born: (Unknown)—Date of Death: 28 April 1899
Place: Hill County
Event: Legal Execution/Hanged

Tom Robinson, a black man, was the first ever to go to the gallows at Hill County. He had committed an outrage on a little black girl and was subsequently tried, found guilty and sentenced to death for his actions.

Robinson's hanging was to be private, but the town was packed with would-be spectators, many of whom had climbed onto the roofs of building in hopes of catching a glimpse of the event. Just before midday on Friday, 28 April 1899, Robinson had his final bath and dressed for the upcoming occasion. He bade his family farewell and, accompanied by Sheriff Bell began his trip to the gallows at half past the hour. The Reverend Oliver offered a prayer, at the conclusion of which Robinson exclaimed, "Jesus have mercy." When asked if he wished to speak Robinson acknowledged, and asked that he might have twenty minutes in which to do so. His request was acknowledged, at which point the condemned man launched into a lengthy and disjointed oration during which he reinforced his claim of innocence.

At the conclusion of Robinson's speech Reverend Oliver led the crowd in the hymn "Nearer My God to Thee." As his hands and feet were being bound and the black cap pulled down over his head Sheriff Bell, once again, gave Robinson an opportunity to confess his crime, telling him "Don't die with a story on your lips." Again Robinson professed his innocence, and asked if someone would please bring him a cup of water. A person in the crowd met his request and the cap was pulled up enough so that he might take a drink.

As he felt the noose tighten around his neck Robinson said, "Mr. Bell you are choking me." The sheriff pulled the trigger and Robinson shot through the trap. His death was almost instantaneous.
1090

Little, Charles "Charley"
Born: (Unknown)—Date of Death: 4 May 1899
Place: Hunt County
Event: Legal Execution/Hanged

On 12 November 1897, Charles Little, a field hand, robbed and murdered L. B. Stonecipher. The incident had taken place at the J. J. Roach farm. Little had murdered Stonecipher in an old house that they had taken shelter in, then set the building ablaze to disguise his work. Stonecipher's death had been the result of several blows to the head with a blunt instrument, administered by Little. Little confessed to the killing, claiming that the men had stopped at the abandoned building to taken shelter and play a game of cards. Stonecipher had cheated, and when caught at it reached for a shotgun and pointed it at Little. Little claimed that he had fallen backwards, grabbed an iron bar and stove in Stonecipher's head in self-defense.

Forensic evidence discovered later at the scene did not support Little's story. The iron bar that Little claimed he had used was still firmly attached to the wagon from which it was supposed to have come. Stonecipher was on his way to south Texas to be married at the time of the killing, and had $109.50 in cash which Little relieved him of.

Little came from a respected family. His father had a large ranch near Caddo. Little was married, and had two young daughters aged five and six years, described as "bright little creatures," all came to call on him at the jail prior to his execution.

His appeals to the governor exhausted, Little went to the gallows on Friday, 4 May 1899. Baptist Preachers S. J. Anderson, W. T. Hardy, Reverend Campbell and Reverend Henson all attended to the condemned man in his cell and accompanied him to the hanging. Dinner was fed at 11:45 am, but Little scarcely touched the meal. He was shaved and prepared for presentation as Reverend Tardy prayed and led those present in the hymn "Jesus, Lover of My Soul."

To the rhythm of the tune "Shall We, Shall I" Little marched to the platform and scaled the stairs. He shook hands with the sheriff and his deputies, the cap was placed over his head and, at his request a bandana over his eyes for good measure. The trap was quickly sprung and Little was no more. After hanging for sixteen minutes Little's body was cut down and placed in a casket for burial at Elm Cemetery at Caddo.[1091]

Humphreys, George Washington
Born: 2 July 1871—Date of Death: 26 May 1899
Place: Henderson County
Event: Lynching/Hanged

Humphreys, James Knox Polk
Born: 3 October 1847—Date of Death: 26 May 1899
Place: Henderson County
Event: Lynching/Hanged

Humphreys, John Sharp
Born: 12 November 1866—Date of Death: 26 May 1899
Place: Henderson County
Event: Lynching/Hanged

James Humphreys and his two sons, George and John, were dragged from their home and lynched near Tool on Friday, 26 May 1899. Their crime, according to the ten or so vigilantes who committed this act, was that the men had refused to reveal the identity of a local person named Patison who had killed a constable.[1092]

According to John's wife Cora, a crowd came to their home at about 1:00 am. The family was asleep. James Humphreys was questioned about Patison. The mob soon left, but returned at around 2:30 am with a renewed vengeance and lynched the threesome.[1093]

Newspapers reported that on Monday, 10 July 1899, ten individuals who were involved in the killings were taken into custody at Athens. The Assistant Attorney General, District Attorney and Texas Rangers were dispatched to aid in the apprehension and trial. Sometime later, Ed Cain and Walter Wilkerson were tried and convicted of the killing of Humphreys. Based on the circumstances of the case a favorable recommendation for pardon was made for Wilkerson but not for Cain. On 20

October 1909, the governor pardoned only one of the nine men who were charged with the lynching. It was Walter who got his walking papers that day, based largely on his age at the time of the crime.[1094]

Family genealogists record the killings of all three men as having occurred on 23 May 1899.[1095]

Thomas, Allie
Born: (Unknown)—Date of Death: 28 June 1899
Place: Harrison County
Event: Lynching/Hanged

Between 10:00 and 11:00 am on Wednesday, 28 June 1899, a farmer named A. Fuller went to a neighbor's house and left his fifty-eight year old wife at home with a black field hand named Allie Thomas. When he returned in about an hour he discovered his wife prostrate on the floor and bleeding. She claimed Thomas propositioned her and threatened to kill her husband if she did not consent. She alleges she fought back but Thomas overpowered and outraged her.

Fuller called the sheriff, who came to the scene with bloodhounds. Thomas was captured at about 2:00 pm. He was brought to Waskom, where Mrs. Fuller had been taken for medical treatment. She identified him as her assailant. Thomas confessed his crime and was tied to a stake at the M. C. Abney's store. A crowd soon gathered, intending to lynch Thomas, but they decided to delay their actions and wait for the train that was scheduled to arrive at 5:14 pm as it was bringing more people who wanted to witness the execution.

Sheriff Munden and ten deputies arrived at the scene at about 3:50 pm. The mob surrounded the lawmen. The sheriff agreed to wait for the train, and to plead with the much larger crowd for law and order to take its course. At about 7:00 pm a woman addressed the assembled group saying that it was the duty of the men of Waskom to protect the women. She called the men cowards, and offered to hang Thomas herself. The sheriff and his deputies rushed through the crowd and placed Thomas on a horse then made their escape. All was going well until the sheriff and his deputies reached a point along the road where a group of pursuing mobsters, masked to disguise their identity, shot and killed Thomas as they rode by.

Newspapers claimed that Thomas was about twenty-two years old, and that his parents lived in Marshall. He had been working for Mr. Fuller for three months.[1096] Curiously, tabloids of the day seemed more focused on the fact that there was a lynching than on what the man's crime had been.[1097]

One Unidentified Black Man
Born: (Unknown)—Date of Death: 14 July 1899
Place: Grimes County
Event: Lynching/Hanged

On 25 July 1899, a Georgia newspaper reported that a black man had been lynched at Iola in Grimes

County about two weeks earlier. This unidentified black man had apparently murdered a white boy while out squirrel hunting. The implication was that the man had probably not mistaken the lad for a squirrel.[1098]

Brown, Abe
Born: (Unknown)—Date of Death: 14 July 1899
Place: Washington County
Event: Lynching/Shot

Abe Brown, a black man, had outraged and afterwards murdered a Bohemian woman (white woman of German ancestry) near Gilead. He did the killing with a knife. Not long after the crime Brown was tracked down by a posse and, when he attempted to escape he was shot to death.[1099]

Ford, Clay
Born: circa 1875—Date of Death: 20 July 1899
Place: Fayette County
Event: Legal Execution/Hanged

Clay Ford, a black man, was tried and convicted of robbery and murder. He was executed by hanging at LaGrange on Thursday, 20 July 1899. The *Hallettsville Herald* reported that the same rope that had been used at Cleburne to hang John Shaw on 25 November 1898, was used to dispatch Ford.[1100]

Hamilton, Henry
Born: (Unknown)—Date of Death: 25 July 1899
Place: Grimes County
Event: Lynching/Shot

On 24 July 1899, a "race riot," as newspapers of the day described it, occurred in Grimes County. A white church was burned and a black man named Henry Hamilton was lynched.

Hamilton was said to have been "armed and defiant" when he led the mob that carried out the burning. When confronted he opened fire, wounding two white farmers named Randolph Wright and Lockroy Moodey. A posse of white men tracked Hamilton, eventually overtaking him at about 10:00 am on 25 July 1899. A gunfight took place before he was overpowered, during which Hamilton was wounded in the right hand and left leg. Once in their control, the posse lynched him from a nearby oak tree. Some newspapers reported that Hamilton's given name was John.[1101]

Darlington, James
Born: circa 1874—Date of Death: 28 July 1899
Place: Tarrant County
Event: Legal Execution/Hanged

On the night of Thursday, 21 July 1898, James Darlington and his accomplices robbed the Atchison, Topeka and Santa Fe Railroad train near Saginaw killing the train's fireman, identified only as Mr. Whittaker, and wounding the engineer, identified as Mr. Williams. Darlington was tried and convicted of the robbery and sentenced to death.

At about 1:10 pm on Friday, 28 July 1899, Darlington was hanged at Fort Worth. The execution took place in the presence of about fifty witnesses. Darlington was the first person to be put to death under the new Texas State law allowing for capital punishment of train robbers.[1102]

Ford, Walter
Born: circa 1875—Date of Death: 27 October 1899
Place: McLennan County
Event: Legal Execution/Hanged

On Sunday, 25 June 1899, Walter Ford, a twenty-four year old black man, murdered his fifteen-year old spouse Lucinda Moore. He was tried and convicted of the slaying and sentenced to death.

On Friday, 27 October 1899, Ford bravely met his fate. He scaled the gallows stairs with a smile on his face and greeted those he knew with a cheerful salute. He asked to be allowed to examine the black cap before it was pulled down over his head. The executioner complied, and when the garment was placed on his head he remarked, "It fits alright." Shortly after noon Sheriff John Baker sprung the trap and Ford fell six feet. His neck was broken. Ford was pronounced dead several minutes afterwards.[1103]

Fords body was handed over to relatives who shipped his remains to Franklin for burial.

Morrison, George E.
Born: (Unknown)—Date of Death: 27 October 1899
Place: Wilbarger County
Event: Legal Execution/Hanged

At Austin on Saturday, 6 May 1899, a state court of appeals found Reverend George E. Morrison guilty of the diabolical murder of his wife, Minnie Brady. Morrison had used strychnine poison to commit the act. The incident took place at Panhandle on 10 October 1897, some months earlier.[1104]

Morrison was pastor of the Panhandle Methodist Church, and had been raised in Massachusetts where he and his wife were married. The highly esteemed preacher had traveled to Kansas City a year or so earlier for medical treatment. There he had a liaison with a young woman named Anna

Whittlesey who had been one of his schoolmates. Not telling her that he was married, Morrison invented a story about how he was a wealthy cattleman from Texas and owned a large ranch.[1105]

Morrison returned to Panhandle but continued a correspondence with his new sweetheart, posting letters from neighboring cities to avoid being discovered. He conceived a carefully considered plan whereby he would wait until the local physician was out of town then kill his wife by poisonings her. On Sunday, 10 October 1897, he executed his plan.

Immediately following the funeral Morrison left for Kansas City where he reunited with his paramour. Hearing of an investigation into his wife's murder he fled to several western states, then ultimately to Old Mexico where he was eventually captured on 26 November. Morrison was returned to Kansas City for trial. When he had been taken into custody in Mexico Morrison had in his possession forged deeds to a ranch in Texas that he had used to convince his new lover of his prosperity.[1106]

On the day of his execution his sister came to see him, accompanied by Mrs. W. B. Townsend and others. After a few commonplace words were exchanged Morrison suggested that religious services be held. Mrs. Townsend rendered "Nearer My God to Thee." Reverend Tant then made a fervent prayer on Morrison's behalf. The doomed man sang softly. Promptly at the prescribed hour, Sheriff Williams appeared. He entered the jail cell and was in the act of speaking when Morrison arose, perfectly calm, and addressed him saying, "Mr. Williams, you have your duty to do." The death warrant was read. Morrison was handed a new, neat-fitting overcoat, which he put on. Taking his hat he accompanied the officers downstairs, out the back door and up the gallows steps.

There was a certain ominous stillness in the small crowd of fifty persons that were permitted to witness the execution. For a moment it seemed as though all hesitated to speak. Reverend Morrison himself broke the silence by saying, "Well, I am ready to make my talk: I don't expect to detain you long." In his palmist days he never addressed a congregation with more deliberation than he did in that oration from the scaffold.

When finished he turned, grasped Sheriff Williams by the hand, thanked him warmly and told him that he regarded him highly and bore him no ill will for what he was about to do. Next he told Jailer Shrive good-by, asking him to forgive him for attempting to abuse his kindness by trying to escape, assuring him that he had no intention of harming him and that he was only actuated by a desire to regain his liberty if he could. Shrive took his hand and said: "I don't blame you one bit; if I had been in your place, I would have done the same thing."

Morrison removed his overcoat, stepped on the trap and remained perfectly at ease while the black cap and noose was placed about his neck. "Let me know when you are ready," he remarked to Sheriff Williams.

At 12:55 pm precisely the rope was pulled and the Morrison's body shot downward like a flash. His neck was broken by the fall. At 1:07 pm his pulse ceased to beat and Drs. J. E. Dodson, H. H. Rhoads and G. E. Blackman of Vernon, Albert of Childress and Farrington of Chillicothe pronounced life extinct.

Watrous, Sam
Born: circa 1869—Date of Death: 27 October 1899
Place: Travis County
Event: Legal Execution/Hanged

Sam Watrous was a black man about twenty-seven year of age. He was blind in his left eye, that being a consequence of having been kicked in the head by a horse. Watrous looked the brute he was, and took very little interest in his trial. [1107]

Watrous and his partner, Jim Davidson, another black man, were tried and convicted of the horrific murder of Mr. and Mrs. George W. Engburg. The crime took place near Manor on Thursday, 2 June 1898.

Apparently Watrous had the idea that the Engburg's had a large sum of money concealed somewhere in their home. He told this to his cousin, Jim Davidson, who lived a short distance from the Engburg place. On the night of the crime Davidson and Watrous left the former's home shortly after supper. Watrous carried a double-barreled, muzzle loading shotgun that he had borrowed from a neighbor. The duo went to the home of the Engburg's, who were Swedes. Watrous was able to speak Swedish. When he called out to the Engburg in their native tongue the unsuspecting man opened the door only to find himself face to face with Watrous and his shotgun. Watrous fired. Engburg fell instantly. His wife, who was in the room, ran to the door, closed and locked it then dashed to an adjacent room to get a pistol. She fired one shot, which was ineffective. Watrous fired a shot through the window at Mrs. Engburg. She fell near the body of her husband. Both Watrous and Davidson climbed through the window and outraged her while she lay dying in a pool of her own blood.
The killers made off with some silverware, several silk handkerchiefs, a pistol and a gold ring taken from the dead woman's finger.

The murder remained a mystery until about a month later when Watrous came to Austin and delivered a gold ring to Sheriff White saying that it had been given him by two black boys named Jim Young and Albert Wilson. He believed it to have been the property of Mrs. Engburg.

The execution of Watrous went smoothly. The doomed man's neck was broken and he was pronounced dead.[1108]

Wright, Thomas Adam
Born: circa 1858—Date of Death: 10 November 1899
Place: Erath County
Event: Legal Execution/Hanged

John A. Adams had come to Texas from Louisiana after the end of the Civil War. He became the Erath Precinct 2 Constable in about 1879. During the course of his tenure there Adams had a disagreement with a local man named Thomas A. Wright, also known as "Little Tom." Wright was a known bootlegger, and on at least one occasions an arsonist.

On 18 December 1897, the quarrel between the two men came to a deadly conclusion. Sometime earlier Constable Adams had threatened to shoot Wright, armed or unarmed, if he saw him in town again. On this night Wright was intoxicated and before coming to town had borrowed a gun from a man named Tom Leslie. Wright ambushed Adams. The first shots from Wright's gun hit the lawman in the back of the head. Adams immediately fell to the ground. Wright fired at the fallen man a second time while Adams was lying on the ground bleeding from the wound to his head. This time the bullets hit him in the body. The results were fatal.

Two other men, Dick McCain and a fellow named McCarty, were implicated for their alleged complicity in this crime. Wright was arrested, convicted, and sentenced to be executed.

On 11 November 1899, that verdict was carried out at Stephenville. At about 8:30 am Wright's wife visited him, trembling with fear as he reached through the bars of his cell. At 1:20 pm he emerged from his confinement, walked down the steps of the jailhouse and passed through the building, out to the platform at the south side of the structure that had been erected for the event. Sheriff R. T. Home and 1st Deputy Harve Kieth bracketed the condemned man. When given his opportunity to speak he took it, exclaiming that his friend Lesley had been rotting in jail for two years now and was completely innocent. He, Wright, had done the killing of Adams and not Lesley. His last statements complete, Wright was prepared for the execution. The trigger was pulled at about 1:51 pm. The drop broken his neck, as it should, and he expired instantly.[1109]

Davidson, Jim
Born: circa 1876—Date of Death: 24 November 1899
Place: Travis County
Event: Legal Execution/Hanged

Jim Davidson was a mulatto, about twenty-three years of age, the son of Edmund Davidson who was a respectable old black man in the community who had farmed in the vicinity of Manor for a number of years. The elder Davidson was known for his honesty and industry, and had always gotten along well with his neighbors. Young Davidson had borne a good reputation until he became involved with Sam Watrous in the horrible murder of George W. Engburg and wife described above. The killing took place on Thursday, 2 June 1898.

On the morning of his execution Davidson attended religious service, confessed his crime and prayed for forgiveness. Afterward, Davidson's father arrived and shook hands with him, bidding his son a last farewell.

At about 11:00 am on Friday, 24 November 1899, the spectators took their seats. Sheriff White announced that Davidson had a few remarks to make. The doomed man stood near the trap, cool and collected and said, "I am before you today, only for a short while; I have to leave you soon. I am guilty of the crime I am accused of. I took part in it. It was a mighty horrible crime; but I am guilty. I hope the Lord has forgiven me; I believe He has and I will go to heaven. I stand here and say I took part in it, but I was led into it. Now my turn has come, God be with you all."[1110]
Having expiated his crimes, Davidson stepped forward onto the trap. Deputy Sheriff Corwin put the

black cap on his head and adjusted the rope. At about 11:11 am Sheriff White pulled the lever. The trap flew open and Davidson was launched into eternity.

Flores, Antonio
Born: (Unknown)—Date of Death: 5 January 1900
Place: El Paso County
Event: Legal Execution/Hanged

Para, Geronimo
Born: (Unknown)—Date of Death: 5 January 1900
Place: El Paso County
Event: Legal Execution/Hanged

On Friday, 5 January 1900, Geronimo Para and Antonio Flores were hanged at El Paso. Both men had been convicted of murder and both were desperate outlaws. Para was accused of killing Texas Ranger Sergeant Charles Fusselman on 17 April 1890.

In a decision by the pair not to go quietly into the night, when their cell door was opened for their walk to gallows Para and Flores sprung upon citizens and officers with dirks they had concealed, or fashioned, in their cells. Wild with frenzy their intense thrusting resulted in injury to a number of officers, including Texas Ranger Ed Bryant. Having had enough of the melee, the sheriff ordered the men to stop or they would be shot on the spot. They complied.

Flores and Para finished their walk to the gallows peacefully, Para clutching a crucifix. The fall from the hangman's platform practically severed his head. Flores passed uneventfully.[1111]

Misher, Ellis "Blackbird"
Born: (Unknown)—Date of Death: 12 January 1900
Place: Guadalupe County
Event: Legal Execution/Hanged

On Friday, 12 January 1900, Ellis "Blackbird" Misher was hung at the poor farm at Seguin. Misher, a black man, had been convicted of outrage. He died thirteen minutes after the trap had been sprung.[1112] "Heaven" was the last word heard spoken by "Blackbird."

On 18 April 1899, "Blackbird" had waylaid a Bohemian girl named Rosa Messka who was on her way home from Catholic Church at Weimar. After beating her with a rock until she was insensible he outraged her. Believing that she was dead, he placed the girl's body on the railroad track for the next train to run over then fled to Eagle Lake. He was arrested there the next day, returned, and identified by the severely injured unfortunate young woman who, much to "Blackbird's" surprise had survived the diabolical episode.

"Blackbird" denied having done the deed, and swore to his dying day that a man named Tom Jones, who was also confined in the jail, had been the culprit.

Pierson, Henderson

Born: (Unknown)—Date of Death: 2 February 1900
Place: Red River County
Event: Legal Execution/Hanged

Henderson Pierson, a black man, was hanged at Clarksville on Friday, 2 February 1900. While on the gallows onlookers had begun to sing a hymn, and Pierson joined in on the singing. The trap was sprung and Pierson went to his maker.

Pierson's crime seemed simple. He had fatally shot his wife and her mother because they refused to obey him when he insisted that they not attend church services.[1113]

Sweeney, James

Born: (Unknown)—Date of Death: 10 February 1900
Place: Jefferson County
Event: Lynching/Hanged

Giving evidence to the fact that on occasion a judge may make an extremely unpopular decision that citizens feel compelled to right, James Sweeney was lynched at Port Arthur for a crime that a court had just acquitted him of. Perhaps it was another example of a lawyer's trickery, invoking some obscure precedent or claiming a foul based on a trivial breach in protocol.

Sweeney, a white man, had been charged with killing Gus Krumbach at Port Arthur on Thursday, 1 February.[1114] Sweeney's trial took place on Saturday, 26 January 1900. He was acquitted and released. Now free, Sweeney rode the train back to Port Arthur.

When he arrived there at 12:30 am on Sunday, 11 February 1900, he was met on the platform by a crowd of about 100 armed vigilantes who lynched him from a nearby telephone pole. Adding drama to the already remarkable scene, the rope broke and Sweeney fell to the ground with a thud. A makeshift repair was made and Sweeney was, once again, hoisted into the air where he dangled for some time before suffocating to death.[1115]

Hopkins, Anthony

Born: circa 1872—Date of Death: 9 March 1900
Place: Jefferson County
Event: Legal Execution/Hanged

Anthony Hopkins, a black man who used the alias Willie Jones, was hanged at Beaumont on Friday, 9 March 1900.

On 3 May 1899, Hopkins had killed his wife Lou. Only a few days previous he had beaten her with a rope and driven her from the house. After the flogging she had taken up residence in a boarding house. On the night of the murder Hopkins made his way to her room and somehow managed to gain entry into his wife's sleeping quarters. After a mortal struggle he cut her throat with a razor so severely that, according to newspaper accounts of the day, "her head was practically severed."

About 6,000 citizens turned out to see Hopkins hang. At 11:05 am Sheriff Langham brought him from the jail. Along for the procession was Deputy Langham, Constable Landry, Reverend William H. Bendford from Galveston, Doctor Levis, and W. L. T. Boulding was Hopkins's spiritual advisor.[1116] Religious services were held on the scaffold. Hopkins made a speech that lasted about fifteen minutes, during which he is said to have been rather "disconnected." At 11:38 am Sheriff Langham sprung the trap. The rope slipped around to the back of Hopkins's head, thus his neck was not broken by the fall. He was finally cut down at 11:56 am and declared dead, having dangled a full eighteen minutes as he writhed and convulsed.

A collection of $100 was taken up by the crowd to send along with his remains to Hopkins' mother at Waco.[1117] He was subsequently buried at the First Street Cemetery at Waco.[1118]

Martin, King
Born: (Unknown)—Date of Death: 16 March 1900
Place: Kaufman County
Event: Legal Execution/Hanged

King Martin, a black man, was tried and found guilty of outraging a fourteen-year old white girl named Lizzie Wilson. Lizzie was the daughter of his employer, James Wilson. Martin had worked for Wilson for about three years, and his actions came as a surprise to all...especially Lizzie.

Martin and his wife were well trusted. When the Wilson family went to town overnight they left Lizzie in the care of the Martin's. At about 9:00 pm King Martin asked his wife to go to their house and make a poultice for his foot. During her absence he violated the young girl, telling her that if she reported the incident he would kill her and her family. The following morning Martin went to work in the field. Meanwhile, Miss Lizzie dutifully went to her mother in confidence and told her mother of the outrage. Mrs. Martin, who was in the next room at the time, overheard their conversation. She fled and alerted King Martin.

King Martin and his wife fled. Being pursued by a mob, they took shelter in an orchard near Terrell where they were eventually captured and taken into protective custody at the Dallas jail by Sheriff Keller. While there, Martin made an attack on the sheriff with an iron bar, beating him so viciously that his life was in danger. Keller shot Martin in the leg in order to stop the assault.[1119]

Martin climbed the gallows stairs on Friday, 16 March 1900. Bishop Chisholm, a black preacher, accompanied him. King Martin sang hymns and showed no nerve right to the end. At 11:08 am the trap was sprung and he dropped seven feet to his death, neck broken. He died four and one half minutes later. The executioner used the same rope for the King execution as had been employed in the hanging of James Darlington and others.

Morris, Neverson
Born: (Unknown)—Date of Death: 23 March 1900
Place: Fannin County
Event: Legal Execution/Hanged

White, Frank
Born: (Unknown)—Date of Death: 23 March 1900
Place: Fannin County
Event: Legal Execution/Hanged

Folks at Bonham were treated to a "two for the price of one" hanging on Friday, 23 March 1900.

Friday is hanging day in Texas. Neverson Morris and Frank White, both black men, stepped to the gallows on the same day. They had risen early, after a good night's sleep, and ate a hearty breakfast. At about 10:30 am jailers removed them from their cells and allowed them to shave, bath and prepare for their big day. Both condemned men put on new suits of clothes, and then attended religious services held for them by Reverends Jones and Davis. Afterward the walk to the gallows commenced.

Although a heavy rain had fallen the preceding night and into the morning a crowd of about 8,000 spectators were undaunted, braving the occasional sprinkles and assorted mud puddles to take their place along the fence that covered an area of about sixty feet and had been erected to control the crowds. Once Morris and White had scaled the stairs religious services were again conducted, then White stepped forward and spoke. He claimed to the end that he had not killed the man named Johnson, whose murder he had been found guilty of committing. Morris, on the other hand, confessed to his guilt, and proclaimed that he had been saved and was thus unafraid to die. Sheriff Ridling pulled the trap at 2:16 pm and both men were catapulted into eternity.

Morris's crime took place on 22 April 1899. He had murdered his wife and four year old child with an ax at Honey Grove, clearly an incident of extreme cruelty. He offered no excuse for his actions apart from extreme jealousy. White, on the other hand, had killed a man named B. Johnson at a festival at Honey Grove on 23 October 1898, by luring him to his home, robbing him of a few dollars and cutting his abdomen open with a razor. The wound was fatal.[1120]

McKinney, Bob
Born: (Unknown)—Date of Death: 16 April 1900
Place: Hunt County
Event: Legal Execution/Hanged

In September 1899 Bob McKinney murdered Simon Smith and Margaret Lesley at Greenville. It is said that jealousy was the motive. He was tried and convicted of the crime, then subsequently sentenced to death.

At 12:30 pm on Monday, 16 April 1900 McKinney scaled the gallows steps and met his fate.

Under a recently enacted law, only fifty people were admitted to the gallows enclosure in the jail yard. To his credit, McKinney died fearlessly.[1121]

Brown, Henry
Born: circa 1882—Date of Death: 7 May 1900
Place: Hunt County
Event: Legal Execution/Hanged

Henry Brown, an eighteen-year old black man, was legally hanged at Hunt County on Friday, 7 May 1900. Brown had murdered his sweetheart, Frances Melton, because of jealousy. That incident had occurred at Commerce in August 1899. [1122]

Spears, Sidney
Born: (Unknown)—Date of Death: 18 June 1900
Place: Grayson County
Event: Legal Execution/Hanged

The orchestra played "Home Sweet Home" as Sidney Spears, a black man who killed his wife, dropped through the trap door at 12:04 pm on Monday, 18 June 1900. Sheriff Shrewsbury did the work.

A completely composed Spears had approached the gallows with more bravery than seen displayed by most on that fateful day. He had risen at about 6:00 am, commenting how it was to be his last. Spears bathed his face. A barber named Frank Bell came to the cell to shave him at about 9:00 am. Around noon Spears stepped from his cell while a string band played the song he had requested as he walked to his appointment with the executioner. At his request a white silk handkerchief was tied over his eyes and the quintessential black cap was pulled down over his head. "May God save my enemies" were his last word as the trap was sprung and he was catapulted into eternity.

Spears and his wife had had domestic difficulties. Early on the morning of 6 July 1899, Spears, who was a barber by trade, cut his wife's throat from ear to ear. She staggered from the house and fell dead in the yard.[1123]

Waggoner, Perry
Born: (Unknown)—Date of Death: 6 July1900
Place: Cherokee County
Event: Legal Execution/Hanged

Perry Waggoner, a black man, was executed in Rusk on Friday, 6 July 1900. The event took place before a mostly black audience comprised of about 5,000 persons. Waggoner was convicted of the murder of a white man named J. J. Davis. That killing had taken place on 10 July 1899. Waggoner, a convict serving a life term for a murder at Van Zandt County, bludgeoned fellow inmate Davis while he sat picking his teeth after dinner. Waggoner was tried, convicted and sentenced to death for the deed.

Unlike most convicts awaiting execution, Waggoner refused all religious consolation. He died cursing on the gallows. His neck was broken in the fall, and he expired instantly. Waggoner refused to give a last statement or to comment on his crime. He had killed Davis over a $.50 debt.[1124]

Renfro, John
Born: circa 1872[1125]—Date of Death: 27 July 1900
Place: Johnson County
Event: Legal Execution/Hanged

John Renfro, a white man, was a member of a respected and well-established Cleburne family. The twenty-eight year old had fallen into an unfortunate crowd of reckless and dissipated men, but it was his own sharp tongue that ultimately caused his undoing.

Renfro had sought the affections of a daughter of M. M. Williams. When the girl turned down his proposal of marriage Renfro set about disparaging her, assailing her character and slandering the woman all around town. Mr. Williams protested, and sought an affidavit against Renfro. On the day set for the hearing Renfro met Williams on the steps of the courthouse, jerked a pistol from his waistband and shot the man four times. Williams tumbled down the stairs and was dead before he hit the bottom step.

The incident took place in front of scores of witnesses. Renfro was arrested and placed in the jail. He was later tried and convicted, then sentenced to death. Miss Williams was one of the principal witnesses against him. His date with the gallows was set for 13 July 1900. Due to an application for trial on the basis of insanity, which failed, the appointment was delayed until Saturday, 27 July 1900.

Renfro's hanging went off as expected. He spoke for about thirty minutes, protesting that he had not been treated fairly. Sheriff Stewart sprung the trap at about 12:12 pm. His neck was snapped by the fall, thus ending Renfro's grousing for eternity.[1126]

Howard, Ewing
Born: (Unknown)—Date of Death: 6 October 1900
Place: Washington County
Event: Legal Execution/Hanged

At 12:45 pm on Saturday, 6 October 1900, the trap was sprung and Ewing Howard dropped to his death. The hanging was preceded by Howard holding forth at great length about his innocence in the matter for which he had been condemned to die. His last audible words were, "The sheriff has my body but God has my soul." He was, of course, quite correct on both counts.[1127]

In a fit of jealousy Howard had killed his wife and a man named Luke Taylor. That incident had occurred on Sunday, 4 March 1900. Although, as he mentioned in his final speech, he felt quite justified in ending the lives of both people apparently the court saw the matter differently.

Three Unidentified Black Men

Born: (Unknown)—Date of Death: 15 November 1900
Place: Marion County
Event: Lynching/Hanged

Three unidentified black men were removed from their jail cell and lynched near Cypress Bayou at Jefferson on Thursday, 15 November 1900.

The men were accused of waylaying Mr. Stallcup and attempting to kill him. They had been arrested and confined to the jail where they had confessed to the crime. A mob overpowered the jailer and cut the telephone line so that a call for help could not be place.[1128]

Henderson, John

Born: (Unknown)—Date of Death: 13 March 1901
Place: Navarro County
Event: Lynching/Burned at Stake

John Henderson, a black man, was jailed and charged with the murder of Mrs. Conway Younger, a white woman. The killing had occurred near Belton, at about 7:00 am on Tuesday, 12 March 1901. Henderson had been confined in the Belton jail. Officers were taking him to Fort Worth when Sheriff Baker of Waco refused him lodging there.

There was great local interest in Henderson's crime. The telegraph wires had been tapped at Hillsboro, and a citizens' posse kept themselves constantly informed of the movements of both Henderson and his jailers. Under a heavy guard, Henderson boarded a train at Hillsboro. No attempt was made to capture him until the train neared Itasca. When the endeavor was undertaken the train's conductor tried to prevent the act, attempting to make the run to Fort Worth without stopping. Unsuccessful, the vigilantes entered the car and took the Henderson along with the officers in charge of him. A Johnson county officer pulled a revolver on the vigilantes, but was disarmed before he could shoot.

After a lively fight Henderson was taken to Corsicana, a distance of forty-five miles. The party of kidnappers changed horses and teams at Frost. Henderson made a full confession after arriving at Corsicana, telling how he went to the Younger home and of the attempt he made to outrage Mrs. Younger. He told of how Mrs. Younger fought for her honor, and of how he had attacked her with his knife. Henderson described in detail how the two Younger children screamed in fright when they saw their mother's blood on the walls and floors of the room.

After Henderson's graphic confession his captors decided it would be most appropriate to burn him at the stake. The event was to take place at 2:00 pm that same day. News reached town, however. Soon Texas Rangers and troops were alerted and were making their way from Dallas. With their anticipated arrival time at Corsicana being near noon, hurried preparations were undertaken to burn Henderson before the lawmen could intervene.

By around 11:00 am the small group of vigilantes had grown to a mob of about 2,000 strong. Forty men made a rush for the jail to remove Henderson. Once in hand they formed a circle, holding on to a chain that completely surrounded Henderson and prevented any attempt of the enraged people from getting at him and tearing him to pieces. The doomed man was rushed to the pile of wood that had been prepared for his funeral fire. Next they tied him fast to an iron rail with wire and chains. Cans of kerosene were splashed over his clothes and dozens of lighted matches cast onto the flammable pile. Stores throughout the city were deserted. The streets were full of men and women rushing to the courthouse to witness the man burning.

Just before the pyre was ignited Conway Younger, husband of the murdered woman, jumped at Henderson and slashed him across the face with a knife. At no time during the macabre episode did Henderson give any indication of pain or suffering, nor did he make an outcry other than a groan.

The northbound Central train arrived promptly at noon, crowded with people from the southern part of the county who were disappointment that they had come too late to witness the show. By then the man that was once John Henderson had been reduced to a handful of ashes.[1129]

Davis, Augustus "Gus"
Born: (Unknown)—Date of Death: 14 March 1901
Place: Austin County
Event: Legal Execution/Hanged

Augustus "Gus" Davis, a mulatto living with his mother near Bellville, was legally hanged at Austin for having committed a murder.[1130]

On 22 December 1900, Davis shot and killed Herman Schluens. The act was clearly premeditated, and seeming without cause. At the time of the incident Schluens was standing at the corner of the True Blue Saloon in Bellville, innocently talking with friends. Davis stepped up behind him and fired one shot from a pistol into Schluens head, killing him instantly. Sheriff's deputies J. B. Minton and Thomas Bethany, who were standing nearby at the time, immediately grabbed Davis and took him into custody. At the trial it was revealed that Davis had intentionally followed Schluens to town that day, tracking him the entire time until delivering the fatal, unexpected gunshot. No reason of any kind for Davis's actions was discovered.

The trap was sprung at 2:12 pm on Friday, 14 March 1901. The execution was a private one, witnessed by a handful of spectators who had obtained the requisite passes. When asked by Sheriff Palm is he had anything to say, Davis replied "No." Satisfied that he had done his duty, the sheriff replied "Goodbye Gus" then immediately wheeled and pulled the lever, catapulting Davis into eternity. The drop of seven feet, or more accurately the abrupt stop at the end, did the job. Davis was pronounced dead fourteen minutes later.

Two Unidentified Mexican Men
Born: (Unknown)—Date of Death: June 1901
Place: Gonzales County
Event: Lynching/Hanging and Shot

Newspaper accounts of the day claim that a posse numbering upwards of 500 men was scouring south Texas for Mexican outlaws. The outlaws had come over the border and committed several murders. Among the dead were Sheriff Brack Morris of Karnes County, Sheriff Richard Glover of Gonzales County and Henry Schnabel, a wealthy rancher in the area. Three of the outlaws were captured, one shot to death and one fatally lynched in an effort to get the names of his compatriots.

Morris was shot and killed while questioning a Mexican man about a stolen horse. During the interrogation the suspect's brother, Gregorio Cortez, rushed at Morris. Morris opened fire, wounding Cortez. Cortez then opened fire at Morris, hitting him four times. After the sheriff had already fallen to the ground, mortally wounded, Cortez shot him a fifth time.

Two days later Cortez was involved in another incident with lawmen during which he shot and killed Glover and a posseman named Henry Schnabel. The lawmen were in the process of arresting Cortez for the murder of Morris.

Although most historians have followed the party line on this case and listed Glover's given name as Robert, more recent research appears to establish conclusively that his name was actually Richard Martin Glover Jr., son of Richard Martin Glover and Delilah "Della" Bundick.

Cortez was charged and convicted of the killings, but was eventually pardoned by the governor. Two of his associates were less fortunate.[1131]

One Unidentified Black Man
Born: (Unknown)—Date of Death: 1 August 1901
Place: Tyler County
Event: Lynching

According to one unverified source, a black man was said to have been lynched at Mobile in Tyler County on Thursday, 1 August 1901 for insulting a white woman.[1132] No confirmation of this claim has been discovered.

Rocha, Juan
Born: circa 1841—Date of Death: 2 August 1901
Place: Bexar County
Event: Legal Execution/Hanged

On Friday, 2 August 1901, a frail, grey haired old man laboriously scaled the gallows stair at San Antonio. From the appearance of this aged Mexican man one might wonder what crime he could possibly have committed that would lead him to the gallows.

Sixty-year old Juan Rocha had been tried and convicted of murdering John Grimsinger, his employer. The incident took place in January at San Antonio.

Grimsinger was a thirty one year old bartender. He had married an attractive Mexican girl named Guadalupe Rodriguez. The couple had one child, a five-year old girl. Rocha was a peon, a Mexican day laborer or unskilled farm worker, who had been employed by the Rodriguez family for many years. He came along with Guadalupe to the marriage as part of her dowry. Rocha was a true peon in every sense, faithful, reliable and loyal in all regards, eager to do the bidding of the young woman. The new Mrs. Grimsinger was not happy in the marriage, which she shared in confidence with Rocha. Eager to help as always, Rocha was open to aiding in a plot to murder Mr. Grimsinger, which the two hatched over about a two week period.

Grimsinger's profession occasioned him to work at night. On the fatal day of the planned execution Grimsinger slept until noon, then rose briefly to eat a meal then returned to bed. Rocha crept into his sleeping chamber and, using an ax handle that he had fashioned himself, stove in Grimsinger's head. Rocha returned to the kitchen and informed Mrs. Grimsinger that the thing had been done. She dressed her husband and, when evening fell, Rocha carried the corpse out of the house with the intention of depositing it on the railroad tracks where a train would strike it and destroy the evidence. Owing perhaps to the fact that Rocha was frail and old, he dropped the body some distance short of the intended destination along the railroad tracks.

Finished with that aspect of the chore, Rocha returned to the house and assisted Mrs. Grimsinger in washing the blood stained clothing. When the scrubbing failed to yield the desired result they set fire to the building, hoping to destroy the evidence. Unfortunately for them the fire department responded promptly and saved the day...or perhaps not.

Meanwhile, the following morning a passerby discovered the body of Mr. Grimsinger and sounded the alarm. Both Mrs. Grimsinger and Rocha were arrested and tried. Rocha received the death sentence. Guadalupe Grimsinger received life in prison.[1133]

Wilder, Abe

Born: (Unknown)—Date of Death: 20 August 1901
Place: Red River County
Event: Lynching/Hanged and Burned

Elizabeth Ann "Bessie" Bullard married a well-known young Grayson County farmer named of John M. Caldwell on 8 May 1901. John and Bessie lived on a farm about two miles from the Bullard farm, on the old Caruthers Place. On Friday, 16 August 1901, she was murdered. A black man named Abe Wilder slit her throat while she was at home alone.

Bessie had been taught to help the needy. It was not unusual for her to give food to anyone who came by asking for a handout. When she answered a knock at her door about 10:00 am that day she found a homeless black man asking to be fed. Bessie left the man standing in the yard, went into the house, prepared him food, and sent him on his way. At about 4:00 pm her husband told her that he needed to check something in the field and would return later. After he left, Bessie being in the early stages of pregnancy and feeling the oppressive heat of an August afternoon, decided to take a break. She went out on the porch where she could feel a light breeze and sat down to read. Hearing a noise, she looked up and was seized by an intruder. It was the same man that she had treated with charity earlier in the day.

Bessie put up a desperate resistance and was about to overpower her attacker when he seized an ax and struck her on the head, knocking her senseless. When husband John returned from the field at approximately 6:30 pm he found no one at home. He went to the rear of the house and discovered the scene of a struggle, complete with bloodstains on the floor. John followed the trail outside to the stone cellar where he found a bloodstained ax laying near the opening. He went down into the basement and discovered the body of his wife, crumple on the floor. Death had come in a horrendous way. Her throat had been cut. The carotid artery and jugular vein were severed. In addition, she had been dealt several blows to the head. The debauchery had included outrage.

Clues pointed to the assailant being Abe Wilder. At about 1:00 pm on Tuesday, 20 August 1901, a posse crossed the Red River into Indian Territory and captured Abe. According to family lore, when Abe was apprehended he was wearing a coat that belonged to John Caldwell. The *Whitesboro News* claimed that a Barlow knife belonging to Caldwell was found on Abe's person as well.

The citizens' posse planned to go to the Bullard place near Sadler, home of the dead woman, and lynch Wilder there. Crowds began flocking into Whitesboro to witness the reckoning. By 7:30 pm it was claimed that 10,000 people had congregated. The town mayor addressed the mob, asking them to lay their weapons down and not to interfere with the posse or the prisoner. The vigilante mob, which at that point was en route to Whitesboro with Wilder, was tipped off. They changed their plan and decided to handle their business with the killer nearby, escorting Wilder to a thicket about two miles southwest of the Red Branch community at the Nelson Ranch.[1134]

The posse obtained a confession from Wilder. He admitted to the crime, in detail, after which he was taken to a tree and swung in the air by means of a rope attached to his neck. Wood and fodder were piled beneath him and a fire was built. Someone suggested that he ought not be allowed to die too quickly, thus Wilder was let down to the ground for a time while a party went to Dexter to procure coal oil. When they returned with the accelerant an ample quantity was thrown on the flame and the task of burning Wilder alive was completed. [1135]

Martinez, Felix
Born (Unknown)—Date of Death: 25 August 1901
Place: Karnes County
Event: Lynching/Shot

According to unverified reports, on Sunday, 25 August 1901, a Mexican man named Felix Martinez answered a knock at the door of his home near Kenedy and was shot to death.[1136]

Two Unidentified Black Men

Born: (Unknown)—Date of Death: 28 September 1901
Place: Harrison County
Event: Lynching/Beaten and Hanged

Walker, Thomas "Tom"

Born: (Unknown)—Date of Death: 28 September 1901
Place: Harrison County
Event: Lynching/Beaten to Death

Two Unidentified Black Men

Born: (Unknown)—Date of Death: 29 September 1901
Place: Harrison County
Event: Lynching/Hanged

Muckleroy, George

Born: (Unknown)—Date of Death: 29 September 1901
Place: Harrison County
Event: Lynching/Beaten to Death

Unidentified Black Woman

Born: (Unknown)—Date of Death: 4 October 1901
Place: Harrison County
Event: Lynching

A race riot of some sorts broke out near Hallsville on Saturday night, 28 September 1901. A mob of white men beat one black man so severely that he died. Next, the ruffians tried to break into the home of a black man named Thomas Walker who lived on the plantation of Julian Atwood. Walker shot and killed Atwood during his escape. Another black man was caught and allegedly hanged. Some reports indicate that this man was Walker.

On Sunday, 29 September 1901, two unidentified black men were taken out into the timber near the Gregg County line at Hallsville and lynched. George Muckleroy, a black man, was taken out and whipped to death near Marshall.[1137]

Undocumented sources claimed that an unknown black woman was lynched near Marshall on Friday, 4 October 1901, for having committed an assault. It is possible that she was one of the blacks lynched during the race riots that started on 28 September 1901.[1138]

Some newspapers claimed that the trouble had begun over crop mortgages, alleging that the blacks had secured advances against their harvest and refused to fulfill the contracts. Another newspaper claims that the race troubles started on Tuesday, 24 September 1901, when a black man named Rufus Bonner assaulted a white overseer on a road gang named Charles Livingston. Louis

Atwood, brother of Julian, was the constable and arrested Bonner. Bonner was publicly whipped at Hallsville. Threats were also made to whip Muckleroy and Walker.[1139]

Triggs, Judge
Born: (Unknown)—Date of Death: 8 October 1901
Place: McLennan County
Event: Unknown

Judge Triggs, a black man, was found dead near the Missouri, Kansas and Texas railroad tracks. Trigg's transgression or the means of his death were not mentioned.[1140]

Pearl, John "Little Johnny"
Born: 25 January 1876—Date of Death: 22 October 1901
Place: Coleman County
Event: Legal Execution/Hanged

John "Little Johnny" Pearl was tried and found guilty of the murder of Ed Tucker in December of 1900.

The victim, Tucker, was a cotton farmer who had a place south of Bangs. In December 1900, he disappeared. No one had seen him since 4 December 1900, and his friends and neighbors soon began to wonder where he had gone. A hired hand, Pearl, said Tucker had decided to move to back to his native Germany.

Pearl sold some of Tucker's cotton and cottonseed in Brownwood. He said Tucker had left him his wagon and team, along with other equipment and a bill of sale for some property. Tucker's friends and acquaintances had heard nothing of any such plan to return to the Fatherland. Finally someone checked the Tucker place and, on the second day of dragging the pond, uncovered Tucker's body. The corpse had been weighted down with a large rock.

Pearl was hanged on Tuesday, 22 October 1901. Sheriff Goodfellow reluctantly sprung the trap. The county called on Doctor T. M. Hays from nearby Santa Anna to certify the condemned man's death. Hays said that when he first put his stethoscope to Pearl's chest, "My heart was beating so hard that I couldn't be sure whether it was mine or his." Even though he had no doubt that Pearl was guilty, his role in springing the trap bothered Goodfellow for the rest of his life. He served as sheriff until 6 November 1906, and did not run again.

Right to the end Pearl maintained his innocence, insisting that he had helped to hide the body but did not do the killing. The man who actually killed Ed Tucker is said to have confessed on his deathbed some years later.[1141]

Pearl is buried at the Coleman City Cemetery.

Gordon, Gaines

Born: (Unknown)—Date of Death: 25 October 1901
Place: Wood County
Event: Lynching/Hanged

John W. Shoemaker, a farmer, was robbed and beaten to death near Quitman on Friday, 25 October 1901. The murderer, a black highwayman, stole about $200 in cash that Shoemaker had obtained from the sale of cotton.

Gaines Gordon was arrested under suspicion of having committed the murder. He was confined in the jail at Mineola. By evening a crowd of about 600 men had gathered, demanding that officers release Gordon to them. Their efforts were thwarted by the lawmen. Not long afterwards a mob of seventy-five armed and masked riders stormed the jail, beat the door in and removed Gordon. Such a formidable force was too great to resist. He was lynched from the water tower at the public well nearby.[1142]

King, Will

Born: circa 1879—Date of Death: 25 October 1901
Place: McLennan County
Event: Legal Execution/Hanged

On Saturday, 27 October 1900, Will King, a black man, had been causing a drunken disturbance at a local saloon owned by L. P. Hanna. Waco policeman William Davis Mitchell responded to the call for help and was dismounting from his horse when King opened fire on him with a pistol, hitting him with at least three shots. One bullet entered Mitchell's chest. Another hit him in the stomach, and the third in the shoulder. The wounds were fatal.

King was drunk at the time of the incident, and had threatened to shoot the first officer who tried to arrest him. He followed through on that oath. Mitchell fired several times at King and struck him once in the leg. Mitchell's body was brought across the street and his wife and children were summoned. He died about an hour later with his family by his side. King was apprehended, tried and convicted of Mitchell's murder. He was sentenced to death.

At 1:45 pm on Friday, 25 October 1901, Will King went to the gallows at Waco. In spite of eyewitness reports to the contrary, all the way to his appointment with the hangman King adamantly maintained that he did not shoot Mitchell nor did he even know him. He also claimed that it had been a man named Will Cook who shot him in the leg that day, not Mitchell. King said that he had been under the influence of intoxicants and had not realized anything that took place until the following morning. When asked how he was doing just prior to the trap door being sprung, King replied, "Oh, I am as well as could be expected under the circumstances."[1143]

King is buried at the First Street Cemetery.

McClinton, J. N.
Born: (Unknown)—Date of Death: 25 December 1901
Place: Lamar County
Event: Lynching/Shot

On Christmas Day 1901, Reverend J. N. McClinton answered a knock at the door at his residence in Paris. He was met by two armed persons who shot him dead.[1144] McClinton, a black man, had greeted his callers armed with a shotgun, however. A horse said to have belonged to one of the assailants was found nearby, sporting buckshot wound to the shoulder.

Owing to the fact that McClinton was a black man, this incident is being included under the presumption that his killing was some sort of vigilante act.

Norris, Anderson
Born: circa 1883—Date of Death: 10 January 1902
Place: McLennan County
Event: Legal Execution/Hanged

Anderson Norris, a black man, was tried and convicted of murdering Mrs. Emma French. The crime had taken place on 5 December 1900, in Navarro County, two miles from Barry.

Norris worked for the French family on their farm. He turned up sick that day and, in the afternoon, went to Mrs. French and asked for a target rifle that he had bartered for from her husband as compensation for the work that he had not yet finished. Mrs. French refused because Norris had not yet fulfilled his part of the bargain. Norris wrenched the gun from her hands and hit her in the head with it, killing her.

Norris began his walk to the gallows at Waco at 12:40 pm on Friday, 10 January 1902. He strode with a firm step, and when there spoke to the crowd, rambling on occasion and giving the impression that he was bargaining for time. Norris maintained his innocence to the end. James French, husband of the murdered woman, stood front and center beneath the gallows. He addressed French and said, "Mr. French you think that I killed your wife and I am going to hang for it, but the last thing I say is I did not do it. I hope that you will not hold anything against me for I am not guilty." Powerful words for a man but minutes from his death.

The black cap was pulled down and adjusted over his head. Breaking his vow that his address to Mr. French was to be the last thing he said, Norris uttered, "Oh my God. Goodbye everybody." And so it was. At 1:05 pm the trigger was pulled and Norris dropped to his death.[1145]

Morris, Thomas
Born: (Unknown)—Date of Death: 31 January 1902
Place: Navarro County
Event: Legal Execution/Hanged

Thomas Morris, a white man, was tried and convicted of murdering W. G. Broome. The incident took place on Thursday, 7 June 1900, near Corsicana. Broome had been a roommate of Morris. Broome's body was found in a tank of water weighted down with iron. Morris had disposed of Broome's belongings the day preceding the discovery of the body.

Although the evidence was purely circumstantial, Morris was convicted and sentenced to hang. At 12:30 pm on Friday, 31 January 1902, Morris's judgment was carried out. The drop was successful on the first try. Morris's neck was broken in the fall.[1146]

Bird, Carlbert
Born: circa 1886—Date of Death: 7 March 1902
Place: Caldwell-Guadalupe County
Event: Lynching/Presumed Hanged

Bird, Nathan
Born: March 1853—Date of Death: 7 March 1902
Place: Caldwell-Guadalupe County
Event: Lynching/Shot

On Friday evening, 7 March 1902, a group of ruffians went to the home of Nathan Bird, a black man, living near Prairie Lea and demanded his sixteen year old son Carlbert. The young man had apparently been involved in a brawl with a white boy, the latter having sustained a severe whipping and a broken arm. Mr. Bird refused, and was taken from his home and shot to death. The mob then took Carlbert. It is presumed that they lynched him, although no evidence of that claim has been found thus far. No trace of Carlbert was ever found.[1147]

Roan, John
Born: circa 1874—Date of Death: 19 April 1902
Place: Falls County
Event: Legal Execution/Hanged

John Roan, a black man, was tried and convicted of having outraged a woman. He was sentenced to death at the fall term of court in July 1901.

Roan maintained his innocence to the bitter end. During the morning hours of Saturday, 19 April 1902, black ministers attended to his spiritual needs, telling him that he had been forgiven by God and that he had nothing to fear. The B. C. Clark Light Guard, under the command of Captain George H. Carter, was requested by the sheriff and was posted around the jail at Marlin thirty minutes before the hanging.

At about 11:32 am Roan was taken from his cell and descended the narrow stairway to the gallows, then scaled the hangman's platform with a nervous tread. After a few brief remarks to the crowd he uttered a fervent prayer and reinforced his innocence while the sheriff adjusted the black cap on his head. At 12:20 pm the lever was pulled. Eight minutes afterwards Roan was declared dead.[1148]

de la Cerda, Ramon
Born: (Unknown)—Date of Death: 15 May 1902
Place: Cameron County
Event: Lynching/Shot

Robuck, William Emmett
Born: (Unknown)—Date of Death: 9 September 1902
Place: Cameron County
Event: Lynching/Shot

de la Cerda, Alfredo
Born: (Unknown)—Date of Death: 3 October 1902
Place: Cameron County
Event: Lynching/Shot

Rancher and suspected cattle thief Alfredo de la Cerda and his brother Ramón owned the Francisco de Asís Ranch. Their land bordered the expansive King Ranch. A Brownsville policeman had killed Alfredo's father in 1900. In 1901 Alfredo and Ramón de la Cerda were arrested and charged with rustling cattle from the King Ranch.

Texas Ranger Sergeant A. Y. Baker, Privates William E. Robuck and Harry Wallis were investigating cattle rustling when they came upon Ramón de la Cerda who was at the time in the process of branding cattle on the King Ranch property. Baker reported that de la Cerda fired at him and killed his horse, so he returned fire and shot de la Cerda in the head and killed him. All three rangers were arrested and charged with murder and released on $10,000 bond each. Miller, an employee of Mrs. M. H. King, was charged as an accessory. He was also released on a $10,000 bond.

The rangers were supported financially and legally by Richard King, former ranger captain John B. Armstrong and the Lyman brothers. The results of an inquest into the incident determined that Baker had acted in self-defense.

At about 10:00 pm on Tuesday, 9 September 1902, Baker, Robuck and a man named Jesse Miller, who has been reported as a ranger private, were riding their horses back to the ranger camp near Brownsville when several men ambushed them. Shots were fired from concealment. The assailants used shotguns loaded with buckshot. Robuck was struck and mortally wounded. He rode about 150 yards before he collapsed and died. Baker was slightly wounded. Miller was unscathed, although he had had his horse shot out from under him. The attackers escaped.

After an investigation by ranger Captain John A. Brooks Alfredo de la Cerda and five other men who were suspected of the ambush were arrested. A man named Heroulano Berbier, who was scheduled to testify against de la Cerda, was killed before he could do so. Robuck was buried by the Knights of Honor at the cemetery next to the Episcopal Church in Brownsville. His remains were later moved to the Bunton Cemetery in Dale, Caldwell County. Robuck was not married, and was survived by seven siblings. In some newspaper accounts his surname is spelled Robuck or Roebuck, but his ranger enlistment papers indicate that his name was Robuck.

Alfredo de la Cerda was released on bond. He swore that he would kill Baker or pay $1,000 to anyone who would do it for him. Baker was a tough lawman. Rather than spend the remainder of his days looking over his shoulder he acted first.

Shortly before 5:00 pm on Saturday, 3 October 1902, Baker caught Alfredo de la Cerda trying on a pair of gloves at a Brownsville store. He shot him through the store window with a Winchester rifle. Predictably, a rifle bullet at close range did the job. Baker contended that Alfredo was reaching for his pistol at the time, and that he had acted self-defense. Using money provided by the King family, and others, Baker was soon free on bond. On Tuesday, 13 October 1903, Baker was acquitted of the killings of Ramón and Alfredo de la Cerda. The jury was only out for deliberation for twenty minutes.

The twenty-five year old William Emmett Robuck, who hailed from Caldwell County, had been a ranger less than a year, having taken the oath in July 1901. It seems somewhat incomprehensible that Alfredo de la Cerda's death would be recorded as an assassination and Robuck's, which occurred under practically identical circumstances, would not.[1149]

Morgan, Dudley
Born: (Unknown)—Date of Death: 22 May 1902
Place: Harrison County
Event: Lynching/Burned to Death

Dudley Morgan, a black man, had assaulted and attempted to outrage Mrs. McKee, wife of the Texas and Pacific Railroad foreman at Lansing.

Morgan was captured and taken to Lansing by train. An appropriate execution site that was bordered by large trees was selected, consisting of a grassy area 200 yards wide and 300 yards long. Spectators arrived by the trainload, anxious to witness the festivities. Morgan was taken to the railroad section house where he was positively identified by Mrs. McKee. That formality dispensed of, he was escorted to the intended place of execution and chained to a stake by about 200 men armed with Winchesters. Once securely fastened thereto Morgan confessed to the crime, whereupon spectators took burning sticks from a fire that had already been prepared for the purpose and poked out his eyes. Such punishment might seem sufficient, even to the most ardent haters in the crowd, but this scene of macabre debauchery had only just begun.

The crowd slowly tortured the pitiful man, burning off his clothing and slowly roasting every square inch of his body as he cried out in agony to be shot in mercy. The victim, Mrs. McKee, was brought to the scene by carriage to see her assailant punished. Due to the vastness of the crowd the driver was unable to maneuver the hack close enough for her to get a good look. After a protracted episode of torture and burning Morgan's body had been so completely devoured by the flames that only the trunk remained.

Mrs. McKee's husband had been the one to strike the first match and set the mortal inferno loose on Morgan.[1150]

Olivarez, Andres
Born: circa 1884—Date of Death: 2 June 1902
Place: Nueces County
Event: Legal Execution/Hanged

According to reports, a Mexican man named Andres Olivarez was legally executed near Corpus Christi in Nueces County on Monday, 2 June 1902.

    Olivarez had been tried and convicted of murdering Mrs. James Hatch Jr., who was just eighteen years old at the time. A bloodstained hatchet found near the Hatch home was undoubtedly the murder weapon. The incident took place about two miles west of Corpus Christi. A farmhand named John Priour who was looking for a drink of water discovered the body, lying on the kitchen floor of the Hatch residence covered with blood while the woman's two infant children stood by crying. Five other Mexican men had been arrested along with Olivarez, who ultimately paid the price for the crime.[1151]

Warren, John
Born: (Unknown)—Date of Death: 15 August 1902
Place: Limestone County
Event: Legal Execution/Hanged

According to reports, a black man named John Warren, alias Will Bryan, was executed at Groesbeck in Limestone County on Friday, 15 August 1902. Warren had been tried and convicted of murder and robbery. On 1 November 1901, he had brutally murdered Doc Stephens, a black merchant, at his store near Mexia. Warren had overpowered Stephens and cut his throat with a knife, then robbed him.

    The trap was sprung at 2:13 pm. A crowd of nearly 5,000 looked on. Warren, who was neatly dressed, made his way to the gallows in a dignified manner. Although he declined to confess to his crime he addressed the crowd for practically thirty minutes, making a rambling oration touching on a variety of points. Songs were sung and prayers made. At the culmination the black cap was fitted, the trap sprung, and the thing done. Prior to the execution he had sold his body to research for $5.00.[1152]

Bailey, Walter
Born: (Unknown)—Date of Death: 22 August 1902
Place: Dallas County
Event: Legal Execution/Hanged

Walter Bailey, a black man, had been tried and convicted of the murder of Robert Hunter, another black man. That killing had taken place near Orrville about two years earlier. Bailey had designs on Hunter's wife. He had crept up to Hunter's home in the dark of night, slipped the barrel of a shotgun through a crack in the logs and fired a load of buckshot into Hunter. Not surprisingly, the wounds proved fatal.

During his trial, once the guilty verdict had been read, Bailey made a desperate attempt to escape. Afterwards he feigned insanity, and then began a hunger strike during which he diminished his health to the point where jailers had to force feed him in order that he might live to make his date with the executioner. Seems ironic.

At about 9:30 am on Friday, 22 August 1902, Bailey was hanged in the Dallas County jail. Few were in attendance. About fifty blacks gathered outside to satisfy their morbid curiosity. Held in private, Sheriff Blackwell robbed the hanging of all sensational features, saying that he was "...hoping to have a dampening effect on those emotional Negro murderers who think the surest and straightest route to heaven is straight from the gallows at the end of an inch [diameter] hemp rope."[1153]

Walker, Jesse
Born: circa 1880—Date of Death: 4 September 1902
Place: Waller County
Event: Lynching/Hanged

Jesse Walker, a mulatto man, was suspected of having outraged Mrs. Henry Loggins on Sunday night, 31 August 1902. The incident took place near Howth Station. Walker was arrested on Monday evening when Mrs. Loggins's little daughter positively identified him as the assailant. Mrs. Loggins herself became very faint and ill when she was asked if she recognized Walker as her despoiler.

Now certain of Walkers guilt, at about 7:30 pm on Thursday evening, 4 September 1902, a crowd of several hundred citizens forcibly removed the man from the jail at Hempstead and lynched him from a telephone pole in front of Robinson's Store. Walker made a full confession before he expired. Newspaper reports of the day emphasized that the crowd was very orderly, and that not a single shot was fired. The good people of Waller County made no attempt to disguise themselves. Everything was done in the open.[1154]

Saucedo, Vincente
Born: circa 1875—Date of Death: 19 September 1902
Place: Bexar County
Event: Legal Execution/Hanged

Vincente Saucedo, a Mexican man, was tried and convicted of having criminally assaulted his ten-year old stepdaughter. His case had been appealed, claiming that he blamed ardent spirits for all his troubles, and if he had done the terrible thing he was charged with that it had been accomplished while he was under the influence of whiskey. His excuse making convinced no one, and Saucedo was found guilty. He was sentenced to be executed for the heinous deed.

A hanging date of 5 September had been set, but was stayed until 19 September. On 11 September he was notified that Governor Joseph D. Sayers had ruled that his death sentence be carried out.[1155]

At about noon on Friday, 19 September 1902, Saucedo scaled the gallows stairs at San Antonio not looking at all like the person who had committed the vicious crime for which he was convicted. Saucedo was composed and confident, and carried himself in the manner of the bravest of men. During the reading of the death warrant he stood still, hands clasped in credulity and without a nervous shake, afterwards saying to the Sheriff, "All right Mr. Tobin."

He delivered a brief talk from the gallows in a voice that did not betray any hint of uneasiness. Then, as if concerned that he may pass un-forgiven, he begged for mercy from all present. At 12:08 pm Sheriff Tobin tripped the lever and Saucedo dropped through the trapdoor and into eternity.[1156]

Saucedo's memorial service was claimed by one newspaper of the day to have been, "the most remarkable funeral ever held in San Antonio." It was said that over 1,000 persons, mainly Mexicans, were in attendance. Dignitaries included Sheriff Tobin, the judge, the doctor who declared him dead at the hanging, and Saucedo's attorney F. A. Chapa. The funeral procession, led by a brass band playing a dirge, marched the three miles from the funeral home to San Fernando Cemetery.[1157]

Duncan, Utt
Born: (Unknown)—Date of Death: 4 October 1902
Place: Colorado County
Event: Lynching/Hanged

Late on the night of Friday, 3 October 1902, an improperly clad Utt Duncan, a black man, entered the telephone office at Eagle Lake where Miss Lena Harris was on duty as night operator. It is presumed that he had removed a portion of his livery for the purpose of outraging the young woman. Whether he succeeded or failed at that undertaking was not mentioned in the newspaper accounts, only that he had showed up missing some garments.

Duncan was apprehended, and in an effort to avoid a lynching was taken by freight train to Columbus and housed in the jail. The following morning about 100 men from Eagle Lake made their way to Columbus, intent on removing Duncan from the jail and settling the mater outside of court. After several failed attempts the mob finally managed to penetrate the jail and forcibly remove Duncan at around 6:00 pm. A speedy lynching followed.[1158]

Buchanan, Jim
Born: (Unknown)—Date of Death: 16 October 1902
Place: Nacogdoches County
Event: Legal Execution/Hanged

The title of the newspaper article of 19 October 1902, summed it up rather succinctly by simply saying, "The Texas Way."

The trial, conviction and execution of Jim Buchanan, a black man, probably sets an all time record for speedy hangings. The second placeholder is John Hood Prince of San Augustine County who made it to the gallows in twenty-four hours on 23 March 1920.

Buchanan was a self-confessed murderer, having killed three members of the Hicks family at Nacogdoches. On two occasions vigilante mobs had tried to lynch Buchanan but the sheriff, who displayed unusual and uncommon bravery, had managed to evade their efforts. Waiving his right to a thirty-day delay, Buchanan was brought to trial in the morning where he was found guilty almost instantly. A crude scaffold was erected outside the court building and the matter was settled for eternity.[1159]

The name of the undaunted sheriff, which no source found important enough to mention, was W. J. Campbell. He had been elected on 8 November 1898, and served until 6 November 1900. Such stalwart conduct in the face of the racial prejudices of the day is noteworthy.[1160]

Barton, Reddick "Reddish"
Born: (Unknown)—Date of Death: 21 October 1902
Place: Waller County
Event: Lynching/Hanged

Wesley, Joseph (Jim)
Born: (Unknown)—Date of Death: 21 October 1902
Place: Waller County
Event: Lynching/Hanged

Reddick Barton and Joseph Wesley were both black men. Barton was tried for the murder of Mrs. Susan Lewis, age sixty-three. That incident had taken place on Sunday, 12 October 1902. A jury, comprised in part of blacks had quickly returned a guilty verdict. A death sentence was sure to follow. Wesley was also tried for assault and murder. He too was found guilty, and once again the death penalty was virtually a certainty. During Wesley's trial an angry mob broke into the courtroom and attempted to remove him so they might speed up the process of his hanging.

A district judge had requested that the militia be summoned to aid in transporting both men to the jail at Houston for safekeeping. Judge Thompson countermanded that order, and when it was clear that no troops were going to arrive the mob overpowered Sheriff Lipscomb and took both men to the town square for some home grown justice. Sheriff Sparks of Lee County was accidentally shot and injured by a participant during the melee. Sheriff Lipscomb's back was severely injured in the affray.

Wesley and Barton were swiftly lynched from the cross arm of a telephone pole. Burning had been considered, but the mob thought that remedy might take too long to apply.[1161]

Mikel, Jeff
Born: (Unknown)—Date of Death: 13 December 1902
Place: Lee County
Event: Legal Execution/Hanged

Jeff Mikel, a black man, was tried and convicted of murdering his wife. The incident took place at Giddings on Friday, 12 April 1901. After killing her he tried to commit suicide by cutting his own throat. Although he did a yeoman like job, nearly severing his windpipe, Mikel managed to survive.

It seems that he had been working around the old mill for a time and his wife had refused to live with him, citing his cruel treatment as her reason. He would follow her to her places of work, and on the day of the killing trailed her to the home of Anderson Gamble, a black man. When she refused to go home with her he shot the woman with a pistol. The bullet failed to take effect, so Mikel picked up a grubbing hoe that was laying in the yard and struck her in the head with it, breaking the handle in two. He fled, but immediately returned and tried to take his own life.

Mikel scaled the gallows stairs at Giddings on Saturday, 13 December 1902, smoking a cigar and aided by Sheriff Scarborough. He delivered a speech, saying in part, "Well friends, I am about to leave you now. Let this be a warning to you all; mind how you stray away from home and who you stray with. This is [has] come to me all on account of marrying. I tell you friends let this be a warning to you. She might be mighty neat and nice, but if she don't treat you right you see where I am." Mikel went on to praise his wife's family for their kind treatment and forgiveness. At 1:40 pm Sheriff Scarborough pulled the lever and the trap door fell. The condemned man dropped seven feet before the hangman's rope plaid out. His neck was snapped and he died without a struggle.[1162]

Harris, John
Born: (Unknown)—Date of Death: 19 December 1902
Place: Lamar County
Event: Legal Execution/Hanged

John Harris, a black man, was tried and convicted of murdering City Marshal Benjamin Hill of Blossom.

Hill died from gunshot wounds he received when he attempted to detain John Harris who had been firing a gun at an outdoors church festival. During the arrest Harris shot Hill three times. It remains unclear as to why Hill thought it was a good idea to discharge a firearm at a church bazaar.

Harris was convicted of Hill's murder on 27 October 1902. He received the death sentence. Harris's hanging date was set, but a petition for commutation of his sentence was filed thus postponing the event. On 18 December 1902, the governor turned down the petition and released Harris for execution.

Hill went to the gallows at Paris shortly after noon on Friday, 19 December 1902. He delivered a brief speech from the platform, encouraging both blacks and whites to live better, saying that ardent spirits and gambling had brought his life to an early conclusion. At precisely 2:22 pm Sheriff Carpenter pulled the trigger and the trap door fell, launching Harris into the ever after.[1163]

O'Neal, Random
Born: (Unknown)—Date of Death: 14 January 1903
Place: Brazoria County
Event: Lynching/Shot

Tunstall, Charles
Born: (Unknown)—Date of Death: 14 January 1903
Place: Brazoria County
Event: Lynching/Shot

Random O'Neal and Charles Tunstall, both black men, had been confined in the jail at Angleton awaiting trial for the murder of County Attorney Edward C. Smith. That incident had taken place some months earlier while Smith was attempting to arrest another black man. Under cover of darkness person or persons unknown crept into the jail at Angleton and shot both men, setting fire to the bedclothes, which practically burned one man's leg off. The killings were not discovered until the following morning.[1164]

Ransom, John
Born: circa 1864—Date of Death: 3 April 1903
Place: Williamson County
Event: Legal Execution/Hanged

John Ransom, a black man, was tried and convicted of the murder of Leslie Rucker, a black farmer. The incident took place near Circleville. Ransom was sentenced to death.

On Friday, 3 April 1903, the condemned man ate a hearty breakfast as prospective spectators began to gather outside the jail. The hanging was to be private, so only a handful of witnesses were allowed in to observe the event. His eyes twinkled as if it were the happiest day of his life while he looked through bars. Ransom had confessed to his crime, before God and man, so he was prepared to meet his maker.

At about 8:00 am Reverend T. S. Barkus, a Methodist preacher, baptized Ransom. As he stepped onto the trap he asked a fellow black inmate named Lon Crayton to lead a prayer, which he did in a very intelligible manner. As the cap was pulled over Ransom's head he was observed to tremble a bit. Sheriff Sam Connell pulled the trigger and Ransom shot into eternity.[1165]

Johnson, Hensley
Born: circa 1885—Date of Death: 25 April 1903
Place: Panola County
Event: Lynching/Hanged

On Saturday, 25 April 1903 Hensley Johnson, an eighteen-year old black man, was lynched at Carthage for having molested a four-year old girl white girl. The victim was the daughter of a very respectable family in the area. A mob caught up with him and strung him up from a telephone pole at the public square where he remained until the following morning.[1166]

Johnson, Rip
Born: (Unknown)—Date of Death: 14 May 1903
Place: Walker County
Event: Legal Execution/Hanged

Rip Johnson, a black man, was tried and convicted of the murder of Mose Washington, another black man. The incident had taken place in June 1902. Johnson received the death sentence.

At about 1:00 pm on Thursday, 14 May 1903, Johnson began his walk from the penitentiary to the scaffold, which had been erected alongside the railroad track about one half mile from Huntsville. He was asked if he wished to speak and he declined. One of the preachers in attendance announced that he had spoken with Johnson and he had made his peace with God. The condemned man asked permission to remove his shoes, which was granted. As Sheriff Brooks pulled the black cap over his head and adjusted the ropes and bindings Johnson said, "Be sure and send my things to my mother." At 2:15 pm, in front of 2,000 witnesses, the trap was pulled and Johnson dropped to his death, neck broken and throat severely lacerated.[1167]

Green, Charley
Born: (Unknown)—Date of Death: 23 May 1903
Place: Fort Bend County
Event: Legal Execution/Hanged

Charley Green, a black man, was tried, convicted and sentenced death for a criminal assault that occurred near Duke on 23 October 1902. Green was a convict on the House plantation, and had been released from custody two days earlier. He assaulted a sixty-five year old black woman named Flora Jones who was a housekeeper for Wesley Fay. After Fay had left for his blacksmith shop, Green entered the home and committed the outrage. A convict guard sergeant at the House plantation, identified as Mr. Boykin, started in pursuit with bloodhounds. Green shot and wounded Boykin, but was captured shortly thereafter.

On Saturday, 23 May 1903, Green made a short walk from the jail to the gallows. He said he was a child of God and wanted to meet all good people in heaven. At 3:30 pm Green was escorted to the scaffold where Reverend Nathan Powell, pastor of the white Methodist church, led a prayer. Sheriff Pearson read the death warrant and asked Green if he wished to make a statement. Green made a rambling and disconnected speech, claiming innocence and blaming others for a conspiracy against him. At the end of his oration he became nervous and begged for mercy. At 4:02 pm the trap was sprung. Green was pronounced dead from strangulation at 4:20 pm. The newspaper said this was Sheriff Pearson's first execution and that he had conducted himself like a veteran. [1168]

Shutt, J. E.

Born: (Unknown)—Date of Death: 29 May 1903
Place: Bowie County
Event: Legal Execution/Hanged

J. E. Shutt, a prominent white businessman, was tried and convicted of murdering J.C. Whitener at Boston. Shutt was executed by hanging on Friday, 29 May 1903.[1169]

Johnson, Henry

Born: (Unknown)—Date of Death: 30 May 1903
Place: Kaufman County
Event: Legal Execution/Hanged

Henry Johnson, a black man, was tried and convicted of having outraged a white woman named Mrs. Charles Whitworth.

Johnson was tried, found guilty, and sentenced to death. For his hanging the gallows was erected at the railroad yards at Kaufman, in plain view of thousands of onlookers. Sheriff Henderson's force, along with the Terrell Rifles, brought Johnson directly to the spot from the jail. The sheriff placed the noose around the condemned man's neck and carefully adjusted it. Before the black cap was pulled over his head Johnson made a brief speech, confessing his guilt and imploring other blacks not to follow his path. At 1:04 pm the trap was sprung and Johnson dropped eight feet, snapping his neck as the rope plaid out. Within minutes of this nasty business having been concluded the throng quietly dispersed. The town returned to its usual, tranquil appearance.[1170]

The following day, newspaper headlines proclaimed that, "Black Cap for Negro Johnson - [The] Brute Who Criminally Assaulted Mrs. Whitworth is Hanged."

Harkey, George
Born: (Unknown)—Date of Death: 30 June 1903
Place: Camp County
Event: Legal Execution/Hanged

The headlines read, "Condemned Negro Advises Colored People to Quite Carrying Pistols and Be Good."

George Harkey, a black man, was tried and convicted of killing his neighbor, Grip Wright, on 24 September 1902. Wright was also a black man. Harkey used a shotgun to do the work. The incident took place near his home, located about twelve miles southwest of Pittsburg. It seems that Harkey's cotton harvest had been levied upon for debts owed and Wright had been contracted to haul it to town. When Harkey learned of this he went hunting for the man, overtaking him on a lane not far distant. He fired a blast into Wright, then reloaded and fired a second time as he let out a yell. Satisfied, he returned home

About 7,000 people flocked to Pittsburg throughout the course of the day to witness the hanging, which was the first such legal event of its kind in Camp County. A gallows had been set up in an open field about 400 yards southwest of the old mill. At 3:00 pm Harkey was escorted to a hack by Sheriff Stafford and driven to the intended spot, three quarters of a mile from the jail. The condemned man was in good spirits, smiling and joining in with enthusiasm in an animated way as several religious songs were rendered. From the gallows Harkey made a five minute speech, emphasizing that God had forgiven him and warning Colored People to, "...Quite Carrying Pistols and Be Good." At 3:53 pm the sheriff sprung the trap. Harkey was pronounced dead in fifteen minutes.[1171]

Allen, Mooney
Born: (Unknown)—Date of Death: 23 July 1903
Place: Jefferson County
Event: Lynching/Shot

Mooney Allen, a black man, had shot his wife the previous year and was known by lawmen to be a desperate character. At about 11:00 am on Thursday, 23 July 1903, neighbors called the police about a family disturbance at Allen's house. When an officer arrived Allen shot at him with a Winchester rifle. The officer quickly retreated to safety.

Beaumont Police Officer Walter W. Stansbury lived near where the incident was taking place and responded to the shooting. As he approached the house Allen shot him once in the chest, mortally wounding him. Stansbury was taken to the hospital where he died at 4:50 pm.

Allen fled the scene, but was later located by the sheriff and a deputy who were on horseback at the time. Allen refused to surrender, so the sheriff told him that officer Stansbury was not seriously wounded and that he could make bail if he returned to town peacefully. Allen agreed. The sheriff and the deputy rode in front of Allen on the way back to town. Allen was still armed. He stopped along the way at a saloon and had four shots of whiskey.

As the group entered the downtown area they saw that a crowd had assembled. At that point the sheriff tried to position himself behind Allen to prevent him from breaking and running. Allen is said to have pointed his gun at the sheriff. Gunfire erupted. During the melee the sheriff shot Allen in the right arm, rendering him unable to operate his rifle. According to reports, during the shooting exchange the sheriff fired five times and Allen fired four times...all at close range.

Allen fled down a city street with the crowd of angry citizens hot on his heels, shooting at him as they ran. Eventually a bullet from the mob hit Allen, and he fell to the ground mortally wounded. Several members of the now highly excited horde fired numerous times into Allen's lifeless body before finally regaining composure and returning to civilized conduct.[1172]

One Unidentified Black Man
Born: (Unknown)—Date of Death: 31 July 1903
Place: Cherokee County
Event: Lynching

Newspaper reports of the day claimed that an unidentified black man had cursed and insulted a group of white women as he rode past their home on horseback. He followed up his verbal assault by firing a gunshot through the Findley home.

A crowd quickly formed and captured the man. He was taken to the river bottoms near Alto, about sixty-five miles south of Tyler on the Tyler Southwestern Railroad. Nothing had been seen or heard of the fellow since his disappearance.[1173]

Subsequent articles seem to indicate that the black man involved in this incident was dealt a sound whipping and released. Other sources claim that he was lynched. There is no conclusive evidence of the man's death. The authors have chosen to list this case in the interest of completeness.

Two Unidentified Black Men
Born: (Unknown)—Date of Death: 12 August 1903
Place: Grayson County
Event: Lynching

Newspaper accounts of the day speak of a racial incident at Whitesboro. A plot by black people to kill whites was uncovered there, which initiated an uprising during which blacks were flushed from their homes and maltreated. The lynching of two black was implied, but in none of the several reports by newspapers of the day are those claims clear enough to substantiate the veracity of the hangings. None-the-less, this incident is being included in the interest of completeness. [1174]

Davis, Walter
Born: (Unknown)—Date of Death: 1 October 1903
Place: Harrison County
Event: Lynching/Hanged

On Thursday morning, 1 October 1903, Harrison County Precinct 4 Constable Charles Lott Hays and Deputy Constable Sid Keasler went to a farmhouse to arrest a black man named Mich Davis. Davis was wanted on a warrant they were holding. Davis's brother Walter said that Mich was not there, and that he had been working in a nearby cotton field.

Hays and Keasler galloped their horses to the field to prevent Walter Davis from arriving ahead of them and warning his brother of their presence. Mich saw the officers coming and attempted to get his gun from a nearby building. Hays and Keasler beat him to the gun and made the arrest. After the lawmen had left the farmhouse Walter took his shotgun and went to the road to intercept the group. When the lawmen approached with Mich in custody Walter raised his shotgun and demanded that they release his brother. Walter Davis fired a load of buckshot into Hays's side. Keasler fired at Walter Davis, striking him in the side. Walter was only slightly injured. Hays fell from his horse mortally wounded.

Walter Davis was arrested and placed in the jail at Marshall. Mich Davis as well as Nathan Hilton, the Davis' stepfather, was also arrested. Mob violence was feared. Sure enough, a number of men from Haleyville, Longview and the western part of the county soon began to arrive. By 7:00 pm it was clear to all that an attempt was going to be made on the jail. Lawmen tried to call the governor and request that the militia be called out. That initiative failed. Sheriff Calloway requested Major G. P. Rains and the Marshall militia to respond. By 7:30 pm a detachment of six soldiers had made their way to town and were seen near the jail. On the signal from a man that no one seemed to know the gathered mass moved off towards the jail, practically in unison. Along the way they picked up a telephone pole to use as a battering ram, and in medieval fashion broke down the jail door and entered Davis's cell. A rope was strung around his neck and the doomed man was dragged into the street. The mob's first intention was to hang Davis, so he was walked west on Fannin Street the south on Bridge Street to Russell's Mill where the thing was done. A number of shots were fired into his body for good measure. [1175]

Reyna, Marguerito
Born: (Unknown)—Date of Death: 4 December 1903
Place: Lavaca County
Event: Legal Execution/Hanged

Marguerito Reyna, a Mexican man, was executed at Hallettsville for having outraged a young girl. Newspaper reports of the day describe the victim as "a child."

No doubt there were few who pitied Reyna, given the nature of his debauchery. To the end he professed his innocence. When asked by Sheriff Noble if he wished to speak he declined, saying that although he was not guilty the law had ordered his hanging and therefore it would have to be done. On the gallows Reyna removed his shoes and gave them to a young Mexican boy who was among the onlookers. He bid everyone farewell and shook hands all around. A thirty foot high fence had been erected to ensure the privacy of the hanging. At the prescribed time the thing was done.[1176]

Fugett, Henry
Born: (Unknown)—Date of Death: 12 February 1904
Place: Johnson County
Event: Legal Execution/Hanged

"Cleburne Wife Murderer Executed..." was the headline announcing the hanging of Henry Fugett, a black man with a very unfortunate surname who, as the banner exclaimed, had killed his wife. The reason for Fugett having ending his wife's life prematurely was not given.

Fugett was smiling as he scaled the gallows at Cleburne and the black cap was pulled down over his head. He had shaken hands and was quite reserved. At 12:25 pm Sheriff Long cut the rope and sprung the trap. Fugett's neck was broken and he was pronounced dead in six minutes.[1177]

Maynard, John
Born: (Unknown)—Date of Death: 21 March 1904
Place: Montgomery County
Event: Lynching/Hanged

John Maynard, a black man, was found hanging from a telephone pole near Montgomery Station, about 100 miles from Houston on the tracks of the Santa Fe railroad. It was presumed that he had not gotten himself into that condition on his own. Maynard had confessed to having been involved in the beating and robbery of a group of railroad workers, one of whom had died afterwards.[1178]

Smith, Brozier
Born: circa 1884—Date of Death: 25 March 1904
Place: Ellis Oak County
Event: Legal Execution/Hanged

Brozier Smith, a twenty-one year old black man, shot and killed his wife at Waxahachie in a most brutal and heartless manner during February 1904. He was tried and convicted of the killing and sentenced to death. That judgment was carried out on Friday, 25 March 1904.[1179]

Murray, Will
Born: (Unknown)—Date of Death: 25 April 1904
Place: Jefferson County
Event: Legal Execution/Hanged

Will Murray, a black man, was tried and convicted of murdering Josephine Baker, his sweetheart. The incident had taken place at Beaumont. Murray was sentenced to death.

Murray's verdict was carried out on Monday, 25 April 1904, when he was publically hanged for his crime.[1180]

Simmons, Henry
Born: circa 1874—Date of Death: 2 May 1904
Place: Travis County
Event: Legal Execution/Hanged

In a trial that took less than three hours from start to finish Henry Simmons, a black man who used the alias Williams, was tried and convicted of the outrage and murder of Miss Lulu Sandberg, a white woman. The incident had taken place at Austin. Simmons waived his right to a thirty-day delay between sentencing and execution, and selected Monday, 2 May 1904 as his hanging date.

Simmons kept his date with the hangman in an unusually uneventful display at Austin.[1181]

Kenny, George
Born: (Unknown)—Date of Death: 28 May 1904
Place: Anderson County
Event: Legal Execution/Hanged

George Kenny, a black man, was hanged on Saturday, 28 May 1904. The event occurred at Palestine, before a crowd of 3,000 people. The procession started from the jail at 1:30 pm, with the prisoner riding in a wagon followed by a mixed crowd of several thousand people. Kenny walked firmly up the gallows. He spoke for three minutes, protesting his innocence and warning young people of his race to lead a right life. He said he was at peace with God, and would go straight to heaven. Strangely he urged all blacks to vote for Henry Watts for sheriff. The black cap was placed over his head and the noose around his neck. At 1:46 pm the trap was sprung. The fall was seven feet and it did not break his neck. He was pronounced dead about twelve minutes later.

Kenny was hanged for the alleged criminal assault of three-year old Ethel Hawkins, The outrage had occurred near Elkhart, on 13 August 1903. Kenny had been severely wounded by a posse and later arrested by Sheriff Watts. He was tried, convicted, and sentence to death. Appeals were denied. He had requested a public execution. [1182]

Losario, Basente
Born: circa 1886—Date of Death: 16 June 1904
Place: Live Oak County
Event: Legal Execution/Hanged

Basente Losario, a sixteen-year old Mexican man, who is referred to in some newspaper articles as Vicente Lisono, was convicted of murdering a man named C. Soir.

Losario had killed Soir with an ax, and robbed him of some assorted garments and $18.00 in cash. After the killing Losario fled to Rio Grande City where he was eventually captured by Sheriff Wash Shelly of Starr County. When he was taken into custody he was wearing the murdered man's shoes, undershirt, hat and trousers.

Losario went to the gallows at Oakville on Thursday, 16 June 1904. He ascended the stairs with a firm and steady gate, made a few farewell remarks and asked for forgiveness. Losario thanked Sheriff Lewis for the kind treatment he had been accorded during his confinement. The black cap was fitted and at 11:20 pm the trap was sprung. Losario met his fate with dignity and composure.[1183]

Larremore, Jonathan W. "John"
Born: (Unknown)—Date of Death: 26 July 1904[1184]
Place: Caldwell County
Event: Lynching/Shot

Eight or ten white men took Jonathan Larremore, a black schoolteacher and Chairman of the Caldwell County Republican executive committee, from his home at Lockhart under force of arms and shot him to death. The incident took place at about 2:00 am on Wednesday, 26 July. They dragged Larremore as far as the gate then shot him with a .38 caliber pistol. Mrs. Larremore fired three times at the mob, causing them to disperse. She claimed to have hit one of the culprits. [1185]

Tom Catherton (Coperton), another black man and a friend of Larremore, was "whitecapped" on the same evening. Both were accused of acting "arrogant" towards whites, particularly since the Republican Party had adopted a race plank.[1186]

State records show Larremore's date of death as 26 July 1904, while newspaper accounts indicate that the incident occurred on 27 July 1904. It is unclear which is correct.

Tucker, Oscar Lee
Born: circa 1887—Date of Death: 31 August 1904
Place: Colorado County
Event: Lynching/Hanged

Oscar Tucker (Turner), a seventeen-year old black man, had attempted to outrage Minnie Schultz, the nineteen-year old daughter of a wealthy white farmer. Tucker was apprehended and confined in the jail at Weimar pending arraignment. When officers went to the cell to remove him for trial they discovered him dead, hanging from a forty-foot long rope that had drawn the man up to a hole in the ceiling of his cell. No one seemed to have a clue as to how the cell had been breached, or for that matter how Tucker wound up in that condition. There were no signs of forced entry.[1187]

One Unidentified Mexican Man
Born: (Unknown)—Date of Death: 30 November 1904
Place: McLennan County
Event: Unknown

In Carrigan's book *The Lynching Culture* the author claims that an unidentified Mexican man was found dead along the Texas and Central railroad tracks. His means of death or his transgression were not mentioned. This case, although unconfirmed, is being included in the interest of completeness.[1188]

Hernandez, Appolonario
Born: (Unknown)—Date of Death: 23 December 1904
Place: Nueces County
Event: Legal Execution/Hanged

On Tuesday, 16 February 1904, Appolonario Hernandez, a Mexican man, murdered his wife in a field near Bluntzer.[1189] She had been shot twice, and when authorities arrived she was still barely alive and able to identify her husband as the killer. Hernandez was found two days later in Alice.

    Catholic Priests Father Jailett and Father Comer arrived at about 1:00 pm on Friday, 23 December 1904, and for several minutes prayed with the condemned man. At 1:55 pm the walk to the gallows commenced. Hernandez, calm and collected, bid his jailers "adios" as the black cap was adjusted and his hands and feet bound. At exactly 2:00 pm the trap door was sprung and Hernandez flew into eternity.[1190]

One Unidentified Black Man
Born: circa 1859—Date of Death: 28 December 1904
Place: McLennan County
Event: Unknown

In Carrigan's book *The Lynching Culture* the author claims that an unidentified forty-five year old black man was found dead in a caboose at the Missouri, Kansas and Texas railroad yard. His means of death or his transgression were not mentioned by the source. This case, although unconfirmed, is being included in the interest of completeness.[1191]

McNeil, Wilson
Born: (Unknown)—Date of Death: circa 1905
Place: Travis County
Event: Legal Execution/Hanged

According to sources, a white man named Wilson McNeil was legally executed at Travis County sometime during 1905. McNeil had been tried and convicted of murder.[1192]

By means of background, on 19 July 1878, Travis County Deputy Sheriff Edgar Maurice Bowie Moore, Williamson County Deputy Sheriff Ahilah W. "Caige" Grimes and a group of Texas Rangers were in Round Rock to stake out the bank. An informant, Jim Murphy, reported that the Bass Gang was planning to pull off a hold up at the Williamson County Bank.

Deputies Grimes and Moore observed Frank Jackson Sam Bass and Seaborn Barnes hitch their horses in the alley north of Georgetown Avenue and make their way towards the Kopperal's General Store. When Grimes approached one of the gang members who were purchasing tobacco, claimed by most to have been Sam, he asked him "do you have a pistol?" Sam replied, "I'll let you have it", at which point Sam shot him. Frank and Seaborn are also said to have opened fire. Moore, who had been waiting outside the store, began shooting as well. He wounded Sam Bass in the hand before being shot in the chest that took him out of the affray. In all there were six bullet holes in Moore's body.

As the gang attempted to flee from town Seaborn Barnes was shot and killed as he attempted to make his getaway. Some claim Texas Ranger George Herold shot him, and others believe that a local citizen named Conner fired the fatal bullet. Sam Bass was also shot and fatally wounded as he fled the town. Several have taken credit for firing that shot as well.

Almost a decade later, on 10 November 1887, Moore was shot and killed while attempting to arrest a man on a warrant. When Moore entered the man's home he produced a rifle and a struggle took place. An unknown person, believed to have been Wilson McNeil, entered the house and shot Moore with a shotgun.

McNeil is said to have been hanged in 1905 for another murder, although verification of that execution has not been found.

Munoz, Carlos
Born: (Unknown)—Date of Death: 16 February 1905
Place: Caldwell County
Event: Lynching/Hanged

On Thursday, 16 February 1905, a mob took a Mexican man named Carlos Munoz away from a constable and sheriff deputies by force of arms near the town of Dale in Caldwell County. Munoz had been arrested for having molested Mrs. Miers, the wife of a local farmer. He was spirited off into the woods and lynched.[1193]

Johnson, William

Born: (Unknown)—Date of Death: 17 February 1905
Place: Bastrop County
Event: Lynching/Shot

William Johnson, a black man, had been captured in connection with the criminal assault of Mrs. Powell Tiffany. Johnson confessed, and indicated that there were three women who were also involved in the crime.

None of the alleged female accomplices were ever located. During his capture Johnson was shot to pieces by a mob. While in pursuit of Johnson the posse discovered the body of a Mexican who had been lynched in Caldwell County (see Carlos Munoz above). The unfortunate fellow was still hanging from a tree where the thing had been done.[1194]

Reeves, John H.

Born: (Unknown)—Date of Death: 17 February 1905
Place: Red River County
Event: Legal Execution/Hanged

John H. Reeves, a white man, was convicted in the district court at Clarksville of murdering his twenty-eight year old wife, Minnie Mahala McCuiston. The incident took place during the night of 30 March–1 April 1904. Family genealogists cite the date as 1 April 1904.[1195]

The couple lived on a farm near Avery. Mrs. Reeves was the daughter of a wealthy farmer and had one young female child by a previous marriage. When Reeves, who had previously been a farmhand working for the elder S. J. McCuiston, had wed Minnie the couple were given a farm and some stock to get them started. The pair had apparently cohabitated happily, until John Reeves decided to break her neck and bury her in an onion patch.

Reeves was convicted of the crime on 22 June 1904. His sentence was death. At about 2:03 pm on Friday, 17 February 1905, Sheriff Dinwiddie sprung the trap and that judgment was carried out. Reeves was declared dead after about twelve minutes. His body was cut down and taken to Avery for burial.[1196]

Minnie Mahala McCuiston is buried at the Garland Cemetery at Annona in Red River County.[1197]

Schwartz, Conrad

Born: circa 1885—Date of Death: 22 March 1905
Place: DeWitt County
Event: Legal Execution/Hanged

Conrad Schwartz, a white man, was tried and convicted of murdering William E. Earle, a telegraph operator. Schwartz had tried to rob the railroad station at Yorktown where Earle was employed.

Before going to the gallows Schwartz made a second confession. His first had been in a letter he had written to his victim's wife, on 11 March 1905. Schwartz was hanged at Cuero on Wednesday, 22 March 1905.[1198]

Young, John Henry
Born: circa 1885—Date of Death: 31 March 1905
Place: Ellis County
Event: Legal Execution/Hanged

John Henry Young, a black man, was tried and convicted of murder. The gallows were erected on the same spot where Brozier Smith had been hanged about a year earlier. He was executed at Waxahachie on Friday, 31 March 1905.[1199]

Sheriff Minnick used the rope belonging to former Sheriff W.A. Stewart of Johnson County, which had been used in eighteen hangings. Stewart had it made in St. Louis in 1898, to be used in the execution of John B. Shaw. The rope was made by a German and was hand twisted, constructed of the very best quality hemp available at the time. The thing was eighteen feet long and cost $12.50. The hangman's knot that had originally been made for use with Shaw had never been changed. [1200]

Stevens, Julius
Born: (Unknown)—Date of Death: 14 April 1905
Place: Gregg County
Event: Lynching/Shot

Julius Stevens, a black man, was accused of assaulting Carl Anderson, a sawmill operator at Longview. He was arrested and taken to the jail to await a hearing.

On Tuesday, 14 March 1905, a mob forcibly entered the jail at Longview, compelling the jailer to surrender the keys. Stevens was removed from his cell and given a chance to confess. He requested paper and pencil with which to write a final note to his mother. Vigilantes fatally shot him, hitting him in the heart with a .44 caliber bullet.[1201]

Vann, Holly
Born: circa 1875—Date of Death: 12 May 1905
Place: Dallas County
Event: Legal Execution/Hanged

Holly Vann, a thirty-year old white man, was tried and convicted of murdering a merchant named Sol Aranoff. The incident occurred at Oak Cliff on 29 November 1904. He was tried immediately, convicted in December and appealed in January. Meanwhile he escaped from jail but was quickly captured and returned.

On the day preceding his hanging Vann was baptized into the Catholic Church by Father James M. Hays of the Sacred Heart Cathedral. Afterwards the priest administered communion and remained with Vann while he prayed. A crowd of about 4,000 turned out to see Vann off. Decked out in a clean black suit, white shirt, black tie and white chrysanthemum pinned to his lapel Vann scaled the gallows stairs at Dallas on Friday, 12 May 1905, professing his innocence to the end. Holding his bible in his left hand he delivered a brief address, saying in part, "Boy's, read this book and follow all its teachings. In an hour when no friend on earth can aid you, the things that are in this old book will give you strength to bear what God has sent upon you." Vann went on to add, "It was keeping bad associates and using strong drink that has brought me to this and they will ruin any man." Vann's calmness seemed to permeate the crowd as he underwent the pinning of his hands and feet and the fitting of the black cap.

On balance, a calmer, more polite and pious condemned man had never stepped on a gallows. At 1:15 Sheriff Ledbetter pulled the lever and the trap was sprung. Holly Vann went home to meet his God. Vann is buried at the Oak Cliff Cemetery in Dallas.[1202]

Collins, Sam
Born: (Unknown)—Date of Death: 19 May 1905
Place: Harrison County
Event: Legal Execution/Hanged

Sam Collins, a black man who used the alias Sam Fite, was employed as a gravedigger at Marshall. He had a wife and several children, but abandoned them in favor of a mistress he took up with at Jonesville, sixteen miles from Marshall. Collins's new paramour was a black woman named Maria Jacobs who hailed from Greenwood, Louisiana.

The couple rented a cabin from W. S. Curry at Jonesville. On Saturday, 2 September 1905, Curry saw Collins, who owed him $3.00 rent. Collins claimed that his wife had died and that he needed money to buy a coffin so he could ship her body back to Greenwood. Curry was suspicious, so he sent a doctor and D. L Hill, justice of the peace, to investigate. They found the body of Maria Jacobs at the cabin, badly bruised and battered.

Collins was charged with murder. A grand jury was in session, so he was rapidly convicted. The only witness to the crime, other than Collins, was the four year old son of Maria Jacobs. Collins had used a freshly cut gumwood branch to beat Jacobs to death. The weapon proved very effective. Collins was sentenced to death. He maintained his innocence all the way to the gallows.

Collins arrived at the prison farm on Friday, 19 May 1905. He scaled the gallows stairs with the aid of deputies. Reverends M. J. Johnson and Noah Murphy assisted Collins with prayer, and lead in the singing of hymns which Collins joined in on. Sheriff Munden cut the rope and the trap door was sprung on Collins, alias, Fite, at 12:37 pm. [1203]

Manning, Will T.
Born: (Unknown)—Date of Death: 7 July 1905
Place: Hunt County
Event: Legal Execution/Hanged

On Thursday, 29 December 1904, Will Manning, a white man, murdered his wife by poisoning her. The incident took place just twenty-four hours after she had given birth to a daughter. The woman, Eva McGuire, was from one of the most respected families in the county. No one suspected that Manning had killed her until several months later when his peculiar actions gave him away.

Apparently Manning wanted to marry his wife's fifteen-year old sister, Ida. Her father found out about the proposed nuptials, discovered a forged note by Manning, and had him arrested. In jail Manning bragged to deputies about how he had been intimate with the underage girl while his wife was still alive. Somehow Manning believed that his father-in-law would drop the forgery charge and let him marry Ida. After interviewing Ida deputies learned that Manning had told her that his wife would not live long and that they would soon be married.

An autopsy was ordered. Traces of strychnine were found in the woman's stomach. Manning was convicted of the criminal assault of his late wife's sister, Ida McGuire, and forgery. He was sentenced to life for prison. A grand jury indicted him for murder. He was tried, convicted, and sentenced to death. Manning requested that his judgment not be appealed.

Manning was executed by hanging at Greenville on Friday, 7 July 1905.[1204] While in jail awaiting the inevitable day he read the bible and sang to crowds who gathered nightly outside the jail. He spent his last night on earth peacefully, and slept until 10:00 am. More than 1,000 people stood outside and listened to Manning speak for thirty minutes. Deputies took him from his cell at 1:30 pm. As his arms and legs were being pinned Manning remarked, "You do not know what it is to look death in the face." At 2:15 pm the trap was sprung and Manning dropped seven feet, breaking his neck. He was buried in the city cemetery.

King, Sam
Born: circa 1889—Date of Death: 20 July 1905
Place: Comal County
Event: Lynching/Shot

Sam King, a sixteen-year old black man, was accused of having attacked the four-year old daughter of a German farmer named William Karbach. The crime had occurred Tuesday night, 18 July 1905, at Comaltown near New Braunfels. King was an employee of Karbach's. He was captured and taken to the Comal County jail.

At about 1:00 am on Thursday, 20 July 1905, a mob of vigilantes broke into the Comal County jail at New Braunfels and shot King to death in his cell. They had patiently waited all day for the sheriff, who was guarding King, to leave. No sooner had he departed than the mob forced their way into the building and tried to remove the man. Unable to open the locked cell door, the mob fired through the bars killing King. The city marshal tried to save King but his efforts were frustrated causing his intervention to be ineffective.

New Braunfels was home to a small German farming community numbering about 3,000. The village was famous for being among the most law abiding in the state.[1205]

Unidentified Black Man
Born: (Unknown)—Date of Death: 29 July 1905
Place: Red River County
Event: Lynching/Hanged

An unidentified black man attempted to assault two white women near Avery on Thursday, 27 July 1905. Their screams eventually frightened the man away. The assailant hid out until Thursday, 29 July 1905, when he was captured by a posse at the Sulphur River. After being positively identified by his would-be victims his captors apparently decided that there was no need to wait for the formality of a trial. The fellow was taken into the woods and lynched straight away.[1206]

Majors, Sank (Hank)
Born: (Unknown)—Date of Death: 8 August 1905
Place: McLennan County
Event: Lynching/Hanged

Sank Majors, a black man, was charged with outraging the wife of a farmer living near Goliad named Mrs. B. Roberts. Once captured he was assured by neighbors that the law would be allowed to take its course and that he would receive a trial.

A grand jury was schedule to meet and review his case on 28 July 1905. Majors was tried and found guilty, but he appealed his case to Governor Lanham. A new trial was granted, based on a technicality. Citizens apparently thought that since they were sure that Majors had outraged Mrs. Roberts the delay of having to wait for a new trial would have little impact on the jury's decision.

Vigilante justice was dispensed of at the end of a sisal hemp rope when Majors was taken from the jail by a mob of about 500 persons and lynched from the beams of the bridge over the Brazos River on Tuesday, 8 August 1905. The mob was divided over hanging or burning the man. Majors pleaded that he not be burned. Once the decision was made to hang him Majors was calm, and followed the orders of the mob leaders. The rope that the vigilantes used was too short to reach Majors while seated on a horse. He was told to stand in the saddle, which he did. The horse was led from under him and he slowly strangled to death. The body dangled for two hours until the county undertaker cut him down at about 3:30 am.[1207]

Williams, Thomas "Tom"
Born: circa 1875—Date of Death: 11 August 1905
Place: Hopkins County
Event: Lynching/Burned at Stake

Thomas Williams, a thirty-year old black man, was lynched and burned on the public square at Sulphur Springs on the morning of Friday, 11 August 1905.

Williams had attempted to criminally outrage Miss Nettie Griggs, who lives two miles southwest of town. The incident occurred at about 6:00 am on the morning of Friday, 11 August 1905. Nettie, who had been handled roughly in the doing, was badly frightened but not in a dangerous condition. She had started to a nearby pasture to drive the calves to the holding lot for the morning's milking. When she had gone about 200 yards from the house she looked over her shoulder and saw Williams about ten steps behind her. He sprang upon her immediately with an open knife in his hand, and told her if she screamed or made any noise he would cut her throat. Never the less, the brave girl let out a blood- curdling howl that alerted he sister who was in the house. Frightened, Williams ran away before accomplishing his purpose.

News of the attempted assault was telephoned to officers immediately after the occurrence. People began leaving the town in squads, hunting for Williams. Soon a large force of armed citizens was scouting the country for the man. City Marshal Hail, Wilbur Chaney and Gran Corbin soon apprehended Williams. He was found walking along the Katy Railroad track about two miles east of town and five miles from the scene of the crime.

A mob consist of about 3,000 persons carried Williams to the scene of the crime for identification. Upon arriving they found that Miss Griggs was suffering from nervous prostration, thus Williams could not be taken to her for identification until after a physician had arrived and administered a potion to quiet her nerves. Griggs was a nineteen-year old single woman who was living with her married sister, Mrs. J. E. Ellis. Her father, Jesse Griggs, resides near Como. Her mother was deceased. After Dr. Smith had quieted the young woman's nerves with opiates she was able to identify Williams, saying "Yes, that's him; my God! My God! That's him!"

That was enough for the waiting multitude. The procession to town with Williams in tow began, gathering participants along the way like a Crusade from the middle ages. The crowd continued to increase in numbers as they made their way to toward their destination. At a point about a mile from the square Sheriff Jerry Lewis met them. Lewis implored the mob, asking that the dignity of the law be upheld and that the process be allowed to take its course with no further violence being done. According to newspaper journalists of the day, a thousand voices shouted, "No. He is in our hands, and he shall not be given a courthouse trial. The safety of our wives and daughters will not permit that such brutes be allowed to live. We can take no chances." It is unlikely that the crowd had rehearsed that rather lengthy response and actually recited it in unison as this reporter claimed. None-the-less, the words seem to accurately capture the sentiment of the moment.

Realizing that he was powerless against such odds, Sheriff Lewis fell back to the rear of the procession as the march to town was resumed. Now replete with two thousand guns glistening in the early morning's sun the parade was a bizarre scene, like a rabble army on the march. When they arrived at city hall nearly 5,000 more people met the party that had Williams in tow.

Williams was dragged to the bandstand in the center of the square by means of the rope around his neck. Coal oil was poured over his body and a match stuck to ignite him while he was being hanged. He was burned as he swung in midair. Before long the rope seared in two and his body fell. More oil was poured over him. The blaze continued to be replenished with additional accelerant each time the flames dwindled until all the flesh was burned from his body.[1208]

Tankersley, Presley
Born: circa 1874—Date of Death: 1 September 1905
Place: Williamson County
Event: Legal Execution/Hanged

The headlines read, "Pres Tankersley expiates crime...Killed on Gallows for Wife Murder." The article went on to say that Tankersley, a black man, killed his wife Lou for infidelity, and that he had always been an industrious, hardworking and law abiding Negro.

Tankersley had been born and raised in Williamson County. He, his wife and six children, live at A. T. Irvin's farm, twelve miles east of Georgetown, where he was employed. The crime occurred on Wednesday, 20 July 1904, when he was on a visit about three miles away. When he returned home he discovered his wife Lou locked in conjugal endearment with another man. Tankersley grabbed a six-shooter and killed his wife, then went after the black man she had been with. He was stopped before shooting him as well.

Tankersley fled, and managed to stay on the lam for five days before being captured by officers about ten miles from where the incident had taken place. He was tried and convicted of the killing, and sentenced to death. His employer, A. T. Irvin, tried in vain to petition the governor to reduce the death sentence to prison time.

At 1:45 pm on Friday, 1 September 1905, Tankersley scaled the gallows stairs at Georgetown. He made a brief speech, acknowledging that he had killed his wife. His only regret was that he had not managed to kill the man she had committed adultery with. Had he done so he would have been satisfied. For most in attendance it was difficult to disagree with that statement. Hymns were sung and the trap was sprung. Presley Tankersley was no more.[1209]

Davis, Stephen "Steve"
Born: (Unknown)—Date of Death: 7 September 1905
Place: Ellis County
Event: Lynching/Burned to Death

Stephen Davis, a black man, had brutally outraged Mrs. S. P. Norris, wife of a local farmer. A crowd comprised of friends of the victim's family apprehended him and took Davis before her for identification. Mrs. Norris, who was in critical condition after the assault and rough handling, positively identified Davis.

After admitting his guilt to an ad hoc council of mob leaders they quickly decided to burn Davis at the stake. The time of the ghoulish event was set for 7:00 pm, presumably so the onlookers could have a fine view of the medieval episode silhouetted against the setting sun. Davis begged to be hanged. A vote was taken. Unfortunately for Davis they decided to stick with the original plan of man burning.

Davis was allowed to telephone his sister and brother who lived about eight miles from Howard. They too pleaded with the vigilante mob for mercy, but to no avail.

At about 8:00 pm, in view of about 3,500 persons including his brother and sister who had rushed to the scene, Davis was lashed to a post and set on fire. The husband of the outraged victim lit the first match and ignited the pyre.[1210]

One Unidentified Black Man
Born: (Unknown)—Date of Death: 11 November 1905
Place: Rusk County
Event: Lynching/Hanged

Askew, Robert
Born: (Unknown)—Date of Death: 11 November 1905
Place: Rusk County
Event: Lynching/Hanged

Reese, John
Born: (Unknown)—Date of Death: 11 November 1905
Place: Rusk County
Event: Lynching/Hanged

The headline, "Texas Mob Takes Quick Vengeance on Murder of Farmer" pretty much sums up this story.

Robert Askew, John Reese, and another unidentified man, all black men, were arrested on suspicion of murdering a farmer about ten miles from Henderson. A force of about 200 armed men on horseback charged the jail and took all three prisoners to the public square and lynched them.[1211]

Bates, Henry
Born: (Unknown)—Date of Death: 8 December 1905
Place: Colorado County
Event: Legal Execution/Hanged

On Saturday night, 15 July 1905, someone entered the residence of Mr. and Mrs. Fred Kuhlee, located about five miles from Eagle Lake in Colorado County. After bludgeoning the couple with a heavy object the intruder robbed them of $9.50 in cash and a .45 caliber revolver.

Henry Bates, a former employee of Kuhlee, was suspect of having done the deed. He was arrested and brought to trial on 9 October 1905. A guilty verdict was rendered and the death sentence was read on 12 October 1905.

On Friday, 8 December 1905, Bates walked quietly to the gallows smoking a cigar. He had eaten a modest lunch, and apart from confessing his crime had little to say before climbing the gallows stairs. Bates added that he had, "made his peace with God." The scaffold was located along the county road, about a mile and a half from town. An immense crowd was present, including Mr. and Mrs. Kuhlee, the victims. At 2:30 pm the sheriff sprung the trap and Bates dropped to his death.[1212]

Turner, George H.
Born: circa 1862—Date of Death: 22 December 1905
Place: Bexar County
Event: Legal Execution/Hanged

Extra precautions were being taken by Sheriff Tobin as early as a month before the scheduled execution of George Turner, a forty-three year old white man who had been convicted of the murder of Mrs. Lynch. James Lynch, husband of the murdered woman, had asked permission to witness the hanging and bring a couple of friends along. The sheriff had graciously conceded, and did not want Turner to spoil his own show.[1213]

Turner was condemned and hanged for the 9 March 1905, decapitation murder of Mrs. Elizabeth Lynch. He went to the gallows at San Antonio on Friday, 22 December 1905.

Harris, Benjamin "Ben"
Born: (Unknown)—Date of Death: 10 January 1906
Place: Polk County
Event: Lynching/Hanged

Shortly after midnight on Wednesday, 10 January 1906, a mob of about seventy-five men overpowered the sheriff, removed Benjamin Harris from jail at Livingston and left town.
Harris, a black man, had been charged with the murder of G. O. Polk, commissioner of the Behring Manufacturing Company of Houston. Apparently Polk, a white man, had disciplined Harris the day preceding the crime.

Harris was taken to Borings Mill at Moscow, about thirteen miles away. The lynch mob, apparently unprepared for the task at hand, had to wait at the railroad station for someone to locate a rope. Harris, apparently bored with the delay, began singing songs. When questioned why he had killed Polk he first answered that it had been an accident, then said because he wanted to, and lastly claimed that he had done it out of meanness.

Harris was lynched at about 1:00 am.[1214] His hands were handcuffed and one foot was tied to the manacles.

Henderson, Sam
Born: (Unknown)—Date of Death: 19 March 1906
Place: McLennan County
Event: Unknown

Sam Henderson, a black man, was found dead near the Cotton Belt railroad bridge. His neck and shoulder were broken. The nature of his death, or his transgression, is not known. He may have died from an accidental fall. The case is included in the interest of possible completeness. The only source, which is unverified, is Carrigan's *Lynching Culture*.[1215]

Johnson, Albert
Born: (Unknown)—Date of Death: 30 March 1906
Place: Ellis County
Event: Legal Execution/Hanged

Albert Johnson, a black man, was executed at Waxahachie for the murder of J. H. Taylor, a white man. The Taylor murder had taken place near the city on 3 July 1905. Johnson robbed Taylor of $67.00 then smashed in his skull. Taylor never regained consciousness and died the next day. Johnson's first trial ended in a hung jury. During the second trial Johnson changed his testimony, claiming that Taylor had attempted to assault him. On cross-examination, however, Johnson eventually admitted to having assaulted Taylor. He was convicted and sentenced to death. Thousands of people turned out for the hanging.[1216]

Young, John Thomas "Tom"[1217]
Born: November 1861—Date of Death: 30 March 1906
Place: Williamson County
Event: Legal Execution/Hanged

John Thomas "Tom" Young, a white man, was tried and convicted of assaulting and murdering a sixteen-year old girl he had adopted named Alma Reece.

Young's hanging drew a grand crowd, estimated at 10,000. Families came on horseback to see the event, which took place on a prairie about thirty miles from Austin at Georgetown.[1218]

Through the diligent work for Mrs. Neal, wife of the City Attorney, Young had come to know

God in his final days. He expressed a desire to be baptized and the sheriff granted permission. The ceremony was performed at the jail, in the bathtub where the usual full immersion rite took place. Reverend J. S. Huckabee of the Northtown church along with Mrs. Neal and Mr. Hewett were gathered around his cell as they sang "Oh Happy Day" and "Are You Washed in the Blood..." At the conclusion of the reading of the death warrant by Sheriff Connell, Young responded by saying, "Yes sir" then followed with "Come and let's finish this thing."

Dressed in a neat black suit, a small bunch of violets in his left lapel, Young strode to his execution chatting and humming "Happy Land, Happy Land." The sheriff remarked, "That's a nice suite of clothes you've got on." Young replied, "I will have a better one in heaven."[1219]

Young is buried at the Elmwood Cemetery at Bowie.[1220]

Porter, Lincoln
Born: (Unknown)—Date of Death: 24 April 1906
Place: Limestone County
Event: Lynching/Shot

Lincoln Porter, a black man, was accused of having entered the bedchambers of a young white girl named Esterling. The incident took place at about 11:00 pm at the Esterling home near Delia. When Porter was discovered in the girl's room he fled. A posse, of about 150 men, which included the girl's father, tracked him down in a field near Groesbeck. When Porter admitted that he had planned to chloroform the young woman and outrage her Mr. Esterling leveled his double barrel shotgun at the man and emptied both barrels, killing him instantly.[1221]

One Unidentified Black Man
Born: circa 1889—Date of Death: 25 April 1906
Place: Freestone and Leon Counties
Event: Lynching/Hanged

On Wednesday, 25 April 1906, an unidentified seventeen-year old black man was lynched at Oakwood, eighteen miles south of Palestine. He had attempted to outrage a white woman at her own residence.[1222]

The man had been taken into custody by lawmen, but a mob numbering over 100 strong took him from the officers and carried him to a place along the International and Great Northern railroad tracks and lynched him.[1223]

Wilkerson, Jack
Born: September 1861—Date of Death: 29 June 1906
Place: Polk County
Event: Legal Execution/Hanged

Jack Wilkerson, a white man who hailed from Brazos and had come to Livingston by way of Oklahoma, was tried and convicted of murdering his own wife, Mrs. Hooker. She was Wilkerson's second wife.

Wilkerson confessed to the killing, but refused to say what his reason had been. He reinforced that "only God knew..." and that although the sheriff thought he did, he was mistaken. On Friday, 29 June 1906, the forty-four year old Wilkerson scaled the gallows stairs. He spoke to the crowd briefly, denying all of the charges leveled against him but confessing to the murder of his wife, for which he was exceedingly sorry. His speech was calm and deliberate, and he faced his fate in a resolute and dignified manner, apologizing to the crowd by saying, "People, it is an awful thing to witness, but I am prepared to meet my God."[1224]

Wilkerson left behind eight children.

Martin, Rufus
Born: circa 1877—Date of Death: 12 July 1906
Place: Tarrant County
Event: Legal Execution/Hanged

Rufus Martin, a black man, was tried and convicted of robbing and murdering Charles L. Swackhammer, a farmer of German ancestry from Arlington in Tarrant County.

Martin and another black man named Jordan Thompson had been in his employ as cotton pickers. The incident took place near Cupp's Store on Saturday, 28 October 1905. The case was first brought on 30 October 1905. Martin received the death sentence. His attorneys alleged discrimination and appealed the case.

Martin's case eventually went all the way to the United States Supreme Court before the sentence was affirmed. On 7 July 1906, less than a week before his scheduled execution Martin wrote a letter to his mother in which he confessed to the killing and begged her forgiveness, saying, "Mama, I killed the man but God did forgive me for it..."

Before 11:00 am a crowd had begun to form near the gallows. Whistles were blowing the hour of 1:00 pm when the black cap was pulled down over Martin's head at Fort Worth on Thursday, 12 July 1906.[1225] He had scaled the gallows earlier, and delivered a lengthy talk, taking as text Romans 14:11,"For it is written, as I live, saith the Lord, every knee shall bow to me, and every tongue shall confess to God" exhorting repentance by all. He smiled and walked briskly to the designated spot where his hands and feet were bound. Scripture was read up to the last minute. When the sheriff had positioned his foot against the trap he said, "Goodbye Rufus" and let the lever free. Martin dropped, snapping his neck when the hangman's tether reached its end.[1226]

Johnson, Bob
Born: circa 1876—Date of Death: 20 July 1906
Place: Erath County
Event: Legal Execution/Hanged

Bob Johnson, a thirty-year old black man, was tried and convicted of the murder of Alfred Berry, a white man. The incident took place in the seed house at the Dublin Oil Mill at Hamilton. Johnson had stopped there for the night while en route from Stamford to Hamilton.

Johnson was arrested in the Tehuacana Bottoms, about five miles from Waco on Sunday, 16 December 1905. He confessed to the killing, saying that he had taken $3.00 in cash and a suit of clothes from Berry's grip. The two men had ridden down to Dublin in a boxcar together. Johnson had plans of heading to Oklahoma. Berry had claimed that he had $150.00 on his person. The two men had asked permission to sleep in the seed house and had burrowed into a pile for the night when Johnson, unable to sleep, arose. He picked up a large fork handle and hit Berry in the front of the head with it, smashing his skull. He retrieved Berry's valise and walked down the Texas Central railroad tracks a distance before opening the case and putting on a suit of Berry clothing, leaving his own tattered garment behind in the grip.

Johnson's first hearing ended in a mistrial when the jury could not agree on a verdict. His second trial ended in a conviction, with the death sentence as penalty. After a series of appeals the conviction and verdict were upheld.

Bob Johnson rose in fine spirits at Stephenville on Friday, 20 July 1906. After a hearty breakfast of spring chicken, French fried potatoes, scrambled eggs, toast and butter, brown gravy, two oranges, orange wine and hot chocolate he asked to be shown through the new jail that had just been turned over to the county that day. Johnson examined the gallows, placing his foot on the trap and asking if it had been tested.

At noon he ate another hearty meal of fried chicken, ice cream, cake and milk. At 1:00 pm sharp Sheriff Mack Creswell announced that Johnson had decided not to give a speech, turning away roughly 6,000 persons who had gathered to hear him hold forth. The condemned man said goodbye to his wife and friends and was taken directly to the gallows where he asked to have his shoes removed. He stepped onto the trap and as the sheriff was adjusting the noose said goodbye to everyone present. At 1:29 pm the trap was sprung. The rope was a little long and the drop a little short, thus his neck was not broken in the fall. Johnson was declared dead about twenty minutes afterward.[1227]

Frazier, Mitchell
Born: (Unknown)—Date of Death: 15 September 1906
Place: Falls County
Event: Lynching/Hanged

Mitchell Frazier, a black man, had slashed a white man named Frank Hess across the abdomen with a knife at Rosebud. The wound was so serious that Hess later expired. According to some versions of the story Hess had pushed Frazier from a walk, which spawned the confrontation. A group of white men gave chase, overtaking him about a mile from town where they lynched him from a tree.

In another version of the lynching, Frazier is said to have been confined in the jail where he was removed by force by a mob of 100 men, then strung up from the supporting structure of the town's water tower. There is no way to reconcile the conflicting versions of this tale. All one can say is that the report made by the *Boston Herald* stands in stark contrast to other versions, and implies that Hess was the cause of the affray.[1228]

Davis, Anthony
Born (Unknown)—Date of Death: 9 October 1906
Place: Bowie County
Event: Lynching/Hanged

Blacks lynched Anthony Davis, a black hack driver, at Texarkana, Texas, on Tuesday, 9 October 1906. Davis had been arrested, fined and released on appeal for the attempted outrage of a fifteen-year old black girl. His body was found near the Cotton Belt roundhouse, one half mile from the center of town. Davis was reportedly lured to the scene where he was beaten and strangled to death.[1229]

Pitts, "Slab"
Born: (Unknown)—Date of Death: 26 October 1906
Place: Reeves County
Event: Lynching/Shot

"Slab" Pitts, a black man, was convicted of a violation of the Edmunds Act and was run out of town at Roswell, New Mexico after serving ninety days for the crime. His accessory, a white woman, followed him to Texas.[1230]

Cowboys at Toyah snuck up on Pitts while he was sleeping, placed a rope around his neck then dragged him behind a horse for a while before finishing the job by hauling him up a tree and lynching him.[1231]

Garrett, Dick
Born: (Unknown)—Date of Death: 21 November 1906
Place: Shelby County
Event: Legal Execution/Hanged

Dick Garrett, a black man, shot and killed Doctor M. M. Paul on the streets of Center on Saturday, 17 November 1906, when Paul spotted Garrett displaying a weapon.

Following the letter of the law, Garrett received a speedy trial, rapid verdict and almost instantaneous hanging. A grand jury returned an indictment on Tuesday, 20 November 1906. The gallows was quickly prepared in the public square overnight, and the trial took place between 9:00 and 11:00 am on the 21st. By 2:00 pm the matter had been settled, and Garrett was swinging from the gibbet.[1232]

Brown, Henry

Born: circa 1873—Date of Death: 30 November 1906
Place: Medina County
Event: Legal Execution/Hanged

Henry Brown, a black man, murdered Albert Taylor, another black man, at D'Hanis. The killing had taken place on Friday, 25 July 1902, while both men who were serving life sentences. The pair were laboring together on a chain gang when the killing took place.

Brown was tried and convicted of the crime. His sentence was death. On Friday, 30 November 1906, that judgment was carried out. Brown's hanging was the first in Medina County since the territory had been organized in 1848.

Sheriff Joe Ney read the death warrant at 11:00 am and walked Brown to the gallows at Hondo. The large crowd that had gathered for the event sang hymns as the condemned man made his way to the platform. Brown made a few brief comments, then at 11:20 the trap was sprung and Brown dropped into history.[1233]

Jones, Jesse

Born: circa 1880—Date of Death: 30 November 1906
Place: McLennan County
Event: Legal Execution/Hanged

Jesse Jones, alias Jesse Washington, who was a twenty-six year old black man, had murdered his employer, Matthias Block, on Sunday, 9 September 1906. Jones attacked Block, a white man who was the wealthy owner of a grocery and meat market, while he napped at his desk. Jones struck the dozing man repeatedly with the butt of a heavy ax then robbed the store of between $200 and $300.

Jones was apprehended the day following the incident. Most of the stolen cash was recovered, unlike the life of Block, which had been spent for eternity. He went to trial on 18 September 1906. Jones was found guilty and sentenced to hang.

At about midday on Friday, 30 November 1906, Jones scaled the gallows steps at Waco. He faced the crowd, bowed and smiled widely displaying his unusually white teeth. In a rambling talk that lasted about ten minutes Jones described how ardent spirits, gambling and other vices had led to his downfall, compelling those in the gallery to abstain. At about 12:30 pm Sheriff Tilley sprung the trap and Jones dropped seven feet, broke his neck and died easily.[1234]

Vargas, Alberto
Born: circa 1889—Date of Death: 4 January 1907
Place: Callahan County
Event: Legal Execution/Hanged

On Friday, 19 October 1906, Alberto Vargas murdered Miss Emma Blakely at Baird. Blakely was employed as a waitress at the Signal Hotel where Vargas held a job as a dishwasher. Blakely had been working at the inn for several years, while Vargas had only recently arrived in town. Apparently Vargas, who had little command of the English language, imagined himself deeply infatuated with the young woman. She, on the other hand, was engaged to a respectable railroad man and about to be married, thus she fended off his advances indignantly. Vargas was determined to get even. He concealed himself behind the dining room door between the kitchen and the eating area. When Blakely opened the portal he stabbed her in the heart with a long bladed pocketknife. Death came almost instantly.

Vargas' victim was the stepdaughter of a wealthy rancher named C. H. Willeford from Callahan County. She had four brothers and was in fact scheduled to have been married in a just few weeks.

Vargas was taken into custody shortly after the incident. Fearing that a mob would lynch the man, Sheriff T. A. Irvin spirited him away to the jail at Abilene as soon as night had fallen and their escape could be concealed from view. Vargas was returned to Baird for trial on 5 November 1907. The jury deliberated briefly before returning a guilty verdict.

On Friday, 4 January 1907, the eighteen-year old Vargas made his way to the gallows. He delivered a speech in Spanish before a packed house with tickets at a premium. Sheriff Irvin pulled the trap and Vargas swung into eternity, saying that he had made his peace with God.[1235]

Campos, Ramon Felix
Born: (Unknown)—Date of Death: 1 February 1907
Place: Karnes County
Event: Legal Execution/Hanged

Ramon Felix Campos, a Mexican man, was charged with the murder of his girlfriend Juana McHaney. Campos had also killed the woman's younger sister.

Campos had divorced his wife in anticipation of marrying McHaney. Apparently McHaney had second thoughts and turned him down. On Monday morning, 26 March 1906, Campos met Juana, her twenty-year old sister and their little brother who were traveling along in a hack. They asked Campos if he wanted to ride with them. He said that he did, and climbed into the back of the buggy. After a short distance Campos began to implore McHaney to change her mind and consent to marrying him. She again declined, which enraged Campos. At that Campos withdrew a razor from his pocket and slashed McHaney's throat, killing her instantly. The younger sister screamed. Campos drew his pistol and tried to shoot her but the girl took hold of the gun. A desperate struggle began.

When the young woman finally broke free and ran Campos shot her in the head, killing her instantly. He next turned his attentions to the boy, firing several shots at him in the wagon but the lad escaped unscathed.

Campos was tried, convicted, and sentenced to death. That verdict was to be carried out on 18 January 1907. As he remained on deathwatch on 16 January Campos was unrepentant so far as Juana McHaney was concerned, but sorry that he had killed the younger sister. Campos finally went to the gallows at Karnes City on Friday, 1 February 1907. The trap was sprung at 12:10 pm. Only thirty persons were admitted to witness the execution.[1236]

Washington, Abraham B.
Born: (Unknown)—Date of Death: 14 February 1907
Place: Bastrop County
Event: Legal Execution/Hanged

Abraham Washington, a black man, was tried and found guilty of murdering a black woman at Bastrop. He was sentenced to death for his crime.

Immediately following the trial, which took place on Thursday, 14 February 1907, Washington was hanged. He addressed the crowd from the gallows, claiming that ardent spirits had led to his ruin.[1237]

Powell, Felix
Born: (Unknown)—Date of Death: 2 April 1907
Place: Victoria County
Event: Legal Execution/Hanged

Felix Powell and two other black men, Monk Gibson and Harry Howard, were arrested for the murder of Mrs. A. J. Condit and her four children at Edna, Jackson County, in September of 1905. Gibson was tried first on a change of venue to San Antonio. Powell and Howard were witnesses for the prosecution against Gibson. The state's case was that Gibson was the sole perpetrator of the crime. The state's attorneys even tried to establish alibis for Powell and Howard to shore up their case against Gibson. The trial resulted in a hung jury and a mistrial.

Former Texas Ranger captain Bill McDonald, now a state revenue officer, believed that Powell was the killer, and that Gibson and Howard were accessories. He was sent to Edna to investigate the crime and ultimately arrested Powell and Howard. Powell and Howard were indicted, and Gibson re-indicted, for the murders. Powell was tried on a change of venue in Victoria, convicted and sentenced to death. Without making a statement he was hanged at 12:30 pm on Tuesday, 2 April 1907 in Victoria, before a crowd of three thousand people.[1238]

The hanging of Felix caused quite a stir in the Powell family. Felix's brother, Arthur, swore to kill Sheriff Egg, the man who was responsible for Felix's arrest. Arthur and his father-in-law, George

Alexander, came to town in person to confront the sheriff but he was away at the time. Upon his return Alexander warned him that Arthur had sworn a death pledge.

Egg began a search for Arthur, locating him at Koppas's Grocery sitting on a sugar barrel with a double barrel shotgun. Egg approached. When Arthur turned to fire Egg opened up with a Winchester semi-automatic rifle, hitting him six times at close range. As one might expect, the wounds were fatal.[1239]

Monk Gibson was tried on a change of venue at Cuero, Dewitt County, convicted and sentenced to death. He was hanged on Saturday, 27 June 1908, in that city.[1240] It does not appear that Howard was ever prosecuted for the murders.

Armstrong, John
Born: (Unknown)—Date of Death: 26 April 1907
Place: Colorado County
Event: Legal Execution/Hanged

John Armstrong, a black man, was tried and convicted of murdering his wife. On Friday, 26 April 1907, that sentence was carried out at Columbus. Due to a miscalculation in the length of the hangman's line, when the trap was sprung and Armstrong had traveled the length of the rope his feet reached the ground. It was necessary for officers to hold him up while he struggled wildly for about four minutes before the spirit finally flew from its mortal host.[1241]

Wilson, Fred
Born: (Unknown)—Date of Death: 14 July 1907
Place: Val Verde County
Event: Lynching/Shot

Fred Wilson, a black man, had shot and killed a fellow named Early Smart at Del Rio on Sunday, 14 July 1907. Smart had interfered in a dispute Wilson was having with some boys and wound up being shot in the head for his trouble.

A posse was quickly formed, and after a search was undertaken he was found in less than two hours, hiding in a barrel in a warehouse. When the fugitive showed fight the posse opened fire, killing him instantly.[1242]

Hall, Thomas "Tom"
Born: (Unknown)—Date of Death: 6 August 1907
Place: Goliad County
Event: Lynching/Hanged

One day earlier Tom Hall, a black man, was arrested at Goliad for the attempted assault of two young white women. Hall was placed in the city jail, but when the sun rose on Tuesday, 6 August 1907, he had disappeared from the lockup. Hall's body was discovered hanging from a tree near the jail, quite dead. No one could explain how it got there and how Hall had managed to get himself in that condition. Several blacks who expressed their displeasure with the sight were ordered to leave town.[1243]

Johnson, Alexander

Born: (Unknown)—Date of Death: 4 November 1907
Place: Milam County
Event: Lynching/Hanged

Alexander Johnson, a black man, was charged with the assaulting and outraging a white woman named Miss Hailey. The incident took place on Wednesday, 30 October 1907. A grand jury returned an indictment of assault with intent to commit criminal assault, a charge that does not carry a death penalty.

At about 4:00 pm on Monday, 4 November 1907, Johnson was taken from the jail at Cameron by a force of nearly 500 men who were armed with sledgehammers. They battered their way in to the building, pummeling the doors until the locks were rendered ineffective. Sheriff Holtzclaw and his deputies were feckless against the mob. The prisoner was lynched from a large oak tree in the courthouse yard.

Influential citizens including Judge Scott pleaded with the crowd to not hang the man, all to no avail. The governor called out the militia, but not in time to save Johnson.[1244]

Bailey, Dock

Born: (Unknown)—Date of Death: 7 November 1907
Place: Nacogdoches County
Event: Legal Execution/Hanged

Dock Bailey, a black man, was tried and convicted of the robbery and murder of a man named Owens.

On Thursday, 7 November 1907, Sheriff Blackburn brought Bailey back to Nacogdoches from Rusk on the early train. Crowds gathered to witness the hanging. Reverend Wiley Harris, a black preacher, ascended the gallows to speak and pray with Bailey. As the cap was being pulled down over his head Bailey made a brief talk, during which he confessed that he and he alone had killed Owens. The sheriff sprung tripped the lever at 2:03 pm. At 2:12 pm Doctor A. A. Nelson pronounced Bailey dead.[1245]

Calloway, Anderson

Born: (Unknown)—Date of Death: 26 December 1907
Place: Leon County
Event: Lynching/Hanged

It seems that early Christmas morning Anderson Calloway had broken into the home of W. J. Dean, a farmer who lived about two miles from town. Calloway, a black man, was apparently looking for something special for his Christmas present, and made his way to the bedroom that was normally occupied by Dean's young granddaughter, Miss Buchanan. As he shed his livery and crept between the sheets in gleeful anticipation of finding the buxom and fetching Buchanan girl he was startled to discover the bed occupied by a neighbor boy. The young man was aroused with a start and caused quite a commotion. Calloway fled, but was quickly apprehended. He was taken to the jail at Marques where he remained for only one day.

On the night of Thursday, 26 December 1907, vigilantes removed Calloway, the midnight creeper, from the jail under force of arms. After confessing to the break-in, and to his intention to outrage Miss Buchanan, he was lynched from a nearby tree.[1246]

Scott, Charles

Born: circa 1890—Date of Death: 28 February 1908
Place: Montgomery County
Event: Lynching/Hanged

Charles Scott, an eighteen-year old black man, was found hanging from a tree at Conroe on Friday, 28 February 1908. Attached to his feet was a handmade sign saying, "Warning to negroes found prowling in white folks' houses."

Scott had been arrested earlier and place under bond for the assault and outrage of Miss Alloy, a white woman. The newspaper account of the day offered no explanation as to how Scott had gotten from the jail to the hanging tree unaided.[1247]

Campbell, John

Born: (Unknown)—Date of Death: 9 March 1908
Place: Grimes County
Event: Lynching/Shot

John Campbell, a black man, was charged with slashing county commissioner J. T. Berry with a knife. He was taken to the jail at Navasota where a crowd of men removed him by force and lynched him from a telephone pole. Campbell's body remained hanging until the following morning.[1248]

Two Unidentified Black Men
Born: (Unknown)—Date of Death: 16 March 1908
Place: Montgomery County
Event: Lynching/Shot

On Monday, 16 March 1908, a young white woman reported that a black man had attempted to assault her at Magnolia. The sheriff went to the scene and found that one black had been killed and another mortally wounded by a person or persons unknown. One of the pair was identified as the girl's attacker.[1249]

One Unidentified Black Man
Born: (Unknown)—Date of Death: 22 March 1908
Place: Montgomery County
Event: Lynching/Shot

Early on Sunday morning, 22 March 1908, Mrs. Wright, a resident of Timber, was awakened by the sound of someone trying to enter her bedroom. She produced a revolver and fired several shots at the intruder through the window. Her aim was good. The prowler, a black man, died from the gunshot wounds a few hours later.[1250]

Brown, John
Born: (Unknown)—Date of Death: 27 March 1908
Place: DeWitt County
Event: Legal Execution/Hanged

According to sources, a black man named John Brown criminally assaulted a black woman at Cuero. He was tried and found guilty of the crime, then subsequently sentenced to death. Brown's lawyers appealed the case. On 27 March 1908, governor refused to commute the sentence.
    Brown was subsequently executed on 28 March 1908. The lever was tripped at 3:13 pm and Brown was catapulted into eternity. His neck was broken by the fall. Family members took his body to Yoakum for burial.[1251]

Fields, Albert
Born: circa 1888—Date of Death: 9 April 1908
Place: Gregg County
Event: Lynching/Hanged

Albert Fields, a black man, charted a direct course to the hangman's tree when he insulted the honor of, and attempted to outrage, Miss May Morris, a white woman. The incident took place at Longview on Thursday, 9 April 1908. At about 6:15 pm the attractive Miss Morris was coming home from a visit with a neighbor and was just outside the city limits. Fields met her just as she passed a stretch of deep woods about a quarter mile in length. Fields asked her age, name and weight then began to lift her up in his arm. The girl let out a scream and fled.

At about 10:00 pm, and less than four hours after the alleged act occurred, Fields had already been lynched from a tree. He had fled when an elderly black man rushed to the aid of Miss Morris who, at the time, was screaming loudly after Fields had grabbed her arm. Both she and the elderly fellow positively identified Fields, who eventually confessed to having been the attacker.

A large crowd of unmasked citizens quietly gathered to witness justice being done. Fields was taken to the courthouse yard at about 10:05 pm where a rope was tied around his neck and he was hauled up a tree by use of a horse. The crowd dispersed, but the poor fellow was left dangling there for some time.[1252] Miss Morris was very badly frightened by the event.

Douglas, Jasper
Born: (Unknown)—Date of Death: 19 April 1908
Place: Cass County
Event: Lynching/Hanged

Jasper Douglas, a black man, was charged in a criminal warrant on Saturday, 18 April 1908, for assault upon his twelve-year old stepsister. The following day his body was found hanging from a tree limb near his home at Atlanta. The verdict of the coroner's jury was that Douglas, "...came to his death at the hands of unknown persons."[1253]

Williams, John
Born: (Unknown)—Date of Death: 6 May 1908
Place: Morris County
Event: Lynching/Hanged

John Williams, a black man who was charged with robbery and assault to commit murder on a white man named J. T. Warrick, was lynched at Naples on Wednesday, 6 May 1908.

The crime had occurred on Friday, 20 March 1908. Williams had escaped, but was captured at Pensacola, Florida and returned for trial. The district judge ordered the transporting officer not to take him to Naples as he feared reprisal. The lawmen ignored the order. Williams was given a hearing, but as the judge had foretold, immediately following he was taken by a mob and lynched from a tree near the depot.[1254]

Cason, James B.
Born: 15 August 1872—Date of Death: 22 May 1908
Place: Parker County
Event: Legal Execution/Hanged

The headlines read, "James B. Cason Hangs; Last Words are Prayers." James Cason, a white man, had been accused of killing Mr. L. F. McLemore in the Eddleman pasture. The place is located about six miles south of Kaufman. The killing took place on February 1907. Cason, who was tried and convicted of the killing, was sentenced to die on Friday, 22 May 1908.

Cason, who was called "Major Cason," and McLemore had left the Cason farm in January 1907 by wagon, traveling to some point in New Mexico where they intended to locate on government land. McLemore was a bachelor, about fifty years old, who had just sold his farm at Kaufman and was traveling with around $1,000 in cash on his person with which he planned to establish himself at his new location.

Cason and McLemore had known each other for several years. Cason had warned him against traveling with that much cash, recommending that the money be placed in a bank upon which a draft could later be drawn. McLemore promised to do so, but failed to follow through. The men left on their journey. No word of them was received once they had passed Weatherford until 19 February 1907, when J.B. Eddleman's son discovered McLemore remains in their pasture, mutilated and partially burned. The site of the crime was found, where posts had been cut from Eddelman's fence and used to make a fire with which to destroy the evidence of the killing. McLemore's body had been cut nearly in two at the waist to facilitate the burning. The remains were placed in a small ravine.

Cason's movements were traced to where he had fed the team at a local wagon yard. He sold the outfit then departed for New Mexico, Oklahoma, Kansas, Hot Springs, and finally returning to Kaufman County.

In spite of strong petition for the commutation of his sentence Cason went to the gallows on schedule.[1255] The hanging took place at the outskirts of Weatherford, near the gun club grounds. An enclosure had been erected to assure a private hanging. In spite of the fact that only a handful of people were allowed to witness the actual event, a crowd of thousands of men, women and children packed the surrounding grounds. Sheriff Pope and his deputies left the jail promptly at 1:30 pm with Cason and headed to the site where Reverend R. B. Morgan, Baptist Preacher, and a quartet had already set up shop and were performing. Upon arrival, Reverend Morgan led a prayer at the wagon that was participated in by the condemned man and Texas Rangers who were present. After prayer the attending pastor recited the 23rd Psalm and three congregants rendered a song.

Cason delivered a lengthy speech. At 2:36 pm Sheriff Pope sprung the trap and the condemned man dropped to his death at the end of a hangman's rope. Cason never moved a muscle, his neck broken from the fall he died almost instantly.[1256] He is buried at Cedar Grove Cemetery at Kaufman.[1257]

Jones, Thomas "Tom"
Born: (Unknown)—Date of Death: 20 June 1908
Place: Fort Bend County
Event: Legal Execution/Hanged

Thomas Jones, a black man, was tried and convicted of murdering an eighty year old black man named Morris Lemon at Richmond. The killing took place on Wednesday, 19 March 1908. After robbing and killing the old gentleman he set the man's cabin on fire in an attempt to conceal his evil deed.

Jones was taken to jail when he foolishly showed up in town several days after the incident with a wagon that had belonged to Lemon. He was tried, convicted, and sentenced to death.

The verdict was carried out on Saturday, 20 June 1908, when Jones was hanged at Richmond. Several thousand persons turned out to see the execution.[1258]

Evans, Jerry
Born: circa 1886—Date of Death: 21 June 1908
Place: Sabine County
Event: Lynching/Hanged

Evans, Hardy
Born: (Unknown)—Date of Death: 21 June 1908
Place: Sabine County
Event: Lynching/Shot

Johnson, Will
Born: circa 1884—Date of Death: 21 June 1908
Place: Sabine County
Event: Lynching/Hanged

Manual, William "Will"
Born: circa 1873—Date of Death: 21 June 1908
Place: Sabine County
Event: Lynching/Hanged

McCoy, William "Bill" or "Rabbit"
Born: circa 1868—Date of Death: 21 June 1908
Place: Sabine County
Event: Lynching/Shot

Spellman, Will "Mose or Moss"
Born: circa 1884—Date of Death: 21 June 1908
Place: Sabine County
Event: Lynching/Hanged

Williams, Cleveland "Cleve"
Born: circa 1871—Date of Death: 21 June 1908
Place: Sabine County
Event: Lynching/Hanged

Williams, Frank
Born: circa 1886—Date of Death: 21 June 1908
Place: Sabine County
Event: Lynching/Shot

One Unidentified Black Man
Born: (Unknown)—Date of Death: 21 June 1908
Place: Sabine County
Event: Lynching/Shot

On Saturday 6 June 1908, several white men visited the Rockhill Church near Geneva, a black place of worship where a dance was in progress. Allegedly the men were looking to buy liquor. A confrontation occurred during which Hugh Dean, one of the white men, was killed. The crime was not reported until the following morning. Dean's body was left on the floor overnight. Six black men were arrested. At the preliminary hearing that followed evidence revealed that the men had plotted to kill Dean.

On Saturday 20 June 1908, a prominent white farmer named Aaron M. "Artie" Johnson was assassinated while seated at the dining table with his wife and child. Another report claimed that he was lying on a cot playing with the child. A black man named Perry Price was arrested. Price implicated another black man, Robert Wright. Wright was related to one of the men who was being held for the Dean murder.

At about 1:00 am on Sunday, 21 June 1908, a mob of approximately 200 men stormed the jail at Hemphill and overpowered the guards. The six men held for the murder of Dean were seized by the mob. They were taken about a mile from the courthouse where Jerry Evans age twenty-two, Will Johnson age twenty-four, Moss Spellman age twenty-four, Cleve Williams age twenty-seven, and Will Manuel age twenty-five were hanged from the same dogwood tree. Frank Williams, age twenty, was shot and killed while trying to escape. Later that same night a black man named Bill "Rabbit" McCoy was shot and killed while standing at the gate of the Johnson home. A cocked and loaded pistol was found beside his body. The following morning two more black men were discovered shot to death and left in the creek bottoms. One newspaper account claimed that the dead man was Hardy Evans, who was considered a principal in the murder of Dean.

Robert Wright, who allegedly confessed to the murder of Aaron Johnson, and his accomplice were transferred to the jail at Beaumont for safekeeping.[1259]

Gibson, Monk
Born: circa 1889—Date of Death: 27 June 1908
Place: DeWitt County
Event: Legal Execution/Hanged

Felix Powell and two other black men, Monk Gibson and Harry Howard, were arrested for the murder of Mrs. A. J. Condit and her four children at Edna, Jackson County. That incident had taken place in September of 1905. Gibson was tried first on a change of venue to San Antonio. Powell and Howard were witnesses for the prosecution against Gibson. The state's case was that Gibson was the sole perpetrator of the crime. The state's attorneys even tried to establish alibis for Powell and Howard to shore up their case against Gibson. The trial resulted in a hung jury and a mistrial.

Former Texas Ranger captain Bill McDonald, now a state revenue officer, believed that Powell was the killer and that Gibson and Howard were accessories. He was sent to Edna to investigate the crime. McDonald ultimately arrested Powell and Howard. Powell and Howard were indicted and Gibson re-indicted for the murders. Powell was tried on a change of venue in Victoria, convicted and sentenced to death. Without making a statement he was hanged at 12:30 pm on Tuesday, 2 April 1907 in Victoria, before a crowd of three thousand people.[1260]

Monk Gibson was tried on a change of venue at Cuero, Dewitt County, convicted and sentenced to death. Gibson's luck ran out when Governor Campbell refused to interfere with his execution. The hanging came off as planned, at Cuero, on the afternoon of Saturday, 27 June 1908.[1261] A crowd of three thousand people witnessed the event, including about 200 who arrived on a special train from Edna. At exactly 2:44 pm the trap was sprung, jerking him into eternity. Gibson made no confession and simply said he was not guilty[1262]

Macklin, Willis
Born: (Unknown)—Date of Death: 2 July 1908
Place: Polk County
Event: Legal Execution/Hanged

Willis Macklin, a black man, was tried and found guilty of the murder of Jack Darden.

At about 1:40 pm on Thursday, 2 July 1908, Sheriff Chapman escorted Macklin to the foot of the gallows at Livingston. The condemned man was decked out in a brand new black suit. The pair quietly scaled the stairs. Macklin had little to say. When asked if he had killed another man named T. S. Spurlock he nodded his head yes, and then followed with a verbal refutation. A crowd of about 2,000 watched as Sheriff Chapman pulled the trap and Macklin dropped six feet, breaking his neck as the rope plaid out.[1263]

Smith, Tad
Born: circa 1890—Date of Death: 28 July 1908
Place: Hunt County
Event: Lynching/Burned to Death

During the afternoon of Monday, 27 July 1908, Tad Smith, an eighteen-year old black man, assaulted and violated Miss Viola DeLancey at Clinton. Smith fled, but was captured at about 2:00 am the following day.

After being positively identified by DeLancey, and while en route to the Greenville jail, a mob of citizens' overpowered officers, took Smith and prepared to hang him. Someone in the rabble held forth the suggestion that it would be more appropriate to burn the man at the stake, given that he had outraged a white girl. The proposition took hold, and Smith was taken to the square at Greenville. There he was placed in the midst of bundles of sticks and twigs that had been bound together and dowsed with kerosene. A match was struck and tossed on the pile, which immediately ignited.

A crowd, estimated to number one thousand, watched as the young black man slowly burned to death.[1264]

Williams, J. "Dock"
Born: (Unknown)—Date of Death: 31 July 1908
Place: Bexar County
Event: Legal Execution/Hanged

"Dock" Williams, a black man, was tried and convicted of the murder of a white chicken peddler named Thomas J. Turner. The incident occurred along the Lavernia road, about sixteen miles from San Antonio. Williams had robbed Turner then attempted to conceal the crime by cremating Turner's remains. The following day passersby found the smoldering corpse lying near the road. Williams, the last man seen with Turner, was charged the next day.

Williams' execution date was set for Friday, 31 July 1908. On Saturday night, 18 July 1908, he managed to escape from the jail at San Antonio after feigning suicide and overpowering the jailer. Williams was soon captured, safe and sound apart from a broken ankle that he suffered when he leaped from the roof of a shed during his flight. He was well enough to keep his date with the executioner.[1265]

Mitchell, Frank
Born: (Unknown)—Date of Death: 1 August 1908
Place: Burleson County
Event: Legal Execution/Hanged

On Thursday, 21 March 1907, Frank Mitchell, a black man, murdered a black woman named Charity Bradley. He was tried and convicted of the crime and sentenced to death.

Originally that sentence was scheduled to be carried out on Monday, 29 June 1908, but a stay of execution was granted after a claim was filed on Mitchell's behalf alleging that he was mentally imbalanced.[1266] The disorder was said to have resulted from a severe blow to the head that Mitchell had received some years earlier. Eventually Mitchell's luck ran out and his sentence was ordered to be carried out.

The hanging took place about a quarter of a mile from Caldwell, on Saturday, 1 August 1908.[1267]

Jackson, Moses
Born: (Unknown)—Date of Death: 15 August 1908
Place: Austin County
Event: Legal Execution/Hanged

A black man named Moses Jackson was allegedly lynched at Bellville in Austin County on Saturday, 15 August 1908. The source did not provide any information concerning Jackson's crime. No record to confirm this incident has been located.[1268]

Newton, Daniel (Raymond)
Born: (Unknown)—Date of Death: 12 September 1908
Place: Waller County
Event: Lynching/Hanged

Daniel (Raymond) Newton, a black man, was charged with complicity in the murder of Judge John Buchtorn, a wealthy white farmer and rancher who had been shot to death near his plantation home at Brookshire. Newton, his father and his brother were all placed in jail at Brookshire awaiting arraignment.

On Saturday night, 12 September 1908, Daniel Newton was forcibly taken from the jail and lynched by a vigilante mob. Fearing for their safety, his father and brother were moved to the jail at Hempstead.[1269]

Some sources list Newton's given name as Raymond. The spelling of the victim's surname varies widely from one newspaper account to the next, and in one instance within the same article.[1270]

Clark, George
Born: (Unknown)—Date of Death: 22 September 1908
Place: El Paso County
Event: Lynching/Hanged

George Clark, a black man, had created a disturbance at Ulmer during which he shot Constable W. H. Taylor. Taylor had chased Clark for two miles when Clark picked up a rock and struck the officer. Taylor drew his pistol, which Clark took from him and used to shoot Taylor with. Taylor was hit in the leg twice. Clark escaped into the woods but was captured by a citizen's posse at Shero.

At about 3:00 am on Tuesday, 22 September 1908, an agitated mob took control of Clark and lynched him from a tree. The following morning the mob's prescription was found not to have worked when Clark was discovered, still clinging to life, dangling from the limb where he had been left. Their calculation of rope length had been faulty, thus leaving Clark with the ability to touch the ground with his toes.

Clark was cut down and taken to jail where a second group of vigilantes, determined to finish the job, tried to remove him from custody.[1271] Unfortunately the newspaper article failed to confirm whether Clark was successfully lynched on the second attempt or by some miracle managed to dodge the vigilante's rope. Clark's case is being included in the interest of completeness.

Price, Ben
Born: (Unknown)—Date of Death: 5 October 1908
Place: Wharton County
Event: Lynching/Hanged

Ben Price, a black man, was confined in the jail at Glen Flora for outraging his own daughter. On Monday, 5 October 1908, a mob rushed the jail and took Price to the center of town where he was lynched from a pecan tree.[1272]

Parker, Will
Born: circa 1886—Date of Death: 7 January 1909
Place: Limestone County
Event: Lynching/Hanged

Will Parker, a black man, committed a stunning outrage on the three-year old daughter of his employer, Mr. N. O. Bailey. The girl was harshly dealt with in doing. Parker fled, but was captured hiding in a corncrib near Mexia where he was lynched on Thursday, 7 January 1909, by the posse that had pursued him. [1273]

Boyd, John
Born: circa 1886—Date of Death: 8 January 1909
Place: Fayette County
Event: Legal Execution/Hanged

John Boyd, a black man, was tried and convicted of committing an outrage at LaGrange. He was sentenced to death. That verdict was to have been carried out on 3 April 1908, but Governor Campbell granted a stay of execution while he was waiting for a verdict from the Supreme Court. Boyd's luck finally ran out. He was hanged on Friday, 8 January 1909.[1274]

Wyatt, Rolly
Born: circa 1849—Date of Death: 9 February 1909
Place: Robertson County
Event: Lynching/Hanged

Rolly Wyatt, a black man, was lynched by a band of about 200 vigilantes at Hearne on Tuesday, 9 February 1909, on the property of the Planters Oil Mill. Wyatt and another man named Alex McKenzie had shot and killed a section foreman named J. A. Kessler earlier in the day.

Kessler had been checking a house on land that he had recently rented and discovered Wyatt and McKenzie trying to move into the place. A dispute arose, during which the two black men, armed with a shotgun, relented and left. When they returned a short time later they had a load of furniture with them. Kessler once again tried to dissuade the pair from occupying the house that he had rented. His effort ineffective, he sent his brother home to get a shotgun. When the man returned Wyatt and McKenzie shot Kessler in the abdomen without saying a word.

Kessler left behind a family. The status of Alex McKenzie is not known.[1275]

Golden, Claude
Born: circa 1864—Date of Death: 12 February 1909
Place: Jasper County
Event: Lynching/Shot

During the night of Tuesday, 14 July 1908, a posse of about 1,000 men frantically scoured the woods near Beaumont searching for the black man who had attacked and beaten a thirteen-year old white girl named Ada Bell Furlong Hopkins insensible. Her injuries were of a nature that she was not expected to survive.

Emotions were running high. The mob shot and killed an elderly black man who they had mistakenly identified as their targeted prey. The same horde of searchers burned two black amusement parks to the ground and threatened to torch other buildings occupied by blacks near the scene of the crime. [1276]

A black man named Claude Golden was eventually apprehended and sent to jail awaiting trial, which was to have taken place on 3 August 1908. That trial was postponed until 2 December 1908, when Golden was indicted and a change of venue granted. Another black man named Matthew Finnels was also charged in the crime. He went to trial in August and was released on $2,500 bond.

Golden was eventually convicted, and went to the gallows at Jasper on Friday, 12 February 1909. Just before 1:00 pm he was led to a jail window where he addressed the crowd that had gathered outside to witness his hanging. Golden proclaimed his innocence, and asked for those of his race that were present to pray for him. Next he publically thanked Sheriff Brown and his deputies for the kind way in which he had been treated while in jail. Golden asked that the black cap that had been placed over his head be removed. Once done he made another statement, proclaiming that only a doctor could testify that a woman had been outraged and that he was about to be hanged on the testimony of a nurse. Sheriff Brown pulled the lever releasing the trap door. Golden dropped through the floor and shot into eternity.[1277] Golden's body was turned over to friends for shipment to Beaumont for burial.

No further mention was made of poor Ada Bell Hopkins or her condition after the ordeal. On 17 July 1908, an operation was performed to relieve a blood clot on her brain. At that time her status was reported as "not better and not worse." Upon further research it was learned that the girl did recover, and went on to live a long and productive life, finally expiring in October 1972 at Milwaukie, Clackamas County Oregon.[1278]

Green, Johnny

Born: circa 1889—Date of Death: 25 February 1909
Place: Bastrop County
Event: Legal Execution/Hanged

Johnny Green, a black man, was tried and convicted of the murder of an old black man named W. P. Green. That incident took place over one year earlier.

On Thursday, on 25 February 1909, Johnny Green walked to the gallows at the Bastrop jail, smoking a cigarette. He stepped to an open window and addressed the crowd that had gathered outside to witness the event, saying "Hello People. Boys, I want to warn you boys, be good; don't get into trouble. Stay home. You see where I am. I am going to heaven and want to meet you all there." Green finished his smoke while the straps and black cap were being adjusted. At about 1:00 pm Sheriff Townsend sprung the trap and Johnny Green dropped, snapping his neck when the rope plaid out.[1279]

Ellis, Anderson

Born: (Unknown)—Date of Death: 7 March 1909
Place: Rockwall County
Event: Lynching/Burned to Death

On Friday morning, 5 March 1909, a black farmhand named Anderson Ellis outraged Mrs. Arthur McKinney of Rockwall. Ellis was an employee of the woman's husband. Some have alleged that this incident was the result of a forbidden but consensual affair gone badly.

The alarm spread quickly and the entire section turned out for the hunt. During the quest a black man named Will Clark was shot and killed when his father, Andrew Clark, refused the posse permission to search his place for Ellis. As it turns out, Ellis was concealed there, but managed to flee. Hounds were put on the trail and at about 8:00 pm and the fugitive was captured at a place about three miles from Cado Mills.

Ellis was armed, and exhausted his supply of ammunition into the posse without effect. He was immediately wrestled to the ground and secured with ropes. Ellis had been wounded twice in the shootout, once in the back and once in the arm. He was taken to the jail at Rockwall for safekeeping where Mrs. McKinney positively identified him as the man who had attacked her. He later confessed to the crime.

When it became generally known that he was there in the jail a crowd began to quietly gather, eventually numbering in the hundreds of men. The mob overpowered the jailer, took the keys and removed Ellis by force of arms and chained him to an iron stake that had been driven into the ground at the public square. A pile of cordwood saturated in kerosene was placed around him and ignited. Bravely, Ellis never made a sound. He was dead in about nine minutes.[1280] A crowd of more than 1,000 souls attended the man burning.

Afterwards, the *Waco Morning News* wrote, "Resembling the forefathers who dared anything for their country's sake, the determined band of farmers and neighbors last night declared to the sheriff that they didn't want trouble, but that their blood would not stand for a fiendish brute to trample the chastity and sacredness of life and their women folk."

Redden, Joe
Born: (Unknown)—Date of Death: 29 March 1909
Place: Navarro County
Event: Lynching/Hanged

At about 8:00 pm on Monday, 29 May 1909, a crowd of 200 men took a black man named Joe Redden from the city jail at Dawson and hanged him from a telephone pole near the post office. Earlier that day Redden had allegedly insulted a white woman. He was captured by a neighbor and brought to town. A mob gathered and watched the jail. As the force of vigilantes grew, and darkness fell, they decided to take action. After the lynching was concluded the group quietly dispersed.[1281]

Chase, Hill "Pie"
Born: (Unknown)—Date of Death: 30 April 1909
Place: Harrison County
Event: Lynching/Hanged

Chase, Matthew
Born: (Unknown)—Date of Death: 30 April 1909
Place: Harrison County
Event: Lynching/Hanged

Mose, Creole
Born: (Unknown)—Date of Death: 30 April 1909
Place: Harrison County
Event: Lynching/Hanged

Shortly after midnight on Monday, 26 April 1909, Deputy Sheriff Lewis Markham Huffman was shot and killed and Deputy Constable Alex Cargill was injured when the lawmen went to a railroad camp near Marshall to investigate a crap game that was reportedly taking place there. The men in the camp extinguished the lamps and opened fire on the officers as they approached the encampment. Both lawmen were hit. Huffman was shot in the right side. The bullet traveled through his body and exited his left arm. He staggered away about forty feet and died at the scene. His partner, Constable Alex Cargill, was shot through the left arm but survived. He returned to town for help. [1282]

All three suspects, "Creole" Mose, Hill Chase and Mat Chase were eventually apprehended. Mose, said to be a "yellow Louisiana negro," a light skinned mulatto, was apprehended near Waskom.[1283]

At about midnight on Friday, 30 April 1909, Sheriff Cargill went to the jail and told the militia who had been stationed there for about a week that they were relieved. The men began to pack up their belongings and leave almost at once as someone in the crowd began to sing, "God Be With You Till We Meet Again."

Between 2:00 and 3:00 am a mob of about thirty or forty persons formed outside the building. At first they tried to deceive the jailer, Jesse Stotz, in order to gain entry. Their ruse did not work, so the rabble charged the jail and broke a hole through the wall with a long ramming post that they had cut from a telephone pole. They cut the telephone wires then removed Hill, Chase and Mose and lynched them from a large willow tree near Pope's gin in the south section of town.[1284]

Hodges, James "Jim"
Born: circa 1884—Date of Death: 1 May 1909
Place: Smith County
Event: Lynching/Hanged

According to sources, a black man named James Hodges was lynched at Tyler in Smith County on Saturday, 1 May 1909. Hodges had assaulted a young woman named Winnie Harmon the preceding evening, inflicting serious injury from the rough handling. The incident occurred between 5:00 and 6:00 pm. Miss Hodges, the eighteen year old daughter of M. J. Harmon, a truck grower living three miles south of the city, was snatched from here home by Hodges who had come calling for her father.

He carried the girl to the barn, tied and gagged her then grabbed her around the waist and throat. At that point Miss Harmon lost consciousness. Frightened, Hodges ran off before culminating the outrage. At least that is the story that her mother was sticking with. Her brother and sister discovered the girl some time afterwards.

The search for Hodges had lasted through the night. A pair of shoes belonging to the man was found at the Jim Reese home, where Hodges hiding place was revealed.

Great excitement prevailed. Scores of citizens who had joined the search gathered in town. By about 8:00 am news had spread, and by 10:30 am more than 3,000 souls had massed on the town square. When the 11:30 am International and Great Northern train arrived reinforcements poured out. The doors of the jail were breached, Hodges was removed, and at the stroke of noon was run up a tree and lynched. Sheriff Smith had wired the governor, but that alert had come far too late to have any effect. Once the thing had been done the crowd disbursed quietly, and the town was returned to propped order.[1285]

Shelton, Edmund

Born: (Unknown)—Date of Death: 14 May 1909
Place: Galveston County
Event: Legal Execution/Hanged

Edmund Shelton, a black man, was tried and convicted of murdering Ephraim Bass, another black man. That incident took place in October 1907. He was sentenced to death. After several appeals and two reprieves by Governor Campbell Shelton's time ran out.

At about 3:00 pm on Friday, 14 May 1909, that sentence was carried out at Galveston. Sheriff Thomas pulled the trap.[1286]

Barrett, Tom

Born (Unknown)—Date of Death: 28 May 1909
Place: Taylor County
Event: Lynching/Shot

On Friday, 28 May 1909, a mob charged the county jail at Abilene and fatally shot a convicted murderer named Tom Barrett while the man was still in his cell. Barrett, a white man, had been convicted of the murder of Alexander Sears, a prominent cattleman. He was sentenced to ninety-nine years in prison. Barrett was in the county jail pending an appeal of his conviction. The killers escaped. Judge Blanton empanelled a grand jury to investigate the murder and return indictments against the mob members.[1287]

Juareque, Refugio
Born: (Unknown)—Date of Death: 11 June 1909
Place: Wilson County
Event: Legal Execution/Hanged

Refugio Juareque, a Mexican man, who had been tried and convicted of outrage, was sentenced to hang on Friday, 11 June 1909.

Juareque kept his date with the hangman, but he had a few surprises in store for his executioners as well as the onlookers when his judgment day arrived. As Sheriff William Wright attempted to adjust the black cap over Juareque's head he produced a metal spoon that had been sharpened into a point and stabbed the sheriff. The blade entering his chest, just above the heart. A struggle ensued during which Wright was able to break free. Fortunately Juareque's blade struck a rib, deflecting the blade so as to miss the sheriff's vital organs. When the trap was finally sprung Juareque dropped sideways over the opening, making it necessary to repeat the process. The second try was a success. Juareque had professed his innocence to the end.[1288]

Thomas, Marcellus
Born: (Unknown)—Date of Death: 3 September 1909
Place: Harris County
Event: Legal Execution/Hanged

Marcellus Thomas, a black man, was tried and convicted of murdering Thomas Blair and another white man near Spring nearly three years previous. Thomas was tried and convicted of the murder of Blair. The case went all the way to the United States Supreme Court, which failed to rule based on a lack of jurisdiction.

Thomas was a well to do black man, but spent his fortune trying to avoid hanging. Obsessed with dodging the gallows, he attempted to escape and kill Sheriff Anderson by slashing the lawman's throat with a knife he had made from the fragment of a pie plate he had fashioned into a weapon.

In spite of his best efforts to dodge the inevitable, Thomas climbed the gallows at Houston on Friday, 3 September 1909, and kept his date with the hangman.[1289]

One Unidentified Black Man
Born: (Unknown)—Date of Death: 13 September 1909
Place: Unknown County
Event: Lynching

According to Carrigan's book *The Lynching Calendar*, on Monday, 13 September 1909, vigilantes murdered an unidentified black man at Bellamy. One additional source also lists this incident. There is, however, no town named Bellamy in Texas thus raising some question as to the veracity of this claim. There is, however, a Bellmead located in McLennan County.[1290]

Keyes, Jake
Born: circa 1859—Date of Death: 17 September 1909
Place: Brazoria County
Event: Lynching

Nobles, Charles
Born: (Unknown)—Date of Death: 17 September 1909
Place: Brazoria County
Event: Lynching

On Sunday, 12 September 1909, two black men identified as Charles Delaney and John Cooper escaped from the county jail at Angleton. There may have been a third black man involved in the jailbreak. The men were armed, and headed to the rail station to catch a train to Houston. At the depot they encountered stationmaster, J.T. "Tut" Hardin, who they shot and killed. Hardin was also a wealthy stockman.

On Wednesday, 15 September 1909, the sheriff and a posse of five men located Steve Hayes, a cousin of Delaney, at Sandy Point. The search party employed two packs of bloodhounds to locate the group of men. Hillen Armour Munson, a wealthy rancher, joined the posse because he had employed Hayes and knew him. Munson approached the cabin. Either Delaney or Hayes fatally shot him with a shotgun. Delaney and Hayes fled the scene. Hayes was later killed. Delaney was captured and jailed in Houston.

On Friday, 17 September 1909, a posse of 200 heavily armed men shot and killed Jake Keyes, an armed black man, when he allegedly refused to surrender. A man named Charles Nobles was shot and killed by mistake. He was an innocent young white man from Navasota who just happened to be traveling through the region. [1291]

Some sources list Nobles's surname as Knoble and DeLancy is sometimes listed as Delaney.[1292]

McIntosh, Will
Born: (Unknown)—Date of Death: 1 October 1909
Place: Lamar County
Event: Legal Execution/Hanged

Lamar County Deputy Constable William Draper was shot and killed when he and Constable Matthews attempted to serve a warrant on a man named Bill (Will) McIntosh. At about 8:00 pm on Friday, 5 February 1909, Draper and Matthews went to the home of McIntosh in Paris to place him under arrest for assault. When they arrived McIntosh was not at home. The lawmen were talking with a woman at the residence when McIntosh returned. Draper and Matthews told him that they had come to place him in custody. McIntosh grabbed a rifle from inside the back door of his home and shot Draper at point blank range, killing him instantly. After the shooting McIntosh fled.

McIntosh was captured at Wister, Oklahoma on 9 February 1909, and returned to Paris.

He was tried and convicted of Draper's murder, and sentenced to be executed by hanging on 7 October 1909.

The widow of Draper, as well as a handful of acquaintances, attended the hanging on the date prescribed. McIntosh had had a shave on his last morning, administered by a white barber named Nelson who was serving time for bigamy. The sheriff gave McIntosh a quarter in order to compensate the barber. For his last meal McIntoch requested fish and half a dozen eggs. Claiming to have been a Baptist since age sixteen he requested no special services, claiming that he felt no more converted now than he did when he joined up.

Sheriff Walker pulled the lever to actuate the trap at about 11:30 am, sending McIntoch to the hereafter. He never flinched on the gallows and never confessed to having done the crime.[1293]

Russell, Lee
Born: (Unknown)—Date of Death: 1 October 1909
Place: Houston County
Event: Legal Execution/Hanged

Lee Russell, a black man, was tried and found guilty of the murder of Mollie Harris, a black woman, who had been found dead in a well at Crockett a few weeks previous. He was sentenced to hang for his crime.

On Friday, 1 October 1909, eight thousand people gathered at Crockett to see Lee Russell hanged. A black preacher spoke, and then Russell gave a fifteen minute speech telling the crowd to be good and to meet him in heaven. Russell continued to protest his innocence. He remained calm until the black cap was placed over his head, then he fainted. At 2:00 pm the lever was pulled and Russell was catapulted into the next life.[1294]

Williams, Frank
Born: (Unknown)—Date of Death: 21 October 1909
Place: Hunt County
Event: Lynching/Hanged

Surname Unknown, Louis
Born: (Unknown)—Date of Death: 21 October 1909
Place: Hunt County
Event: Lynching/Hanged

A company of state militia took a black man accused of assaulting a white woman into custody at Greenville. The victim was identified as Mrs. Boyd. A mob attempted to seize the prisoner but was rebuffed. The group reformed, this time with reinforcements, and managed to take control of the accused fellow. Once in their hands they lynched him without delay.[1295]

Williston, Tom

Born: (Unknown)—Date of Death: 22 October 1909
Place: Newton County
Event: Legal Execution/Hanged

Tom Williston, alias T. W. Butler, was found guilty of the murder of county attorney A. K. Nicks. The incident took place at Turpentine Camp, in the north end of Newton County. Williston, a black man, received the death penalty.

At about 1:30 pm on Friday, 22 October 1909, Williston paid the price for his crime on the gallows at Newton. A large crowd had gathered, however few were actually able to witness the hanging through the limited number of windows in the jailhouse. Williston spoke to the multitude, imploring young black men to stay home and keep out of trouble. Sheriff F. M. Mattox pulled the trap and Tom Williston was all over.[1296]

Wright, Robert

Born: (Unknown)—Date of Death: 17 December 1909
Place: Sabine County
Event: Legal Execution/Hanged

Robert Wright, a white man from Sabine County, was tried and convicted of assassinating his brother-in-law in June 1909. The two men lived within 300 yards of each other on the road between Geneva and Bronson in Sabine County. Wright received a death sentence. He was to have been hanged on 17 December 1909, but the governor issued a series of respites delaying the hanging. According to the records posted by the *Death Penalty Information Center* Wright was executed as scheduled.[1297]

Mills, Louis "Coke"

Born: (Unknown)—Date of Death: 20 December 1909
Place: Falls County
Event: Lynching/Hanged

On Monday, 20 December 1909, a black man named Louis Mills, referred to as "Coke Mills" in one newspaper article, shot and fatally wounded Falls County Constable James Edgar Williams. Williams died two days later on Wednesday, 22 December 1909, from the effects of his wounds. Mills was wanted on a minor charge. When Williams attempted to arrest him the man fled, turned and fired the fatal gunshots.

Rosebud Mayor S. J. Ward joined in the melee and pursued Mills through town in a running gun battle that culminated at the edge of the village where Ward finally wounded Mills in the right leg below the knee.

Mills was placed in the city jail at about 6:00 pm. Shortly afterwards a mob of about fifty angry citizens removed him under force and lynched him from the tower of the fire station.[1298]

One Unidentified Black Man
Born: (Unknown)—Date of Death: 24 January 1910
Place: Jefferson County
Event: Lynching/Shot

On Monday, 24 January 1910, an unidentified black man was lynched for attacking Mrs. L. P. Jones, wife of a farmer near Beaumont. In this context the term "attacked" is presumed to have meant outraged.

A posse led by Mr. Jones, the woman's husband, captured the man. While en route to the jail at Beaumont the accused is aid to have tried to escape, at which time the armed posse opened fire. His corpse was taken to Beaumont and a report was filed.[1299]

Thomas, Gus
Born: circa 1886—Date of Death: 26 February 1910
Place: Wharton County
Event: Legal Execution/Hanged

Washington, Sam
Born: circa 1876—Date of Death: 26 February 1910
Place: Wharton County
Event: Legal Execution/Hanged

Gus Thomas and Sam Washington, both black men, were tried and found guilty of the murder of two black women. The pair was hanged at Wharton on Saturday, 26 February 1910.[1300]

The men became the first to meet their end on the gallows at Wharton in many years, causing all to recall the last, and most unfortunate incident that involved a Mr. Farrell. That incident had taken place several years earlier when a miscalculation of rope length resulted in the poor fellow's decapitation.

Brooks, Allen
Born: (Unknown)—Date of Death: 3 March 1910
Place: Dallas County
Event: Lynching/Hanged

At about midnight on Thursday, 3 March 1910, Allen Brooks, a black man who had been charged with criminally assaulting a two year old white child, was forcibly removed from his jail cell at Dallas and lynched. Dozens of angry citizens tore the jail door down, grabbed Brooks from his cell and threw him through a window, down to the waiting throng below. Brooks was marched to a place known as Elk's Arch and strung up.

Apparently not yet ready to leave his mortal host, Brooks' ghost is claimed to roam the Dallas jail, making himself manifest to black inmates there on a routine basis. One such black prisoner claimed that he was awakened during the night by the apparition of Brooks, walking through his cell with the hangman's rope around his neck, head cocked to one side, crying out in pain. He always appears at around midnight, witnesses' claim, which was the approximate hour of his launching. Some level of credibility has been assigned to the allegations of Brooks' supernatural wanderings, as many of the witnesses had no idea who the man was until they were told afterwards.

In May 1920, the sheriff was forced to convert the section of the jail involved into a storeroom in order to bring a halt Brooks' frequent visits.[1301]

Bates, Frank
Born: (Unknown)—Date of Death: 5 April 1910
Place: Leon County
Event: Lynching/Hanged

Frank Bates, a black man, along with his son Dolly Bates, were confined to the Centerville jail for being a ringleader in a nefarious group of malefactors. Following an escape attempt during which Jailer Jeff St. John was seriously wounded (perhaps fatally) Frank Bates was lynched at the Centerville jail on Friday, 5 April 1910. His son Dolly was also strung up, but was cut down before he expired.[1302]

Robertson, Julius R. "Bubber"
Born (Unknown)—Date of Death: 13 May 1910
Place: Dallas County
Event: Legal Execution

On 11 November 1908, Frank Wolford, a white farmer at Rose Hill, along with his stepson and a neighbor boy were walking down Main Street in Dallas heading to their wagon when three black men approached them. Robertson and two accomplices named Eugene "Gene" Jones and Walter "Shine" West ordered them to throw up their hands. Wolford pulled a knife and cut Robertson slightly. Robertson asked Wolford if he was going to give up his money. When he did not reply Robertson shot and killed him. The men fled, but Jones and West were captured and confessed. Robertson was captured some time later.

Jones turned state's evidence against the other two men. He was charged in the robbery of Wolford and the murder of another man. West was convicted and sentenced to death but died in jail.

On Friday, 13 May 1910, Julius R. Robertson, alias Bubber Robinson, was hanged at Dallas for the murder of Frank Wolford. More than 3,000 people attended his funeral and viewed his body at a Dallas funeral home. Robertson's remains were shipped to Paris for burial.[1303]

Miller, G. R.
Born: (Unknown)—Date of Death: 3 June 1910
Place: Donley County
Event: Legal Execution/Hanged

G. R. Miller, a black man, was tried and convicted of having robbed and murdered Floyd Autrey and for shooting Fred Garrett. Autrey was killed in a boxcar on the Fort Worth and Denver freight train between 3:00 and 4:00 am on Saturday night, 20 March 1909. Miller was also accused of having killed a second man on that same train and having tossed his body from the railcar into the Red River near Estelline. In addition to Autrey, Miller shot Garrett, Autrey's cousin, in the course of the same incident. Garrett escaped further harm by leaping from the moving train car.

Autrey and Garrett had bought a ticket to ride as passengers from Fort Worth to Childress. From that point they decided to save a few pennies and ride in a boxcar, which is where they encountered Miller. The latter entered the same conveyance the pair was traveling in. He appeared friendly, and was soon sharing their tobacco with them. All went swimmingly well until Miller produced a revolver and opened fire.

Miller was tried and convicted on 22 March 1910. He received the death sentence.[1304] On Friday, 3 June 1910, the sentence was carried out at Clarendon. A large crowd watching from a distance. At 11:06 am Sheriff Patmon pulled the lever and Miller dropped through the trap, breaking his neck when he reached the end of his rope.[1305]

Lemon, Douglas
Born: (Unknown)—Date of Death: 5 June 1910
Place: Orange County
Event: Lynching/Shot

Moore, Rankin
Born: (Unknown)—Date of Death: 5 June 1910
Place: Orange County
Event: Lynching/Shot

Early in the day on Sunday, 5 June 1910, Douglas Lemon, a black man, was shot down on the streets of Orange. Later the same day another black man, Rankin Moore was killed in a fusillade of gunshots said to have been fired by three white men. The local sentiment was that serious trouble between the races could boil over at any time.[1306]

Wynne, John
Born: (Unknown)—Date of Death: 24 June 1910
Place: Walker County
Event: Legal Execution/Hanged

John Wynne, a black man convicted of murder, had cheated the hangman twice, successfully having his execution reprieved by the Governor on two occasions. On Friday, 24 June 1910, his luck ran out. Wynne was hanged at Huntsville. [1307]

Johnson, Leonard
Born: (Unknown)—Date of Death: 26 June 1910
Place: Cherokee County
Event: Lynching/Hanged

On Monday, 20 June 1910, Miss Maude Redden, a white girl and the daughter of Constable Redden, was murdered at Rusk while her father was away at a political meeting. Leonard Johnson, a black man, who had been working near the Redden place, was arrested under suspicion of having done the act. Officers did their best to protect him from vigilantes who wanted to lynch him on the spot.[1308] Their efforts came up short. Johnson was lynched at Rusk on Sunday, 26 June 1910.

One Unidentified Black Man
Born: (Unknown)—Date of Death: 5 July 1910
Place: Navarro County
Event: Lynching/Hanged

On Monday, 4 July 1910, a black man entered the home of Hub Bailey, a merchant living at Rodney near Corsicana. The man brandished a knife, threatening Mrs. Bailey, bride of three months. The woman grappled with the fellow until he dropped the knife and fled. A posse of mounted vigilantes caught up with the would-be molester at Richland Creek bottom and lynched him on the spot.[1309]

Cannon, John W.
Born: (Unknown)—Date of Death: 8 July 1910
Place: Polk County
Event: Legal Execution/Hanged

John Cannon, a black man who had been tried and convicted of murdering Warren Perryman, another black man, was executed at Livingston on Friday, 8 July 1910. That killing had taken place near Camden nearly a year ago

Cannon walked deliberately to the gallows, scaled the stairs and joined in the singing that was being led by two black preachers. He shook hands with Sheriff Chapman, thanking him for his kind treatment during his stay in jail. Cannon also shook hands with all of the deputies, bidding them farewell. After his final salutation to the crowd the black cap was pulled down over his head and the noose affixed. Chapman pulled the lever and Cannon dropped to his death, neck broken from his trip through the gallows floor.[1310]

Henderson, Henry "Slick"

Born: circa 1887—Date of Death: 8 July 1910
Place: Rusk County
Event: Legal Execution/Hanged

Newspapers of the day indicated that Henry "Slick" Henderson, a twenty-three year old black man who had been raised at Hubbard City, was convicted of the murder of E. C. Landrum on 8 December 1909. Henderson did the deed with a hammer, at Landrum's own store, where he struck him nine times with the blunt instrument, caving in his head. Once he was convinced that Landrum was dead he rifled the man's pockets and robbed the store of about $75. Henderson was arrested at Alto, about seven miles from the site of the killing.

Henderson ate a hearty breakfast and supper on his last morning. He went to the gallows on Friday, 8 July 1910. At about 1:30 pm Sheriff Norwood left the jail with the condemned man in tow, taking Henderson about one half mile north of town to the prescribed location. Reverends Turner Brown and Sam Love ascended the platform with the condemned man, making prayers as they went. Henderson spoke for about five minutes, letting all know that he would meet them in heaven. As the black cap was being fitted over his head he thanked jailer E. C. Martin for the man's kind treatment while he was locked up. The trap was sprung at 2:16 pm

Henderson's surname is incorrectly referenced as Roberson in some newspaper articles of the day.[1311]

Gentry, Henry

Born: circa 1892—Date of Death: 22 July 1910
Place: Bell County
Event: Lynching/Shot and Burned to Death

Henry Gentry, an eighteen-year old black man, was charged with the murder and the attempted outrage of a white woman.

Gentry had tried to force his way into the home of Mrs. Lamb, a widow, but was frightened away by a gunshot delivered by the woman's daughter. Several hours later a posse headed up by Constable James Mitchell was in hot pursuit. A person or persons unknown fired a shot at Mitchell from ambush, inflicting a fatal wound. When the mob surrounded Gentry he made a dash for freedom but was wounded by a gunshot fired by one of the vigilantes.

Gentry was dragged behind an automobile back to Belton then taken to the public square where he was bound tightly and placed on a makeshift pyre. A torch was applied and the bonfire ignited. As he was being burned to death several hundred shots were fired into Gentry's body, just for good measure.

Some sources provide a slightly different account, claiming that Gentry was shot to death in a cornfield where he murdered Mitchell, then taken to Belton by the posse where his body was dragged around the square behind a wagon and burned until nothing remained of him but ashes. In that telling the bonfire is said to have been at the courthouse flagpole.[1312]

The frenzied mob made a dash for the city jail with designs on doing the same for two men who had aided Gentry in the killing of Mitchell, but a show of force by the sheriff halted their advance.[1313]

Baker, Sam
Born: (Unknown)—Date of Death: 29 July 1910
Place: Anderson County
Event: Lynching/Shot

Burley, Will
Born: (Unknown)—Date of Death: 29 July 1910
Place: Anderson County
Event: Lynching/Shot

Dancer, Ben
Born: (Unknown)—Date of Death: 29 July 1910
Place: Anderson County
Event: Lynching/Shot

Forman, William
Born: (Unknown)—Date of Death: 29 July 1910
Place: Anderson County
Event: Lynching/Shot

Hays, John
Born: (Unknown)—Date of Death: 29 July 1910
Place: Anderson County
Event: Lynching/Shot

Holly, Alex
Born: (Unknown)—Date of Death: 29 July 1910
Place: Anderson County
Event: Lynching/Shot

Larkin, Cleve
Born: (Unknown)—Date of Death: 29 July 1910
Place: Anderson County
Event: Lynching/Shot

Larkin, Ned
Born: (Unknown)—Date of Death: 29 July 1910
Place: Anderson County
Event: Lynching/Shot

Wilson, Abe
Born: (Unknown)—Date of Death: 29 July 1910
Place: Anderson County
Event: Lynching/Shot

Wilson, Dick
Born: (Unknown)—Date of Death: 29 July 1910
Place: Anderson County
Event: Lynching/Shot

Wilson, Jeff
Born: (Unknown)—Date of Death: 29 July 1910
Place: Anderson County
Event: Lynching/Shot

Two Unidentified Black Men
Born: (Unknown)—Date of Death: 29 July 1910
Place: Anderson County
Event: Lynching/Shot

Newspapers of the day tell the chilling tale of black men being hunted down like wild animals in the woods near Palestine.

As accurately as Sheriff Black could relate the incident, about 300 men from the Slocum and Dennison Springs neighborhoods were roaming about the woods terrorizing and killing black people. The entire region was in a state of high excitement as blacks fled for their lives. As far as a cause is concerned, Sheriff Black was unable to cite one, apart from speculating that a disagreement over a promissory note may have ignited the melee. In total, twelve to fifteen blacks were killed.[1314]

The *Fort Worth Star Telegram* claimed that armed white men had traveled over a section that was heavily populated by black people, shooting them down. Many were said to have been elderly and defenseless. Eleven in all were killed, "many" wounded. Some houses and barns were torched. The whole ugly affray is said to have sprung from a quarrel between a white farmer and a black tenant.[1315]

On Friday night, 29 July 1910, a white mob of 200 or more drove black residents into a heavily wooded area and killed them. The incident took place near the village of Slocum, about fourteen miles south of Palestine. Cutting the telephone lines along the way, the rabble assured that news of the violence would be difficult to confirm. Scattered bands clashed. At least eighteen black people were killed. The bodies were left as they fell, in the woods and on the roads. Some of the news accounts reported the number of deaths as thirty or forty.

Texas Rangers arrived the day after the incident, under the command of Captain Godfrey Rees Fowler, a local son and former Army officer recently returned from Nicaragua. The presence of militia seemed to bring the violence under control, but only after it had spread to the towns of Denson Springs and Elkhart. The state militia guarded the county jail in Palestine, where the first prisoners were placed.

Tension had been building in the weeks prior to the riot. Black farmers had begun to protest the peonage system. A black man, Henry Gentry, had declined to pay a debt sponsored by a white farmer named Redin Alford. Alford had to pay it. Then, a white man, according to some accounts named James Spurger, refused to work under a black supervisor when assigned to a road crew. There were rumors of secret meetings among black residents, and a black man allegedly confessed to a plan to kill Spurger and his family.

On the night of the riot, a black man, believed to be carrying a shotgun, was declared to be advancing on Spurger. When he refused to surrender a posse shot him. The rioting followed shortly thereafter. Farmers and other white citizens stocked up on weapons before County Judge B. H. Gardner ordered the sale of firearms to be discontinued and dictated that all saloons closed as well.

Sheriff William Black's description of the situation was later quoted widely by major newspapers, including the *Washington Post, New York Times, and Atlanta Constitution,* "Men were going about and killing Negroes as fast as they could find them...without any real cause. These Negroes have done no wrong that I could discover....It will be difficult to find out just how many were killed....Some will probably never be found."

A grand jury was formed that included District Attorney Harris and District Judge Gardner. The names of fourteen of the dead were established. In this account eleven have been confirmed, and cited by name (twelve counting Henry Gentry). There were sixteen white men arrested in connection with the riots, including James Spurger, Reagon McKenzie, and S. F. Jenkins. All were held without bail.[1316]

Rodriguez, Antonio
Born: (Unknown)—Date of Death: 2 November 1910
Place: Edwards County
Event: Lynching/Burned to Death

On Wednesday afternoon, 2 November 1910, Mrs. Lem Henderson, the wife of a rancher who lived with her husband about eighteen miles northeast of Rocksprings, was murdered. Apart from her two small children she was alone at the time when Antonio Rodriguez, a Mexican man, rode up and, for reasons unknown, murdered her on the porch of her house. When Mr. Henderson returned home the eldest child told him that "a bad Mexican had killed mama."

Mr. Henderson sounded the alarm. Rodriguez, who seemed to fit the description provided, was apprehended some miles away by another rancher named Jim Hunter. Rodriguez confessed to the killing, giving no other reason than that Mrs. Henderson had "spoke mean to him." He was taken to the jail at Rocksprings.

Later the same day a crowd of Mexicans and whites gathered. They eventually removed Rodriguez from the jail under force of arms and took him to a clump of trees a mile or two outside of town where he was lashed to a mesquite tree, logs piled around him, dowse with kerosene and set ablaze. The angry crowd, none of whom made any attempt to conceal their identity with a mask or such, stared at the man as flames licked around him and he was reduced to ash. All the time Rodriguez stared back at them from the inferno, it is said, expressionless like Lucifer himself.[1317]

Cassaway, Louis
Born: (Unknown)—Date of Death: March 1911
Place: Bexar County
Event: Lynching/Ax Murder

Cassaway, Mrs. (Given Name Unknown)
Born: (Unknown)—Date of Death: March 1911
Place: Bexar County
Event: Lynching/Ax Murder

Cassaway, Three Children
Born: (Unknown)—Date of Death: March 1911
Place: Bexar County
Event: Lynching/Ax Murder

Louis Cassaway, his wife and three children, were all mysteriously murdered at their home on Olive Street in San Antonio. One child was a six-month old infant. The other two were three and six respectively. The incident occurred during the night. The Cassaway family, who were black, were asleep when a person or persons unknown crept into their home and attacked them with an ax.

Cassaway was a janitor at a local black school. He was highly regarded. Mrs. Cassaway is said to have been light skinned, perhaps a white woman, quadroon or octoroon. She had been divorced from a cowboy to whom she had been married in her girlhood, about ten years previous. [1318] The Cassaway killing was but the first in a string of such incidents that occurred throughout Texas and Louisiana. Before the ax killings were over about fifty poor souls would fall victim.

One Unidentified Man

Born: (Unknown)—Date of Death: 30 May 1911
Place: Ward County
Event: Lynching/Shot

According to sources, an unidentified Mexican man was shot to death in the Black Bridge area of Barstow in Ward County for shouting "Viva Diaz." The incident is said to have taken place during a celebration of the victories of Madero. Apparently that alone will get one shot in Texas.

Reliable newspaper accounts are clear on the point that the reports of this incident are unconfirmed. Carrigan's *Forgotten Dead*, does not make that distinction.[1319]

Gomez, Antonio

Born: circa 1897—Date of Death: 19 June 1911
Place: Milam County
Event: Lynching/Hanged

Antonio Gomez, a Mexican youth, was beaten and lynched at Thorndale on Monday, 19 June 1911.

Gomez was suspected of murdering Charles Ziechung, who is said to have insulted the lad. According to newspaper reports of the day, Ziechung's outburst contained unprintable words. In short, Ziechung had said, "If that_____little_____ever comes down in front of my place of business whittling on shingles I will whip the_____." One's imagination might fill in the blanks in several different ways, but whatever was said it was sufficiently derogatory in Gomez's opinion to warrant shooting Ziechung.

Five or six men went to the house where Gomez was staying and took him into custody, padlocking a chain around his neck. Unable to find an automobile, they attached the chain to a horse and more or less dragged Gomez to town where, according to Judge English, he was already practically dead upon arrival.

Four men were arrested and charged with the murder of Gomez, Z. T. Gore, Jr., Ezra Stephens, G. P. Noach and Harry Wuenche. Gore was acquitted of the killing on Tuesday, 14 November 1911, in a trial at Cameron. G. P. Noack, Erza Stephens and H. W. Wuenehe, were tried at Georgetown for having participated in the killing. Noack was acquitted on 2 March 1912, but the disposition of the charges against Stephens and Wuenche is not clear.[1320] Afterwards, Judge E. F. English proclaimed that the youth was but fourteen years of age and weighted no more than fifty pounds. Some sources list Gomez's given name as Fernando.

Jones, Commodore
Born: (Unknown)—Date of Death: 11 August 1911
Place: Collin County
Event: Lynching/Hanged

Commodore Jones, a black man who had lived in the Farmersville area for about two years, was confined in the jail there for having insulted a white widow woman named Woodward. A group of unknown parties, all wearing masks to conceal their identity, broke down the door of the jail, removed Jones, and then lynched him from a telephone pole. About 500 people, including City Marshal D. H. Foster, witnessed the spectacle. Jones hung for about thirty-five minutes before someone cut him down.[1321]

Ollie, Will
Born: (Unknown)—Date of Death: 29 October 1911
Place: Harrison County
Event: Lynching/Hanged

On Friday, 27 October 1911, Will Ollie, a black man, is said to have attacked a white woman at a spot about five miles west of Marshall. The woman was entering a field on her farm when Ollie descended upon her, throttling her and attempting to hang her and set fire to her clothing. The sounds of the woman's screams frightened Ollie away. He fled to Longview where another black man turned him in to the city marshal.

Shortly after midnight, on Sunday 29 October 1911, Ollie was taken from officers who were transporting him to Marshall and lynched him from a tree near the sight of the crime.[1322]

Johnson, Riley
Born: (Unknown)—Date of Death: 6 November 1911
Place: Red River County
Event: Lynching/Shot

Riley Johnson, a black man, entered a farmhouse near Clarksville and attacked a young woman. He clubbed the girl's mother practically insensible when she responded to the calls of her struggling daughter and came to her aid. A neighbor who approached the house interrupted Johnson's evil work while the deed was in progress.

Johnson fled, but was captured by an impromptu posse. He attempted to gain his freedom from the lawmen, breaking loose for an instant before armed citizens who had accompanied the search party shot him dead.[1323]

Johnson, Louis
Born: circa 1892—Date of Death: 30 January 1912
Place: Polk County
Event: Legal Execution/Hanged

The *Death Penalty Information Center* claims that a twenty-year old black man named Louis Johnson was legally executed at Polk County on 30 January 1912. He had been tried and convicted of committing an outrage. Thus far no documentation to support this claim has been located.[1324]

Jackson, Mary
Born: circa 1872—Date of Death: 13 February 1912
Place: Harrison County
Event: Lynching/Hanged

Saunders, George
Born: circa 1852—Date of Death: 13 February 1912
Place: Harrison County
Event: Lynching/Hanged

A white man named Paul Strange was shot and killed from ambush on Monday, 29 January 1912. A black man named Tennie Sneed was arrested and placed in the county jail at Marshall. Sneed confessed, and said that he had he gotten the gun from a black female named Mary Jackson who lived with a black man named George Saunders (or Sanders). Sneed, Saunders and Jackson all lived in the same house.

Shortly before midnight on Monday, 12 February 1912, a party of eight to ten white men went to the jail asking for Sneed. They were told he had been transferred to the jail at Rusk. The following night the men returned, taking Saunders and Jackson from the jail and hanging them from the same tree. Sneed was later tried for the murder of Strange but the outcome of that court case is not known.[1325]

Varner, Albert
Born: (Unknown)—Date of Death: 16 February 1912
Place: Guadalupe County
Event: Legal Execution/Hanged

A black man named Albert Varner was legally executed at Seguin in Guadalupe County on Friday,

16 February 1912. He had been tried and convicted of committing an outrage in Colorado County in October 1911.

Varner went to the gallows at Seguin at about noon, escorted by Sheriff Phil P. Medlin. He scaled the stairs of the gibbet and paused to address the gathered crowd, extolling the virtues of a good life and stating that bad company was the cause of his troubles. Varner prayed long and hard for forgiveness. The actual hanging was done in private. Sheriff Mays of Colorado County pulled the lever and sprung the trap, causing Varner to drop to his death. Varner's execution was the first in the county since 1900.[1326]

Dove, Hattie
Born: (Unknown)—Date of Death:19 February 1912
Place: Jefferson County
Event: Lynching/Ax Murder

Dove, Ernest
Born: (Unknown)—Date of Death: 19 February 1912
Place: Jefferson County
Event: Lynching/Ax Murder

Dove, Ethel
Born: (Unknown)—Date of Death: 19 February 1912
Place: Jefferson County
Event: Lynching/Ax Murder

Quirk, Jessie
Born: (Unknown)—Date of Death: 19 February 1912
Place: Jefferson County
Event: Lynching/Ax Murder

On Sunday, 18 February 1912, four blacks were murdered at Beaumont. It was the seventh in a series of similar murders of black persons to occur in the area. All of the previous killings had taken place in western Louisiana, near Crowley, and resulted in a total of twenty-six deaths in just six families. Among those killed at Beaumont was the mother, Hattie Dove, her son, Ernest Dove aged fourteen, daughter Ethel Dove aged sixteen, and a married daughter named Jessie Quirk aged eighteen (identified as Mrs. Jim or Jeff Burks). They were found in their beds, beaten to death with an ax during the night.

One newspaper account attributed the murders to a religious fanatic from the "Church of Sacrifice." Each case involved victims being killed in their beds while asleep with the murder weapon, an axe, left behind. None of the dead had been robbed. In one incident, the murderer chopped off the heads of the victims. Police believe that the same person committed all of these heinous slayings. [1327]

Compton, James Barney
Born: circa 1886—Date of Death: 15 March 1912
Place: Webb County
Event: Legal Execution/Hanged

James Barney Compton, a white man, was tried and convicted of the murder of G. J. Levytansky, a jeweler.

The incident occurred at Laredo on Friday, 22 December 1911. Compton had sought to have his sentence commuted to life in prison. On 11 March 1911, Governor Colquitt refused the appeal. Compton's execution went off as planned, in the barn at the county jail at about 11:00 am on Friday, 15 March 1912.[1328]

Compton's wife had preceded him in death. He is buried at the City Cemetery at Laredo.[1329]

Finucane, Lyle
Born: circa 1875—Date of Death: 27 March 1912
Place: Colorado County
Event: Lynching/Ax Murder

Monroe, Alberta
Born: circa 1904—Date of Death: 27 March 1912
Place: Colorado County
Event: Lynching/Ax Murder

Monroe, Dewey
Born: circa 1900—Date of Death: 27 March 1912
Place: Colorado County
Event: Lynching/Ax Murder

Monroe, Ellen
Born: circa 1866—Date of Death: 27 March 1912
Place: Colorado County
Event: Lynching/Ax Murder

Monroe, Jessie
Born: circa 1901—Date of Death: 27 March 1912
Place: Colorado County
Event: Lynching/Ax Murder

Monroe, Willie
Born: circa 1896—Date of Death: 27 March 1912
Place: Colorado County
Event: Lynching/Ax Murder

On 28 March 1912, six unidentified blacks were jailed in connection with the gruesome ax murder of Lyle Finucane and five members of the Monroe family; Alberta, Dewey, Jessie, Willie and the mother, Ellen. Some of the victims were found in their beds and some on the floor. There was no evidence of a struggle. The ax used in the killing belonged to the Monroe family. On 13 April 1912, one of the men, Jim Fields, was indicted on six counts for the crime, but after deliberating only one hour a jury returned a verdict of not guilty.[1330]

Some sources list the surname as Munroe, not Monroe.

McCline, Dan
Born: circa 1886—Date of Death: 29 March 1912
Place: Falls County
Event: Legal Execution/Hanged

Dan McCline, a black man, was tried and convicted of the murder of Rosa Tubbs, a black woman. McCline shot the woman in the back about two years earlier. Jealousy was cited as the cause.

McCline appealed his case to Governor Colquitt twice without success. He was hanged on Friday, 29 March 1912 at Marlin.[1331]

Burton, William
Born: (Unknown)—Date of Death: 11 April 1912
Place: Bexar County
Event: Lynching/Ax Murder

Burton, Mrs. William (Given Name Unknown)
Born: (Unknown)—Date of Death: 11 April 1912
Place: Bexar County
Event: Lynching/Ax Murder

Burton, Unidentified Child #1
Born: (Unknown)—Date of Death: 11 April 1912
Place: Bexar County
Event: Lynching/Ax Murder

Burton, Unidentified Child #2
Born: (Unknown)—Date of Death: 11 April 1912
Place: Bexar County
Event: Lynching/Ax Murder

Evers, Leon
Born: (Unknown)—Date of Death: 11 April 1912
Place: Bexar County
Event: Lynching/Ax Murder

The Burton, family, along with Mrs. Burton's brother, Leon Evers, all blacks, were found murdered in their home at San Antonio. The killer had used an ax to perform the morbid chore. The hatchet-wielding attacker entered the residence sometime between midnight and daybreak on Thursday, 11 April 1912.

Newspaper accounts of the day claimed that the killing bore similarities to the Cassaway murders, which had occurred at San Antonio a year earlier and the recent slaughter of a black family in Louisiana.[1332]

McClennan, Charles (Charlie)
Born (Unknown)—Date of Death: 13 April 1912
Place: Washington County
Event: Legal Execution/ Hanging

Charles McClennan was convicted of the murder of Herbert Hughes. He was sentenced to be hanged at Brenham on Saturday, 6 April 1912. Just hours before the execution was to take place he received a reprieve from Governor O.B. Colquitt. Unfortunately for McClelland the governor did not commute the death sentence, and he was hanged on Saturday, 13 April 1912. Reverends McGill and Coleman, both of whom were black, along with McClelland's mother were with him before his execution.[1333]

Three or Four Unidentified Black Men
Born: (Unknown)—Date of Death: 14 April 1912
Place: Waller County
Event: Lynching/Ax Murder

Newspaper accounts of the day claim that a person or persons unknown murdered three or four unidentified black men at Hempstead. The killer used an ax, which had been the weapon of choice in the recent serial killings of roughly forty-five black men, women and children throughout Texas and Louisiana.

Some blacks blamed it on a devil, or demons. Others thought that whites were responsible for the slayings. The "ax man," as he had been called, had struck terror in the hearts of blacks throughout the region.[1334] Anonymous "red ax" letters had been received at some towns and turned over to authorities for investigation. White newspapers attempted to blame certain black "cult" religions for the heinous crimes. Most remarkable, it seems is that the killer had been able to slay multiple members of a family while they slept...without waking anyone.

Davis, Daniel "Dan"

Born: (Unknown)—Date of Death: 25 May 1912
Place: Smith County
Event: Lynching/Burned to Death

On Saturday, 25 May 1912, Dan Davis, a black man, was arrested at Athens for attacking and outraging a sixteen-year old white girl named Carrie Johnson. The young woman was the daughter of a local farmer.

The incident had taken place on Monday, 13 May 1912, while Miss Johnson was walking along the railroad tracks near Tyler. Davis knocked her to the ground, outraged the girl, then slashed her throat with a knife. The assailant(s) left the scene thinking the girl was dead. Carrie, barely clinging to life, was discovered by a search part the following morning.

A sheriff's posse brought Davis to the jail at Tyler where he confessed to taking part in the assault. He had done it with another black man who was later identified as George Price. Although Miss Johnson failed to positively identify Davis as her assailant, another man who saw him in the area at the time identified him.

Amid the strong protest lodged by officers and many citizens, Davis was finally surrendered to a mob whose numbers made further remonstration useless. From the jail the prisoner was taken to the public square where several wagonloads of wood had been piled. He was tied to a rail, and after he reiterated his confession, a match was applied and the flames enveloped him. Davis repeated his guilt before he died, crying, "I am guilty" as the flames were leaping high around his head. The mob stood around the fire until it had died down and little was left of the man but charred bones and ashes.

The work of the lynch mob was done quickly and quietly. One newspaper reporter penned that, "The determination of the men who had the execution in charge appeared to have a sobering effect upon them."[1335]

George Price, Davis's alleged accomplice in the Carrie Johnson attack, was captured and confined in the jail at Waco on Sunday, 26 May 1912. A group of 200 men traveled by train to that place to carry out a second round of vigilante justice. The lawless horde attempted to break him out and lynch him, but when they had breached the confines of the lock up they discovered that Price was already gone. Lawmen had removed him to a safer location. Price's fate is unknown.[1336]

Henry, John

Born: (Unknown)—Date of Death: 12 July 1912
Place: Travis County
Event: Legal Execution/Hanged

John Henry, a black man, was tried and convicted of murdering his wife. Henry's attorney tried unsuccessfully to have the Governor intervene.

The execution went off as planned, on Friday, 12 July 1912. Henry made a thirty minute speech from the gallows during which he expressed great sorrow for his crime and resignation to his fate. He went on to beg the young men present to learn from his mistakes and not repeat them. At 4:10 pm the trap was sprung and Henry dropped through the floor, swinging for thirteen minutes before being declared dead.[1337]

Maxey, Wood

Born: (Unknown)—Date of Death: 9 August 1912
Place: Grayson County
Event: Legal Execution/Hanged

Vines, Sellers

Born: circa 1894—Date of Death: 9 August 1912
Place: Grayson County
Event: Legal Execution/Hanged

Wood Maxey and Sellers Vines, both black men, spent time in their jail cells joking about who would go to the gallows first. Both men had been tried, convicted of murder, and sentenced to be executed. Both verdicts were to be carried out on the same day.

On Wednesday, 27 September 1911, Grayson County Precinct 1 Constable Thomas Frederick "Fred" Mounger was shot and killed by Sellers Vines while he was responding to a report of a man trespassing in a boxcar. When Mounger approached, Vines drew a .45 caliber pistol and shot him. The wound was fatal. Vines was later arrested.

Maxey had been convicted of murdering Ernest Johnson. That killing took place on 16 October 1910, over a year previous, when Johnson had put Maxey out of a restaurant for misbehaving.

As if the entire spectacle had been orchestrated by the Almighty Himself, on the eve of the pair's date with the hangman the skies were illuminated with the most spectacular lightning display that many could ever recall seeing. Terrified by the exhibit of nature's electricity gone wild, both condemned men got down on their knees and prayed that they would be saved. Maxey asked to be awakened every hour during the night to make certain that the jail had not been destroyed with him in it. His request was complied with. Maxey got out of his cot and prayed at each reveille. Vines, on the other hand, went to bed and slept through until morning.

On Friday, 9 August 1912, both men scaled the gallows at Sherman and met their fate. At about 2:00 pm the lever was pulled. Maxey won the bet. He got to go first.[1338]

Jones, Sam

Born: circa 1867—Date of Death: 16 October 1912
Place: Grayson County
Event: Legal Execution/Hanged

Sam Jones, a black man, was tried and convicted of murdering his divorced wife Eddie Jones. That incident took place on Friday, 16 August 1912.

Jones began the fatal attack on his wife with a pick, but she overpowered him and took the tool away. As she fled from the house he caught up with her, choked her to near unconsciousness, then picked up an ax and finished the job. When questioned, Jones claimed that he had murdered her because she refused to live with him again. If she would not live with him she would not live with anyone.

When convicted and sentenced to death Jones asked that his hanging be set for 16 October, the same day of the month upon which he had killed his wife, and at 10:00 am, the same time of day that he had done the murderous deed.

Jones's appeal was granted. At precisely 10:00 am on Wednesday, 16 October 1912, he scaled the gallows stairs to meet his end. Owing to a miscalculation in either rope length or Jones's weight, the fall from the gallows practically snapped the man's head from his body, spattering blood in every direction and providing a most spectacularly grizzly scene for the spectators.[1339]

Oates, Burrell

Born: (Unknown)—Date of Death: 29 November 1912
Place: Ellis County
Event: Legal Execution/Hanged

Burrell Oates, a black man, spent a great deal of time bragging from his jail cell at Waxahachie that he would never be hanged. Apparently his exuberance stemmed from the belief that Governor Colquitt would either stay his execution or commute his sentence. Oates based that hypothesis on the fact that only eighty-four out of eighty-five jurors during his seven trials had voted for him to be hanged for a murder he and a man named Holly Van had committed several years ago. Oates and Van had held up a white man and his wife, stealing the money from their cash drawer. When the woman resisted Oates and Van opened fire, killing the woman's husband.[1340]

"They's going to wear out these Texas jails with me, yet" Oates claimed, as he bragged to fellow inmates. On Friday, 29 November 1912, Oates's luck ran out. He scaled the gallows steps and learned, as we all do in the end, that all men must accept responsibility for their actions and settle up at the final reckoning.

The self-proclaimed "immortal" Burrell Oates was tried seven times. His cases were responsible for two changes in Texas statutes.

Robinson, John "Bubber"

Born: (Unknown)—Date of Death: 10 January 1913
Place: Dallas County
Event: Legal Execution/Hanged

On Thursday night, 4 May 1911, Otto Kahlkhoff and his wife were returning home when they were waylaid and robbed by John "Bubber" Robinson, a black man.

The incident happened just as the couple passed Chestnut and Dawson Streets in southeast Dallas. Otto Kahlkhoff was struck over the head with a coupling pin (also called a king pin, or king bolt) and left for dead. His wife was also beaten and left for dead. Otto did expire, at the hospital a few days later. His wife recovered. Robinson was captured on the Houston and Texas Central railroad tracks, near Commerce Street.

Robinson went to trial on 13 December 1911 and was immediately found guilty. The death penalty was assessed. His case was appealed on 6 November 1912, and the mandate to uphold the death penalty issued on 28 December 1912. During his hearing at Dallas Judge Seay had said to him. "I point you to the crucifixion of Christ as your only hope in this terrible emergency." A sarcastic Robinson replied, "Thanks you judge, I ain't afraid of no harm from Christ."

Robinson was anything but the model prisoner during his stay at the jail. He attacked a black trustee and cut Sheriff Brandenburg with a piece of a glass milk bottle while attempting an escape.[1341]

In his closing moments Robinson showed a ravenous appetite, devouring his last meal as if... well...as if it were his last meal. He died game, wearing the insignia of the 9th Cavalry on his coat at his hanging, the unit he had served with in the Santiago Campaign of 1898 at San Juan Hill when his outfit rescued Theodore Roosevelt and his Rough Riders. Robinson walked to the gallows at Dallas briskly, where the trap was sprung at about half past noon on Monday, 10 January 1913. Three other black men in north Texas had also met their fate at the end of the same hangman's rope.

Monson, Henry

Born: (Unknown)—Date of Death: 17 January 1913
Place: Lamar County
Event: Lynching/Hanged and Burned

Henry Monson, a black man, was accused of having attacked a twelve-year old white girl named Mary Merrill. He was lynched from a telegraph pole at Cooper late in the day on Friday, 17 January 1913, by a mob of about 1,000 men.

Monson is said to have hidden behind some shrubberies near Pecan Gap and shot at the young woman and her brother as they were walking home. Miss Merrill was killed. Her brother was only wounded.

The mob reportedly had no trouble taking Monson from the custody of Sheriff Frazer and his deputies. Once night had fallen Monson's body was cut down and placed on an impromptu pile of railroad ties, dowse with kerosene and set ablaze.[1342]

Stanley, Richard "Dick"
Born: circa 1897—Date of Death: 23 January 1913
Place: Red River County
Event: Lynching/Hanged

Dick Stanley, a sixteen-year old black man, was accused of having attempted to outrage a four-year old white girl at Fulbright. While Sheriff McChristian was escorting Stanley to jail a lynch mob overpowered him and took the young black man and hung him from a nearby tree.[1343]

Wilson, Vine
Born: circa 1895—Date of Death: 23 January 1913
Place: Lamar County
Event: Lynching/Hanged and Shot

Vine Wilson, an eighteen-year old black man, was lynched at Deport on Thursday, 23 January 1913. Wilson had attacked and outraged the three-year old daughter of Charles Devlin, a farmer near Gintown.

Only fifty men were in the mob that took Wilson from the sheriff by force. For a moment Wilson gave the mob the slip, and attempted to avoid lynching by slashing his own wrists with a knife. His efforts were ineffectual. Wilson was recaptured, strung up and shot full of holes for good measure.

Miss Devlin was seriously injured from being handled so harshly at such a young age.[1344]

Anderson, Given Name Unknown
Born: (Unknown)—Date of Death: 24 February 1913
Place: Harrison County
Event: Lynching/Hanged

Perry, Robert
Born: (Unknown)—Date of Death: 24 February 1913
Place: Harrison County
Event: Lynching/Shot

On Monday, 24 February 1913, two black men were lynched and a third wounded by mobs in Harrison County. A man named Anderson was hanged by a mob about ten miles from Elysian Fields.

Robert Perry and George Redden were prisoners of Constable Ed Odom of Karnack. They were brought before Justice W. S. Baldwin on a hog stealing charge. En route to the county jail a mob overwhelmed the constable and seized the men. Perry was riddled with bullets and died shortly thereafter. Redden was shot in the left leg, both bones were shot off.[1345]

Perry, Diggs
Born: (Unknown)—Date of Death: 21 April 1913
Place: Matagorda County
Event: Lynching/Hanging

A black man named Diggs Perry was tried and convicted of robbing and murdering a man named of Jack Simmons at Matagorda. Perry's sentence was appealed, and had been reprieved twice while Governor Colquitt investigated the matter.[1346]

Subsequent to the last reprieve in March Perry's luck at litigation seemed to have been exhausted. He was ultimately hanged for his crime at Bay City at precisely 1:16 pm on 21 April 1913. Perry professed his innocence to his final breath.

Ortiz, Abraham
Born (Unknown)—Date of Death: 2 May 1913
Place: Hidalgo County
Event: Legal Execution/Hanged

According to claims by *The Death Penalty Information Center* a man named Abraham Ortiz was hanged on Friday, 2 May 1913, in Hidalgo County for the crimes of outrage and murder.[1347]

Finley, Gus
Born: (Unknown)—Date of Death: 13 May 1913
Place: Morris County
Event: Lynching/Hanged

At about 5:00 am on Tuesday, November 26, 1912, Morris County Constable George Tucker, along with Ed Boozer, were attempting to serve a civil writ of sequestration on a white man named Gus Finley, alias Will Taylor. The order included picking up a mule that Finley had traded for some time earlier. When Tucker approached Finley the man opened fire. Tucker was hit twice, and died from his wounds. Boozer escaped unscathed from the shooting affray.

Finley fled to Louisiana where he was captured and transferred to the jail in Shreveport. The killer told lawmen that he shot Tucker because Tucker was in the process of pulling a gun on him.

Finley was tried and convicted of murder. He was sentenced to death, and scheduled to be hanged on Tuesday, 6 May 1913. Governor Colquitt granted a thirty-day stay of execution. Morris County residents were not pleased with the Governor's actions. While Finley was being transferred out of the Daingerfield jail on Monday, 5 May 1913, irate citizens burned two churches and a residence in protest. Finley was later lynched by a vigilante mob there on Tuesday, 13 May 1913, thus saving the State of Texas the trouble of a legal execution.

The mob that did the work was very quiet that day. Few people know that the lynching had occurred until after daybreak. The sheriff found the body of Finley at around 8:00 am, hanging up a tree along a public road and filled with lead. The agitated state that had existed in the community immediately calmed once Finley's fate was made known.[1348]

Brock, Henry

Born: (Unknown)—Date of Death: 30 May 1913
Place: Travis County
Event: Legal Execution/Hanged

Henry Brock, a white man, was tried and found guilty of the murder of Mollie King, a white woman. The incident took place on Thursday, 24 April 1912. Brock, a saloonkeeper, was tried and convicted of the crime.

Brock was sentenced to death. He appealed on the basis of insanity, but the ruling was upheld. At about 3:30 pm on Friday, 30 May 1913, Brock was hanged at the jail at Austin.[1349]

Brock walked to his death with Sheriff George S. Matthews and Deputy Schmidt each taking an arm, working their way through the crowd. As he reached the gallows he stumbled, then quickly recovered and scaled the steps. Three ministers prayed and sang hymns, at the conclusion of which Brock clenched his hands and held them behind him to be tied. The trap was sprung, and three minutes afterwards he was pronounced dead.[1350]

Galloway, Richard "Dick"

Born: (Unknown)—Date of Death: 4 June 1913
Place: Newton County
Event: Lynching/Shot

Richard Galloway, a black man, along with two other black men, were accused of attacking a party of white men who had been observing a black picnic near Newton on Saturday, 31 May 1913. All three were taken to jail at Beaumont. Galloway unwisely posted bail rather than wait until sentiment in the community had calmed down. His bullet-riddled body was found alongside the railroad tracks with a rope lying nearby forty miles north of Beaumont at Newton on Friday, 6 June 1913.[1351]

No attempt was made to molest his companions, who were still sitting in the jail.

Asbeck, William F.

Born: March 1869—Date of Death: 28 June 1913
Place: Victoria County
Event: Legal Execution/Hanged

William Asbeck was tried and convicted of the murder of his wife, Susan Josephine Powers. The killing had occurred on Wednesday, 4 December 1912. The Asbeck family was playing cards or dominoes at their home when William Asbeck called his wife into the bedroom. He was holding a gun. She grabbed the barrel and tried to divert it. Mr. Asbeck fired, hitting Susan in the knee. The wound was serious, practically severing the limb. Susan's brother Jim Powers took her to the hospital where she eventually bled to death.

Asbeck fled, sprinkling acid behind him as he went in an effort to throw off the tracking dogs. He was ultimately captured, tried and convicted of the killing. Asbeck received a death sentence.

At about 1:40 pm on Saturday, 28 June 1913 Asbeck walked to the gallows at Victoria with a cigarette in his mouth. According to reports he had been the most jovial prisoner in the jail, constantly laughing and playing pranks on other inmates. The black cap was pulled down over his head as Reverend J. F. Penny of the Victoria Methodist Church offered a prayer. Sheriff Welsiger sprung the trap, and in minutes he was pronounced dead. The execution took place in the courtyard adjoining the jailhouse.[1352]

Stanton, Floyd

Born: (Unknown)—Date of Death: 1 August 1913
Place: Dallas County
Event: Legal Execution/Hanged

On Thursday, 5 December 1912, Floyd Stanton, a black man, murdered his wife Naomi. The killing took place at Dallas. No reason for Stanton's action was offered by the newspaper who seemed more interested in the hanging than the crime from which the retribution flowed.

As is so often the case with condemned men, Stanton waited until several days before his hanging was scheduled to profess his faith and find Jesus. Stanton was converted to the Catholic religion with the aid of Father McSweeney. Afterwards he said," I am going to be brave because I know I am going to heaven." "I am the resurrection and the life: he that believeth in me, though he were dead, yet shall he live."[1353]

As Stanton climbed the stairs, dressed in a new black gallows suit, he addressed the crowd, saying, "Dear friends, I am guilty and I am willing to pay for my crime. Don't follow in my footsteps..." Just moments past noon on Friday, 1 August 1913, Sheriff Brandenburg sprung the trap and Stanton was no more.[1354]

Fowler, Paul
Born: (Unknown)—Date of Death: 7 August 1913
Place: Tarrant County
Event: Legal Execution/Hanged

Harrison, Ernest
Born: (Unknown)—Date of Death: 7 August 1913
Place: Tarrant County
Event: Legal Execution/Hanged

On Monday night, 1 July 1912, Robert Knetsch, a thirty five year old sculptor and interior decorator, was robbed and murdered at East Front Street and Kentucky Avenue in Fort Worth.

Paul Fowler and Ernest Harrison, both black men, were arrested in Hill County on suspicion of the murder. They confessed to having fired two fatal shots into Knetsch's body and robbing him.

On Thursday, 7 August 1913, Sheriff William Rea stood by each man as they climbed the gallows and took their respective place. Hands and feet were strapped and the hood pulled down over their heads. Fowler was the first to meet his maker when the trap was sprung at 11:13 am. Harrison followed, at 11:48 am. Both men had been baptized in their cells before making the one-way trip to the gallows.[1355]

Harrison was the tenth man to be hanged by the rope used that day, which belonged to Sheriff Lee McAfee of Sherman. It had most recently been used at Waxahachie on 29 November 1912, in the hanging of Burrell Oats, another black man executed for robbery and murder.

Davis, William "Will"
Born: (Unknown)—Date of Death: 21 September 1913
Place: Robertson County
Event: Lynching/Hanged

Several men were playing cards at a house located at Petteway, about eight miles from the county seat at Bremond. Some sort of quarrel took place during which a black man named William "Will" Davis shot and killed Luther Hodge. As Davis fled the scene he shot and wounded another man named Tom Maxwell.

Robertson County Sheriff's Deputy Charles Thomas "Tom" Rushing, who was riding his horse nearby, heard the gunfire. He rode to the home and ordered Davis to surrender his gun. Rather than surrender, Davis shot Rushing in the stomach. The wounded Rushing dismounted, pulled his pistol, and tried to return fire. Before he was able to get off a shot Davis fired again, this time hitting him in the heart and killing him instantly.

A large posse of citizens located Davis. After he had admitted to having murdered Rushing and Hodge they wasted no time and lynched him from the nearest tree.[1356]

Long, Ed
Born: (Unknown)—Date of Death: 19 December 1913
Place: Dallas County
Event: Legal Execution/Hanged

Texas and Pacific Railroad Police Officer Thomas Bennett was shot and killed while investigating a railroad boxcar burglary at Dallas. Three black men were involved, Ed Long, Ed Christian and George Williams.

On Saturday, 10 September 1910, Bennett came upon three suspicious men who he believed to be burglars. One of the men shot him in the chest. Bennett died from the gunshot wound the following day. According to some sources his murderers were apprehended, tried and convicted. Other sources claim that only Long and Christian were tried. In any case, Long was tried separately, convicted and received a death sentence. The other two were also sentenced to death. However, based on Texas execution records it does not appear that their sentence was ever carried out.

Ed Long did keep his appointment with the hangman on Friday, 19 December 1913, at Dallas. He was still professing his innocence when the trap was sprung at twenty minutes past noon. The execution went off without incident.[1357]

Thompson, Dave
Born: (Unknown)—Date of Death: 3 January 1914
Place: Marion County
Event: Lynching/Hanged

During the evening hours on Saturday, 3 January 1914, fifteen masked men removed David Thompson, a black man, from the Marion County jail at Jefferson and lynched him from a bridge. Thompson was charged with wounding Matt Taylor, a constable, in a shooting affray.[1358]

Lee, Thomas "Tommie"
Born: circa 1896—Date of Death: 9 March 1914
Place: Tarrant County
Event: Legal Execution/Hanged

Fort Worth Police Officer John Ogletree was shot and killed while attempting to arrest a black man for firing a gun in public.

Ogletree confronted the man, Thomas "Tommie" Lee, who had discharged his firearm in public. Ogletree ordered Lee to drop the gun. Rather than complying with the order Lee opened fire, hitting Ogletree in the chest. In spite of being mortally wounded Ogletree was able to return fire, but his shots went wild and had no effect. Ogletree made it to the steps of a nearby saloon. He was taken to the St. Joseph Infirmary where he died from his injuries.

Lee was eventually arrested. He was never tried for Ogletree murder, but for that of another victim named Walter Moore. That incident took place during the same evening of mayhem. Lee had gone to McCampbell's Bar-B-Q on East 8th Street where, after a disagreement over a crap game, he shot a black man named Pete Soles. He left the restaurant and proceeded to McGar's Pool Hall on Jones Street where he shot and killed Moore.

Lee was found guilty and sentenced to hang. He was confined to the jail awaiting the outcome of his appeal to Governor Colquitt. Outside, a frustrated mob that had tried repeatedly to penetrate the jail and lynch Lee brooded and stubbornly awaited the long sought after event. On Monday, 9 March 1914, a smug Tommie Lee laid in repose on his comfortable cot in his jail cell smoking a cigar and joking with fellow inmates as he awaited his execution. Lee received religion and was baptized in his cell by Reverend J. H. Winn of the Baptist faith.

On the platform Lee bowed and said farewell as the black cap was pulled down over his head. Sheriff William Rea sprung the trap at 11:20 am and Lee was pronounced dead ten minutes later. [1359]

Williams, William "Bill"

Born: (Unknown)—Date of Death: 12 March 1914
Place: Robertson County
Event: Lynching/Hanged

William "Bill" Williams, a black man, was captured by a posse of citizens and lynched near Hearne on Thursday, 12 March 1914. Williams was suspected of wounding a local plantation manager named J. R. Robertson.[1360]

Martinez, Jr., Leon Cardenas

Born: circa 1896—Date of Death: 11 May 1914
Place: Reeves County
Event: Legal Execution/Hanged

Leon Cardinez Martinez was tried and convicted of having stabbed and shot to death a young woman named Emma Brown.

The incident took place three years earlier, on Saturday, 22 July 1911, and occurred while Brown was driving along in a buggy near Saragossa, in Reeves County. Miss Brown lived with her sister and was headed home from Saragossa. When she never arrived her sister posted the alarm. The girl was found, with the buggy, alongside the road. She had been shot several times and stabbed repeatedly in the back and chest.

Initially Martinez confessed, but later recanted. He was scheduled to meet his fate on 18 January 1914, but the hanging was postponed. Martinez was executed at Pecos, around noon on Monday, 11 May 1914.[1361]

Robertson, William "Will"
Born: (Unknown)—Date of Death: 5 June 1914
Place: Grimes County
Event: Lynching/Shot

On Wednesday, 4 March 1914, a white planter named Jesse Johnson was killed at the Whitehall settlement. He had been discussing some aspect of farming with William Robertson, a black field hand, when Robertson produced a revolver and shot him.

Robertson surrendered and was in the process of being taken to Anderson by officers when, about two miles north of Navasota near the public highway leading to Anderson, persons unknown forcibly removed him from custody and shot him to death. The body was filled with bullet holes.[1362]

Torres, Portirio
Born: (Unknown)—Date of Death: 14 August 1914
Place: Atascosa County
Event: Legal Execution/Hanged

Portirio Torres (also reported as Torrez) was arrested, tried and convicted of the murder of a man named Ike Hill. That incident had taken place on 25 October 1913, at Fowlerton. Torres appealed his death sentence, but all were denied.

On Friday, 14 August 1914, Portirio Torres was hanged at Pleasanton. At 11:25 am the trap was sprung and Torres dropped through the gallows floor. He was declared dead thirteen minutes later. The Spanish language newspaper at San Antonio reported Torres resisted being executed.[1363] In various newspaper articles one will find his surname spelled "Tores or "Torrez."

Durfee, Joseph "Joe"
Born: (Unknown)—Date of Death: 14 October 1914
Place: Brazoria County
Event: Lynching/Hanged

On Tuesday, 13 October 1914, the liberal leaning Governor Oscar Branch Colquitt commuted the death sentence of Joe Durfee, a black man, for his role in the murder of a white woman named J. M. Seitz. The incident took place at Angleton, on Thursday, 9 July 1914. Her badly mutilated body had been found in an alley near a rooming house where she had engaged lodging. There were stab wounds visible, and bite marks on her shoulder as well as bruises from fingerprints on her throat from having been throttled. The woman's parasol and handbag, which she had been carrying when she left her room, were gone. Her shoes were missing and her stocking feet were soiled.

On Wednesday, 14 October 1914, an angry mob, fuming over the Governor's decision, took justice into their own hands and removed Durfee by force from the jail. The vigilantes dragged

Durfee to the edge of town and lynched him. It took surprisingly little effort to overpower the feckless jailer. With only modest encouragement Durfee confessed to the crime before he went to meet his maker.[1364]

Wilson, Henry
Born: (Unknown)—Date of Death: 14 December 1914
Place: Calhoun County
Event: Legal Execution/Hanged

Henry Wilson, a black man, was tried and convicted of outraging a young woman at Calhoun County. He was given the death sentence, which was carried out in the presence of a small group of lawmen on Monday, 14 December 1914, at Port Lavaca.[1365]

Argijo, Alejos
Born: (Unknown)—Date of Death: 23 December 1914
Place: Live Oak County
Event: Lynching/Hanged and Shot

A Mexican man, claimed by some sources to have been Alejos Argijo, was tortured, shot and lynched at Oakville in Live Oak County. Argijo was suspected of having been involved in the killing of Oakville jailer Harry Hinton (see summary below). Numerous bullets were fired into his body and the corpse left hanging from the tree in which he was lynched.[1366]

Falcon, Felipe
Born (Unknown)—Date of Death: circa Late Summer/Early Fall 1915
Place: Cameron County
Event: Lynching/Shot

According to unverified sources, sometime in the late summer or early fall of 1915 a Mexican named Felipe Falcon is claimed to have been shot and killed by Texas Rangers. The man had been captured by U.S. soldiers at Las Yescas Ranch, then turned over to rangers who are said to have killed him. No confirmation of this killing has been located.[1367]

Gonzalez, Ysidro
Born: (Unknown)—Date of Death: 1 February 1915
Place: Live Oak County
Event: Legal Execution/Hanged

Deputy Sheriff Harry Hinton died after being beaten and suffocated with bedclothes by two inmates during an escape attempt at the county jail at Oakville. An accomplice had passed up an iron bar to two Mexican prisoners. The man had attached a length of fishing line to the piece of metal so the inmates could haul it up to their cell window from the street below.

The two men escaped. A reward of $500 was offered for their arrest. Tensions ran high in the community as a result of the brutal killing. Hinton was a member of a prominent family in the area and was well liked in the community. A major manhunt was immediately organized involving hundreds of citizens, many of whom were provided by local rancher George West. Information obtained from a local man led to the arrest of Ysidro Gonzales, one of the murderers. Gonzales was captured in the Mexican section of Oakville on Wednesday, 23 December 1915.

On Tuesday, 29 December 1914, fifty men and boys of Oakville defended the jail against 100 armed Mexican men who had come with the intent of liberating Gonzalez and his accomplice Federico Sanchez.

The twice lucky Gonzalez lived to see another day. However, after a foiled jailbreak attempt and having cheated fate at the hands of a would-be lynching party, he was hanged at Oakville on Monday, 1 February 1915.[1368]

Ballard, Henry
Born: circa 1894—Date of Death: 19 February 1915
Place: Red River County
Event: Legal Execution/Hanged

Henry Ballard, a black man, was tried and convicted of murdering an elderly white man near Clarksville in the fall of 1914. Ballard was sentenced to death. That verdict was carried out on Friday, 19 February 1915, when at about 1:49 pm Sheriff Martin sprung the trap and Ballard's short life of twenty-one years ended, a consequence of his own misdeeds.[1369]

Hemphill, Will
Born: (Unknown)—Date of Death: 26 February 1915
Place: Guadalupe County
Event: Legal Execution/Hanged

Will Hemphill a black man was convicted of outraging a white woman. The crime took place two years earlier. Hemphill's first conviction was reversed, and the case was remanded to a lower court. His second trial affirmed his guilt. Surprisingly, Governor James Edwards Ferguson refused to intervene. Hemphill was hanged at the Seguin poor house at half past noon on Friday, 26 February 1915.[1370]

Sanchez, Federico
Born: circa 1900—Date of Death: 3 March 1915
Place: Live Oak County
Event: Legal Execution/Hanged

Federico Sanchez was tried and found guilty of the murder of jailer Harry Hinton at Oakville (see Gonzalez above). He was sentenced to be hanged. On Wednesday, 3 March 1915, that sentence was carried out when Sanchez, a native of Mexico who was only fifteen years old, was executed by hanging.[1371]

Mexican General Carranza is said to have filed a protest with Washington, D.C. over the hanging of this youth, claiming "discrimination against our [his] race."[1372]

Guerrero, Benignio
Born: (Unknown)—Date of Death: 9 April 1915
Place: Hays County
Event: Legal Execution/Hanged

Benignio Guerrero, a Mexican man, was tried and convicted of the murder of a fourteen-year old Mexican girl named Isabel Morales. He was executed at San Marcos on Friday, 6 April 1915. Guerrero holds the distinction of being the first man to be legally executed by hanging in Hays County.[1373]

Oliver, Carl
Born: (Unknown)—Date of Death: 16 April 1915
Place: Grayson County
Event: Legal Execution/Hanged

Carl Oliver, a black man, was hanged at Sherman at two minutes past noon on Friday, 16 April 1915. He had been convicted of the 18 June 1910, murder of Robert D. Stanley of Mount Vernon.

Oliver's hanging took place at the county jail, and only admitted witnesses consisting primarily of lawmen were allowed to witness the event. Oliver strode calmly to his end, and declined an opportunity to address those present.[1374]

Larkins, Joe
Born: (Unknown)—Date of Death: 17 April 1915
Place: Ellis County
Event: Legal Execution/Hanged

On Saturday night, 27 February 1915, Joe Larkins, a black man, murdered a white man named Jack

Jones at Waxahachie. Jones was employed as a collector and night watchman at a local garage. His body was discovered the morning after the crime on the floor of his bedroom at the business where he was employed, covered with bedclothes. Jones's body bore evidence of bruises from having been bludgeoned by a heavy object. The blood stained front axle from an automobile was found nearby. Robbery was apparently Larkins' motive, since the cash register had been breached and Jones' suitcases had been rummage though.

Suspecting that he had been involved, officers went to Larkins' home that same night where they discovered blood stained clothing along with a pair of tan shoes, watch and a wallet belonging to Jones. The following afternoon "Red" Watson, a jitney car operator, and Constable Hickman of Ennis, arrested Larkins in the eastern part of the city.

The hanging of Larkins was eagerly anticipated. The event was expected to draw a crowd. So many in fact that the original site, near the pumping station, had to be changed as authorities feared that the roof covering the large reservoir nearby might collapse if spectators decided to observe from that elevated vantage point. Now built about a mile from the courthouse, the new gallows was prepared to receive Larkins. The large crowd tore down an obstruction that had been specially constructed to block their view. Larkins scaled the edifice alone, amid applause from the crowd that lasted about ten minutes. A final religious service had been carried out at the jail where he had been baptized. Larkins spoke for nearly ten minutes, continuing to deny his guilt in the murder. He did, however, admit to having been involved but claimed that someone else had done the killing. At 11:40 am the trap was sprung, Larkins' neck was broken in the fall, and all discussion on the matter ended. He was buried at the potters filed at the expense of the county.[1375]

One Unidentified Black Man
Born: (Unknown)—Date of Death: 9 May 1915
Place: Upshur County
Event: Lynching/Hanged

Sometime around midnight on Sunday, 9 May 1915, an unidentified black man fatally shot Julius A. Philmon, a thirty-year old car inspector for the Texas and Pacific Railroad named. The killer snatched Philmon's purse containing $1.75. When Philmon gave chase the black man wheeled and fired, inflicting a wound that would become fatal. Philmon died on Monday, 10 May 1915. He is buried at the Grange Hall Cemetery at Marshall.[1376]

A posse was quickly organized. The black man was discovered about an hour and a half later, asleep in a cabin. He was taken to the jail at Big Sandy where, at about 9:00 pm on the same day as the incident a vigilante mob pried the door of the jail open with a crow bar, removed Philmon's suspected killer and lynched him.[1377]

Jackson, Cornelius
Born: (Unknown)—Date of Death: 2 July 1915
Place: Wharton County
Event: Legal Execution/Hanged

In January 1915 Cornelius Jackson, Alton Owens and Nathan Hughes, all black men, murdered an elderly store owner named Asa Ray at Wharton. Jackson's fourteen-year old son was present at the affray, having been compelled to attend by his father.

At trial all three men were convicted. Only Jackson received a death sentence. At 1:48 pm on Friday, 2 July 1915, the will of the court was carried out before a large crowd at Wharton.[1378]

Two Unidentified Mexican Men
Born: (Unknown)—Date of Death: 7 July 1915
Place: Hidalgo County
Event: Lynched/Shot

On Wednesday, 7 July 1915, two unidentified Mexican men who were a part of the band that had been observed raiding in Hidalgo County recently were shot and killed by a posse led by Cameron County Sheriff W. T. Vann. Other members of the gang escaped, and were being chased by Vann and his men.

No verification of these cases has been found. The authors have elected to include this uncorroborated case for purposes of completeness.[1379]

Manriquez, Gorgonio
Born: (Unknown)—Date of Death: 24 July 1915
Place: Hidalgo County
Event: Lynched/Shot

Manriquez, Lorenzo
Born: (Unknown)—Date of Death: 24 July 1915
Place: Hidalgo County
Event: Lynched/Shot

Two Mexican men named Gorgonio and Lorenzo Manriquez were shot by a posse at Hidalgo County on Saturday, 24 July 1915. Perhaps the foregoing case is related to the Wednesday, 7 July 1915 incident noted above.[1380]

Munoz, Adolfo (Rodolfo)

Born: (Unknown)—Date of Death: 28 July 1915
Place: Cameron County
Event: Lynching/Hanged

During the evening hours of Wednesday, 28 July 1915, Adolfo Munoz, a Mexican man, was forcibly removed from the custody of City Marshal J. F. Carr and hanged from a tree about two miles from San Benito. Apparently unwilling to allow the law to take its own course, the vigilantes dispatched Munoz who was suspected of having been involved in a number of nefarious acts including the murder of an elderly merchant in the Sebastian section of town two years earlier. Munoz and his confederates were accused of burning a railroad bridge and cutting all the telephone lines running past the place last Saturday night.[1381]

Stanley, Will

Born: (Unknown)—Date of Death: 30 July 1915
Place: Bell County
Event: Lynching/Burned to Death

An incident that drew statewide attention over a three-day period began on Wednesday, 28 July 1915. It started with the murder of three children on the William Grimes farm outside of Temple. Seven-month old twins along with an older boy, William Jr., who was seven, were killed. The parents, William and Annie were savagely beaten but managed to survive. A transient black man named Will Stanley was arrested in Rogers, roughly thirty-six hours after the bodies were discovered. Stanley did the work with a hammer while the family were asleep.

When Stanley was captured he was wearing a pair of trouser pants with the name Will Grimes sewn into the waistband. Stanley told lawmen that two men, who he identified as Rodell Harrison and Dicey Wells, had given him the trousers the previous day. Harrison and Wells were also arrested.

Word of the apprehensions spread quickly throughout the county. Intent on a lynching, a convoy of automobiles headed to Belton while another set out for Rogers. Hearing that an angry mob had gathered at Belton, lawmen took the suspects to Temple. Citizens were already gathering there, outside the office of Justice of the Peace R. L. Cooper. The crowd grew rapidly, until more than 5,000 people assembled in downtown area, determined to carry out their own brand of justice.

Authorities tried to outwait the mob, creating a standoff that lasted about seven hours. By midnight the frenzied multitude stormed the building and dragged Will Stanley, still in chains, outside. He tried unsuccessfully to blame Harrison and Wells for the murders. Both had already been freed. According to one source, before Stanley could finish giving his account of the incident someone in the crowd shot him. He was dragged to the town square where a hastily constructed pyre had been constructed. Stanley was set ablaze, remaining there until he was reduced to ashes. The incident was viewed by hundreds of men, women and children. Once Stanley had been burned beyond recognition spectators hung him from a telephone pole and collected souvenirs from the ashes.[1382]

Flores, Antonio
Born: (Unknown)—Date of Death: 3 August 1915
Place: Willacy County
Event: Lynched/Shot

Flores, Desiderio
Born: (Unknown)—Date of Death: 3 August 1915
Place: Willacy County
Event: Lynched/Shot

Flores Jr., Desiderio
Born: (Unknown)—Date of Death: 3 August 1915
Place: Willacy County
Event: Lynched/Shot

Three Mexican men named Antonio, Desiderio and Desiderio Jr. Flores were shot by a posse at Paso Real in Willacy County 3 August 1915. The men were suspected of murder. Although there are a number of cases that occurred during this time period, no record of the Flores killings has been located.[1383]

Williams, Clint
Born: (Unknown)—Date of Death: 5 August 1915
Place: Tarrant County
Event: Legal Execution/Hanged

Clint Williams, a black man, was executed by hanging at Fort Worth on Thursday, 5 August 1915. He had been tried and found guilty of the murder of a messenger boy named Oscar Sproggins.

Just before going to meet his maker Williams, in an attempt to hedge his bets, was baptized in the Baptist faith.[1384]

Hernandez, Eusebino
Born: (Unknown)—Date of Death: 8 August 1915
Place: Cameron County
Event: Lynched/Shot

Salinas, Abraham
Born: (Unknown)—Date of Death: 8 August 1915
Place: Cameron County
Event: Lynched/Shot

Tobar, Juan
Born: (Unknown)—Date of Death: 8 August 1915
Place: Cameron County
Event: Lynched/Shot

According to various reliable reports, three Mexican men who were refugees and outlaws, suspected of having committed a murder, were executed by a posse at Cameron County on Sunday, 8 August 1915. Eusebino Hernandez was killed at the El Suaz Ranch near Raymondville. Juan Tobar and Abraham Salinas were both executed at the Norias Division of the King Ranch, at Raymondville.[1385]

One Unidentified Mexican Man
Born: (Unknown)—Date of Death: 10 August 1915
Place: Willacy County
Event: Lynched/Shot

Becanegra, Francisco
Born: (Unknown)—Date of Death: 10 August 1915
Place: Willacy County
Event: Lynched/Shot

One unidentified Mexican man and another Mexican named Francisco Becanegra were shot to death at Sebastian in Willacy County on Tuesday, 10 August 1915. Both were suspected outlaws.[1386]

Three Unidentified Mexican Man
Born: (Unknown)—Date of Death: 12 August 1915
Place: Hidalgo County
Event: Lynched/Shot

On Thursday, 12 August 1915, a posse killed three Mexican outlaws near Mercedes and seized twenty-two horses belonging to the raiders.

The article notes that although they could not be certain which, it was either U.S. troops, Texas Rangers or other lawmen that did the work. In all likelihood there is some duplication of entries made during this time period in Carrigan's book *The Forgotten Dead.* [1387]

One Unidentified Mexican Man
Born: (Unknown)—Date of Death: 12 August 1915
Place: Hidalgo County
Event: Lynched/Shot

One unidentified Mexican outlaw was reported to have been shot and killed by a citizen's posse near Mercedes on Thursday, 12 August 1915. This incident allegedly occurred just hours after the killing of the three Mexican outlaws cited above. The posse came upon the man sleeping in the brush, and when awakened, he drew his pistol to fire and was killed instantly.[1388]

Flores, Given Name Unknown
Born: (Unknown)—Date of Death: 12 August 1915
Place: Willacy County
Event: Lynched/Shot

A posse comprised of peace officers and regular US Army soldiers went to Lyford on Thursday, 12 August 1915, in search of a Mexican man identified only as Flores. He was accused of wounding Lyford night watchman Fritz Georgie a week earlier. Flores was arrested and was shot when he allegedly made a break to escape.[1389]

Nine Unidentified Mexican Men
Born: (Unknown)—Date of Death: 17 August 1915
Place: Hidalgo County
Event: Lynched/Shot

According to unverified sources, as many as nine unidentified Mexican men who were all suspected of being outlaws were shot by a posse somewhere in Hidalgo County on Tuesday, 17 August 1915.[1390]

Two Unidentified Mexican Men
Born: (Unknown)—Date of Death: 18 August 1915
Place: Cameron County
Event: Lynched/Shot

Two unidentified Mexican men who were being held in the San Benito jail under suspicion of the Austin killing in the Sebastian raid were taken out in the absence of a guard and shot at Brownsville in Cameron County on Wednesday, 18 August 1915.[1391]

Six Unidentified Mexican Men
Born: (Unknown)—Date of Death: 20 August 1915
Place: Cameron County
Event: Lynched/Shot

Six unidentified Mexican men who were all suspected of being outlaws were shot by a posse at San Benito in Cameron County on Friday, 20 August 1915.[1392]

One Unidentified Mexican Man

Born: (Unknown)—Date of Death: 26 August 1915
Place: Cameron County
Event: Lynched/Shot

According to several reliable sources, one unidentified Mexican men who was suspected of being an outlaw was shot to death at the Norias Division of the King Ranch at Raymondville in Cameron County on 26 August 1915.[1393]

One Unidentified Mexican Man

Born: (Unknown)—Date of Death: 29 August 1915
Place: Cameron County
Event: Lynched/Shot

According to several reliable sources, one unidentified Mexican men who was suspected of murdering a man named Austens was shot to death by a posse at Raymondville in Cameron County on Thursday, 29 August 1915.[1394]

It is thought that this case, cataloged in *The Forgotten Dead*, is a duplicate of the 18 August 1915 incident.

Richmond, Joe

Born: (Unknown)—Date of Death: 29 August 1915
Place: Hopkins County
Event: Lynching/Burning

Richmond, King

Born: (Unknown)—Date of Death: 29 August 1915
Place: Hopkins County
Event: Lynching/Burning

In a case where the hunter suddenly became the hunted, Hopkins County Sheriff's Office Chief Deputy Nathan A. Flippin and the Sheriff J.B. Butler were ambushed by two suspects that the lawmen had been diligently searching for.

Among the charges against this pair was the burning of the sheriff's home, the shooting death of his wife and the theft of his horses at Honey Grove. Making the crime all the more heinous, the pair had burned the sheriff's wife in the fire. Perhaps that fact alone helps explain the surprising and hideous outcome of the capture.

Two black men were involved, King Richmond and his brother Joe. They were wanted for having committed a variety of crimes including murder, arson, and horse theft. A man named Seawright Jones had tipped off the officers as to the whereabouts of the Richmond brothers. As Flippin and Butler approached their cabin near Tazwell the pair hid out in an orchard near the home and waited. The two men ambushed the officers, rushed out from cover and shot Flippin in the head, sending a bullet through his brain and killing him instantly. Next they shot Butler in the neck. A desperate hand-to-hand fight commenced between the Richmond brothers and Butler, during which Butler was shot through the arm and grazed across the top of his head. The two attackers' then pistol whipped and thrashed Butler for good measure, crushing his skull in three places in the process.

Amazingly Butler's injuries were not fatal. The pair of killers grabbed Butler by the collar and were in the process of dragging him to a nearby wooded area, presumably to finish him off, when a neighbor named John Stribling intervened and rescued Butler from almost certain death.

Now having in their possession the pistols of both Flippin and Butler, the Richmond brothers fled. After being notified of the incident at about 8:35 am Constable Sam Smith, deputies Grover Williams and Bob Gafford headed for the scene immediately. Crowds of armed citizens began to gather near the courthouse as word of the crime spread through the town like wildfire. Heavily armed bands of twos and fours took to the field and joined the chase. Word spread by wire. Soon lawmen from Hunt, Delta, Franklin and Rains Counties joined the search. Makeshift posse members converged near Burks Creek where the Richmond brothers were believed to be hiding. An estimated 2,000 searchers responded.

At around 11:00 am King and Joe Richmond were surrounded in a pasture that belonged to Don Campbell, located about two to three miles south of Tazwell. Bloodhounds struck the trail at about 11:30 am and followed the escapees to a cabin near Jim Copelin's farm where they continued the search to a sandy creek bottom area nearby where the pair were found hiding in a clump of willows. When commanded to come out with their hands up one of the men failed to comply. A barrage of gunfire immediately followed, resulting in the instantaneous death of one Richmond brother and the wounding of the other.

The two killers, one now dead and one wounded and unconscious, were loaded into a wagon and brought to Sulphur Springs at about 4:30 pm. Almost at once a crowd, estimated to number upwards of 8,000 citizens, began to assemble near the bandstand at Buford Park. Ignoring the prudent counsel of a handful of influential townspeople, the angry multitude seemed bent on a "man burning." In spite of the fact that only one of the men was dead, they doused the pair with coal oil and burned their bodies. An estimated 1,500 to 2,000 onlookers remained to watch the revolting spectacle. [1395]

Orozco, Pascual
Born: (Unknown)—Date of Death: 30 August 1915
Place: Green River Canyon
Event: Lynched/Shot

Four Unidentified Mexican Men
Born: (Unknown)—Date of Death: 30 August 1915
Place: Green River Canyon
Event: Lynched/Shot

According to unverified sources, four unidentified Mexican men and another Mexican man named Pascal Orozco were accidentally shot to death by a posse who mistook them for outlaws. Reports indicate that this incident occurred at Green River Canyon on Monday, 30 August 1915. The only place name that might fit this vague report is Gruene, Texas that is located on the Guadalupe River near New Braunfels.[1396]

Fourteen Unidentified Mexican Men
Born: (Unknown)—Date of Death: September 1915
Place: Hidalgo County
Event: Lynched/Shot

As many as fourteen unidentified Mexican men who were all suspected of being outlaws were shot by a posse at Donna in Hidalgo County sometime in September 1915. [1397]

Bazan, Jesus
Born: (Unknown)—Date of Death: September 1915
Place: Hidalgo County
Event: Lynched/Shot

Longoria, Given Name Unknown
Born: (Unknown)—Date of Death: September 1915
Place: Hidalgo County
Event: Lynched/Shot

Two Mexican men named Jesus Bazan and Longoria (given name unknown) are said to have been executed at Hidalgo County in September 1915 for giving shelter to fugitive Mexican outlaws. This claim is unverified. The only reference that has been located thus far that may be a match to this sources claim involved a Daniel Longoria and his son Ventura who were taken into custody but not killed on 16 September 1915.[1398]

Three Unidentified Mexican Men
Born: (Unknown)—Date of Death: 2 September 1915
Place: Hidalgo County
Event: Lynched/Shot

According to unverified sources, three Mexican men who were suspected of murder and resisting arrest were executed near Edinburg in at Hidalgo County on Thursday, 2 September 1915.[1399]

Three Unidentified Mexican Men
Born: (Unknown)—Date of Death: 2 September 1915
Place: Cameron County
Event: Lynched/Shot

According to unverified sources, three Mexican men who were suspected of murder and resisting arrest were killed near Los Cuates in Cameron County on Thursday, 2 September 1915 by county officers. The alleged bandits had burned a railroad bridge and murdered two white men named Earl Donaldson and J. S. Smith.[1400]

Guerra, Francisco
Born: (Unknown)—Date of Death: 9 September 1915
Place: Cameron County
Event: Lynched/Shot

According to unverified reports, a Mexican man named Francisco Guerra who was a bill collector was shot to death by five unidentified Mexican outlaws at Cameron County on Thursday, 9 September 1915. [1401]

Rincones, Ygnacio
Born: (Unknown)—Date of Death: 14 September 1915
Place: Cameron County
Event: Lynched/Shot

Rivera, Angel
Born: (Unknown)—Date of Death: 14 September 1915
Place: Cameron County
Event: Lynched/Shot

Vela, Alejos

Born: (Unknown)—Date of Death: 14 September 1915

Place: Cameron County

Event: Lynched/Shot

On Monday, 13 September 1915, U.S. Army troops were fired upon by a group of Mexican men. Three members of the band were subsequently arrested and placed in the jail at San Benito. Claims of the fate vary depending upon the source. One indicated that the three men, whose names were Ygnacio Rincones, Angel Rivera (A. Bala) and Alejos Vela, were shot and killed while trying to escape from the custody of lawmen during transport. Another report indicated that a lone Mexican man was shot to death by lawmen while being transported to jail on 13 September 1915. A third indicated that the men were already in the jail, and had escaped on Tuesday, 14 September 1915. When their bodies were found they had both been shot in the back. Regardless of the version one chooses to believe, it seems that they were murdered.

Adding further to the confusion, some reports of the incident cite Friday, 10 September 1915, as the day it occurred.[1402]

Three Unidentified Mexican Men

Born: (Unknown)—Date of Death: 14 September 1915

Place: Willacy/Cameron County

Event: Lynched/Shot

In Carrigan's book *The Forgotten Dead* the author claims that three Mexican men who were suspected of being thieves were fatally shot on Tuesday, 14 September 1915. From the ambiguous wording it is difficult to determine if there was only one Mexican man shot and the incident was reported as having taken place at three different locations, or if there were actually three Mexicans killed. Various locations of the incident were reported, including Lyford, Sebastian in Willacy county and Lacoma in Cameron County. It would seem that this case is a duplicate of the foregoing one that involved Ygnacio Rincones, Angel Rivera (A. Bala) and Alejos Vela.[1403]

Cantu, Alberto

Born: (Unknown)—Date of Death: 17 September 1915

Place: Willacy County

Event: Lynched/Shot

A Mexican man named Alberto Cantu who was suspected of being an outlaw was shot to death near Lyford in Willacy County on Friday, 17 September 1915.[1404]

Perez, Refugio L.
Born: circa 1870—Date of Death: 17 September 1915
Place: Willacy County
Event: Lynched/Shot

According to reports, a Mexican man named Refugio Perez who was mistaken for the outlaw Jesus Perez was shot to death by Texas Rangers near Lyford in Willacy County on Friday, 17 September 1915. Family genealogists claim that he died at Ojo de Agua in Hidalgo County, not Willacy.[1405]

Rodriguez, Juan Nepemuceno
Born: (Unknown)—Date of Death: 17 September 1915
Place: Unknown County
Event: Lynched/Shot

A Mexican Man named Juan Nepemuceno Rodriguez was dragged to death behind a horse with a wire fastened around his neck. Rodriguez was suspected of being an outlaw. This incident took place on Friday, 17 September 1915. Although newspaper reports of the day indicate that Rodriguez was taken into custody at San Antonio in September 1915, and it would seem logical that this treatment would have been fatal, no verification of his death has been located.[1406]

One Unidentified Mexican Man
Born (Unknown)—Date of Death: 20 September 1915
Place: Cameron County
Event: Lynching/Hanged

On or about Monday, 20 September 1915, an unidentified Mexican man was taken from lawmen while he was being transported from San Benito to Brownsville. Once the mob had him under their control they lynched him. Newspaper reports of the day claimed that three unidentified Mexican men were shot a week earlier while they were being taken to Harlingen for safekeeping. Two others had been killed in a similar manner, and all were reported to have been attempting to escape when the killings took place.

Two other Mexican men were killed near San Benito after they were reported to have broken out of jail. Reporters hastened to inform readers that all of the men had been shot from the front, not from behind, apparently believing that the murder of three Mexican persons would be easier to justify as long as they had been killed in a dignified and gentlemanly manner.[1407]

Twelve Unidentified Mexican Men
Born: (Unknown)—Date of Death: 28 September 1915
Place: Hidalgo County
Event: Lynched/Shot

In Carrigan's book *The Forgotten Dead*, the author claims that at least twelve Mexican men were executed near Ebenoza in Hidalgo County on Tuesday, 28 September 1915. Members of the group had all been suspected of being outlaws.[1408]

Garcia, Arturo
Born: (Unknown)—Date of Death: October 1915
Place: Hidalgo County
Event: Lynched/Shot

In Carrigan's book *The Forgotten Dead*, the author claims that a Mexican man named Arturo Garcia was removed by force and shot to pieces in the street like a dog sometime in October 1915. Garcia had been held at the jail in Mercedes for an unknown crime.[1409]

Nieto, Juan
Born: (Unknown)—Date of Death: October 1915
Place: Willacy County
Event: Lynched/Shot

Robles, Manuel
Born: (Unknown)—Date of Death: October 1915
Place: Willacy County
Event: Lynched/Shot

Two Mexican men named Juan Nieto and Manuel Robles, both of whom were suspected of being outlaws, were shot to death in two separate incidents. Nieto was killed near Lyford, close to the Norias Division that is now in Kenedy County. Robles was shot to death in his home at Sebastian.[1410]

Six Unidentified Mexican Men
Born: (Unknown)—Date of Death: 19 October 1915
Place: Cameron County
Event: Lynching/Shot

Garcia, Severe
Born: (Unknown)—Date of Death: 19 October 1915
Place: Cameron County
Event: Lynching/Shot

Salas, Santiago
Born: (Unknown)—Date of Death: 19 October 1915
Place: Cameron County
Event: Lynching/Shot

Ybarra, Manuel
Born: (Unknown)—Date of Death: 19 October 1915
Place: Cameron County
Event: Lynching/Shot

Ybarra, Trinidad
Born: (Unknown)—Date of Death: 19 October 1915
Place: Cameron County
Event: Lynching/Shot

On Tuesday night, 19 October 1915, a group of unidentified Mexican men wrecked the St. Louis, Brownsville and Mexico passenger train near Brownsville. Three white men were killed and four other wounded in the incident. A posse caught up with the group, killing ten, lynching four from trees. Among the men that were positively identified were Santiago Salas, Severe Garcia, Manuel Ybarra and Trinidad Ybarra.

According to newspaper reports of the day as many as 1,500 cavalry troops were involved in the search, augmenting local lawmen. The entire region was in quite an uproar.[1411]

Tevar, Juan
Born: (Unknown)—Date of Death: November 1915
Place: Willacy County
Event: Lynching/Shooting

In Carrigan's book *The Forgotten Dead*, the author claims that a Mexican man named Juan Tevar was shot to death by a posse near the Las Norias in November 1915. Tevar was suspected of being an outlaw.[1412]

One Unidentified Mexican Man
Born: (Unknown)—Date of Death: 10 November 1915
Place: Willacy County
Event: Lynching/Shooting

In Carrigan's book *The Forgotten Dead*, the author claims that an unidentified Mexican man was killed by a mob of whites at Sebastian on Wednesday, 10 November 1915. The unfortunate fellow's crime is not known.[1413]

Myers, C.A.
Born: circa 1855—Date of Death: 10 November 1915
Place: Tarrant County
Event: Legal Execution/Hanged

C.A. Myers, a white man, was tried and convicted of the murder of A. W. Montague, superintendent of terminals for the Texas and Pacific Railroad. That incident had taken place on Wednesday, 20 January 1915. Myers was sentenced to death. That verdict was carried out on Wednesday, 10 November 1915.

Myers, who earlier had been caught digging at his own arteries in an attempt to cheat the gallows, climbed the stairs to meet his fate at Fort Worth. Due to a miscalculation on the part of the executioner, when Myers fell through the trap and reached the end of his tether the force severed his head from his body. Witnesses to this macabre display were mortified by what they saw.[1414]

Collins, John
Born: (Unknown)—Date of Death: 24 November 1915
Place: Bowie County
Event: Lynching/Hanged

On Wednesday, 24 November 1915, a black man named John Collins was lynched at Dalby Springs, ten miles south of DeKalb. Newspaper accounts indicated that Collins had killed a merchant named U. S. Shaw with an ax. Sometime between midnight and dawn a mob overpowered jailers and removed Collins, running him up a tree at the end of a hangman's noose.[1415]

Thompson, Floyd
Born: (Unknown)—Date of Death: 6 January 1916
Place: Freestone County
Event: Legal Execution/Hanged

In May 1914 Floyd Thompson, a black man, murdered Jim Casey, a white man, near Fairfield. Thompson's crime was described by newspapers of the days as having been, "...the most atrocious in the history of Freestone County."

Just before the hanging Thompson declared that he wanted to make a statement. Sheriff Burleson took him out of the jail and placed him in an automobile but Thompson tried to make a getaway, revealing his true intentions. It took a dozen deputies to restrain the man as he struggled to gain freedom.

At about 3:54 pm on Thursday, 6 January 1916, Sheriff Burleson pulled the lever and the trap door fell. Thompson's neck was broken in the fall and he was declared dead by Doctors Snead and Bradford. The only witnesses to the event, which took place inside the jail, were the usual deputies, physicians and newspapermen.[1416]

Mayfield, William. J.
Born: circa 1872[1417]—Date of Death: 25 January 1916
Place: Bowie County
Event: Lynching/Hanged

William J. Mayfield, a white man, killed his father Thomas J. Mayfield, his mother Frances C. Silva, and his forty-six year old brother Luther L. Mayfield. He did the work with an ax, at their home near Boston on Thursday, 30 December 1915.

On Saturday, 22 January 1916, a jury was discharged in the trial after having failed to reach a verdict during the deliberations that they had begun five days earlier, on Tuesday. Apparently frustrated and impatient with the legal process, at a few minutes before midnight a mob overpowered the jailer and managed to extract the keys from him. They then liberated Mayfield and lynched him from a tree about a half-mile south of town near Texarkana. Few persons knew of the hanging as it took place at about 1:00 am.[1418]

Utley, Louis
Born: (Unknown)—Date of Death: 1 February 1916
Place: Harris County
Event: Legal Execution/Hanged

Precinct 7 Deputy Constable William Clinton Harless died of a gunshot wound he received while attempting to serve a burglary arrest warrant on Louis Utley, a black man.

The incident took place at about 5:00 pm on Wednesday, 14 April 1915, at Spring. Utley fired a shot from a Winchester rifle through the front window of the house, hitting Harless in the neck. Harless died the following day.

Utley was arrested, tried, convicted, and sentenced to death. That judgment was carried out at about 11:07 am on Tuesday, 1 February 1916, when Utley climbed the gallows stairs at Houston and was executed by hanging.[1419]

Sampson, Henry
Born: (Unknown)—Date of Death: 15 February 1916
Place: Harris County
Event: Legal Execution/Hanged

"I ain't [am not] afraid to die. Go ahead and let her drop" were Henry Sampson's last words, a black man who was hanged at Houston on Tuesday, 15 February 1916. His death sentence was scheduled earlier, but was appealed and had been postponed by the Governor.[1420] Sampson had murdered J. C. Bourgeois, a white storekeeper, sometime earlier.

Mikeska, Frank B.
Born: (Unknown)—Date of Death: 10 March 1916
Place: Harris County
Event: Legal Execution/Hanged

Frank B. Mikeska, a white man, was hanged at Houston on Friday, 10 March 1916. Mikeska had murdered his wife. The killing took place at Crosby a year earlier.[1421]

Mikeska's death sentence had also been scheduled for some time earlier, but was postponed by the Governor, James E. "Pa" Ferguson, who along with his wife Miriam A. "Ma" Ferguson held the post of Texas' chief executive. The pair were notorious for putting criminals back on the streets.

Jernigan, Sam
Born: (Unknown)—Date of Death: 11 March 1916
Place: Trinity County
Event: Legal Execution/Hanged

Sam Jernigan, a black man, was tried and convicted of outraging a fourteen-year old white girl.

At about 11:00 am on Saturday, 11 March 1916, in the jail yard at Groveton Sam Jernigan scaled the steps and mounted the gallows. He joked with the sheriff, telling him to "brace up" amid the tension of the moment. Jernigan delivered a lengthy address to the numerous onlookers, professing his innocence. After the trap door had been sprung and Jernigan dropped to his death a deputy sheriff made the surprising announcement that the man had confessed to outraging the girl just before his sentence was read, but wanted to wait until after he was hanged to reveal his admission of guilt. Since it was his hanging he was entitled to see the thing done his way.[1422]

Williams, Chester

Born: (Unknown)—Date of Death: 18 March 1916
Place: Brazoria County
Event: Legal Execution/Hanged

Chester Williams, a black man and a barber, was hanged at the prison at Angleton on Saturday, 18 March 1916. Williams was a double murderer. He had chopped off his wife's head after accusing her of accepting five cents worth of cake from another man. That crime only got him a prison sentence. He ultimately received the death penalty for slashing the throat of a man in his barber chair while serving his prison sentence.

Williams delivered a fifteen minute talk as he stood on the gallows, cautioning other not to follow his example. He added that he should have been hanged for killing his wife in the first place. He was correct.[1423]

Wade, John

Born: (Unknown)—Date of Death: 9 April 1916
Place: Val Verde County
Event: Lynching/Shot

Army Private John Wade, a black man attached to the 24th Infantry, was shot and killed at Del Rio when two Texas Rangers and Sheriff Almond attempted to arrest sixteen blacks in a sporting house in the restricted district of town. The black soldiers shot out all the windows in the establishment while the women fled, scattering like quail and seeking shelter at the courthouse until the matter had been settled.

Three black men, including Wade, attacked the lawmen while they were attempting to take the group to jail. Wade jumped on Ranger W. L Barler, a forty-two year old man who was only 5 feet 8 inches tall, and began clubbing him on the head with a revolver. Barler drew his pistol and fired over his shoulder, killing Wade.

A formal protest was filed requesting the removal of all black troops from Del Rio in the wake of this incident. Ranger Barler recovered, and went on to be appointed a Captain two years later on 10 September 1918.[1424] This case was reported as a "lynching" by *The Lynching Calendar*. From the data it is unclear how that conclusion could have been reached.

Burgess, Robert H.

Born: circa 1881—Date of Death: 29 April 1916
Place: Jefferson County
Event: Legal Execution/Hanged

Robert H. Burgess, a traveling man, was tried and found guilty of the murder of his wife May. The killing took place on Wednesday, 27 January 1915 at Beaumont.

Burgess went to the gallows on Saturday, 29 April 1916, at Beaumont. He tried to cheat the hangman by ingesting poison just before the scheduled time. His attempt was frustrated by a guard.[1425]

Dixon, Thomas "Tom"
Born: circa 1894—Date of Death: 5 May 1916
Place: Waller County
Event: Lynching/Hanged

Thomas Dixon, a black man, was accused of having outraged a fourteen-year old white girl at Hempstead. The young woman was returning from school at the time the incident took place. Her screams quickly alerted nearby citizens, who formed a mob, caught Dixon and lynched him on the spot.[1426]

Washington, Jesse
Born: (Unknown)—Date of Death: 15 May 1916
Place: McLennan County
Event: Lynching/Hanged and Burned

Jesse Washington, a black man, was accused of the murder and outrage of his white employer's wife, Lucy Fryer. The incident took place at Robinson. There were no witnesses to the crime. During an interrogation by the sheriff Washington signed a confession and described the location of the murder weapon.

Washington was tried in a Waco courtroom in front of a crowd of angry onlookers. He pled guilty, and was quickly sentenced to death. Immediately following the court proceedings Washington was forcibly taken from the courtroom and lynched in the presence of about 10,000 citizens.

There was a celebratory atmosphere about, and many attended the show during their lunch hour. Some members of the mob castrated Washington, cut off his fingers then draped his body over a bonfire. Once the flames beneath the poor man had gone cold his charred corpse was dragged through town and parts were sold as souvenirs.[1427]

Buenrostro, Jose
Born: circa 1891—Date of Death: 19 May 1916
Place: Cameron County
Event: Legal Execution/Hanged

Chapa, Melquiades
Born: circa 1893—Date of Death: 19 May 1916
Place: Cameron County
Event: Legal Execution/Hanged

Jose Buenrostro and Melquiades Chapa, both Mexican men, were hanged at Brownsville on Friday, 19 May 1916. The pair had been convicted of the murder of A. L. Austin and his son Charles during the Mexican raid that took place in the fall of 1915. The reader might recall that in 1915 several Mexican men, thought to be the killers of Mr. Austin, were executed.

As if the event had been choreographed, the men were tied together on the gallows, fell through the double trap simultaneously and expired at almost the exact same moment. Prior to meeting their maker the pair issued a joint statement thanking every one of the community for what they had done for them. The presence of about 100 peace officers and three dozen U.S. Cavalry troops assured that the event went off without incident.[1428]

Morin, Louis
Born: (Unknown)—Date of Death: 22 May 1916
Place: Kleberg County
Event: Lynching/Shot

Ponce, Victoriano
Born: (Unknown)—Date of Death: 22 May 1916
Place: Kleberg County
Event: Lynching/Shot

Two Mexican men, Colonel Jose Morin, a former Villista officer, and Victoriano Ponce, were shot to death by Texas Rangers after being taken into custody at Kingsville for suspicion of being train wreckers. The pair had planned an uprising, which was first scheduled for 5 May then postponed to 10 May. A force estimated to number 1,000 supporters who were scattered throughout the area were claimed to have been ready to fight when given the signal. Morin was heavily armed when captured and said to have had important papers on his person. He left San Antonio by train on Monday, 8 May 1916. Special Agent Howard P. Wright and US Marshal Hanson, who were trailing him, boarded the train as well and made the arrest at Saspamco when he tried to disembark.

Morin and Ponce were killed on Monday, 22 May 1916.[1429]

Lerma, Geronimo
Born: (Unknown)—Date of Death: 20 June 1916
Place: Cameron County
Event: Lynching/Shot

Geronimo Lerma, a Mexican man, suspected of the knife wielding assault on Mrs. W. U. Kuykendall, was shot and killed by a posse who had been pursuing him. Lerma had done the work while Mrs. Kuykendall was sleeping at her residence in Brownsville. This case, reported as a shooting by various newspapers, was claimed to have been a lynching by Carrigan's *The Forgotten Dead.* [1430]

Brown, Stephen
Born: (Unknown)—Date of Death: 6 August 1916
Place: Baylor County
Event: Lynching/Shot and Burned

Stephen Brown, a black man, shot and killed Sheriff William Louis Ellis at Seymour on Monday, 6 August 1916. Brown was a prisoner being transported to the jail the time of the incident.

The shooting took place at about noon on 6 August 1916. Ellis had arrested Brown in connection with a theft from a local store and was bringing him to town. At a point about two miles south of Seymour Brown struck Ellis with his handcuffs, stunning him. Brown took the Ellis' pistol and shot him, then fled the scene. Ellis died at 2:30 pm the same day.

A posse was assembled and caught up with Brown, shot him to death and burned him at the stake. He was still wearing the handcuffs and carrying Ellis' pistol when he was apprehended.

Newspaper reports of the day made the outrageous claim that all of the black residents of Seymour packed up and left town on the train. Based on the last census 83% of the population were white, 14% were Hispanic (Mexican) and slightly over 2% were black.[1431]

Lang, Edward
Born: (Unknown)—Date of Death: 19 August 1916
Place: Navarro County
Event: Lynching/Hanged

Edward Lang, a black man, was charged with the outrage of a young white girl while she was picking cotton on her father's farm. Lang was taken into custody and locked in the jail, but a second contingent of angry citizens took charge of him and lynched the man from a telephone pole at Rice. [1432]

Spencer, William "Will"
Born: (Unknown)—Date of Death: 5 October 1916
Place: Upshur County
Event: Lynching/Hanged

William "Will" Spencer, a black man, was lynched near Graceton, about twenty miles from Longview.

Spencer had had a difficulty with Constable Ed Harrell over some cotton during which gunshots were exchanged. Spencer made bond in the affair, but sometime during the night of Wednesday, 4 October 1916, a mob of angry citizens went to his home and, after a considerably struggle, drug him from his residence and lynched him.[1433]

Cooley, Clarence
Born: circa 1895—Date of Death: 18 October 1916
Place: Harris County
Event: Legal Execution/Hanged

Clarence Cooley, a black man with an impressive criminal record, was captured on Saturday, 12 August 1916.

Cooley, who used the alias George Washington or Clarence Wise, was wanted for the double murder of Johannes Hansen, age thirty-two. He had also killed Louis Teten, age seventeen. The murders took place on Thursday, 10 August 1916, near Aldine, about twelve miles from Houston. Cooley shot the men then robbed them. At the time of the homicides Cooley was also facing five burglary charges.

Cooley met his end on Wednesday, 18 October 1916, when he was hanged at Houston. He is buried at the College Memorial Park Cemetery at Houston.[1434]

Williams, John
Born: (Unknown)—Date of Death: 27 October 1916
Place: McLennan County
Event: Legal Execution/Hanged

John Williams, a black man, was tried and convicted of the murder of Allison Criner, another black man. Williams shot and killed Criner in July 1916 at Waco.

Sheriff S.S. Fleming had planned on hanging Williams on 28 August 1916. Governor James E. "Pa" Ferguson interfered with those plans by delaying the execution. Fleming was busy trying to secure a silk rope that was in the possession of the sheriff at Cleburne for Williams' hanging. That fine tool had been used successfully on fifteen occasions, at Dallas, Fort Worth, Waco, Waxahachie and Cleburne. It always produced a good result.

On Friday, 27 October 1916, time ran out for Williams. While on the gallows he requested that he be allowed to speak to the Governor on the long distance telephone. His request was denied. Williams urged the crowd to never get into trouble. At 11:27 am the trap was sprung. Williams dropped through the gallows floor and was dead in seven minutes. He had requested that his body be sent to Mount Calm for burial.[1435]

Johnson, Joseph "Joe"
Born: (Unknown)—Date of Death: 5 November 1916
Place: Matagorda County
Event: Lynching/Hanged

Joseph Johnson, a black man, had killed a fellow named Thomas Fitzmaurice, a white farmer. That incident occurred on Saturday night, 4 November 1916.

On Sunday night, 5 November 1916, Johnson was forcibly removed from the custody of Sheriff Carr and lynched from a railroad bridge near the city. Carr was en route to Wharton at the time to place Johnson in the jail there for safekeeping until his trial. Roughly fifty masked men overtook the vehicle and spirited Johnson off to his lynching.[1436]

Thomas, Buck
Born: (Unknown)—Date of Death: 29 November 1916
Place: Red River County
Event: Lynching/Hanged

Buck Thomas, a black man, was charged with having entered the home of Austin Bishop on Thursday, 23 March 1916. During the break-in he attacked Bishop and his wife with a club. At about 9:00 pm on 29 November 1916, Thomas was forcibly taken from Sheriff Will Lum and removed to a place four miles west of Clarksville where he was lynched.[1437]

Jefferson, Robert
Born: (Unknown)—Date of Death: 7 June 1917
Place: Bell County
Event: Lynching/Shot

Robert Jefferson, a black man, was shot and killed while resisting arrest for draft dodging. Reports claim that he assaulted the lawman who was trying to apprehend him.[1438]

The circumstances of Robert Jefferson's death are outside the normal criteria for this book in that he was not legally executed, lynched, burned, shot by a firing squad, or otherwise tracked down and killed with malevolence. Although his name has been included on several "lynching" rosters his name should probably not be listed.

Harper, Benjamin
Born: (Unknown)—Date of Death: 22 June 1917
Place: Grimes County
Event: Lynching/Hanged

While returning to Houston from Brenham where the group was celebrating emancipation, eight black men riding in two automobiles struck a horse that was being ridden by twelve-year old Ollie May Goodrum. The second car hit the girl, killing her. All eight men were arrested and taken to the jail at Anderson. In route Ben Harper, who was the driver of the car that hit the girl, managed to escape. He was discovered the following day hanging from a tree near where the incident had taken place.[1439]

Hays, Elijah
Born: (Unknown)—Date of Death: 23 June 1917
Place: McLennan County
Event: Lynching/Beaten to Death

Elijah Hays, a black man, was charged with assaulting a woman who owed him $.75. A man named O. E. Courtade was the first to strike Hays. In all, a dozen men participated in beating him to death with pieces of cordwood.[1440] The incident took place at Riesel, fourteen miles south of Waco.

Two days after Hays's death six white men were arrested and charged with the killing, including O. E. Courtade, A.H. Courtade, W. T. Mullins, All Bettes and Clint Roberson. Bond for O. E. Courtade was fixed at $3,000. The rest had to post $2,500.[1441]

Sawyer, Charles
Born: (Unknown)—Date of Death: 25 June 1917
Place: Galveston County
Event: Lynching

Charles Sawyer, a black man, had been accused of outraging the wife of a dairyman six weeks earlier. He was forcibly removed from the jail at about 2:30 am on Monday, 25 June 1917, and lynched at the western boundary of Galveston city. The mob, which was comprised of only a few men, had gained access to the jail by means of a clever ruse.[1442] Sawyer was hanged from a signpost. Although his abductors wore hoods it was obvious from the parts of their body that were exposed that they were all white men.[1443]

Some sources list his surname as Sawyer and his given name as Chester or Henry.

Guidry, Gilbert
Born: circa 1887—Date of Death: 3 July 1917
Place: Orange County
Event: Lynching/Shot

On Monday, 2 July 1917, Gilbert Guidry, a black man, was accused of having attempted to outrage the five-year old daughter of a wealthy Vinton, Louisiana plantation owner.

Guidry was employed at the farm as a yardman and had attacked the girl in an outbuilding. Her screams attracted her parents to the scene and frightened Guidry away. There was a delay in organizing a posse as the family of the girl had wished to keep the matter private, thus Guidry had a good head start. He had covered a distance of about six miles and managed to reach the Sabine River by the time the posse was organized.

Before daybreak on Tuesday, 3 July 1917, a watchman at the Echo Bridge notified officers that he had spotted Guidry crossing over to Texas. Deputy Harvey and several men from Vinton picked up his trail and captured him in the woods. In the process of transporting Guidry to jail by automobile it was claimed that he tried to escape, and was shot to death by Harvey.[1444]

Jones, Will
Born: (Unknown)—Date of Death: 29 July 1917
Place: McLennan County
Event: Lynching/Shot

Private Will Jones, a black man and a member of the 24th Infantry just recently posted at Camp McArthur, was shot in the head and killed during a melee between white citizens and black soldiers on Sunday, 29 July 1917.

It all began when crowds of armed white citizens gathered at the town square to aid officers in keeping the peace should the black troops consider another "uprising."[1445] In spite of their preparations, trouble soon began when black soldiers of the 24th ordered white proprietors of a restaurant to take down a sign in the establishment. In another version of this same incident the source indicated that black troops refused to allow whites to pass in front of a black motion picture theater. In either case, officers fired shots when the black soldiers showed signs of being game for a fight. The riotous blacks fled, being pursued by lawmen and white troops from Camp McArthur. The situation calmed down when twenty of the most militant soldiers were arrested.[1446]

One week later six black soldiers of Jones's outfit went before a general court martial. Five members of the group were sentenced to serve five years at hard labor at the Federal Penitentiary at Leavenworth, Kansas. The sixth man received a ten year sentence. All were given a dishonorable discharge and had to forfeit all pay and allowances due them.[1447]

Jones, Charles
Born: (Unknown)—Date of Death: 22 August 1917
Place: Harrison County
Event: Lynching/Hanged

Charles Jones, a black man, was taken from the jail at Marshall by five men and rushed away in an automobile. At a point halfway between Marshall and Elysian Fields his captors hoisted him up a tree and lynched him. Jones had been jail for entering the bedchambers of a white woman. That incident had taken place on Monday night, 20 August 1917.[1448]

Two Unidentified Black Men
Born: (Unknown)—Date of Death: 23 August 1917
Place: Harris County
Event: Lynching/Hanged

According to sources that have often proven unreliable, two unidentified black men were lynched at Houston on Thursday, 23 August 1917.[1449]

The alleged incident is claimed to have been part of the well documented Houston Race Riot, or Camp Logan Incident, which began on 23 August 1917. This sources claim is questionable, considering that the episode has been well documented and painstakingly researched.[1450]

Jenning, Charles
Born: (Unknown)—Date of Death: 3 September 1917
Place: Jefferson County
Event: Lynching/Hanged

In another report by sources that have often proven unreliable, a black man named Charles Jenning was lynched at Beaumont on Monday, 3 September 1917. There was no mention of his crime.[1451]

There are records of a man named Charles Jennings who died by means other than vigilante intervention at Jefferson County on Saturday, 25 August 1917. There is not sufficient information available to link him to this incident, however.[1452]

Smith, Bertram
Born: (Unknown)—Date of Death: 21 September 1917
Place: Harris County
Event: Lynching/Hanged

Bertram Smith, a black man who was employed as a camp cook in the oil fields, was charged with having outraged the wife of an oilfield worker near Goose Creek. He was forcibly taken from the jail by a mob of several hundred and lynched.[1453]

Baltimore, Charles W.
Born: (Unknown)—Date of Death: 11 December 1917
Place: Bexar County
Event: Legal Execution/Hanged

Brackenridge, William
Born: (Unknown)—Date of Death: 11 December 1917
Place: Bexar County
Event: Legal Execution/Hanged

Brown, Larsen
Born: (Unknown)—Date of Death: 11 December 1917
Place: Bexar County
Event: Legal Execution/Hanged

Davis, Ira
Born: (Unknown)—Date of Death: 11 December 1917
Place: Bexar County
Event: Legal Execution/Hanged

Divine, James
Born: (Unknown)—Date of Death: 11 December 1917
Place: Bexar County
Event: Legal Execution/Hanged

Hawkins, Thomas
Born: (Unknown)—Date of Death: 11 December 1917
Place: Bexar County
Event: Legal Execution/Hanged

Johnson, Frank
Born: (Unknown)—Date of Death: 11 December 1917
Place: Bexar County
Event: Legal Execution/Hanged

McWharter, Pat
Born: (Unknown)—Date of Death: 11 December 1917
Place: Bexar County
Event: Legal Execution/Hanged

Moore, Jesse
Born: (Unknown)—Date of Death: 11 December 1917
Place: Bexar County
Event: Legal Execution/Hanged

Nesbit, William
Born: (Unknown)—Date of Death: 11 December 1917
Place: Bexar County
Event: Legal Execution/Hanged

Snodgrass, Carlos
Born: (Unknown)—Date of Death: 11 December 1917
Place: Bexar County
Event: Legal Execution/Hanged

Wheatley, James
Born: (Unknown)—Date of Death: 11 December 1917
Place: Bexar County
Event: Legal Execution/Hanged

Young, Rosley
Born: (Unknown)—Date of Death: 11 December 1917
Place: Bexar County
Event: Legal Execution/Hanged

The violence that occurred during the night of Thursday, 23 August 1917, is oftentimes referred to as the Camp Logan Riot, although the actions of the mutinous soldiers assigned to the camp took place away from the actual premises of the military base. Two locations were involved. First, along Buffalo Bayou in the suburban residential community of Brunner, which is on the north side of Buffalo Bayou and at the intersection of Washington Avenue and the modern Shepherd Drive. The second riot scene was on the south side of Buffalo Bayou, along San Felipe Road (now known as West Dallas Avenue) in a residential area of the Fourth Ward known as the San Felipe District.

The events began when army Corporal Charles W. Baltimore, an off duty military policeman from the 3rd Battalion, was arrested and reportedly treated roughly by a Houston policeman. Rumors circulated that Baltimore had been killed, provoking anger and frustration among the troops. The disquiet continued to build during the early evening. To avoid an armed confrontation the commandant, Major Kneeland S. Snow, ordered all the rifles and ammunition collected. As the weapons were being gathered troops sighted a mob that was advancing toward the camp. Someone fired a shot. Chaos broke out. The soldiers raided the supply tent for their guns. They began shooting indiscriminately into the residential neighborhood. A mob of over 100 black soldiers spilled out of the camp and on to the streets of the Brunner community, determined to march to the Fourth Ward jail and release their imprisoned comrade.

Officers Rufus Daniel, W. C. Wilson, Horace Moody and C. E. Carter had commandeered a vehicle to ride to the action. They stopped the car when they heard shots fired. Mob leader Sergeant Vida Henry ordered his men to take cover in the City Cemetery, located on the south side of the street. Officer Daniels unwisely decided to charge the troops in the cemetery, armed only with his service revolver. He was instantly killed. Carter, Wilson and Moody took cover in a nearby garage. Moody was shot in the leg and severely injured. He later died while doctors were amputating the limb. The firing ceased, and the soldiers mutilated the corpse of Daniels, battering his face and bayoneting his body. Next the frenzied mob advanced toward downtown Houston.

At Heiner Street, four blocks into their route, the throng encountered a seven passenger touring car driven by James E. Lyon. The vehicle had two civilian passengers along with police officers John E. Richardson and Ira Raney. They had hitched a ride to get to the area where the violence was taking place. The mob disarmed the group in the vehicle and held them, hands raised in the air. Richardson inadvertently let his hands drop and was hit over the head with the butt of a rifle by one of his captors. At that point Raney and the civilian passenger, Eli Smith, decided to take off running in hopes of reaching safety. Smith was shot. His body was later found in the ditch at Heiner Street. Smith had also been bayoneted in the hip and the left armpit. Raney was also shot. His body was beaten and bayoneted. Asa Bland, the other civilian passenger in the touring car, was wounded by a gunshot as well. The bullet grazed him just over his left eye.

A second car arrived at the Heiner Street intersection. That vehicle carried Captain Joseph Mattes from Camp Logan, three enlisted soldiers and Police Officer Edwin Meinke. When Captain Mattes stood up in the car to address the out of control horde about forty of the black troops took aim at the vehicle and opened fire. Both Mattes and Meinke were killed immediately.

During the melee detective T. A. Binford received a minor wound to the knee. In little more than two hours of violent rioting the mob had killed their own captain and five Houston police officers.

The now deflated rabble retreated a few blocks to the south and re-formed ranks near the railroad tracks on the eastern edge of the Fourth Ward. By that time most of the soldiers had lost interest in their savage crusade and slowly drifted back to camp. No doubt fearing reprisal for his role in the affray, Sergeant Henry took his own life at about 2:05 a.m. the following morning.

On 24 August 1917, Governor James E. Ferguson declared martial law in Houston and placed Brigadier General John A. Hulen, commander of the Texas National Guard, in charge of the city. In an effort to restore order 350 Coast Guard servicemen were dispatched from Galveston, along with 600 infantrymen from San Antonio. By 9:30 a.m. on Saturday 25 August 1917, all of the troops of the 3rd Battalion had been loaded on trains and sent to either San Antonio or New Mexico to await trial. Order was restored to the city on Monday 27 August 1917.

A total of eleven citizens and five police officers were killed during this unspeakable disaster. Thirty citizens suffered severe wounds. Four of the rioting black soldiers were killed. Two fell at the hands of their own men, who had mistaken them for citizens. One soldier who had been shot by a citizen died in a hospital. Sergeant Vida Henry died by his own hand.

Three separate courts martial were convened at Fort Sam Houston in San Antonio 1917. The magistrate indicted one hundred eighteen men of I Company, 24th Infantry, 3rd Battalion. Seven of the soldiers who rioted testified against the others in exchange for clemency. One hundred ten of the mutinous soldiers were found guilty of at least one charge. Nineteen of them were hanged and sixty-three of them received life sentences. Two officers of Camp Logan faced courts martial, but were released. Thirteen of the men, named above, were hanged on Tuesday, 11 December 1917.[1454]

Castanedo, Antonio
Born: circa 1846—Date of Death: 28 January 1918
Place: Presidio County
Event: Lynching/Shot

Flores, Longoria
Born: circa 1874—Date of Death: 28 January 1918
Place: Presidio County
Event: Lynching/Shot

Garcia, Alberto
Born: circa 1883—Date of Death: 28 January 1918
Place: Presidio County
Event: Lynching/Shot

Gonzalez, Eutemio
Born: circa 1881—Date of Death: 28 January 1918
Place: Presidio County
Event: Lynching/Shot

Hernandez, Ambrosio
Born: circa 1897—Date of Death: 28 January 1918
Place: Presidio County
Event: Lynching/Shot

Herrera, Pedro
Born: circa 1893—Date of Death: 28 January 1918
Place: Presidio County
Event: Lynching/Shot

Herrera, Viviano
Born: circa 1895—Date of Death: 28 January 1918
Place: Presidio County
Event: Lynching/Shot

Herrera, Severiano
Born: circa 1900—Date of Death: 28 January 1918
Place: Presidio County
Event: Lynching/Shot

Huerta, Macedonio
Born: circa 1888—Date of Death: 28 January 1918
Place: Presidio County
Event: Lynching/Shot

Jacquez, Tiburcio
Born: circa 1868—Date of Death: 28 January 1918
Place: Presidio County
Event: Lynching/Shot

Jiminez, Juan
Born: circa 1902—Date of Death: 28 January 1918
Place: Presidio County
Event: Lynching/Shot

Jiminez, Pedro
Born: circa 1891—Date of Death: 28 January 1918
Place: Presidio County
Event: Lynching/Shot

Jiminez, Serapio
Born: circa 1893—Date of Death: 28 January 1918
Place: Presidio County
Event: Lynching/Shot

Morales, Manuel
Born: circa 1871—Date of Death: 28 January 1918
Place: Presidio County
Event: Lynching/Shot

Nieves, Roman (Ramone)
Born: circa 1870—Date of Death: 28 January 1918
Place: Presidio County
Event: Lynching/Shot

The fifteen Mexican men listed above were killed during an incident known as The Porvenir Massacre. It was one of a series of clashes between men of Mexican descent and the Texas Rangers that had been ignited by the Mexican Revolution.

The incident was one of the most serious acts of ranger misconduct ever cited. In November 1917, ranger captain J. M. Fox noted that a few cattle and horses had been stolen. He suspected "Mexican Bandits" from the Carranistas and Villistas near Presidio County to be the culprits. On 25 December 1917, Mexicans had perpetrated the Brite Ranch Raid, an incident in which several Mexicans and whites were killed, horses were stolen, and the ranch store was robbed. Several days later Ranger Company B, which included eight men under Fox, Troop G of the Eighth Cavalry from Camp Evetts under Captain Henry H. Anderson along with local ranchers Buck Pool, John Pool, Tom Snider, and Raymond Fitzgerald all arrived at the ranch of Manuel Morales in Porvenir. Reports conflict as to the precise date of their arrival. After a bloody confrontation with persons they thought to be the Mexican bandits the party left Porvenir. In their wake fifteen Mexican men lay dead. None were Mexican outlaw. All were Texas residents. Family members and friends buried the fallen at El Comidor in Mexico.

Exactly what happen at that place is unclear. Although most of the white participants, as well as noted historian Walter Prescott Webb, found "Mexicans" responsible for the confrontation, Henry Warren, Captain Anderson, and Porvenir residents of Mexican descent offer a different account. Not until 18 February 1918, did Fox explain to the adjutant general what had happened that day. He claimed that as the Mexicans were being marched to the edge of town some of their comrades fired at the rangers. Rangers, in turn, returned the fire. Fox went on to claim that some of the Mexicans had been found with pocketknives, soap, and shoes belonging to the Brite Ranch. He also claimed that one dead man had "sent word" some nine months earlier that a raid would be made on "Texas Gringos" and that looting and burning would also occur. Anderson, however, called some official versions of the story "white-washed," and claimed that he, his sergeant, the twelve men he sent out with the rangers along with the widows and family members could testify to the truth.

According to Webb, agreement was unanimous among the rangers and ranchers on the "culpability of the Mexicans." Webb noted that in a preliminary visit by rangers and federal agents to Pilares and Porvenir, "Mexicans" were found wearing Hamilton Brown shoes from the Brite Ranch. In corroboration of Fox's version, Colonel George T. Langhorne and the rangers said the party was fired on from the brush while gathering evidence, allegedly by the "Mexicans," and that the whites fired back. Raymond Fitzgerald told Webb that some Porvenir residents were "thieves, informers, spies, and murderers." Webb based his assessment of the incident on the testimony of whites however, ignoring the affidavits by Mexican-descent women in Canales's investigation.

Henry Warren, whose father-in-law, Tiburcio Jáquez, was killed in the incident, wrote a different version of the story in an undated manuscript written sometime after June 1918. He sought to explain what he called a "massacre" and the "wholesale destruction of these Mexicans." Warren blamed the rangers. Several elderly Mexican men were spared, as were all women and children. John J. Bailey, a white man living in the village on the ranch, was also spared. Warren claimed he saw the bodies on 29 January 1918. He made a list of the deceased, including their names, ages, spouses, and children, and noted that the rangers' actions had orphaned forty-two children. Warren sought to explain the incident by suggesting that rancher Tom Snider had stolen and sold horses belonging to Porvenir residents, told the rangers that the "Mexican bandits" who conducted the Brite Ranch raid were in Porvenir, and thus had planned the killings so his own crime would not be discovered.

The role of the United States Cavalry is unclear. Press reports claimed that the army had nothing to do with the affair. On 4 June 1918, Governor William P. Hobby disbanded Company B of the Texas Rangers and dismissed five officers for their actions. Eulalia Gonzales Sánchez gave Warren power of attorney and sought to recover damages for the murder of her husband. In 1919 Canales highlighted the Porvenir Massacre in the investigation of the rangers. About 140 Porvenir residents abandoned their homes and fled to Mexico. The community ceased to exist for several years.[1455]

The victims, ranging in age from sixteen to seventy-two, were Manuel Morales age forty-seven, Roman Nieves age forty-eight, Longino Flores age forty-four, Alberto Garcia age thirty-five, Eutimio Gonzales age thirty-seven, Macedonio Huertas age thirty, Tiburcio Jaques age fifty, Ambrosio Hernandez age twenty-one, Antonio Castanedo age seventy-two, Pedro Herrera age twenty-five, Viviano Herrera age twenty-three, Severiano Herrera age eighteen, Pedro Jimenez age twenty-seven, Serapio Jimenez age twenty five, and Juan Jimenez age sixteen.[1456]

Mann, John B.
Born: (Unknown)—Date of Death: 5April 1918
Place: Harris County
Event: Legal Execution/Firing Squad

Matthews, Walter
Born: (Unknown)—Date of Death: 5 April 1918
Place: Harris County
Event: Legal Execution/Firing Squad

Both John Mann and Walter Matthews were black soldiers, rank of private. They had been tried and convicted of the murder of a fellow soldier named Ralph M. Foley from Company G, 130th Infantry. The incident occurred while Foley was guarding Mann and Matthews who were picking up trash around the camp. After the incident they fled, but were quickly captured.

Their execution by firing squad took place at Camp Logan. The condemned wretches went to meet their fate quietly. Apart from a handful of newspaper reports, and of course the necessary military personnel to carry out the death sentence, no one attended.[1457]

Garcia, Florencio
Born: (Unknown)—Date of Death: 5 April 1918
Place: Cameron County
Event: Lynched/Shot

A Mexican man named Florencio Garcia who was suspected of theft was taken from his jail cell at Port Isabel and shot to death on Friday, 5 April 1918. No records can be found to support this claim.[1458]

Dodd, Leonard
Born: (Unknown)—Date of Death: 24 May 1918
Place: Dallas County
Event: Legal Execution/Hanged

Stevenson, Walter
Born: (Unknown)—Date of Death: 24 May 1918
Place: Dallas County
Event: Legal Execution/Hanged

Walter Stevenson and Leonard Dodd, both white men, were tried and convicted of committing and outrage on a woman. They were found guilty and sentenced to death.

Dodd tried to cheat the hangman by attempting to take his own life in his cell prior to the prescribed time of his execution. He was unsuccessful. A doctor ordered him sufficiently well to keep his date with the hangman, that being perhaps the most peculiar diagnosis a physician has ever issued. The order was carried out at Dallas on Friday, 24 May 1918, when both Dodd and Stevenson dropped through the trap door and reached the end of the line...literally.[1459]

Goolsbee, Kirby
Born: circa 1899—Date of Death: 27 May 1918
Place: Tyler County
Event: Lynching/Hanged

Kirby Goolsbee, a nineteen-year old black man, was accused of committing and outrage on a white girl. For that he was taken out and lynched by an angry mob near Woodville.

Newspapers were quick to point out the "white brutes" that had done the lynching but made no mention of the young white girl who had been viciously molested, nor did they bother to identify the victim by name.[1460]

Cabaniss, Sarah
Born: (Unknown)—Date of Death: 1 June 1918
Place: Walker County
Event: Lynching/Shot

Cabaniss, Bessie
Born: (Unknown)—Date of Death: 1 June 1918
Place: Walker County
Event: Lynching/Shot

Cabaniss, Cute
Born: (Unknown)—Date of Death: 1 June 1918
Place: Walker County
Event: Lynching/Shot

Cabaniss, Lena
Born: (Unknown)—Date of Death: 1 June 1918
Place: Walker County
Event: Lynching/Shot

Cabaniss, Peter "Pete"
Born: (Unknown)—Date of Death: 1 June 1918
Place: Walker County
Event: Lynching/Shot

Cabaniss, Tenola
Born: (Unknown)—Date of Death: 1 June 1918
Place: Walker County
Event: Lynching/Shot

George Cabaniss, a black man, repeatedly refused to register for the draft. He was eventually arrested and taken to Houston where he was compelled to comply with the law and register. Once registered, Cabaniss refused to answer two draft calls. He sent word to the Sheriff T. E. King that he would have to come and get him.

On Thursday, May 30, 1918, Cabaniss met the sheriff's brother-in-law, P. W. Allen. He reprimanded Cabaniss for resisting the draft. Cabaniss pulled a revolver on Allen and threatened to kill him. Allen swore out a warrant. The sheriff and his deputies went to the Cabaniss' cabin at Dodge and attempted to arrest him. The posse was met by George, his mother and sister, all of whom were carrying shotguns. Gunfire quickly erupted. When the smoke cleared George was dead and his mother and sister were both wounded.

A black man alerted the sheriff that Cabaniss' relatives were threatening revenge. In a preemptive move, six Cabaniss clansmen were killed and their cabin burned down at daybreak on Saturday, 1 June 1918. There is some confusion as to the actual names of the dead family members. It appears that the list included George's mother Sarah, his sister Bessie and brothers Pete, Cute, Tenola and Lena.

One newspaper claimed that it was unclear if the family was killed by a mob or shot as a result of resisting arrest by the sheriff's deputies. Another newspaper claimed that it was clear that the sheriff and his deputies had shot the six family members. The sheriff reported that the Cabaniss clan had fired 200 rounds at the posse during the affray. Curiously, none of the bullets managed to hit a single posseman. [1461]

Hoffman, Nat
Born: circa 1893—Date of Death: 11 July 1918
Place: McLennan County
Event: Legal Execution/Hanged

Army Private Nat Hoffman, a twenty five year old black man who was formerly a member of the supply company, 19th Field Artillery, 5th Brigade, was hanged at Fort McArthur at 5:38 am on Thursday, 11 July 1918. Hoffman had been tried by a military court martial for the criminal outrage of an eleven-year old white schoolgirl near the post. That incident took place in April 1918.

No witnesses were permitted. According to reports his only comment was that he deserved his fate.[1462]

Brown, Gene (Jim)
Born: (Unknown)—Date of Death: 27 July 1918
Place: Limestone County
Event: Lynching/Hanged

Gene Brown, a black man, was lynched by a mob of about 150 men on Saturday, 27 July 1918. Brown was suspected of having attempted to outrage a white woman at Ben Hur. The woman was asleep when a man entered her bedroom and threw acid on her in the mistaken belief that it was a drug to induce unconsciousness. She screamed, and the man escaped. A citizen's posse caught Brown and the sheriff was notified. When the lawman arrived he discovered that a mob had beaten him to the punch and had already strung Brown up from a nearby tree. The vigilantes who did the work had already disbursed.[1463]

Brown, Steve
Born (Unknown)—Date of Death: 2 August 1918
Place: Kaufman County
Event: Legal Execution/Hanged

At 12:14 pm on Friday, 2 August 1918, a black man named Steve Brown was hanged at Kaufman for the murder of another black man named George Jackson. Brown and Jackson were roommates at Terrell when Brown killed Jackson while he was sleeping. Brown nearly severed Jackson's head when he struck him with an ax. At his trial Brown claimed that Jackson, an old crippled man, had threatened him with the ax first. The jury did not believe his claim. Brown was only twenty-three years old.[1464]

Franklin, James
Born (Unknown)—Date of Death: 16 August 1918
Place: Hardin County
Event: Legal Execution/Hanged

The *Death Penalty Information Center* claims that a black man named James Franklin was executed by hanging in Hardin County on Friday, 16 August 1918. This incident has not been independently verified.[1465]

Hubert, Harvey
Born: circa 1884—Date of Death: 23 August 1918
Place: Travis County
Event: Legal Execution/Hanged

Harvey Hubert, a black man, was tried and convicted of murdering a seventeen-year old white boy. Hubert was tried twice, and convicted both times. After his second appeal the court affirmed the case. Hubert was hanged at the jail at Austin on Friday, 23 August 1918.[1466]

Jones, Will
Born: circa 1889—Date of Death: 30 August 1918
Place: Dallas County
Event: Legal Execution/Hanged

Will Jones, a black man, was tried and convicted of an outrage committed against Mrs. Anna Wolford of Dallas. Immediately following the brutal attack on Wolford neighbors and citizens mobbed the jailhouse, intent on lynching the man. They were only subdued when authorities agreed to give Jones a speedy trial and a humane hanging. Numerous witness attended Jones's hanging, including his victim Mrs. Wolford.[1467]

Collier, Babe
Born: (Unknown)—Date of Death: 17 September 1918
Place: Bexar County
Event: Legal Execution/Hanged

McDonald, Thomas
Born: (Unknown)—Date of Death: 17 September 1918
Place: Bexar County
Event: Legal Execution/Hanged

Robinson, James
Born: (Unknown)—Date of Death: 17 September 1918
Place: Bexar County
Event: Legal Execution/Hanged

Smith, Joseph
Born: (Unknown)—Date of Death: 17 September 1918
Place: Bexar County
Event: Legal Execution/Hanged

Wright, Albert
Born: (Unknown)—Date of Death: 17 September 1918
Place: Bexar County
Event: Legal Execution/Hanged

Five black soldiers of Company I, 24th Infantry, were sentenced to death by hanging for their participation in the Houston Riots of August 1917. On Tuesday, 17 September 1918, that verdict was carried out in private at Fort Sam Houston at San Antonio.

The event was shrouded in secrecy. No civilians were allowed to attend. Ten additional troops of the 24th had been condemned to hang, but their sentences were commuted to life in prison.[1468]

O'Neal, Abe
Born: (Unknown)—Date of Death: 19 September 1918
Place: Grimes County
Event: Lynched/Hanged

According to *The Lynching Calendar*, a black man named Abe O'Neal was lynched at a place called Buff Lake, which is east of Navasota in Grimes County on Thursday, 19 September 1918.[1469]

Boone, William
Born: (Unknown)—Date of Death: 24 September 1918
Place: Bexar County
Event: Legal Execution/Hanged

Army Private William Boone, a black man, formerly of Company I, 24th Infantry, was tried and convicted of playing a role in the deaths that occurred during the Houston Race Riot. He was hanged on Tuesday, 24 September 1918. Boone's death marked the sixth in Texas that month arising from the same incident.[1470]

Coats, Rufus
Born: circa 1898— Date of Death: 8 November 1918
Place: Tarrant County
Event: Legal Execution/Hanged

Rufus Coats, a white man, was tried and convicted of having murdered his seventeen-year old sweetheart, Zella Faulk. That incident took place on Monday, 4 June 1917. Miss Faulk's body was discovered in the woods near the city.

Coats was sentenced to death. Governor W. P. Hobby issued a stay of execution on three occasions, finally relenting and allowing the sentence to be carried out. Coats's execution took place at Fort Worth on Friday, 8 November 1918.[1471]

Shipman, Charles
Born: (Unknown)—Date of Death: 14 November 1918
Place: Fort Bend County
Event: Lynching

According to *The Lynching Calendar*, a black man named Charles Shipman was lynched at Fort Bend County on Thursday, 14 November 1918. A Black newspaper in Washington, DC reported that the National Association for the Advancement of Colored People (NAACP) had sent a letter to Texas Governor William P. Hobby requesting an investigation into the incident. The document included a report from their San Antonio Branch that five men had lynched a black man at a plantation where Shipman lived.[1472]

Almost twenty years after the time when death certificates were mandatory in Texas there is no records of any kind of this incident.

Williams, Bragg
Born: (Unknown)—Date of Death: 30 January 1919
Place: Hill County
Event: Lynching/Burned to Death

Bragg Williams, a black man who murdered Mrs. George Wells and her infant child, was burned to death at Hillsboro by a mob numbering in the hundreds.[1473]

Williams had already been tried and convicted in a courtroom, packed with Texas Rangers for security. He was sentenced to be hanged on Friday, 21 February 1919. Shortly after 1:00 pm on Thursday, 30 January 1919, a mob quietly formed. County officials are said to have tried to hold back the crowd, but the vigilantes had cut down a telephone pole and used it as a battering ram to gain entry to the jail. Williams was taken to the town square where boxes, barrels and other assorted flammable materials were piled around him and set on fire.[1474]

Surname Unknown, "Shag"

Born: (Unknown)—Date of Death: May 1919
Place: Gregg County
Event: Lynching

A black man known only as "Shag" was lynched north of Kilgore. Newspaper articles of the day provided no insight into "Shag's" crime, but did focus on the racial disturbance that the event caused at nearby Longview. In the face of the anticipated racial insurgence, National Guardsmen and Texas Rangers began disarming citizens, right down to the Boy Scouts who had to give over their little rifles to authorities. National Guardsmen and Rangers patrolled the town all the way into the month of July.[1475]

Walters, Lemmel

Born: (Unknown)—Date of Death: 17 July 1919
Place: Gregg County
Event: Lynching/Shot

Lemmel Walter, a black man who was accused of having carried on a romance with a white woman, was lynched at Longview on Thursday, 17 July 1919.

Walters was removed from the jail by a mob that, according to reports, encountered no resistance from the sheriff who acknowledged and greeted the individual members by name as they passed. Walters was taken to the edge of town and shot to pieces, his naked corpse left alongside the road as food for the birds of prey. Later, a group of blacks took charge of his remains and gave the wretch a proper burial.

The event caused an uproar. His white paramour was said to be "prostrate," and under the care of a physician at Kilgore. As in the case of the black man named "Shag," Governor James A. "Pa" Ferguson once again called out the National Guard troops and sent Texas Rangers to the town to quell the disturbance. Again, even the Boy Scouts were disarmed. [1476]

Several days after the incident three brothers of the white woman who had been accused by a local black man named Jones of having had the romantic relationship with Walters went to Jones's home and beat him senseless, leaving him with a warning that he had better leave town for good.

Still in an uproar about the false accusations, fifteen or twenty white men from the Longview community started into the black neighborhood to set things right. Jones was already gone, but the mob was fired on from concealment. In all, five white men were wounded. After dark another mob formed, returning to the black neighborhood and setting fire to the Jones home along with several other buildings including the Men's League, a grocery store, drug store and dance hall.[1477]

Jennings, Chilton
Born: (Unknown)—Date of Death: 24 July 1919
Place: Upshur County
Event: Lynching/Hanged

On Thursday, 24 July 1919, a black man named Chilton Jennings was forcibly removed from the jail at Gilmer and lynched. Jennings was accused of assault to commit an outrage on a white woman.

    Generally, the perpetrators of vigilante lynching's are never identified and never brought to justice. In this case, among the first in Texas, Charley Lansdale, Willie Long, and Tom Lay were brought under the examining light of a trial on Thursday, 22 April 1920, at Canton. All three were given a two year suspended sentence.[1478]

Price, John Hood
Born: circa 1877—Date of Death: 23 March 1920
Place: San Augustine County
Event: Legal Execution/Hanged

Setting a new record for the State of Texas, John Price, a black man, was legally hanged at San Augustine for the murder of John Kennedy, a white man. The affair took less than twenty-four hours from the time the crime took place until Price was legally hanged.

    Kennedy, a farmer, had quarreled with Price recently. On Monday, 22 March 1920, Price shot him through the window of his home using a double barrel shotgun.

    Price was captured at about 4:30 pm. A night session of court was convened. Price was found guilty and sentenced to death. By 11:00 am the following day, 23 March 1920, he had already been hanged in the town square in front of about 2,000 witnesses.[1479]

Five Unidentified Mexican Men
Born: (Unknown)—Date of Death: 8 April 1920
Place: El Paso County
Event: Lynching

According to newspaper reports, five unidentified Mexican men, thought to be outlaws and members of a larger party numbering fifteen or more, recently raided the mining camp of John Hicks in the

Guadalupe Mountains. According to reports, the Mexican outlaws rode up to the Hicks camp, disarmed all of the Americans and made off with $6,000 in silver bars. The loss so enraged the miners that they formed a posse and gave chase, eventually overtaking the group. They captured the leader and four of his men, and then lynched the lot from a convenient tree. The silver was recovered but the remaining ten escaped and, according to reports, joined Villa.[1480]

Anderson, Elijah
Born: circa 1890—Date of Death: 29 June 1920
Place: Wharton County
Event: Lynching/Hanged

Gordon, Jodie
Born: circa 1886—Date of Death: 29 June 1920
Place: Wharton County
Event: Lynching/Burned

Wharton County Deputy Sheriff Harry McCormick was shot and killed near Diamond Mound when he went to help Constable Pitman serve a warrant on a white man named Washington Giles.

Giles had first agreed to go along quietly with the officers, but then began to resist. During a struggle that took place Giles was able to gain control of Pitman's pistol. In the midst of the skirmish Osborne Giles, the brother of the suspect, emerged with a Winchester rifle in hand. While McCormick tried to assist the other officer Osborne Giles shot him in the head. McCormick was taken to the Caney Valley Hospital but he never regained consciousness. He expired at about 10:30 pm.

A posse said to have numbered 250 strong surrounded the two Giles brothers near Diamond Mound. Although given an opportunity to surrender the pair decided to shoot it out. Both were killed. Two other men who had aided in the original escape, Jodie Gordon and Elijah Anderson, were lynched from trees by a vigilante mob about six miles from Wharton. Their only crime, according to one newspaper source, had been providing a change of clothing to the killers. Others cite the fact that the men had gone to town to purchase ammunition and supplies for the fugitives. The bodies were discovered the following day hanging from a tree about six miles east of Wharton.[1481]

Washington Giles's wife Lottie was tried, convicted and sentenced to twenty-five years in prison. The case was reversed on appeal.

Arthur, Herman
Born: (Unknown)—Date of Death: 6 July 1920
Place: Lamar County
Event: Lynching/Burned to Death

Arthur, Irving
Born: (Unknown)—Date of Death: 6 July 1920
Place: Lamar County
Event: Lynching/Burned to Death

On Tuesday, 6 July 1920, a Paris mob murdered brothers Herman and Irving Arthur, black sharecroppers accused of killing their landlords, father and son.

Herman Arthur, a black World War I veteran of combat in France, had convinced his eighteen year old brother Irving, that the family should not continue to sharecrop because of the constant debt necessitated by advances from the landlord. The entire family was planning to move.

The landowner, Will Hodges, and his father J. H. Hodges had a different view of the sharecropping Arthur family. The Hodges' perceived the Arthur family to be lazy and "slack about work." The *Paris News* account claimed that a conflict had arisen about the failure of the Arthur family to work on the Saturday prior to 1 July. The Hodges family became concerned that the Arthurs were preparing to leave town while still owing them a huge debt on the advances they were made under the sharecropping system. Feeling that their concerns were legitimate, they decided to confront the Arthur clan.

On Thursday, 1 July 1920, Will Hodges and his father appeared at the family's shack on Stillhouse Road and forced their way inside. The only persons present were the women. The Hodges kicked over the cook stove and food thereon, then said they would return the next day to talk to the brothers. They did. This time with guns.

Herman and Irvin Arthur were at home when the Hodges's showed up. The verbal conflict erupted into gunfire. In differing accounts of the same story it is said that one side or the other began shooting first. In the end, both Will and J. H. Hodges lay mortally wounded.

Herman and Irvin knew they would not be well treated by Lamar County authorities, so they fled to Oklahoma. A posse spread out across Northeast Texas and Southeast Oklahoma searching for the pair. Finally, on Tuesday, 6 July 1920, lawmen arrested the Arthur brothers in Oklahoma.

In spite of caution otherwise, Herman and Irvin Arthur were returned to Paris and placed in the Lamar County jail. A crowd began to gather almost immediately. From the courthouse steps, District Judge Denton begged the mob to disperse. The crowd, using sledgehammers, broke into the jail, and according to newspaper reports of the day, faced a "compliant sheriff" who allowed the brothers to be taken from their cell and removed to the fairgrounds.

Before a crowd of about 3,000, the Arthur brothers were chained to a flagpole and burned to death. With the bodies still warm, the mob attached the pair to a pickup truck and a caravan of vehicles drove the corpses through the streets and yards of the black sections of Paris.

Two intense days of near riotous conditions followed. The *Paris News* reported rumors that the "Negroes were assembling and would seek revenge with miscellaneous shootings throughout the evening." On Wednesday evening, 7 July 1920, the town square filled with dozens of armed white men. Hardware stores throughout the city were looted of ammunition and guns. Finally, the men were organized into squads using Pine Bluff as a black/white dividing line and ordered to stop all movement across the line.[1482]

The *Paris News* claimed the bodies of Herman and Irvin Arthur were recovered separately, one the night of 6 July and the other on 7 July. Both were buried at an undisclosed location in Lamar County.

A later account of the incident claimed that five people were indicted for participation in the lynchings. All of them were found not guilty.[1483]

Hunter, Green
Born: (Unknown)—Date of Death: 9 July 1920
Place: Dallas County
Event: Legal Execution/Hanged

Green Hunter, a black man, was hanged at the Dallas County jail on Friday, 9 July 1920.

Hunter was convicted of assaulting a white woman at Hale Station on Friday, 28 May 1920. He also admitted to having been the one who had attacked another white woman, a crime for which Ben Perry, another black man, had been convicted and sentenced to life in prison.

"Friday has always been my Hoodoo," said Perry. He was born on a Friday, committed the crime on a Friday, convicted on a Friday and was to be hung on a Friday.[1484]

Daniels, Lige
Born: circa 1904—Date of Death: 3 August 1920
Place: Shelby County
Event: Lynching/Hanged

Lige Daniels, a sixteen-year old black youth accused of having murdered a white woman, was lynched in the town square at Center.

Daniels reportedly beat the forty-two year-old widow about the head with a hoe for no reason. When a local doctor arrived, he had the dying woman taken to the local hospital and delivered Daniels to the sheriff. Word of the incident spread rapidly, and a mob was soon demanding that the boy be hanged. The throng of vigilantes were talked out of the notion, but reconvened later when the sheriff left town.

The chief lawman had departed with the keys to his jail, thinking that he could thus discourage further attempts to get at the accused. He was mistaken. During his absence the mob once again formed up, and broke into the jail. Members dragged Daniels to an oak tree where he was lynched. According to observers, Daniels was wearing "a white shirt, torn pants and no shoes." Over the objections of a court official who had mounted the scaffold and delivered an ardent plea, fate would soon intervene for the mob's benefit. The official spokesperson's oration was cut short when the makeshift scaffold that he and some of the vigilantes were standing on collapsed, and all on it but Daniels landed on the ground. Daniels, who had already had the hangman's noose placed around his neck, was lynched by fate, not by vigilante force. He was left dangling there all day.

Douglas, Fred
Born: circa 1877—Date of Death: 27 August 1920
Place: Dallas County
Event: Legal Execution/Hanged

"Hanging takes all the pep out of a victim" was the rather peculiar tagline of an article in the *Bellingham Herald* (Bellingham, Washington). The piece referred to Fred Douglas, a black man, who was strung up on Friday, 27 August 1920, for the murder of I. P. Williams, manager of a local Dallas oil station. The journalist who penned this piece had to add, "He [Douglas] refused offers of watermelon and fried chicken and requested that for his last breakfast he be given a large cherry pie."[1485]

Beasley, Oscar
Born: (Unknown)—Date of Death: 16 September 1920
Place: Brazoria County
Event: Lynching/Hanged

On Saturday, 15 September 1920, forty-eight year old Sheriff Joe Snow was shot and killed by Oscar Beasley, a black man. The incident took place while Snow was attempting to arrest Beasley for theft of a horse.

Snow had been to Beasley's farm the day before to investigate a fire. Beasley was under indictment for theft of cowhides at the time. While he was there he noticed his own saddle and a group of horses that had been stolen from his farm a few days earlier. The following day Snow returned to arrest Beasley. As it turned out the plan did not work out to well for him. Beasley shot Snow with a shotgun at close range. The wound was fatal. Snow died almost immediately.

After a protracted manhunt that lasted practically two days Beasley was captured near Danburry, five miles from Angleton. He was arrested and taken to jail. Before he could stand trial a mob of about 300 citizens took justice into their own hands and lynched him from a tree in front of the jailhouse. Beasley's body was left hanging in the tree all day in a grotesque display of homemade justice.[1486]

Vickery, Thomas W.
Born: 24 May 1871—Date of Death: 22 December 1920
Place: Tarrant County
Event: Lynching/Hanged

On Monday, 20 December 1920, Fort Worth Police Officer Jeff C. Couch was shot and killed by Thomas Vickery. Vickery, a service car driver, was arrested and charged with the murder. He claimed that the incident was the result of a disagreement over money. Vickery apparently settled the score by shooting Cough five times.

Vickery was apprehended and confined in the jail on Wednesday, 22 December 1920. Later the same night a mob of about twenty-five masked and angry citizens, believed to have been comprised largely of members of the police department, forcibly removed Vickery and lynched him from a tree. Clad only in his nightclothes, the unfortunate man was dragged to a grove of trees in the packinghouse district. The rabble then shot him for good measure.[1487]

Vickery is buried at Mount Olivet Cemetery, Tarrant County.[1488]

Black, Albert

Born: 3 April 1901—Date of Death: 18 March 1921
Place: Gonzales County
Event: Legal Execution/Hanged

A black man named Albert Black, alias Albert Howard, was legally executed at Gonzales on Friday, 18 March 1921. Howard, who had been a jail breaker, went to the gallows for the robbery and outrage of an elderly white woman at Harwood on Thursday, 27 October 1920.[1489] He was but days away from his twentieth birthday when he went to meet his maker.[1490]

Flores, Jose

Born: circa 1904—Date of Death: 21 July 1921
Place: Falls County
Event: Legal Execution/Hanged

Israel, Jordan

Born: (Unknown)—Date of Death: 21 July 1921
Place: Falls County
Event: Legal Execution/Hanged

Falls County Deputy Sheriff Oscar Sharp was shot and killed by Israel Jordan, a black man, and Jose Flores, a Mexican, during an escape attempt at the county jail.

Sharp had just opened the cell doors to give the inmates their midday meal when Israel and Flores attacked him. The pair managed to gain control of Sharp's gun and used it to shoot him. Although mortally wounded Sharp was able to prevent the escape by throwing the jail keys through an open window.

Israel and Flores were tried and convicted of the murder. They were both sentenced to death. That sentence was carried out on Thursday, 21 July 1921. Both men were executed by hanging. Notable among Isreal's last quotes was, "Ise [I am] gwine [going] to die; gimme [give me] what I wants [sic] to eat."[1491]

Although Pedro Sanches was convicted, and also sentenced to death for the murder, Israel made a confession just minutes before his hanging in which he claimed that Sanches was not guilty. The Sanches case was on appeal. The outcome is not known.

Winn, Alexander

Born: (Unknown)—Date of Death: 15 August 1921
Place: Limestone County
Event: Lynching/Hanged

Alexander Winn, a black man, was suspected of having outraged a seven-year old white girl. He met his predicted fate at the hands of a lynch mob at Datura. After Winn had expired his body was turned over to an undertaker for burial.

Not satisfied that the lynching had been adequate punishment, vigilantes removed Winn's corpse from the funeral home at Coolidge and set it ablaze. [1492]

McNeely, Wylie

Born: (Unknown)—Date of Death: 10 October 1921
Place: Camp County
Event: Lynching/Hanged and Burned

Wylie McNeely, a black man, was accused of having outraged an eight-year old white girl.

A mob numbering about 500 formed on Sunday night, 9 October 1921, bent on lynching McNeely. By the time they had finished the job on Monday morning, 10 October 1921, members of the group decided to burn the man as well.

Reporters were quick to blame authorities for not taking enough action to prevent the burning. Pundits opined that had their leaders been arrested before the mob was allowed to disperse then perhaps the events of Monday, 10 October 1921, would not have followed. Writers also mused about the relative ease with which the sheriff had allowed access to McNelly in the jail.[1493]

Rouse, Fred

Born: (Unknown)—Date of Death: 11 December 1921
Place: Tarrant County
Event: Lynching/Hanged and Beaten

A packinghouse worker named Fred Rouse, a black man, was beaten and lynched for being a strikebreaker. Two men, Tom and Tracy Maclin were shot and wounded during the same incident. They later recovered.

Rouse's assailants were claimed to have been Henry Tiller and William H. "Bill" Atherton, both Niles City police officers. Another man, M. B. Morgan, was also involved. In October 1921, Bugger Red Cantrell, John Roberts, Bud Maclin and Tom Howell were charged with the murder.[1494]

Rouse was hanged from the same tree where Thomas Vickery had been lynched one year earlier on Wednesday, 22 December 1920. For that reason, and perhaps superstition as well, some locals wanted the tree to be removed. Cutting down the massive thing was not that easy. Soon a controversy developed regarding whether the old oak stood on county property or on private land. A judge subsequently ruled that if the tree was on private land it would remain, otherwise it could be removed. The outcome of the challenge is not known.[1495]

Newsome, Lonnie
Born: (Unknown)—Date of Death: 12 December 1921
Place: Gregg/Upshur Counties
Event: Lynching/Hanged

Lonnie Newsome, a black man, was lynched at Gladewater on Sunday, 12 December 1921. Authorities could find no clue as to the identity of the persons responsible for helping Newsome reach his untimely end. Newspaper accounts of the day failed to mention the reason for the hanging.[1496]

Hackney, Curley
Born: circa 1891—Date of Death: 13 December 1921
Place: McLennan County
Event: Lynching/Hanged

"Curley" Hackney, a white man, was suspected of having outraged a woman. He was taken from the jail by force and driven by automobile to an appropriate spot about three miles from town where he was lynched. A mob numbering about 300 strong did the work at Waco on Tuesday, 13 December 1921.[1497] After the hanging he was shot repeatedly for good measure.[1498]

Hackney directed his own execution. Objecting to the use of a drag chain, he waited until a suitable rope could be located then instructing the mob on how to position the hangman's rope for a good result. "Put the knot under my left ear and do this thing right" were among his last mortal words.[1499]

Many of Hackney's final comments were noteworthy. Among the most poignant was, "No need to argue with a mob buddy, they are holding aces and I hold trumps." He followed by saying, "One consolation boys, I get to shake hands with several of you in Hell." One of the bystanders commented, "You certainly are the gamest condemned man I have ever heard of", to wit Hackney replied, "There never was a gamer sucker."[1500]

Hackney's death certificate lists 14 December 1921, as the date of his passing. One newspaper account claimed that the lynching took place on 13 December 1921, and another cites 14 December 1921.[1501]

Newspapers claimed that Hackney was the second victim of a lynch mob at McLennan County in recent years and the third man lynched in Texas that week.[1502]

Grace, George McKinley

Born: (Unknown)—Date of Death: 6 January 1922
Place: Bexar County
Event: Legal Execution/Hanged

George Grace, a black man, was tried and convicted of criminally outraging a white woman. He was sentenced to die for his crime.

On Friday, 6 January 1922, that verdict was carried out at the county jail at San Antonio. Thousands of people jammed the streets, straining to get a glimpse of the hanging.[1503]

Duarte, Manuel

Born: circa 1892—Date of Death: 2 February 1922
Place: Cameron County
Event: Lynching/Shot

Blanket indictments charging murder and conspiracy to murder in connection with the shooting death of Manuel Durate, a Mexican citizen, were returned by the grand jury against twenty men on Thursday, 2 February 1922. Their names were withheld pending their arrest.

Durate was the foreman of a ranch and had been warned to leave. Four men came to his home at night and shot him to death. Officers believed that twenty-five men participated in the conspiracy to murder Durate. Durate was thirty years old.[1504]

Norman, P.

Born: (Unknown)—Date of Death: 11 February 1922
Place: Bowie County
Event: Lynching/Hanged and Shot

On Saturday night, 11 February 1922, four masked men removed P. Norman, a black man, from the custody of Deputy Sheriff W. T. Jordan and lynched him at about 10:00 pm.

Norman had been brought by automobile to Texarkana to be jailed on a misdemeanor charge. The man's body was found not far from Spring Lake Park bearing the evidence of a lynching. He had also been shot three times in the head and once in the chest. His death certificate indicates that the cause of death was from gunshot wounds, not from a lynching as newspapers have reported however.

The vigilante actions that resulted in the Norman lynching spawned a fierce reaction, followed by a probe into Ku Klux Klan activities in northeast Texas.[1505]

Hornsby, George F.
Born: 20 July 1891—Date of Death: 14 April 1922
Place: Bell County
Event: Legal Execution/Hanged

On Monday, 11 October 1920 George Hornsby, a white man, murdered thirty-six year old John Norman Weatherby, an automobile dealer from Brownwood. He was arrested, charged and convicted of the crime. Many local citizens believed that Hornsby was innocent, however.

Curious onlooker peered in to watch the hanging of Hornsby, which took place behind a high wall that had been erected at Belton to prevent the stares of unwanted spectators. Hornsby met his maker on Friday, 14 April 1922.[1506]

Hornsby is buried at the Hillcrest Cemetery at Temple in Bell County. A crowd of 3,000 to 4,000 persons attended his funeral.[1507]

Weatherby is buried at the Goldthwaite Cemetery.

Parker, Carl
Born: circa 1891—Date of Death: 4 May 1922
Place: Harris County
Event: Legal Execution/Hanged

Carl Parker, a white blacksmith who had come to Texas from West Virginia, was tried and found guilty of the murder of Mordie Conroy, rent car driver. A court of law assessed the death penalty, which was to be carried out on Thursday, 4 May 1922.

Timing is everything. It seems that Federal Judge J. V. Hutchingson's stay of execution order reached the jail at Houston three minutes after the trap door at the gallows had been sprung and Carl Parker had already been shot into eternity.[1508]

Cornish, John
Born: circa 1898—Date of Death: 6 May 1922
Place: Freestone County
Event: Lynching/Burning

Curry, McKinley "Snap"
Born: circa 1898—Date of Death: 6 May 1922
Place: Freestone County
Event: Lynching/Burning

Jones, Mose
Born: circa 1878—Date of Death: 6 May 1922
Place: Freestone County
Event: Lynching/Burning

Cornish, Tom
Born: (Unknown)—Date of Death: 8 May 1922
Place: Freestone County
Event: Lynching/Hanged

Green, Frederick (Shadrick)
Born: circa 1899—Date of Death: 8 May 1922
Place: Freestone County
Event: Lynching/Hanged

On Thursday, 4 May 1922, a seventeen-year old girl named Eula Ausley was assaulted, outraged and brutally murdered at Kirvin. Miss Ausley was an orphan girl being raised by her grandfather, Otis King, who was a local farmer.

Drew King, Eula's uncle, found her body in a pool of blood lying in a ditch with her throat slashed. The attack had been so savage that the young woman's head was practically severed.
Armed men gathered at Waco, Corsicana, Mexia, Teague, and a dozen more small towns rushing to join in the hunt for the perpetrators. A group numbering about 1,000 strong searched for her, combing through the woods while heavily armed with whatever weapons they could find. Early into the search, the disgruntled wife of a black search party member alerted neighbors that her husband, McKinley "Snap" Curry, had come home on the afternoon of the murder bloodied from what he claimed was a rabbit hunt.

Despite the fact that Sheriff Horace Mayo already had two white suspects who were enemies of Eula's family in custody, Curry became the hunted. Mayo arrested Curry and apparently forced a statement from him that implicated two other persons, nineteen-year old John Cornish and forty-six year old Mose Jones. A mob consisting of most of the original search party reassembled outside the jail looking for vengeance. In the end, the three black men were the only ones suspected of having done the evil deed.

Vigilante justice was swift. After midnight on Saturday, 6 May 1922, the mob forced its way into the jail and dragged the three black suspects out of their cells. They were driven to a lot between the old Baptist Church and the Methodist Church in Kirvin where a gruesome ritual began. Approximately fifty men started gathering wood. A heavy plow was dragged into the lot to act as an anchor for the soon to be burned black men. As the props were being prepared the crowd became anxious for a quicker punishment. "Snap" Curry, Mose Jones and John Cornish were taken from the cars and thrown to the ground in front of the mob.

A knife appeared in the hands of one of the vigilantes. Accounts vary as to what happened next, but all agree that Curry was castrated. Cornish may have suffered the same fate. When enough wood was available, the bloodied Curry was bound to the plow's seat and doused in gasoline. That done, wood was stacked around Curry and a match was applied. The flames consumed him in short order. Within ten minutes he was dead, and his flesh was burned to a crisp.

Next, Jones was brought forward. As the metal of the plow was too hot to touch, a water soaked rope was used to tie up Jones hands and drag him back and forth through the fire. Supposedly, Jones made one attempt to break free from the ropes and ran directly into Eula's uncle, Otis King. King then hit him with a radius rod from a Model T Ford, dislodging an eye from the socket. Jones was pulled back into the fire and soon died. Cornish, having seen the slow, painful deaths of his friends, grabbed the plow and stuck his head deep into the fire, inhaled, and died. The three dead bodies were then tossed in a pile, doused with kerosene, and lit a fire.

Tom Cornish and Frederick Green were the lucky ones. They were found lynched, hanging from a tree between Kirvin and Fairfield, on Monday, 8 May 1922. Green was found hanging naked, with his neck broken and his body filled with bullets.

Two detachments of Texas Rangers were ordered to Freestone County by Governor Neff to assist Sheriff W. M. Mayo. Terror reigned for days afterwards, as the shock of the three burnings claimed more lives. On Monday morning, 8 May 1922, Shadrick Green, a friend of John Cornish and Jones who was said to have been fishing with the two on Thursday, 4 May 1922, was found hanging from a tree. He was naked with his neck broken and his body shot full of holes. Hanging from the same tree was John's brother, Tom Cornish. [1509]

Afterwards it is claimed that mobs roamed the streets killing any blacks they could find. Survivors said that lynched blacks were found daily, and that other bullet-ridden bodies were discovered in outhouses, fields and shallow graves. By Tuesday, 9 June 1922, the rash of murder and lynching had ended. The effects on Kirvin were grim and lasting. Many of the town's workers disappeared, as nearly the whole black population left the area. Recent census data confirms that the ethnic breakdown of Kirvin today is 94.6% white and 5.4% black, which is in stark contrast to the state average of 80.3% white versus 12.4% back. [1510]

It is worth mentioning that a recent investigation, although some claim inaccurate and bias, concluded that Mose Jones and Johnny Cornish were innocent. McKinley "Snap" Curry is said to have accepted $15 to assist two men in murdering Miss Ausley. Those men, Claude and Audey Prowell, were the same two fellows who were in custody when Curry was arrested. Their bloody tracks had led the sheriff from the murder site to their house, but they were released after the four black men were arrested.

Miss Ausley is buried at the Shanks Cemetery at Kirvin.

Surname Unknown, "Early"

Born: circa 1897—Date of Death: 17 May 1922
Place: Grimes County
Event: Lynching/Hanged

A young black man known only as "Early" was captured Monday night, 15 May 1922, when the screams of a young white girl he was about to outrage attracted the attention of neighbors.

Early was placed in the jail at Anderson, from which he escaped the following day. The man was again apprehended on Wednesday night, 17 May 1922, and lynched by his captors thus preventing further jailbreak attempts. Farmers in the area found him on Thursday, 18 May, hanging from a tree near Plantersville and quite dead.[1511]

Bozier, Mose
Born: circa 1862—Date of Death: 20 May 1922
Place: Angelina County
Event: Lynching/Hanged

Mose Bozier, a black man age sixty, was forcibly taken by a mob of about 300 persons near Alleyton.[1512] He had been arrested near Fretzburg at about 9:00 am on the charge of having assaulted a twelve-year old white girl. That crime took place about twelve miles from Columbus. Bozier was hanged from an oak tree near the scene of the outrage on Saturday, 20 May 1922.

Winters, Jim (Joe)
Born: circa 1903—Date of Death: 20 May 1922
Place: Montgomery County
Event: Lynching/Burned to Death

Jim Winters, a nineteen-year old black man, was accused of having outraged a young white girl. He was forcibly taken from the custody of lawmen by a mob of 500 men, women and children then burned at the stake in the town square at Conroe.[1513] His victim, twelve-year old Ida Matthews, daughter of H. G. Matthews of Conroe, had been so harshly handled during the affair that she was not expected to recover.[1514] The girl had been attacked in a rural area and discovered afterwards by a passerby.

Winters, who confessed to having committed the act upon young Miss Matthews, was dragged to Conroe where he was fastened to an iron stake that had been driven into the ground. The mob piled brush and logs around him then douse the wood with kerosene and lit it afire. Winters was quickly burned to a crisp. The date was Saturday, 20 May 1922.

Rudolph Manning, another black men suspected of having been involved in the assault, was in custody. Some sources list Winters's age as sixteen.[1515]

Wilson, Gilbert
Born: (Unknown)—Date of Death: 23 May 1922
Place: Brazos County
Event: Lynching/Beaten to Death

On Tuesday, 23 May 1922, Gilbert Wilson, a black man who was suspected of cattle theft, was beaten to death by a mob at Bryan. Some sources show the date of this incident as the 24 May, not the 23 May.[1516]

Thomas, Jesse

Born: (Unknown)—Date of Death: 26 May 1922
Place: McLennan County
Event: Lynching/Shot and Burned

On Sunday, 7 May 1922, William Driskell, a cotton buyer and part-time constable in Waco was killed with an ax in his own garage. Driskell's pistol, watch, and a ring were taken.

Homicide investigators had no clues as to the identity of his killer, and were making no progress in the case when the murderer struck again. Harvey Bolton, age twenty-five, was parked with his twenty-six year old girlfriend, Margaret Hays, just outside Waco on Thursday, 25 May 1922, when a black man emerged from the bushes brandishing a pistol. The man shot Bolton three times, killing him instantly, then dragged the woman out of the automobile and outraged her. The next day the woman, still shaken up by the incident, identified Jesse Thomas as the one who had done the deed.

Hearing that, Thomas was shot seven times by the woman's father, Sam Hays. The wounds were fatal. Thomas's body was carried to downtown Waco where it was publicly burned by a lynch mob. The mob's morbid enjoyment had not yet been satisfied. They dragged the burned corpse through the black section of Waco while some participants picked up parts for souvenirs.

Unfortunately for Thomas, deceived by her hysteria Margaret Hays had made a mistake.

On Wednesday, 10 January 1923, a black gunman leaped onto the running board of an automobile passing through Cameron Park, jabbing a shotgun through the passenger's window. He was knocked to the ground without firing a shot, but left behind a checkered cap. On Saturday, 20 January 1923, W. E. Holt and Ethel Denecamp were parked five miles from Waco when a gunman appeared from nowhere. He killed Holt with a shot to the head and beat Denecamp to death, dumping her body in a nearby field. Their car was recovered in Waco the following morning, abandoned by the killer.

Lawmen got a break when a witness identified the checkered cap's owner as thirty-year old Roy Mitchell, a Louisiana native currently living in Waco. Mitchell was arrested on Tuesday, 30 January 1923, on a gambling charge. A search of his home turned up Driskell's handgun and holster along with a watch fob stolen from another victim. After three days in jail, Mitchell confessed to five murders, however he recanted those admissions before his trial in March 1923.

Convicted on all counts and sentenced to die, he was hanged before a cheering crowd of 8,000 spectators on Monday, 30 July 1923.[1517]

Unidentified White Man
Born: circa 1903—Date of Death: 2 June 1922
Place: Limestone County
Event: Lynching/Shot

Gibson, Ally
Born: (Unknown)—Date of Death: 2 June 1922
Place: Freestone County
Event: Lynching

Gibson, LeRoy
Born: circa 1903—Date of Death: 2 June 1922
Place: Freestone County
Event: Lynching

On Friday, 2 June 1922, an unidentified white man was killed, and three other whites seriously injured by a mob of blacks at the John King farm near Mexia, two and a half miles north of Kirvin. This action came in retaliation for the lynching and burning of several black men in connection with the Eula Ausley murder (see summary above). Miss Ausley's grandfather is said to have been among the wounded. The tally of blacks involved in this mob action was said to have been "a good many."

Four automobile loads of lawmen were dispatched to assist in quelling the disturbance.[1518] The riot came in the wake of the arrest of LeRoy Gibson. As officers were removing Gibson from his house the lawmen were fired at by a group of blacks brandishing military rifles. Leroy Gibson and his brother Ally were killed during the melee. Shortly after, another mob of forty or fifty blacks formed ranks and took up refuge in an abandoned home on the Powell farm located four and a half miles south of Kirvin. They were said to have been armed with high-powered rifles.

LeRoy and Ally Gibson were the grandchildren of Moses Gibson, one of the wealthiest black farmers in Texas. He owned 300 acres of land in the Mexia area. Some northern newspapers claimed that a "cracker lynch mob" was more interested in getting Gibson's land than they were in justice.

Newspaper accounts of the day claimed that at about 1:00 am on Friday, 2 June 1922, a heavily armed mob of between 750 and 1,000 whites left the town of Kirvin on a trek to the nearby black settlement at Simsboro, four miles south. Members of the angry throng were determined to burn the residences of blacks there and shoot them as they fled. [1519] Other similar mobs from Streetman, Corsicana and Wortham have left to join in the hunt. The Corsicana hardware was called upon to provide arms and ammunitions for the impromptu posse. It is unclear how much of the foregoing account is accurate.

Lewis, Warren
Born: circa 1904—Date of Death: 23 June 1922
Place: Montgomery County
Event: Lynching/Hanged

Warren Lewis, a black man, was captured and lynched after attempting to outrage a young, married white woman at New Dacus Friday, 23 June 1922.

According to reports, Lewis approached the woman's house at about 11:00 am Friday and asked if he might trouble her for a drink of water, which she gave him. Lewis returned about fifteen minutes later with more than water on his mind. He demanded a watch, which was refused, then lit a cigarette at the kitchen stove. Next he grappled with the woman. She managed to fight him off until her screams for help attracted a nearby woodchopper who came to her rescue.

Lewis fled to his home on horseback, located about three miles away. There he was captured and lynched at about 3:30 pm by a posse of around 300 Montgomery County citizens.[1520]

Johnson, O. J.
Born: (Unknown)—Date of Death: 7 September 1922
Place: Newton County
Event: Lynching/Hanged

O. J. Johnson, a black man, had been tried in a court of law twice for the murder of a turpentine plant foreman near Hemphill. The killing had taken place four years earlier. Apparently frustrated with the speed of justice, Johnson was removed from the jail at Newton by a mob of vigilantes at about 1:00 am on Thursday, 7 September 1922, and lynched from a tree limb. Afterwards, to make certain that the man was dead, they peppered his body with bullets.[1521]

Johnson, Abe
Born: circa 1866—Date of Death: 22 September 1922
Place: Liberty County
Event: Legal Execution/Hanged

Abe Johnson, a black preacher, was tried and convicted of the murder of W. L. Saxon, mill foreman of Ragland's Mill near Carmon. He was sentenced to death for the crime.

Johnson was hanged at Liberty on Friday, 22 September 1922.[1522]

Zarate, Elias Villareal
Born: (Unknown)—Date of Death: 18 November 1922
Place: Hidalgo County
Event: Lynching/Hanged

Elias Zarate, a Mexican man, was lynched at Weslaco after he had an altercation with a white man. The Mexican Embassy filed a protest. Unfortunately Zarate was already dead by the time their complaint arrived.[1523]

Gay, George
Born: circa 1897—Date of Death:11 December 1922
Place: Freestone County
Event: Lynching/Hanged

George Gay, a twenty five year old black man, was charged with attempted outrage and assault on a white woman at Streetman. Streetman is located only a few miles from Kirvin, where three black men were burned at the stake and one lynched a few months earlier.

Gay is said to have stuffed the girl's mouth full of cotton and pulled a burlap sack over her head so she could not scream. Although the victim was unable to positively identify Gay as her assailant, a mob estimated to number 1,500, decided that "close enough is good enough" and lynch him anyway.[1524]

At about 2:50 pm on Monday, 11 December 1922, Gay was forcibly taken from the custody of Sheriff Mayo, chained to a tree and shot. He suffered an estimated 300 bullet wounds. Gay's corpse remained attached to the tree where he died for quite some time after the incident. The killing took place about three miles south of Streetman.[1525]

Two Unidentified Black Men
Born: (Unknown)—Date of Death:14 December 1922
Place: Denton County
Event: Lynching/Disappeared

Two unidentified black men who were wanted in connection with the theft of two horses were found missing from the jail at Pilot Point on Thursday, 14 December 1922. In their place was a note that read, "Let this be a warning to all Negro loafers. Negroes get a job or leave town."

Two other black men had disappeared recently from that same jail, which was left unguarded at night.[1526]

Hughes, Harvey L.
Born: circa 1903—Date of Death: 7 April 1923
Place: Brewster County
Event: Legal Execution/Hanged

On Friday, 20 October 1922 Harvey Hughes a youth from Detroit, surrendered to authorities at Alpine. His only commented was that it was, "...much easier to face the gallows than the wilds of Texas."

Hughes had been convicted of murdering C. H. Rogers. That incident had taken place on Tuesday, 24 January 1922. Robbery was the motive. The two men had just alighted from a train en route to California when the killing took place. The fatally wounded Rogers commented, "Its hell to feed a man and then have him shoot you in the back for $20.00." A watch and other personal items were recovered soon after the crime.[1527]

Hughes had been in jail awaiting execution when, on Monday, 9 October 1922, he seized a chance to escape by pouncing on the wife of the deputy sheriff from behind when she was distracted. The woman, Mrs. T. I. Morgan, was making the rounds of the jail during her husband's absence. Hughes dragged Mrs. Morgan down the stairs by her hair while she fought valiantly to prevent his escape.

For three days Hughes wandered the wilderness of the Big Bend Country until he was practically delirious from hunger and thirst, to say nothing of being intimidated by the vastness of the barren terrain. Ultimately Hughes staggered into a train station at Toronto and surrendered, saying the he had had enough of starvation and thirst and was ready to meet his fate.[1528]

Hughes got his wish, and was executed by hanging on Saturday, 7 April 1923. Sheriff Tobin of Bexar County had loaned the rope that was used in the hanging to Sheriff Townsend.[1529]

Bullock, Jesse
Born: circa 1899—Date of Death: 4 July 1923
Place: Fayette County
Event: Lynching/Hanged

Jesse Bullock, a black man, made the fatal mistake of outraging a twelve-year old white girl at her parent's home near Schulenburg shortly before noon on 4 July 1923.

At about 4:00 pm on Independence Day 1923 a mob of about 200 angry vigilantes from Fayette, Lavaca and Colorado Counties sought him out and forcibly removed Bullock from the custody of City Marshal C. W. Swinkey then strung him up from an oak tree on Main Street, near the city jail. As the noose was fitted around Bullock's neck he admitted his wrong deed.[1530]

Johnson, Sol
Born: (Unknown)—Date of Death: 20 July 1923
Place: Bowie County
Event: Legal Execution/Hanged

On the night of 9 February 1922, a black man named Sol Johnson robbed and murdered an elderly white farmer named G. W. Landers at Elyau.

On Friday, 20 July 1923, Johnson virtually ran up the nine gallows stairs at New Boston, reaching the top ahead of the sheriff and whistling all the way. He professed his innocence to the end, but affirmed that he was ready to meet his maker. At about 11:15 am the trigger was pulled and Johnson dropped through the trap floor. His passing was without event, and he was declared dead thirteen minutes afterward. [1531]

Mitchell, Roy
Born: (Unknown)—Date of Death: 30 July 1923
Place: McLennan County
Event: Legal Execution/Hanged

A long career of crime including the murder and outrage of white women in and around Waco came to an end when Sheriff Phil Hobbs finally caught up with Roy Mitchell, a black man.

Mitchell was charged with, and convicted of murdering, more people than anyone in Texas to date. His most recent trial was for the killing of four white men and two white women. The rather impressive list of homicides includes, but is probably not limited to:

W. P. Driskill: 7 May 1922
Harrell Bolton: 25 May 1922
Grady Skipworth: 20 November 1922
W. E. Holt: 19 January 1923
Mrs. Ethel Denecamp: 19 January 1923
Mrs. Lula Barker: 12 February 1923
W. H. Barker: 12 February 1923
Homer Turk: 12 February 1923

Mrs. Driskill, Mrs. Barker and the Turk boy were all killed with an ax. The others were done up more neatly and were shot to death.

On Friday, 19 January 1923, the State of Texas put an end to the crime spree of Roy Mitchell for all time. He refused the new suit of clothing offered him by the county and went to the gallows wearing the same outfit he had been sporting while incarcerated. A barefoot Mitchell read his own death warrant. After bidding everyone farewell he mumbled, "Take me home." Sheriff Stegall sprung the trap at 11:02 am and Mitchell dropped, breaking his neck in the fall.[1532]

Lee, Nathan
Born: circa 1888—Date of Death: 31 August 1923
Place: Brazoria County
Event: Legal Execution/Hanged

Nathan Lee, a black man, was tried and convicted of the murder of James Spurgeon, a local farmer. Spurgeon had been found dead near his home on Thursday, 7 September 1922.

Lee went to the gallows at 11:20 am, admitting his crime and saying that no one else had anything to do with it.[1533]

Lee holds the distinction of being the last person to swing from a hangman's rope on a Texas gallows. After Lee, all legal execution in Texas were done by means of electrocution until 30 July 1964 when Joseph Johnson Jr. became the 361's person to meet that fate in Texas. Afterwards, capital punishment was outlawed until 1982. When it resumed in the method was changed to lethal injection. The first to die by that means was Charles Brooks Jr., on 7 December 1982.

Martinez, Matiax
Born: (Unknown)—Date of Death: 28 November 1923
Place: Duval County
Event: Lynching/Shot

Sometime in November 1923, a prominent Duval County rancher named Gregg Gibson was shot to death from ambush while riding his horse through a pasture on his ranch near that place. The killer, a Mexican man named Matiax Martinez, escaped to Mexico on Gibson's horse. On Wednesday, 28 November 1923, Martinez was shot and killed by officers in a running gun battle as he tried again to escape. In Carrigan's book *The Forgotten Dead* the author makes an unconfirmed claim that Martinez was lynched, not shot, thus this case has been included in the interest of completeness.[1534]

Cases Occurring After 1923
(In Chronological Order)

Gonzalez, Cinco
Born: (Unknown)—Date of Death: 9 September 1926
Place: Willacy County
Event: Lynching/Shot

Nunez, Tomas
Born: (Unknown)—Date of Death: 9 September 1926
Place: Willacy County
Event: Lynching/Shot

Nunez, Jose
Born: (Unknown)—Date of Death: 9 September 1926
Place: Willacy County
Event: Lynching/Shot

Nunez, Delancio
Born: (Unknown)—Date of Death: 9 September 1926
Place: Willacy County
Event: Lynching/Shot

Zaller, Matt
Born: (Unknown)—Date of Death: 9 September 1926
Place: Willacy County
Event: Lynching/Shot

Willacy County Deputy Sheriff Louis "Slim" May, Willacy County Precinct 1 Deputy Constable "Red" Shaw, and four other lawmen were assigned to keep peace at and around several Mexican dances. Sometime between 2:00 and 3:00 am on Sunday, 5 September 1926, a shot was fired near where one of the events had been held. The six lawmen split up into groups of three each and went to investigate.

The officers had not gone very far when one lawman told May and Shaw that he had seen a weapon pointed at them. A moment later gunfire erupted. Shaw was shot between the eyes and died instantly. May was shot in the heart and suffered a fatal injury. The third lawman in the group was slightly wounded in the stomach.

Local officers theorized that the first shots had been fired to lure the lawmen into a fatal trap in retaliation for a previous arrest they had made. Sheriff Teller and his deputies rounded up twenty to twenty four persons who were in and around the area and placed them in custody for questioning.

On Tuesday, 7 September 1926, the father of a man named Jose Nuñez, who was one of the suspects being held in the shooting, was allowed to talk with his son at the jail. After doing so the father told the sheriff that his son confessed, and would assist in locating the weapons that were used in the murder of Mays and Shaw. Later that afternoon five deputies took Jose and Delancio Nuñez, Cinco Gonzalez, Matt Zaller, and Tomas Nuñez from the jail to a brushy area eight miles west of Raymondville. Reportedly, Jose Nunez pointed out to the deputies where they would find the gun that had been used in the murder. The officers claim that when they led the prisoners into the underbrush they were ambushed, and met with a hail of gunfire. According to this extraordinary chronicle given by the lawmen, all of the officers ducked, return fire, and accidentally killed all five prisoners in the crossfire.

Not surprisingly, there were many in the community who did not accept the lawmen's far-fetched narrative. On its face, it appeared as though the officers had simply marched the group out of town at gunpoint, and in an act of unspeakable vengeance summarily executed them.

The Nuñez family made claims to the Mexican Consul General that the body of Tomas Nuñez had been beheaded during the incident. At the request of the U.S. State Department the governor ordered the Texas Rangers to investigate the shooting. The beheading rumors turned out to be false, but Sheriff Teller was accused of allowing a mob into the jail, thus permitting the group to remove the five prisoners and execute them.

A Willacy County grand jury investigated the case and indicted Teller, and others, charging them with the murders of the five men. Teller was tried in 1927 as an accessory to the murders but was acquitted.[1535]

Brown, Robert
Born: (Unknown)—Date of Death: 11 November 1926
Place: Fort Bend County
Event: Lynching/Shot

Brown, Sally
Born: (Unknown)—Date of Death: 11 November 1926
Place: Fort Bend County
Event: Lynching/Shot and Burned

Evans, Scott
Born: (Unknown)—Date of Death: 11 November 1926
Place: Fort Bend County
Event: Lynching/Shot

Robert Brown, Sally Brown and Scott Evans, all black, were taken out and shot alongside the roadway at Fort Bend County on the night of 10-11 November 1926. Sally Brown's body was burned for good measure. The reason for the lynching was not mentioned. Five young white men had done the work. They were later apprehended and charged at Houston on 19 November 1926. Included on the dishonor roll were H. B. Crowder, John Crowder, "Buster" Roberts, W. H. Holden and Joe Rose.[1536]

Authorities hypothesized that the death of the three blacks had grown out of the murder of H. B. Crowder's brother, Wallace Crowder. That killing occurred at a dance some time earlier, and involved a black tenant farmer named Tanner Evans (Ivans).

Powell, Robert
Born: (Unknown)—Date of Death: 20 June 1928
Place: Harris County
Event: Lynching/Hanged and Shot

Houston Police Detective Albert Davis was shot and killed by a black man named Robert Powell while he was attempting to disperse a crowd in the early morning hours of Sunday, 17 June 1928.

Powell, a member of the rabble fled down Robin Street with Davis in hot pursuit. A running gun battle broke out between Davis and Powell during which Powell shot Davis in the head and shoulder. The wounds proved fatal. Davis died at the Baptist Hospital at about 11:45 am.

The wounded Powell was arrested and placed in custody. He refused to make a statement. On 20 June 1928, eight unidentified men forcibly removed Powell from the hospital. His hands and feet were bound as he was dragged into the street he was shot in the stomach and lynched for good measure. A witness, a hospital orderly named Jackson McCarter, testified that Powell's last words were, "Oh Lord have mercy." Powell's lifeless body was discovered at about 6:30 am that day by detectives John Gambill and Ira Nix, hanging from a bridge about eight miles from town.

A reward of $1,250 was offered for information leading to the arrest of the person or persons who lynched Powell. There were no takers. A $10,000 fund was raised to conduct a probe into the incident. Texas Ranger Captain Frank Hamer was assigned to the case and came to Houston later in the day on 20 June. Hamer learned little that lawmen did not already know.[1537]

Hernandez, Jose
Born: (Unknown)—Date of Death: 17 September 1928
Place: Henderson County
Event: Lynching/Shot

At about 1:15 am on Monday, 17 September 1928, Henderson County Deputy Sheriff John Reeves was on duty and working at a dance in Malakoff. He asked a Mexican man named Jose Hernandez who had been causing a disturbance to leave the dance platform. Without warning Hernandez pulled a pistol and shot Reeves in the head, killing him instantly. Hernandez left the dance, but returned a short time later and surrendered.

Using Mr. Melvin Dodd's automobile, Henderson County Constable White and Dodd left the dance with Hernandez in custody to deliver him to the county jail in Athens. Before getting out of the City of Malakoff the car was intercepted by a group of local citizens. White was pulled from the vehicle while two of the citizens shot Hernandez seven times, killing him instantly. Neither White nor Dodd were injured by the gunfire. The local newspaper reported that White and Dodd did not know the identity of the men who had shot Hernandez.[1538]

Ratliff, Marshall Field
Born: 26 March 1903—Date of Death: 19 November 1929
Place: Eastland County
Event: Lynching/Hanged

It all began around noon on Friday, 23 December 1927 when the foursome consisting of Marshall Ratliff, Henry Helms, Robert Hill and Louis Davis held up the First National Bank of Cisco. While the robbery was in progress Mrs. B. P. Blassengame and her six-year-old daughter Francis had entered the bank. Realizing the danger, and in spite of warnings from the robbers that they would shoot her, the undaunted Mrs. Blassengame led her daughter through the bookkeeping department to the side door that emptied into the alley, forcibly crashed through the portal and dashed across a vacant lot to report the incident to Chief of Police George Emory "Bit" Bedford.

In minutes practically the whole town had heard the news. Bedford, who grabbed a riot gun, positioned himself at the head of the alley alongside the bank that opened onto Main Street. Deputy City Marshal George Carmichael took up a position in the alley running behind the bank, which intersected the other escape route that the chief was covering. Both were directing crossfire at the back door of the bank where one of the robbers had emerged with a semi-automatic pistol in each hand, blazing away at both lawmen as he rushed from the building. Both Bradford and Carmichael eventually died from their wounds.

After a protracted chase that lasted for days the outlaws were captured. Ratliff went to trial on Monday, 16 January 1928. He was first convicted of armed robbery on Friday, 27 January 1928, and sentenced to serve 99 years in prison. He was moved to the jail at Eastland County to stand trial for another charge when he attempted to escape. In the process of that failed adventure he killed Jailer Tom Jones. The following morning a crowd began to gather. By nightfall the mob had grown to over 1,000 outraged citizens. The crowd demanded that Ratliff be handed over to them. Jailer Kilbourn refused, but was eventually overpowered as the horde of vigilantes rushed the jail and pulled Ratliff out into the street. They promptly tied Ratliff's hands and feet and headed for a nearby utility pole to carry out the death sentence that the State of Texas had failed to prescribe. Their first attempt to lynch Ratliff failed when the amateur hangman's knot gave way, causing Ratliff to tumble to the ground. After a fifteen-minute wait for a second rope the crowd made another attempt. This time the noose did not come undone. Ratliff was pronounced dead at 9:55 pm on Monday, 19 November 1928.[1539]

Hughes, George

Born: (Unknown)—Date of Death: 9 May 1930
Place: Grayson County
Event: Lynching/Burned to Death and Hanged

The Sherman riot of 1930 was one of the major incidents of racial violence that occurred in the United States at the onset of the Great Depression, and it initiated a flurry of racial violence in Texas.

A black farm hand named George Hughes, described by acquaintances as "crazy," was accused of the criminal outrage of a young white woman, who was never publicly identified. Hughes admitted that he had come to the farm five miles southeast of Sherman on Saturday, 3 May 1930, in search of the woman's husband who owed him wages. Hughes left when the woman said that her husband was in Sherman. He soon returned with a shotgun, demanding his wages. It was at that time that the outrage occurred.

Hughes fled, and fired at unarmed pursuers and a patrol car driven by the deputy sheriff who later arrived to investigate the disturbance before he finally surrendered. On Monday, 5 May 1920, Hughes was indicted for criminal assault. In the days preceding the trial rumors spread about the case, among them that Hughes had mutilated the woman's throat and breasts and that she was not expected to live. However, a medical examination of the woman and of Hughes showed the claims to be false. Officers removed Hughes from the jail to an undisclosed location as a precaution against mob violence.

In the early morning of Friday, 9 May 1930, Texas Ranger Captain Frank Hamer, two other rangers and one police sergeant, escorted Hughes to the county courthouse. A crowd began to gather outside the building, filling the corridors from the main entrance to the courtroom doors. Hamer announced that he did not believe that the trial could be held in Sherman without bloodshed. At about 2:30 pm two youths threw an open can of gasoline through a broken window into the county tax collector's office. A fire started and quickly spread through the building. It was claimed that when the deputies guarding Hughes offered to escort him out, but he chose to remain locked in the vault. Rangers attempted to rescue him but were cut off by flames. The mob held the firemen back and cut their hoses. By 4:00 pm only the walls of the building and the fireproof vault remained.

With dynamite and acetylene torches, the leaders of the mob worked on the vault until they opened it just before midnight. More than 5,000 people filled the courthouse yard and lined an adjacent street. Hughes's body was thrown from the vault then dragged behind a car to the front of a drugstore in the black business section where it was hanged from a tree. The store furnishings were used to fuel a fire under the hanging corpse. The mob also burned down the drugstore and other businesses in the area and prevented firemen from saving the burning buildings. By daybreak of 10 May 1930, most of the town's black businesses and residential area lay in ashes.

Martial law was eventually declared. Nine Texas Rangers and 430 national guardsmen were sent to the scene to keep peace. It was weeks before the town settled down, and generations before the event faded from the memory of most.[1540]

Johnson, George
Born: circa 1900—Date of Death: 16 May 1930
Place: Fannin County
Event: Lynching/Burned

Fifty miles from Sherman, where George Hughes had been burned to death on 9 May 1930, and while martial law was still in effect in that county, a second mob gathered at Honey Grove in Fannin County on Friday, 16 May 1930. A white landowner named E. E. Fortenberry employed a black man named George Johnson. Fortenberry, who was also a deputy sheriff, went to collect a debt from Johnson. Johnson shot Fortenberry three times, killing him then fleeing with the man's gun.

Johnson barricaded himself in a cabin. Officers surrounded the house and kept up a steady barrage of fire until Johnson's gun was silent. The crowd of several thousand rushed the cabin and found Johnson lying on the floor, his body pierced with bullets numerous times.

Johnson's body was lashed to the back of a truck and dragged two miles to Honey Grove where the corpse was hung from a tree and burned.[1541]

Rowan, Bill
Born: (Unknown)—Date of Death:18 June 1930
Place: Brazos County
Event: Lynching/Hanged

A posse was seeking Bill Roan, a black man, for the attempted outrage of a white woman named Mrs. Henry Bowman. The incident occurred at Benchly, on Monday, June 16 1930. Mrs. Bowman claimed that Roan, who worked on the farm, attempted to attack her and that she beat off his advances. On Wednesday, 18 June 1930, Roan was found, shot full of buckshot and quite dead.[1542]

Mendiola, Higinio
Born: (Unknown)—Date of Death: 29 December 1931
Place: Hidalgo County
Event: Lynching/Hanged

On Tuesday, 29 December 1931, assistant section foreman Higinio Mendiola was found hanging far out on the branch of a tree near his home at Edinburg. Officers suspected from the condition of the body that he had not committed suicide. An inquest conducted by the justice of the peace ruled that his death was by strangulation or asphyxiation. A wet towel found at the scene was apparently used to suffocate Mendiola, and then afterwards he was hanged with a small rope. Seven people were arrested after an investigation. The outcome of any charges filed is not known.[1543]

Tillis, Dave

Born: circa 1882—Date of Death: 1 April 1932
Place: Houston County
Event: Lynching/Hanged

Dave Tillis, a black tenant farmer who lived at the Arch Maples farm about nineteen miles from Crockett, was lynched on Friday, 1 April 1932 at that place. It seems that Tillis had been an uninvited guest in the bedchambers of a white woman. Maples turned Tillis over to officers, but four unidentified men took him from custody and lynched him from a blackjack oak.[1544]
According to newspaper accounts of the day, the Tillis incident had been the first such lynching since that of Will Rowan on 17 June 1930.

Lovell, W. C.

Born: (Unknown)—Date of Death: 23 May 1935
Place: Panola County
Event: Lynching/Hanged

According to a claim made by *The Lynching Calendar,* a black man named W. C. Lovell was lynched at Carthage on 23 May 1935. No record of this incident, or the passing of Mr. Lovell, has been located.[1545]

Four Unidentified Black Men

Born: (Unknown)—Date of Death: 22 June 1935
Place: Anderson County
Event: Lynching/Hanged

One Unidentified Black Woman

Born: (Unknown)—Date of Death: 22 June 1935
Place: Anderson County
Event: Lynching/Hanged

One source has claimed that four black men and one black woman were lynched at Elkhart on Saturday, 22 June 1935. According to that report the group had committed the brutal outrage and murder of the young wife of the constable. Author Kerry Segrave in his book, *Lynchings of Women in the United States,* cites his source as the *Galveston Daily News* of 22 June 1935. Unfortunately the archives for that year were destroyed, thus verification of the incident is impossible unless one happens to have a physical copy of the article.[1546]

Collins, Ernest
Born: (Unknown)—Date of Death: 12 November 1935
Place: Colorado County
Event: Lynching/Hanged

Mitchell Jr., Benny
Born: (Unknown)—Date of Death: 12 November 1935
Place: Colorado County
Event: Lynching/Hanged

Two black youths named Ernest Collins and Benny Mitchell, Jr. were charged with the slaying of a young white woman. The incident had taken place on Thursday, October 17, 1935. The woman had accused the pair of stealing pecans. Sometime after midnight on Tuesday, 12 November 1935, the young men were seized by a mob at Altair, eleven miles south of Columbus, and hanged from a live oak tree. The site of the hanging was about a mile from the girl's home. About 600 people made up the mob who took the youths from the custody of the sheriff and his men when they had stopped their patrol car on a bridge over the Colorado River.

     The county attorney refused to prosecute the mob members. Instead, he applauded and condoned their actions, claiming that it was an "expression of the will of the people."[1547]

     Both Mitchell's and Ernest Collins's death certificates indicates that they passed on 12 November 1935, claiming that their death was the result of a broken neck received during the hanging.[1548]

Williams, Elbert
Born: (Unknown)—Date of Death: 22 June 1940
Place: Cameron County
Event: Lynching/Hanged

A black man named Elbert Williams was said to have been lynched at Brownsville on 22 June 1940. No further information has been located about this incident thus far.[1549]

     No record of the passing of a black man named Elbert Williams in Texas has been located however. There was a black man named Albert Williams who died on 1 July 1940, at Anderson County. He was seventy-two years old and pass away of natural causes after being ill for four weeks.[1550] The only person with the name Elbert Williams to ever die in Cameron County was a white man who passed on 7 December 1959.[1551]

Vinson, Willie
Born: 22 November 1910—Date of Death: 13 July 1942
Place: Bowie County
Event: Lynching/Hanged

Willie Vinson, a thirty-one year old black man from Texarkana, became the last man to be lynched in Texas when he fell victim to mob violence at that place on Monday, 13 July 1942.

Vinson had been charged with the assault and attempted outrage of a twenty-two year old white woman named Jayson Talley. She was the wife of a defense ordnance plant worker in that town. According to reports, Vinson had dragged the woman from her trailer camp bed where she was sleeping with her nineteen-month old child early Sunday morning, 12 July 1942. He tried to outrage her. When neighbors heard the commotion Vinson fled, and ran to a café where he worked as a dishwasher. A bystander named C. L. Roberts chased Vinson and struck him with the butt of his pistol, which discharged wounding Roberts. Vinson then pulled a butcher knife. At that point Roberts shot him in the stomach and subdued him.

Afterward Mrs. Talley tentatively identified Vinson as the attacker. The critically injured Vinson was taken to an infirmary where he probably would have died without the aid of vigilantes. Never the less, at about half past midnight on Monday, 13 July 1942, a small group of men removed the accused rapist from the hospital, lynched him from the rafters of a cotton gin outside town then dragged the corpse behind an automobile to insure his death.

Many newspapers of the day incorrectly claimed that Vinson was twenty-five. His death certificate indicates that he was born 22 November 1910. Vinson was married, and hailed from Jefferson, Texas. His wife, Lucile Ownes, had what remained of his body removed to Shreveport, Louisiana for burial.[1552]

594

Epilogue

This book covers the nearly 1,900 cases of legal hanging, lynching, man burning or execution that took place between 1819 and 1942. In those incidents the authors can document at least 2,600 persons killed. Given the ambiguity of some accounts, the actual tally may be well over 3,000. Over 1,000 of the victims, 40.2%, were black. Nearly 900 were white, or 33.5%, while nearly 500, or 19.3%, were Mexican. The remaining 7%, just fewer than 200 souls, were not identified by race by the reporting source.

Knowing these statistics the casual reader might inquire, what can one glean from that information? As Horace, a major lyric Latin poet of the Augustan Age wrote, *Pale Death with impartial tread beats at the poor man's cottage door and at the palaces of kings*. In other words, death by hanging or lynching came to all races in Texas between 1819 and 1923. Some more frequently than others.

By 1920 the state's population had grown to nearly 4.7 million.[1553] Of that number about 635,000 were reported to have been black, or 13.6%. Roughly 3.9 million were white, or 83.7%. Persons claiming their birthplace as Mexico accounted for another 17,500 persons, or just .04%. Based on these numbers the category of "other" accounts for 97, 394 persons, or over five times the population of Mexican persons.[1554] It does not take a mathematics wizard to see that, on balance, black and Mexican persons were hanged or lynched in numbers disproportionate to their segment of the overall population, thus a black man was almost four time more likely to be hanged, lynched or burned alive in Texas than was a white man. Those of Mexican lineage were only slightly more fortunate.

There is no real "conclusion" to a non-fiction history account of this nature. One can only wonder how civilized persons could have done some of the deeds the authors have chronicled. Thought provoking...certainly. Shocking...without question. A lesson to all...hopefully.

Notes

1. Tolnay, Stewart E. and Beck, E. M. 1995. *A Festival of Violence*. Urbana and Chicago, Illinois: University of Illinois Press. p ix.

2. *Oregonian* (Portland, Oregon). 3 October 1906. p 6.

3. The two of the deserters were Nicaragua Smith and E. P. Allen. The third man's name is not known.

4. Richmond, Douglas W. and Haynes, Sam W. 2013. *The Mexican Revolution, Conflict Consolidation, 1910–1940*. College Station, Texas: Printed for the University of Texas at Arlington by Texas A & M University Press. p 15.

5. *Dallas Morning News* (Dallas, Texas). 2 August 1899. p 6.

6. The Indian Wars in Texas resulted in countless deaths of settlers, militias, rangers and the various Indian tribes. Although death by hanging was the fate suffered by many of these individuals, a conscious decision was made to exclude most such cases from this manuscript in order to maintain the integrity of the books theme.

7. In regard to the term "Hispanic," it is a category created by the United States Government for the purpose of neatly classifying persons who were neither white, black, or Indian for purposes of the census. Hispanic persons would have come from Hispaniola, a major Caribbean Island where Christopher Columbus first landed in 1492. The island is divided into two nations, the Dominican Republic and Haiti. A person identified as a "Hispanic" would have to have come to the United States from either of those places. Once again, not only is the term poorly chosen but it also fails to identify the origin of the specific persons one is attempting to identify. Illegal, or undocumented immigration from Mexico was not much of a problem during the period covered by this book. Smuggling was. Most persons coming into the United States from Mexico were Mexicans. Thus the term "Mexican" is respectfully chosen in lieu of Hispanic. Condemned First Nations persons of the Mongoloid race, now generally referred to as Native Americans, are respectfully listed as "Indians." If their specific tribe of origin is know that fact is also listed.

8. Warren, Harris Gaylord. "Aury, Louis Michel." *Handbook of Texas Online*. Texas State Historical Association. 2013.

9. *Galveston Daily News* (Galveston, Texas). 9 September 1888.

10. Block, W. T. "Myth of Texas Executions Debunked." *Beaumont Enterprise* (Beaumont, Texas). 13 September 1978. p 9-C.

11. *Galveston Daily News* (Galveston, Texas). 9 September 1888. Also see *Alexandria Gazette* (Alexandria, Virginia). 29 December 1819. p 2.

12. *Commercial Advertiser* (New York, New York). 12 May 1834.

13. Raines, C. W. 1901. *The Year Book of Texas 1901*. Austin, Texas: Gammel Book Company. pp 81-82.

14. Barker, Eugene Campbell. 1924–1928. *The Austin Papers, Annual Report of the American Historical Association for the year 1919, 1920*. Three Volumes. Washington, DC: Government Printing Office. Also see Bugbee, Lester G. "The Old Three Hundred: A List of Settlers in Austin's First Colony." *Quarterly of the Texas State Historical Association*. October 1897. Also see Kuykendall, J. H. "Reminiscences of Early Texans." *Quarterly of the Texas State Historical Association* 6-7. January, April, July 1903. Also see Ray, Worth Stickley. 1949. *Austin Colony Pioneers*. Austin, Texas: Jenkins.

15. Jenkins, John Holland. 1958. *Recollections of Early Texas*. Austin, Texas: University of Texas Press. pp 24-26.

16. Carrigan, William D. 2004. *The Making of a Lynching Culture: Violence and Vigilantism in Central Texas 136-1916*. Urbana and Chicago: University of Illinois Press.

17. *Macon Weekly Telegraph* (Macon, Georgia). 26 April 1870. p 2.

18. *Weekly Houston Telegraph* (Houston, Texas). 31 March 1838. p 2. Also see *Arkansas Weekly Gazette* (Little Rock, Arkansas). 25 April 1838.

19. Linn, John J. 1986. *Reminiscences of Fifty Years in Texas*. Austin, Texas: State House Press.

20. Grimes, Roy. 1968. *300 Years in Victoria County*. Victoria, Texas: Victoria Advocate.

21. *Times (Hartford, Connecticut)*. 10 November 1838. Also see *The Caledonian* (St. Johnsbury, Vermont). 13 November 1838. p 3.

22. 1st. Regiment, Texas Infantry.

23. *Philadelphia Inquirer* (Philadelphia, Pennsylvania). 31 December 1839. p 2. Also see (*Charleston Courier* (Charleston, South Carolina). 28 December 1839. Also see Ladd, Kevin. 1994. *Gone to Texas: Genealogical Abstracts from The Telegraph and Texas Register 1835–1841.* Bowie, Maryland: Heritage Books.

24. *August Chronicle* (Augusta, Georgia). 11 April 1843. p 2. Also see by Kelsey, M., Bishop, Floyd, N. G., Parsons, Floyd, G. G. 2007. *Miscellaneous Texas Newspaper Abstracts - Deaths. Volume 2.* Berwyn, Maryland: Heritage Books. p 93.

25. *Galveston Daily News* (Galveston, Texas). 9 September 1888.

26. Block, W. T. "Myth of Texas Executions Debunked." *Beaumont Enterprise* (Beaumont, Texas). 13 September 1978. p 9-C. Also see *Galveston Daily News* (Galveston, Texas). 9 September 1888.

27. *Galveston Daily News* (Galveston, Texas). 9 September 1888.

28. *Spectator* (New York, New York). 16 February 1842. p 1.

29. *New Hampshire Sentinel* (Keene, New Hampshire). 8 December 1841. p 3. Also see *Norwich Courier* (Norwich, Connecticut). 8 December 1841. p 3. Also see Wooster, Robert. "Pine Island, Texas (Jefferson County)". *Handbook of Texas Online.* Texas State Historical Association.

30. *Weekly Herald* (New York, New York). 13 November 1841. p 62.

31. *Ibid*

32. *Ibid*

33. *Liberator* (Boston, Massachusetts). 19 November 1841. p 187.

34. *National Gazette* (Philadelphia, Pennsylvania). 10 June 1841. p 3.

35. *Albany Argus* (Albany, New York). 5 October 1841. Also see *Caledonian* (St Johnsbury Vermont). 5 October 1841.

36. *Daily National Intelligencer* (Washington, DC). 6 December 1841.

37. The University of Texas Institute of Texan Cultures. 1984. *Residents of Texas, 1782–1836.* St. Louis, Missouri: The University of Texas Institute of Texan Cultures.

38. *Wabash Courier* (Terre Haute, Indiana). 11 December 1841. p 2.

39. *Massachusetts Spy* (Worcester, Massachusetts). 17 November 1841. p 2. According to this source, at the time of Texas Independence in 1835 the center of present day Shelby County was in the village of White Cottage of the Tenaha Municipality in the Nacogdoches Department, within the Mexican state of Texas y Coahuila in the Republic of Mexico. See "Shelby County, At the Beginning of the Republic." *We The People of Shelby County.* Unique Publishing. Spring 2012.

40. Kelsey. *Miscellaneous Texas Newspaper Abstracts - Deaths.* Volume 2. p 93.

41. *Gloucester Telegraph* (Gloucester, Massachusetts). 10 November 1841. p 2.

42. *Barre Gazette* (Barre, Massachusetts). 8 July 1842. p 3.

43. *Southern Patriot* (Charleston, South Carolina). 20 June 1842. Also see *Philadelphia Inquirer* (Philadelphia, Pennsylvania). 23 June 1842. Also see Kelsey. *Miscellaneous Texas Newspaper Abstracts - Deaths.* Volume 2. p 9.

44. *Commercial Advertiser* (New York, New York). 2 May 1841. Also see *Daily Herald* (New Haven, Connecticut). 3 May 1841. Also see *Augusta Chronicle* (Augusta, Georgia). 18 April 1843. Also see *Spectator* (New York, New York). 31 May 1843.

45. *Galveston Daily News* (Galveston, Texas). 9 September 1888.

46. Carrigan. *Lynching Culture.* Appendix B - Unconfirmed.

47. *Newport Mercury* (Newport, Rhode Island). 22 June 1844. p 3. Also see Kelsey. *Texas Newspaper Abstracts - Deaths.* Volume 2. p 160. Carrigan. *Lynching Culture.* Appendix B - Unconfirmed.

48. Ancestry. Tree# 7025851. Person # 1179961828.

49. *Muskegon Chronicle* (Muskegon, Michigan). 12 January 1891. Also see Kelsey. *Texas Newspaper Abstracts - Deaths.* Volume 2. p 161.

50. *Galveston Daily News* (Galveston, Texas). 9 September 1888.

51. *Alexandria Gazette* (Alexandria, Virginia). 14 October 1844. p 3. Also see Kelsey. *Texas Newspaper Abstracts - Deaths.* Volume 2. p 97.

52. *Daily National Intelligencer* (Washington, DC). 4 July 1844. p 3. Also see Kelsey. *Texas Newspaper Abstracts - Deaths.* Volume 2. p 36.

53. "Southwestern Historical Quarterly." January 1951. Volume LIV. pp 275-278.

54. *Daily Union* (Washington, DC). 11 August 1845. p 3. Also see Kelsey. *Texas Newspaper Abstracts - Deaths*. Volume 2. p 101.

55. *The Red-Lander* (San Augustine, Texas). 11 December 1845. Ancestry. Tree# 26279456. Person # 1813051955.

56. Kelsey. *Texas Newspaper Abstracts - Deaths*. Volume 2. p 165.

57. *Philadelphia Enquirer* (Philadelphia, Pennsylvania). 3 July 1847. *The Spectator* (New York, New York). 28 April 1847. *The Richmond Whig* (Richmond, Virginia). 30 April 1847. *The Southern Patriot* (Charleston, South Carolina). 10 May 1847.

58. *Richmond Whig* (Richmond, Virginia). 29 June 1847.

59. Kelsey. *Texas Newspaper Abstracts - Deaths*. Volume 2. p 198. *Evening Post* (New York, New York). 20 July 1847. p 2

60. *Mississippi Free Trader* (Natchez, Mississippi). 9 June 1847. *Age* (Augusta, Maine). 25 June 1847. *Commercial Advertiser* (New York, New York). 12 June 1847. p 1. Kelsey. *Texas Newspaper Abstracts - Deaths*. Volume 2. p 198.

61. *Sun* (Baltimore, Maryland). 12 October 1847.

62. *Standard* (Clarksville, Texas). 10 June 1848. p 2. Swenson. *Early Texas News 1831–1848*. p 71.

63. *Trenton State Gazette* (Trenton, New Jersey). 8 December 1848.

64. *Trenton State Gazette* (Trenton, New Jersey). 19 September 1848.

65. *Spectator* (New York, New York). 15 November 1849.

66. Ancestry. Tree #1150700. Person #1661916764.

67. *Times Picayune* (New Orleans, Louisiana). 18 September 1849. Also see Ancestry. Tree# 46939831. Person # 6701690461.

68. *Massachusetts Spy* (Worchester, Massachusetts). 1 August 1849. p 4.

69. Carrigan. *Lynching Culture*. Appendix B - Unconfirmed. Limmer, E.A. 1988. *Story of Bell County, Texas, Volume 1*. Woodway, Texas: Eakin Press. pp 17-19. Wilbarger, J.W. 1889. *Indian Depredations in Texas*. Austin, Texas: Hutchings Printing House.

70. Carrigan. *Lynching Culture*. Appendix A - Confirmed.

71. *Daily Illinois State Register*. (Springfield, Illinois). 24 May 1850.

72. *Plain Dealer* (Cleveland, Ohio). 5 August 1850.

73. Ancestry. U.S. Federal Census Mortality Schedules Index, 1850–1880. Provo, Utah: Ancestry. 1999.

74. *Plain Dealer* (Cleveland, Ohio). 5 August 1850.

75. *Evening Post* (New York, New York). 26 August 1850. p 1.

76. *Daily National Intelligencer* (Washington, DC). 13 August 1850.

77. Ancestry. Tree# 10844809. Person # 1781535300.

78. *New London Daily Chronicle* (New London, Connecticut). 7 June 1851. p 2.

79. *Massachusetts Spy* (Worcester, Massachusetts). 11 June 1851. p 3.

80. *New Hampshire Sentinel* (Keene, New Hampshire). 30 January 1851. p 2.

81. *Charleston Courier* (Charleston, South Carolina). 2 April 1851. p 2. Also see *Alexandria Gazette* (Alexandria, Virginia). 21 April 1851. p 2.

82. Fandango is a term for a lively couple's dance that had its origins in Spain. The Fandango was widely popular in Mexico and south Texas. The dance is usually done in triple meter and traditionally accompanied by guitars and castanets or hand-clapping ("palmas" in Spanish). Fandango can both be sung and danced. The term Fandango is applied to the venue (event) as well as the dance form (artistic non-verbal communication) itself.

83. *Charleston Courier* (Charleston, South Carolina). 2 April 1851. p 2.

84. *Charleston Courier* (Charleston, South Carolina). 2 April 1851. p 2. Also see *Alexandria Gazette* (Alexandria, Virginia). 21 April 1851. p 2.

85. Geue, Chester W., and Geue, Ethel Hander, compilers. 1972. *A New Land Beckoned: German Immigration to Texas 1844–1847*. Waco, Texas: Texian Press. Reprinted by Genealogical Publishing Co., Baltimore, 1982. Ancestry. *Texas, Compiled Census and Census Substitutes Index, 1820–1890*. Provo, Utah: Ancestry. 1999.

86. *Daily Union* (Washington, DC). 12 July 1851.

87. *Daily Union* (Washington, DC). 5 August 1851. p 3.

88. *National Era* (Washington, DC). 28 August 1851. p 138. Kelsey. *Texas Newspaper Abstracts - Deaths*. Volume 2. p 107.

89. *Times-Picayune* (New Orleans, Louisiana). 20 August 1851.

90. *Times-Picayune* (New Orleans, Louisiana). 26 December 1851. Also see Ancestry. Tree# 10929035. Person # 541929212.

91. There are several versions of how wild, unbranded cattle came to be known as "Mavericks." Nearly all of them involve Samuel A. Maverick. Maverick was a native of South Carolina who came to Texas in 1835. He moved his family to the gulf coast in Matagorda County between 1844 and 1847. Maverick had apparently accepted a herd of 400 cattle in lieu of repayment for a $1,200 loan. When the family returned to San Antonio, he left the animals in the care of a local family. The cattle were neglected, and many of the calves were not branded. Residents soon began to refer to any unbranded cow as "one of Maverick's." Soon any unbranded cattle were claimed as "Mavericks" and branded. By 1855 Maverick had sold his entire herd to his neighbor Pierre Gustave Toutant De Beauregard. By 1857 people around San Antonio were referring to unbranded cattle over one year in age as "Mavericks." Unbranded calves under that age and still suckling were considered to be the property of whoever owned the mother. See Caldwell, Clifford R. 2013. *Robert Kelsey Wylie, Forgotten Cattle King of Texas.* Privately Published. p 38.

92. *Trenton State Gazette* (Trenton, New Jersey). 12 May 1852.

93. *Liberator* (Boston, Massachusetts). 11 June 1852.

94. *Evening Post* (New York, New York). 20 May 1852.

95. Kelsey. *Texas Newspaper Abstracts - Deaths.* Volume 2. p 176.

96. *Richmond Whig* (Richmond, Virginia). 18 May 1853.

97. *Dallas Daily Herald* (Dallas, Texas). 17 July 1853. p 4. Also see Biffle, Kent. 1993. *A Month of Sundays.* Denton, Texas: University of North Texas Press. pp 102-104.

98. *Mississippi Free Trader* (Natchez, Mississippi). 12 July 1853.

99. *Plain Dealer* (Cleveland, Ohio). 12 September 1853. Also see *The Standard* (Clarksville, Texas). 13 August 1853. Also see *Missouri Courier* (Hannibal, Missouri). 22 September 1853.

100. *Daily Union* (Washington, DC). 10 September 1853.

101. *Washington Reporter* (Washington, Pennsylvania). 26 October 1853. p 1. Also see *Nacogdoches Chronicle* (Nacogdoches, Texas). 6 September 1853. p 3. *Nacogdoches Chronicle* (Nacogdoches, Texas). 13 September 1853. Also see *The Standard* (Clarksville, Texas). 13 August 1853. p 2. *The Standard* (Clarksville, Texas). 20 August 1853. p 2. *Boston Herald* (Boston, Massachusetts). 15 September 1853. p 4.

102. *Ledger and Texan* (San Antonio, Texas). 15 September 1853. p 3. Also see Nicklas, Linda Cheves. 1994. *Abstracts of Early East Texas Newspapers, 1839–1856.* Greenville, S.C.: Southern Historical Press, Inc. p 44.

103. *Charleston Courier* (Charleston, South Carolina). 24 December 1853. p 1. *Times Picayune* (New Orleans, Louisiana). 27 December 1853. p 4.

104. *St. Alban's Messenger* (St. Alban, Vermont). 4 January 1855.

105. *Evening Star* (Washington, D.C.). 20 January 1854.

106. "Death Penalty Information Center". ESPY File. Accessed 8 August 2014.

107. Kelsey. *Texas Newspaper Abstracts - Deaths.* Volume 2. p 201.

108. *Ibid.* Also see *Ledger and Texan* (San Antonio, Texas). 23 March 1854. p 2.

109. Carrigan. *Forgotten Dead.* Appendix B - Unconfirmed.

110. *Portland Weekly Advertiser* (Portland, Maine). 25 July 1854.

111. "Death Penalty Information Center". Espy File. 1608-202. Accessed 8 August 2014.

112. *Liberator* (Boston, Massachusetts). 2 June 1854.

113. *Liberator* (Boston, Massachusetts). 19 January 1855. p 12. Also see *Daily Union* (Washington, DC). 29 November 1854. Also see Kelsey. *Texas Newspaper Abstracts - Deaths.* Volume 2. p 206.

114. Kelsey. *Texas Newspaper Abstracts - Deaths.* Volume 2. p 70.

115. *Centinel of Freedom* (Newark, New Jersey). 15 May 1855. p 2. Carrigan. *Forgotten Dead.* Appendix A - Confirmed.

116. *Charleston Courier* (Charleston, South Carolina). 2 June 1855. Also see *Times-Picayune* (New Orleans, Louisiana). 13 May 1855.

117. *Daily National Intelligencer* (Washington, DC). 2 July 1855. p 3.

118. *Vermont Journal* (Windsor, Vermont). 10 August 1855.

119. *Galveston Daily News* (Galveston, Texas). 11 June 1899.

120. *Galveston Daily News* (Galveston, Texas). 9 September 1888.

121. Moore, John Trotwood. 1923. *Tennessee, The Volunteer State 1769–1923*. Chicago, Illinois: S. J. Clark Publishing Co. Also see *Ledger and Texan* (San Antonio, Texas). 6 July 1854.

122. Kelsey. *Texas Newspaper Abstracts - Deaths*. Volume 2. p 209. Also see Ancestry. Tree# 5228006. Person # 1042200550. Also see *Sun* (Baltimore, Maryland). 4 October 1855.

123. *Daily Advocate* (Baton Rouge, Louisiana). 23 August 1855. Carrigan. *Forgotten Dead*. Appendix B - Unconfirmed.

124. "Death Penalty Information Center". Espy File. 1608-2002. Accessed 8 August 2014.

125. *Charleston Courier* (Charleston, South Carolina). 2 November 1855.

126. *Alexandria Gazette* (Alexandria, Virginia). 15 November 1855.

127. *Philadelphia Inquirer* (Philadelphia, Pennsylvania), 9 December 1855. p 1. Carrigan. *Forgotten Dead*. Appendix A - Confirmed.

128. "Death Penalty Information Center". Espy File. 1608-2002. Accessed 8 August 2014.

129. Barrett, Thomas. 1961. *The Great Hanging at Gainesville*. Texas: Texas State Historical Association. p 3.

130. *Daily National Intelligencer* (Washington, DC). 16 July 1856.

131. *Daily Union* (Washington, DC). 2 July 1856.

132. *Public Ledger* (Philadelphia, Pennsylvania). 19 November 1856. p 4.

133. Kelsey. *Texas Newspaper Abstracts - Deaths*. Volume 2. p 51. Also see Ancestry. Tree# 50650411. Person # 13405719023.

134. *Public Ledger* (Philadelphia, Pennsylvania). 19 November 1856. p 4. Also see Ancestry. Tree# 1060393. Person # 944192531. Also see *Charleston Courier* (Charleston, South Carolina). 30 June 1856. p 2. Also see Caldwell/DeLord. *Texas Lawmen 1835–1899*. p 182. Also see National Park Services. "Database of Civil War Soldiers and Sailors." Accessed 30 August 2014. File M-227 Roll 1. There is a man named Samuel Ashworth who enlisted in Company B of Ragsdale's Battalion, Texas Cavalry but he does not appear to be the same man who was involved in the Deputy killing.

135. *Sun* (Baltimore, Maryland). 26 July 1856. p 1.

136. *Centinel of Freedom* (Newark, New Jersey). 23 September 1856. p 3. Also see *Delaware State Reporter* (Dover, Delaware). 26 September 1856. p 2.

137. *Times-Picayune* (New Orleans, Louisiana). 13 November 1856.

138. Ancestry. Tree# 1060393. Person # 944192531.

139. One source claims that the execution took place on 23 November 1856. See *New York Herald* (New York, New York). 21 December 1856. p 8.

140. *Daily National Intelligencer* (Washington, DC). 21 October 1857. p 3.

141. Yancy, Karen. 1983. *San Saba County History*. San Saba, Texas: San Saba County Historical Commission.

142. *Times-Picayune* (New Orleans, Louisiana). 21 March 1857. Also see Ancestry. Tree# 48474781. Person # 20117555944.

143. *Ledger and Texan* (San Antonio, Texas). 21 March 1857. p 2.

144. *Daily Statesman* (Columbus, Ohio). 31 March 1857. p 3.

145. Carrigan. *Forgotten Dead*. Appendix A - Confirmed.

146. Kelsey. *Texas Newspaper Abstracts - Deaths*. Volume 2. p 218.

147. *Ibid*. p 138.

148. *Albany Evening Journal* (Albany, New York). 19 June 1857. p 2. Kelsey. *Texas Newspaper Abstracts - Deaths*. Volume 2. p 58. Also see Caldwell/DeLord. *Texas Lawmen, 1835–1899*. p 198.

149. *Sunday Delta* (New Orleans, Louisiana). 21 June 1857. p 2.

150. *Ledger and Texan* (San Antonio, Texas). 13 June 1857. p 2.

151. *Press* (Philadelphia, Pennsylvania). 3 August 1857. p 4.

152. Carrigan. *Forgotten Dead*. Appendix A - Confirmed.

153. *Liberator* (Boston, Massachusetts). 2 October 1857. p 160.

154. Carrigan. *Forgotten Dead*. Appendix B - Unconfirmed. Also see *Ledgerand Texas, San Antonio, Texas* (26 September 1857) and *Ledger and Texas, San Antonio, Texas* (19 September 1857).

155. Kelsey. *Texas Newspaper Abstracts - Deaths*. Volume 2. p 138. Also see *Ledger and Texan* (San Antonio, Texas). 19 September 1857. p 2. Also see *Times-Picayune* (New Orleans, Louisiana). 26 September 1857. Ancestry. Tree 53398938. Person 13503152133.

156. *Columbian Register* (New Haven, Connecticut). 9 January 1858. p 2.

157. *Wisconsin Free Democrat* (Milwaukee, Wisconsin). 15 January 1858. p 4.

158. *Daily True Delta* (New Orleans, Louisiana). 28 February 1858. p 3.

159. *Galveston Daily News* (Galveston, Texas). 8 September 1888.

160. *Ledger and Texas* (San Antonio, Texas). 22 May 1858. Reynolds, Donald E. 2007. *Texas Terror, The Slave Insurrection Panic of 1860 and The Secession of the Lower South*. Baton Rouge, Louisiana: Louisiana State University Press. p 15.

161. Carrigan. *Forgotten Dead*. Appendix A - Confirmed.

162. *Connecticut Currant* (Hartford, Connecticut). 12 June 1858.

163. Caldwell, Clifford R. 2012. *An Anthology of Old West Tales, Selected Works of Clifford R. Caldwell*. Privately Published. pp 193-209.

164. *Lowell Daily Citizen and News* (Lowell, Massachusetts). 7 June 1858. p 2. Also see *Southern Intelligencer* (Austin, Texas). 2 June 1858.

165. *Sun* (Baltimore, Maryland). 6 August 1858. p 1.

166. *Sun* (Baltimore, Maryland). 21 July 1858. p 1.

167. *Weekly Houston Telegraph* (Houston, Texas). 28 July 1858. p 2.

168. *Lowell Daily Citizen and News* (Lowell, Massachusetts). 16 July 1858. p 2.

169. *Weekly Houston Telegraph* (Houston, Texas). 28 July 1858. p 3.

170. *Uvalde County Texas* (Uvalde, Texas). 10 August 1858.

171. *Richmond Whig* (Richmond, Virginia). 10 August 1858. p 1.

172. *Weekly Houston Telegraph* (Houston, Texas). 14 July 1858.

173. *Richmond Whig* (Richmond, Virginia). 10 August 1858. p 1. Also see *New York Herald* (New York, New York). 13 August 1858. p 3.

174. *Weekly Houston Telegraph* (Houston, Texas). 15 September 1858.

175. *Weekly Houston Telegraph* (Houston, Texas). 15 September 1858. Also see *Ledger and Texas* (San Antonio, Texas). 4 September 1858.

176. *New York Tribune* (New York, New York). 24 September 1858. Also see Ancestry. Tree# 59907327. Person # 44050594956.

177. *Trenton State Gazette* (Trenton, New Jersey). 4 December 1858. p 2.

178. *Lowell Daily Citizen and News* (Lowell, Massachusetts). 20 December 1858. p 2. Ancestry. Tree# 45134445. Person # 6312041986.

179. *Alexandria Gazette* (Alexandria, Virginia). 27 January 1859.

180. *Texas State Gazette* (Austin, Texas). 6 August 1859.

181. *Commercial Advertiser* (New York, New York). 21 January 1861.

182. *Weekly Wisconsin Patriot* (Madison, Wisconsin). 28 May 1859. p 4.

183. *New Mexican* (Santa Fe, New Mexico). 12 January 1895. p 1.

184. *Springfield Republican* (Springfield, Massachusetts). 9 March 1858.

185. *Standard* (Clarksville, Texas). 5 March 1859. p 2.

186. *Lowell Daily Citizen and News* (Lowell, Massachusetts). 26 March 1859.

187. *Massachusetts Spy* (Boston, Massachusetts). 13 April 1859.

188. *Waco Southern* (Waco, Texas). 8 June 1858. Also see *Alexandria Gazette* (Alexandria, Virginia). 15 June 1859. p 2.

189. Thompson, Jerry Don. 1971. *Colonel John Robert Baylor: Texas Indian Fighter and Confederate Soldier*. Hillsboro, Texas: Hill Junior College Press.

190. *Philadelphia Enquirer* (Philadelphia, Pennsylvania). 18 May 1859.

191. Ancestry. Tree# 36457505. Person # 18938759967.

192. *Standard* (Clarksville, Texas). 25 June 1859.

193. *American Traveler* (Boston, Massachusetts). 16 July 1859.

194. Find-A-Grave Memorial# 80912268.

195. *New York Ledger* (New York, New York). 6 August 1859.

196. *New York Tribune* (New York, New York). 2 August 1859. p 3.

197. *Texas State Gazette* (Austin, Texas). 6 August 1859. Also see Ancestry. Tree# 475675. Person # 2078491530.

198. Clark, Pat B. 1937. "The History of Clarksville and Old Red River County." Also see Ancestry. Tree #293575. Person #1856913418. Story #6208531.

199. *Daily Confederation* (Montgomery, Alabama). 8 September 1859. p 2.

200. *Houston Tri-Weekly Telegraph.* 18 October 1860. p 2.

201. Ancestry. Tree# 18876856. Person # 1824042081.

202. *San Francisco Bulletin* (San Francisco, California). 15 December 1859. p 1.

203. *Public Ledger* (Philadelphia, Pennsylvania). 26 October 1859.

204. During the Mexican War John Salmon "RIP" Ford (1815–1897) was adjutant of Hays's regiment and in command of a spy company. He acquired the nickname "RIP" from his habit of including the message "Rest in Peace" when sending out notices of deaths to family of his fallen men. Later, under the exigencies of battle conditions, Ford's message was shortened to "R.I.P." The nickname stuck with him for a lifetime.

205. Caldwell/DeLord. *Texas Lawmen 1835–1899.* p 47.

206. Carrigan. *Lynching Culture.* Appendix B - Unconfirmed.

207. *Ibid.*

208. Carl W. Matthews, Jr. Navarro County, Texas. 8 August 2014.

209. *Bonham News* (Bonham, Texas). 17 October 1913.

210. Ancestry. Tree# 9626204. Person # 637841706. "Death Penalty Information Center." Espy File. 1608-2002. Accessed 8 August 2014.

211. *Boston Herald* (Boston, Massachusetts). 17 May 1860. p 1. Marten, James. 1990. *Texas Divided: Loyalty and Dissent in the Lone Star State 1856-1874.* Lexington, Kentucky: University of Kentucky Press, p 7.

212. *Galveston Daily News* (Galveston, Texas). 8 September 1888. Gregory, Peggy H. 1976. *Records of Interments of the City of Galveston 1859–1872.* Privately Published.

213. Reynolds, Donald E. 2007. *Texas Terror, The Slave Insurrection Panic of 1860 and The Secession of the Lower South.* Baton Rouge, Louisiana: Louisiana State University Press. p 23.

214. *Sun* (Baltimore, Maryland). 14 June 1860. p 4. *Centinel of Freedom* (Newark, New Jersey). 19 June 1860. p 2. Reynolds. *Texas Terror.* p 23. This source cites the C. B. Moore Diary. University of North Texas Library. Denton, Texas.

215. *Weekly Houston Telegraph* (Houston, Texas). 26 June 1860. Kelsey. *Texas Newspaper Abstracts - Deaths.* Volume 2. p 72.

216. *Ibid.* Ancestry. Tree# 62014567. Person # 44079241747.

217. *Constitution* (Washington, DC). 16 June 1860. p 2.

218. *Commercial Advertiser* (New York, New York). 7 August 1860.

219. *Commercial Advertiser* (New York, New York). 7 August 1860. Also see Barry, James Buckner. 1984. *Buck Barry, Texas Ranger and Frontiersman.* Lincoln, Nebraska: University of Nebraska Press. pp 121-123.

220. The song is about the difficulties of getting to heaven. Chorus: "(So) take off your overcoats and roll up your sleeves; Jordan am [is] a hard road to travel, I believe." The original contains assorted political references to the 1850s. The author of the tune is Daniel D. Emmett, and the words are believed to have been written by T. F. Briggs. The earliest date that this song appears in sheet music is 1853.

221. Ancestry. Tree# 46158431. Person # 24047018910.

222. *Richmond Whig* (Richmond, Virginia). 17 August 1860. p 4.

223. *Constitution* (Washington, DC). 4 August 1860. Also see *The Liberator* (Boston, Massachusetts). 7 September 1860.

224. Carrigan. *Lynching Culture.* Appendix B.

225. *Richmond Whig* (Richmond, Virginia). 17 August 1860. p 4.

226. *Ibid.* Also see *Liberator* (Boston, Massachusetts). 7 September 1860. p 142.

227. *Constitution* (Washington, DC). 4 August 1860. p 5.

228. *Ibid. Richmond Whig* (Richmond, Virginia). 17 August 1860. p 4.

229. *Richmond Whig* (Richmond, Virginia). 17 August 1860. p 4. Also see *Camden Democrat* (Camden, New Jersey). 18 August 1860. p 3.

230. Ibid.

231. *Massachusetts Spy* (Worcester, Massachusetts). 22 August 1860. p 4.

232. *Springfield Republican* (Springfield, Massachusetts). 7 Sept 1860.

233. *Springfield Republican* (Springfield, Massachusetts). 7 Sept 1860.

234. *San Antonio Daily Ledger and Texas* (San Antonio, Texas). 15 August 1860. Reynolds. *Texas Terror.* p 79. This source cites Mann, W. L. Billums Creek, Tyler County to Thomas B. Hulling, Lampasas. 24 August 1860.

235. Reynolds. *Texas Terror.* p 74.

236. *Evening Post* (New York). 20 August 1860. p 4.

237. *Commercial Advertiser* (New York, New York). 7 August 1860.

238. *Liberator* (Boston, Massachusetts). 7 September 1860. p 141.

239. *Wisconsin Daily Patriot* (Madison, Wisconsin). 18 August 1860. p 2.

240. *New York Tribune* (New York, New York). 15 September 1860. p 8. Also see *Philadelphia Inquirer* (Philadelphia, Pennsylvania). 19 September 1860. p 2.

241. *New York Tribune* (New York, New York). 15 September 1860. p 8.

242. Gregory. *Records of Interments of the City of Galveston.*

243. *Sun* (Baltimore, Maryland). 18 August 1860. p 1. Also see *Evening Post* (New York). 20 August 1860. p 4.

244. Correspondence of Don Price. Beaumont, Texas. Southwest Historical Quarterly. Vol. LII. No. 3. January 1949. Also see Ancestry. Tree# 161350. Person # 1332979837.

245. *Liberator* (Boston, Massachusetts). 7 September 1860. p 142.

246. *Ibid.*

247. *New York Tribune* (New York, New York). 15 September 1860. p 8. Also see *Daily National Intelligencer* (Washington, DC). 15 September 1860. Also see Barry, James Buckner. 1984. *Buck Barry, Texas Ranger and Frontiersman.* Lincoln, Nebraska: University of Nebraska Press. pp 121-123.

248. Ancestry. Tree# 20994647. Person # 1011895734.

249. *Daily National Intelligencer* (Washington DC). 15 September 1860.

250. Ancestry. Tree# 877725. Person # 1672120529.

251. *Liberator* (Boston, Massachusetts). 7 September 1860. p 142.

252. *Daily Ohio Statesman* (Columbus, Ohio). 19 September 1860. p 2. Also see *Philadelphia Inquirer* (Philadelphia, Pennsylvania). 19 September 1860. p 2.

253. *New York Times* (New York, New York). 27 August 1860.

254. *Philadelphia Inquirer* (Philadelphia, Pennsylvania). 19 September 1860. p 2.

255. *Daily National Intelligencer* (Washington, DC). 15 September 1860.

256. US Census. Year 1860. Census Place: Beat 2, Anderson, Texas. Roll M653_1287. Page 14. Image 31. Family History Library Film 805287.

257. Barry. *Buck Barry.* pp 121-123.

258. *Desert News* (Salt Lake City, Utah). 21 November 1860.

259. Find-A-Grave Memorial. # 24418914. Also see Reynolds, Donald E. "Bewley, Anthony," *Handbook of Texas Online.* Also see *Plain Dealer (Cleveland, Ohio).* 17 October 1860. p 1.

260. *Sun* (Baltimore, Maryland). 19 October 1860. p 1. Also see *Sandusky Register* (Sandusky, Ohio). 18 October 1860. p 3.

261. *New York Tribune* (New York, New York). 27 October 1860. p 10.

262. *Pennsylvania, Church and Town Records, 1708–1985.* Provo, Utah: Ancestry. 2011. Original data from *Historic Pennsylvania Church and Town Records.* Philadelphia, Pennsylvania: Historical Society of Pennsylvania.

263. *New York Herald* (New York, New York). 22 October 1860. p 1.

264. *Dallas Weekly Herald* (Dallas, Texas). 28 November 1860. p 2. *Constitution* (Middletown, Connecticut). 19 December 1860. p 2.

265. *Dallas Weekly Herald* (Dallas, Texas). 28 November 1860. p 2.

266. *Times-Picayune* (New Orleans, Louisiana). 7 December 1860. p 5.

267. *Albany Evening Journal* (Albany, New York). 11 December 1860.

268. Marten, James. 1990. *Texas Divided, Loyalty and Dissent in the Lone Star State 1856–1874*. Louisville, Kentucky: University of Kentucky Press. p 14. Also see Wish, Harvey. "The Slave Insurrection Panic of 1856." *Journal of Southern History*. 5 May 1939. p 208. Also see Ledbetter, Bill. "Slave Unrest and White Panic, The Impact of Black Republicanism In Antebellum Texas." *Texana 10*. 1972. p 340. Also see Grimsted, David. 1998. *American Mobbing, 1828–1861*. New York, New York: Oxford Press. p 174.

269. *Times Picayune* (New Orleans, Louisiana). 31 May 1867.

270. *San Antonio Express* (San Antonio, Texas). 7 December 1903.

271. *Springfield Republican* (Springfield, Massachusetts). 1 June 1861.

272. Scott, Zelma. 1998. *A History of Coryell County Texas*. Texas State Historical Association. p 60.

273. *Texas Republican* (Marshall, Texas). 17 August 1861.

274. Kelsey. *Texas Newspaper Abstracts - Deaths*. Volume 2. p 78.

275. Ancestry. Tree# 10025935. Person # 6133110039.

276. Kelsey. *Texas Newspaper Abstracts - Deaths*. Volume 2. p 79. Also see *Philadelphia Inquirer* (Philadelphia, Pennsylvania). 9 October 1861. Also see *Wisconsin Daily Patriot* (Madison, Wisconsin). 11 December 1861. Also see *Times-Picayune* (New Orleans, Louisiana). 18 September 1861. p 1.

277. Ancestry. Tree# 16219818. Person # 363896069.

278. *Daily True Delta* (New Orleans, Louisiana). 4 October 1861. p 1.

279. *Daily True Delta* (New Orleans, Louisiana). 4 October 1861. p 1.

280. Cox, Mike .2008. *Historic Photos of Texas Lawmen*. Nashville, Tennessee: Turner Publishing Company. p 9.

281. *Daily True Delta* (New Orleans, Louisiana). 2 October 1861. p 1.

282. *Dallas Weekly Herald* (Dallas, Texas). 13 November 1861. p 1.

283. Kelsey. *Texas Newspaper Abstracts - Deaths*. Volume 2. p 80.

284. Carrigan. *Lynching Culture*. Appendix A - Confirmed.

285. *Ibid.*

286. Find-A-Grave Memorial# 81677759.

287. Marten, James. 1990. *Texas Divided: Loyalty and Dissent in the Lone Star State, 1856–1874*. Lexington, Kentucky: The University Press of Kentucky. p 120

288. U.S. Census Year 1860. Census Place Beat 3, Henderson, Texas. Roll M653_1297. Page 49. Image: 102.

289. Harper Centennial Year Committee, Harper, Texas. 1963. *Here's Harper*. Fredericksburg, Texas: Also see U.S. Census Year 1860. Census Place Beat 3, Henderson, Texas. Roll M653_1297. Page 49. Image: 102. Also see Caldwell, Clifford R. 2011. *A Day's Ride From Here Volume II, Noxville, Texas*. Charleston, South Carolina: History Press.

290. *Daily True Delta* (New Orleans, Louisiana). 5 February 1862. p 1.

291. *Daily True Delta* (New Orleans, Louisiana). 5 February 1862. p 1.

292. *Ibid.*

293. *Bellville Countrymen* (Bellville, Washington). 31 May 1862. Also see Ancestry. Tree #41935785. Person # 19699840848. Find-A-Grave Memorial #36036618. Ancestry. 16270573. Person # 355861233.

294. *Daily True Delta* (New Orleans, Louisiana). 17 April 1862. p 2. Also see Gregory. *Records of Interments of the City of Galveston 1859–1872*.

295. *Bellville Countrymen* (Bellville, Washington). 31 May 1862.

296. *Philadelphia Inquirer* (Philadelphia, Pennsylvania). 25 July 1862. p. 2.

297. "Death Penalty Information Center". Espy File. 1608-2002. Accessed 8 August 2014.

298. Luther, Joseph. 2012. *Camp Verde, Texas Frontier Defense*. Charleston, South Carolina: History Press.

299. Ransleben, Guido E. 1974. *A Hundred Years of Comfort in Texas*. San Antonio: Underwood, Rodman L. 2002. *Death on the Nueces: German Texans Treue der Union*. Austin: Eakin Press.

300. Fritz Lange is honored as one of those who died at the Rio Grande. His name was not been placed on the monument because his involvement was not verified until many years after his death. Treuer Reue Der Union Monument on High Street, between 3rd and 4th Sts. Comfort, Kendall County, Texas.

301. *Galveston Daily News* (Galveston, Texas). 6 May 1880.

302. The majority of this text, apart from some edits and deletions, has been taken from Dr. Richard B. McCaslin's summary of the "Great Hanging at Gainesville." *Handbook of Texas Online.* Published by the Texas State Historical Association.

303. Ancestry. Tree #11290363. Person #12515020371.

304. Ancestry. A total of 106 trees, including Tree #36465196. Person #19702593246.

305. Ancestry. Tree #839918. Person #24114285215.

306. *Massachusetts Spy* (Worcester, Massachusetts). 17 December 1862. p 2.

307. "Death Penalty Information Center". Espy File. 1608-2002. Accessed 8 August 2014.

308. *Rock River Democrat* (Rock River, Illinois). 11 March 1863. *Connecticut Current* (Hartford, Connecticut). 21 February 1863. p 2.

309. *Albany Evening Journal* (Albany, New York). 17 March 1863.

310. *Connecticut Current* (Hartford, Connecticut). 21 February 1863. p 2.

311. *Connecticut Courant* (Hartford, Connecticut). 28 February 1863.

312. *Albany Evening Journal* (Albany, New York). 17 March 1863. Also see *The Galveston Daily News* (Galveston, Texas). 2 January 1863. *The Galveston Daily News* (Galveston, Texas). 1 August 1898.

313. *Connecticut Courant* (Hartford, Connecticut). 21 February 1863. p 2.

314. Moneyhon, Carl H. "Davis, Edmund Jackson." *Handbook of Texas.* Ancestry. Tree# 2124151. Person # 214993282.

315. Kelsey. *Texas Newspaper Abstracts - Deaths.* Volume 2. p 127. Ancestry. Tree# 36991541. Person # 19020058294.

316. Kelsey. *Texas Newspaper Abstracts - Deaths.* Volume 2. p 128.

317. *New York Tribune* (New York, New York). 15 December 1863.

318. Ancestry. Tree # 13286753. Person #12045746083. Ancestry. Tree #13520930. Person #376996835. Story #6122f56.

319. Underwood, Marylyn. "Rodriguez, Josefa [Chipita]," *Handbook of Texas Online.* Published by the Texas State Historical Association.

320. *Ibid.* Also see Abernethy, Francis Edward. "Legendary Ladies of Texas." *Texas Folklore Society 43.* Dallas: E-Heart 1981. Also See *Dallas Morning News* (Dallas, Texas). 13 November 1994. McDaniel, Ruel. "The Day They Hanged Chipita." *Texas Parade.* September 1962. Smylie, Vernon. "A Noose for Chipita." *Texas News Syndicate Press.* 1970). Winegarten, Ruthe. *Finder's Guide to the 'Texas Women: A Celebration of History" Exhibit Archives.* Denton: Texas. Woman's University Library 1984.

321. *Connecticut Courant* (Hartford, Connecticut). 16 April 1864. p 3.

322. *Galveston Daily News* (Galveston, Texas). 9 September 1888.

323. Marten, James. 1990. *Texas Divided, Loyalty and Dissent in the Lone Star State 1856–1874.* Louisville, Kentucky: University of Kentucky Press. p 112.

324. *Ibid.*

325. Marten, James. 1990. *Texas Divided, Loyalty and Dissent in the Lone Star State 1856–1874.* Louisville, Kentucky: University of Kentucky Press. p 60.

326. *Houston Tri Weekly Telegraph* (Houston, Texas). 22 January 1864. p 1.

327. *Plain Dealer* (Cleveland, Ohio). 1 February 1864.

328. Caldwell/DeLord. 2011. *Texas Lawmen: 1835–1899.* p 316.

329. Caldwell/DeLord. 2011. *Texas Lawmen: 1835–1899.* p 316.

330. Historical Data Systems. *U.S., Civil War Soldier Records and Profiles, 1861–1865.* Provo, Utah: Ancestry. Original data compiled by Historical Data Systems of Kingston, Massachusetts. Also see *Big Blend Magazine's Way Back When.*

331. *Dallas Weekly Herald* (Dallas, Texas). 14 October 1865. Caldwell/DeLord. *Texas Lawmen 1835–1899.* pp 54-55.

332. Kelsey. *Texas Newspaper Abstracts - Deaths.* Volume 2. p 82

333. Wilson, R. Michael. "Desertion during the Civil War." *Big Blend Magazine's Way Back When.*

334. *Austin Republican* (Austin, Texas). 9 October 1868. p 3. *Houston Telegraph* (Houston, Texas). 28 October 1864. Also see *Houston Telegraph* (Houston, Texas). 28 October 1864. p 1.

335. Sonnischsen, C. L. 2000. *Ten Texas Feud.* Albuquerque, New Mexico: University of New Mexico Press. 2nd Revised Edition. p 69. *Austin Republican* (Austin, Texas). 9 October 1868.

336. Ancestry. Tree# 1063005. Person #2005373242.

337. Carrigan. *Lynching Culture.* Appendix B.

338. *Galveston Daily News* (Galveston, Texas). 9 September 1888.

339. *Dallas Morning News* (Dallas, Texas). 9 August 1905.

340. Headsman. 2012. "1865 Galveston Deserter - Antone Richers." *Execution Today.com.* Accessed 13 October 2013.

341. Marten. *Texas Divided.* p 112.

342. *New York Tribune* (New York, New York). 13 May 1865. p 8.

343. National Archives and Records Administration (NARA). *Carded Records Showing Military Service of Soldiers Who Fought in Confederate Organizations. Compiled 1903–1927, documenting the period 1861–1865.* Catalog ID *586957.* Record Group *#109.* Roll *# 126.*

344. Jayhawkers is a term adopted by militant bands affiliated with the free-state cause. They were guerrilla fighters who often clashed with pro-slavery groups. After the Civil War the word "Jayhawker" became synonymous with people from Kansas.

345. *Houston Tri-Weekly Telegraph (Houston, Texas).* 21 June 1865. p 3.

346. Marten. *Texas Divided.* p 159.

347. Wilbarger, J. W. 1889. *Indian Depredations in Texas.* Austin, Texas: Hutchings Printing House.

348. *Austin Republican* (Austin, Texas). 9 October 1868. p 3.

349. *Ibid.*

350. *Ibid.*

351. *Austin Republican* (Austin, Texas). 9 October 1868. p 3.

352. Carrigan. *Lynching Culture.* Appendix B.

353. Marten. *Texas Divided.* P 113.

354. *Austin Republican* (Austin, Texas). 9 October 1868. p 3.

355. Ancestry. Tree# 31864462. Person # 18138730973.

356. *Cincinnati Daily Gazette* (Cincinnati, Ohio). 23 February 1866. p 4.

357. Historical Data Systems *U.S., Civil War Soldier Records and Profiles, 1861–1865.* Provo, Utah: Ancestry. Operations Inc., 2009. Original data compiled by Historical Data Systems of Kingston, Massachusetts.

358. *Galveston Daily News* (Galveston, Texas). 15 April 1866.

359. Ancestry. Tree# 9338548. Person # 815941028.

360. *Galveston Daily News* (Galveston, Texas). 15 April 1866.

361. Kelsey. *Texas Newspaper Abstracts - Deaths.* Volume 2. p 225. Also see *New Orleans Times* (New Orleans, Louisiana). 5 June 1866. p 9

362. *Flake's Bulletin* (Galveston, Texas). 28 July 1868. Vol. IV. Issue 32. p 1. Also see *Galveston Tri-Weekly News* (Galveston, Texas). 5 November 1869.

363. Ancestry. Tree# 41902379. Person # 19694596063.

364. *Flake's Bulletin* (Galveston, Texas). 28 July 1868. p 1. Also see Roell, Craig H. Harsdorff-Lees, Linda. "Hill, Benjamin F.," *Handbook of Texas.*

365. *Galveston Daily News* (Galveston, Texas). 28 June 1866. Also See *Austin Republican* (Austin, Texas). 9 October 1868. p 3.

366. Ancestry. Tree# 9360573. Person # 562765603.

367. *Albany Evening Journal* (Albany, New York). 20 July 1866. p 3.

368. *Galveston Daily News* (Galveston, Texas). 25 July 1866. Also see *Austin Republican* (Austin, Texas). 9 October 1868. p 3.

369. Ancestry. Tree# 31051364. Person # 13873045942.

370. *Galveston Daily New* (Galveston, Texas). 28 June 1866. Also see *Galveston Daily News* (Galveston, Texas). 25 July 1866. *Galveston Daily News* (Galveston, Texas). 31 July 1866. *Galveston Daily News* (Galveston, Texas). 7 April 1867. The incident was the subject of a two page political cartoon by Thomas Nast in *Harper's Weekly.* 23 March 1867. pp 184-185.

371. Carrigan. *Lynching Culture*. Appendix A.

372. Kelsey. *Texas Newspaper Abstracts - Deaths*. Volume 2. p 2.

373. *Flake's Bulletin* (Galveston, Texas). 23 June 1868. p 5.

374. *Austin Republican* (Austin, Texas). 9 October 1868. p 3.

375. *Ibid.*

376. *Flake's Bulletin* (Galveston, Texas). 23 June 1868. p 5.

377. *Ibid.*

378. *Ibid.*

379. *Ibid.*

380. *Ibid.*

381. *Ibid.*

382. *Ibid.*

383. *Ibid.*

384. *Ibid.*

385. *Ibid.*

386. *Ibid.*

387. *Ibid.*

388. *Ibid.* Also see "Death Penalty Information Center." Espy File. 1608-2002. Accessed 8 August 2014.

389. *Ibid.*

390. *Ibid.*

391. *Ibid.* p 6.

392. *New Orleans Times* (New Orleans, Louisiana). 28 January 1867.

393. *Austin Republican* (Austin, Texas). 9 October 1868.

394. Ancestry. *Texas, Muster Roll Index Cards, 1838–1900*. Provo, Utah.

395. Find-A-Grave Memorial# 9446461. Also see Vol. 19. 2001. Probate Minutes, Coryell County, Texas. p 107.

396. Carrigan. *Forgotten Dead*. Appendix B.

397. Ochoa, Ruben E. "San Miguel, Texas." *Handbook of Texas Online*.

398. Carrigan. *Lynching Culture*. Appendix A.

399. *Times Picayune* (New Orleans, Louisiana). 12 March 1867.

400. *Daily Eastern Argus* (Portland, Maine). 19 April 1867.

401. *New Orleans Tribune* (New Orleans, Louisiana). 2 May 1867. p 4. Kelsey. *Texas Newspaper Abstracts - Deaths*. Volume 2. p 243.

402. Carrigan. *Lynching Culture*. Appendix B.

403. *Flake's Bulletin* (Galveston, Texas). 8 June 1867. *Flake's Bulletin* (Galveston, Texas). 17 July 1867. p 6. Kelsey. *Texas Newspaper Abstracts - Deaths*. Volume 2. p 247.

404. Carrigan. *Lynching Culture*. Appendix A.

405. Find-A-Grave Memorial# 16393280.

406. *Austin Republican* (Austin, Texas). 9 October 1868.

407. *Ibid.*

408. *Ibid.*

409. *Ibid.*

410. *Austin Republican* (Austin, Texas). 28 May 1868. p 2.

411. *Flake's Bulletin* (Galveston, Texas). 8 July 1868. p 6.

412. *Ibid.*

413. *Austin Republican* (Austin, Texas). 28 May 1868. p 2.

414. *Ibid.*

415. *Ibid.*

416. Carrigan. *Lynching Culture*. Appendix B.

417. *Dallas Weekly Herald* (Dallas, Texas). 29 February 1868. p 1. Also see Ancestry. Tree# 47952902. Person # 13212956927. Kelsey. *Texas Newspaper Abstracts - Deaths.* Volume 2. p 355.

418. *Austin Republican* (Austin, Texas). *31 March 1868.* p 2.

419. *Austin Republican* (Austin, Texas). 7 April 1868.

420. *Austin Republican* (Austin, Texas). 28 May 1868. p 2. Also see *Flake's Bulletin* (Galveston, Texas). 8 July 1868. p 6. Also see *Austin Republican* (Austin, Texas). 7 April 1868. p 2.

421. *Austin Republican* (Austin, Texas). *31 March 1868.* p 2.

422. *Austin Republican* (Austin, Texas). *31 March 1868.* p 2.

423. Ancestry. Tree# 34333209. Person # 18627160851.

424. Carrigan. *Lynching Culture.* Appendix A.

425. Kelsey. *Texas Newspaper Abstracts - Deaths.* Volume 2. p 364.

426. *Flake's Bulletin* (Galveston, Texas). 8 May 1868. Also see *New York Herald* (New York, New York). 14 May 1868. p 10.

427. *Austin Republican* (Austin, Texas). 28 May 1868. p 2.

428. *Flake's Bulletin* (Galveston, Texas). 25 June 1868. Also see *Austin Republican* (Austin, Texas). 3 August 1868.

429. *Flake's Bulletin* (Galveston, Texas). 18 June 1868.

430. Carrigan. *Lynching Culture.* Appendix A. Also see *Austin Republican* (Austin, Texas). 28 May 1868. p 2.

431. *Times-Picayune* (New Orleans, Louisiana). 2 June 1868. p 2.

432. Kelsey. *Texas Newspaper Abstracts - Deaths.* Volume 2. p 370.

433. *Flake's Bulletin* (Galveston, Texas). 6 June 1868. p 7.

434. *Flake's Bulletin* (Galveston, Texas). 25 June 1868.

435. *Flake's Bulletin* (Galveston, Texas). 6 June 1868. p 7. Also See *Austin Republican* (Austin, Texas). 9 October 1868. p 3.

436. *Flake's Bulletin* (Galveston, Texas). 12 June 1868. p 5.

437. Carrigan. *The Making of a Lynching Culture.* Appendix A.

438. *Philadelphia Inquirer* (Philadelphia, Pennsylvania). 1 September 1868. p 4.

439. Ancestry. Tree# 47588910. Person # 6827197010.

440. *Philadelphia Inquirer* (Philadelphia, Pennsylvania). 1 September 1868. p 4.

441. *Canton Repository* (Canton, Ohio). 22 July 1868. p 8.

442. Caldwell/DeLord. *Texas Lawmen 1835–1899.* p 63. Also see *Flake's Bulletin* (Galveston, Texas). 30 July 1868.

443. *Mobile Register* (Mobile, Alabama). 7 August 1868. Kelsey. *Texas Newspaper Abstracts - Deaths.* Volume 2. p 376

444. *New York Tribune* (New York, New York). 4 August 1868.

445. *Flake's Bulletin* (Galveston, Texas). 8 August 1868.

446. *Ibid.*

447. *Ibid.*

448. *Ibid.*

449. *Daily Constitutionalist* (Atlanta, Georgia). 30 July 1868. p 4. Also see *New York Tribune* (New York, New York). 4 August 1868. p 1. Also see *Evening Post* (New York, New York). 20 August 1868. p 4. Also see *Richmond Enquirer* (Richmond, Virginia). 31 July 1868. p 1.

450. *Cleveland Leader* (Cleveland, Ohio). 3 September 1868. Carrigan. *Lynching Culture.* Appendix A. Also see *Flake's Bulletin* (Galveston, Texas). 8 August 1868.

451. *Austin Republican* (Austin, Texas). 7 April 1868. 28 May 1868.

452. *New York Tribune* (New York, New York). 23 October 1868. p 2. Also see *Austin Republican* (Austin, Texas). 31 August 1868. p 2.

453. *New York Tribune* (New York, New York). 23 October 1868. p 2.

454. Carrigan. *Lynching Culture.* Appendix A.

455. *Austin Republican* (Austin, Texas). 16 September 1868. p 2.

456. Carrigan. *Lynching Culture.* Appendix A.

457. *Ibid.*

458. *Flake' Bulletin* (Galveston, Texas). 7 October 1868. p 5. Kelsey. *Texas Newspaper Abstracts - Deaths.* Volume 2. p 382.

459. *Flake' Bulletin* (Galveston, Texas). 7 October 1868. p 5.

460. *Austin Republican* (Austin, Texas). 15 October 1868. p 3.

461. *Flake's Bulletin* (Galveston, Texas). 7 October 1868. p 7. *Mobile Register* (Mobile, Alabama). 19 October 1868.

462. *Austin Republican* (Austin, Texas). 29 October 1868. p 2. Kelsey. *Texas Newspaper Abstracts - Deaths.* Volume 2. p 384.

463. Carrigan. *Lynching Culture.* Appendix A.

464. *Ibid.*

465. *New York Tribune* (New York, New York). 13 November 1868.

466. *Times Picayune* (New Orleans, Louisiana). 7 December 1868.

467. *Flake's Bulletin* (Galveston, Texas). 6 December 1868.

468. *Times-Picayune* (New Orleans, Louisiana). 26 June 1868.

469. Barry. *Buck Barry, Texas Ranger.* p 209.

470. Texas State Police Records. Entry 871. Ancestry. Tree# 46545585. Person # 6933753390.

471. *Union* (Houston, Texas). 17 March 1869.

472. Carrigan. *Lynching Culture.* Appendix B.

473. *Union* (Houston, Texas). 17 March 1869. p 1.

474. *Ibid.*

475. *Flake's Bulletin* (Galveston, Texas). 6 March 1869. p 8.

476. *Union* (Houston, Texas). 17 March 1869.

477. *Flake's Bulletin* (Galveston, Texas). 3 April 1869. Also see Carrigan. *Lynching Culture.* Appendix A.

478. *San Antonio Express* (San Antonio, Texas). 4 April 1869. p 1. *Galveston Daily News* (Galveston, Texas). 2 April 1869.

479. *Flake's Bulletin* (Galveston, Texas). 27 February 1869. *New York Herald* (New York, New York). Also see 4 March 1869. *Dallas Weekly Herald* (Dallas, Texas). 10 April 1869. Also see Ancestry. Tree# 30564408. Person # 12355959052.

480. *New York Herald* (New York, New York). 21 April 1869. Also see *Cleburne Times-Review* (Cleburne, Texas). 30 October 2009.

481. Kelsey. *Texas Newspaper Abstracts - Deaths.* Volume 2. p 183. *Galveston Tri-Weekly* (Galveston, Texas). 4 June 1869. p 4.

482. *Flake's Bulletin* (Galveston, Texas). 24 April 1869. p 5. Kelsey. *Texas Newspaper Abstracts - Deaths.* Volume 2. p 90.

483. *Commercial Advertiser* (New York, New York). 21 April 1869. p 4. *Flake's Bulletin* (Galveston, Texas). 24 April 1869. p 5.

484. *Flake's Bulletin* (Galveston, Texas). 5 May 1869. p 6. Also see *Commercial Advertiser* (New York, New York). 21 April 1869. p 4.

485. *Commercial Advertiser* (New York, New York). 24 May 1869.

486. *Galveston Tri-Weekly* (Galveston, Texas). 21 June 1869. p 2. Also see Ancestry. Tree #6943531. Person # 984913540.

487. *Flake's Bulletin* (Galveston, Texas). 31 July 1869. Also see *Denton Monitor* (Denton, Texas). 17 July 1869.

488. *Flake's Bulletin* (Galveston, Texas). 7 August 1869.

489. *New York Herald* (New York, New York). 26 August 1869. p 6.

490. *New York Herald* (New York, New York). 1 September 1869. p 5.

491. *Washington Reporter* (Washington, Pennsylvania). 27 October 1869.

492. Carrigan. *Lynching Culture.* Appendix A.

493. Carrigan. *Lynching Culture.* Appendix B.

494. Carrigan. *Lynching Culture.* Appendix A.

495. *Union* (Houston, Texas). 11 March 1870. p 3.

496. *Flake's Bulletin* (Galveston, Texas). 20 April May 1970.

497. Ancestry. Tree# 51183906. Person # 13160171584. Also see Ancestry. *U.S., Federal Census Mortality Schedules Index, 1850–1880.* Provo, Utah.

498. *Flake's Bulletin* (Galveston, Texas). 18 May 1970.

499. Kelsey. *Texas Newspaper Abstracts - Deaths.* Volume 2. p 156.

500. *Flake's Bulletin* (Galveston, Texas). 12 May 1870.

501. *New York Herald* (New York, New York). 30 July 1870. p 3.

502. *Texas State Police Records.* Austin, Texas: State Archives. Entry 1099.

503. *Ibid.*

504. *New York Herald* (New York, New York). 30 August 1870.p 5. Also see Kelsey. *Texas Newspaper Abstracts - Deaths.* Volume 2. p 192.

505. *Union* (Houston, Texas). 3 May 1871. p 2.

506. *New York Herald* (New York, New York). 29 July 1871. p 6.

507. Brown, Frank. *Annals of Travis County and the City of Austin.* Manuscript. Frank Brown Papers. Dolph Briscoe Center for American History. University of Texas at Austin. Also see *Union* (Houston, Texas). 20 December 1871. p 2.

508. Carrigan. *Forgotten Dead.* Appendix A.

509. Carrigan. *Forgotten Dead.* Appendix A. *Galveston Tri-Weekly News* (Galveston, Texas). 9 February 1872. p 1.

510. Caldwell/DeLord. *Texas Lawmen: 1835–1899.* p 108.

511. *Quincy Whig* (Quincy, Illinois). 24 May 1872. p 4.

512. Carrigan. *Forgotten Dead.* Appendix B. *Auburn Daily Bulletin* (Auburn, New York). 30 September 1872. p 2. *Portland Daily Press* (Portland, Maine). 24 August 1872. p 2.

513. *Times-Picayune* (New Orleans, Louisiana). 22 October 1872. p 9.

514. *Plain Dealer* (Cleveland Ohio). 4 October 1872.

515. Carrigan. *Forgotten Dead.* Appendix A - Carrigan. *Lynching Culture.* Appendix A. Also see *McKinney Messenger* (McKinney, Texas). 9 November 1872.

516. *Duluth Minnesotan* (Duluth, Minnesota). 18 January 1873. p 1.

517. *Critic-Record* (Washington, DC). 25 February 1873.

518. Carrigan. *Lynching Culture.* Appendix B.

519. Ancestry. Tree# 3176659. Person # 6925760071.

520. *San Francisco Bulletin* (San Francisco, California). 5 May 1873. p 4.

521. *Indianapolis Sentinel* (Indianapolis, Indiana). 16 June 1873.

522. *Dallas Weekly Herald* (Dallas, Texas). 12 July 1873. p 1. Johnson, David. 2014. *The Horrell Wars: Feuding in Texas and New Mexico.* Denton, Texas: University of North Texas Press. p.136

523. *San Antonio Express* (San Antonio, Texas). 29 July 1873. p 1. Also see Caldwell, Clifford R. 2011. *A Day's Ride From Here, Volume I Mountain Home, Texas.* Charleston, South Carolina: The History Press.

524. *Jackson Citizen* (Jackson, Michigan). 30 September 1873. p 1.

525. Carrigan. *Forgotten Dead.* Appendix A.

526. *San Francisco Bulletin* (San Francisco, California). 5 November 1873.p 1. Also see *Dallas Weekly Herald* (Dallas, Texas). 25 October 1873. p 1.

527. Statement of Miguel Martinez. Coroner's Inquest. Justice of the Peace. Precinct 3. Nueces County. 8 December 1873.

528. *Jackson Citizen Patriot* (Jackson, Michigan). 30 December 1873.

529. Caldwell/DeLord. *Texas Lawmen: 1835–1899.* p 131.

530. US Census. Census Year 1870. Census Place Precinct 5, Hunt, Texas. Roll M593_1593. Page 420A. Image 231.

531. *New York Herald* (New York, New York). 17 July 1875.

532. *St. Albans Daily Messenger* (St. Albans, Vermont). 13 February 1874.

533. *Cincinnati Daily Times* (Cincinnati, Ohio). 26 September 1876. p 3. *Weekly Louisianan* (New Orleans, Louisiana). 31 October 1874. p 1. *Times-Picayune (New Orleans, Louisiana).* 18 June 1874. p 2.

534. *Richmond Whig* (Richmond, Virginia). 24 April 1874.

535. *St. Albans Daily Messenger* (St. Albans, Vermont). 4 June 1874.

536. *New York Herald* (New York, New York). 13 April 1874. *Macon Weekly Telegraph* (Macon, Georgia). 21 April 1874.

537. *Morning Republican* (Little Rock, Arkansas). 21 May 1874.

538. *Times Picayune* (New Orleans, Louisiana). 17 May 1874. Carrigan *Forgotten Dead.* Appendix A.

539. Ancestry. Tree# 878117. Person # 1546437223.

540. Ancestry. Tree# 10715357. Person # 6138517211.

541. Some sources, including the tombstones of all of the men who were slain, cite 25 May 1874, as the correct date of the incident. Find-A-Grave Memorial. Memorial # 92958969.

542. Atkison, Bertha. 1929. *The History of Bell County, Texas*. M.A. Thesis. University of Texas. Bell County Historical Society.

543. *Daily Inter Ocean* (Chicago, Illinois). 24 June 1874. p 2.

544. *New York Herald* (New York, New York). 17 July 1875. *Daily Inter Ocean* (Chicago, Illinois). 24 June 1874. *Times Picayune* (New Orleans, Louisiana). 17 June 1874.p 2. Carrigan. *Forgotten Dead*. Appendix A.

545. *San Antonio Daily Express* (San Antonio, Texas). 2 July 1874.

546. *Indianapolis Sentinel* (Indianapolis, Indiana). 26 June 1874.

547. Ancestry. Tree# 27405843. Person # 12272480294.

548. *Daily Inter Ocean* (Chicago, Illinois). 24 August 1874. p 5.

549. Carrigan. *Forgotten Dead*. Appendix A.

550. *Ibid.*

551. *San Antonio Daily Express* (San Antonio, Texas). 11 July 1874

552. *Dallas Weekly Herald* (Dallas, Texas). 5 September 1874. p 1.

553. *Cincinnati Daily Times* (Cincinnati, Ohio). 20 August 1874. p 3.

554. See...Givens, Murphy. "Peñascal Killers Left Trail of Brown Sugar." *Corpus Christi Caller Times* (Corpus Christi, Texas). 30 July 2008. Apparently between his earlier article in 1999 and the 2008 update Mr. Murphy deduced that there were eleven bandits, and the location was Peñascal, not Penscal.

555. Givens, Murphy. "Hanging Times Part 2." *Corpus Christi Caller Times* (Corpus Christi, Texas). 7 April 1999.

556. "Death Penalty Information Center". Espy File. 1608-2002. Accessed 8 August 2014.

557. Carrigan. *Forgotten Dead*. Appendix A.

558. *Times* (Troy, New York). 8 November 1874.

559. *New York Tribune* (New York, New York). 3 January 1874.

560. Caldwell/DeLord. *Texas Lawmen 1835–1899*. pp 15-16.

561. *New York Herald* (New York, New York). 17 July 1875.

562. *Dallas Weekly Herald* (Dallas, Texas). 2 March 1878. p 3. Also see *Galveston Weekly News* (Galveston, Texas). 4 March 1878.

563. Marten. *Texas Divided*. p. 177.

564. *New York Herald* (New York, New York). 17 July 1875.

565. David Johnson. E-mail message to author. 29 December 2013.

566. The Coinage Act of 1792 authorized the minting of the half-cent coin on 2 April 1792. The coin was produced in the United States from 1793 to 1857. The half-cent piece was made of 100% copper and was only slightly smaller than a modern U.S. quarter. All were produced at the Philadelphia Mint.

567. *Quincy Whig* (Quincy, Illinois). 6 January 1875. p 2.

568. *Indianapolis Centennial* (Indianapolis, Indiana). 23 January 1875. p 1.

569. The term "brain fever" was used in those days to describe what is now more accurately called meningitis, or encephalitis. It is an infectious disease characterized by inflammation of the meninges (the tissues that surround the brain or spinal cord) usually caused by a bacterial infection. The symptoms include headache, stiff neck, fever and nausea. All of these symptoms would have fit those claimed to have been experienced by Scott Cooley as witnesses later described them. See Caldwell. *A Day's Ride From Here, Mountain Home, Texas Volume I*.

570. Ancestry. Tree# 47410748. Person # 6764686106.

571. *Hartford Daily Courant* (Hartford, Connecticut). 1 April 1875. p 6.

572. *Evening Post* (New York, New York). 30 March 1875. p 3. Also see *Times Picayune* (New Orleans, Louisiana). 7 April 1875. *Cincinnati Daily Gazette* (Cincinnati, Ohio). 30 March 1875. p 1. Carrigan. *Forgotten Dead*. Appendix A.

573. Carrigan. *Forgotten Dead*. Appendix A.

574. *Ibid.*

575. *Ibid.*

576. "Death Penalty Information Center". Espy File. 1608-2002. Accessed 8 August 2014.

577. Caldwell/DeLord. *Texas Lawmen 1835–1899*. p 126.

578. *Galveston Daily News* (Galveston, Texas). 28 May 1875.

579. *Daily Inter Ocean* (Chicago, Illinois). 25 June 1875. p 2.

580. *Salt Lake Tribune* (Salt Lake, Utah). 5 June 1985. p 1.

581. *Daily Inter Ocean* (Chicago, Illinois). 14 June 1875.

582. "Death Penalty Information Center". Espy File. 1608-2002. Accessed 8 August 2014.

583. *Austin Daily Democratic Statesman* (Austin, Texas). 31 July 1875. Also see *Iredell Times* (Iredell, Texas). 5 March 1876. Find-A-Grave Memorial# 33772808.

584. Ancestry. Tree# 901248. Person # 1719183624. Story 619735.

585. Sonnischsen, C. L. 1984. *Outlaw on the Dodge with Baldy Russell*. Athens, Ohio: Swallow Press. Also see Follett, Jay C. Nelson A. "Cooney" Mitchell 1796–1875. Only man ever legally hanged in Hood County". *Hood County Genealogical Society Newsletter*. No. 21. February 1989. Also see the *Cincinnati Daily Enquirer*. 13 October 1975.

586. *Daily Inter Ocean* (Chicago, Illinois). 14 June 1875. p 2.

587. *Philadelphia Inquirer* (Philadelphia, Pennsylvania). 18 July 1876.

588. *Times Picayune* (New Orleans, Louisiana). 19 January 1876.

589. *San Francisco Bulletin* (San Francisco, California). 15 February 1876. p 4. Also see *New Orleans Times* (New Orleans, Louisiana). 26 January 1876. p 3. Also see *The Patriot* (Harrisburg, Pennsylvania). 3 February 1876.

590. Carrigan. *Forgotten Dead*. Appendix A.

591. *New Orleans Times* (New Orleans, Louisiana). 18 February 1876. p 1.

592. *Ibid.*

593. *Ibid.*

594. Carrigan. *Forgotten Dead*. Appendix A.

595. *Ibid.*

596. *Evening Post* (New York, New York). 6 March 1876. p 4.

597. *New York Herald* (New York, New York). 18 August 1876. p 5. Also see *Cincinnati Daily Times* (Cincinnati, Ohio). 20 September 1876. p 2. *Daily Times* (Cincinnati, Ohio). 26 September 1876. p 3 Tise. *Texas Sheriffs*. p 528.

598. Carrigan. *Lynching Culture*. Appendix B.

599. *Territorial Enterprise* (Virginia City, Nevada). 27 August 1876.

600. *New York Herald* (New York, New York). 12 August 1876.

601. Caldwell/DeLord. *Texas Lawmen 1835–1899*. Also see *The Murder of Captain W. H. Sim*. That account is provided by Mrs. Lewis Alexander of Uvalde, Texas, a former longtime resident of Burnet County. The incident occurred on the night of 31 August 1876, in the northwestern section of the county [Burnet] near Morgan Creek. Also see Burnet County History. 1979. *A Pioneer History 1847–1979; Darrell Debo*. Vol. I, p. 274. (2 vols.). Burnet, Texas: Eakin Press.

602. Ancestry. Tree# 24919530. Person # 12633565772.

603. *Albany Evening Journal* (Albany, New York). 28 September 1876. p 2. Also see Kelsey. *Texas Newspaper Abstracts - Deaths*. Volume 2. p 127.

604. Carrigan. *The Making of a Lynching Culture*. Appendix A.

605. *Galveston Weekly News* (Galveston, Texas). 30 October 1876. p 5. Also see Caldwell/DeLord. *Texas Lawmen: 1835–1899*. p 45. p 407.

606. *New Orleans Times* (New Orleans, Louisiana). 15 November 1876. p 8.

607. "Death Penalty Information Center". Espy File. 1608-2002. Accessed 8 August 2014.

608. *New York Herald* (New York, New York). 15 December 1878. p 7.

609. *Times Picayune* (New Orleans, Louisiana). 8 May 1877. Also see *Macon Weekly Telegraph* (Macon, Georgia). 22 May 1877. p 5. *Galveston Weekly News* (Galveston, Texas). 30 April 1877. Times Picayune (New Orleans, Louisiana). 8 May 1877. Also see *Macon Weekly Telegraph* (Macon, Georgia). 22 May 1877.

610. Carrigan. *Forgotten Dead*. Appendix A.

611. *Ibid.*

612. *Ibid.*

613. *Times-Picayune* (New Orleans, Louisiana). 20 August 1870. p 5.

614. *Galveston Weekly News* (Galveston, Texas). 27 August 1877.

615. Johnson, David. 2006. *The Mason County "Hoo Doo" War, 1874–1902.* Denton, Texas: University of North Texas Press. pp 212-217.

616. *Galveston Weekly News* (Galveston, Texas). 3 September 1877. p 6.

617. Ancestry. Tree #13407965. Person #12796709673.

618. Caldwell/DeLord. *Texas Lawmen: 1835–1899.* pp 223-224.

619. *Evening Star* (Washington, DC). 6 September 1877.

620. *Macon Telegraph* (Macon, Georgia). 6 September 1877. p 2.

621. *New York Herald* (New York, New York). 9 November 1877. p 11.

622. Cool, Paul. 2008. *Salt Warriors, Insurgency on the Rio Grande.* College Station, Texas: Texas A & M University Press.

623. Caldwell/DeLord. *Texas Lawmen: 1835–1899.* pp 332-334.

624. Find-A-Grave Memorial# 10621196.

625. *Jackson Citizen* (Jackson, Michigan). 15 April 1878. p 2. *Jackson Citizen* (Jackson, Michigan). 16 April 1878. p 4.

626. Parsons, Chuck. "Personal Reminiscences of Brown Bowen". Unpublished Manuscript. 23 July 2013. Text edited. Also see *Gonzales Inquirer* (Gonzales, Texas). 18 May 1878. *Gonzales Inquirer (Gonzales, Texas).* 25 May 1878. *Galveston Weekly News* (Galveston, Texas). 20 May 1878.

627. *Daily Commercial* (Vicksburg, Mississippi). 1 June 1878. p 1.

628. Caldwell/DeLord. *Texas Lawmen 1835–1899.* pp 201-202.

629. *Jackson Citizen* (Jackson, Mississippi). 9 July 1878. p 7.

630. *Ibid.*

631. *Jackson Citizen* (Jackson, Michigan). 16 July 1878. p 7.

632. *Philadelphia Inquirer* (Philadelphia, Pennsylvania). 31 August 1878.

633. Caldwell, Clifford R. 2011. *A Day's Ride from Here, Volume I - Mountain Home Texas.* Charlotte, South Carolina: History Press. pp 35-42. Also see...Bartholomew, Ed Ellsworth. 1953. *Wild Bill Longley: A Texas Hard-Case.* Houston Frontier Press. Also see Fuller, Henry Clay. 1983. *The Adventures of Bill Longley,* Nacogdoches, Texas: S. Malone. Also see Miller, Rick. 2002. "Boastful Bill Longley: Cold-blooded Texas Killer". *Wild West Magazine.* Also see *Galveston Daily News* (Galveston, Texas). 16 September 1877. *Galveston Daily News* (Galveston, Texas). 7 September 1878. *Galveston Daily News* (Galveston, Texas). 1 August 1877. *Galveston Daily News* (Galveston, Texas). 10 March 1870.

634. Carrigan. *Forgotten Dead.* Appendix A.

635. *Jackson Citizen Patriot* (Jackson, Michigan). 22 November 1878.

636. *Illinois State Journal* (Springfield, Illinois). 13 December 1878. p 1. *Galveston Daily News* (Galveston, Texas). 16 December 1878. p 1. *New York Herald* (New York, New York). 18 December 1878. p 7. Johnson. *The Horrell Wars.* pp 138-155.

637. The term "darkie" is a disparaging term for a Black person.

638. *New York Herald* (New York, New York). 15 December 1878. p 7.

639. Caldwell, Clifford R. 2009. *Guns of the Lincoln County War.* Mountain Home, Texas: Privately Published. p 1

640. Johnson, David. 2014. *The Horrell Wars, Feuding in Texas and New Mexico.* Denton, Texas: University of North Texas Press.

641. *Ibid.* Jerry Scott's saloon is often referred to at the Gem Saloon or the Matador Saloon.

642. O'Neal, Bill. 1979. *Encyclopedia of Western Gunfighters.* Norman, Oklahoma: University of Oklahoma Press. p 140. Gillett. *Six Years with The Texas Rangers.* p 113

643. Caldwell, Clifford R. "The Horrell-Higgins Feud" *The Journal of the Wild West History Association.* Volume IV. Number 2. February 2011.

644. David Johnson. E-mail to author. 3 March 2014. Also see *San Antonio Daily Express* (San Antonio, Texas). 16 December 1878. *Galveston Daily News* (Galveston, Texas). 17 December 1878. *Austin Daily Democratic Statesman* (Austin, Texas). 19 December 1878. Interview of Uncle Ed Nichols by C. L. Sonnichsen at Lampasas, Texas. 15 July 1944. Sonnichsen Collection. University of Texas at El Paso.

645. Menardville was the original name for the town of Menard, in Menard County, Texas. Interestingly enough the name was shortened at the request of the railroad when they were unable to fit the entire name on their new sign. See Caldwell, Clifford R. 2012. *Fort McKavett, and Tales of Menard County.* Privately Published. p 1.

646. *New York Herald* (New York, New York). 24 December 1878. p 3.

647. *Repository* (Canton, Ohio). 17 April 1879. p 1. Johnson, David, 2006. *The Mason County "Hoo Doo" War, 1874–1902.* Denton, Texas: University of North Texas Press. P.226. Johnson. *The Horrell Wars.* p 161.

648. Merriam-Webster defines "grogshop" as a usually low-class barroom. "Tenpins" as a bowling game using ten pins and a large ball 27 inches in circumference. Each player bowls two balls in each of ten frames.

649. *New York Herald* (New York, New York). 3 May 1879. p 4.

650. *New York Herald* (New York, New York). 8 July 1879. p 3.

651. *Times Picayune* (New Orleans, Louisiana). 23 January 1879.

652. *New York Herald* (New York, New York). 12 July 1879. p 4.

653. *New York Herald* (New York, New York). 9 August 1879. p 7.

654. *New York Tribune* (New York, New York). 23 August 1879. p 3.

655. *Philadelphia Inquirer* (Philadelphia, Pennsylvania). 13 September 1879. p 1.

656. Ancestry. Tree# 846490. Person # 6002831126.

657. "Hallettsville Hanging Tree". *Texas A & M University Forest Service.* Texas A & M University. 2012.

658. *San Francisco Bulletin* (San Francisco, California). 13 October 1879. p 4.

659. *Worcester Daily Spy* (Worcester, Massachusetts). 7 November 1879. p 1. *New York Herald* (New York, New York). 7 November 1879. p 5.

660. *The New York Sun* (New York, New York). 15 November 1879.

661. *Galveston Daily News* (Galveston, Texas). 22 November 1879.

662. *The Denton Record-Chronicle* (Denton, Texas). 4 July 1976. Section E. Image 38.

663. *Daily Inter Ocean* (Chicago, Illinois). 28 November 1879.

664. Smith, Matt. *Cleburne Times Review.* "A Falsely Accused Son and a Hell Bound Father." 1 November 2009. Also see *New York Herald* (New York, New York). 22 March 1880. p 4.

665. *New York Herald* (New York, New York). 27 March 1880. p 5. Also see *Galveston Weekly News* (Galveston, Texas). 1 April 1880.

666. *New York Herald* (New York, New York). 27 March 1880. p 5.

667. *New York Herald* (New York, New York). 16 April 1880. p 4.

668. *Ibid.*

669. *Cincinnati Commercial Tribune* (Cincinnati, Ohio). 1 May 1880. p 1.

670. Carrigan. *Forgotten Dead.* Appendix A.

671. *New York Herald* (New York, New York). 8 May 1880. p 4.

672. *Macon Telegraph* (Macon, Georgia). 9 May 1880. p 1.

673. *Cincinnati Commercial Tribune* (Cincinnati, Ohio). 12 June 1880. p 1.

674. *New York Herald* (New York, New York). 19 June 1880. p 5.

675. *Philadelphia Inquirer* (Philadelphia, Pennsylvania). 3 July 1880. p 1.

676. *Galveston Weekly News* (Galveston, Texas). 26 August 1880. p 4.

677. *Galveston Daily News* (Galveston, Texas). 28 August 1880. Also see *New Hampshire Patriot and State Gazette* (Concord, New Hampshire). 2 September 1880.

678. *Times-Picayune* (New Orleans, Louisiana). 21 August 1880. p 1.

679. *Galveston Weekly News* (Galveston, Texas). 18 November 1880. p 4.

680. *San Francisco Bulletin* (San Francisco, California). 5 February 1881. p 1.

681. Carrigan. *Forgotten Dead.* Appendix A.

682. Carrigan. *Forgotten Dead.* Appendix B.

683. *Cincinnati Daily Gazette* (Cincinnati, Ohio). 30 June 1881. p 3. *Times* (Troy, New York). 30 June 1881. p 3. *Indianapolis Sentinel* (Indianapolis, Indiana). 1 July 1881. p 4. *Huntsville Gazette* (Huntsville, Alabama). 9 July 1881. p 1.

684. *Dallas Weekly Herald* (Dallas, Texas). 7 July 1881. p 7.

685. *Daily Gazette* (Rockford, Illinois). 30 July 1881. p 1.

686. *Plain Dealer* (Cleveland, Ohio). 26 August 1881. p 2.

687. US Census. Census Year 1880. Census Place Orange, Texas. Roll 1322. Family History Film 1255322. Page 120D. Enumeration District 059.

688. *Dallas Weekly Herald* (Dallas, Texas). 14 July 1881. p 8.

689. *Galveston Weekly News* (Galveston, Texas). 20 October 1881. p 8. *Births Deaths and Marriages from El Paso Newspapers through 1885 for Arizona Texas New Mexico Oklahoma and Indian Territory.* Beard, Jane. Complier. (Greenville, South Carolina: Southern Historical Press 1982). p 97.

690. *Galveston Weekly News* (Galveston, Texas). 3 November 1881. p 4.

691. Find-A-Grave Memorial# 41954059.

692. *Births Deaths and Marriages from El Paso Newspapers through 1885 for Arizona Texas New Mexico Oklahoma and Indian Territory.* Beard, Jane. Complier. (Greenville, South Carolina: Southern Historical Press 1982). p 144

693. Carrigan. *The Making of a Lynching Culture.* Appendix B.

694. *Portland Daily Press* (Portland, Main). 6 February 1882. p 2.

695. Find-A-Grave Memorial# 9046304

696. *Standard* (Clarksville, Texas). 24 February 1882. p 3. *New York Herald* (New York, New York). 20 February 1882. p 7. *Daily Inter Ocean* (Chicago, Illinois). 20 February 1882. p 2.

697. *New York Herald* (New York, New York). 9 June 1882. p 6.

698. *Plain Dealer* (Cleveland, Ohio). 9 June 1882.

699. *San Francisco Bulletin* (San Francisco, California). 29 July 1882. p 1.Carrigan. *Forgotten Dead.* Appendix A.

700. *Wheeling Register* (Wheeling, West Virginia). 29 July 1882. p 1. Caldwell/DeLord. *Texas Lawmen 1835–1899.* p 181.

701. *Dallas Weekly Herald* (Dallas, Texas). 10 August 1882. p 5. *Births Deaths and Marriages from El Paso Newspapers.* Beard. p 133.

702. Carrigan. *Forgotten Dead.* Appendix B.

703. *New York Herald* (New York, New York). 12 August 1882. p 3.

704. *Ibid.*

705. *Salt Lake Tribune* (Salt Lake City, Utah). 26 August 1882. p 6.

706. *New York Herald* (New York, New York). 19 August 1882. p 3.

707. *New York Herald* (New York, New York). 22 August 1882. p 4.

708. *Cincinnati Daily Gazette* (Cincinnati, Ohio). 19 December 1882. p 1. *Times* (Troy, New York). 21 December 1882. p 2.

709. *Jackson Citizen* (Jackson, Michigan). 5 December 1882. p 1. *Times-Picayune* (New Orleans, Louisiana). 5 December 1882. p 1. *Births Deaths and Marriages from El Paso Newspapers.* Beard. p 163.

710. *New York Herald* (New York, New York). 6 January 1883. p 3.

711. *New York Herald* (New York, New York). 9 January 1883. p 4. *Repository* (Canton, Ohio). 15 January 1883. p 2.

712. *Cleveland Leader* (Cleveland, Ohio). 1 March 1883.

713. *Times-Picayune* (New Orleans, Louisiana). 24 March 1883. p 1. Also see Caldwell/DeLord. *Texas Lawmen, 1835–1899.* p 195.

714. Carrigan. *Lynching Culture.* Appendix A. Also see *Dallas Weekly Herald* (Dallas, Texas). 19 April 1883. p 7.

715. *Times-Picayune* (New Orleans, Louisiana). 24 March 1883. p 1. Also see Caldwell/ DeLord. *Texas Lawmen, 1835–1899.* p 195.

716. Carrigan. *Forgotten Dead.* Appendix A.

717. Carrigan. *Forgotten Dead.* Appendix A.

718. *Times Picayune* (New Orleans, Louisiana). 6 June 1883.

719. *Waco Daily Examiner* (Waco, Texas). 2 June 1883. *Dallas Weekly Herald* (Dallas, Texas). 7 June 1883. p 6.

720. *Trenton Evening Times* (Trenton, New Jersey). 7 June 1883.

721. *Trenton Evening Times* (Trenton, New Jersey). 18 June 1883.

722. *Repository* (Canton, Ohio). 27 June 1883. *Times Picayune* (New Orleans, Louisiana). 3 July 1883. *New Hampshire Patriot and State Gazette* (Concord, New Hampshire). 5 July 1883. Also see *Jackson Citizen* (Jackson, Michigan). 3 July 1883.

723. *New York Herald* (New York, New York). 8 July 1883. p 8. Also see *New York Tribune* (New York, New York). 7 July 1883.

724. *Galveston Weekly News* (Galveston, Texas). 12 July 1883.

725. Carrigan. *Lynching Culture*. Appendix A. Also see *Times Picayune* (New Orleans, Louisiana). 14 August 1883. Also see *The Times* (Troy, New York). 2 August 1883. p 2.

726. *Births Deaths and Marriages from El Paso Newspapers*. Beard. p 5.

727. *San Francisco Bulletin* (San Francisco, California). 18 August 1883. p 3.

728. *New Haven Register* (New Haven, Connecticut). 24 September 1884. p 1.

729. *New York Herald* (New York, New York). 20 October 1883. p 3. *Births Deaths and Marriages from El Paso Newspapers*. p 58, Beard. p 144.

730. *New York Herald* (New York, New York). 20 October 1883. p 8. *Cleveland Leader* (Cleveland, Ohio). 20 October 1883. p 3.

731. Caldwell /DeLord. *Texas Lawmen 1835–1899*. pp 379-380. Also see *Jackson Citizen* (Jackson, Michigan). 20 November 1883.

732. Carrigan. *Forgotten Dead*. Appendix B.

733. *Patriot* (Harrisburg, Pennsylvania). 10 December 1883. p 2. Carrigan. *Forgotten Dead*. Appendix A

734. *Dallas Weekly Herald* (Dallas, Texas). 13 December 1883. p 1.

735. Luke. 23:34.

736. *Dallas Weekly Herald* (Dallas, Texas). 27 December 1883. p 8.

737. Caldwell/DeLord. *Texas Lawmen: 1835–1899.*p 155.

738. *Cleveland Leader* (Cleveland, Ohio). 26 December 1883. p 1.

739. *New York Herald* (New York, New York). 23 January 1884.

740. *Critic-Record* (Washington, DC). 20 October 1884. *Repository* (Canton, Ohio). 21 October 1884.

741. Caldwell/DeLord. *Texas Lawmen 1835–1899*. pp 127-128. Also see *New York Herald* (New York, New York). 4 February 1884. p 3.

742. *New Haven Register* (New Haven, Connecticut). 8 March 1884.

743. *Critic Record* (Washington, DC). 26 March 1884.

744. *New York Herald* (New York, New York). 9 April 1884. p 6.

745. Carrigan. *Lynching Culture*. Appendix A. *Waco Daily Examiner* (Waco, Texas). 16 July 1885.

746. *Cincinnati Post* (Cincinnati, Ohio). 7 June 1884.

747. *Times-Picayune* (New Orleans, Louisiana). 9 June 1884.

748. *Whitney Messenger* (Whitney, Texas). 27 June 1884. Also see *Augusta Chronicle* (Augusta, Georgia). 26 June 1884.

749. *New Haven Register* (New Haven, Connecticut). 9 August 1884. p 1.

750. *Times-Picayune* (New Orleans, Louisiana). 14 August 1884. p 1. *Repository* (Canton, Ohio). 18 August 1884. p 5. *San Francisco Bulletin* (San Francisco, California). 23 March 1885. p 1. *Births Deaths and Marriages from El Paso Newspapers*. Beard. p. 103.

751. Carrigan. *Lynching Culture*. Appendix A. Also see *New York Herald* (New York, New York). 24 August 1884.

752. Ancestry. Tree 15386458. Person # 780148529.

753. *Galveston Daily News* (Galveston, Texas). 8 September 1888.

754. *Daily Inter Ocean* (Chicago, Illinois). 30 May 1889.

755. Caldwell/DeLord. *Texas Lawmen: 1835–1899*. p 194. *Births Deaths and Marriages from El Paso Newspapers*. Beard. p. 140

756. *Bridgeport Evening News* (Bridgeport, Connecticut). 13 September 1884.

757. *Daily Advocate* (Baton Rouge, Louisiana). 30 September 1884. p 2. *Births Deaths and Marriages from El Paso Newspapers*. Beard. p. 68.

758. *Daily Illinois State Journal* (Springfield, Illinois). 8 October 1884. p 4. *Births Deaths and Marriages from El Paso Newspapers*. Beard. p 49.

759. *Times-Picayune* (New Orleans, Louisiana). 1 November 1884. *Dallas Weekly Herald* (Dallas, Texas). 6 November 1884. p 6.

760. *New York Herald* (New York, New York). 4 November 1884. p 5. *Births Deaths and Marriages from El Paso Newspapers.* Beard. p 144.

761. Carrigan. *Forgotten Dead.* Appendix B.

762. *Philadelphia Inquirer* (Philadelphia, Pennsylvania). 24 January 1885. p 1. *Jackson Citizen* (Jackson, Michigan). 27 January 1885. p 1.

Campbellite is a mildly pejorative term referring to a 19th century religious group having historic roots in the Restoration Movement. Its leaders were Thomas and Alexander Campbell. Members of the group generally consider the term "Campbellite" inappropriate, claiming that they are followers of Jesus, not Campbell. Their beliefs are somewhat in parallel with those of Martin Luther's and the Anabaptist movement.

763. *Jackson Citizen* (Jackson, Michigan). 10 February 1885. p 8. *Births Deaths and Marriages from El Paso Newspapers.* Beard. p.74.

764. *Charleston News and Courier* (Charleston, South Carolina). 5 March 1885. p 3. *Births Deaths and Marriages from El Paso Newspapers.* Beard. p 56.

765. *Daily Advocate* (Baton Rouge, Louisiana). 27 April 1885. p 1.

766. Find-A-Grave Memorial #15753712. Also see *Dallas Daily Herald* (Dallas, Texas). 9 June 1885. Caldwell/DeLord. *Texas Lawmen: 1835–1899.* pp 96-98. Find-A-Grave Memorial #15757447. Ancestry. Tree# 26169836. Person # 12574206394. Ancestry. Tree# 26169836. Person # 12574205946.

767. *Galveston Daily News* (Galveston, Texas). 8 September 1888.

768. *New York Herald* (New York, New York). 31 May 1885. p 14.

769. *New Hampshire Patriot and State Gazette* (Concord, New Hampshire). 11 June 1885.

770. *Cincinnati Commercial Tribune* (Cincinnati, Ohio). 30 June 1885. p 1.

771. *Daily Advocate* (Baton Rouge, Louisiana). 23 June 1885. p 2.

772. *Daily Advocate* (Baton Rouge, Louisiana). 27 June 1885. p 2. *Kansas City Times* (Kansas City, Missouri). 26 June 1885. p 1.

773. *Boston Herald* (Boston, Massachusetts). 28 June 1885. p 1. *Dallas Morning News* (Dallas, Texas). 28 November 1885. p 2. *Births Deaths and Marriages from El Paso Newspapers.* Beard. p 83. p 103.

774. *Waco Daily Examiner* (Waco, Texas). 19 July 1885.

775. *Summit County Beacon* (Akron, Ohio). 8 July 1885. p 2. *Births Deaths and Marriages from El Paso Newspapers.* Beard. p 71.

776. Carrigan. *Lynching Culture.* Appendix A.

777. *Critic-Record* (Washington, DC). 15 August 1885. p 1.

778. *Daily Star* (Atchison Kansas). 28 August 1885. Also see *Daily Advocate* (Newark, Ohio). 31 August 1885. Also see *The New Era* (Humeston, Iowa). 3 September 1885. *Kansas City Star* (Kansas City, Kansas). 28 August 1885. p 1.

779. *Ibid.*

780. Caldwell/DeLord. *Texas Lawmen: 1835–1899.* p. 184

781. *Times-Picayune* (New Orleans, Louisiana). 12 October 1885. *Dallas Morning News* (Dallas, Texas). 11 October 1885.

782. *Dallas Morning News* (Dallas, Texas). 14 November 1885.

783. *Plain Dealer* (Cleveland, Ohio). 17 December 1885. p 1.

784. *Deseret News* (Salt Lake City, Utah). 23 December 1885. p 7.

785. *New York Herald* (New York, New York). 16 January 1886. p 3.

786. *Daily Inter Ocean* (Chicago, Illinois). 16 January 1886. p 3.

787. Find -A-Grave #15622728. *New York Herald* (New York, New York). 23 January 1886. p 3.

788. *Macon Weekly Telegraph* (Macon, Georgia). 16 February 1886. p 5. Also see *Austin Daily Statesman* (Austin, Texas). 9 February 1886.

789. *August Chronicle* (Augusta, Georgia). 16 March 1886. p 5.

790. Find-A-Grave Memorial #15622932. Also see Carrigan. *Lynching Culture.* Appendix A. Ancestry. Tree# 8940124. Person # 6602890941.

791. *Dallas Morning News* (Dallas, Texas). 16 March 1886.

792. *Kansas City Star* (Kansas City, Missouri). 1 April 1886. p 2.

793. *Times Picayune* (New Orleans, Louisiana). 17 April 1886.

794. Carrigan. *Forgotten Dead.* Appendix A. Also see *New York Herald* (New York, New York). 20 April 1886. p 10. *Daily Advocate* (Baton Rouge, Louisiana). 21 April 1886. p 2. *Daily Advocate* (Baton Rouge, Louisiana). 30 April 1886. p 2.

795. Carrigan. *Forgotten Dead.* Appendix A. p 10.

796. *Daily Advocate* (Baton Rouge, Louisiana). 28 April 1886. p 1.

797. Carrigan. *Forgotten Dead.* Appendix B.

798. *New York Herald* (New York, New York). 5 May 1886. p 4.

799. *Dallas Morning News* (Dallas, Texas). 9 May 1886. p 6.

800. *Dallas Morning News* (Dallas, Texas). 18 June 1886. p 7.

801. *New York Herald* (New York, New York). 30 June 1886. p 10.

802. Find-A-Grave Memorial # 15623038. Also see Carrigan. *Lynching Culture.* Appendix A. Also see, *Dallas Morning News* (Dallas, Texas). 14 July 1886. p 5. *Dallas Morning News* (Dallas, Texas). 4 August 1886. p 2.

803. Find-A-Grave Memorial# 63602286.

804. *Evening Star* (Washington, DC). 27 July 1886. p 1. Also see *Omaha World Herald* (Omaha, Nebraska). 27 July 1886. p 1.

805. Find-A-Grave Memorial # 15623121. Also see Carrigan. *Lynching Culture.* Appendix A. Also see *Dallas Morning News* (Dallas, Texas). 4 August 1886. p 2.

806. *Columbus Daily Enquirer* (Columbus, Ohio). 4 September 1886.

807. *New York Herald* (New York, New York). 11 September 1886. p 5. Also see *Dallas Morning News* (Dallas, Texas). 22 January 1886. *Dallas Morning News* (Dallas, Texas). 11 September 1886.

808. *Kansas City Times* (Kansas City, Kansas). 6 October 1886. p 1. Also see *Dallas Morning News* (Dallas, Texas). 5 October 1886.

809. *Cincinnati Commercial Tribune* (Cincinnati, Ohio). 18 October 1886. p 1.

810. *Omaha World Herald* (Omaha, Nebraska). 30 October 1886. p 1. Also see *New York Herald* (New York, New York). 31 October 1886. p 13.

811. *Dallas Morning News* (Dallas, Texas). 2 November 1886. p 7.

812. *Kansas City Times* (Kansas City, Missouri). 2 December 1886. p 2.

813. *Kalamazoo Gazette* (Kalamazoo, Michigan). 4 December 1886. Also see *Dallas Morning News* (Dallas, Texas). 3 December 1886.

814. *Daily Inter Ocean* (Chicago, Illinois). 17 December 1886. p 2.

815. Carrigan. *Forgotten Dead.* Appendix A. Also see *New York Herald* (New York, New York). 4 February 1887. p 5.

816. *Kansas City Star* (Kansas City, Missouri). 3 February 1887. p 1.

817. *Patriot* (Harrisburg, Pennsylvania). 18 February 1887. p 1.

818. Find-A-Grave Memorial # 15630399. *Dallas Morning News* (Dallas, Texas). 5 March 1887.

819. *Kansas City Star* (Kansas City, Missouri). 14 May 1887. p 1. Also see *Dallas Morning News* (Dallas, Texas). 14 May 1887.

820. Find-A-Grave Memorial # 15631272. Also see *New York Tribune* (New York, New York). 26 July 1887. p 1. Also see *Dallas Morning News* (Dallas, Texas). 24 July 1887.

821. *Jackson Citizen* (Jackson, Michigan). 4 October 1887. Borders, Gary B. 2006. *A Hanging in Nacogdoches: Murder, Race, Politics and Polemics in Texas's Oldest Town 1870–1916.* Austin, Texas: University of Texas Press.

822. Carrigan. *Forgotten Dead.* Appendix B.

823. *Cincinnati Post* (Cincinnati, Ohio). 17 October 1887. *Dallas Morning News* (Dallas, Texas). 15 October 1887. p 2.

824. *Dallas Weekly Herald* (Dallas, Texas). 22 October 1887. p 5.

825. Carrigan. *Forgotten Dead.* Appendix A. Also see *Dallas Morning News* (Dallas, Texas). 10 December 1887.

826. *Dallas Morning News* (Dallas, Texas). 2 April 1887.

827. Carrigan. *Forgotten Dead.* Appendix A. *Kansas City Times* (Kansas City, Missouri). 17 December 1887. p 1.

828. *New York Herald* (New York, New York). 31 December 1887. p 10. *Saginaw News* (Saginaw, Michigan). 31 December 1887. p 2. *Daily Illinois State Register* (Springfield, Illinois). 31 December 1887. p 1.

829. *Denver Rocky Mountain News* (Denver, Colorado). 31 December 1887. p 1.

830. *Kansas City Times* (Kansas City, Missouri). 5 January 1888.

831. *Daily Advocate* (Baton Rouge, Louisiana). 7 March 1888. Kelsey. *Texas Newspaper Abstracts - Deaths*. Volume 2. p 63. *Dallas Morning News* (Dallas, Texas). 10 January 1888. p 6. *Augusta Chronicle* (Augusta, Maine). 5 January 1888. p 1.

832. Carrigan. *Forgotten Dead*. Appendix A. *Oregonian* (Portland, Oregon). 18 January 1888. p 4.

833. *Oregonian* (Portland, Oregon). 18 January 1888. p 4. *New York Herald* (New York, New York). 25 January 1888. p 4.

834. *Trenton Evening News* (Trenton, New Jersey). 1 March 1888.

835. Find-A-Grave Memorial# 15702386.

836. Find-A-Grave Memorial# 92469822. *Plain Dealer* (Cleveland, Ohio). 1 March 1888. *Times Picayune (New Orleans, Louisiana).* 5 March 1888. p 4. *Dallas Morning News* (Dallas, Texas). 29 February 1888. p 1.

837. *New York Herald* (New York, New York). 14 April 1888.

838. Caldwell/DeLord. *Texas Lawmen 1835–1899*. pp 224-225.

839. *St. Louis Republic* (St. Louis, Missouri). 9 June 1888. p 1. *Dallas Morning News* (Dallas, Texas). 9 June 1888. p 1.

840. *Dallas Morning News* (Dallas, Texas). 11 July 1888. p 3. *Muskegon Chronicle* (Muskegon, Michigan). 13 July 1888. p 1. *Daily Illinois State Journal* (Springfield, Illinois). 13 July 1888. p 1.

841. *Cincinnati Commercial Tribune* (Cincinnati, Ohio). 18 July 1888. p 1.

842. Find-A-Grave Memorial #15677476.

843. *Dallas Morning News* (Dallas, Texas). 23 July 1888.

844. Mitchell, Joe H. 2009. *The Strangest Fruit: Forgotten Black-on-Black Lynchings 1835–1935*. Privately Published.

845. *Morning Star* (Rockford, Illinois). 4 September 1888.

846. *Daily Inter Ocean* (Chicago, Illinois). 1 September 1888. p 3.

847. *Philadelphia Enquirer* (Philadelphia, Pennsylvania). 3 September 1888. p 8.

848. *Dallas Morning News* (Dallas, Texas). 28 September 1888.

849. *Macon Telegraph* (Macon, Georgia). 6 October 1888. p.1.

850. *Dallas Morning News* (Dallas, Texas). 18 October 1888. p 6. *Cleveland Gazette* (Cleveland, Ohio). 3 November 1888. p 1.

851. *Evening Star* (Washington, DC). 16 October 1888. p 5.

852. *Morning Star* (Rockford, Illinois). 20 October 1888. p 1.

853. *Macon Telegraph* (Macon, Georgia). 23 October 1888. p 1.

854. Find-A-Grave Memorial #15685503.

855. *Dallas Morning News* (Dallas, Texas). 26 October 1888.

856. *St. Louis Republic* (St. Louis, Missouri). 8 December 1888.

857. *St. Louis Republic* (St. Louis, Missouri). 22 December 1888. p 1.

858. *Dallas Morning News* (Dallas, Texas). 22 December 1888.

859. *Dallas Morning News* (Dallas, Texas). 30 December 1888. Also see *Dallas Morning News* (Dallas, Texas). 14 January 1888.

860. Shirley, Glenn. 1994. *The Fighting Marlows: Men who wouldn't be lynched*. Fort Worth, Texas: Texas Christian University Press.

861. *San Diego Union* (San Diego, California). 31 January 1889.

862. *Births Deaths and Marriages from El Paso Newspapers*. Beard. p 4.

863. Find-A-Grave Memorial# 94620351

864. Ancestry. Tree #486419. Person #6088663180.

865. *Wheeling Register* (Wheeling, West Virginia). 22 February 1889. p 2.

866. Mitchell. *30 Years of Lynching*. p 95.

867. *St. Louis Republic* (St. Louis, Missouri). 5 April 1889. p 2.

868. Find-A-Grave Memorial #15703074. Also see *St. Louis Republic* (St. Louis, Missouri). 15 April 1889. p 3. *New Mexican* (Santa Fe, New Mexico). 17 April 1889. p 1.

869. Mitchell. *30 Years of Lynching*. p 95.

870. *Dallas Morning News* (Dallas, Texas). 30 July 1899.

871. Carrigan. *Lynching Culture.* Appendix A. Also see *Waco Weekly Stock and Farm News* (Waco, Texas). 29 July 1889.

872. *Dallas Morning News* (Dallas, Texas). 15 July 1889.

873. *Weekly Pelican* (New Orleans, Louisiana). 20 July 1889. p 3. *Births Deaths and Marriages from El Paso Newspapers.* Beard. p 73.

874. *Huntsville Gazette* (Huntsville, Texas). 24 August 1889.

875. Ancestry. Tree# 16216594. Person # 354444018.

876. *Dallas Morning News* (Dallas, Texas). 28 July 1889. *Dallas Morning News* (Dallas, Texas). 2 August 1889.

877. *New York Herald* (New York, New York). 15 August 1889. p 3.

878. Ancestry. Tree# 1847840. Person # 1824437167.

879. Caldwell/DeLord. *Texas Lawmen: 1835–1899.* p 152. Also see *New York Herald* (New York, New York). 24 August 1889. p 2.

880. Find-A-Grave Memorial # 10083915. Also see *Austin Statesman* (Austin, Texas). 24 August 1889.

881. *Elkhart Daily Review* (Elkhart, Indiana). 28 September 1889.

882. *Clarion Ledger* (Jackson, Mississippi). 31 October 1889. p 4.

883. *Dallas Morning News* (Dallas, Texas). 2 November 1889.

884. *Chicago Herald* (Chicago, Illinois). 31 January 1890.

885. Carrigan. *The Making of a Lynching Culture.* Appendix A. Mitchell. *30 Years of Lynching.* p 95.

886. *Births Deaths and Marriages from El Paso Newspapers.* Beard. p 6.

887. Mitchell. *30 Years of Lynching.* p 95.

888. Find-A-Grave Memorial # 15684136. Also see *Dallas Morning News* (Dallas, Texas). 7 January 1890. *Dallas Morning News* (Dallas, Texas). 7 January 1890.

889. Find-A-Grave Memorial #15684319. Also see *Dallas Morning News* (Dallas, Texas). 20 March 1890.

890. *New York Herald* (New York, New York). 29 March 1890. p 10.

891. *Waco Daily News.* 5 April 1890. Also see *Daily Journal and Journal and Tribune* (Knoxville, Tennessee). 5 April 1890.

892. Mitchell. *30 Years of Lynching.* p 95.

893. *St. Louis Republic* (St. Louis, Missouri). 24 April 1890. p 3.

894. Mitchell. *30 Years of Lynching.* p 95.

895. *New Mexican* (Santa Fe, New Mexico). 14 May 1890. p 1. *Dallas Morning News* (Dallas, Texas). 11 May 1890. p 9.

896. *Evansville Courier and Press* (Evansville, Indiana). 3 June 1890. p 1.

897. *Wheeling Register* (Wheeling, West Virginia). 8 June 1890. p 1.

898. *Births Deaths and Marriages from El Paso Newspapers.* Beard. p 130.

899. Carrigan. *Forgotten Dead.* Appendix A.

900. *Philadelphia Inquirer* (Philadelphia, Pennsylvania). 20 June 1890. p 1.

901. Mitchell. *30 Years of Lynching.* p 95.

902. *St. Louis Republic* (St. Louis, Missouri). 3 July 1890. p 9. Mitchell. *30 Years of Lynching.* p 95.

903. *Idaho Statesman* (Boise, Idaho). 22 July 1890. p 1. Also see the *Macon Telegraph* (Macon, Georgia). 22 July 1890.

904. Carrigan. *Forgotten Dead.* Appendix B. Also see *Daily Illinois State Register* (Springfield, Illinois). 24 July 1890.

905. Mitchell. *30 Years of Lynching.* p 95.

906. *Kalamazoo Gazette* (Kalamazoo, Michigan). 8 August 1890.

907. Mitchell. *30 Years of Lynching.* p 95.

908. Carrigan. *Lynching Culture.* Appendix B.

909. *Wheeling Register* (Wheeling, West Virginia). 4 December 1890. p 1.

910. *New York Tribune* (New York, New York). 18 December 1890. *Elkhart Daily Review* (Elkhart, Indiana). 19 December 1890. p 1. *Births Deaths and Marriages from El Paso Newspapers.* Beard. p 91.

911. *Jackson Citizen Patriot* (Jackson, Michigan). 3 January 1891. p 3. Also see Ancestry. Tree# 12107890. Person # 333886705.

912. *Waco Daily News* (Waco, Texas). 9 January 1890.

913. *Dallas Morning News* (Dallas, Texas). 6 January 1891. p 1. Carrigan. *Lynching Culture.* Appendix A.

914. *Daily Journal and Journal and Tribune* (Knoxville, Tennessee). 10 January 1891. p 4.

915. *Patriot* (Harrisburg, Pennsylvania). 9 February 1891.

916. *Dallas Morning News* (Dallas, Texas). 17 February 1891. p 1. *Fresno Morning Republican* (Fresno, California). 19 February 1891. p 2.

917. Carrigan. *Lynching Culture.* Appendix A. *Dallas Morning News* (Dallas, Texas). 28 February 1891.

918. *Omaha World Herald* (Omaha, Nebraska). 7 March 1891. p 1. *Kansas City Times* (Kansas City, Missouri). 7 March 1891. p 4.

919. *Kalamazoo Gazette* (Kalamazoo, Michigan). 29 March 1891.

920. *Freeman* (Indianapolis, Indiana). 2 May 1891. p 2.

921. Mitchell. *30 Years of Lynching.* p 95.

922. Mitchell. *The Strangest Fruit.* p 101.

923. *Fort Worth Gazette* (Fort Worth, Texas). 9 June 1891. p 1.

924. *Leavenworth Advocate* (Leavenworth, Kansas). 20 June 1891. p 2. Also see Carrigan. *Lynching Culture.* Appendix A.

925. *Denver Rocky Mountain News* (Denver, Colorado). 27 June 1891. p 1.

926. *Elkhart Weekly Review* (Elkhart, Indiana). 30 July 1891. p 2.

927. *State* (Columbia, South Carolina). 1 August 1891. p 1. Also see Caldwell/DeLord. *Texas Lawmen: 1835–1899.* pp 265-266.

928. Carrigan. *Lynching Culture.* Appendix A.

929. *Chicago Herald* (Chicago, Illinois). 19 September 1891. p 3. Also see *The San Saba News and Star* (San Saba, Texas). 16 October 1975. *The Eagle Pass News Guide* (Eagle Pass, Texas). 16 September 1971.

930. *Daily Inter Ocean* (Chicago, Illinois). 30 September 1891. p 3.

931. *Cleveland Plain Dealer* (Cleveland, Ohio). 10 October 1891. p 2.

932. *Dallas Morning News* (Dallas, Texas). 7 November 1891.

933. *Daily Inter Ocean* (Chicago, Illinois). 27 October 1891. p 6.

934. Find-A-Grave Memorial# 75273899

935. *St. Louis Republic* (St. Louis, Missouri). 31 October 1891. p 2. *Also see the Dallas Morning News* (Dallas, Texas). 31 October 1891.

936. *Jackson Citizen Patriot* (Jackson, Michigan). 13 November 1891. p 3.

937. *New York Herald* (New York, New York). 12 November 1891. p 12.

938. *Galveston Daily News* (Galveston, Texas). 25 January 1891.

939. The Christina hymn "What a Friend We Have in Jesus" was originally written as a poem, by Joseph M. Scriven. Scriven was born into a prosperous Irish family on 10 September 1819. As a young man he graduated from Trinity College and became engaged to be married. Sadly his fiancée drowned the night before they were to be wed. After the loss of his bride to be Scriven emigrated to Canada. There he became engaged to Eliza Roche, a relative of the family he was tutoring. She died shortly before the wedding. Scriven then joined the Plymouth Brethren and helped the elderly members of the community. He was known as a selfless man who never refused help to anyone in need. In 1855, Scriven learned that his mother was seriously ill in Dublin, Ireland. He was unable to travel there to be with her. Instead, he wrote her a letter and enclosed a poem. Later, when he himself was ill, a friend came to visit and happened to see the scribbled sonnet. Although Scriven had not intended to publish the poem, it was included in a small collection of his works in 1869. The composer, Charles C. Converse, was a Christian who wrote articles on many subjects under the pen name Karl Reden. He had many of his musical works performed by leading orchestras and choirs, but he is best remembered for this tune. Ira D. Sankey discovered the hymn in 1875 and included it in *Sankey's Gospel Hymns Number One.* Since that time, "What a Friend We Have in Jesus" has become one of the most loved hymns of all time.

940. *St. Louis Republic* (St. Louis, Missouri). 21 November 1891. p 6.

941. *Denver Rocky Mountain News* (Denver, Colorado). 23 November 1891.

942. *St. Louis Republic* (St. Louis, Missouri). 28 November 1891. p 2.

943. *Dallas Morning News* (Dallas, Texas). 11 December 1891.

944. *Daily Inter Ocean* (Chicago, Illinois). 30 January 1892. p 3.

945. *Daily Inter Ocean* (Chicago, Illinois). 14 March 1892. p 1.

946. *Ibid.*

947. *Dallas Morning News* (Dallas, Texas). 21 April 1892. p 3. *Kansas City Times* (Kansas City, Missouri). 23 April 1892. Also see, *New Orleans Item* (New Orleans, Louisiana). 23 April 1892. p 4. Carrigan. *Lynching Culture.* Appendix A.

948. *St. Louis Republic* (St. Louis, Missouri). 28 May 1892. p 7.

949. *Kansas City Times* (Kansas City, Missouri). 28 May 1892.

950. *Albuquerque Morning Democrat* (Albuquerque, New Mexico). 12 June 1892.

951. *St. Louis Republic* (St. Louis, Missouri). 12 June 1892. p 15.

952. *St. Louis Republic* (St. Louis, Missouri). 25 June 1892. p 7.

953. *Boston Journal* (Boston, Massachusetts). 28 June 1892. p 2.

954. *Dallas Morning News* (Dallas, Texas). 9 July 1892. p 1. *Galveston Daily News* (Galveston, Texas). 9 July 1892. Also see Caldwell/DeLord. *Texas Lawmen: 1835–1899.*pp 24-25.

955. Ancestry. Tree #27174811. Person #13932849507. Ancestry. Tree #1705853. Person #255376878. Ancestry. Tree #26393491. Person #26098702688. Ancestry. Tree # 5267129. Person #24065101415. Ancestry. Tree #46108624. Person #6479728335. Ancestry. Tree #9414568. Person #803237098. Ancestry. Tree #25521378. Person #12213579764. Ancestry. Tree #6716324. Person #332690286.

956. *Daily Inter Ocean* (Chicago, Illinois). 16 July 1892. p 3.

957. Caldwell/DeLord. *Texas Lawmen: 1835–1899.* pp 184-185. Also see *Idaho Statesman* (Boise, Idaho). 27 July 1892. p 1.

958. Caldwell/DeLord. *Texas Lawmen 1835–1899.* p 130.

959. *Langston City Herald* (Langston, Oklahoma). 24 September 1892.

960. *Riverside Independent Enterprise* (Riverside California). 21 September 1892. p 1. *Dallas Morning News* (Dallas, Texas). 21 September 1892. p 6. *Cleveland Gazette* (Cleveland, Ohio). 10 September 1892. p 1. *Freeman* (Indianapolis, Indiana). 26 November 1892. p 7. Mitchell. *The Strangest Fruit.*

961. "Death Penalty Information Center". Espy File. 1608-2002. Accessed 8 August 2014.

962. *Dallas Morning News* (Dallas, Texas). 15 October 1892.

963. *St. Louis Republic* (St. Louis, Missouri). 1 July 1892. p 7. Also see *The New Mexican* (Santa Fe, New Mexico). 26 November 1892. p 1.

964. *Kalamazoo Gazette* (Kalamazoo, Michigan). 27 November 1892.

965. *Plain Dealer* (Cleveland, Ohio). 4 December 1892. p 9.

966. *Trenton Evening Times* (Trenton, New Jersey). 2 February 1893. p 4. Also see *New York Sun* (New York, New York). 2 February 1893.

967. *Trenton Evening News* (Trenton, New Jersey). 8 February 1893. *Sun* (Baltimore, Maryland). 8 February 1893. p 6.

968. *Philadelphia Inquirer* (Philadelphia, Pennsylvania). 24 February 1893.

969. *Idaho Statesman* (Boise, Idaho). 16 April 1893.

970. *Morning Olympian* (Olympia, Washington). 29 April 1893. p 1.

971. *Idaho Statesman* (Boise, Idaho). 29 April 1893.

972. *St. Louis Republic* (St. Louis, Missouri). 13 May 1893. p 13.

973. *Charlotte Observer* (Charlotte, North Carolina). 11 June 1893. p 5.

974. *Plain Dealer* (Cleveland, Ohio). 17 July 1893.

975. *Dallas Morning News* (Dallas, Texas). 26 July 1893. Also see *Charlotte Observer* (Charlotte, North Carolina). 30 July 1893. p 3.

976. *Charlotte Observer* (Charlotte, North Carolina). 30 July 1893. p 3.

977. *Dallas Morning News* (Dallas, Texas). 29 July 1893.

978. *San Antonio Daily Express* (San Antonio, Texas). 29 July 1893. Also see *Galveston Daily News* (Galveston, Texas). 29 July 1893.

979. Find-A-Grave Memorial# 27885447.

980. *Sun* (Baltimore, Maryland). 4 August 1893. p 6.

981. *Idaho Statesman* (Boise, Idaho). 2 August 1893. p 1.

982. *Dallas Morning News* (Dallas, Texas). 26 July 1893.

983. "Death Penalty Information Center". Espy File. 1608-2002. Accessed 8 August 2014.

984. *Elkhart Weekly Review* (Elkhart, Indiana). 23 November 1893. Also see *Dallas Morning News* (Dallas, Texas). 17 November 1893.

985. *Dallas Morning News* (Dallas, Texas). 9 December 1893.

986. *Galveston Daily News* (Galveston, Texas). 13 January 1894. Also see *San Antonio Daily Express* (San Antonio, Texas). 13 January 1894. *Dallas Morning News* (Dallas, Texas). 13 January 1894.

987. *Dallas Morning News* (Dallas, Texas). 11 February 1894.

988. *Times Picayune* (New Orleans, Louisiana). 31 March 1894.

989. *Waco Evening News* (Waco, Texas). 11 April 1894. Also see Ancestry. Tree# 22290639. Person # 1222084356.

990. Find-A-Grave Memorial #41602396.

991. Caldwell, Clifford R. 20143. *Robert Kelsey Wylie, Forgotten Cattle King of Texas*. Privately Published.

992. Carrigan. *Lynching Culture*. Appendix A.

993. "Death Penalty Information Center". Espy File. 1608-2002. Accessed 8 August 2014.

994. *Dallas Morning News* (Dallas, Texas). 17 May 1894

995. *New Mexican* (Santa Fe, New Mexico). 25 May 1894.

996. *State* (Columbia, South Carolina). 26 May 1894.

997. *Columbus Daily Enquirer* (Columbus, Ohio). 12 June 1894. p 4.

998. *Omaha World Herald* (Omaha, Nebraska). 30 June 1894.

999. *New Orleans Item* (New Orleans, Louisiana). 20 July 1894. Also see *Dallas Morning News* (Dallas, Texas). 18 July 1894.

1000. Had the author taken the time to verify he/she would have found that in the Choctaw language the word "drunk" most directly translates to *chukf oloha*. The slang term *haksi* is also used to describe the inebriated condition. Byington, Cyrus. 1915. *A Dictionary of the Choctaw Language*. Washington, DC: Government Printing Office. p 132.

1001. *Dallas Morning News* (Dallas, Texas). 29 September 1894. p 1.

1002. *Riverside Daily Press* (Riverside, California). 6 October 1894.

1003. *Elkhart Weekly Review* (Elkhart, Indiana). 27 December 1894.

1004. *Parsons Weekly Blade* (Parsons, Kansas). 2 February 1895.

1005. *St. Louis Republic* (St. Louis, Missouri). 19 January 1895.

1006. Carrigan. *Forgotten Dead*. Appendix B.

1007. "Death Penalty Information Center". Espy File. 1608-2002. Accessed 8 August 2014.

1008. *Times Picayune* (New Orleans, Louisiana). 13 April 1895.

1009. *St. Louis Republic* (St. Louis, Missouri). 13 April 1895.

1010. *New Mexican* (Santa Fe, New Mexico). 25 May 1895. p 1. Segrave, Kerry. 2010. *Lynchings of Women in the United States: The Recorded Cases, 1851–1946*. Jefferson, North Carolina: McFarland and Company, Inc. Publishers. pp 79-80.

1011. *St. Louis Republic* (St. Louis, Missouri). 12 June 1895.

1012. *Times Picayune* (New Orleans, Louisiana). 12 June 1895.

1013. Carrigan. *Forgotten Dead*. Appendix B. *Waco Morning News* (Waco, Texas). 12 June 1895.

1014. *Waco Post* (Waco, Texas). 25 July 1895. Segrave. *Lynchings of Women*. pp 79-80.

1015. *Dallas Morning News* (Dallas, Texas). 21 July 1895.

1016. Segrave. *Lynchings of Women*. pp 79-80.

1017. *Repository* (Canton, Ohio). 26 July 1895.

1018. *St. Louis Republic* (St. Louis, Missouri). 3 August 1895.

1019. *Wheeling Register* (Wheeling, West Virginia). 3 August 1895. Segrave. *Lynchings of Women*. pp 79-80.

1020. *Morning Olympian* (Olympia, Washington). 14 August 1895.

1021. *Kansas City Times* (Kansas City, Missouri). 24 August 1895.

1022. *Dallas Morning News* (Dallas, Texas). 22 August 1895. Caldwell/DeLord. *Texas Lawmen: 1835–1899*.p 233.

1023. Ancestry. Tree #9927674. Person #6993567212.

1024. *Cherokee Advocate* (Tahlequah, Oklahoma). 25 September 1895.

1025. *St. Louis Republic* (St. Louis, Missouri). 12 October 1896. p 2.

1026. *St Louis Republic* (St. Louis, Missouri). 13 October 1895. p 7. *State Ledger* (Topeka, Kansas).11 October 1895. p 2. *Philadelphia Inquirer* (Philadelphia, Pennsylvania).11 October 1896. p 1. Segrave. *Lynchings of Women.* p 82. Carrigan. *Forgotten Dead.* Appendix A.

1027. *Omaha World Herald* (Omaha, Nebraska). 15 October 1895. p 1. Also see *St. Louis Republic* (St. Louis, Missouri). 15 October 1895.

1028. "Death Penalty Information Center". Espy File. 1608-2002. Accessed 8 August 2014.

1029. *St. Louis Republic* (St. Louis, Missouri). 26 October 1895.

1030. *New York Herald* (New York, New York). 10 November 1895. p 3.

1031. Romans 12:19.

1032. *St. Louis Republic* (St. Louis, Missouri). 22 November 1895.

1033. *Dallas Morning News* (Dallas, Texas). 18 December 1895.

1034. Carrigan. *Lynching Culture.* Appendix B.

1035. *Plain Dealer* (Cleveland, Ohio). 31 January 1896. Carrigan. *Forgotten Dead.* Appendix A.

1036. *Leavenworth Herald* (Leavenworth, Kansas). 29 February 1896.

1037. Find-A-Grave Memorial # 46166991.

1038. *Dallas Morning News* (Dallas, Texas). 19 March 1896.

1039. *Daily Journal and Journal Tribune* (Knoxville, Tennessee). 28 March 1896. p 8. Also see *The State* (Columbia, South Carolina). 28 March 1896.

1040. *Duluth News-Tribune* (Duluth, Minnesota). 4 May 1896.

1041. *Kalamazoo Gazette* (Kalamazoo, Michigan). 22 May 1896.

1042. *Dallas Morning News* (Dallas, Texas). 11 June 1896.

1043. *Dallas Morning News* (Dallas, Texas). 20 June 1896.

1044. *Dallas Morning News* (Dallas, Texas). 27 June 1896.

1045. *Freeman* (Indianapolis, Indiana). 11 July 1896.

1046. "Death Penalty Information Center". Espy File. 1608-2002. Accessed 8 August 2014.

1047. Mitchell. *30 Years of Lynching.* p 96.

1048. *Sioux City Journal* (Sioux City, Iowa). 22 August 1896. p 3. *Freeman* (Indianapolis, Indiana). 29 August 1896. p 4. *St. Louis Republic* (St. Louis, Missouri). 1 October 1896.

1049. *Sioux City Journal* (Sioux City, Iowa). 5 September 1896. p 1.

1050. Carrigan. *Forgotten Dead.* Appendix B.

1051. *Daily Journal and Journal and Tribune* (Knoxville, Tennessee). 28 November 1896. Also see Ancestry. Tree# 35848571. Person # 19145231665. *Dallas Morning News* (Dallas, Texas). 28 September 1896.

1052. *Omaha World Herald* (Omaha, Nebraska). 24 January 1897. Also see *Wheeling Register* (Wheeling, West Virginia). 24 January 1897. p 1.

1053. *Emporia Gazette* (Emporia, Kansas). 6 March 1897. Also see *Dallas Morning News* (Dallas, Texas). 6 March 1897.

1054. *Dallas Morning News* (Dallas, Texas). 3 April 1897.

1055. *Dallas Morning News* (Dallas, Texas). 29 April 1897.

1056. *Charlotte Observer* (Charlotte, North Carolina). 1 May 1897.

1057. Carrigan. *Forgotten Dead.* Appendix A.

1058. *Dallas Morning News* (Dallas, Texas). 16 May 1897. *Colorado Springs Gazette* (Colorado Springs, Colorado). 15 May 1897. p 1.

1059. *Worcester Daily Spy* (Worcester, Massachusetts). 24 May 1897.

1060. *Dallas Morning News* (Dallas, Texas). 6 May 1897.

1061. *Dallas Morning News* (Dallas, Texas). 11 June 1898.

1062. *Fort Worth Morning Star* (Fort Worth, Texas). 11 July 1897. Also see *Dallas Morning News* (Dallas, Texas). 10 July 1897.

1063. *New Mexican* (Santa Fe, New Mexico). 30 July 1897. Also see *The Denver Post* (Denver, Colorado). 30 July 1897.

1064. *St. Louis Republic* (St. Louis, Missouri). 8 August 1897. p 5.

1065. Find-A-Grave Memorial# 46700733.

1066. *Fort Worth Morning Register* (Fort Worth, Texas). 28 August 1897. p 2.

1067. *Austin Daily Statesman* (Austin, Texas). 28 August 1897. Also see *Omaha World Herald* (Omaha, Nebraska). 28 August 1897.

1068. *Daily Register Gazette* (Rockford, Illinois). 11 October 1897. Caldwell/DeLord. *Texas Lawmen: 1835–1899.* p 230.

1069. *Muskegon Chronicle* (Muskegon, Michigan). 18 November 1897. Mitchell. *The Strangest Fruit:* pp 156-157.

1070. *Dallas Morning News* (Dallas, Texas). 19 February 1898.

1071. Caldwell/DeLord. *Texas Lawmen: 1835–1899.* pp 48 - 50. Carrigan. *The Forgotten Dead.* Appendix A.

1072. Find-A-Grave Memorial # 52261381

1073. *St. Louis Republic* (St. Louis, Missouri). 28 May 1898.

1074. Caldwell/DeLord. *Texas Lawmen: 1835–1899.*p 61. Also see *Plain Dealer* (Cleveland, Ohio). 11 June 1898. p 3.

1075. *Dallas Morning News* (Dallas, Texas). 11 June 1898. p 4. *Births Deaths and Marriages from El Paso Newspapers.* Beard. p 403.

1076. *Dallas Morning News* (Dallas, Texas). 11 June 1898.

1077. *Dallas Morning News* (Dallas, Texas). 15 June 1898. p 10. *Dallas Morning News* (Dallas, Texas). 20 June 1898. p 4. *Births Deaths and Marriages from El Paso Newspapers.* Beard. p 68.

1078. *Morning Herald* (Lexington, Kentucky). 9 August 1898. p 8.

1079. *St. Louis Republic* (St. Louis, Missouri). 3 September 1898.

1080. *San Antonio Express News* (San Antonio, Texas). 8 October 1898.

1081. Find-A-Grave Memorial # 82131505

1082. *Age-Herald* (Birmingham, Alabama). 28 October 1898. p 2.

1083. *Anaconda Standard* (Anaconda, Montana). 6 February 1899. p 4. *Daily Illinois State Journal* (Springfield, Illinois). 19 November 1898. p 1.

1084. *St. Louis Republic* (St. Louis, Missouri). 3 December 1898. p 5.

1085. *San Antonio Express* (San Antonio, Texas). 14 January 1899. Also see *Augusta Chronicle* (Augusta, Georgia). 14 January 1899. *Dallas Morning News* (Dallas, Texas). 14 January 1899.

1086. *Bay City Times* (Bay City, Michigan). 4 June 1899. p 2.

1087. *Times Picayune* (New Orleans, Louisiana). 27 February 1899.

1088. *Age-Herald* (Birmingham, Alabama). 25 March 1899. p 5.

1089. *Age Herald* (Birmingham, Alabama). 1 April 1899. p 3.

1090. *Dallas Morning News* (Dallas, Texas). 29 April 1899. Also see *Cleveland Plain Dealer* (Cleveland, Ohio). 29 April 1899.

1091. *Dallas Morning News* (Dallas, Texas). 5 May 1899

1092. *New Haven Register* (New Haven, Connecticut). 10 July 1899. p 6.

1093. *Dallas Morning News* (Dallas, Texas). 29 May 1899.

1094. *Fort Worth Telegram* (Fort Worth, Texas). 9 December 1908. *Dallas Morning News* (Dallas, Texas). 21 October 1909.

1095. Ancestry. Tree# 16257323. Person # 359629155.

1096. *Dallas Morning News* (Dallas, Texas). 29 June 1899. p 1

1097. *Dallas Morning News* (Dallas, Texas). 6 July 1899.

1098. *Augusta Chronicle* (Augusta, Georgia). 26 July 1899. *Arkansas Gazette* (Little Rock, Arkansas). 15 July 1899.

1099. *Arkansas Gazette* (Little Rock, Arkansas). 15 July 1899. .

1100. *Dallas Morning News* (Dallas, Texas). 2 August 1899. p 6.

1101. *Fort Worth Morning Register* (Fort Worth, Texas). 26 July 1899. Also see *Augusta Chronicle (Augusta, Georgia).* 26 July 1899. *Charleston News and Courier* (Charleston, South Carolina). 26 July 1899. p 1.

1102. *Sedan Lance* (Sedan, Kansas). 3 August 1899. p 6.

1103. *San Antonio Express* (San Antonio, Texas). 28 October 1899.

1104. *Dallas Morning News* (Dallas, Texas). 28 October 1899. p 4.

1105. *Fort Worth Morning Register* (Fort Worth, Texas). 28 October 1899. p 2. Also see *Albuquerque Citizen* (Albuquerque, New Mexico). 27 October 1899. p 1.

1106. *Columbus Daily Enquirer* (Columbus, Georgia). 7 May 1899. p 2.

1107. *Fort Worth Morning Register* (Fort Worth, Texas). 28 October 1899. p 2. Also see *Evening News* (San Jose, California). 24 November 1899. p 1.

1108. *Fort Worth Morning Register* (Fort Worth, Texas). 28 October 1899. p 2.

1109. *San Antonio Express* (San Antonio, Texas). 11 November 1899. Also see Caldwell/DeLord. *Texas Lawmen: 1835–1899.* p 92.

1110. *San Antonio Express* (San Antonio, Texas). 28 October 1899. p 9.

1111. *Grand Forks Herald* (Grand Forks, North Dakota). 6 January 1900. p 1. Caldwell/DeLord. *Texas Lawmen: 1835–1899.* pp 347-348.

1112. *Arkansas Gazette* (Littlerock, Arkansas). 13 January 1900. p 5.

1113. *Age-Herald* (Birmingham, Alabama). 3 February 1900. p 3.

1114. Block Jr., W. T. "Cannonball Express". *Texas Escapes.* 19 June 2006.

1115. *Age-Herald* (Birmingham, Alabama). 12 February 1900. p 1.

1116. *Dallas Morning News* (Dallas, Texas). 10 March 1900.

1117. *Plain Dealer* (Cleveland, Ohio). 11 March 1900.

1118. Find-A-Grave Memorial# 84761488.

1119. *San Antonio Express* (San Antonio, Texas). 17 March 1900. p 4.

1120. *American Citizen* (Kansas City, Kansas). 25 March 1900. p 1. Also see *Dallas Morning News* (Dallas, Texas). 24 March 1900. *Honey Grove Signal* (Honey Grove, Texas). 23 March 1900.

1121. *Columbus Daily Enquirer* (Columbus, Georgia). 17 April 1900. p 5.

1122. *Columbus Daily Enquirer* (Columbus, Georgia). 17 April 1900.

1123. *Dallas Morning News* (Dallas, Texas). 19 June 1900.

1124. *Dallas Morning News* (Dallas, Texas). 9 July 1900. p 1.

1125. Ancestry. Tree# 32150187. Person # 18193582044.

1126. *Fort Worth Morning Register* (Fort Worth, Texas). 28 July 1900. p 3.

1127. *Age-Herald* (Birmingham, Alabama). 7 October 1900. p 8.

1128. *Idaho Statesman* (Boise, Idaho). November 1900. p 3.

1129. *Times Herald* (Corsicana, Texas). 13 March 1901.

1130. *Dallas Morning News* (Dallas, Texas). 15 March 1901.

1131. *Evening News* (San Jose, California). 18 June 1901. p 1. Also see Caldwell/DeLord. *Texas Lawmen: 1900–1940.* p 162.

1132. Mitchell. *30 Years of Lynching.* p 97.

1133. *Kansas City Star* (Kansas City, Missouri). 2 August 1901.

1134. *Sherman Daily Register* (Sherman, Texas). 17 August 1901. *Sherman Daily Register* (Sherman, Texas). 21 August 1901. *The Whitesboro News* (Whitesboro, Texas). 21 August 1901.

1135. Ancestry. Tree# 4905878. Person # 1056459794. *The American Citizen* (Kansas City, Kansas). 23 August 1901.

1136. Carrigan. *Forgotten Dead.* Appendix A.

1137. *Ibid.*

1138. *Pawtucket Times* (Pawtucket, Rhode Island). 2 October 1901. *Dallas Morning News* (Dallas, Texas). 1 October 1901. Carrigan. *Waco Times Herald* (Waco, Texas). 8 October 1901.

1139. *Omaha World Herald* (Omaha, Nebraska). 30 September 1901. Also see *Pawtucket Times* (Pawtucket, Rhode Island). 2 October 1901. Daily *People* (New York, New York). 3 October 1901. p 1. *Dallas Morning News* (Dallas, Texas). 3 October 1901. p 3.

1140. *Waco Times Herald* (Waco, Texas). October 1901. *The Waco Times Herald* (Waco, Texas). 8 October 1901.

1141. Find-A-Grave Memorial. # 34876282. Also see Cox, Mike. "Pearl". *Texas Escapes.* July 2003.

1142. *Daily Herald* (Biloxi, Mississippi). 27 October 1901.

1143. *Dallas Morning News* (Dallas, Texas). 26 October 1901. Also see Caldwell/DeLord. *Texas Lawmen: 1900–1940.* p 362.

1144. *Springfield Republican* (Springfield, Massachusetts). 30 December 1901. p 12. Also see *Dallas Morning News* (Dallas, Texas). 28 December 1901.

1145. *Fort Worth Morning Register* (Fort Worth, Texas). 11 January 1902. p 5.

1146. *Times Picayune* (New Orleans, Louisiana). 1 February 1902.

1147. *Dallas Morning News* (Dallas, Texas). 9 March 1902.

1148. *San Antonio Express* (San Antonio, Texas). 20 April 1902. p 9.

1149. Caldwell/DeLord. *Texas Lawmen: 1900–1940.* pp 342–343.

1150. *Philadelphia Enquirer* (Philadelphia, Pennsylvania). 23 May 1902. p 2.

1151. *Tiempo* (Las Cruces, New Mexico). 3 May 1902. Also see *Times-Picayune* (New Orleans, Louisiana). 22 April 1902.

1152. *Montgomery Advertiser* (Montgomery, Alabama). 16 August 1902. Also see *Dallas Morning News* (Dallas, Texas). 16 August 1902.

1153. *Montgomery Advertiser* (Montgomery, Alabama). 23 August 1902. p 3.

1154. *San Antonio Express* (San Antonio, Texas). 5 September 1902. p 3. Also see *Dallas Morning News* (Dallas, Texas). 5 September 1902. p 3.

1155. *Dallas Morning News* (Dallas, Texas). 12 September 1902.

1156. *San Antonio Express* (San Antonio, Texas). 20 September 1902. p 5.

1157. *Dallas Morning News* (Dallas, Texas). 22 September 1902.

1158. *Montgomery Advertiser* (Montgomery, Alabama). 5 October 1902. p 1.

1159. *Columbus Daily Enquirer* (Columbus, Ohio). 19 October 1902. p 12.

1160. Tise. *Texas County Sheriffs.* p 387.

1161. *Colorado Springs Gazette* (Colorado Springs, Colorado). 22 October 1902. p 1.

1162. *Dallas Morning News* (Dallas, Texas). 14 December 1902.

1163. *Fort Worth Star Telegram* (Fort Worth, Texas). 19 December 1902. Caldwell/DeLord. *Texas Lawmen: 1900–1940.* p 45. Also see *Austin Daily Statesman* (Austin, Texas). 4 December 1902.

1164. *Dallas Morning News* (Dallas, Texas). 15 January 1903.

1165. *Dallas Morning News* (Dallas, Texas). 4 April 1903.

1166. *Jackson Citizen* (Jackson, Michigan). 28 April 1903. p 2. Also see *Dallas Morning News* (Dallas, Texas). *27 April 1903.*

1167. *Dallas Morning News* (Dallas, Texas). 15 May 1903.

1168. *Dallas Morning News* (Dallas, Texas). 24 May 1903. Page 9.

1169. *Montgomery Advertiser* (Montgomery, Alabama). 30 May 1903.

1170. *Fort Worth Star Telegram* (Fort Worth, Texas). 31 May 1903. p 1.

1171. *Dallas Morning News* (Dallas, Texas). 1 July 1903.

1172. Caldwell/DeLord. *Texas Lawmen: 1900–1940.* p 33. Also see *Omaha World Herald* (Omaha, Nebraska). 24 July 1903.

1173. *Dallas Morning News* (Dallas, Texas). 1 August 1903. Also see *Dallas Morning News* (Dallas, Texas). 2 August 1903. Mitchell. *30 Years of Lynching.* p 97.

1174. *Idaho Statesman* (Boise, Idaho). 13 August 1903. Also see *Dallas Morning News* (Dallas, Texas). 13 August 1903. *Times Picayune* (New Orleans, Louisiana). 14 August 1903. *Montgomery Advertiser* (Montgomery, Alabama). 14 August 1903.

1175. Caldwell/DeLord. *Texas Lawmen: 1900–1940.* p 182. Also see *Ann Arbor Daily Times* (Ann Arbor, Michigan). 2 October 1903. Also see *The Times-Clarion* (Longview, Texas). 8 October 1903.

1176. *Fort Worth Star Telegram* (Fort Worth, Texas). 5 December 1903. p 5.

1177. *Fort Worth Star Telegram* (Fort Worth, Texas). 12 February 1904.

1178. *State* (Columbia, South Carolina). 22 March 1904.

1179. *Fort Worth Star Telegram* (Fort Worth, Texas). 23 February 1904.

1180. *Macon Telegraph* (Macon, Georgia). 26 April 1904.

1181. *Columbus Ledger* (Columbus, Ohio). 2 May 1904. p 7. *Fort Worth Star-Telegram* (Fort Worth, Texas). 30 April 1904. p 1.

1182. *Dallas Morning News* (Dallas, Texas). 29 May 1904. p 22.

1183. *Fort Worth Star Telegram* (Fort Worth, Texas). 16 June 1904. p 10. Also see *Dallas Morning News* (Dallas, Texas). 17 June 1904.

1184. Ancestry.com. *Texas Death Index, 1903–2000*. Provo, Utah: Ancestry.com Operations Inc., 2006.

1185. *Montgomery Advertiser* (Montgomery, Alabama). 30 July 1904.

1186. *Trenton Evening Times* (Trenton, New Jersey). 30 July 1904.

1187. *Bellingham Herald* (Bellingham, Washington). 31 August 1904.

1188. Carrigan. *Lynching Culture.* Appendix B. *Waco Times Herald* (Waco, Texas). 30 November 1904.

1189. Bluntzer had been a stop on the San Antonio-Brownsville stagecoach line. The place had been known as Santa Margarita Crossing before Nicholas Bluntzer moved into the area about 1860.

1190. *Dallas Morning News* (Dallas, Texas). 24 December 1904.

1191. Carrigan. *Lynching Culture.* Appendix B. *Waco Times Herald* (Waco, Texas). 28 December 1904.

1192. Caldwell/DeLord. *Texas Lawmen: 1835–1899.* pp 214-215.

1193. Carrigan. *Forgotten Dead.* Appendix A. *Montgomery Advertiser* (Montgomery, Alabama). 17 February 1905. p 3. *Oregonian* (Portland, Oregon). 18 February 1905. p 15.

1194. *Daily Recorder* (Olympia, Washington). 17 February 1905. p 1.

1195. Ancestry. Tree# 8243486. Person # 971369195.

1196. *San Antonio Express* (San Antonio, Texas). 18 February 1905. p 4.

1197. Find-A-Grave Memorial # 65036847

1198. *Columbus Daily Enquirer* (Columbus, Georgia). 23 March 1905.

1199. *Fort Worth Star Telegram* (Fort Worth, Texas). 30 March 1905. Also see *Dallas Morning News* (Dallas, Texas). 14 March 1905.

1200. *August Chronicle* (Augusta, Georgia). 28 April 1905. p 3.

1201. *Times Picayune* (New Orleans, Louisiana). 15 March 1905.

1202. Find-A-Grave Memorial #22971492. *Fort Worth Star Telegram* (Fort Worth, Texas). 12 May 1905. Also see *Dallas Morning News* (Dallas, Texas). 13 May 1905.

1203. *Dallas Morning News* (Dallas, Texas). 20 May 1905.

1204. *Fort Worth Star Telegram* (Fort Worth, Texas). 8 July 1905. p 6. Also *Dallas Morning News* (Dallas, Texas). 8 July 1905.

1205. *Fort Worth Star Telegram* (Fort Worth, Texas). 20 July 1905.

1206. *Springfield Republican* (Springfield, Massachusetts). 30 July 1905. p 1.

1207. *Fort Worth Star Telegram* (Fort Worth, Texas). 10 August 1905. p 4. Also see *Waco Weekly Tribune* (Waco, Texas). 12 August 1905. *Fort Worth Star Telegram* (Fort Worth, Texas). 26 July 1905. *Plain Dealer* (Cleveland, Ohio). 15 July 1905. *Dallas Morning News* (Dallas, Texas). 9 August 1905. p 2.

1208. *Galveston Daily News* (Galveston, Texas). 12 August 1905. p 1.

1209. *Dallas Morning News* (Dallas, Texas). 2 September 1905. Also see *San Antonio Express* (San Antonio, Texas). 2 September 1905.

1210. *Grand Rapids Press* (Grand Rapids, Michigan). 8 September 1905. p 2.

1211. *Oregonian* (Portland, Oregon). 12 November 1905.

1212. *Dallas Morning News* (Dallas, Texas). 9 December 1905.

1213. *Fort Worth Star Telegram* (Fort Worth, Texas). 23 November 1905. *The Sunday Light* (San Antonio). 12 March 1905. *Dallas Morning News* (Dallas, Texas). 23 December 1905.

1214. *St. Albans Daily Messenger* (St. Albans, Vermont). 10 January 1906. p 1. Also see *Fort Worth Star Telegram* (Fort Worth, Texas). 10 January 1906. p 1.

1215. Carrigan. *Lynching Culture.* Appendix B. Also see *Waco Times Herald* (Waco, Texas). 19 March 1906.

1216. *Fort Worth Star-Telegram* (Fort Worth, Texas). 30 March 1906. Also see *San Antonio Express News* (San Antonio, Texas). 31 March 1906. *Charlotte Observer* (Charlotte, North Carolina). 31 March 1906.

1217. Ancestry. Tree #38210535. Person #19200775569.

1218. *Duluth News Tribune* (Duluth, Minnesota). 31 March 1906. p 1.

1219. *Williamson County Sun* (Georgetown, Texas). 5 April 1906.

1220. Ancestry. Tree #38210535. Person #19200775569.

1221. *Waco Semi-Weekly Tribune* (Waco, Texas). 28 April 1906. *Beaumont Enterprise* (Beaumont, Texas). 26 April 1906.

1222. *Daily Illinois State Register* (Springfield, Illinois). 31 December 1906.

1223. The 6th Amendment Right to Trial by Jury Clause is the Bill of Rights' second mention of the right to trial by jury. There are three in total. The other two are in the 5th and 7th Amendments. In addition to this, the original Constitution itself mentions the right to trial by jury in Article 3, Section 2. Obviously the Founding Fathers considered due process, and being tried by a jury of one's peers, to be an essential element of fair governance.

1224. *Fort Worth Star Telegram* (Fort Worth, Texas). 30 June 1906.

1225. *Fort Worth Star Telegram* (Fort Worth, Texas). 3 June 1906.

1226. *Fort Worth Star Telegram* (Fort Worth, Texas). 12 July 1906. p 1. Also see *Fort Worth Star Telegram* (Fort Worth, Texas). 7 July 1906.

1227. *Dallas Morning News* (Dallas, Texas). 21 July 1906.

1228. *Waco Weekly Tribune* (Waco, Texas). 16 September 1906. *Dallas Morning News* (Dallas, Texas). 16 September 1906. Also see *Boston Herald* (Boston, Massachusetts). 17 September 1906.

1229. *Fort Worth Star Telegram* (Fort Worth, Texas). 10 October 1906. p 10. *Tucson Daily Citizen* (Tucson, Arizona). 10 October 1906. p 1. Mitchell. *The Strangest Fruit.* p 237.

1230. During the administration of President Chester A. Arthur, Senator George F. Edmunds of Vermont took up the cause of polygamy in Washington. The Edmunds Act of 1882 made "unlawful cohabitation" illegal, thus removing the need to prove that actual marriages had occurred. More than 1,300 men were imprisoned under the terms of this measure. The act did declare births in Mormon polygamous marriages prior to 1 January 1883, to be legitimate.

1231. *Daily Illinois State Register* (Springfield, Illinois). 31 December 1906. The Edmunds Act, also known as the Edmunds Anti-Polygamy Act of 1882, is a United States federal statute, signed into law on 23 March 1882, which declared polygamy a felony. The act is named for U.S. Senator George Edmunds of Vermont. The Edmunds Act also prohibited "bigamous" or "unlawful cohabitation" (a misdemeanor), thus removing the need to prove that actual marriages had occurred. Also see *Augusta Chronicle (Augusta, Georgia).* 27 October 1906.

1232. *Oregonian* (Portland, Oregon). 22 November 1906.

1233. *Evening News* (San Jose, California). 30 November 1906. *Dallas Morning News* (Dallas, Texas). 1 December 1906.

1234. *Dallas Morning News* (Dallas, Texas). 1 December 1906.

1235. *Fort Worth Star Telegram* (Fort Worth, Texas). 4 January 1907. p 1.

1236. *Fort Worth Star Telegram* (Fort Worth, Texas). 17 January 1907. p 1. Also see *Dallas Morning News* (Dallas, Texas). 2 February 1907.

1237. *Fort Worth Star Telegram* (Fort Worth, Texas). 15 February 1907.

1238. *Fort Worth Star-Telegram* (Fort Worth, Texas). 2 April 1907. Also see *Charleston News and Courier* (Charleston, South Carolina). 3 April 1907. p 5.

1239. *Fort Worth Star Telegram* (Fort Worth, Texas). 1 May 1907. p 2.

1240. *Fort Worth Star-Telegram* (Fort Worth, Texas). 28 June 1907. Also see *Fort Worth Star-Telegram* (Fort Worth, Texas). 28 June 1908.

1241. *August Chronicle* (Augusta, Georgia). 27 April 1907. p 1.

1242. *Lexington Herald* (Lexington, Kentucky). 15 July 1907.

1243. *Augusta Chronicle* (Augusta, Georgia). 7 August 1907. p 10.

1244. *Duluth News-Tribune* (Duluth, Minnesota). 5 November 1907. Also see *Fort Worth Star Telegram* (Fort Worth, Texas). 5 November 1907.

1245. *Fort Worth Star Telegram* (Fort Worth, Texas). 8 November 1907. p 4.

1246. *Macon Telegraph* (Macon, Georgia). 27 December 1907. p 3.

1247. *Duluth News-Tribune* (Duluth, Minnesota). 29 February 1908. p 1.

1248. *Fort Worth Star Telegram* (Fort Worth, Texas). 9 March 1908. *Oregonian* (Portland, Oregon). 19 March 1908. p 4.

1249. *Montgomery Advertiser* (Montgomery, Alabama). 25 March 1908. p 2.

1250. *Ibid.*

1251. *Fort Worth Star Telegram* (Fort Worth, Texas). 27 March 1908. *Dallas Morning News* (Dallas, Texas). 28 March 1908.

1252. *Fort Worth Star Telegram* (Fort Worth, Texas). 10 April 1908. p 4.

1253. *State* (Columbia, South Carolina). 20 April 1908. p 1.

1254. *Fort Worth Star Telegram* (Fort Worth, Texas). 7 May 1908. *Dallas Morning News* (Dallas, Texas). 7 May 1908. p 1.

1255. *Wichita Daily Times* (Wichita, Texas). 7 April 1908.

1256. *Dallas Morning News* (Dallas, Texas). 23 May 1908.

1257. Find-A-Grave Memorial # 27560941

1258. *Montgomery Advertiser* (Montgomery, Alabama). 21 June 1908. *Dallas Morning News* (Dallas, Texas). 21 June 1908.

1259. *Plaindealer* (Topeka, Kansas). 26 June 1908. p 4. Also see *Repository* (Canton, Ohio). 23 June 1908. p 10. *Jonesboro Weekly Sun* (Jonesboro, Arkansas.) 24 June 1908. p 2. *Dallas Morning News* (Dallas, Texas). 23 June 1908. p 2.

1260. *Fort Worth Star-Telegram* (Fort Worth, Texas). 2 April 1907. Also see *Charleston News and Courier* (Charleston, South Carolina). 3 April 1907. p 5.

1261. *Fort Worth Star Telegram* (Fort Worth, Texas). 3 July 1908. p 1.

1262. *Fort Worth Star-Telegram* (Fort Worth, Texas). 28 June 1907. Also see *Fort Worth Star-Telegram* (Fort Worth, Texas). 28 June 1908.

1263. *Fort Worth Star Telegram* (Fort Worth, Texas). 3 July 1908. p 9.

1264. *Columbus Daily Enquirer* (Columbus, Georgia). 29 July 1908. p 1.

1265. *Times Picayune* (New Orleans, Louisiana). 1 August 1908. p 8.

1266. *Fort Worth Star-Telegram* (Fort Worth, Texas). 3 August 1908. p 7.

1267. *Fort Worth Star-Telegram* (Fort Worth, Texas). 3 August 1908. p 2.

1268. Mitchell. *30 Years of Lynching.* p 98.

1269. *Trenton Evening Times* (Trenton, New Jersey). 14 September 1908. p 12.

1270. *Grand Forks Daily Herald* (Grand Forks, Nebraska). 16 September 1908. Mitchell. *30 Years of Lynching.* p 98.

1271. *Seattle Daily Times* (Seattle, Washington). 22 September 1908. p 12

1272. *Aberdeen Daily News* (Aberdeen, South Dakota). 7 October 1908.

1273. Carrigan. *Lynching Culture.* Appendix A. Also see *State* (Columbia, South Carolina). 9 February 1908. Also see *Duluth News-Tribune* (Duluth, Minnesota). 9 February 1909. p 1.

1274. *Fort Worth Star-Telegram* (Fort Worth, Texas). 3 April 1908. p 12.

1275. *Fort Worth Record* (Fort Worth, Texas). 10 February 1909.

1276. *Baltimore American* (Baltimore, Maryland). 16 July 1908. Also see *Dallas Morning News* (Dallas, Texas). 11 September 1908.

1277. *Dallas Morning News* (Dallas, Texas). 13 February 1909.

1278. Ancestry. Tree #77223297. Person #44372797166.

1279. *Dallas Morning News* (Dallas, Texas). 26 February 1909.

1280. *Augusta Chronicle* (Augusta, Georgia). 8 March 1909.

1281. *Fort Worth Star Telegram* (Fort Worth, Texas). 30 March 1909. p 3.

1282. Caldwell, Clifford R. and DeLord, Ron. 2012. *Texas Lawmen: 1900–1940.* p 185.

1283. *Fort Worth Star Telegram* (Fort Worth, Texas). 26 April 1909. p 2.

1284. *Evansville Courier and Press* (Evansville, Indiana). 1 May 1909. p 1. Also see Caldwell/DeLord. *Texas Lawmen: 1900–1940.* p 185. Also see *Dallas Morning News* (Dallas, Texas). 1 May 1909.

1285. *Fort Worth Record* (Fort Worth, Texas). 2 May 1909.

1286. *Fort Worth Star Telegram* (Fort Worth, Texas). 14 May 1909.

1287. *Montgomery Advertiser* (Montgomery, Alabama). 1 June 1909. p 1.

1288. *Idaho Statesman* (Boise, Idaho). 12 June 1909.

1289. *Times Picayune* (New Orleans, Louisiana). 4 September 1909.

1290. Mitchell. *30 Years of Lynching.* p 98.

1291. Caldwell/DeLord. *Texas Lawmen: 1900–1940.* p 53. Also see *Dallas Morning News* (Dallas, Texas). 18 September 1909. p 2. *Times Picayune* (New Orleans, Louisiana). 24 September 1909.

1292. *Macon Telegraph* (Macon, Georgia). 18 September 1909. Also see *Fort Worth Star Telegram* (Fort Worth, Texas). 19 September 1909. p 1.

1293. *Dallas Morning News* (Dallas, Texas). 10 June 1909. Also see *Daily Texas* (Dallas, Texas).1 October 1909. Also see *Paris Morning News* (Paris, Texas). 1 October 1909.

1294. *Dallas Morning News* (Dallas, Texas). 20 July 1909. *Dallas Morning News* (Dallas, Texas). 2 October 1909.

1295. *Hobart Daily Republican* (Hobart, Oklahoma). 22 October 1909

1296. *Dallas Morning News* (Dallas, Texas). 23 October 1909.

1297. *Dallas Morning News* (Dallas, Texas). 10 June 1909.

1298. *Fort Worth Star Telegram* (Fort Worth, Texas). 21 December 1909. p 4. Also see *Daily State* (Baton Rouge, Louisiana). 23 December 1909. Also see *Dallas Morning News* (Dallas, Texas). 24 September 1909.

1299. *Montgomery Advertiser* (Montgomery, Alabama). 25 January 1910.

1300. *Albuquerque Journal* (Albuquerque, New Mexico). 27 February 1910. p 1.

1301. *Grand Forks Herald* (Grand Forks, North Dakota). 2 May 1920. p 22.

1302. *Olympia Daily Record* (Olympia, Washington). 5 April 1910. p 1.

1303. *Dallas Morning News* (Dallas, Texas). 14 May 1910. p 16. *Beaumont Enterprise* (Beaumont, Texas). 5 April 1910. *Beaumont Enterprise* (Beaumont, Texas). 11 May 1910.

1304. *Fort Worth Star Telegram* (Fort Worth, Texas). 22 March 1910.

1305. *Fort Worth Star Telegram* (Fort Worth, Texas). 3 June 1910. p 1.

1306. *Duluth News Tribune* (Duluth, Minnesota). 7 June 1910. p 2.

1307. *Beaumont Journal* (Beaumont, Texas). 9 June 1910.

1308. *Times Picayune* (New Orleans, Louisiana). 21 June 1910. p 9.

1309. *Idaho Statesman* (Boise, Idaho). 6 July 1910.

1310. *Fort Worth Star Telegram* (Fort Worth, Texas). 9 July 1910.

1311. *Fort Worth Star Telegram* (Fort Worth, Texas). 7 July 1910. Also see *Dallas Morning News* (Dallas, Texas). 2 January 1910. *Dallas Morning News* (Dallas, Texas). 9 July 1909.

1312. The Townsend Memorial Library. University of Mary Hardin-Baylor.

1313. *Albuquerque Morning Journal* (Albuquerque, New Mexico). 23 July 1910. Find-A-Grave Memorial #76874552. *Montgomery Advocate* (Montgomery, Alabama). 23 July 1910.

1314. *Albuquerque Journal* (Albuquerque, New Mexico). 1 August 1910. p 1.

1315. *Fort Worth Star Telegram* (Fort Worth, Texas). 4 June 1911. p 12.

1316. Rucker, Walter C. and Upton, James N. 2006. *Encyclopedia of American Race Riots*. Westport, Connecticut: Greenwood Publishing Group, Inc.

1317. *Charlotte Observer* (Charlotte, North Carolina). 16 November 1910.

1318. *Daily Oklahoman* (Oklahoma City, Oklahoma). 26 March 1911. p 10.

1319. Carrigan. *Forgotten Dead*. Appendix A. Also see *Dallas Morning News* (Dallas, Texas). 30 May 1911. Also see *Patriot* (Harrisburg, Pennsylvania). 31 May 1910. *Idaho Statesman* (Boise, Idaho). 30 May 1910.

1320. *Fort Worth Star Telegram* (Fort Worth, Texas). 1 March 1912. p 5. Also see *Fort Worth Star Telegram* (Fort Worth, Texas). 28 February 1912. Also see *Tampa Tribune* (Tampa, Florida). 25 June 1911. *Fort Worth Star Telegram* (Fort Worth, Texas). 14 November 1911. p 1. *Anaconda Standard* (Anaconda, Montana). 3 March 1912. p 10.

1321. *Cleburne Morning Review* (Cleburne, Texas). 12 August 1911.

1322. *State* (Columbus, South Carolina). 30 October 1911. p 1.

1323. *Anaconda Standard* (Anaconda, Montana). 7 November 1911. p 1.

1324. "Death Penalty Information Center". Espy File. 1608-2002. Accessed 8 August 2014.

1325. *Macon Telegraph* (Macon, Georgia). 16 February 1912. p 6. Segrave. *Lynchings of Women.* pp 118-119.

1326. *Dallas Morning News* (Dallas, Texas). 17 February 1912.

1327. *Dallas Morning News* (Dallas, Texas). 20 February 1912. p 11. *New Orleans Item* (New Orleans, Louisiana). 20 February 1912. p 1.

1328. *Dallas Morning News* (Dallas, Texas). 12 March 1912.

1329. Ancestry. Tree# 55152308. Person # 13774236767. Also see *Dallas Morning News* (Dallas, Texas). 15 March 1912.

1330. *Fort Worth Star Telegram* (Fort Worth, Texas). 28 March 1912. p 11. *Cleveland Gazette* (Cleveland, Ohio). 20 July 1912.

1331. *Fort Worth Star-Telegram* (Fort Worth, Texas). 29 March 1912. p 1.

1332. *Fort Worth Star Telegram* (Fort Worth, Texas). 12 April 1912. p 9.

1333. *Dallas Morning News* (Dallas, Texas). 15 April 1912. p 4. *Fort Worth Star Telegram* (Fort Worth, Texas). 7 April 1912. p 9.

1334. *Greensboro Daily News* (Greensboro, North Carolina). 5 May 1912. *Cleveland Gazette* (Cleveland, Ohio). 25 May 1912.

1335. *Tulsa World* (Tulsa, Oklahoma). 26 May 1912. p 1.

1336. *Times Picayune* (New Orleans, Louisiana). 27 May 1912.

1337. *Cleburne Morning Review* (Cleburne, Texas). 14 July 1912. Also see *Daily Oklahoman* (Oklahoma City, Oklahoma). 13 July 1912.

1338. *Fort Worth Star Telegram* (Fort Worth, Texas). 8 August 1912. Also see Caldwell/DeLord. *Texas Lawmen: 1900–1940*. p 165. Also see *Fort Worth Star Telegram* (Fort Worth, Texas). 9 August 1912.

1339. *Cleburne Morning News* (Cleburne, Texas). 17 October 1912. p 2.

1340. *Fort Worth Star Telegram* (Fort Worth, Texas). 11 November 1912. p 12. Also see *Evening News* (San Jose, California). 23 November 1912.

1341. *Dallas Morning News* (Dallas, Texas). 10 January 1913. Also see *Fort Worth Star Telegram* (Fort Worth, Texas). 10 January 1913.

1342. *Tampa Tribune* (Tampa, Florida). 19 January 1913. Also see *Daily People* (New York, New York). 19 January 1913. Find-A-Grave Memorial # 22976780.

1343. *Richmond Times Dispatch* (Richmond, Virginia). 24 January 1913. Also see *Tulsa World* (Tulsa, Oklahoma). 24 January 1913.

1344. *Fort Worth Star Telegram* (Fort Worth, Texas). 24 January 1913.

1345. *Dallas Morning News* (Dallas, Texas). 26 February 1913. p 16. *Montgomery Advertiser* (Montgomery, Alabama). 26 February 1913. p 10.

1346. *Fort Worth Star Telegram* (Fort Worth, Texas). 18 March 1913. Also see *Dallas Morning News* (Dallas, Texas). 22 April 1913.

1347. "Death Penalty Information Center". Espy File. 1608-2002. Accessed 8 August 2014.

1348. Caldwell/DeLord. *Texas Lawmen: 1900–1940*. p 274. *The Daily Times Herald (Dallas, Texas)*. 18 May 1913.

1349. *Cleburne Morning Review* (Cleburne, Texas). 4 February 1913.

1350. *Dallas Morning News* (Dallas, Texas). 31 May 1913.

1351. *Times Picayune* (New Orleans, Louisiana). 6 June 1913. Also see *Tulsa World* (Tulsa, Oklahoma). 6 June 1913.

1352. *Victoria Advocate* (Victoria, Texas). 28 June 1913. Also see *Dallas Morning News* (Dallas, Texas). 29 June 1913.

1353. John 11:25.

1354. *Dallas Morning News* (Dallas, Texas). 2 August 1913. p 18.

1355. *Dallas Morning News* (Dallas, Texas). 8 August 1913.

1356. *Duluth News Tribune* (Duluth, Minnesota). 23 September 1913. Also see Caldwell/DeLord. *Texas Lawmen: 1900–1940*. p 312.

1357. *Fort Worth Star Telegram* (Fort Worth, Texas). 19 December 1913. p 7.

1358. *Idaho Statesman* (Boise, Idaho). 4 January 1914. p 7. *Tampa Tribune* (Tampa, Florida). 4 January 1914. p 27.

1359. *Fort Worth Star Telegram* (Fort Worth, Texas). 8 March 1914. Also see Caldwell/DeLord. *Texas Lawmen: 1900–1940*. p 139. *Dallas Morning News* (Dallas, Texas). 26 July 1913.

1360. *San Diego Union* (San Diego, California). 13 March 1914. p 3. *Fort Worth Star Telegram* (Fort Worth, Texas). 13 March 1914. p 9. *Dallas Morning News* (Dallas, Texas). 13 March 1914. p 8.

1361. *Plain Dealer* (Cleveland, Ohio). 12 May 1914. p 7. Also see *Fort Worth Star Telegram* (Fort Worth, Texas). 17 January 1914.

1362. *Fort Worth Star Telegram* (Fort Worth, Texas). 6 June 1914. p 1.

1363. *La Prensa* (San Antonio, Texas). 20 August 1914. p 5. *Fort Worth Star Telegram* (Fort Worth, Texas). 1 April 1914. p 9. *Fort Worth Star Telegram* (Fort Worth, Texas). 8 April 1914. p 3. *Fort Worth Star Telegram* (Fort Worth, Texas). 29 April 1914. p 5. *Fort Worth Star Telegram* (Fort Worth, Texas). 6 May 1914. p 2.

1364. *Fort Worth Star Telegram* (Fort Worth, Texas). 14 October 1914. p 1.

1365. *Cleburne Morning Review* (Cleburne, Texas). 16 December 1914.

1366. *Grand Forks Daily Herald* (Grand Forks, North Dakota). 24 December 1914.

1367. Carrigan. *Forgotten Dead.* Appendix B.

1368. Caldwell/DeLord. *Texas Lawmen: 1900–1940.* p 252. Also see *Augusta Chronicle* (Augusta, Georgia). 30 December 1914.

1369. *Dallas Morning News* (Dallas, Texas). 20 February 1915.

1370. *Dallas Morning News* (Dallas, Texas). 27 February 1915. p 3.

1371. *Ibid.*

1372. *Oregonian* (Portland, Oregon). 6 March 1915. p 4. Similar incidents of this nature continue. Humberto Leal, a Mexican citizen who was convicted of raping and killing a sixteen-year old girl was executed in Texas on 7 July 2011. Edgar Tamayo, a Mexican national, was executed on 22 January 2014, for the 1994 shooting death of a Houston police officer. In spite of the protests, in virtually every case the condemned man's execution goes forward as planned.

1373. *Dallas Morning News* (Dallas, Texas). 5 March 1915. p 10. *Dallas Morning News* (Dallas, Texas). 10 April 1915. p 15.

1374. *Dallas Morning News* (Dallas, Texas). 17 April 1915. p 6.

1375. *Dallas Morning News* (Dallas, Texas). 18 April 1915. p 10.

1376. Find-A-Grave Memorial # 7769522

1377. *Dallas Morning News* (Dallas, Texas). 10 May 1915. Also see *Fort Worth Star Telegram* (Fort Worth, Texas). 10 May 1915.

1378. *Tulsa World* (Tulsa, Oklahoma). 3 July 1915. p 3.

1379. Carrigan. *Forgotten Dead.* Appendix B. Also see *Cleburne Morning News* (Cleburne, Texas). 11 July 1915. *San Jose Mercury News* (San Jose, California). 9 July 1915. p 15.

1380. Carrigan. *Forgotten Dead.* Appendix A.

1381. *Dallas Morning News* (Dallas, Texas). 30 July 1915.

1382. *Temple Daily Telegraph* (Temple, Texas). 31 July 1915. Also see *Fort Worth Record* (Fort Worth, Texas). 31 July 1915. Also see Wilson, Carol O'Keefe. 2014. *In the Governor's Shadow, The True Story of Ma and Pa Ferguson.* Denton, Texas: University of North Texas Press. pp 62-63.

1383. Carrigan. *Forgotten Dead.* Appendix A.

1384. *Jonesboro Evening Sun* (Jonesboro, Arkansas). 7 August 1915. p 4.

1385. *Dallas Morning News* (Dallas, Texas). 8 August 1915. *Montgomery Advertiser* (Montgomery, Alabama). 9 August 1915. p 1. Carrigan. *Forgotten Dead.* Appendix A .

1386. *Tulsa World* (Tulsa, Oklahoma). 13 August 1915. pp 1-3. Carrigan. *Forgotten Dead.* Appendix B.

1387. Carrigan. *Forgotten Dead.* Appendix A. Also see *Fort Worth Star Telegram* (Fort Worth, Texas). 12 August 1915.

1388. Carrigan. *Forgotten Dead.* Appendix B. *Fort Worth Star Telegram* (Fort Worth, Texas). 13 August 1915. *Times-Picayune* (New Orleans, Louisiana). 13 August 1915.

1389. Carrigan. *Forgotten Dead.* Appendix B. Also see *Columbus Ledger* (Columbus, Ohio). 13 August 1915. *Evening Star* (Washington, DC). 13 August 1915.

1390. Carrigan. *Forgotten Dead.* Appendix B.

1391. *Albuquerque Journal* (Albuquerque, New Mexico). 19 August 1915. Carrigan. *Forgotten Dead.* Appendix A.

1392. Carrigan. *Forgotten Dead.* Appendix A.

1393. Carrigan. *Forgotten Dead.* Appendix B

1394. *Ibid.*

1395. Caldwell/DeLord. *Texas Lawmen: 1900–1940.* p 194. Also see *Fort Worth Star Telegram* (Fort Worth, Texas). 30 August 1915. p 2.

1396. Carrigan. *Forgotten Dead.* Appendix B.

1397. Carrigan. *Forgotten Dead.* Appendix A.

1398. *Ibid.* Also see *Prensa* (San Antonio, Texas). 17 September 1915. *Boston Herald* (Boston, Massachusetts). 25 September 1915. p 2.

1399. Carrigan. *Forgotten Dead.* Appendix A.

1400. *Ibid.* Also see *Boston Journal* (Boston, Massachusetts). 4 September 1915. p 5.

1401. Carrigan. *Forgotten Dead.* Appendix B. Also see *Prensa* (San Antonio, Texas). 14 September 1915.

1402. Carrigan. *Forgotten Dead.* Appendix A. Also see *Dallas Morning News* (Dallas, Texas). 16 September 1915. *Augusta Chronicle* (Augusta, Georgia). 15 September 1915. p 2.

1403. Carrigan. *Forgotten Dead.* Appendix A. Also see *Dallas Morning News* (Dallas, Texas). 16 September 1915.

1404. Carrigan. *Forgotten Dead.* Appendix A.

1405. Johnson, Benjamin Heber Dr. 2005. *Revolution in Texas: How a Forgotten Rebellion And Its Bloody Suppression Turned Mexicans Into Americans.* Yale University Press. p 117. Also see Ancestry. Tree# 51413331. Person # 13207725767.

1406. Carrigan. *Forgotten Dead.* Appendix A. Also see *Regidor* (San Antonio, Texas). 1 September 1915.

1407. *Fort Worth Star-Telegram* (Fort Worth, Texas). 21 September 1915. p 1.

1408. Carrigan. *Forgotten Dead.* Appendix A.

1409. Carrigan. *Forgotten Dead.* Appendix B.

1410. Carrigan. *Forgotten Dead.* Appendix A.

1411. *Oregonian* (Portland, Oregon). 20 October 1915. p 5. Carrigan. *Forgotten Dead.* Appendix B.

1412. Carrigan. *Forgotten Dead.* Appendix A.

1413. Carrigan. *Forgotten Dead.* Appendix B.

1414. *Times-Picayune* (New Orleans, Louisiana). 11 November 1915. p 3.

1415. *Fort Worth Star Telegram* (Fort Worth, Texas). 26 November 1915. p 1. Also see *Evening Tribune* (San Diego, California). 27 November 1915.

1416. *Dallas Morning News* (Dallas, Texas). 7 January 1916. p 4.

1417. Ancestry. Tree# 24320824. Person # 1506179457.

1418. *Tulsa World* (Tulsa, Oklahoma). 25 January 1916. p 1.

1419. *Dallas Morning News* (Dallas, Texas). 2 February 1916. Caldwell/DeLord. *Texas Lawmen: 1900–1940.* p 175.

1420. *Fort Worth Star Telegram* (Fort Worth, Texas). 7 February 1916. p 1.

1421. *Ibid.*

1422. *Fort Worth Star Telegram* (Fort Worth, Texas). 12 March 1916. p 9.

1423. *Fort Worth Star Telegram* (Fort Worth, Texas). 19 March 1916. p 5.

1424. *Anaconda Standard* (Anaconda, Montana). 10 April 1916. p 1.

1425. *Duluth News Tribune* (Duluth, Minnesota). 30 April 1916. p 1.

1426. *Cleburne Morning Review* (Cleburne, Texas). 5 May 1916.

1427. Glasrud, Bruce A. and Smallwood, James. 2007. *The African American Experience in Texas: an Anthology.* Lubbock: Texas Tech University Press.

1428. *Macon Telegraph* (Macon, Georgia). 20 May 1916. p 1.

1429. *Jackson Citizen Patriot* (Jackson, Michigan). 23 May 1916. Also see *Dallas Morning News* (Dallas, Texas).12 May 1916. p 3. Carrigan. *Forgotten Dead.* Appendix A.

1430. *Olympia Daily Record* (Olympia, Washington). 20 June 1916. Carrigan. *Forgotten Dead.* Appendix A.

1431. *Fort Worth Star Telegram* (Fort Worth, Texas). 7 August 1916. Also see Caldwell/DeLord. *Texas Lawmen: 1900–1940.* p 33. Also see City-Data. Accessed 17 August 2014.

1432. *Oregonian* (Portland, Oregon). 21 August 1916. p 5. Also see *Duluth News-Tribune* (Duluth, Minnesota). 20 August 1916.

1433. *Fort Worth Star Telegram* (Fort Worth, Texas). 5 October 1916. p 3.

1434. *Fort Worth Star Telegram* (Fort Worth, Texas). 13 August 1916.

1435. *Dallas Morning News* (Dallas, Texas). 26 August 1916. *Fort Worth Star Telegram* (Fort Worth, Texas). 27 October 1916. p 7.

1436. *New Orleans Item* (New Orleans, Louisiana). 6 November 1916.

1437. *Fort Worth Star Telegram* (Fort Worth, Texas). 29 November 1916. p 1.

1438. *Fort Worth Star Telegram* (Fort Worth, Texas). 8 June 1917.

1439. *Dallas Morning News* (Dallas, Texas). 23 June 1917.

1440. *Waco Semi-Weekly Tribune* (Waco, Texas). 17 July 1917.

1441. *Dallas Morning News* (Dallas, Texas). 25 June 1917.

1442. *Daily Register Gazette* (Rockford, Illinois). 25 June 1917.

1443. *Wilkes Barre Times Leader* (Wilkes Barre, Pennsylvania). 25 June 1917. p 11.

1444. *New Orleans Item* (New Orleans, Louisiana). 3 July 1917. p 7.

1445. *Montgomery Advertiser* (Montgomery, Alabama). 30 July 1917. p 5.

1446. *Tulsa World* (Tulsa, Oklahoma). 31 July 1917. p 5.

1447. *Charlotte Observer* (Charlotte, North Carolina). 4 September 1917.

1448. *Macon Telegraph* (Macon, Georgia). 23 August 1917.

1449. "Death Penalty Information Center". Espy File. 1608-2002. Accessed 8 August 2014.

1450. Caldwell/DeLord. *Texas Lawmen: 1900–1940*.pp 201-203

1451. Mitchell. *30 Years of Lynching*. p 99. "Death Penalty Information Center". Espy File. 1608-2002. Accessed 8 August 2014.

1452. Ancestry. *Texas Death Index, 1903–2000*. Provo, Utah: 2006. Original data: Texas Department of Health. *Texas Death Indexes, 1903–2000*. Austin, Texas: Texas Department of Health, State Vital Statistics Unit.

1453. *Times Picayune* (New Orleans, Louisiana). 22 September 1917.

1454. Caldwell, Clifford R. 2012. *Fort McKavett, and Tales of Menard County*. Mountain Home, Texas: Privately Published. pp 130-133. Also see *Miami District Daily News* (Miami, Oklahoma). p 1.

1455. Orozco, Cynthia E. 2014. "Porvenir Massacre." *Handbook of Texas Online*

1456. Albarado, Evaristo. *El-Porvenir Ranch "The Truth" of 1918*. 23 April 2009.

1457. *Fort Wayne Sentinel* (Fort Wayne, Indiana). 5 April 1918. p 9.

1458. Carrigan. *Forgotten Dead*. Appendix A.

1459. *Salt Lake Telegram* (Salt Lake City, Utah). 24 May 1918. p 2.

1460. *Cleveland Gazette* (Cleveland, Ohio). 15 June 1918. Also see *Fort Worth Star Telegram* (Fort Worth, Texas). 28 May 1918.

1461. *Montgomery Advertiser* (Montgomery, Alabama). 2 June 1918. p 1. *Cleveland Gazette* (Cleveland, Ohio). 15 June 1918. *Trenton Evening Times* (Trenton, New Jersey). 2 June 1918. p 3.

1462. *Tulsa World* (Tulsa, Oklahoma). 12 July 1918. p 3.

1463. Carrigan. *Lynching Culture*. Appendix A. *Waco Times-Herald* (Waco, Texas). 28 July 1918. Also see *Washington Bee* (Washington, DC). 10 August 1918.

1464. *Dallas Morning News* (Dallas, Texas). 3 August 1918. p 2.

1465. "Death Penalty Information Center". Espy File. 1608-2002. Accessed 8 August 2014.

1466. *Dallas Morning News* (Dallas, Texas). 11 October 1917. p 5.

1467. *Macon Telegraph* (Macon, Georgia). 31 August 1918.

1468. *Broad Ax* (Chicago, Illinois). 28 September 1918. p 3. Also see the *Trenton Evening News (Trenton, New Jersey)*. 18 September 1918. p 3.

1469. "Death Penalty Information Center". Espy File. 1608-2002. Accessed 8 August 2014.

1470. *Augusta Chronicle* (Augusta, Georgia). 25 September 1918.

1471. *Dallas Morning News* (Dallas, Texas). 8 November 19818.

1472. *Washington Bee* (Washington, DC). 28 December 1918. p 2. Carrigan. *Lynching Culture*. Appendix A.

1473. *Dallas Morning News* (Dallas, Texas). 21 January 1919.

1474. *Springfield Republican* (Springfield, Illinois). 21 January 1919.

1475. *Dallas Morning News* (Dallas, Texas). 16 July 1919.

1476. *Ibid.*

1477. *New Orleans Statesman* (New Orleans, Louisiana). 11 July 1919.

1478. *Tulsa World* (Tulsa, Oklahoma). 22 April 1920. p 10.

1479. *Lexington Herald* (Lexington, Kentucky). 24 March 1920. p 1.

1480. *Fort Worth Star Telegram* (Fort Worth, Texas). 8 April 1920.

1481. Caldwell/DeLord. *Texas Lawmen: 1900–1940.* p 370. Also see *San Jose Mercury News* (San Jose, California). 1 July 1920. Also see *The Wharton Spectator* (Wharton, Texas). 2 July 1920, *The Houston Chronicle* (Houston, Texas). 30 June 1920. *The Daily Times Herald* (Dallas, Texas). 30 June 1920.

1482. "Arthur lynchings in Paris were 87 years ago." Staff reports. *The Paris News.* 6 July 2007.

1483. *Fort Wayne News Sentinel* (Fort Wayne, Indiana). 7 July 1920.

1484. *Macon Telegraph* (Macon, Georgia). 10 July 1920. p 2.

1485. *Bellingham Herald* (Bellingham, Washington). 28 August 1920.

1486. *Dallas Morning News* (Dallas, Texas). 17 September 1920. p 12. Also see Caldwell and DeLord. *Texas Lawmen: 1900–1940.* p 54.

1487. *Idaho Statesman* (Boise, Idaho). 24 December 1920. p 3. Also see Caldwell/DeLord. *Texas Lawmen: 1900–1940.* p 143.

1488. Find-A-Grave Memorial # 11322654

1489. *Dallas Morning News* (Dallas, Texas). 21 March 19121, P. 2

1490. Ancestry. *Texas, Death Certificates, 1903–1982.* Provo, Utah: Ancestry.com. Original data from Texas Department of State Health Services. Texas Death Certificates, 1903–1982. Orem, Utah.

1491. Caldwell/DeLord. *Texas Lawmen 1900–1940.* p 31. Also see *Dallas Morning News* (Dallas, Texas). 21 July 1921.

1492. *Montgomery Advertiser* (Montgomery, Alabama). 17 August 1921. Also see *Jonesboro Daily Tribune* (Jonesboro, Arkansas). 16 August 1921.

1493. *Dallas Morning News* (Dallas, Texas). 13 October 1921.

1494. *Dallas Morning News* (Dallas, Texas). 3 October 1922. *Dallas Morning News* (Dallas, Texas). 14 February 1922.

1495. *Fort Worth Star Telegram* (Fort Worth, Texas). 12 December 1921. p 2.

1496. *Fort Worth Star Telegram* (Fort Worth, Texas). 16 December 1921.

1497. *Waco Times-Herald* (Waco, Texas). 14 December 1921. Find

1498. Ancestry. *Texas, Death Certificates, 1903–1982.* Provo, Utah: Ancestry. Operations, Inc. 2013.

1499. *San Jose Mercury News* (San Jose, California). 15 December 1921. p 1.

1500. *Jonesboro Daily Tribune* (Jonesboro, Arkansas). 15 December 1921.

1501. *Dallas Morning News* (Dallas, Texas). 23 December 1921.

1502. *Miami District Daily News* (Miami, Oklahoma). 15 December 1921. p 5.

1503. *Times Picayune* (New Orleans, Louisiana). 7 January 1922. p 7.

1504. Ancestry. *Texas, Death Certificates, 1903–1982.* Provo, Utah: Ancestry Operations, Inc. 2013. Original data from Texas Department of State Health Services. Texas Death Certificates, 1903–1982. Archives, Orem, Utah; Carrigan. *Forgotten Dead.* Appendix B.

1505. *Denver Post* (Denver, Colorado). 22 February 1922. Also see *Dallas Morning News* (Dallas, Texas). 21 February 1922.

1506. *Fort Worth Star Telegram* (Fort Worth, Texas). 13 April. 1922. p 1.

1507. Find-A-Grave Memorial # 31304775.

1508. *Kalamazoo Gazette* (Kalamazoo, Michigan). 5 May 1922. Texas Department of State Health Services. Texas Death Certificates, 1903–1982. LDS Archives. Orem, Utah.

1509. *Tulsa World* (Tulsa, Oklahoma). 10 May 1922. Find-A-Grave Memorial # 49377812. Also see *Evening News* (San Jose, California). 8 May 1922. p 1.

1510. City-Data.com. Accessed on 17 August 2014.

1511. *Tulsa World* (Tulsa, Oklahoma). 19 May 1922. p 1. Also see *Augusta Chronicle* (Augusta, Georgia). 19 May 1922. p 5.

1512. *Fort Worth Star Telegram* (Fort Worth, Texas). 21 May 1922. p 1.

1513. *Fort Worth Star Telegram* (Fort Worth, Texas). 21 May 1922. p 1.

1514. It appears as though Ida Mae survived the ordeal. She later married a man named Dancy and moved to California, where she died at Sacramento on 1 August 1997 at the age of eighty-eight. State of California. *California Death Index, 1940–1997.* Sacramento, CA: State of California Department of Health Services. Center for Health Statistics.

1515. *Daily Illinois State Register* (Springfield, Illinois). 21 May 1922. p 1.

1516. *Daily Illinois State Journal* (Springfield, Illinois). 4 June 1922. p 24.

1517. *New York Times (New York, New York).* 28 May 1922. Also see *Dallas Morning News* (Dallas, Texas). 15 February 1998.

1518. *Tulsa World* (Tulsa, Oklahoma). 3 June 1922. p 11.

1519. *Ibid.*

1520. *Tulsa World* (Tulsa, Oklahoma). 24 June 1922. p 17.

1521. *Miami District Daily News* (Miami, Oklahoma). 7 September 1922.

1522. *Dallas Morning News* (Dallas, Texas). 24 September 1922. Texas Department of State Health Services. *Texas Death Certificates, 1903-1982.* Archives. Orem, Utah.

1523. *Salt Lake Telegram* (Salt Lake City, Utah). 20 November 1922. p 5.

1524. *Elkhart Truth* (Elkhart, Indiana). 11 December 1922.

1525. *Tulsa World* (Tulsa, Oklahoma). 12 December 1922. p 3.

1526. *Miami District Daily News* (Miami, Oklahoma). 14 December 1922.

1527. *San Antonio Express* (San Antonio, Texas). 8 April 1923.

1528. *Salt Lake Telegram* (Salt Lake City, Utah). 20 October 1922. p 11.

1529. *San Antonio Express* (San Antonio, Texas). 7 April 1923.

1530. *State Times Advocate* (Baton Rouge, Louisiana). 4 July 1923. p 12.

1531. *Dallas Morning News* (Dallas, Texas). 21 July 1923.

1532. *Dallas Morning News* (Dallas, Texas). 31 July 1923. Section 2. p 13.

1533. *Dallas Morning News* (Dallas, Texas). 1 September 1923.

1534. *Dallas Morning News* (Dallas, Texas). 29 November 1923. Carrigan. *Forgotten Dead.* Appendix B

1535. *Dallas Morning News* (Dallas, Texas). 18 September 1926. Also see Caldwell/DeLord. *Texas Lawmen: 1900-1940.* p 381.

1536. Henrietta Vinton Davis website. Accessed 8 August 2014. *Macon Telegraph* (Macon, Georgia). 14 November 1926.

1537. Caldwell/DeLord. *Texas Lawmen: 1900-1940.* p 210.

1538. Caldwell/DeLord. *Texas Lawmen: 1900-1940.* p 189.

1539. Caldwell/DeLord. *Texas Lawmen: 1900-1940.* p 77. Also see Greene, A. C. 1958. *The Santa Claus Bank Robbery.* Cisco, Texas: First National Bank of Cisco. p 27. *Abilene Morning Reporter-News* (Abilene, Texas). 1 January 1928.

1540. *Dallas Morning News* (Dallas, Texas). 10 May 1930. Thompson, Thompson. "Sherman Riot of 1930," *Handbook of Texas.*

1541. *Trenton Evening Times* (Trenton, New Jersey). *17 May 1930.* p 3.

1542. *Trenton Evening Times* (Trenton, New Jersey). 19 June 1930. p 10. Also see *Dallas Morning News* (Dallas, Texas). 3 April 1932.

1543. *Dallas Morning News* (Dallas, Texas). 3 January 1932. p 6.

1544. *Dallas Morning News* (Dallas, Texas). 3 April 1932.

1545. "Death Penalty Information Center". Espy File. 1608-2002. Accessed 8 August 2014.

1546. Segrave. *Lynchings of Women.* p. 162

1547. *Dallas Morning News* (Dallas, Texas). 15 November 1935. Also see *Richmond Times Dispatch* (Richmond, Virginia). 13 November 1935. p 2. *Greensboro Record* (Greensboro, South Carolina). 18 November 1935. p 6. .

1548. Ancestry. *Texas, Death Certificates, 1903-1982.* Provo, Utah: Ancestry.com Operations, Inc. 2013. Original data at Texas Department of State Health Services. Texas Death Certificates, 1903-1982. iArchives, Orem, Utah.

1549. *Plaindealer* (Kansas City, Kansas). 25 October 1940. p 2.

1550. Ancestry. *Texas, Death Certificates, 1903-1982.* Certificate #30810. Provo, Utah. Ancestry, Inc. 2013.

1551. Ancestry. *Texas, Death Certificates, 1903-1982.* Certificate #66628. Provo, Utah. Ancestry, Inc. 2013.

1552. *Dallas Morning News* (Dallas, Texas). 15 July 1942. Also see *Plaindealer* (Kansas City, Kansas). 24 July 1942, *Advocate* (Baton Rouge, Louisiana). 14 July 1942, *Richmond Times Dispatch* (Richmond, Virginia). 14 July 1942. Ancestry. *Texas, Death Certificates, 1903-1982.* Certificate #29862. Provo, Utah. Ancestry, Inc. 2013.

1553. US Census Data. 1920. Texas. 4,670,892 total persons.

1554. Ancestry lists 635,185 as the total count of black persons living in Texas at the time of the 1920 census. An additional 3,920,864 were white. About 17,449 reported their birthplace as having been Mexico. The database is an index of individuals enumerated in the 1920 United States Federal Census, the Fourteenth Census of the United States.

Source Materials

Abernathy, Francis Edward, ed. 1981. *Legendary Ladies of Texas*. Publication of the Texas Folklore Society. Dallas, Texas: E-Heart.

Atkison, Bertha. 1929. "The History of Bell County, Texas." M.A. Thesis. University of Texas. Bell County Historical Society.

Barker, Eugene Campbell. 1924–1928. *The Austin Papers, Annual Report of the American Historical Association for the year 1919, 1920*. Three Volumes. Washington, DC: Government Printing Office.

Barrett, Thomas and George Washington Diamond. 2012. *The Great Hanging at Gainesville, 1862: The Accounts of Thomas Barrett and George Washington Diamond."* Denton, Texas: Texas State Historical Association.

Barry, James Buckner. 1984. *Buck Barry, Texas Ranger and Frontiersman*. Lincoln, Nebraska: University of Nebraska Press.

Borders, Gary B. 2006. *A Hanging in Nacogdoches: Murder, Race, Politics and Polemics in Texas's Oldest Town 1870–1916*. Austin, Texas: University of Texas Press.

Bartholomew, Ed Ellsworth. 1953. *Wild Bill Longley: A Texas Hard-Case*. Houston, Texas: Frontier Press.

Beard, Jane A. 1982. *Births, Deaths, and Marriages from El Paso Newspapers through 1885 for Arizona, Texas, New Mexico and Indian Territory*. El Paso Genealogical Society. Easley, South Carolina: Southern Historical Press.

Beard, Jane. 1992. *Births, Deaths, and Marriages from El Paso Newspapers from 1886–1890 for Arizona, Texas, New Mexico and Indian Territory, Vol. II*. El Paso Genealogical Society. Greenville, South Carolina: Southern Historical Press.

Beard, Jane. 1995. *Births, Deaths, and Marriages from El Paso Newspapers from 1891–1895 for Arizona, Texas, New Mexico and Indian Territory, Vol. III*. El Paso Genealogical Society Greenville, South Carolina: Southern Historical Press.

Beard, Jane Alida. 2000. *Births, Deaths, and Marriages from El Paso Newspapers from 1896–1899 for Arizona, Texas, New Mexico and Indian Territory, Vol. IV*. El Paso Genealogical Society Provo. Utah: Brigham Young University.

Biffle, Kent. 1993. *A Month of Sundays*. Denton, Texas: University of North Texas Press.

Block Jr., W. T. "Cannonball Express". Texas Escapes. 19 June 2006.

Block, W. T. "Myth of Texas Executions Debunked." Beaumont Enterprise. 13 September 1978.

Brown, Frank. *Annals of Travis County and the City of Austin*. Manuscript. Frank Brown Papers. Dolph Briscoe Center of American History. University of Texas at Austin.

Bugbee, Lester G. "The Old Three Hundred: A List of Settlers in Austin's First Colony." Quarterly of the Texas State Historical Association. October 1897.

Burnett County History Association. 1979. A Pioneer History 1847–1979; Darrell Debo. Vol. I. Burnett, Texas: Eakin Press.

Miller, Rick. "Boastful Bill Longley: Cold-blooded Texas Killer". Wild West Magazine.2002

Caldwell, Clifford R. 2011. *A Day's Ride from Here, Volume I Mountain Home, Texas*. Charleston, South Carolina: The History Press.

Caldwell, Clifford R. 2011. *A Day's Ride from Here Volume II, Noxville, Texas*. Charleston, South Carolina: The History Press.

Caldwell, Clifford R. 2012. *An Anthology of Old West Tales, Selected Works of Clifford R. Caldwell.* Privately Published.

Caldwell, Clifford R. 2012. *Fort McKavett, and Tales of Menard County. Mountain Home, Texas:* Privately Published.

Caldwell, Clifford R. 2013. *Robert Kelsey Wylie, Forgotten Cattle King of Texas.* Privately Published.

Caldwell, Clifford R. and DeLord, Ron. 2011. *Texas Lawmen 1835–1899, The Good and the Bad.* Charleston, South Carolina: The History Press.

Caldwell, Clifford R. and DeLord, Ron. 2012. *Texas Lawmen 1900–1940, More of the Good and the Bad.* Charleston, South Carolina: The History Press.

Caldwell, Clifford R. 2012. *An Anthology of Old West Tales, Selected Works of Clifford R. Caldwell.* Privately Published.

Caldwell, Clifford R. 2009. *Guns of The Lincoln County War. Mountain Home, Texas:* Privately Published.

Caldwell, Clifford R. "The Horrell-Higgins Feud." *The Journal of the Wild West History Association.* Volume IV. Number 2. February 2011.

Carrigan, William D. 2006. *The Making of a Lynching Culture, Violence and Vigilantisms in Central Texas, 1836–1916.* Champaign, Illinois: University of Illinois Press.

Carrigan, William D. and Webb, Clive. 2013. *Forgotten Dead: Mob Violence against Mexicans in the United States, 1848–1928.* Oxford University Press.

Cool, Paul. 2008. *Salt Warriors, Insurgency on the Rio Grande.* College Station, Texas: Texas A&M University Press.

Cox, Mike. 2008. *Historic Photos of Texas Lawmen.* Nashville, Tennessee: Turner Publishing Company.

Follett, Jay C. "Nelson A. 'Cooney' Mitchell 1796–1875. Only man ever legally hanged in Hood County". *Hood County Genealogical Society Newsletter.* No. 21. February 1989.

Fuller, Henry Clay. 1983. *The Adventures of Bill Longley.* Nacogdoches, Texas: S. Malone.

Geue, Chester W., and Geue, Ethel Hander, Compilers. 1972. *A New Land Beckoned: German Immigration to Texas 1844–1847.* Waco, Texas: Texian Press.

Gillett, James B. 2007. *Six Years With The Texas Rangers.* New York, New York: Cosimo Classics.

Givens, Murphy. "Peñascal Killers Left Trail of Brown Sugar." Corpus Christi Caller Times. 30 July 2008.

Givens, Murphy. "Hanging Times Part 2." Corpus Christi Caller Times. 7 April 1999. Reprinted by Genealogical Publishing Co., Baltimore, 1982.

Glasrud, Bruce A. and Smallwood, James. 2007. *The African American Experience in Texas: an Anthology.* Lubbock: Texas Tech University Press.

Gowens, William. "Magnis's Famous Texans". 12 July 2013.

Green, A.C. 1958. *The Santa Claus Bank Robbery.* Cisco, Texas: First National Bank of Texas.

Gregory, Peggy H. 1976. *Records of Interments of the City of Galveston 1859–1872.* Privately Published.

Grimes, Roy. 1968. *300 Years in Victoria County.* Victoria, Texas: Victoria Advocate.

Grimsted, David. 1998. *American Mobbing, 1828–1861.* New York, New York: Oxford Press.

"Hallettsville Hanging Tree". Texas A&M University Forest Service. Texas A&M University. 2012.

Harper, Texas Centennial Year Committee. 1963. *Here's Harper. Harper, 1863–1963.* Fredericksburg, Texas: The Radio Post.

Headsman (The). 2012. "1865 Galveston Deserter - Antone Richers." *Execution Today.com.*

Jenkins, John Holland. 1958. *Recollections of Early Texas.* Austin, Texas: University of Texas Press.

Johnson, Benjamin Heber Dr. 2005. *Revolution in Texas: How a Forgotten Rebellion And Its Bloody Suppression Turned Mexicans Into Americans.* New Haven, Connecticut: Yale University Press.

Johnson, David. 2006. *The Mason County "Hoo Doo" War, 1874–1902.* Denton, Texas: University of North Texas Press.

Johnson, David. 2014. *The Horrell Wars: Feuding in Texas and New Mexico.* Denton, Texas: University of North Texas Press.

Kelsey, Michael and Floyd, Nancy Graff and Parsons, Ginny Guinn. 1995. *Miscellaneous Texas Newspaper Abstracts - Deaths. Volume I*. Bowie, Maryland: Heritage Books, Inc.

Kelsey, Michael and Floyd, Nancy Graff and Parsons, Ginny Guinn. 1997. *Miscellaneous Texas Newspaper Abstracts - Deaths. Volume II*. Bowie, Maryland: Heritage Books, Inc.

Kuykendall, J. H. "Reminiscences of Early Texans." *Quarterly of the Texas State Historical Association*. 6-7. January, April, July 1903.

Ladd, Kevin, ed. 1994. "Gone to Texas: Genealogist Abstracts from The Telegraph and Texas Register 1835–1841". Bowie, Maryland: Heritage Books, Inc.

Ledbetter, Bill. "Slave Unrest and White Panic, The Impact of Black Republicanism in Antebellum Texas." Texana 10. 1972.

Limmer, E. A. 1988. *Story of Bell County, Texas- Volume I*. Woodway, Texas: Eakin Press.

Linn, John J. 1986. *Reminiscences of Fifty Years in Texas*. Austin, Texas: State House Press.

Luther, Joseph. 2012. *Camp Verde, Texas Frontier Defense*. Charleston, South Carolina: The History Press.

Marten, James. 1990. *Texas Divided: Loyalty and Dissent in the Lone Star State 1856–1874*. Lexington, Kentucky: The University of Kentucky.

McCaslin, Richard B. "Great Hanging at Gainsville," Handbook of Texas Online. Texas State Historical Association.

McDaniel, Ruel. "The Day They Hanged Chipita." Texas Parade. September 1962.

Miller, Rick. 2002. "Boastful Bill Longley: Cold-blooded Texas Killer." Wild West Magazine.

Mitchell, Joe H. 2010. *The Strangest Fruit: Black-On-Black Lynchings in America 1835–1935*. Privately Published.

Moneyhon, Carl H. "Davis, Edmund Jackson." Handbook of Texas.

Moore, John Trotwood. 1923. *Tennessee, The Volunteer State 1769–1923*. Chicago, Illinois: S. J. Clark Publishing Co.

Moore, Stephen L. 2002. *Savage Frontier, Volume I: Rangers, Riflemen, and Indian Wars in Texas, 1835–1837*. Plano, Texas: Republic of Texas Press.

Moore, Stephen L. 2006. *Savage Frontier, Volume II: Rangers, Riflemen, and Indian Wars in Texas, 1838–1839*. Denton, Texas: University of North Texas Press.

Moore, Stephen L. 2007. *Savage Frontier, Volume III: Rangers, Riflemen, and Indian Wars in Texas, 1840–1841*. Denton, Texas: University of North Texas Press.

Moore, Stephen L. 2010. *Savage Frontier, Volume IV: Rangers, Riflemen, and Indian Wars in Texas, 1842–1845*. Denton, Texas: University of North Texas Press.

Mitchell, Joe Henry. 2010. *30 Years of Lynching in the United States 1889–1918*. Baltimore, Maryland: National Association for the Advancement of Colored People.

Nicklas, Linda Cheves, ed. 1994. *Abstracts of Early East Texas Newspapers, 1839–1856*. Greenville, South Carolina: Southern Historical Press, Inc.

Ochoa, Ruben E. "San Miguel, Texas." Handbook of Texas Online.

O'Neal, Bill. 1979. *Encyclopedia of Western Gunfighters*. Norman, Oklahoma: University of Oklahoma Press.

Orozco, Cynthia E. 2014. "Porvenir Massacre." Handbook of Texas Online.

Parsons, Chuck. "Personal Reminiscences of Brown Bowen". Unpublished Manuscript. 23 July 2013.

Ransleben, Guido E. 1974. *A Hundred Years of Comfort in Texas*. San Antonio, Texas: Naylor Company.

Ray, Worth Stickley. 1949. *Austin Colony Pioneers*. Austin, Texas: Various.

Reynolds, Donald E. "Bewley, Anthony." Handbook of Texas Online.

Reynolds, Donald E. 2007. *Texas Terror, The Slave Insurrection Panic of 1860 and The Secession of the Lower South*. Baton Rouge, Louisiana: Louisiana State University Press.

Richmond, Douglas W. and Haynes, Sam W. 2013. *The Mexican Revolution, Conflict, Consolidation, 1910–1940*. College Station, Texas: University of Texas at Arlington by Texas A&M University.

Roell, Craig H. and Linda Harsdorff-Lees. "Hill, Benjamin F." Handbook of Texas.

Rucker, Walter C. and Upton, James N. 2006. Encyclopedia of American Race Riots. Westport, Connecticut: Greenwood Publishing Group, Inc.

Scott, Zelma. 1998. A History of Coryell County Texas. Texas State Historical Association.

Segrave, Kerry. 2010. Lynchings of Women in the United States: The Recorded cases, 1851–1946. Jefferson, North Carolina: McFarland and Company, Inc., Publishers.

Shirley, Glenn. 1994. The Fighting Marlows: Men who wouldn't be lynched. Fort Worth, Texas: Texas Christian University Press.

Smith, Matt. "A Falsely Accused Son and a Hell Bound Father." Cleburne Times Review. 1 November 2009.

Sonnichsen, C. L. 1984. Outlaw on the Dodge with Baldy Russell. Athens, Ohio: Swallow Press.

Sonnischsen, C. L. 2000. Ten Texas Feud. Albuquerque, New Mexico: University of New Mexico Press. 2nd Revised Edition.

Sowell, A.J. 1986. Texas Indian Fighters: Early Settlers and Indian Fighters of Southwest Texas. Abilene, Texas: State House Press.

Smith, Matt. "A Falsely Accused Son and a Hell Bound Father." Cleburne Times Review. November 2009.

Smylie, Vernon. "A Noose for Chipita." Texas News Syndicate Press. 1970.

Steelwater, Eliza. 2003. The Hangman's Knot: Lynching, Legal Execution, and America's Struggle with the Death Penalty. Boulder, Colorado: Westview Press.

Swenson, Helen Smothers. 1984. Early Texas News 1831–1848. Abstracts from Early Texas Newspapers. Signal Mountain, Tennessee: Mountain Press.

Thompson, Jerry Don. 1971. Colonel John Robert Baylor: Texas Indian Fighter and Confederate Soldier. Hillsboro, Texas: Hill Junior College Press.

Thompson, Thompson. "Sherman Riot of 1930." Handbook of Texas Online.

Tise, Sammy.1989.Texas County Sheriffs. Albuquerque, New Mexico: Oakwood Printing.

Tolnay, Stewart E. and Beck, E. M. 1995. A Festival of Violence. Urbana and Chicago, Illinois: University of Illinois Press.

Underwood, Marylyn. "Rodriguez, Josefa [Chipita]." Handbook of Texas Online.

Underwood, Rodman L. 2002. Death on the Nueces: German Texans Treue der Union. Austin, Texas: Eakin Press.

University of Texas Institute of Texan Cultures. 1984. Residents of Texas, 1782–1836. St. Louis, Missouri. University of Texan Cultures.

Warren, Harris Gaylord. "Aury, Louis Michel." Handbook of Texas Online.

Wilbarger, J. W. 1889. Indian Depredations in Texas. Austin, Texas: Hutchings Printing House.

Wilson, Carol O'Keefe. 2014. In The Governor's Shadow, The True Story of Ma and Pa Ferguson. Denton, Texas: University of North Texas Press.

Wilson, R. Michael. "Desertion During the Civil War." Big Blend Magazine's Way Back When.

Winegarten, Ruthe. 1984. Finder's Guide to the 'Texas Women: A Celebration of History' Exhibit Archives. Denton, Texas: Texas. Woman's University Library.

Wish, Harvey. "The Slave Insurrection Panic of 1856." Journal of Southern History. 5 May 1939.

Wooster, Robert. "Pine Island, Texas (Jefferson County)." Handbook of Texas Online. Texas State Historical Association.

Yancy, Karen. 1983. San Saba County History. San Saba, Texas: San Saba County Historical Commission.

Other Sources

Albarado, Evaristo. "Porvenir Massacre 1918." 1 October 2011.

Ancestry.com.

"Correspondence of Don Price - Beaumont, Texas." Southwest History Quarterly. Vol LII. No. 3. January 1949.

Statement of Carl W. Matthews, Jr. Navarro County, Texas.

Find A Grave Memorial, PO Box 522107, Salt Lake City, Utah .

Harpers Weekly

Interview of Uncle Ed Nichols by C. L. Sonnichsen at Lampasas. 15 July 1944.

Matthews, Carl W. Navarro County, Texas. 8 August 2014. Sonnichsen Collection. University of Texas at El Paso.

Pennsylvania, Church and Town Records, 1708–1985. Provo, Utah: Ancestry. 2011.

Southwest History Quarterly. January 1951. Volume LIV.

Statement of Miguel Martinez. Coroner's Inquest. Justice of the Peace. Precinct 3. Nueces County, Texas. 8 December 1873.

Texas State Police Records. Austin, Texas: State Archives.

Townsend Memorial Library. University of Mary Hardin-Baylor.

U.S. Federal Census Mortality Schedules Index 1850–1880. Provo, UT.

United States Census. Census Years 1850, 1860, 1870, 1880, 1900, 1910, 1920, 1930.

U.S. Civil War Soldier Records and Profiles, 1861–1865. Provo, Utah: Ancestry. Original data compiled by Historical Data Systems of Kingston, Massachusetts.

Newspapers

Aberdeen Weekly (Aberdeen, South Dakota)

Abilene Morning Reporter (Abilene, Texas)

Advocate (Baton Rouge, Louisiana)

Age (Augusta, Maine)

Age-Herald (Birmingham, Alabama)

Albany Argus (Albany, New York)

Albany Evening Journal (Albany, New York)

Albuquerque Citizen (Albuquerque, New Mexico)

Albuquerque Journal (Albuquerque, New Mexico)

Albuquerque Morning Democrat (Albuquerque, New Mexico)

Albuquerque Morning Journal (Albuquerque, New Mexico)

Alexandria Gazette (Alexandria, Virginia)

American Citizen (Kansas City, Kansas)

American Traveler (Boston, Massachusetts)

Anaconda Standard (Anaconda, Montana)

Ann Arbor Daily Times (Ann Arbor, Michigan)

Augusta Chronicle (Augusta, Georgia)

Arkansas Gazette (Littlerock, Arkansas)

Arkansas Weekly Gazette (Littlerock, Arkansas)

Augusta Chronicle (Augusta, Georgia)

Austin Republican (Austin, Texas)

Baltimore Sun (Baltimore, Maryland)

Barre Gazette (Barre, Massachusetts)

Baltimore American (Baltimore, Maryland)

Bay City Times (Bay City, Michigan)

Beaumont Enterprise (Beaumont, Texas)

Beaumont Journal (Beaumont, Texas)

Bellingham Herald (Bellingham, Washington)

Bellville Countrymen (Bellville, Washington)

Bonham News (Bonham, Texas)

Boston Herald (Boston, Massachusetts)

Boston Journal (Boston, Massachusetts)

Bridgeport Evening News (Bridgeport, Connecticut)

Broad Ax (Chicago, Illinois)

Camden Democrat (Camden, New Jersey)

Canton Repository (Canton, Ohio)

Centinel of Freedom (Newark, New Jersey)

Charleston Courier (Charleston, South Carolina)

Charleston News and Courier (Charleston, South Carolina)

Charlotte Observer (Charlotte, North Carolina)

Cherokee Advocate (Tahlequah, Oklahoma)

Cincinnati Commercial Tribune (Cincinnati, Ohio)

Cincinnati Daily Gazette (Cincinnati, Ohio)

Cincinnati Post (Cincinnati, Ohio)

Clarion Ledger (Jackson, Mississippi)

Cleburne Morning Review (Cleburne, Texas)

Cleburne Times-Review (Cleburne, Texas)

Cleveland Plain Dealer (Cleveland, Ohio)

Colorado Springs Gazette (Colorado Springs, Colorado)

Columbus Daily Enquirer (Columbus, Ohio)

Columbus Daily Enquirer (Columbus, Georgia)

Columbian Register (New Haven, Connecticut)

Commercial Advertiser (New York, New York)

Connecticut Currant (Hartford, Connecticut)

Constitution (Middletown, Connecticut)

Constitution (Washington, DC)

Corpus Christi Caller Times (Corpus Christi, Texas)

Critic Record (Washington, DC)

Daily Advocate (Baton Rouge, Louisiana)

Daily Advocate (Newark, Ohio)

Daily Commercial (Vicksburg, Mississippi)

Daily Confederation (Montgomery, Alabama)

Daily Eastern Argus (Portland, Main)

Daily Herald (Biloxi, Mississippi)

Daily Herald (New Haven, Connecticut)

Daily Illinois State Register (Springfield, Illinois)

Daily Inter Ocean (Chicago, Illinois)

Daily Journal and Journal and Tribune (Knoxville, Tennessee)

Daily National Intelligencer (Washington, DC)

Daily Ohio Statesman (Columbus, Ohio)

Daily Oklahoman (Oklahoma City, Oklahoma)

Daily People (New York, New York)

Daily Register Gazette (Rockford, Illinois)

Daily State (Baton Rouge, Louisiana)

Daily Statesman (Columbus, Ohio)

Daily True Delta (New Orleans, Louisiana)

Daily Union (Washington, DC)

Dallas Daily Herald (Dallas, Texas)

Dallas Morning News (Dallas, Texas)

Dallas Weekly Herald (Dallas, Texas)

Delaware State Reporter (Dover, Delaware)

Denton Monitor (Denton, Texas)

Denver Rocky Mountain News (Denver, Colorado)

Desert News (Salt Lake City, Utah)

Duluth News-Tribune (Duluth, Minnesota)

Duluth Minnesotan (Duluth, Minnesota)

Elkhart Daily Review (Elkhart, Indiana)

Elkhart Truth (Elkhart, Indiana)

Elkhart Weekly Review (Elkhart, Indiana)

Emporia Gazette (Emporia, Kansas)

Evansville Courier and Press (Evansville, Indiana)

Evening News (San Jose, California)

Evening Post (New York, New York)

Evening Star (Washington, DC)

Evening Tribune (San Diego, California)

Flake's Bulletin (Galveston, Texas)

Fort Worth Gazette (Fort Worth, Texas)

Fort Wayne News Sentinel (Fort Wayne, Indiana)

Freeman (Indianapolis, Indiana)

Fresno Morning Republican (Fresno, California)

Galveston Daily News (Galveston, Texas)

Gloucester Telegraph (Gloucester, Massachusetts)

Gonzales Inquirer (Gonzales, Texas)

Grand Forks Daily Herald (Grand Forks, Nebraska)

Grand Forks Herald (Grand Forks, North Dakota)

Grand Rapids Press (Grand Rapids, Michigan)

Greensboro Daily News (Greensboro, North Carolina)

Huntsville Gazette (Huntsville, Texas)

Hobart Daily Republican (Hobart, Oklahoma)

Honey Grove Signal (Honey Grove, Texas)

Houston Telegraph (Houston, Texas)

Houston Tri-Weekly Telegraph (Houston, Texas)

Idaho Statesman (Boise, Idaho)

Indianapolis Sentinel (Indianapolis, Indiana)

Illinois State Journal (Springfield, Illinois)

Illinois Weekly State Journal (Springfield, Illinois)

Iredell Times (Iredell, Texas)

Jackson Citizen (Jackson, Mississippi)

Jackson Citizen Patriot (Jackson, Michigan)

Jonesboro Evening Sun (Jonesboro, Arkansas)

Kalamazoo Gazette (Kalamazoo, Michigan)

Kansas City Star (Kansas City, Missouri)

Kansas City Times (Kansas City, Missouri)

La Grange True Issue (La Grange, Texas)

Langston City Herald (Langston, Oklahoma)

Leavenworth Advocate (Leavenworth, Kansas)

Ledger and Texan (San Antonio, Texas)

Lexington Herald (Lexington, Kentucky)

Liberator (Boston, Massachusetts)

Lowell Daily Citizen and News (Lowell,
  Massachusetts)

Marietta Journal (Marietta, Georgia)

McKinney Messenger (McKinney, Texas)

Miami District Daily News (Miami, Oklahoma)

Mobile Register (Mobile, Alabama)

Montgomery Advertiser (Montgomery, Alabama)

Morning Herald (Lexington, Kentucky)

Morning Olympian (Olympia, Washington)

Morning Republican (Little Rock, Arkansas)

Morning Star (Rockford, Illinois)

Macon Telegraph (Macon, Georgia)

Macon Weekly Telegraph (Macon, Georgia)

Massachusetts Spy (Worchester, Massachusetts)

Miami District Daily News (Miami, Oklahoma)

Mississippi Free Trader (Natchez, Mississippi)

Missouri Courier (Hannibal, Missouri)

Muskegon Chronicle (Muskegon, Michigan)

Nacogdoches Chronicle (Nacogdoches, Texas)

National Era (Washington, DC)

National Gazette (Philadelphia, Pennsylvania)

New Hampshire Patriot and State Gazette (Concord,
  New Hampshire)

New Hampshire Sentinel (Keene, New Hampshire)

New Haven Register (New Haven, Connecticut)

New London Daily Chronicle (New London,
  Connecticut)

New Mexican (Santa Fe, New Mexico)

Newport Mercury (Newport, Rhode Island)

New Orleans Item (New Orleans, Louisiana)

New Orleans Times (New Orleans, Louisiana)

New York Herald (New York, New York)

New York Ledger (New York, New York)

New York Tribune (New York, New York)

Norwich Courier (Norwich, Connecticut)

Olympia Daily Record (Olympia, Washington)

Omaha World Herald (Omaha, Nebraska)

Oregonian (Portland, Oregon)

Paris Morning News (Paris, Texas)

Parsons Weekly Blade (Parsons, Kansas)

Pawtucket Times (Pawtucket, Rhode Island)

Philadelphia Inquirer (Philadelphia, Pennsylvania)

Plaindealer (Topeka, Kansas)

Plain Dealer (Cleveland, Ohio)

Portland Daily Press (Portland, Main)

Portland Weekly Advertiser (Portland, Maine)

Prensa (San Antonio, Texas)

Press (Philadelphia, Pennsylvania)

Public Ledger (Philadelphia, Pennsylvania)

Quincy Whig (Quincy, Illinois)

Regidor (San Antonio, Texas)

Repository (Canton, Ohio)

Richmond Times Dispatch (Richmond, Virginia)

Richmond Whig (Richmond, Virginia)

Riverside Daily Press (Riverside, California)

Riverside Independent Enterprise (Riverside,
  California)

Rock River Democrat (Rockford, Illinois)

Salt Lake Telegram (Salt Lake City, Utah)

Salt Lake Tribune (Salt Lake City, Utah)

Sandusky Register (Sandusky, Ohio)

San Antonio Daily Ledger (San Antonio, Texas)

San Antonio Express (San Antonio, Texas)

San Diego Union (San Diego, California)

San Francisco Bulletin (San Francisco, California)

San Jose Mercury News (San Jose, California)Sedan
  Lance (Sedan, Kansas)

Sherman Daily Register (Sherman, Texas)

Sioux City Journal (Sioux City, Iowa)

Southern Patriot (Charleston, South Carolina)

Spectator (New York, New York)

Springfield Republican (Springfield, Massachusetts)

St. Alban's Messenger (St. Alban, Vermont)

State (Columbia, South Carolina)

State Ledger (Topeka, Kansas)

St. Louis Republic (St. Louis, Missouri)

Standard (Clarksville, Texas)

State (Columbia, South Carolina)

Summit County Beacon (Akron, Ohio)

Sun (Baltimore, Maryland)

Sunday Delta (New Orleans, Louisiana)

Tampa Tribune (Tampa, Florida)

Temple Daily Telegraph (Temple, Texas)

Territorial Enterprise (Virginia City, Nevada)

Texas Republican (Marshall, Texas)

Texas State Gazette (Austin, Texas)

The American Citizen (Kansas City, Kansas)

The Caledonian (St. Johns bury, Vermont)

The Daily Times Herald (Dallas, Texas)

The Denton Record-Chronicle (Denton, Texas)

The Denver Post (Denver, Colorado)

The Eagle Pass News Guide (Eagle Pass, Texas)

The Evening Star (Washington, D.C.)

The New Era (Humeston, Iowa)

The Red-Lander (San Augustine, Texas)

The San Saba News and Star (San Saba, Texas)

The Standard (Clarksville, Texas)

The State (Columbia, South Carolina)

The Sunday Light (San Antonio, Texas)

Tiempo (Las Cruces, New Mexico)

The Times-Clarion (Longview, Texas)

The Wharton Spectator (Wharton, Texas)

Times (Troy, New York)

Times (Hartford, Connecticut)

Times Herald (Corsicana, Texas)

Times-Picayune (New Orleans, Louisiana)

Trenton Evening Times (Trenton, New Jersey)

Trenton State Gazette (Trenton, New Jersey)

Tucson Daily Citizen (Tucson, Arizona)

Union (Houston, Texas)

Uvalde County Texas (Uvalde, Texas)

Vermont Journal (Windsor, Vermont)

Victoria Advocate (Victoria, Texas)

Wabash Courier (Terre Haute, Indiana)

Waco Daily Examiner (Waco, Texas)

Waco Post (Waco, Texas)

Waco Semi Weekly (Waco, Texas)

Waco Southern (Waco, Texas)

Washington Bee (Washington, DC)

Washington Reporter (Washington, Pennsylvania)

Weekly Houston Telegraph (Houston, Texas)

Weekly Herald (New York, New York)

Weekly Pelican (New Orleans, Louisiana)

Weekly Wisconsin Patriot (Madison, Wisconsin)

Wheeling Register (Wheeling, West Virginia)

Wilkes Barre Times Leader (Wilkes Barre,
  Pennsylvania)

Williamson County Sun (Georgetown, Texas)

The Whitesboro News (Whitesboro, Texas)

Whitney Messenger (Whitney, Texas)

Wichita Daily Times (Wichita, Kansas)

Wisconsin Daily Patriot (Madison, Wisconsin)

Wisconsin Free Democrat (Milwaukee, Wisconsin)

Worchester Daily Spy (Worchester, Massachusetts)

Name Index

Note: First or last names not known indicated with a blank.

Daniels, Gilbert, 358
Daniels, Henry, 398
Daniels, John, 371
Daniels, Lige, 568
Daniels, Marie, 398
Darden, Jack, 481
Darlington, James, 418, 424
Davidson, Edmund, 421
Davidson, Jim, 420-422
Davila, Andres, 202, 203
Davis, _____, 270
Davis, _____, 425
Davis, Albert, 587
Davis, Anthony, 469
Davis, Arthur, 211
Davis, Augustus "Gus," 428
Davis, Celia L. Tatum, 371
Davis, Clay, 295, 296
Davis, Daniel, 510
Davis, Ed, 205
Davis, Edward Jackson, 124
Davis, G. C., 280
Davis, Henry, 289
Davis, Ira, 551
Davis, J. J., 426, 427
Davis, Jeff, 130
Davis, Jefferson, 114
Davis, Louis, 588
Davis, Mannon, 370, 371
Davis, Mitch, 450
Davis, Morris, 394
Davis, Perry, 226
Davis, Sidney "Sid," 300
Davis, Stephen, 462, 463
Davis, Walter, 450
Davis, William "Bill," 244
Davis, William "Henry," 327
Davis, William, 518
Davis, Zedolph, 364
Daw, _____, 140
Dawson, America Jane, 119
Dawson, Arfaxton R., 119
Dawson, Jane Caroline
  Stalcup, 119
Dawson, Mary Horn, 119
Day, _____, 400, 407
Day, Sam, 304
de la Cerda, Alfredo, 438,
  439
de la Cerda, Ramon, 438,
  439
Dean, Hugh, 480

Dean, W. J., 475
Decker, Tuck, 147
Degener, Hilmar, 107, 112
Degener, Hugo, 107, 112
DeGraffenreid, George,
  190, 191
DeHart, _____, 395
Dehay, _____, 184
DeLancey, Viola, 482
Delaney, Charles, 491
Delgado, Jose Antonio, 65
Delno, Charles, 257, 258
Delno, O. L., 257, 258
Denecamp, Ethel, 578
Denecamp, Ethel, 583
Dening, _____, 229
Denton, _____, 567
Deon, Maggie Boykin, 401
Deon, Prean, 401
Deputy, Samuel, 58-61
Depuy, M. C., 211
Devere, N. E., 305
Devlin, Charles, 514
Dial, Hardy H., 155
Dias, Pablo, 107, 112
Diaz, _____, 240
Diaz, Vivian, 310
Dick, Ben, 280
Dickerson, _____, 349
Dickson, _____, 220
Dickson, James, 114
Diggs, George, 326
Dill, _____, 206
Dillingham, Jessie, 370
Dinwiddie, Seth T., 456
Divine, James, 551
Dixon, David, 77
Dixon, Thomas K. "Tom,"
  199, 200
Dixon, Thomas, 542
Dixon, William A. "Bill,"
  200
Dodd, Belton, 160
Dodd, Leonard, 558
Dodd, Melvin, 587, 588
Dodge, _____, 183
Dodson, J. E., 419
Dolan, _____, 240
Donaldson, Earl, 534
Donegan, John, 69
Doran, George, 252, 253
Doran, W. R., 225

Dorough, John D., 130
Dorsey, Frank, 388
Dougherty, Maria, 66
Douglas, Ephraim, 369
Douglas, Fred, 569
Douglas, Jasper, 270
Douglas, Jasper, 477
Douney, Henry, 394
Dove, Ernest, 506
Dove, Ethel, 506
Dove, Hattie, 506
Dove, Jesse, 185
Dove, John T., 395
Down, _____, 75
Doyle, _____, 148
Drake, _____, 72
Draper, William, 491
Driskell, William, 578
Driskill, W. P., 583
Duarte, Manuel, 573
Duff, James W., 102, 106,
  111, 123
Duncan, George Taplin
  "Tap," 346
Duncan, Mary Ann Griffin,
  140
Duncan, Richard H. "Dick,"
  345, 346
Duncan, Thomas C., 140
Duncan, Utt, 442
Dunlap, _____, 283
Dunn, E. E. _____, 253
Dunn, William J., 55
Dupree, _____, 104
Duran, Juan, 275
Durfee, Joseph, 521, 522
Dwyer, John, 224
Dwyer, Thomas, 391
Dye, George, 139
Dye, Rama, 117
Dyer, Eli P., 285, 286
Dyer, Samuel B., 286
Dyke, Henry, 376

Earle, William E., 457
Eastwood, Frank, 190, 191
Eckles, _____, 181
Eddleman, J. B., 478
Edwards, Frank, 243
Edwards, Pete, 329
Egbart, _____, 100
Egg, _____, 472, 473

El Paso Salt War, 228
Elkins, Jane, 46
Ellerman, Dorah, 265
Elliff, _____, 185
Ellington, Isaac, 155, 156
Elliot, Colonel _____, 51
Ellis, Anderson, 486, 487
Ellis, Charles E., 227, 228
Ellis, Charles, 227, 228
Ellis, Mrs. J. E., 461
Ellis, William Louis, 545
Ellison, Bud, 328
Elstner, Joseph, 110, 112
Ely, Colonel _____, 176
Emshoff, Dora, 389
Engburg, George W., 420
English, E. F., 503
English, Joseph McFerron,
  78
Ensor, Eli, 101
Epperson, _____, 47, 48
Erath, George, 101
Erickson, Albert, 396
Erwin, Thomas, 88
Esman, Hudson John, 119
Esry, _____, 100
Esterling, _____, 466
Estes, William, 166, 167
Eubank, H. T., 225
Euren, John, 44
Evans, _____, 394
Evans, Green, 233
Evans, Hardy, 479, 480
Evans, Jerry, 479, 480
Evans, Sallie, 304
Evans, Scott, 586
Evans, Tanner, 587
Everhart, Dick, 331
Everhart, Nick, 331
Evers, Leon, 509

Falcon, Felipe, 522
Fant, John J., 271
Farley, J. M., 381
Farmer, Aleck, 251
Farmer, R. S., 404
Farrar, S. B., 169
Farrar, Tom, 303
Farrell, Jack, 361, 494
Farrington, _____, 419
Faulk, Zella, 563
Fay, Wesley, 447

McWharter, Pat, 551
Means, William, 126
Mearsfelder, Arthur, 128
Medlin, Phil P., 506
Meers (Mages), _____, 57, 58
Meinke, Edwin, 553
Melena, _____, 337
Melena, Mrs. _____, 337
Melena, Vitolo, 337
Melton, Frances, 426
Mendez, Jose Maria, 351
Mendiola, Higinio, 590
Mendiola, Jose Maria, 295
Mendoza, Bartolo, 178
Merrill, Mary, 513, 514
Messka, Rosa, 422
Meyer, Henry, 413
Meyers, _____, 364
Michael, George W., 257, 258
Micheaux, Henry, 263
Middleton, Thomas Jefferson, 73
Miers, Mrs. _____, 455
Miguel, San Juan, 376
Mikel, Jeff, 444
Mikeska, Frank B., 541
Miller, _____, 151
Miller, _____, 282
Miller, _____, 63
Miller, Caleb B., 178
Miller, Cato "Uncle Cato," 86
Miller, Elvira, 369
Miller, G. R., 496
Miller, George, 157
Miller, Henry, 184
Miller, Henry, 366, 367
Miller, James, 169
Miller, Jesse, 438
Miller, John B., 164
Miller, John M., 120
Miller, Martha Jane Sandusky, 120
Miller, Mary Eubanks, 120
Miller, Nimrod J., 191
Miller, Samuel Cornelius, 138, 139
Miller, Seth, 320
Miller, Tom, 334
Mills, Jack, 37

Mills, Louis "Coke," 493, 494
Mills, W. P., 328
Milton, George, 276
Mims, William C., 62
Minnick, J. P., 411, 457
Minton, J. B., 429
Misher, Ellis "Blackbird," 422
Mitchel, Jules, 183
Mitchell Jr., Benny, 592
Mitchell, _____, 31
Mitchell, _____, 346
Mitchell, Bill alias Bill Russell, 214, 215
Mitchell, Burke, 319
Mitchell, David C., 66
Mitchell, Frank, 482, 483
Mitchell, George, 361
Mitchell, James, 498
Mitchell, Jeff, 214
Mitchell, Mary, 375
Mitchell, Nelson A. "Cooney," 214, 215
Mitchell, Roy, 578, 583
Mitchell, William Davis, 435
Monroe, Alberta, 507, 508
Monroe, Dewey, 507, 508
Monroe, Ellen, 507, 508
Monroe, Jessie, 507, 508
Monroe, Jim, 46
Monroe, Willie, 508
Monson, Henry, 513, 514
Montague, A. W., 539
Monte, _____, 225
Montgomery, Robert, 95
Montgomery, W. F., 343
Montgomery, William W., 124
Moodey, Lockroy, 417
Moody, Horace, 553
Mooney, _____, 96
Mooney, Martin alias John Martin, 347, 348
Moore , Dennis H., 56
Moore, _____, 177
Moore, _____, 226
Moore, _____, 287, 288
Moore, _____, 343
Moore, _____, 409
Moore, C. B., 74

Moore, Dennis H., 56
Moore, Edgar Maurice Bowie, 455
Moore, Edwin Ward, 29
Moore, Jesse, 552
Moore, Lucinda, 418
Moore, Rankin, 496
Moore, Robert, 173
Moore, Tom, 374, 375
Moore, Walter, 520
Mootry, Mat, 389, 390
Morales, Isabel, 524
Morales, Manuel, 555, 557
Morell, _____, 78
Morgan, _____, 166, 167
Morgan, _____, 51
Morgan, Dudley, 439, 440
Morgan, Frank, 287, 288
Morgan, M. B., 571
Morgan, Mrs. T. I., 582
Morgan, R. B., 478
Morin, Louis, 544
Morris Tobe, 211
Morris, _____, 177
Morris, _____, 22
Morris, _____, 229
Morris, _____, 335
Morris, _____, 35
Morris, _____, 35
Morris, _____, 68, 69
Morris, Brack, 430
Morris, Emanuel, 410
Morris, George, 79
Morris, John A., 120
Morris, John W., 117
Morris, Josephine Hornbuckle, 115
Morris, Marguerite, 120
Morris, Mary Carter, 120
Morris, May, 476, 477
Morris, Michael Wesley, 120
Morris, Neverson, 425
Morris, Thomas, 436, 437
Morris, William Washington, 115
Morrison, _____, 89
Morrison, George E., 418, 419
Morrow, Robert S., 245
Morse, C. F., 164
Mortimer, _____, 228
Morton, John, 203

Morton, Michael, 203
Mose, Creole, 488
Mosely, Ben, 251
Mounger, Thomas Frederick, 511
Muckleroy, George, 433
Mullins, W. T., 548
Munden, G. W., 416, 458
Munoz, Adolfo (Rodolfo), 527
Munoz, Carlos, 455
Munson, Hillen Armour, 491
Murchiso, Mattie, 293
Murphy, Jack, 340
Murphy, Jim, 455
Murphy, Noah, 458
Murphy, Sam, 351
Murray, Irvin, 302, 303
Murray, Molly, 302, 303
Murray, Will, 452
Murrell, John A., 53
Murrell, Morgan, 384
Murrell, Thomas, 384
Myers Jr., Samuel Houston "Sam," 247, 248
Myers Sr., Samuel Houston "Sam"
Myers, C.A., 539
Myers, Cynthia Ann Bales, 247, 248
Myers, Martha "Patsy" Wallace, 247
Myers, Thomas Jefferson, 247

Nail, B., 132
Nail, Clark B., 131, 132
Nash, L. T., 151
Nathaniel, Nat, 321
Nations, William, 330
Neal, Benjamin F., 126
Neal, Mrs. _____, 465, 466
Neff, _____, 127
Neff, P. M., 576
Neil, Thomas Jefferson, 218
Neill, Alpheus D., 226
Nelson, _____, 124
Nelson, _____, 36
Nelson, _____, 492
Nelson, _____, 59
Nelson, A. A., 474

Starrett, H. J., 67
Staton, William R., 93
Stegall, Leslie, 583
Stein, Frederick, 408
Stephens, Doc, 440
Stephens, Ezra, 503
Stephens, John, 331
Stephens, Sallie Sarah
   Hulsey, 301, 302
Stephens, William, 382
Stephenson, Charles, 394
Stevens, Heinrich, 108, 112
Stevens, Horace, 385
Stevens, Julius, 457
Stevens, Rom, 213
Stevens, W. A., 405
Stevenson, Walter, 558
Stewart, R. W., 400
Stewart, Sabe, 399
Stewart, W. A., 392, 410,
   427, 457
Stieler, Heinrich, 110, 112
Still, Washington, 129
Stokes, _____, 189
Stokes, J. C., 291
Stonecipher, L. B., 414
Storey, George, 185
Stormer, John, 382, 383
Stotz, Jesse, 488
Strake, Anna, 369
Strange, Paul, 505
Straum, _____, 242
Strawther, Clem, 389
Stribling, John, 532
Strickland, _____, 27
Strickland, Robert, 273
Stuart, R. S., 350
Stull, Anthony, 236
Stull, John, 236
Suaste, Florentino
   (Florentina), 384
Suhr, Mrs. _____, 403
Sullivan, Blackstone B., 222
Sullivan, William "Buck,"
   358, 359
Sutton, Andrew, 337
Sutton-Taylor Feud, 229
Swackhammer, Charles
   L., 467
Swaid, A., 81
Swan, Elisha, 413
Swancey, J. R., 411

Sweat, Thomas, 404
Sweeney, Cornelius, 282
Sweeney, James, 423
Swift, Frank, 199
Swift, Thad, 199
Swink, _____, 384
Swinkey, C. W., 582
Swinney, Charles, 327, 328

Talley, Jayson, 593
Tally, E. J., 148, 151
Tankersley, Lou, 462
Tankersley, Presley, 462
Tant, _____, 419
Tapia, Hypolita, 202, 203
Tattenbaum, William
   Rogers "Russian Bill,"
   260
Taufo, George, 304
Taylor, _____, 153
Taylor, Albert, 470
Taylor, Edwin, 132
Taylor, Francis, 225
Taylor, George, 339, 340
Taylor, J. H., 465
Taylor, James, 275
Taylor, James, 62
Taylor, K. D. "Kid," 380
Taylor, Luke, 427
Taylor, Martha Ann Welch,
   120
Taylor, Matt, 519
Taylor, Price, 392
Taylor, W. H., 484
Taylor, William Allen, 282
Taylor, William B., 120
Tays, Heinrich Frederich
   "Fritz," 110, 112
Tays, John B., 228
Teague, D. E., 349
Tedford, John M., 191
Teel, Jerry, 333
Tegener, Fritz, 111
Tegener, Guss, 106
Tegener, William, 106
Telgmann, Wilhelm, 108, 112
Teller, R. H., 585, 586
Telles, Juan, 299
Templeton, _____, 90
Templeton, Frank, 61
Terly, _____, 60
Terrell, Alexander, 396

Terry, _____, 265
Teten, Louisk, 546
Tevar, Juan, 538
Tharps, _____, 211
Thomas, Aaron, 397, 398
Thomas, Allie, 416
Thomas, Benny, 398
Thomas, Buck, 547
Thomas, Chess, 263, 264
Thomas, Eli Sigler, 120
Thomas, George, 234
Thomas, Gus, 494
Thomas, Harry, 162, 163
Thomas, Henry, 489
Thomas, Jesse, 578
Thomas, Jim, 397, 398
Thomas, Lee, 381
Thomas, Lewis, 397, 398
Thomas, Marcellus, 490
Thomas, Susan Mary
   Hedenberg, 120
Thomason, Thomas, 207
Thompson Charles, 175
Thompson, _____, 104
Thompson, _____, 444
Thompson, _____, 53
Thompson, Adam, 255, 256
Thompson, Cody, 306
Thompson, Dave, 519
Thompson, Floyd, 539, 540
Thompson, John, 173
Thompson, Jordan, 467
Thompson, Josiah, 173, 174
Thompson, Miles, 261
Thompson, Tyre, 198
Thompson, Yance, 347
Thompson's Kid, 319
Thornton, _____, 180
Thornton, _____, 251
Thornton, Thomas H., 130
Throckmorton, James W.,
   114
Tickle, S. A., 79
Tiernan, Richard, 286
Tiffany, Mrs. Powell, 456
Tiller, Henry, 571
Tilley, _____, 130
Tillis, Dave, 591
Tinkle, _____, 258
Tinley, _____, 145
Tinsley, Calvin Thomas,
   103, 104

Tipton, _____, 68, 69
Tobar, Juan, 529
Tobin, John W., 442, 464,
   582
Todd, _____, 56
Toetel (Toettel), Julius, 244,
   245
Torres, Portirio, 521
Towles, Allen, 248, 249
Townsend, E. E., 582
Townsend, Mrs. W. B., 419
Townsend, Woody, 486
Trammell, _____, 268
Treadway, Robert, 213
Trent, Dan, 225
Triggs, Judge, 434
Trimble, Robert, 240
Truan, Carlos F., 126
Truitt, Isaac, 214
Truitt, James, 214, 215
Truitt, Sam, 214
Tubbs, Rosa, 508
Tucker, Ed, 434
Tucker, George, 515
Tucker, Oscar Lee, 453
Tucker, Robert, 91
Tumlinson, Joe, 230
Tunstall, Charles, 445
Turk, Homer, 583
Turknett, Jacob, 102
Turknett, John S.C., 102
Turknett, Philip Brandon,
   102
Turley, Tom, 208
Turner, E. B., 235
Turner, George H., 464
Turner, Norwood, 166
Turner, Thomas J., 482
Tutt, James B., 33
Twichell, _____, 59
Tyson, Benjamin, 29

Underwood, _____, 98, 99
Unidentified by ethnicity:
   American Indian, 20, 21,
   30, 38, 61, 65, 70, 73, 74,
   76, 134, 170, 188
   Black, 32, 33, 38-40, 43,
   47, 50, 59, 64, 73, 77, 79,
   82-90, 92, 93, 97, 104,
   127, 132, 134, 135, 141,
   143-147, 151-154, 157,

County Index

About The Authors

Clifford Caldwell has continually cultivated his interest in western history since boyhood. After a stint in United States Marine Corps during the Vietnam War, and a successful thirty-five-year career working for several Fortune 500 corporations, Cliff is now retired and free to pursue his interests as a historian, writer and lecturer on a full-time basis.

Cliff hold a Bachelor of Science degree in business and is the author of several book and published works, including *Old West Tales: Good Men, Bad Men, Lawmen; Dead Right, The Lincoln County War; Guns of the Lincoln County War; A Day's Ride From Here Volume I and II; John Simpson Chisum: The Cattle King of the Pecos Revisited; Guns of the Lincoln County War; Fort McKavett, and Tales of Menard County; Texas Lawmen 1835–1899; Texas Lawmen 1900–1940;* and his latest work *Robert Kelsey Wylie, Forgotten Cattle King of Texas.*

Cliff is recognized as an accomplished historian and researcher on the American West and period firearms. He has conducted extensive research on the Texas cattle trails, trail drivers and cattle kings. Cliff is a member of Western Writers of America, Inc., the Texas State Historical Association, and The Great Western Cattle Trail Association. When not deeply involved in writing, Cliff volunteers some of his time doing research for the Peace Officers Memorial Foundation of Texas and is a volunteer leader at the Kerr County Christian Men's Job Corps. Cliff and his wife live in the Hill Country of Texas, near Kerrville.

Ron DeLord was a patrol officer for the Beaumont, Texas Police Department from 1969 to 1972. He served as a patrol officer and detective for the Mesquite, Texas Police Department from 1972 to 1977. In 1977, DeLord was one of the founders of the Combined Law Enforcement Associations of Texas (CLEAT) and was elected its first president. After thirty years as president, he retired in 2013. He is a licensed Texas attorney and is a nationally recognized police labor official and author who is known for his leadership style and visionary ideas.

Ron has a Bachelor of Science degree in government from Lamar University (1971), a Master of Arts degree in police science and administration from Sam Houston State University (1982) and a Doctor of Jurisprudence degree from South Texas College of Law (1986). He has been a licensed Texas attorney since 1987. He graduated from the ten-week Harvard University Trade Union Program (1992).

Ron initiated the legislation to create the Texas Peace Officers Memorial on the grounds of the state capitol in Austin. He is the past director of the Peace Officers Memorial Foundation, Inc., a 501(c)(3) charitable corporation dedicated to honoring the memories of Texas law enforcement and corrections officers who have given their lives in the line of duty. He volunteers his time researching historic cases for the Sheriff 's, National, Texas and other state memorials.

Ron is the author and co-author of several book and published works, including *Police Union Power, Politics and Confrontation in the 21st Century: New Challenges, New Issues* (2nd edition). *Navigating Dangerous Waters: The Real World of Police Labor Management Relations; Working Together: A Police Labor-Management Practitioner's Guide to Implementing Change, Making Reforms and Handling Crisis; Police Association Power, Politics and Confrontation: A Guide for the Successful Police Labor Leader;* and *The Ultimate Sacrifice: The Trials and Triumphs of the Texas Peace Officer - Texas Lawmen 1835-1899 and Texas Lawmen 1900-1940.* Ron and his wife live in Georgetown, Texas.

Many and sharp the num'rous ills
Inwoven with our frame!
More pointed still we make ourselves
Regret, remorse, and shame!
And Man, whose heav'n-erected face
The smiles of love adorn, -
Man's inhumanity to man
Makes countless thousands mourn!

—Robert Burns

www.ingramcontent.com/pod-product-compliance
Lightning Source LLC
Chambersburg PA
CBHW080351030426
42334CB00024B/2842